Wade Hampton

CIVIL WAR AMERICA, Gary W. Gallagher, editor

Wade Hampton

CONFEDERATE WARRIOR TO SOUTHERN REDEEMER

Rod Andrew Jr.

The University of North Carolina Press ✹ Chapel Hill

This book was published with the assistance of the Fred W.
Morrison Fund for Southern Studies of the University of North
Carolina Press.

Designed by Kimberly Bryant
Set in Quadraat by Keystone Typesetting, Inc.
Manufactured in the United States of America

The paper in this book meets the guidelines for permanence and
durability of the Committee on Production Guidelines for Book
Longevity of the Council on Library Resources.

The University of North Carolina Press has been a member of the
Green Press Initiative since 2003.

Library of Congress Cataloging-in-Publication Data
Andrew, Rod.
Wade Hampton : Confederate warrior to southern redeemer / Rod
Andrew Jr.
p. cm. — (Civil War America)
Includes bibliographical references and index.
ISBN 978-0-8078-3193-9 (cloth : alk. paper)
1. Hampton, Wade, 1818–1902. 2. Generals—Confederate States
of America—Biography. 3. Confederate States of America. Army—
Biography. 4. United States—History—Civil War, 1861–1865—
Cavalry operations. 5. Governors—South Carolina—Biography.
6. Legislators—United States—Biography. 7. United States.
Congress. Senate—Biography. 8. Reconstruction (U.S. history,
1865–1877) 9. South Carolina—Politics and government—1865–
1950. I. Title.
E467.1.H19A64 2008
973.7'42—dc22
                                                          2007045836

12 11 10 09 08 5 4 3 2 1

CONTENTS

ILLUSTRATIONS

MAPS

PREFACE

Wade Hampton III of South Carolina was one of the most beloved, trusted, hated, and feared men of his time. Though today many Americans outside his native state have no idea who he was, virtually every American of his own day did and had strong opinions about him. His military and political careers, as well as his personal life, illuminate many features of the transition from the Old South to the New. As a Confederate military hero, victor over the Republican government in Reconstruction South Carolina, governor, U.S. senator, and cultural icon of the Lost Cause, Hampton was the most important figure in late nineteenth-century South Carolina.

I have two goals for this book. One is simply a better understanding of Hampton himself. Despite his tremendous impact on the events of his own day, he remains one of the most misunderstood figures of his time. Until at least the middle of the twentieth century, biographies of Hampton were exercises in hero worship written by amateur historians or by Hampton's friends and former Confederate comrades. Later historians have avoided biographical portraits of Hampton and instead studied his political stances and activities, especially as they dealt with race relations. Unfortunately, these scholars, too, have often missed the mark in their analysis of Hampton. Concerned more with broad patterns in southern history than biography, they have not considered how Hampton's background, biases, and personal tragedies may explain his words, actions, and apparent inconsistencies. He has appeared in some studies as a racial "moderate"; in others, as a hypocrite who publicly preached moderation while secretly sponsoring white terrorism. Hampton has emerged as a cutout cardboard figure supporting this position or that, rather than a man driven by noble instincts, painful life experiences, and human failings.[1]

I believe that Hampton's personal life experiences, rather than being irrelevant or incidental to his military and political role, are instead central to it. His personal background, tragedies, humiliations, and search for vindication, in fact, explain much about the history of the American South in the era of the Civil War, Reconstruction, and Redemption. As I relate the story of Hampton's life in a chronological fashion, therefore, my other goal will be to use his story to clarify our understanding of major topics in southern history—paternalism, honor, chivalry, the impact of war on individual soldiers and loved ones at home, the reasons why many Confederate soldiers continued to fight as long as they did, Reconstruction, racism and white supremacy, and the myth of the Lost Cause. The war chapters also serve to trace Hampton's development and maturity as an officer; Hampton was one of the few Civil War officers who had no prior military experience but who advanced to the rank of lieutenant general and were competent combat leaders. My hope is that the biographical perspective, used in the study of a major figure whose lifespan stretched from before the Missouri Compromise of 1820 to the presidency of Theodore Roosevelt, will amplify our understanding of all those topics.

The first chapters of this book rely heavily on three themes to explain the cultural influences and socialization of Hampton in the first half of his life. "Paternalism," "honor," and "chivalry" are terms that historians have often used to define the ideals of men and women of Hampton's class and time. I do not attempt to redefine those terms here, but the reader has a right to know my working definitions of them within the pages of this book.

For some academic readers, my use of the term "paternalism" will prove the most problematic. I am aware that a growing body of current scholarship treats claims of the southern master class to be paternalistic providers and protectors as masks for oppression. White male slaveholders, it is argued, used rhetoric about principled leadership and protection of social inferiors, including slaves and women, to justify their own status and social power.[2] I do not question the notion that many members of the antebellum southern gentry did exactly that. A close study of the life of Wade Hampton III, however, leads to the inescapable conclusion that southern white men were not always cynical and self-serving when they sought to be protectors and providers. Born into a world of wealth, security, and privilege, Hampton believed that elite, educated men like himself had the right and responsibility to lead and govern. In return, they had paternalistic responsibilities to their social inferiors, including white women and dependent black laborers. For Hampton not to treat "the Negro" with humanity, considering their differences in status, social power, and supposed intellectual ability, would reflect dishonor upon himself as a member of the elite. It would put him on a level with the petty, poor whites around him, unrefined by culture, education, and magnanimity; or with unscrupulous "carpetbaggers," who allegedly made irresponsible promises to black men for opportunistic reasons. I argue that, unless we take Hampton's sense of paternalistic obligation seriously, it is impossible to explain his seemingly contradictory postwar political behavior. Frankly telling both black and white audiences that he believed blacks to be culturally and intellectually inferior, he nevertheless went far beyond many of his white contemporaries in promising legal protections and basic civil rights to African Americans. He knew that he risked paying a high political price among would-be allies for obstinately holding this ground, and pay it he did. What was most tragic about paternalism in his case is that no matter how benevolent Hampton might try to be, his speeches and policies could never lead to racial justice or equality, since paternalism itself was built on the assumption of black inferiority.

"Honor" is a less contentious term in today's historical scholarship, but it is a broad one. Most studies in southern history use the word to connote an ethical system that demanded that white men give the appearance that they possessed truthfulness, independence of action, physical and social power, and the will and ability to defend their own public reputations, families, and communities—violently if necessary. The elements of honor that most apply here are the cultural tendencies to venerate forebears; to respect ferocity of will, especially in the defense of home and family; to hail martial valor and ability; and to place immense value on one's public reputation for integrity, dependability, and personal autonomy. To retain his high social position and his own self-respect, Hampton had to convince his fellow citizens that he possessed these traits.[3]

This definition of honor overlaps significantly with, but also differs from, the third ideal—chivalry. My understanding of the term owes much to a cultural study of a quite different Confederate hero, written by my friend and colleague Paul Anderson. The nineteenth-century chivalric ideal shared much with honor in that home defense lay at its core. The chivalric ideal valued, even glorified, martial valor and ferocity when home and dependent family members were threatened. It had martial and aristocratic associations. One sign that a man was "chivalric," for example, was his appearance on horseback, particularly if he was a skilled horseman. There were, however, important differences between "honor" and "chivalry." Most observers treat chivalry as a later addition to southern culture, coming to full flower some time in the first half of the nineteenth century, around or just after the time of Hampton's birth. Chivalry, says Anderson, added a layer of external restraint to men who were accustomed to none. It valued domestic tenderness toward women and children, and magnanimity toward social inferiors and defeated foes. It was more compatible with evangelical religion, honoring Christian piety, humility, and forgiveness as much as vengeance. Finally, chivalry was an elastic ideal. It allowed social space for stern patriarchs, men of "honor," to become benevolent paternalists— men who could be tender within their own home and yet ferocious in defense of it when duty required.[4]

Paternalism, chivalry, and honor, the dominant social ideals affecting Hampton's upbringing, obviously overlapped and interconnected. All three rested on the assumption of white supremacy and/or leadership by elites, and all three influenced who Hampton thought he was supposed to be from the time of his childhood until his death.

For that reason, I do not abandon my use of these three concepts when the narrative reaches the latter half of Hampton's life. I do pick up another theme, however. That theme is "vindication," closely akin to what other scholars have labeled "redemption," "restoration," and "justification." The theme of vindication, I believe, is the one in which I make the most use of the biographical perspective in explaining post–Civil War political events. Until late 1860, Wade Hampton wished to avoid disruption to his antebellum life and the Old South civilization in which he had come of age. Believing that civil war threatened upheaval and uncertainty, he was one of the last antisecessionists in the most secession-eager slave state. War came, nevertheless, and Hampton's middle years were defined by social chaos, violent revolution, personal tragedy, the loss of his entire fortune, and physical and emotional suffering. He gave his wealth, his own blood, and a beloved brother and son in a cause denounced as treasonous by the other side. For the rest of his life, then, Hampton sought not only a return of social peace and stability, but also vindication for all that he had suffered. He wished to redeem the honor of his loved ones, his native state, and his own name. He knew that the Old South was gone and could never be restored, but he hoped to salvage something good and noble from its past, as well as honor for himself, his comrades, and his loved ones. This urge to achieve vindication and self-justification drove Hampton for the rest of his life and explains nearly everything about his postwar political behavior.[5]

Some readers will note that I have not listed "race" or "white supremacy" as central themes of Hampton's life. Previous studies have held Hampton up to more modern yardsticks of racial enlightenment in a one-dimensional way by simply examining his racial policies and

pronouncements. Many historians have been puzzled to find his performance wildly inconsistent by modern standards. Alternately, they have
praised his "moderation" or kind feelings toward blacks, conveniently
glossing over evidence that contradicts that description.

I take a different approach. I do not mean to shift the focus away
from Hampton's stance on racial issues. I do intend to explain his
position on race and apparent inconsistencies by arguing that race was
rarely his primary concern. Hampton spent the second half of his life
dedicated neither to racial equality nor strict racial proscription. He was
most interested, instead, in redemption and vindication—the restoration of "home rule" for South Carolina, political stability, social peace,
and preserving the honor of his home state and its Confederate veterans. The South could achieve this stability, social peace, and vindication, he thought, through humane treatment of the "Negro," the re-
establishment of the traditional ruling elite, a biracial Democratic Party,
and the expulsion of "carpetbaggers," followed by reconciliation with
the North. Thus what Hampton regarded as "humane treatment" of an
inferior race was part of his program, but full racial equality was not. He
was willing to sacrifice racial equality in favor of political stability, native
white leadership, and personal vindication.

That relentless determination to restore, redeem, and justify that
which had been lost was much of the reason why Hampton eventually
became a larger-than-life figure—not during the Civil War but afterward. He became a mythical hero to the white people of South Carolina
and to a large degree of the American South as a whole, even among
those who opposed him politically or disagreed with his racial "moderation." In Hampton's chivalric bearing, personal misfortunes, and
proud refusal to apologize for the past, white southerners thought they
saw themselves. And they liked what they thought they saw. This quest
for vindication, for redemption, for meaning and validation in the face
of tragedy, then, was not only Wade Hampton's story after the Civil
War. It forms a central part of the story line in the saga of the American South.

⭐ I should add a few comments about terminology. First, wherever
possible, I have taken care to avoid the generic term "southerners,"
which in the past has implicitly referred to white people and excluded
black residents of the South. Instead, I have almost always specified
"black southerners," "white southerners," or "southerners, both black
and white." Second, the phrase "Negro rule" appears often in this   xv

manuscript because, to white contemporaries of Hampton's day, the term implied more than any one phrase I could replace it with. It meant more than "African American leadership" in government, as it also implied black social superiority or equality, undue carpetbagger influence, political and social corruption, and the complete overturning of white supremacy. The reader should know that my use of the term does not imply my endorsement of its assumptions.

ACKNOWLEDGMENTS

When I decided seven years ago to write a biography of Wade Hampton, I naively underestimated how long it would take, as well as how many people I would be indebted to once it was complete. I sincerely thank my editor, David Perry, for showing faith in this project once it was under way and for being tolerant with its author. David, Zach Read, Ron Maner, and others at the UNC Press were patient and flexible when a stint of military active duty altered parts of our production schedule. My series editor, Gary Gallagher, believed in this project also and provided indispensable guidance, saving me from numerous errors. He read the entire draft, of course, but so did my former mentor and one of my heroes, Emory Thomas, who did so for no better reason than friendship. Mike Parrish of Baylor University performed the same chore, a very generous act. Both Emory and Mike offered excellent advice, so they cannot be blamed for any of the flaws that remain. My good friends Kyle Sinisi, Charles Smith, and Paul Anderson also read substantial chunks of the manuscript and helped tremendously.

Other friends and senior colleagues greatly encouraged me simply by lending an ear and offering moral support and sound advice, including Nat Hughes, John Inscoe, Roger Grant, Alan Grubb, Tom Kuehn, Steve Marks, Don McKale, David Nicholas, Sylvia Rodrigue, Bill Steirer, Eric Wittenberg, and Bill Fisk. Nat Hughes not only lent his expertise to the chapter covering the Battle of Bentonville, but also donated to me his entire set of volumes of *Official Records* of the "War of the Rebellion."

Many thanks are due to dozens of librarians and archivists in Clemson; Columbia; Charleston; Chapel Hill; Durham; San Marino, California; and Washington, D.C. I regret that it is impossible to list all of them, but I especially thank Henry Fulmer and Allen Stokes of the South Caroliniana Library; Eric Emerson, formerly of the South Carolina Historical Society; and Michael Kohl at the Strom Thurmond Institute in Clemson. Henry Fulmer, in particular, went to great lengths to help with the reproduction of illustrations from the South Caroliniana. Alexis Thompson of the Historic Columbia Foundation was extremely helpful and efficient in the same way, as was Mike Coker of the South Carolina Historical Society.

Chris Cartledge, a good friend and an artistic genius, prepared the maps for this book. He did so for a fee that one could charge only to a friend or to a charity case—I suppose I qualified as both. I thank my parents, Rod Andrew Sr. and Dottie Sauer, for over four decades of love, support, and wisdom. Jessica, Lydia, and Marina Andrew do not remember a time when Daddy was not "working on Wade Hampton." They were determined to push the project along with cries of "Come on, Daddy, Wade Hampton's got to die sometime!" reminding me that indeed this project could not go on forever.

Karmin Heather Andrew is the other person who read every single word of every chapter, and she did much more than that. The people described in this book spoke much of courage, steadfastness, devotion, loyalty, and selflessness, but I am sure that none of them displayed those traits on a daily basis more heroically than my wife does. I thank her for teaching me that the true source of all these virtues is a deep reservoir of love. To her this book, and much more, is affectionately dedicated.

Gloria soli Deo

PART I ★ PATERNALISM

CHAPTER I

THE PATRIARCHS

The intertwining concepts of honor, paternalism, and chivalry together defined everything that Wade Hampton III of South Carolina was supposed to be. When he entered the world on March 28, 1818, and received the name of his father and grandfather, his elders assumed and fervently hoped that he would represent the best of all three ideals—that he would be ferocious in defense of home and family; physically powerful; brave; honest (or at least publicly seen as such); an able master, provider, and protector of women, children, blacks, and poor whites; and zealous in defense of his personal reputation. All three ideals—paternalism, honor, and chivalry—rested on the assumption of his social superiority. He was to protect, lead, and command.

Wade Hampton III was sixteen years old when his grandfather, Wade Hampton I, died. Wade I had been one of the two important male elders in the boy's life. The youngest Wade had no surviving uncles or great-uncles, and his siblings were all younger than he was. "Grandfather," or "General Hampton," as Wade III alternately referred to him, was the source of the family's wealth, reputation, and social prominence. He was undoubtedly the most important authority figure in the Hampton clan, even after Wade III's father reached adulthood and started his own family. Yet, as important as "Grandfather" was to young Wade, he usually exerted his influence from a distance. His plantation was only a few miles away from where the boy grew up, but in later years, his descendant rarely recalled spending time with him. Both in public and in private letters, he referred to his grandfather in terms of pride rather than love. Still, in an Old South society that venerated ancestors and their heroic feats, the story of the first Wade Hampton's life was of the utmost importance to his descendants.[1]

When Wade Hampton I died at his home in Columbia in 1835, many people at the time believed that he was the wealthiest planter and slaveholder in the South. Yet Wade I had not always been wealthy. He had reached his lofty position in the southern aristocracy through a combination of battlefield valor, shrewd opportunism, and ruthless ambition. He was the fifth (surviving) son of Anthony Hampton, a "lesser planter," militia captain, and frontier trader, and he had grown up with his four brothers and two sisters in the North Carolina backcountry. The

Hamptons were landowners but never moved in the top circles of the elite. Though their ancestors were English and had originally settled in Virginia, the Hamptons joined the tide of Scotch-Irish settlers moving southwestward from Pennsylvania and Maryland and filling up the Carolina backcountry. Thus Wade Hampton I, born in 1751, came to manhood in a rugged, dangerous frontier. Scotch-Irish culture had begun evolving in the lawless borderlands between Scotland and England, where law enforcement was weak and kinship loyalties were fierce. It was a culture that valued physical courage, manly feats of strength and horsemanship, and ferocity in the defense of home and family. A young man proved himself by showing that he was willing and able, if not eager, to fight. This culture was perfectly suited to the American frontier, where ordinary men and women had to master a rugged environment as well as threats from hostile Native Americans. Indeed, warfare with local Indians was endemic along the North Carolina frontier between 1755 and 1763. Wade I's father Anthony served as a militia captain during those dangerous times, and his sons joined the ranks as they came of age.[2]

The culture of the frontier also valued rugged self-reliance and individual initiative. While the father acquired wealth through a series of shrewd land transactions, the sons thrived as traders, obtaining deer skins from the Cherokee nation and taking them to market in Charles Town, South Carolina. They eventually moved up-country to be closer to their source of deer skins. Though already in his late fifties, Anthony Hampton and his wife Elizabeth decided to migrate with their sons in the summer of 1773, and the entire clan, including twenty-two-year-old Wade I, moved once again. They settled in the Tyger River Valley in modern-day Spartanburg County, again along the outer fringe of white settlement. Captain Hampton, Wade, and his brothers prospered as farmers, traders, and surveyors, and doubtless hoped for continued peace along the frontier.[3]

But tension was building between the colonies and the British authorities, and it quickly spilled over into the Carolina backcountry. Encouraged by a British agent, a band of Cherokees in May 1775 captured Wade Hampton's brothers, who remained bound until they escaped with the help of white and Indian friends. In the minds of rebellion-minded patriots in South Carolina, the Cherokees and British authorities had joined forces and become a unified threat. The most tragic story in the Hampton saga was that of the family massacre. On June 30 Cherokees and Loyalists, or "Tories," arrived at the home of old Anthony Hampton. Wade I's older brother Preston was there, perhaps to warn his father and mother of impending raids. Also present were Anthony's nine-year-old grandson John Bynum, and an infant, the child of Wade's sister Elizabeth Hampton Harrison and James Harrison.[4]

There are several accounts of what happened next, differing slightly in detail. One of the most well known and probably the most reliable is one written by Wade Hampton II, originally published in the *Magnolia* in 1843 and later reprinted by the *Charleston Mercury*. The only victim to witness and survive the ordeal was young John Bynum, and his version of the story must have been told around Hampton firesides for generations to come. When the Indians arrived at the Hampton home, Preston and Anthony recognized some with whom they had been on good terms. As Anthony was shaking hands with "one of their chiefs," Wade II claimed, a gunshot felled Preston.[5] An instant later, the "very hand" that Anthony had grasped in friendship sent a tomahawk crashing through his skull.[6] Mrs. Hampton suffered the same fate, while young John Bynum "stood perfectly astounded amidst this murder and carnage, having lost all presence of mind, and making no effort to escape." The infant "was dashed against the wall of the house," and just before a warrior raised his weapon to kill Bynum, a chief arrested the blow and took the lad under his protection.[7] Meanwhile, Elizabeth Hampton Harrison was returning from a visit to a neighbor, Mrs. Sadler. Her husband James was with her. They arrived in time to see Elizabeth's father, mother, and brother lying dead, the house in flames, and perhaps to see their baby murdered. Elizabeth's husband stifled her screams and physically prevented her from rushing out of hiding and into the yard as the Indians proceeded to ransack the house.[8]

News of the massacre of the Hamptons and two other frontier families spread quickly across the colony. Any hope the remaining Hampton brothers may have held of staying on the sidelines of the conflict drained away with the blood of their lifeless parents, brother, and baby nephew. Under the prevailing code of the southern frontier, family honor demanded vengeance against both the Indians and their British allies. Even without the grief and rage the news undoubtedly inspired, failure to retaliate would have convicted the Hampton sons, individually and collectively, of cowardice and ruined their reputations forever. Though some of the brothers were already in military service and stationed in Charleston, all of them obtained permission to join one of the militia companies being formed in the upstate and sent to wreak vengeance for the slaughter of the Hampton, Hite, and Hannon families. In several pitched battles, raids, and massacres, the patriot militia exacted its revenge. Edward Hampton was the hero of the first encounter. In a later skirmish, Henry Hampton captured an Indian wearing the coat of his dead brother Preston. Henry then killed the Indian "with his own hand."[9] Every Hampton brother continued to serve the patriot cause. Edward, however, would be murdered by "Bloody Bill" Cunningham's band of Tories in October 1780 while eating a meal in the house of a friendly upstate family. The larger story was that every Hampton brother who survived the massacre of his family spent the years from 1776 to 1781 exacting vengeance, until he died or until the British were defeated. The moral of the tale could not have been lost on Hampton descendants—when tragedy struck, a Hampton responded with a combination of ferocity, patience, and stoic resolve until he achieved vindication.[10]

When war came to South Carolina in 1776, the Hampton brothers had already established themselves as backcountry merchants, with valuable contacts in Charleston. Wade I, in particular, used these connections to build the foundation of his fortune. He became something of a soldier-merchant, alternating and combining the two roles in various ways throughout the Revolution. With Wade's ability to deliver much-needed provisions for patriot forces, he and his brothers provided a valuable service to the patriot cause, while bringing substantial profit to themselves. As Wade's biographer explains, his "civilian pursuits and military duties were not incompatible, but were, in fact, complementary."[11]

Initially, Wade Hampton I was successful as a staff officer and backcountry merchant. No man, however, could accuse him of lacking courage. In later years, it was his patriotism and heroism that contemporaries and descendants remembered about his Revolutionary service, not his business acumen. By the time the war was over, Hampton had established a reputation not only as a loyal patriot, but also as a gallant combat leader. This reputation came from the campaign of 1781, and it was his feats during this stage of the conflict that later inspired his grandson and left a legacy of heroism in battle that he would fight to uphold. Wade III may never have systematically studied and researched Revolutionary history; he could not recite dates, but he knew the stories. In 1870 he responded to historian Lyman C. Draper's request for information about his grandfather. His reply indicated the importance of family oral tradition but suggests that he may have spent little time indeed in intimate conversation with Wade I. "In reference to my grandfather," Hampton wrote, "I can give you little except from family tradition, as all our family records & papers were destroyed, when Sherman burned my father's house. . . . My father told me that his father, was serving with [Thomas] Sumter, when [Nathanael] Greene was in N.C."[12]

First, there were the stories of "Grandfather's" horsemanship. By the spring of 1781 Wade I was a lieutenant colonel and recruiting men for his own regiment of cavalry to serve as state troops. Recruiting was not always easy at this stage of the war, and Hampton resorted to gallant feats of horsemanship to win over potential enlistees. According to one account, he would pick a hat or a sword off the ground while galloping at full speed. He outfitted his regiment at least partially at his own expense, expecting, of course, that the state would eventually reimburse him.[13]

Then there was the thrilling story of Grandfather Hampton's surprise, predawn attack on Fort Granby in early May 1781, when his small force routed a contingent of 250 Tories. A few days later, he participated in the siege and recapture of Orangeburg. Later he performed well in actions near Goose Creek and Monck's Corner, earning Sumter's praise in official reports.[14]

Wade I played his most conspicuous role at the Battle of Eutaw Springs on September 8, 1781. In this engagement, Greene's army of over two thousand men took on a slightly larger British force under the command of Lieutenant Colonel Alexander Stewart. At a critical point in the battle, Hampton rallied three regiments of South Carolina troops, "restoring them to confidence and order," and led two determined assaults on a British position. At another moment, Hampton had a horse killed beneath him. Wade III later related that, as his grandfather was pinned beneath his dying horse, an enemy soldier attempted to bayonet him. Hampton parried the thrusts with his sword until an American sergeant approached and shot his assailant. In his report to Congress, General Greene mentioned Wade Hampton I's prominent role in the battle and approvingly noted that he had captured one hundred enemy troops. Most importantly, Grandfather Hampton had established his reputation as a man of courage and left a legacy of heroism for his descendants—a legacy that his grandson would regard as his duty to uphold. Wade I's feats at Fort Granby, Eutaw Springs, and elsewhere allowed him to don the mantle of the romantic warrior hero, one that, two generations later, would rest even more securely on the shoulders of his grandson.[15]

When later generations of South Carolinians recited Revolutionary lore, they never noted that despite his heroism in battle, Wade Hampton

I had never abandoned his shrewd and materialistic nature. In 1778 he had purchased a great deal of land from merchant William Currie, a Scotsman who was loyal to the king and who had been harassed by the patriot authorities. Currie was forced to leave the state after refusing to sign an oath of allegiance to its Whig-controlled government. Hampton profited from Currie's misfortune. As Currie made arrangements to flee, Hampton bought 175 acres from him for 500 pounds cash, an extraordinarily low price. In another transaction, he bought, on credit, Currie's store and a total of 370 acres for 6,500 pounds. He never paid off the bond for the latter transaction, and Currie was virtually powerless to collect it. Hampton also confiscated the slaves of Loyalist subjects. At a time when Loyalist and British troops did the same and worse to patriot citizens, most patriots would not have condemned these measures. The South Carolina state government, in fact, often paid its troops in the form of confiscated slaves, not money, which was scarcer. Hampton's troops only objected when they thought that he had confiscated more than his share, or that he had taken an inordinate share for himself before dividing it among the soldiers. After the capture of Fort Motte on May 11, 1781, Whig troops complained that their individual booty amounted to no more than a gill of rum per man. One noted bitterly that "Col. Wade Hampton was the commander who is said to have made private property of the spoils on this occasion."[16]

Hampton emerged from the war with land, slaves, and money due him from the state for services rendered. He had also obtained a reputation for courage and ferocity on the battlefield. Neighbors in the Saxe-Gotha (later Richlands) district rewarded this reputation with election to the General Assembly, and he took his seat in January 1782. By 1787 his net worth in land, slaves, and other property probably exceeded ten thousand pounds, making him one of the wealthiest planters in the state.[17]

Besides the acquisition of property and an honorable war record, there was one more path to prominence in Revolutionary-era South Carolina—an advantageous marriage. In 1783 Hampton wed Mrs. Martha Epps Goodwyn Howell, a wealthy widow with important family connections. With this union, he acquired six slaves and over 1,500 acres, the land that became the nucleus of his Woodlands plantation, his principal residence. Martha died in 1784. In 1786 Hampton married Harriet Flud, the daughter of Colonel William Flud, a substantial planter in the Santee region. She bore him two sons, Wade II and Frank, but died in 1794. In 1801 the fifty-year-old Hampton married

Mary Cantey, Harriet's sister-in-law. Again he had married well. Mary Cantey was twenty-two, pretty, and descended from one of the "first families" of South Carolina. She would bear him five daughters and one son.[18]

Yet Hampton cannot be dismissed as a shallow fortune seeker. Even at an advanced age, he retained a patriotic, and sometimes benevolent, impulse. Incensed at British insults to American national honor, he volunteered for military service in 1808, when many thought war with Britain was imminent. Hampton was then fifty-seven. This was a time when he could have had little incentive to parlay military service into financial gain, as he had done in the Revolution—his civilian pursuits were now bringing him an estimated annual income of $50,000. Much of the compensation he did receive for his military service went to charity. When a major fire devastated Charleston in October 1810, Hampton donated $500.00 and then sent a check for $4,456.82, the sum of his military pay and emoluments since being commissioned a brigadier general in 1809. Between 1808 and 1813, he served conscientiously and energetically in New Orleans and along the South Carolina coast. Promoted to major general in March 1813, he took part in General James Wilkinson's botched invasion of Canada the following fall. A British force defeated Hampton's contingent of five regiments at the Battle of Chateaugay on October 25, while the men under Wilkinson's direct control fared no better. In this, Hampton's last campaign, his performance had been mediocre at best. Both men received heavy criticism. While Wilkinson publicly tried to absolve himself and shift the blame to Hampton, Hampton simply resigned and went home.[19]

Wade Hampton I was well established politically and financially in the 1790s and 1800s. He served as a trustee of South Carolina College and as a member of the South Carolina Convention called to vote on ratification of the U.S. Constitution. He served in the General Assembly as well as two terms in Congress. But he was not content to rest on his laurels and his fortune. By fair means and foul, he aggressively continued to build his fortune. Wade I was one of the first South Carolina planters to make a large profit from growing short-staple cotton, made possible by the recent invention of the cotton gin. Meanwhile, he was one of the many beneficiaries of the infamous Yazoo Land scandal, in which well-placed politicians, particularly of the Georgia and South Carolina legislatures, used their influence to obtain millions of acres of western lands at infinitesimal costs. Hampton's involvement hurt his reputation, but in the long run he profited immensely. He obtained

General Wade Hampton I (1751–1835). Planter, congressman, veteran of Revolutionary War and War of 1812. South Caroliniana Library.

property in Mississippi and Louisiana and became the largest sugar producer in Louisiana. He was the builder and owner of toll bridges and ferries. He occasionally invested in the ownership of ships and boats. He bought and sold city lots and made money through the breeding and racing of horses. In 1820 he owned nearly one thousand slaves. By the time of his death in 1835, his estate was worth over $1.6 million.[20]

Wade Hampton I does not easily fit into any of the models historians have created to describe the antebellum southern master class, nor into most popular stereotypes. He was not a born aristocrat, having risen from the ranks of yeomen and small frontier slaveholders. Neither was he a "precapitalist," paternalistic landlord, rejecting the acquisitiveness and moneygrubbing of modern capitalism. Undoubtedly, he was grasping, materialistic, even greedy. When the opportunity came to enrich himself in the Yazoo Land schemes, he did not shrink from compromising his seignorial dignity nor his reputation for a quick dollar. Indeed, he made his start as a backcountry trader and merchant, not a planter. Always seeking more land, more slaves, more wealth, and better investment opportunities, he was as ambitious and shrewd as the stereotypical Yankee merchant.[21]

White southerners often claimed that they sustained a hierarchical, paternalistic structure of family relations in which even slaves were members of an "extended" family. All members of the "family" rendered deference and obedience to the patriarch in exchange for his protection and provision. Such a view often implies a certain amount of paternal care or benevolence on the part of the master toward his slaves. Modern historians have conceded parts of this statement, while insisting that brutality was nevertheless a fundamental part of the master-slave relationship. Still, paternalism recognized the humanity of slaves, who might in turn use the master's paternalism to mitigate the harshness of the system.

At least one planter, however, pushed his slaves to the outer rim of his emotional existence. A British traveler, James Stuart, reported that Wade Hampton I "not only maltreats his slaves, but stints them in food, overworks them, and keeps them almost naked. I have seen more than one of his overseers whose representations gave a dreadful account of the state of slavery on his plantations, and who left his service because they would no longer assist in the cruel punishments inflicted . . . but I do not mention such a fact . . . merely on such authority. General Hampton's conduct toward his slaves is [a] matter of notoriety.[22]

Hampton's alleged inhumanity was indeed "a matter of notoriety" among his fellow slaveholders. Near the height of the sectional crisis, fire-eater and southern nationalist Edmund Ruffin agreed with Stuart's assessment, noting in 1858 that "[Stuart] has exposed, and I am glad of it, some detestible [sic] cruelty of particular southern slaveholders—especially of the late Gen. Wade Hampton."[23] Wade I apparently made little effort to disguise the brutality of slavery with the image of reciprocal obligation—kindness and humane provision by the master in exchange for loyalty and deference from the slave. To him, his slaves were merely capital assets whose sole purpose was to increase his own wealth.

Some endorse this alternative image of the materialistic, ambitious master who regarded his slaves primarily as capital assets, not wards or children. Interestingly, they also argue that while southern slaveholders cared little for their slaves as people, they began, in the nineteenth century, to form closer emotional bonds within tight-knit nuclear families. This trend toward developing nurturing family ties within nuclear households was common at the time throughout Western Europe and the United States, and southerners were very much a part of it. It was a trend toward egalitarianism, not hierarchy, within the family.[24]

Hampton does not fit that interpretation either. There is much evidence that his style of family leadership was hierarchical and authoritarian, not emotionally nurturing. Though Hampton was not brutal toward his wives and children, he apparently did not nurture particularly close emotional ties with them. He did take an interest in the early military careers of his sons Wade II and Frank in the War of 1812, but he developed a reputation for being aloof and distant with nearly everyone around him. George McDuffie, a close friend of the younger Wade, was incredulous that Hampton, though "worth millions," would not lend his son money when he needed it. McDuffie exclaimed that "although his son will probably enjoy the whole of this immense estate after the general's death, yet so capricious is the old man that he not only contributes nothing to relieve his son from his embarrassments, but has been in a measure the cause of them."[25] Similarly, in Wade I's relations with his wife Mary Cantey and his younger children, there is little evidence of a devoted family man tending to the emotional needs of his nuclear family.[26]

Hampton perpetuated the patriarchal, authoritarian structure of family relations in the way he administered and distributed his property. Traditionally, the patriarch retained both his authority and his control of the family's wealth as long as possible. Wade I's biographer explains that Hampton delegated responsibility but not authority to Wade II, even after the lad had reached adulthood. He closely supervised his son's planting and financial affairs, and Wade II always remained under the shadow of his domineering father. Hampton meant for this dominance to pass to his son at his death. Most sources state that when Wade I died, his will specified that all his property would pass to Wade II and none to his widow and daughters. Wade II, however, tore up the will and divided the estate equitably between himself, his stepmother, and his two stepsisters. By leaving all to his oldest and only surviving son, Wade I was attempting to perpetuate his authoritarian and patriarchal style of family relations to the next generation. But Wade Hampton II was a very different sort of man, and times had changed. The custom of primogeniture was disappearing, and more egalitarian methods of providing for one's offspring were replacing it.[27]

Wade Hampton I had many virtues. He was brave, tough, energetic, hard-working, and outwardly moral and sober. He was a bona fide hero of the Revolution. A product of that Revolution, the cotton boom, the expansion of the new republic, and the vast opportunities available to the man of enterprise and energy, he ironically came to symbolize the hard-bitten and stubborn planter aristocrats of the seventeenth and eighteenth centuries. Though a self-made man of the new republic, he curiously resembled the older elites who based their authority on the privileges of birth and class. Greedy, callous, and perhaps even cruel, he was thoroughly disliked by many of his contemporaries. Senator William C. Preston of South Carolina, for example, referred to him as "that wretched old vulture" and "the old villain."[28]

None of Wade Hampton III's surviving letters reveal what his feelings were at his grandfather's death. No doubt he had admired his grandfather, but their relationship seems to have been one of deference and awe on the one hand, and paternal condescension on the other. Indeed, Wade I, as a war hero, a retired general, and one of the wealthiest landlords in the South, inspired more deference and respect than he did love from nearly everyone around him. For Wade III, Grandfather Hampton was a towering figure to which one rendered obeisance. Genuflecting from afar, the young man could clearly see the courage, the fierce will, stubborn pride, sagacity, and patriotism on the face on the monument; propriety and family tradition obscured the flaws of the structure at its base. After the patriarch's death, few contemporaries crossed the bounds of propriety, deference, and good manners boldly enough to speak of his less noble traits publicly or in the presence of his descendants.

★ "Grandfather" died in 1835, but Wade III enjoyed his own father's presence for another twenty-three years. Wade Hampton II had inherited the wealth, courage, and sobriety of the patriarch-general, but little else. He was not overly ambitious and unfortunately exhibited little of his father's business sense. He had few political aspirations. He was kinder, more gracious, and more easygoing. He made a greater effort to be a humane master and an affectionate father. Despite these vast differences between the patriarch and Wade II, however, the life of the son certainly fell within the parameters established for those in his social place.

First, Wade II went to war. The patriarchal, chivalric ideal demanded that men be willing and able to fight in defense of property, family, and home. It contributed to the growth of a military tradition, especially in the slaveholding states. With the knowledge of his father's heroic Revolutionary War service and current high military rank, Wade II probably regarded his own military service as a manly rite of passage. Shortly after his father's promotion to major general in March 1813, Wade II was commissioned as a second lieutenant in the 1st Regiment, Light Dragoons. He served with his father in the ill-fated Canada campaign of 1813. When the elder Hampton resigned the following spring to extricate himself from further intrigues among fellow officers and gossip in the press and the War Department, Wade II returned home with him to Woodlands.[29]

By the fall of 1814, however, young Wade II found himself back at the scene of war. He had gone to Louisiana to handle the sale of his father's sugar crop in New Orleans. A large British naval and land force was headed toward the Louisiana coast, and soon General Andrew Jackson arrived to reinforce the city with his mixed force of regular troops and backwoods militia. The British arrived at the mouth of the Mississippi in December. Wade II offered his services to Jackson, who appointed him "Acting Assistant Inspector General of Troops." The young officer then played the key role in showing Jackson's troops how to move the American artillery pieces across a boggy field so they could be properly emplaced. These cannon would later cut the British force to pieces during the Battle of New Orleans and contribute to a spectacular American victory.[30]

It was then that young Wade II demonstrated another trait of the southern aristocratic ideal—his outstanding horsemanship. Jackson ordered the twenty-three-year-old captain to carry the news of the victory to President James Madison in Washington. In ten days, Hampton rode one extremely sturdy horse the entire 750 miles to Columbia, crossing swamps, swimming rivers, and traveling at night to avoid detection when in hostile Indian territory. He continued on to Washington and soon met with Madison, who informed him that a peace treaty had already been signed. Unknown to the opposing generals at New Orleans, the treaty had been executed in Ghent, Belgium, on December 24. Nevertheless, Wade II received special mention and thanks in Jackson's general orders of January 21.[31]

Wade Hampton II's exploits near the end of the War of 1812 completed a rite of passage. Two years later he married Anne Fitzsimons, the daughter of a wealthy Charleston merchant. He was now ready to settle down and assume his proper place and role as an aristocratic leader of southern society. It is important to describe in detail the social and political role into which he settled, for it was the world in which his son, Wade Hampton III was born and raised. The American South had changed rapidly from the colonial to early republic periods—that is, in the first Wade Hampton's lifetime. By the time the third Wade Hampton came of age in the 1830s, Old South civilization had begun to flow in increasingly predictable and conservative patterns. There was, of course, growing sectional tension and political animosity at the national level

Wade Hampton II (1791–1858). Planter, War of 1812 veteran, "kingmaker" in South Carolina politics. South Caroliniana Library.

over the issue of slavery. But the life of a wealthy South Carolina aristocrat, day to day and year to year, changed little from the time of Wade III's boyhood until the outbreak of the Civil War.

Wade II's Millwood plantation, with its magnificent mansion on the outskirts of Columbia, was a political and social hub for the South Carolina elite. Wade II served only one term in the state senate, and it was the only public office he ever held. Instead, he played a pivotal role behind the scenes, often as a kingmaker with great influence over who won the offices of governor and U.S. senator. He was active and quietly influential in the state's political crises. During the nullification crisis of the early 1830s, he favored South Carolina's nullification of the federal tariff but opposed secession; he also worked to defeat secessionists in the secession crisis of 1850–52. But the South Carolina aristocracy did not gather at Millwood only to conduct political activities. The Hampton estate hosted glamorous balls and other social events. Wade II was also an avid breeder and racer of horses, and his stables were renowned statewide at a time when racing was one of the favorite pastimes of the South Carolina aristocracy.[32]

What anchored Hampton's place in society was his ownership of land and slaves. When the Hamptons divided Wade I's estate in 1835, Wade II left the lucrative sugar plantations in Louisiana to his stepmother and stepsisters, while keeping the Millwood and Woodlands plantations near Columbia for himself. In 1840 those South Carolina lands included over 12,000 acres and 460 slaves. He also retained his own Walnut Ridge tract in Mississippi, consisting of 2,500 acres and several hundred more slaves. He was not as aggressive a businessman as his father, but neither was he totally blind to opportunities. After the defeat of the Indians in the Black Hawk War of 1832, he purchased 2,084 acres in Wisconsin. About the same time, he acquired 8,000 acres in the newly established Republic of Texas. He also invested in railroads.[33]

By the time Wade Hampton II had assumed his father's place as the patriarch, the family's western holdings were the primary source of its wealth. The rich alluvial lands along the Mississippi produced lucrative cotton yields nearly every year, while planters in South Carolina were finding that several decades of intensive cotton cultivation had worn out their soils. Wade II was one of the first to advocate diversification in the state's old cotton fields and grew corn, hay, and grain. The curious pattern that developed for the Hamptons was that while Columbia, South Carolina, was still their home, Mississippi was the source of their wealth.

None of this land would have been worth a dollar without the forced labor of hundreds of African American workers, who held the tragic dual status of both human beings and private property. In capital terms, they were valuable. In 1839 Wade II sold 192 slaves from his Carolina estates for $180,000. In later years he helped his sons Wade III and Christopher "Kit" Hampton acquire hundreds more to get their newly purchased plantations on a profitable footing. One historian has estimated that, between them, Wade Hampton II and his three sons owned approximately 3,000 slaves in the 1850s.[34]

Whether he saw the tragedy in his slaves' situation is doubtful, for in his own mind and in the minds of other whites, Wade Hampton II was a "good" master. So were his sons Wade III, Kit, and Frank. This reflected a key component of the aristocratic planter ethos that was solidifying by the middle decades of the nineteenth century. The ethos began to include a benevolent paternalism that highlighted masters' concerns with their slaves' physical and spiritual needs. This paternalistic ideal was a response in part to the growing attacks on slavery from outside the South, as slaveowners tried to convince themselves and others that they were not the monsters abolitionists often accused them of being. It also drew strength from the growing influence of evangelical religion in the South and probably had its roots in older notions of noblesse oblige.

When Wade Hampton II died in 1858, an obituary in the *Southern Chris-*

tian *Advocate* stressed approvingly that he was known far and wide as a kind master and as one who liberally supported missionary work among slaves in the South. Wade II was the "pioneer," said the article, of the Congaree Mission of the Church, South (South Carolina Conference), and he also contributed greatly to slave missionary work in the Southwest. The writer praised his "humane and considerate treatment of his poor dependents, in such beautiful harmony with his care for their immortal interest."[35]

To Wade II, then, his slaves were not only capital assets, but wards—dependent creatures to be cared for. One way in which masters did this was in providing a holiday, a feast, and presents for their slaves at Christmas. In a revealing letter to his daughter Mary in November 1855, Hampton wrote: "Our crops are good, beyond all description, my cotton is now yielding upwards of two bales to the acre. . . . I have been picking fifteen bales a day. Liza (Dolph's daughter) is among my best pickers, & indeed a first rate hand at all work. I have sent to N. Orleans for supplies, & have ordered presents for all my people. Besides these gifts they shall have a glorious Xmas; & I will do anything to keep them in good spirits."[36] Thus Wade II attributed his success in part to the skill and industry of his "people," and responded with what he felt was generosity.

The Hamptons' attitude toward their slaves is evident in their letters describing sickness and mortality on their plantations. Illness and mortality rates were high in the nineteenth century, particularly in the South, and even more particularly among slaves, especially slaves who worked and lived in hot, damp climates like that of the lower Mississippi River Valley. Like his father, Wade III was aware that illness and death on his plantation potentially threatened the strength and morale of his labor force as well as his own livelihood. But his reports on the loss of his slaves always included a human touch—his own sorrow or that of the other slaves, the name or identity of a particular one. In February 1857 Wade III's Wild Woods plantation in Mississippi suffered a relatively mild, but nonetheless tragic measles epidemic. A letter to Mary Fisher Hampton, his favorite sister, revealed the Hamptons' dual concern for their slaves as both a source of labor and as human beings:

> I did not write to you last Sunday, as I promised to do, because I
> was kept up all Saturday night by the sudden illness of Lizzy, who
> in spite of all that could be done for her, died on Sunday morning.
> Besides the great loss this is to me, I regretted her death very much,

as I really was attached to her, as she had been always a most faithful servant. She leaves two young children; the youngest about a year old. As soon as I can have an opportunity, I will have the little girl taken on for Sally to keep, & the boy shall stay in my house. All the people seem to feel Lizzie's death very much. The measles are of a mild type, & my invalids are doing very well.[37]

Wade III had lost not only a faithful servant, but also one he was "attached" to, one he had stayed up for all night to keep apprised of her condition. On her death, he turned immediately to the question of what to do with her children. One was to go to his eleven-year-old daughter Sally, who lived with her aunts (Wade III's sisters) in Columbia, and the boy was to stay and serve Wade. In one respect it was cruel to separate the two young siblings on the death of their mother, but the practice was common in white families as well. Wade III himself was a widower at the time of this letter, and his daughter Sally and younger children were staying with various relatives or attending boarding schools while he took care of business in Mississippi.

Sickness returned to Wild Woods in November. Wade III wrote Mary Fisher that one of the small children of the aforementioned Lizzy had died, probably the little boy: "The sickness on my place has decreased, but not ceased. There have been two deaths since my arrival: one a fine young man, & the other the youngest child of Lizzy, making in all 37 *deaths this year.* I am greatly disturbed at this mortality. The people seem cheerful now, & I hope soon to see them all well again."[38]

The Hamptons spoke fondly, if condescendingly, of their slaves. Among their favorites were Mauma, or Mom Nelly, childhood nurse and playmate to Wade III and other Hampton babies; and Daddy Carolina, personal servant to Wade II. In August 1857 Wade III wrote Mary Fisher that "yesterday I reached this place [Millwood, in Columbia, where Hampton's sisters usually resided] and found all quite well. . . . Of *your* friends here Mom Nelly, Sarah Gamp, and Anarka have reported themselves as well and all happy except Mrs. G. who is moping. A good feed this morning has however "*sot* her up considerable.' "[39]

When Wade Hampton II died in 1858, it was Daddy Carolina who last saw him alive. The sixty-seven-year-old Hampton had gone riding over his Mississippi plantation on the afternoon of February 9 and returned before sundown, which his servants found unusual. They also noticed that he was riding very slowly. He went into the house, picked up his

Bible, and began reading as Daddy Carolina removed his boots and began to wash his feet. When he finished, the slave said, "Mars' Wade, yo' kin take yo' feet out of de tub now." Hampton did not respond. Daddy Carolina began to repeat the sentence but did not finish before he realized that his master was dead.[40]

The circumstances of the old man's death, if anything, probably enhanced the fondness and trust the rest of the Hamptons felt for their slaves. No doubt the story also reassured other elite southerners who regarded their peculiar institution as one of care and generosity on one side and loyalty and affection on the other. Many slaveholders, like the Hamptons, believed that they presided over a docile, contented, and intellectually simple lot of servants. Their docility and content, they thought, was largely due to their own magnanimity, as well as to the simple, childlike ambitions of African Americans.

Northerners who visited their plantations often were inclined to agree. Agriculturist Solon J. Robinson toured the South in 1849 and stayed at Wade II's Millwood plantation in Columbia. He declared that his journey had dispelled his previous objections to the institution of slavery, as it brought great blessings to the slaves. Robinson continued: "I could tell you facts about the situation of the 300 slaves upon the plantation of Col. Wade Hampton, where I now write this, that would go to show these people to be almost inconceivably better than that of thousands of white 'freedmen' throughout this region."[41] Even more forceful defenses of slavery came from a northern-born woman, Sally Strong Baxter, who married Frank Hampton, brother of Wade III, in 1855. Writing to her father in New York in December 1860 in the heat of the secession crisis, she described the generosity of the Hamptons toward their slaves at Christmastime and followed with a sarcastic denunciation of abolitionists. Sally explained that "Xmas is the Negroes peculiar festival," and for several days the Hamptons allowed them to use the plantation's draft animals to haul their own garden produce to town to sell for personal profit. That year, however, their corn crop had been a small one, and because of a rash of small pox, they were quarantined from Columbia. The Hamptons therefore bought their slaves' corn crop and provided them

> a barrel of whiskey—a Hogshead of molasses—& oxen for a Barbecue are their master's contributions & I am to got out Monday & give out Sugar—Coffee—Rice & Flour to all that want. . . . In these hard times the raising of money is not [an] easy matter but the Negroes will be paid the $500 or so that their crop amounts to,

on Christmas whether money is tight or easy. This looks like "a gigantic system of wickedness & iniquity" does it not—Alas! Alas! they know not what they do nor say—How do they dare overturn a mighty nation—this fanatical sect, for the propagandism of a doctrine . . . founded on ignorance not in knowledge.[42]

It would be foolish and insensitive to accept the mid-nineteenth century romanticized description of slavery as fact. We cannot assume that the Hampton slaves felt the gratitude and loyalty toward their masters that the Hamptons hoped they all shared. A few of them supported Wade III when he ran for governor in 1876, and family members remembered that Mauma Nelly spoke a "long farewell to Marse Wade" when she died in the arms of white Hampton women.[43] But for most of the laborers, no matter how many gifts they received at Christmas, their lives were mainly ones of toil, humiliation, and sorrow, not to mention physical punishment if they tried to stand up to the Hamptons' overseers. Moreover, the Hamptons could have formed close personal attachments to only a few of their thousands of slaves—mostly house servants like Mauma Nelly and Daddy Carolina, or an occasional "picker" like Lizzy. No matter how generous they believed themselves to be, the fact remained that their wealth and social position rested mainly on the forced labor of others. If the Hamptons frequently acknowledged the basic humanity of their servants, they also recognized their economic worth. As will be seen later, Wade Hampton III could speak of slaves not only with affection, but also in terms of how much they were worth and the best time of year to sell them.

The point is that while paternalistic notions may have done little or nothing to improve the lives of his slaves, they did influence the way Wade Hampton III saw himself and the kind of behavior he expected of himself. Equally important, paternalism influenced the way he thought of his slaves. Wade III never consciously felt threatened by black people before Emancipation and only indirectly threatened by them afterward. This point is crucial to understanding his postwar politics, attitudes, and apparent contradictions concerning race. He never doubted that blacks were inferior in intellect to himself and to most whites. He held no commitment to racial equality. He also never doubted that he had a responsibility, as a Christian gentleman, as a patriarch in whom society had invested authority and social duties of a near-sacred nature, to care for their basic needs. Mauma Nelly's gentleness and playfulness with him and his baby sisters, Daddy Carolina's ministrations in his father's last moments, the death of Lizzy, and probably countless other memories—all of them would always temper Hampton's reactions to African Americans during Reconstruction and beyond, even at those times when he came closest to endorsing the more negative view of blacks held by whites whose racist views were more radical and violent. In Hampton's eyes, to deny black people their basic humanity would have been to fall short of his father's reputation as a "Christian" master and to cast dishonor upon himself as an elite white patriarch.

THE YOUNG KNIGHT

Wade Hampton III was born in Charleston on March 28, 1818. His nurse was the favored slave Mauma Nelly, who retained affection for her former charge until her death in 1866. But the earliest stories about Wade III have nothing to do with childhood innocence or childhood nurses. They have to do, instead, with swords. The boy's first mortal enemy was a large gander that "would fly up in his face" and attack him every time he went to play in the yard of the family residence at the Millwood plantation.[1] Sometimes he fled, and sometimes he turned on the gander and chased it. As he approached the age of four, his parents asked him what he would like for his birthday. He replied only that he wanted a sword, and he received a miniature one with a light hilt and a steel blade. On his next trip into the yard, the gander flew at him as usual. The lad held the sword straight out in front of him, and his tormenter skewered itself on the blade.[2]

This is certainly the most well-known story from Hampton's childhood and was apparently told and retold within the family. His elders were undoubtedly elated at the lad's precocious display of courage and warrior spirit. Antebellum southerners always hoped that their male children would develop the proper ferocity of spirit needed to defend hearth, home, and personal and family honor. It was his grandfather especially who seemed to take more interest in young Wade as a future warrior and patriarch than as an innocent child. According to one account, it was he who procured for his grandson the specially made sword that brought an end to the old gander. Wade was still very young when Grandfather Hampton awed him with stories of his Revolutionary adventures and of how he had taken a sword from a British officer and used it for the rest of the war and in the War of 1812. The elder Hampton let the wide-eyed youth hold the weapon and demonstrated how to use it. At the age of seventeen, Wade inherited the sword on his grandfather's death. Hampton also gave his young namesake a pony. By age four the future warrior was handling his mount, boasted his grandfather, "in the usual Hampton tradition."[3]

He entered Rice Creek Academy at the age of ten. By that time, Wade III was not only the designated future patriarch of the Hampton clan, but also the older brother of Christopher, or "Kit," aged 8; Harriet, 5; Catharine (Kate), 4; Ann, 2; and the baby, Caroline. Within a year, he would have another brother, Frank. The last and youngest sibling, Mary Fisher, arrived five years later—on January 13, 1833. Their mother, Ann, never recovered from delivering her seventh child. She died on February 27, one month before young Wade's fifteenth birthday.

We know nothing of Hampton's reaction to his mother's death. He did not keep a diary, and no letters written by him before the age of thirty survive. He did not mention her in later correspondence. Throughout his life, though, Hampton generally suppressed his own grief, a habit that he exercised again and again as he outlived siblings, wives, most of his children, and even grandchildren. He also was extraordinarily close to the female members of his family. Though he established a manly camaraderie with his brothers Kit and Frank, and later with his sons, those bonds lacked a certain tenderness that he reserved for his sisters and daughters. The baby who survived her mother's death, Mary Fisher Hampton, was always his favorite sister. Fourteen years her senior, he addressed her in letters as "My Dear Mary," "darling Mary," or "my own little pet."[4] Surviving family letters suggest that Mary Fisher may have been his closest confidante, though virtually no correspondence survives between him and either of his two wives. Hampton's closest personal relationship was probably with someone he considered a ward, not an equal. Perhaps the death of their mother awakened a protectiveness in Hampton for his younger siblings, particularly his sisters. If so, it was the very protectiveness celebrated by the chivalric ideal. Male camaraderie would always reassure Hampton of his masculinity and of his membership in the fraternity of white men. But except on the death of his father and two oldest sons, his most tender expressions of emotion would always be reserved for females, especially dependents. Of course, this affection and protective instinct toward women and dependents corresponded perfectly with chivalry's ideals. Fate, temperament, and cultural expectations were already combining to create the later Wade Hampton of Old South nostalgia and legend.[5]

Southern boys often began college in their mid-teens, and Wade Hampton III graduated from South Carolina College, his father's alma mater, in 1836, at the age of eighteen. He had a solid record as a scholar and read law for two years after graduation. It was clear, though, that Hampton had little early interest in either the legal profession or politics. Instead, he enjoyed the life of a rural aristocrat and sportsman. Every year his father took him and Kit to Mississippi to oversee the planting of cotton and other operations. They arrived in February or early March and stayed until late April or May. After returning to the family seat near Columbia, they traveled north with most of the family and several slaves to spend the hottest weeks of the summer in Newport, Rhode Island, or, more often, at the stylish White Sulphur Springs resort in the mountains of Virginia. Here they fished, enjoyed the mineral baths, and socialized with other prominent families, some of whom they knew from South Carolina. By November they were back in Mississippi, in time to supervise the final stages of the harvest and the sale of the crop. They usually stayed there through Christmas.

From one perspective, this was a life of idleness. But actually Hampton was fulfilling the expectations of a young planter aristocrat. He was learning the business of planting from his father and helping to administer his father's affairs. He was an attentive older brother to his siblings. He was not frittering away the family fortune on cards or drink, as his deceased Uncle Frank had done. He probably gambled at the racetrack with his father, who was an avid horse racer and breeder, but this could not have aroused any social rebuke, as it was a favored pastime of the aristocracy.

Most of all, though, Hampton fulfilled the social ideal of the mounted warrior knight through his displays of physical courage, strength, and expert horsemanship. By the time he reached manhood, Wade III was roughly six feet tall and powerfully built, with broad shoulders and a deep chest. Contemporaries claimed that his powerful legs could grip a horse like a vise, tightly enough to make it "groan with pain."[6] At eighteen, he joined Richland District's volunteer cavalry company, whose purposes were more social than military, but where young aristocrats could pose as heirs of the cavalier tradition.

Hampton's father's favorite pastime was breeding and racing horses; Wade III's was hunting. He avidly hunted game around Millwood and out in Mississippi. Later, Wade II, Wade III, and Kit bought 2,300 acres in Cashiers Valley in the North Carolina mountains as a hunting and fishing preserve. They built lodges on the property, which became one of Wade III's favorite retreats in the hot summer months. He enjoyed hunting all sorts of game, but especially the largest and most dangerous —that is, bears and then deer. Wade II often wrote Mary Fisher from Mississippi to tell of her brother's success in killing bears and deer. He deferred to his son's greater prowess as a hunter and marksman, writing in 1856: "I want Wade here excessively, the wolves will overrun the country, & his aid, & that of his bear pack, are much needed."[7] Stories began circulating in Mississippi and back home in South Carolina that

Wade III could, while sitting on horseback, lift a small bear off the ground and place him over the pommel of his saddle. His grand-nephew Harry R. E. Hampton explained that this happened once and was a feat "more of horsemanship than of strength, as a horse has a mortal dread of even the scent of a bear, and few riders could make one approach the animal close enough to perform the feat."[8] By the time of his death, Hampton's reputation as a mighty hunter had grown to the level of mythology; even Republicans fell victim to its spell. Theodore Roosevelt once wrote that Wade Hampton had killed "thirty or forty" bears with a hunting knife. Once again, Harry Hampton attempted to inject a dose of reality: "On one occasion, as my father told it to me, a pack of young dogs had a bear at bay, and [Hampton] was afraid the bear might hurt the hounds, so he watched for an opportunity, slipped in behind the animal and cut its throat, a feat which no doubt took considerable strength, as I presume a bear has a rather tough hide. So, he did kill one bear with his knife."[9]

Hampton was also an avid fisherman, and stories abounded of his skill and cleverness as an angler as well. William T. Porter, a friend of Wade II and the editor of the sportsman's publication, Spirit of the Times, also recognized the younger Wade's superiority as an outdoorsman. When Hampton was twenty-eight, Porter dedicated the first American edition of the English publication Guns and Shooting to him with the inscription: "I take the liberty of dedicating to you as the most accomplished sportsman of my acquaintance . . . [this book] . . . in the hope that, like your father, you may distinguish yourself in society as on the turf and in the field . . . that your reputation as a practical planter may be as widely spread as the fame of your exploits as a horseman and a shot."[10]

Hampton's enthusiasm and prowess as a hunter defined him even more clearly as "a paragon of a particularly southern version of [elite] manhood."[11] Hunting, of course, has always been popular in the South. In colonial days, it served as a means of providing meat and hides. But as Nicolas W. Proctor has explained, by the 1830s elite sportsmen, especially in the South, had transformed the hunt into a "form of recreation and public display" that was meant to demonstrate power, mastery, and self-control, and to bolster elite men's claims to social leadership.[12] Hunters and commentators maintained that hunting promoted health, endurance, and manliness. Obeying the "rules of sport" promulgated by the elite additionally demonstrated self-control, the character trait that supposedly separated the white man, the master, from slaves and women. By calling for limits on the quantities of game taken and the methods used to kill them, the slaveholding class asserted that hunting was to be neither an outlet for bloodlust nor a frenzy of killing. Instead, it was to show the white man's calm, masterly control over the meting out of violence and death. White elites often expressed this mastery in terms of chivalrous virtue, claiming that the hunter exemplified the same virtues that made up the chivalric ideal—honesty, loyalty, paternal concern for dependents, and masculinity. Mississippi governor Alexander McNutt summarized this attitude in an 1845 article in Spirit of the Times: "Show me a gentleman devoted to the chase, and I will show you, with rare exception, 'the noblest work of God, an honest man,' respected for manly virtues, a good husband and father, a zealous friend, and an open enemy. 'The rich man's equal, the poor man's benefactor' —richly adorning the pages of his life with the shining virtues of charity and benevolence."[13]

McNutt and many others thus portrayed the hunter as an ideal of white masculinity. By combining the virtues of prowess, self-control, and various elements of mastery, hunting became a display of that white masculinity and mastery. As Proctor concludes, that mastery was "predicated upon control of individual passions . . . [and] potentially included dominion over women, slaves, domestic animals, property, nature, and . . . death. The confidence born of control created the potential for paternalism and a secure justification for patriarchy."[14]

Hampton was fond of recounting his outdoor adventures. It amused him and probably gratified his vanity to report that others did not have his superior ability and endurance on the hunt. In November 1857 he wrote Mary Fisher that a party of English gentlemen who visited his Mississippi plantation to hunt with him simply could not keep up. "Today I took them bear-hunting & we killed four," he boasted. "They are not accustomed to the sport. Lord Althorp / or as Sam calls him 'Lord' / was with me & he literally had his clothes torn off. I had to furnish him with my drawers, so as to enable him to come home decently. To show them the full glory of the country, we had a severe thunderstorm & came home in the hardest rain I ever saw. I fear they will all be knocked up tomorrow. They get on very well, & as Frederic [Hampton's slave] is sick & has been all the time, I just let them take care of themselves."[15] One senses that Hampton enjoyed feeling his superiority in withstanding the rigors of the hunt, as well as having a stronger constitution than his comrades as well as his slaves.

By demonstrating his prowess as a hunter, in fact, Hampton signaled that he was growing into—indeed, excelling in the roles of patriarch, master, and knight. It is in that sense that one should interpret the legends of his hunting prowess. A common practice of hunters, for example, was to return home with their kills draped over the pommels of their saddles.[16] Hampton could confirm his skill and his mastery over nature by draping not just a fox, rabbit, or deer over his saddle, but a bear—a bear that he had lifted onto his saddle without even dismounting, without his feet even touching the ground. Perhaps it was respect for the chivalric ideal and Hampton's reputation for self-control that made younger relatives object to the bloodthirsty claim that he had killed thirty, forty, or even eighty bears with a knife. Hampton had knife-slain one bear, explained his grand-nephew Harry, and he had done it to save his dogs—that is, to rescue creatures less powerful than himself. He possessed enough strength, enough power over violence and death, to slice a bear's throat if he had to, but he chose to do so only in the role of protector and defender of lesser mortals.

In an offhand way, however, William Porter's dedication praising Hampton's skill as a sportsman indicated that he was not yet the perfect cavalier. He had not yet distinguished himself "in society" as his father had, and he was only just becoming a large landowner in his own right. He was a husband and father for several years, as well as an assistant in maintaining his father's estates, before Wade II had helped him buy Wild Woods in Mississippi. And by relying on his father's financial help to purchase his own land, he had still not demonstrated his full independence, yet another defining characteristic of southern manhood.

Nor was Wade III as witty, clever, or popular as his father. For one thing, he was not as physically attractive. Contemporaries often gushed over the dashing good looks of his father, his brother Frank, and his second son, Preston, but no one described Hampton as "dashing." The first thing others noticed when he walked into a room was his size—six feet tall, with broad shoulders, barrel chest, large head, and sinewy neck—and those were initially intimidating. His hair was wavy, but it is difficult to determine the color other than to suppose it was somewhere between dirty blond and brown. Edward L. Wells, a soldier who served under Hampton, noted that his "complexion and hair was [sic] of the Saxon, not the brunette type, but not too markedly so," whereas a later biographer called them "dark."[17] His eyes were large and gray, with a "suspicion" of blue, claimed Wells, and "had a frank, honest, open, kindly look."[18] People who liked Hampton said that he was "genial" and courteous in conversation, but not loud, demonstrative, or a participant

Margaret Preston Hampton (1818–52). Wade Hampton III's first wife. South Caroliniana Library.

in "undignified levity."[19] He never used tobacco and did not drink to excess. Hampton's personality, in other words, did not light up a room. Those who disliked him, especially Union officers or Republican leaders who met him during or just after the war, interpreted his gravity as haughty aloofness or arrogance. Their impressions were probably not unfair. He could be reserved toward strangers. Hampton had a proud bearing, and the bitterness and hatred he carried for Yankees at that stage of his life no doubt made him even more reticent in the company of enemies, without the courtesy or "open, kindly look."[20]

At least one belle found the large, reticent young cavalier a suitable marriage prospect. Sometime in his late teens, Hampton began spending more time at the seat of the Preston family in Abingdon, Virginia. In 1830 Hampton's aunt (his father's half sister Caroline) had married John Smith Preston of Abingdon, the younger brother of U.S. senator William C. Preston of South Carolina. The couple later moved into the Columbia town home that Wade Hampton I had built for his third wife, Caroline's mother. The two families were close, and Wade III fell in love with John Smith Preston's younger sister Margaret, an enchanting brunette who was his half cousin by marriage. Margaret, the tenth and last child of General Francis Smith Preston, had been educated and trained in music by private tutors. She and Wade married in the Preston's stately family mansion in Abingdon on October 10, 1838, both aged twenty.[21]   29

Wade and Margaret Preston Hampton lived at Millwood, his father's house, while a cottage was being built for them nearby. They also spent considerable time at Abingdon. Margaret gave birth to a son, Wade Hampton IV, in 1840 and to another, Thomas Preston Hampton, in 1843. Wade III was now a head of household in his own right. But the social position he occupied was awkward. He had only just become a landowner and slaveholder. Though he was recognized as a fine horseman, sportsman, and respectable young gentleman, it was his father who held all the social authority, save for that exercised over Hampton's own wife and two small children. It was his father's place to protect the family honor, provide for the growing Hampton clan, and steer the course of the Hampton family through the social and political world of South Carolina. Wade Hampton III was a grown man, but he was still under his father's shadow.[22]

No event illustrated this situation more clearly than the family crisis that erupted in 1843. In 1831 Wade III's aunt, Catherine Fitzsimons, had married below her station. Catherine was the younger sister of Hampton's mother, Ann, and against her family's and her brother-in-law Hampton's initial wishes, she had wed an up-and-coming lawyer, planter, and politician, James Henry Hammond. Though his origins were obscure, Hammond was now uncle to Wade III, his two brothers, and four younger sisters, and brother-in-law to their father Wade II. The four older Hampton girls, in particular, came to adore their uncle, and Wade III himself often visited the Hammonds' Silver Bluff plantation near Aiken, South Carolina.[23]

Hammond rose quickly through the ranks of the elite. By the fall of 1840 he was running for governor, and his wife Catherine was pregnant and confined to their home at Silver Bluff. He bought a town house in Columbia from which he could socialize and conduct political activities. Hammond failed to win the governorship in 1840 but was elected in 1842, after which he moved into the governor's mansion. Sometime in 1840 or 1841, however, Hammond's relationship with his Hampton nieces took on a scandalous nature. The girls—Harriet, 18, Kate, 17, Ann, 15, and Caroline, 13—often visited their uncle when he was in Columbia on business, and sometimes his wife was home at Silver Bluff.[24]

No record or mention of the episode appears in family papers or letters of the Hamptons. But five or six years later, Hammond gave his version of what happened in a long diary entry—probably in an attempt to soothe his own conscience and to excuse his own conduct to later readers. Hammond wrote:

Here were four lovely creatures from the tender but precocious girl of 13 to the mature but fresh and blooming woman nearly 19, each contending for my love, claiming the greater share of it as due to her superior devotion to me, all of them rushing on every occasion into my arms and covering me with kisses, lolling on my lap, pressing their bodies almost into mine, wreathing their limbs with mine, encountering warmly every portion of my frame, and permitting my hands to stray unchecked over every part of them and to rest without the slightest shrinking from it, in the most secret and sacred regions, and all this for a period of more than two years continuously.[25]

Apparently these transgressions fell short of sexual intercourse, but Hammond confessed to his diary that he deserved "very great condemnation."[26] It was not Hammond who acted first to halt the activities, however, but Kate, the second oldest girl. On April 13, 1843, the eighteen-year-old Kate took offense at one of Hammond's advances. According to Hammond, he apologized to Kate, and "as I understood received [pardon] from this young lady."[27] For the next eight weeks, Hammond remained in Columbia, socialized with the Hampton family as a whole, but avoided any personal contact with the four sisters. Believing this to be the end of the affair, and relieved that the shameful dalliances that he had lacked the willpower to resist had finally come to an end, he returned to Silver Bluff. But sometime between then and November 1, Kate informed her father of the situation, or at least of some aspect of it.[28]

It is impossible to know what the initial reactions of Wade II and Wade III were. Since the Hamptons left no record of the episode in their letters or memoirs, we are entirely dependent on Hammond's diary. Other prominent South Carolina families soon realized that a deep rift had developed between Hammond and the Hamptons. They whispered that Hammond had apparently committed some grave indiscretion, but few knew or repeated the details. What is clear is that it was up to Wade Hampton II, not his oldest son, to determine the family's response. Wade III, now twenty-five years old, was the most physically powerful Hampton male and undoubtedly eager to avenge his sisters' disgrace. But the patriarchal system left him no choice but to follow his father's lead. His sister Kate showed that she understood that as well as anyone when she informed her father, not her big brother, of what had occurred.

One rumor that reached Hammond several years later was that the story "leaked out" in October 1843 while Wade II was attending horse races in Tennessee.[29] When Hampton returned home and heard the news, Hammond relates, he "armed himself with his gun and was on his way to shoot me when W[illiam] C. Preston interposed, shewed him how such a course would affect his family and induced him to desist."[30] Hammond also heard that Wade III, John Smith Preston, and John Laurence Manning, another brother-in-law of Wade II, "could [only] with difficulty be restrained from attacking me."[31] Hammond was not sure whether to believe this story. He thought it entirely possible but preferred instead to think that Wade II knew the facts well before he let on. Indeed, throughout his diary Hammond wavered between, on the one hand, expecting an armed attack from the Hamptons, and on the other, convincing himself that they were insincere and cowardly, and merely using the scandal to ruin him politically.[32]

Under the antebellum code of honor, Wade II would have been well within his rights to make a violent attack on Hammond. No self-respecting patriarch could tolerate such gross transgressions against his female relatives. He could have demanded a duel with Hammond. But duels were only fought between gentlemen, and such a challenge would have been a tacit admission that Hampton still considered Hammond a gentleman and an equal. Alternately, he could have attacked Hammond with a horsewhip or cane, weapons reserved for social inferiors. There are several reasons why he did neither. First, duels were inherently public events. Accounts of such an action, as well as what prompted it, would appear in every newspaper in South Carolina. This promised to make the disgrace of the Hampton girls fully and irrevocably public, instead of being known only by a few leading families. Wade II would be heaping more disgrace on his own daughters and damaging his family's reputation. Second, Hammond was now the governor, and any violence against him, as well as public knowledge of the behavior that prompted it, would bring public dishonor to the governor's office and to all of South Carolina. Certainly a horsewhipping or caning of the governor would heap disgrace on the state he represented. Indeed, it would ensure that news of the family scandal spread across the nation, ruining the Hampton name along with Hammond's. The normal rules of honor, in other words, simply did not apply in this case. The Hamptons would have to seek their revenge by other means.[33]

What Wade II did instead was attempt to ensure Hammond's social ostracism and political destruction, which were akin to the same thing among South Carolina elites. On November 1, 1843, he sent Hammond a note severing all further contact with him based on his improper advances to Kate on April 13. In response, Hammond wrote to John Smith Preston, brother-in-law to both men. Hammond had been on friendly terms with Preston, and asked him to intercede and help smooth things over. But Preston obviously knew of Hammond's sins, Wade II having already covered that base. Preston's reply arrived within an hour, declaring that "atonement & oblivion were impossible."[34]

At first, Hammond indeed feared an attack by Wade II or one of his sons or allies. He gradually realized, though, that Hampton would try to destroy him politically while keeping the affair itself relatively quiet. When the legislature met in November, rumors spread that a serious quarrel had developed between Wade Hampton II and Governor Hammond. Hammond concluded that "this event deprived me of all satisfaction at the proceedings of the Legislature and will embarrass me through life."[35] With the Hamptons, Prestons, and Mannings doing all they could to isolate him socially, he soon abandoned his residence in Columbia and did not return for any long period for several years. As the General Assembly began to consider Hammond's candidacy for the U.S. Senate in 1846, Hampton struck again. He threatened some of Hammond's supporters that he would make available certain documents to legislators that would prove Hammond's unfitness for office and "prostrate" him forever.[36] Few lawmakers actually read the documents, but the clouds of rumor and suspicion ruined Hammond's bid for the Senate. Hampton and his allies acted similarly when Hammond sought to fill the Senate seat of the recently deceased John C. Calhoun in 1850, and thus thwarted Hammond again. But Hammond did not go away. He remained a prominent South Carolina politician with allies who never deserted him. He finally won election to the Senate in November 1857, three months before Wade II's death. When the legislature had met to fill the vacancy left by the death of Senator Andrew Pickens Butler, Wade II was in Mississippi, ill, and unable to influence events in Columbia. After his death, Wade III was probably too preoccupied with settling in with his new wife, educating his teenage sons, administering his father's estate, providing for his orphaned sisters, and taking stock of the debts his father had left him in Mississippi to pursue the quarrel further.[37]

The Hampton family's silence on the affair, in fact, is deafening. We will never know for sure what Wade III thought, said, or wrote about it. It is possible that he placed some blame on his sisters. They had certainly been indiscreet, especially Harriet, the oldest, with whom Hammond had first had illicit contact. With their mother having been deceased since 1833, and with their Aunt Catherine Hammond away from Columbia, they probably lacked maternal guidance on proper feminine deportment. It was they who suffered the most in the long run. Harriet's death in 1848 saved her from a long life of spinsterhood. Despite their acknowledged beauty and family fortune, none of the girls ever received a marriage proposal; neither did Mary Fisher Hampton, the youngest sister, who was not directly involved. The scandal had not remained secret enough. Perhaps Wade III regretted that his father had not buried the matter completely instead of attempting to use it to injure Hammond. The former course might have saved his sisters' reputations and marriage prospects.[38]

More likely, young Wade directed his disgust and anger against his uncle, the social climber who had wormed his way into the Hampton family and into the social elite, and had proved himself a reprobate and a fraud; the man who had brought disgrace and misery to his sisters and embarrassment to his family. It would have been easier for Wade III to focus his anger on his uncle-by-marriage rather than on his own father and sisters. Besides, by 1850 Hammond's depravity again became obvious when his wife, Wade's Aunt Catherine, discovered that Hammond had had ongoing sexual affairs with two of his female slaves—a mother and her daughter.[39]

In the short run, what Wade III thought scarcely mattered. Regardless of how incensed he may have been, his duty was to follow his father's lead. But one must at least speculate: What lessons did he learn? What was the long-term impact of this tragedy on his attitudes and instincts? Probably there were two lessons to be learned, and one did not necessarily complement the other. In many ways, in fact, they contradicted each other. First, Hampton had followed, and helped execute, his father's policy of slow revenge against the aggressor. Vindication would not come in a day, or even a year. By "steady, patient, and persevering work," said Wade III, he and his would drive out the usurper and work out their own redemption.[40] Interestingly, these words come not from the 1840s, but from 1869, and they refer to an entirely different enemy. Second, Hampton must have seen in his uncle his first vision of effrontery, immorality, and power combined into one hateful specter. The despoiler had once been an outsider, had been admitted into the inner circle, and had proved himself unworthy. But he had also proved to be powerful and difficult to defeat. Later, Wade III would mentally cast other outsiders in the same mold—usurpers who were unprincipled, cowardly, and yet powerful. Ultimate revenge and recompense were impossible, yet so was reconciliation. Perhaps in the end Hampton would simply have to move on and attempt to defend his own from further disgrace.

⭐ Wade Hampton III was beginning his own family in the early 1840s. After the birth of Wade IV in 1840 and Preston in 1842, Margaret bore him a daughter, Sally, in 1845. Almost none of his correspondence from this decade survives. We may deduce that he was very attached to his wife and children, for his later letters are full of expressions of affection and fatherly concern. Yet it seems that Hampton was torn between those domestic bonds and his own love of adventure. He continued to indulge his passion for hunting. Business (as well as hunting) took him, his father, and his brother Kit to Mississippi for months at a time, and often women and small children did not go with the men on these journeys to more unsettled country. From dozens of letters of the 1850s and afterward, it is obvious that Hampton was devoted to his daughter Sally, and yet he may not have been present at her birth. Margaret spent her days of confinement at her parents' home in Abingdon, Virginia, and Sally was born in July 1845. That was the summer that Hampton, his father, and Kit devoted to building a mountain hunting lodge and several cabins at their 2,300-acre preserve in Cashiers, North Carolina.[41]

The following summer Hampton traveled abroad, again without Margaret. John Smith Preston, the husband of Wade II's half sister Caroline, was suffering from anxiety or "nervousness," and Wade II had suggested that the Prestons visit England for relaxation. He asked his son Wade to accompany the Prestons so Caroline would not be alone in a foreign land with an ill husband. Margaret remained at home, for she was pregnant again.[42]

Hampton may have had misgivings about leaving his pregnant wife and young children, but once in England he thoroughly enjoyed himself. The letters he wrote to Margaret—his only surviving correspondence with her—told of his adventures. He met the duke of Wellington, visited Scotland, listened to speeches in the House of Lords, and saw his grandfather's name, "W. HAMPTON," written in a guest book in 1821 in a cottage that once belonged to William Shakespeare. He wrote the same in his own hand next to his grandfather's entry.[43]

Despite all the fun he was having, Hampton longed for his wife and children. "My heart is wholly yours," he wrote Margaret on July 30.[44] 35

The next night he felt "more like pouring out my heart to you than usual for tonight I am sad. I had set my heart on meeting letters here from you and I learn that the steamer is not in. It has been more than a month since I left home and I have not heard from you. . . . God grant we may all be spared to meet soon in health and happiness."[45] "When you write tell me what I must get for you and what for the children," he wrote on August 1. "I will try to get a suit for Wade. Tell him I will not give him anything unless he is a good boy and takes care of Preston and Sally. How I do miss them, especially my little Sally, my dear playfellow. I fear she will forget me. By this time she is walking alone, I hope; and talking too. Make her learn to talk of me."[46] Hampton also wondered about the progress of Margaret's pregnancy. "Have you fattened since I left, or fallen off? Tell me your weight."[47] Hopefully Margaret did not take offense, for he also flattered her on her figure and beauty by comparing her to English ladies, who, he claimed, were rude and "gigantic." He continued: "If you ever get very much larger you must come to London, where you will then be regarded as a sylph. How I did wish that your magnificent beauty could have shone in that great hall to shame the diamond covered brows of the haughty princesses."[48]

Hampton knew that he would have to attend to business matters in Mississippi soon after his return home but was reluctant to make the trip without Margaret. "Will you go with me?" he asked. "I think you could be comfortable at the Houmas until Jan. when I would have more room for you (as it will be needed) at Wildwoods. I will not urge you to go, but wish you to do whatever you prefer. But for this long absence I would rather you should stay in Columbia, but now I would hate to leave you in a week after my return."[49]

Apparently Margaret did accompany Hampton on the western trip after his return from England. The baby, John Preston Hampton, was born on December 12 in Mobile, Alabama, en route from Columbia to the Hamptons' Mississippi holdings. It is remarkable that she was not in Columbia or Abingdon at that stage of her pregnancy.[50]

Hampton was now twenty-eight years old, father of four, heir to a large fortune, and becoming an important planter in his own right. He had a beautiful wife and money and time for leisure. But tragedy was imminent. Death struck close to him in 1847 and would continue to do so for the rest of his life. On October 17, 1847, his baby son, John Preston, died at the age of ten months. Harriet Flud Hampton, the oldest of Hampton's sisters, died at Millwood the following June. Eleven days later Margaret bore Hampton another daughter, who was christened Harriet Flud Hampton after her dead aunt.[51]

Yet a harder blow fell in June 1852, when Margaret herself died. She left the thirty-four-year-old Hampton with four children, aged twelve to four, and a broken heart. It was a devastating, life-changing event for her husband and children. All four of the youngsters went to Millwood to be raised by Hampton's surviving sisters, Kate, Ann, Caroline, and Mary Fisher. These women were now no longer simply dependents, for Hampton now depended on them as allies in the raising of his children. Ann was to take special charge of Sally, while Mary Fisher doted lovingly on Harriet Flud. Tragically, little Harriet died eighteen months later. The two boys were older and would spend some time away at school and some time with their relatives in Abingdon; occasionally they accompanied their father to Mississippi.[52]

Hampton himself seems to have suppressed his grief. We have no record of his initial reaction. Later, though, he poured his heart out in a remarkable letter to his youngest sister, Mary Fisher. It is one of the earliest surviving letters in his handwriting. He had journeyed to Abingdon to visit Margaret's family. When he arrived, he looked out his window to the empty house where he, Margaret, and the children had spent many months together, and the resulting flood of memories nearly overwhelmed him. "All things here, are changed for me," he told Mary Fisher:

> As I look from my window now, at the closed & lonely house, where once all was love & happiness, I realize fully all the great & sad changes which have taken place. Memory, when I shut out external things, in an instant brings up the happy past, again a happy house hold throngs around. . . . Again I hear the voice & see the smile that once were dearer to me than all else on earth. . . . Every scene, every emotion, every memory wrings my heart & I can scarce realize that the weak & broken down man, who mourns here over blasted hopes, & lost happiness, is the same, who years ago, had every dream of joy fulfilled in that house, which like my heart, now seems forsaken & desolate.[53]

These pitiful lines might seem to have come from an anguished man grieving over a recent disaster. In fact, Hampton wrote the letter over three years after Margaret's death. Evidently it took him a long time to face her loss squarely, to grieve fully, and to allow himself the luxury of self-pity. Meanwhile, he had had to struggle on with the practical duties of life. Yet even three years after the event, he was searching his heart for the resolve to begin life anew and to humble himself to God's will:

> May God forgive me for apining. All must be for the best. I hope at some future time to see this clearly. Now I must strive to bear, as all have to do, the burthen placed upon me, & doubtless even these sad memories are not without a . . . purpose, tho they seem grievous for the present. Weak as they make me now, I hope they will leave me a better man. . . .
>
> My heart has been full, & I know yours has been with me. The past & the present alike contribute to make me weak, but I shall hope to gather strength for the future. It is not a bright one, but my duties are many, & so are the blessings still left to me. I shall strive to discharge the one & to be worthy of the other. God bless you all prays
> Your brother
> W. H.[54]

Wade Hampton would indeed need "to gather strength for the future." His tribulations had only just begun.

A FATHER AS WELL AS A BROTHER

Hampton buried his grief initially in politics. Though he had never before sought or held elective office, shortly after Margaret's death he agreed to be a candidate for the post of state representative from Columbia's surrounding Richlands district. He won. He was reelected in 1854 and served in the state senate from 1856 to 1860. As a legislator, Hampton seemed to think that South Carolina should provide paternalistically for its people. He supported improvements to the state's system of free public schools, the establishment of a penitentiary, and expansion of the state lunatic asylum to deal with overcrowding. Meanwhile, he continued to devote attention to his planting interests in Mississippi.[1]

While Wade Hampton III struggled to rebuild his life as a widowed bachelor, his youngest brother Frank was beginning a family of his own. In 1855 Frank married twenty-two-year-old Sally Strong Baxter, the oldest daughter of George Baxter, a prominent merchant of New York City. Sally and Frank settled at Millwood, where Sally quickly grew very fond of her husband's family and her adopted Carolina home. "It is all such a new life," she wrote her father:

> The ease and liberality with which everything is conducted makes it seem so natural that one forgets what is in reality great magnificence. . . . We sit down every day fourteen to twenty at dinner— people come and go, stay or not as they please and it all passes off as a matter of course. But besides all this, which impresses one of course, there is the family, which seems to me the most remarkable of any I every saw—four unmarried sisters—each utterly different from the other and yet it is impossible to say which is the most attractive. Such highbred elegance and with . . . more than ordinary cleverness, such perfect femininity and womanliness.[2]

Sally also grew close to her brother-in-law Wade. She was often sick, and it later became clear that she suffered from a form of tuberculosis. While fighting bouts of illness and trying to make herself at home in her new surroundings, Sally came to appreciate that beneath Wade's reticence lay sincerity and compassion; that "in his way" he was as gentle and kind as her husband Frank. Though his "singularly unpretending manners" might make him seem "indifferent," Sally asserted that "his constant thoughtfulness of others and forgetfulness of self, his thorough goodness of heart and purity of mind warms you in a moment. . . . Half a dozen times in the day brother Wade will come to my [sickroom] to inquire about me and always with some suggestion for my comfort that shows he really thinks about it. Now that I am out and about, tho' still suffering from the pain, he watches me, sees when I am tired and notices the least indication of pain."[3]

By the time of Frank's wedding, Wade himself may have begun to seriously contemplate remarriage. In the early spring of 1853, he had become a financial adviser and friend to Mary Singleton McDuffie, the twenty-four-year-old daughter of Senator George McDuffie and the granddaughter of Colonel Richard Singleton, who had been the closest friend of Wade II. Within the space of two years Mary had lost her father, grandfather, and uncle, and had gone to live with a widowed aunt on the outskirts of Columbia. Mary had inherited a large plantation with hundreds of slaves, but she now had no male relatives to help her manage her estate. Southern society neither expected nor trained most women to handle complex business matters. In short, Mary was in trouble, and the Singleton family asked Colonel Wade Hampton II for advice. Hampton delegated his oldest widowed son to help Mary.[4]

Wade Hampton III thus assumed the role of chivalric protector of a lady. Mary wrote to tell him that she wished to sell all or most of her slaves, probably to clear herself of debts inherited from her father, simplify her estate, and secure a reliable income. In his long, detailed reply of March 1, 1853, Hampton suggested several options for liquidating her estate and provided the names of reputable merchants, slave traders, and attorneys.

Hampton's advice demonstrated that he was experienced in dealing with such matters and that while he had some interest in the slaves' ultimate fate and destination, his primary concern was helping a female member of his own race and class. Hampton explained that Mary could sell all or perhaps one hundred of her slaves immediately, and that he could arrange a sale with "some desirable purchaser, & humane master, in this country." He warned, however, that she would not get the optimal price that late in the season, that the slaves might become ill at that time, and that she would lose her "prospects for a crop" that year. He advised, instead, that she make a "list of your negroes . . . in which the name, age, & qualifications, of each negro, would be accurately given." Hampton would then find a purchaser who was willing to buy on Mary's terms. "I can put a duplicate list," he added, "in the hands of Beard &

May, or some other good auctioneers in N.O. who can also endeavor to find a purchaser." This, he thought, would enable Mary to make an "advantageous sale," perhaps one in which the purchaser made annual payments at interest. "Suppose for example, that you get $75.000 or 100 of your negroes. The interest at 8 pr. Ct. would amount of course to $6000 pr. Ann. If you make the first note payable in five years, & one fifth of the principal payable every year after that, you would receive, besides the interest, $15.000 pr. Ann & the last payment would be made in nine years."[5]

Hampton's letter to Mary McDuffie reveals the limits of planter paternalism and the assumptions about race and white privilege on which it was built. Paternalist slaveholders could make claims about their own benevolence, but such claims would make no sense without the assumption that slaveholders had the unchallenged right to treat human beings like property. Hampton was among the more humane slaveowners, but even he was quite capable of regarding African Americans as capital assets rather than as people. He had no assurance that merchants or auctioneers in New Orleans would try to keep slave families together. More likely, husbands would be separated from their wives and children from their mothers as the auctioneers tried to get the best price for Mary McDuffie and her male adviser. But this was not Hampton's primary concern. His main objectives were protecting Mary's financial security and proving himself a worthy male protector of a white woman. The slaves' welfare and happiness came in a distant second place.[6]

Hampton made several visits to Mary's residence to discuss her financial affairs. She was a shy young lady with delicate features, blue eyes, and long, dark hair cascading in curls onto her shoulders. She did not share Hampton's interest in outdoor activities such as horseback riding, but they both enjoyed books and poetry. It was probably some time, however, before Hampton felt a strong romantic attachment. As seen in his 1855 letter to Mary Fisher, he was still deeply grieving the loss of Margaret two years after beginning a friendship with Mary McDuffie.[7]

But Hampton continued to visit Mary at her aunt's home and eventually began to court her in earnest. He had finally allowed himself to heal from Margaret's death. Moreover, he certainly noticed and probably envied the domestic bliss enjoyed by his brother Frank and his new wife Sally. On Valentine's Day, 1857, Hampton composed a love poem of four stanzas and sent it to Mary from Wild Woods. The first verse

referred to his leaving Columbia for Mississippi the preceding November, anxiously wondering whether her romantic feelings for him would
survive his absence until spring:

When the birds to their southern homes so bright,
Were planning their flight last November,
They promised me, a fair lady to see,
And tell me if she could remember.—

The birds were to tell Mary of his longing for her and gauge her reaction. The fourth verse concluded:

Ah me! Will she listen to day, and believe
In the notes of their musical letters?
Will her smile come to bless? Or must I confess
To the wish—that I never had met her.[8]

By the fall, Hampton and Mary McDuffie had made plans to marry.
On January 27, 1858, the thirty-nine-year-old Hampton and twenty-
eight year-old Mary were wed in her aunt's home. While they honey-
mooned for a few days at the plantation of some of Mary's relatives,
Hampton's father and brother Kit left immediately for Mississippi, accompanied by sisters Ann and Caroline, their black maids, and the elder
Hampton's servant, Daddy Carolina. Hampton and his new bride followed on February 1, arriving in New Orleans by February 12.[9]

There Hampton met some family friends, the Duncans, who gave him
the stunning news that Wade II had died a few days before at his Walnut
Ridge plantation. Hampton had had no chance to tell his father goodbye.
Kit and Daddy Carolina were already taking the body back to Columbia
for burial, while Ann and Caroline mourned at Walnut Ridge.[10]

The death of Colonel Wade Hampton II was an unexpected blow to
all of his children. Hampton's four unmarried sisters had lost not only a
beloved father, but also their primary male protector and provider, and
now would naturally be expected to rely on their brothers, especially
Wade. Hampton, too, had been close to his father and grieved deeply.

He dealt with the situation along two parallel and mutually reinforcing courses of action. First, he put aside his own sadness enough to
quickly move into the role of protector, just as southern society had
always trained him to do. Initially, though, there seemed to be too
many who needed protection, reassurance, and comfort—more than
one mortal could provide. Over the next two months, Hampton wrote at
least twelve letters to Mary Fisher, all of which attempted to comfort his

Mary Singleton McDuffie Hampton (1830–74). Wade Hampton III's second wife. Historic Columbia Foundation.

sisters and children. Besides writing letters, he also had to handle logistics. On hearing of his father's death, Hampton immediately traveled upriver to Walnut Ridge to collect Ann and Caroline, leaving his new wife in New Orleans with the Duncans. He then escorted his sisters to New Orleans and offered to accompany them back to Columbia. They instead went home in the company of their relative John Preston, while Hampton made a fast trip to Wild Woods to see that his vitally important cotton crop was being ginned, baled, and shipped to warehouses. Then he and Mary went on to Columbia for the funeral before returning to Mississippi.[11]

Handling these details and writing letters, however, did not provide enough comfort for either Hampton or his sisters. Hampton therefore pursued another tack as well. Relying on his growing religious faith, he told his sisters, as well as himself, to trust to God for comfort. Within twenty-four hours of hearing the sad news, Hampton wrote to Mary Fisher, immediately assuming the simultaneous roles of pastor and patriarch. His youngest and emotionally closest sister had also been the most dependent on him, while he had trusted her with raising his small children. The protective tone of his February 12 letter may seem condescending to modern readers, but it illuminates the role he expected, and was expected, to play:

You know how dearly I love you, my own little pet. . . . I feel that you *now* belong to me, that it is my duty as well as my happiness to care for you always, to be to you a *father*, as well as a *brother*: to show you always my gratitude for your tender devotion to me & to that dear baby [Harriet] whose memory is so cherished in our hearts. . . . I know that no earthly consolation can now come to any of you, my orphan sisters, but you can feel that you *all* have lived but for *him* who is now I hope with his God. You made his happiness, never for a moment did one of you forget the love & duty you owed to him. It must be a comfort then to know that you have *fully discharged every obligation to him always.* God then, our Merciful Father in heaven, will not leave you comfortless. He will come to you, & give you that peace which the world can not give, or take away. I trust in God, then & to Him do I most fervently commend you. . . .

For *my sake*, Mary, do not give way. Think how it would add to my grief to hear that you were ill or suffering. I *hope* to see you soon & to strive to comfort you. . . . My own heart is wrung with agony & I turn to *you* for comfort. Kiss dear Kate, & the children for me. We must all try to support each other, & place our load on God. Pray for me and may God bless my darling sister.

W. H.[12]

Hampton was clear that he intended to protect and provide for Kate, Caroline, and Ann as well. "I want to do all in my power," he wrote on March 8, "to replace him who has gone: to show my love & reverence *for* him, by my devotion to those dear daughters who made his happiness on earth."[13] He also strove to comfort Mary Fisher with his conviction that their father was now in heaven. "[A man] of purer and nobler impulses never lived," he wrote, "& he had surely become a *Christian*, for he did believe in the Savior & was only withheld from an open profession of his faith by his conscientious fear that he was not *good* enough to become a member of the Church. But his heart was changed, & I hope & think God knew that he was fit to be a member of *his* Church in Heaven, & took him to himself."[14]

Though ready to become a surrogate father to his sisters, Hampton did not assume authority, status, or even inheritance rights over his brothers, Kit and Frank. Colonel Wade Hampton II had died without a will. The Hamptons met at Millwood in June, and, following the example of their father after General Hampton's death, they divided the estate and its debts equitably. Those debts totaled half a million dollars. Wade acquired the largest amount of land, but he also shouldered the largest responsibility for paying his father's debts. He took over the Walnut Ridge estate in Mississippi, along with its slaves and its $400,000 mortgage. Kit renounced any claim to his father's Mississippi or Carolina holdings, but he also assumed none of the debt. Instead, he kept his own holdings and took his father's 2,000 acres in Wisconsin, which he sold for five dollars on the eve of the Civil War. Frank took over most of the Woodlands complex around Columbia, along with $100,000 of debt. The sisters received the Millwood mansion, considered the family seat, along with its 1,079 acres and 39 slaves. Hampton thus emerged as the largest landholder among his siblings, but only time would tell whether the burden of debts would crush him.[15]

With his father's death, Hampton had once again suffered a deep loss. Margaret and little Harriet had been gone for only a few years, and now his father was, too. But there was still much to protect and much to hope for. He had a new wife, and the rest of his family was still intact. His remaining children—Wade IV, Preston, and Sally—were thriving, as were his four sisters and two brothers. Soon Mary McDuffie would bear him a new brood of children. Frank and his wife Sally were happy and producing Hampton nephews and nieces. Moreover, Hampton had his father's name and legacy to carry on. He must continue to be a benevolent provider and protector, a humane master, and prove himself worthy of his name and social status. Maybe, just maybe, his life could now go on with peace and continued prosperity. A few good cotton crops, no major disasters, and life could go on as before—with a healthy wife and children and plenty of time to hunt, fish, and travel. As he assumed the mantle of responsibility for his entire family, Wade Hampton found that he had come to value peace and stability more than ever.

PART II ★ CHIVALRY

CHAPTER 4

THE APPIAN WAY
OF THE CONSTITUTION

As much as Hampton wanted tranquility and stability, there were danger signs on the horizon. For one thing, his financial obligations were increasing. Even before assuming his father's debts, Hampton had borrowed $170,000 from the Bank of Louisiana at New Orleans in 1855. He had overstretched himself in his rapid expansion in Mississippi in the 1840s and early 1850s. Within a decade, he had bought his Wild Woods, Bayou Place, Richland, and Otterbourne plantations in Washington County, for a total of over 8,000 acres. These cotton plantations adjoined his Bear Garden, a 2,085-acre hunting preserve. He had also built, with his father and brother Kit, a lodge and several cottages in Cashiers Valley in the North Carolina mountains. He did not appear to be concerned about his situation until he took over his father's debts of $400,000 in 1858.[1]

Even then, Hampton felt that with a few good cotton crops and a stable economy, he could keep ahead of his creditors and regain financial security. But the 1858 cotton crop was a disappointment. Severe flooding along the Mississippi in April severely delayed planting and at one point threatened to destroy his prospect for any crop at all.[2] There was more flooding in the spring of 1859. His crop that year turned out better than he expected, but not good enough to help his overall financial situation. As he told Mary Fisher, "My places look desolate to the last degree."[3] The year 1860 was no better. As he began planting in February, Hampton realized that "all the objects for which I have labored these last two years, will fail" if he could not make a good crop this time. A heavy frost struck in October, and by November 4 he sadly concluded that "the crops are too far gone to improve. . . . on all these places the cotton is very bad. Tult [Hampton's overseer] is greatly dispirited about this, but says that 'if his life had depended on making a good crop he could not have tried harder.' "[4] Through a combination of unwise investments, his father's debts, and three years of bad weather, Hampton was rapidly heading for financial ruin.

Just as ominous was the worsening political situation of the 1850s, both in South Carolina and in the nation as a whole. Radical secessionists had more influence in South Carolina than in any other state. 49

Known as "fire-eaters," some had been agitating for secession as far back as the nullification crisis, regardless of whether other southern states followed South Carolina's lead.

Hampton was never enthusiastic about secession and only reluctantly supported it once his state was irrevocably committed to leaving the Union. Even then, he hoped that secession would not mean war. For him, disunion could only bring political turmoil, domestic unrest, and possibly war. The Hamptons had thrived within the Union, whatever its imperfections, and saw no need for a political revolution. But the code of chivalry demanded that southern men, especially of Hampton's class, be, above all, patriotic defenders of their homes. If South Carolina seceded, and the federal government attempted to coerce it to remain in the Union, Hampton would have no choice but to fight for his native state. This would particularly be the case if secessionists succeeded in defining patriotism solely as loyalty to South Carolina in opposition to the United States. Unfortunately for Hampton, that is exactly what happened.[5]

South Carolina leaders who opposed disunion never denied that the state had the constitutional right to secede; instead, they asserted that secession was not yet necessary, or that it was foolhardy for the state to leave the Union without coordinating with other slave states. As late as 1852 these conservatives, including Hampton and his father, had fought a successful rearguard action against the fire-eaters, but the latter were gaining strength. An 1852 letter from Hampton to his friend James Chesnut indicates the depth of his fear of the secession movement in South Carolina. In the wake of a recent failed attempt by fire-eaters to take the state out of the Union, Hampton worried that the battle was far from over. After urging continued support for a local antisecessionist newspaper, he asserted: "Unless a strong effort is made by our party, I do not see how we can prevent the secessionists taking the offices of Gov. & Senator, & that such is their purpose, is evident." If the secessionists were successful "when some grave question is submitted to the people," the result would be "ruin."[6]

The fire-eaters gained momentum after 1854 with the passage of the Kansas-Nebraska Act. The new law was a tactical victory for the South, as it opened the possibility of slavery spreading to territories where previously the Missouri Compromise of 1820 had prohibited it. The act infuriated northerners who passionately opposed the introduction of slavery to new territories and led to the formation of the Republican Party, an exclusively northern organization whose main drawing card was opposition to the spread of slavery. North and South also clashed over the fugitive slave law of 1850, which decreed that citizens must assist, not impede, slaveholders in search of their runaway slaves. In response, northern states passed personal liberty laws, specifically designed to counteract the federal law. Slaveholders regarded these northern state laws as violations of federal law, of the Compromise of 1850, and as proof that citizens in the North did not respect their property rights. Meanwhile, violence erupted in the Kansas Territory as antislavery and pro-slavery settlers committed atrocities against each other.

The conflict became personal with the caning of U.S. senator Charles Sumner of Massachusetts in 1856. A committed abolitionist, Sumner grossly insulted Senator Andrew P. Butler of South Carolina in a speech in the Senate. Sumner not only ridiculed the elderly Butler for expectorating when he spoke, but also charged that Butler had "polluted" himself with his "harlot," slavery. Even some of Sumner's allies were shocked at the tone of the address. At the time, Butler was ill in South Carolina, but his younger kinsman, Congressman Preston Brooks, was in Washington. Brooks regarded Sumner's speech as an intolerable attack on his family's honor, and many southerners, once they learned of it, saw it as an attack on the entire South. In fidelity to the southern traditions of honor and violence, Brooks took matters into his own hands. After several days had passed, he approached Sumner's desk as the Senate was adjourning for the day. He coolly informed Sumner that the Massachusetts senator had insulted his kinsman; then he lifted his cane and rained blows on Sumner's head until he was bleeding and barely conscious. The attack shocked the North, while southerners were elated. For once, they crowed, one of those outrageous fanatics got exactly what he deserved.

As the national political climate approached the boiling point, South Carolina moderates like Benjamin F. Perry, James L. Orr, James L. Petigru, James Johnston Pettigrew, and the Hamptons found their positions less tenable. They differed among themselves—some thought that secession was unwise and unwarranted, others felt that it was the proper course but only in coordination with other states, and still others seemed to drift between these two positions. What united them was a general caution and unease in the face of the growing strength of the secessionists. The central problem was that by appealing to caution, they made themselves vulnerable to several charges from the fire-eaters, usually implied rather than made directly. Fire-eaters insinuated that the moderates, or "submissionists," lacked patriotic devotion to South Carolina, that they could not be counted on to defend slavery from northern fanatics, and that they did not have the moral courage to defend their rights and the state's honor.

Such an atmosphere bred personal animosities among the South Carolina elite. The Hamptons and their relatives, William C. Preston and John Smith Preston, sometimes complained that the most radical fire-eaters were nouveaux riches striving to make names for themselves by stirring up trouble. Others, though, represented the leading families of South Carolina. Hampton came to despise Francis W. Pickens, the grandson of South Carolina Revolutionary War hero Andrew Pickens. Francis Pickens had vacillated throughout his political career from being a moderate states' rights politician to one who advocated South Carolina's immediate secession whether other slave states joined it or not. After winning the governor's seat in 1860, he led the state's angry response to Federal moves in the Fort Moultrie–Fort Sumter crisis. In a letter to Mary Fisher in late 1861, Hampton referred to him as "that fool Pickens."[7] Some of these animosities even survived the war. Many years later, Wade's son-in-law noted bitterly that, unlike Hampton, the blowhards who had questioned Hampton's patriotism during the secession crisis had done virtually nothing when the time came for fighting.[8]

One of the moderates' ideas was to have South Carolina work within the national Democratic Party to protect the state's interests. Led by upstate lawyer James Orr and Greenville editor Benjamin Perry, Hampton and others called themselves "Union Democrats." South Carolina, which had remained relatively aloof from the national parties for several decades, sent its first delegation to the Democratic National Convention in 1856.[9]

It was also in 1856 that the fire-eaters returned to their tactic of seeking to reopen the Atlantic slave trade, banned by federal law in 1808. Governor James H. Adams endorsed the revival of the slave trade in his message to the legislature in November. Few "slave-traders," as opponents called them, seriously believed that Congress would ever repeal its ban on the slave trade, as the idea faced strong opposition even in the South. They raised the issue mainly to excite more sectional tension and secessionist fervor in the South. It would give pro-slavery advocates ideological consistency, they thought; it would also heighten the South's sense of indignation and wounded pride as northern leaders denounced the idea as yet another example of southern depravity.

Governor Adams told the legislature that the increased supply of slave labor would lower the price of southern cotton and help the South compete against producers in India and Egypt who relied on coolie labor. The reduced cost of slaves would also benefit nonslaveholding whites by giving them more opportunity to afford slaves. Benjamin Perry's newspaper, the *Southern Patriot*, retorted that the slave trade movement was a disunionist plot. Other conservatives were hesitant to speak out. William C. Preston, a former U.S. senator and Hampton's elderly half uncle, noted the central dilemma of the conservatives. "No one dares denounce [the slave trade] in a high tone of indignation for fear of being suspected of abolitionism," Preston complained. "In truth we are under a reign of terror."[10]

But a few conservatives did speak out. The house referred Adams's recommendation to a committee composed of slave trade advocates. By subtle maneuvering, however, James Orr arranged the resignation of one committee member so planter-scholar James Johnston Pettigrew could take his place and write a minority report. Pettigrew's thorough, well-researched account devastated the slave traders' arguments; even his opponents conceded its logic. He began his speech with comments aimed at the secessionists' entire agenda. It was unwise, he said, to raise new issues with the North out of spite or combativeness. Southern-ers should retain the moral high ground and stick to arguments that were fortified "by both justice and expediency."[11] They should resist the temptation to pick a fight with their northern adversaries; instead, they should abide by their deepest convictions, "the only source of true moral strength."[12]

Pettigrew's speech was a huge success. Despite the majority report's endorsement of reopening the slave trade, the house tabled the issue without debate, and the senate postponed its consideration. Pettigrew received praise and congratulations throughout the state, including a letter from Wade Hampton, who was in the state senate. The agitation, however, did not cease. Between 1856 and 1859 slave trade advocates continued to push their idea at southern commercial conventions in Savannah, Montgomery, and Vicksburg.[13]

Wade Hampton played a larger role in the slave trade debate than he did on any other antebellum issue. He offered his own resolution against the slave trade in the South Carolina Senate in 1858. The leg-islature virtually ignored it but also struck down a resolution in favor of the slave trade by a vote of 63 to 47. Hampton offered several other anti–slave trade resolutions in 1859, only the mildest of which the sen-ate's Committee on Federal Relations adopted and presented to the larger body.[14]

The reasons for Hampton's opposition to reopening the slave trade were threefold. First, the idea offended his basic conservatism. Like other opponents, as well as supporters of the slave trade, he saw the measure as a means to exacerbate sectional tensions and propel the South out of the Union. This was the Union his grandfather had helped build and his father had helped defend. Hampton dreaded war and instability, and to him it was secession, not union, that threatened to bring those about. He deplored what he considered the fanaticism of northern abolitionists but saw it as only as an indirect threat to slavery, the South, and his own prosperity. The abolitionists were dangerous only in that they insulted his fellow southerners' sense of honor and fed secessionist sentiment in the South. Indeed, the arrival of many thousands of "uncivilized" Africans on southern plantations seemed more of a threat to the South's social stability than the rantings of distant abolitionists. As Hampton confided to University of South Carolina professor Francis Lieber, "What number of negroes will be in Ama. in 1870, 1880 or 1900? About 400,000 were imported & there are 4 millions now."[15] Hampton may also have heeded Pettigrew's warning that an increased supply of slave labor would hurt established planters like himself by making his slave property less valuable. Since Hampton's finances were far from secure at this time, it must have crossed his mind.

A second consideration was one of basic humanity. Paternalistic slaveholders like Hampton liked to consider themselves humane, whereas events in South Carolina were a vivid reminder of the inhumanity of the Atlantic slave trade before its abolition in 1808.

The first such event was the arrival of the slave ship *Echo* in Charleston Harbor in 1858. The *Echo*, based in New Orleans, had been sailing off the Cuban coast when it was captured by a U.S. Navy vessel, the USS *Dolphin*, and taken to the South Carolina port. The captain of the vessel was tried in Boston, but the rest of the crew was imprisoned in Charleston. Prominent secessionists and pro–slave traders defended the crew members in federal court, and a Charleston jury found them not guilty in April 1859. Meanwhile, South Carolina newspapers ran lurid stories of the appalling condition of the survivors. In the holds of the ship, the slave traders had packed approximately 318 Africans, nude, in the "spoon fashion." One hundred seventy died on the journey; the survivors were emaciated, "skeletonlike," and diseased.[16]

The appearance of the *Echo* created a sensation. Even some former pro–slave traders were horrified. The shocking condition of the Africans on board offended Hampton's brand of paternalism, as well as that of many others who desperately wished to convince themselves that slavery was a humane institution. Hampton told the legislature in 1859 that it would be not only impolitic but also immoral to repeal the ban on the Atlantic slave trade. It would be unwise to reestablish the slave trade even if "the public voice of christendom [sic], which has so loudly, unitedly and justly stigmatized this traffic as unholy, could be silenced, or [if] the still, small voice, which is continually speaking to our hearts, could be hushed."[17]

As one study has shown, however, many South Carolinians, even antisecessionists, did not wish to condemn the slave trade as immoral, but only as "inexpedient."[18] Some pro–slave trade lawyers gladly took up the legal defense of the *Echo*'s crew. In the spring 1859 session of the General Assembly another lawmaker once again raised the issue, proposing that the legislature resolve that it would be expedient for the state of South Carolina to reopen the slave trade. Hampton offered an opposing resolution, then moved successfully that consideration of both proposals be delayed until the fall session. In the fall, slave trade advocates held meetings in Charleston and Mount Pleasant.[19]

At the fall session, the slave traders submitted a different resolution —one that went further than the last one by claiming that the federal law of 1807 prohibiting the importation of slaves was not just inexpedient for South Carolina, but in fact unconstitutional. Hampton proposed an opposing motion: "*Resolved*, That if it were practicable to reestablish this trade, it should not be done, because it would be disastrous to the slaveholding States of the Confederacy; would institute a traffic which would necessarily involve cruel and inhuman practices; and would, by the introduction of barbarians from Africa, demoralize the slaves now owned in the United States, and infect, with evil influences, the whole system of domestic slavery as now established and existing in the United States."[20]

The senate referred the issue to the Committee on Federal Relations, in which the pro–slave trade resolution became the minority report. The committee rejected Hampton's first resolution cited above, but accepted a milder one from him that ignored moral considerations and restricted itself to the constitutional and practical objections to reopening the slave trade.[21]

A third reason for Hampton's steadfast opposition to reopening the slave trade was his belief that the issue touched on basic notions of honorable behavior among gentlemen. Congress' law banning the Atlantic slave trade was based on an agreement reached by the Constitution's founders in 1787. Honor and chivalry demanded that gentlemen stand by the agreements and pledges they had made. For Hampton, along with many other Americans, the Constitution was simply that—a series of agreements and bargains that thirteen states and thousands of gentlemen had sworn to honor.

This was the thrust of Hampton's speech to the state senate on December 10, 1859—his most well-known antebellum speech and the only one extant from his service in the legislature. He argued that not only did Congress have the power to prohibit the Atlantic slave trade after 1808, but also that that prohibition "was intended by the framers of the Constitution. . . . The clause in the Constitution which gives this power to Congress, was the result of a compromise between the North and the South that the South agreed to close her ports against the importation of Africans after 1808, on condition that the traffic should be allowed until that time; while the North was compensated for this concession by the abrogation of the clause in the Constitution relating to a Navigation Act."[22] Hampton correctly asserted that southern and northern leaders who helped form the republic understood, accepted, and defended the compromise involving the slave trade as a "compact between the Representatives of conflicting interests."[23] He cited several founders and their contemporaries, North and South, including Robert Barnwell and Charles Cotesworth Pinckney of South Carolina, as acknowledging and defending the deal that had been struck. He also quoted the greatest of the next generation of South Carolina statesmen, John C. Calhoun, who not only accepted the prohibition of the slave trade, but also expressed shame that "that odious traffic" lasted as long as it did.[24] The fact that the prohibition was part of a "compact" between sovereign states with "conflicting interests" led Hampton to what he considered the central point: abiding by the agreement was a matter of honor and integrity. As a compact, "it possesses almost the sanctity of a constitutional provision, urging us, by every principle of honor and good faith, to abide by it fully and unhesitatingly."[25]

Hampton's 1859 speech reveals much about his attitudes toward the sectional crisis. While arguing against the slave trade, he took the opportunity to explain his beliefs on the Union, states' rights, abolitionism, slavery, and the importance of maintaining southern unity. First, Hampton put himself on record as a defender of states' rights. "The States forming this Confederacy were sovereign," he asserted, "and each State still retains, as is declared in the Constitution, all the powers not delegated to the United States by the Constitution, nor prohibited, by it, to the States." But those sovereign states "*intended* to vest in Congress" the right to regulate the slave trade.[26]

Hampton feared the breakup of the Union, "consecrated by the blood of patriots and sanctified by woman's blessings," "bequeathed to us by our fathers, and established by their prayers and their swords." That Union was endangered by northern and southern fanatics, including greedy slave trade advocates. Both groups, out of arrogance and selfishness, claimed adherence to a "higher law" greater than the received wisdom of the Founding Fathers and true Christianity. Both groups consisted of "ignorant, reckless, or wicked men" who were capable of wrecking "in an hour" what it had taken years of blood and toil to build. Once the Union was gone, its virtues could never be called back. It would never be the same again; it could never again protect the liberty and prosperity of the South as it had for so long.[27]

The true source of northern agitation over slavery, Hampton argued, was not enlightened principle but hatred. "I have always believed," he said, "that the great battle we are waging with the black cohorts of Abolitionism could best be won by us, fighting in the Union and under the Constitution." With "profound regret," however, Hampton warned that unless "the good and true men of the North" rebuked the spirit of hostility that was growing against the South, and unless memories of the Revolution and respect for the Constitution revived the older fraternal feelings between North and South, "I do not see how the Union *can be* or *should be* preserved." "Mr. President," Hampton continued, "I have heard this sentiment spoken exultingly, but I confess that I utter it mournfully. . . . The ark of freedom may be overthrown . . . and liberty herself be forced to weep over the untimely grave of her youngest and fairest child."[28]

Hampton expressed disgust for fanatic southerners as well, especially those who claimed the moral right to buy and sell African slaves regardless of federal law. They were recklessly "ignoring all constitutional, legal or moral obligations" when they appealed to a "higher law" than that of the federal government. " 'Slaves of the accused thirst of gold,' " he charged, "do not hesitate to advocate the violation of the laws against the slave trade; and placing themselves on the platform of the '*higher law*,' they eulogize those as *patriots* whom the law more justly pronounces *pirates*. With this party—if they may be dignified by the name of a party—I have and can have no sympathy; for I regard them as the worst enemies the South has to contend with."[29]

Clearly, Hampton regarded any philosophy—abolitionism, free trade, secession—that claimed superiority over the wisdom of the Founding Fathers as heresy and humbuggery. Advocates of such philosophies "trampl[ed] the Constitution and Bible alike under their feet."[30] Implied also was Hampton's belief that the Constitution sanctioned slavery.

His speech ended with a simultaneous call for southern unity, a plea for the Constitution, and a rhetorical flourish appealing to personal duty and faith in God. With the Union in such grave danger, he placed his dwindling hopes of its preservation in the remaining "good and true men of the North" and in southern unity. Earlier he had acknowledged that some advocates of the slave trade were "sincere and patriotic."[31] They took their stand because they feared the collapse of the Union and reasoned that the South's safest course was to leave it as soon as possible; advocating the reopening of the slave trade would bring that about more quickly. Hampton respectfully disagreed. The slave trade issue actually divided the South rather than united it. Was there not some other platform, consistent with the Constitution, on which all the South could unite? "The South," he argued, "should studiously avoid making any new issue that might divert her from the only true one, which is the union of the South for the preservation of the South and the Constitution."[32] Hampton concluded:

> Mr. President, some years ago it was my good fortune to hear one of the most distinguished and eloquent of British statesmen defend the constitution of his country from what he regarded as an attack upon it. In the course of his speech he used these striking words, "I stand on the Appian way [sic] of the Constitution!" I would have every son of South Carolina to place himself on the Appian Way of the Constitution; and occupying that strong and proud position, let each of us adopt, as his motto, that noble sentiment which was uttered by one of her most patriotic sons, and which was, during a life of devotion to his State, the ruling principle of his life, "Do your duty, and leave the consequences to God."[33]

Hampton's speech brought him accolades, even from the North. Horace Greeley's *New York Tribune* called it "a masterpiece of logic, directed by the noblest sentiments of the Christian and patriot."[34] In South Carolina, it nailed the coffin shut on further agitation for the slave trade. Though Georgia, Alabama, and Louisiana had already enacted laws to revive the "unholy traffic," South Carolina fire-eaters gave up on the idea. They decided that other tactics were more likely to unite the state in the cause of secession.[35]

Hampton won the battle against reopening the slave trade, but in his broader purpose of checking the secessionist impulse in South Carolina, he was fighting against the tide, as he himself recognized. South Carolina radicalism on the larger issue of secession was rising to fever pitch even as Hampton worked within the General Assembly to stop the slave trade agitation. John Brown's raid on the federal arsenal at Harpers Ferry, Virginia, stoked the flames even higher. With donations from northern abolitionists, Brown launched an expedition on October 16, 1859, to capture weapons from the arsenal, arm the slave population, and incite a slave rebellion. The news sent a shock wave through the entire South, touching the deepest fear of a slaveholding society: rebellion. The realization that many northerners regarded Brown as a hero and martyr compounded white southerners' shock and outrage. "Are we really safer in this Union than out of it?" politicians asked their constituents. "Do we really want to share this Union with countrymen who would arm our slaves?" The Constitution was supposed to "secure domestic tranquility." Instead, they concluded, thousands of Yankees wished to see their southern countrymen murdered in their beds by their own servants.

In the wake of John Brown's raid, it became harder and harder for South Carolina Unionists to stand against the tide. Mary Boykin Chesnut of Columbia confided to her diary that "nobody could live in [South Carolina] unless he were a fire-eater."[36] Hampton's close relative and good friend, John Smith Preston, gravitated toward secession, as did the old family enemy, James Henry Hammond. Hammond thundered in the U.S. Senate that "you do not dare make war on Cotton. Cotton is King!" Preston did one better by responding that "slavery is our king—slavery is our truth—slavery is our Divine Right."[37] Hampton's sentiments were closer to those of John Preston's older brother, former U.S. senator William C. Preston. In 1857 William wrote that "the fanaticism of abolitionism has generated an equal fanaticism in our own section."[38] But the elder Preston also believed that the North had no right to interfere with slavery. Doing so would destroy southern property rights, domestic order, and "everything we hold dear in our society. . . . Altho I think the institution of slavery is a most unfortunate one, yet no foreign panacea can be permitted to meddle with it. Blood and burning and unuterrable [sic] calamity would be the inevitable consequence. . . . We are a magazine round which crackers are exploding."[39]

Occasionally even the most cautious conservatives and dedicated Unionists exploded with indignation. In November 1859, only weeks before Hampton's anti–slave trade speech, Benjamin Perry offered a resolution defending slavery, "which [South Carolinians] are prepared to protect and defend at any and every sacrifice of their political relations with the Federal Government and the Northern States, should it be invaded or assailed in any manner."[40] Perry later regretted the fervor of this statement, but it reflected the climate of opinion in the state as a whole, especially as it came in the immediate wake of John Brown's raid. Nearly a year later, Unionist James Orr reacted vehemently to the possibility of Abraham Lincoln becoming the next president of the United States: "No Black Republican President . . . should ever execute any law within our borders unless at the point of the bayonet and over the dead bodies of our slain sons."[41]

Other than his December 1859 speech on the slave trade, Hampton remained virtually silent on the question of secession, at least in public. Friends knew that he still opposed disunion, but he stayed out of the limelight for most of the momentous year of 1860. By early February he was back in Mississippi, desperately hoping for a decent cotton crop and fretting over the health of his one-year-old son McDuffie, who, he learned, was not well. "My heart has been very sad since I heard of my boy's sickness," he wrote Mary Fisher, "but I pray to God to have mercy on me. I will go home just as soon as I can."[42] Hampton struggled to reconcile his desire to be with McDuffie with his need to oversee the planting of his cotton crop. Knowing that such operations were reaching a crisis point, he simply could not neglect his business in Mississippi. "Everything is at stake now, so that it is important for me to make a crop this year," he explained.[43]

Within a few days, Hampton received word that McDuffie, "my dear boy," was well. He rejoiced that "God has indeed been merciful to me in restoring the dear little fellow."[44] He returned to Columbia in the spring. In May the national Democratic Party held its convention in Charleston, the hotbed of secessionist sentiment in the South. Hampton did not attend. John Smith Preston, however, was elected chairman of the South Carolina delegation. Delegates from the Deep South states insisted that the party adopt a plank in its platform protecting slavery in the territories. When the convention rejected their demand they walked out, breaking up the convention. The Democratic Party then split, with the southern faction holding a new convention in Richmond and the other faction meeting in Baltimore. The southerners nominated John C. Breckenridge, a states' rights advocate and a relative of the Prestons, as their presidential candidate. The National Democrats chose Stephen A. Douglas of Illinois. A third-party candidate, John Bell, also emerged. With the Democrats divided, it seemed likely that Abraham Lincoln, the Republican, would win.[45]

Hampton's reaction to these events is unrecorded. In June he took his wife Mary to Washington to have some dental work done. He soon escorted her back to Columbia but departed again for Mississippi in October to oversee the harvest and its sale. Again family and business matters occupied his mind. Hampton was concerned about Mary, who was six months' pregnant. He also inquired about little McDuffie. "No doubt McDuffie misses me more than anyone else does," he teased his sister, "and when I get back, we shall see whether he loves you the best."[46] Despite his playfulness in letters, Hampton was once again disappointed in his crops. This was the year when a heavy October frost had damaged his cotton, prompting him to write on November 4 that his crop was "very bad."[47]

During this period Hampton tried to follow the political situation, which was even less encouraging. By autumn it was becoming obvious that Abraham Lincoln of Illinois would win the national election. In South Carolina, therefore, much depended on whether unilateral secessionists or cooperationists would gain control of the legislature in the October state elections. This was because conditional unionism in South Carolina was dead. Assuming Lincoln won the presidency, the immediate question would not be whether the state would secede, but whether it would do so alone or in conjunction with other southern states. Once the legislature met and chose presidential electors, would it adjourn? Or would it stay in session long enough to learn whether Lincoln had won, then call for a state convention to vote on secession? Hampton wanted to know, and in late October he commissioned Mary Fisher to be his political informant—"Try . . . to find out about the Legislature & let me know what it is thought will be done."[48] In early November he told her: "I am in expectation of hearing very soon what the Legislature will do and if the Session is continued until the fourth Monday in Nov. I must go on [home] though I shall dislike to do so. If they only remain in Session, for a few days, then there will be no necessity for me to be there."[49]

Even before Lincoln's victory, many South Carolinians had already decided that his success would justify secession, whether other states followed the Palmetto State's lead or not. The personal liberty laws passed years before by northern states, they reasoned, were already proof that northerners were willing to violate the Constitution in order to deny southerners their property rights in slaves. Years of bitter feuds, insults, and accusations had convinced most that most Yankees not only despised them, but also wished them ill. Most South Carolinians associated Abraham Lincoln and all Republicans with abolitionism and the radicalism of John Brown. For them, a Republican victory meant the triumph of abolitionism and the end of sectional neutrality within the national government. As a result, white yeoman farmers and laborers would be forced to compete with thousands of black freedmen for land, economic independence, and status. For many citizens, abolitionism was synonymous with social equality and racial mixing. Greenville's Reverend Richard Furman warned fellow whites that Lincoln's election would mean that "if you are tame enough to submit, abolition preachers will be at hand to consummate the marriage of your daughters to black husbands."[50]

The South Carolina legislature did indeed remain in session after receiving the news of Lincoln's victory—long enough to call for a state convention in Columbia on December 17. By that time Hampton had been back in the city for several weeks. Meanwhile, he signaled that though he had once opposed secession, he too believed that South Carolina's rights as a state were not safe under a Republican administration. In that situation, he refused to act as a traitor to South Carolina. Hampton was then captain of the Richland Light Dragoons, a volunteer company whose social functions were more important than its military ones. In late November the company met and unanimously resolved "That the Captain of the Richland Light Dragoons be and is hereby requested to tender the services of this troop, to His Excellency, the Governor of So. Car." Hampton dutifully transmitted the resolution in a short note to Governor William H. Gist on November 24, adding only, "I take very great pleasure, Sir, in transmitting this resolution to Your Excellency."[51] Two days later he spoke to a pro-secession group called the Columbia Minute Men and firmly but calmly asserted that he now supported secession. The resolution of the Light Dragoons and Hampton's speech to the minutemen were relatively mild considering the temper of the times. They indicate, though, that Hampton had reluctantly gone over to the secessionist position. Above all, he wanted to be seen as a patriot. After explaining his recent absence in Mississippi, he assured his secessionist audience that he had rushed home as soon as he learned that the legislature would call an extra session to move toward secession. He was determined, he declared, "to be here in time to share any danger that might threaten" his state.[52]

As soon as the secession convention met in Columbia on December 17, it agreed to move to Charleston, the hotbed of secessionist sentiment. On December 20 the convention in Charleston voted 169 to 0 to take South Carolina out of the Union. Hampton, as a member of the legislature, went to Charleston as well but took no role in the convention.[53]

It is difficult to know Hampton's precise thoughts after the convention's action. One expert on the period notes that he "seemed unsettled and unsure of what role he should play."[54] Almost none of his letters from the months after the state seceded survive. He certainly did not share in the wave of euphoria sweeping over South Carolina. The correspondence of his sister-in-law, however, provides excellent clues about his political opinions and anxieties during this period.

Sally Baxter Hampton had become a southern apologist to her New York relatives and friends since settling with Frank in Columbia. Not only did she love her husband's family and home, but she also came to regard slavery as an unfortunate, though benign institution, and to look fondly but condescendingly on African American slaves—"the happy, quiet, lazy people," she called them. Accordingly, she bitterly resented the "fanatical sect" of abolitionists.[55]

Sally's letters to her father, other family members, and male friends of her father during the height of South Carolina's secession crisis are revealing for several reasons. First, she was obsessed with political developments and, being in constant contact with the Hamptons and Prestons, very familiar with the latest rumors and views, particularly those of the moderates. She followed the secession of her adopted state with anguished fascination. Second, Sally Hampton's opinions on the issues seem to match closely those of her husband and male relatives. This was a natural result of living in the same household, as well as the fact that the Hamptons' opinions were moderate enough to be reconciled with the views of a transplanted northern woman who had come to love her southern home. Finally, and most interestingly, Sally was consciously seeking to act as a mediator between moderate South Carolina leaders—her male in-laws—and influential men in the North. She explicitly told her father this in her letter of December 22: "I have written the foregoing sheets dear Papa not entirely (as you may conjecture) 'on my own hook'[;] lucky it is for me in this juncture, when I am so often called upon as a mouthpiece, that I can so easily avail myself of other people's ideas & information. I think it would be very much liked if you would make it public in some shape—either by showing it to 'inquiring friends' or thro' the newspapers."[56]

Sally's letters make it clear that Wade Hampton had reluctantly come around to support secession. He still hoped, however, that South Carolina would not act unilaterally but in cooperation with other southern states. As the secession convention debated in Charleston and the legislature was in session there, Sally reported to her northern family that "the party to which Mr Lowndes—the Prestons—Manning—Wade Hampton—Memminger—Orr—& Pettigrew belong, advocate secession but at a later date & greater moderation in all movements. They would like to hear what the North will have to say or to do."[57] The conservatives' desire "to hear what the North will have to say or to do" suggests that even then they still hoped for some conciliatory gesture from the North that would make secession unnecessary.

Sally and her Hampton relatives believed that the primary blame for the crisis rested on radical abolitionists, the arrogant "fanatical sect" that was destroying "a mighty nation . . . for the propagation of a doctrine of which the chiefs confess their presumptive ignorance. . . . When a leading abolitionist says 'I thank my God Sir that my foot has never trod slaveholding soil' does he not bring proof against himself that the belief he avows is founded on ignorance not in knowledge[?]"[58] The Hamptons also believed, though, that their South Carolina brethren were acting precipitously. While Hampton and others advocated "greater moderation in all movements," Sally acknowledged that they were fighting a losing battle. "There is no doubt a very strong tide of public opinion here which drives all the legislators *on on* more rapidly than their own judgements would allow—Wagner said 'no man would dare to postpone the day of secession—*even a month.*' They feel & say that it will not do to allow the impulse to grow cold."[59]

From December 1860 through the Fort Sumter crisis, Sally's letters reflected her own and her male friends' deep sense of foreboding and sadness. Hampton and others of his party expressed fears of "anarchy and confusion" should the Union fall apart. They feared the same results, however, under a Republican-controlled federal government of what Sally called "abolitionists and co-ercionists." Once secession occurred, she believed, as Hampton may have, that South Carolina had made a mistake, but that the decision had resulted from an instinct of self-protection. "It is useless to say," she argued, "that the South has been rash or precipitate—what she has done has been a positively essential precaution—it was a question of existence, & self-preservation is the first instinct of humanity."[60] But they mourned the death of the Union even before the deed was officially done. Sally wrote on December 14 that while the legislature was still meeting in Columbia, many members [presumably moderates] came to her and Frank's Millwood home "to open their hearts." Every one of them, she reported, expressed "heavy sorrow. . . . There are few voices that do not falter—few eyes that are not dimmed as day after day passes & all own that on the 18th this great nation will cease to have existence."[61]

After South Carolina seceded, Sally's letters began to speak of the idea of "re-union"—sometimes hopefully, sometimes despairing that it was impossible unless other northern leaders silenced the abolitionists. On January 11, in a letter to her mother, Sally mentioned that she overheard Frank, Wade, and two other political leaders talking; they "seemed to think if the Southern Constituent Convention met there would be a re-adjustment & all would go back."[62] The day before, Frank had written to his mother-in-law: "After we go out & the South unites, we may offer terms to the North—if you take them we may be reunited but if there is war we will never come back so long as we have a handful of acorns to live on."[63] Sally, Frank, and Wade probably hoped that at least war might be avoided. Still, if it did come, Wade Hampton III was determined to be in the front rank. He and his sons thus enlisted as privates in the Congaree Mounted Riflemen.[64]

Hampton also hoped for moderation on the part of his own state's leaders. Governor Francis Pickens, whom Hampton despised, had taken a very militant stance over the occupation of Fort Sumter in Charleston Harbor by Federal troops under Major Robert Anderson. Pickens and others claimed that the fort was now the property of South Carolina and insisted on Anderson's evacuation, while Anderson and U.S. authorities refused. President James Buchanan attempted to resupply the garrison via a civilian steamer, the Star of the West, flying the flag of the United States. When it entered the harbor on January 9, 1861, Citadel cadets, in obedience to orders, fired artillery rounds at the vessel and forced it to sail away.[65]

The decision to fire on the U.S. flag appalled Hampton. This was not the moderation that would facilitate reunification. Sally Hampton feared that "the enthusiasm & excitement of so many unoccupied men [around Charleston Harbor] will get beyond control & so I think do many of the cooler heads in Charleston." She reported that "Wade Hampton reprobates most strongly the firing on the 'Star of the West' & is entirely disgusted with the manner in which matters [sic] conducted down there."[66]

Obviously Sally Hampton's letters provide compelling insight into her brother-in-law's state of mind as he anxiously watched his native state leave the Union. He still counseled moderation and caution, and he still held a desperate, faint hope that the North would make adequate guarantees and concessions to the South—concessions that would cool the ardor of southern nationalists. He felt that the last thing that was needed was southern artillery shells lobbed at ships flying the U.S. flag. Yet he was determined to leave no room for fellow South Carolinians to charge him with being less than a patriot.

Those who dreaded the prospect of war must have been relieved at the U.S. government's failure to react to the *Star of the West* incident. Months passed with no more overtly hostile acts, and President Buchanan did nothing to retaliate for South Carolina's firing on the U.S. flag. Hoping for the best, Wade Hampton journeyed back to Mississippi. As other Deep South states seceded, South Carolinians felt that their position vis-à-vis Washington was stronger. In February and March 1861 delegates from South Carolina, Mississippi, Florida, Alabama, Georgia, Louisiana, and Texas, meeting in Montgomery, formed the Confederate States of America. Sally Baxter Hampton wrote several letters to her parents and brother in a much lighter tone, discussing tea parties and a fox hunt. When she did turn to politics, she seemed more confident that war could be averted. "You see that the Southern Confederacy is started," she wrote her brother Wyllys, "& on what basis. No *slave trade*—being the most important. I don't see now any excuse for war, but the Fort Sumter business is an ugly one."[67]

By March 19, 1861, well after the inauguration of Abraham Lincoln, Sally considered the Confederacy an established political fact, and it is likely that her brother-in-law Wade did as well. She reported that "everyone feels that it has been very well conducted. Quietly & yet with infinite labor—simply & with great fore-thought. Carolina is more than content —indeed a little inclined to self-glorification because she started the work."[68] Wade Hampton, meanwhile, became a loyal Confederate citizen. As he headed back to Mississippi in the spring, he anticipated "some very pleasant quarrels" with his pro-Union Mississippi neighbors, the Duncans.[69] Frank Hampton—Wade's brother and Sally's husband—was in Charleston organizing the city's defenses, as was twenty-four-year-old Willie Preston, Wade and Frank's young cousin.

Yet with all the preparation for war, some still hoped for peace. According to Sally Hampton, the men busily making military preparations in Charleston "find it hard to believe . . . that there will be no war but I think we 'up-country' people are rather more credulous of the possibility of peace."[70] Amid all this military activity, Wade Hampton still waited. Knowing that his sons, particularly Preston, were eager for military service, he wrote Mary Fisher from Mississippi that seventeen-year-old Preston "must enter college."[71] Clearly Hampton still hoped for peace.

Those hopes shattered in mid-April 1861 while Hampton was in Mississippi. The standoff at Fort Sumter reached an impasse and, in the early morning hours of April 13, Confederate forces around Charleston Harbor fired on Major Robert Anderson's U.S. Army garrison. The fort surrendered thirty-four hours later. In Washington, President Abraham Lincoln immediately switched from a policy of conciliation to coercion, calling for a naval blockade of all southern ports and for the Union's remaining states to provide seventy-five thousand volunteers to suppress the "rebellion" of the seven seceded states.

Wade Hampton hesitated no longer. There was now no possibility of preserving the peace and stability that he longed for. The only way to regain it, in fact, was with the sword. Maybe a successful revolution would remove the discord, instability, and constant agitation from South Carolina politics by eliminating once and for all the northern threat to slavery. Besides, Lincoln had essentially declared war on Hampton's native state to coerce its return to the union. Hampton had never really wanted South Carolina to secede but was always adamant that it had the right to do so. Hundreds of thousands of southerners, not only in the seven Deep South states, but now also in North Carolina, Virginia, Tennessee, and Arkansas, found Lincoln's actions an intolerable insult to their honor. To allow coercion by outside forces was the very definition of slavery, and white southern honor, manhood, and independence defined themselves in opposition to slavery. A man who did not assert his own independence and that of his native state was neither honorable nor free, and the absence of honor and freedom was slavery itself.[72]

If those reasons were not enough, home defense was at the core of the chivalric code. A true knight could never sit idly by while armed men invaded his native land, stole his political independence, and disarmed him, thereby leaving his women and children defenseless. In such a situation, any man raised under the code of chivalry, but particularly a grandson of Wade Hampton I, sought to transform himself into a warrior lest he dishonor himself and his family.

For Hampton, chivalry, honor, and patriotism allowed no other course but war after Lincoln's proclamation in April 1861. Many other white southerners reached the same conclusion, and the Upper South states of Virginia, North Carolina, Tennessee, and Arkansas, where moderates—like Hampton—had previously been in control, now seceded and joined the Confederacy.

Hampton had always considered himself a patriot and a true South Carolinian. If there was going to be a new nation, it would not do for a Hampton to be any less the warrior and founding father than Wade I had been. Hampton's grandfather had proven his patriotism on the battlefield, and so had his father. Yet during the secession crisis, some South Carolina politicians had quietly questioned the patriotism and state loyalty of Wade Hampton III. Now that war had come, Hampton resolved that no one would ever be able to do that again.

MANASSAS BAPTISM OF FIRE

Wade Hampton III was in Mississippi when he heard the electrifying news of Fort Sumter. Eager to prove his patriotic devotion was worthy of a Hampton, he took several steps to place himself at the center of the Confederate revolution. "I trust that I may yet have the opportunity of proving that I can do the State some service," he wrote his youngest sister. "I want a place where I can do real hard work; not one where the only duty is to wear a uniform."[1] First, he left his Mississippi lands in the hands of overseers and traveled east, stopping in the Confederate capital of Montgomery, Alabama, along the way to confer with President Jefferson Davis. Hampton offered to form a "legion" of approximately one thousand South Carolina recruits, to consist of six companies of infantry, four troops of cavalry, and one artillery battery. He would equip the unit largely at his own expense. Davis would officially authorize the raising of the legion on April 27. Hampton additionally offered his entire 1861 cotton crop to the Confederacy, an incredibly generous act considering his own financial woes. Then he stopped in the upstate South Carolina town of Greenville to confer with his old political ally, former Unionist Benjamin Perry, who now declared his unconditional support for the Confederacy. Next Hampton rejoined his wife Mary at their Diamond Hill residence in Columbia; from there, the couple proceeded to Charleston, where Hampton began placing advertisements for recruits to fill the ranks of his new legion. Though he had offered his services to Governor Pickens as a private, everyone involved, including Pickens, Hampton, and Davis, operated on the assumption that Hampton would soon hold a colonel's commission. It would not do for a man of Hampton's wealth and social position to waste his presumed abilities in the ranks.[2]

Hampton spent late April and May feverishly working to organize and equip his legion. By the first week of May, he had drawn more volunteers than he was authorized to accept. He established "Camp Hampton" on the grounds of Frank's Woodlands plantation and began to inspect the volunteer companies that reported, select the ones he found most promising, choose his field-grade officers, and oversee the election of captains and lieutenants by the men. He specified that his cavalrymen would provide their own horses and weapons, while en- 69 deavoring to obtain the most modern firearms (Enfield rifles) for his infantry. He also ordered rifled cannon to be shipped from England. Hampton's enthusiasm spread to his relatives. "All the Hamptons & Prestons & Mannings," wrote Captain James Conner, "do nothing but think and talk and work for the Legion."[3] The young officer boasted that he had drilled his company "pretty hard and you would scarcely know them, they have improved so much."[4]

Meanwhile, the training of the legion became as much a social event as a military one. Most of the officers and even the enlisted men were from the finest families of South Carolina; the Hampton Legion became the socially correct unit to join. Hampton's wife and sisters provided food, books, parties, and dances. Conner reported that "the ladies pet us terribly."[5] Meanwhile, Hampton was fortunate to commission some very capable officers. His second-in-command was Lieutenant Colonel B. J. Johnson, whose ability was widely respected, but who would not survive the first battle. The artillery battery was led by Captain Stephen D. Lee, a West Point graduate. The company commanders included Captain Conner, a thirty-one-year-old Charleston lawyer who had led Company A of the prestigious Washington Light Infantry; Edgefield lawyer Matthew Calbraith Butler; Harvard honor graduate Martin W. Gary of Abbeville; Thomas C. Taylor, and T. M. Logan. Lee, Conner, Butler, and Gary would eventually become Confederate generals. Another member of the legion was seventeen-year-old Private Thomas Preston Hampton. Though his father could no longer restrain the eager youngster, he could at least keep an eye on him in his own command. Wade IV was already an aide-de-camp to Brigadier General P. G. T. Beauregard and on his way to Virginia.[6]

At the age of forty-three, Hampton had no real military experience. Though social convention dictated that he be given a post of great authority, only time would tell whether he would prove to be a capable commander. Initially, his men respected him but did not idolize him. He was neither dashing nor charismatic on a first meeting. He wore a rather plain uniform, refrained from dramatic speeches, and was openly warm only to a select few who gained his trust. Decades later, many men described their first impressions of him fondly, but this was only after he had become a southern hero. Private John Coxe wrote that Hampton's "bearing was distinctly military, but without pompousness or egotism. His hair and beard were dark, and so were his eyes, which had a peculiar natural snappy motion that attracted attention."[7] James Conner spoke respectfully of him to his mother and was gratified that Hampton seemed to have a high opinion of him, but neither he nor many others gushed over their middle-aged commander during the first months of the war.

No one doubted that Hampton was physically capable. He was still powerfully built and well known as an excellent horseman, bear hunter, and outdoorsman. Nor did many doubt that he possessed the proper warrior spirit; if they did, Hampton seems to have been eager to prove them wrong. The blade of his sword was so flexible that Hampton could embed it in the porch at Millwood, then bend it over until the hilt touched the deck. When he released the hilt, it would spring back with the hilt touching the deck on the other side. Someone openly doubted whether such a supple blade could actually cut anything. Hampton answered by striding into the yard and, with one backhand swipe, felling a young pine as thick as a man's forearm.[8]

More importantly, Hampton instinctively grasped early on two fundamentals of military leadership. First, he was willing to lead from the front. "You must not believe a word about my being 'reckless,' " he told his wife's aunt, Mrs. Singleton, after the Battle of Manassas. "I am the personification of discretion. But to make men fight well the officers must lead."[9] Second, over time Hampton endeared himself to his men by doing all he could to accommodate their needs. Military service in wartime means frequent hunger, thirst, extreme fatigue, and exposure to the elements. Some officers' leadership extended only to protecting their reputation for courage on the battlefield, whereas Hampton constantly strove to ensure that his men had adequate food, clothing, and shelter. Years after the war Private Coxe remembered that Hampton was "ever . . . solicitous for the comfort of his men."[10] Heros von Borcke, a German native and Confederate volunteer who knew Hampton well, later asserted that Hampton "took inexhaustible interest in the care of his people, both during and after a fight, and for that they were completely devoted to him."[11] As the war progressed, Hampton sometimes annoyed his superiors with his constant demands to see that his men's basic needs were met. Douglas Southall Freeman's detailed examination of leadership in the Civil War is just one study that confirms what military officers have long recognized—soldiers who know that their leaders will "look out" for them feel more loyalty to their unit and usually perform better in combat. Both of these traits—physical courage and paternalistic concern for subordinates—were supposed trademarks of the planter class that led the Confederate war effort. Hampton's

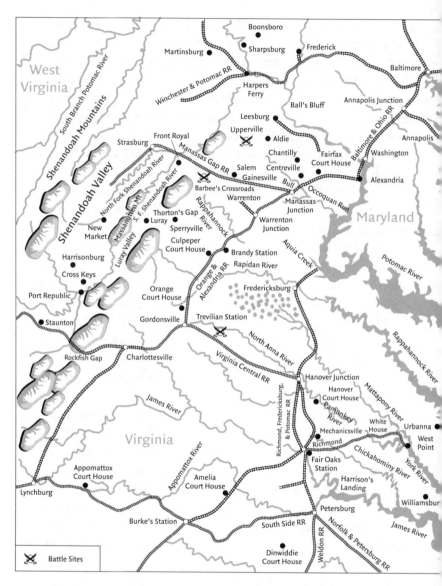

Selected Virginia Battle Sites

men expected nothing less from their aristocratic officers. Hampton expected nothing less of himself.[12]

He was conscious, in fact, not only of his own social status but also of the legacy he had inherited from his father and grandfather. The reputation of General Wade Hampton I, especially, as a South Carolina Revolutionary hero undoubtedly gave Wade III added incentive not to fail as a leader and a fighter. He carried that legacy in a very tangible way. One of the swords he would use in the Civil War had been captured by his grandfather from a redcoat serving under the brutal and hated British officer, Banastre Tarleton. Wade I had bequeathed to his grandson not only a sword, but also a moral imperative: he must not fail to be valiant.[13]

★ In early July 1861 the War Department ordered the Hampton Legion to Richmond, where it would become part of General Joseph E. Johnston's army now positioned in the Shenandoah Valley. The legion left by train to cheering crowds and waving flags. Now it was time for Wade Hampton to say good-bye. Going off to defend his country meant that he would have to rely on others to protect his hearth and home. Left behind was Mary, fifteen-year-old Sally, two-year-old McDuffie, and the baby, Daisy. Frank Hampton's cavalry company was still in Columbia, which allowed him to tend to two small children of his own and his wife Sally, who was pregnant and collapsing into bouts of bloody coughing from her tuberculosis. Kit Hampton also stayed behind to help the four Hampton sisters oversee Millwood and to keep an eye on his and Wade's planting interests in Mississippi.[14]

Arriving in Richmond on July 4, the legion set up camp just outside the city. By mid-July Brigadier General Irvin McDowell's 35,000 Union troops were advancing toward Manassas Junction, where Major General P. G. T. Beauregard waited for him with 24,000 Confederates. Farther west, Johnston held the valley town of Winchester with about 9,000 effective troops; opposite him were General Robert Patterson's 15,000 Federals. Soon news of fighting at Blackburn's Ford, near Manassas Junction, reached Richmond. Beauregard and the Confederate government feverishly worked to gather more troops at Manassas, including those around Richmond. Meanwhile, Beauregard and Johnston devised a plan by which Johnston could slip away from Patterson without his knowledge and travel quickly by rail to Manassas to reinforce Beauregard. Rumors abounded in Richmond—some thought a "terrible battle" was already raging to the north.[15]

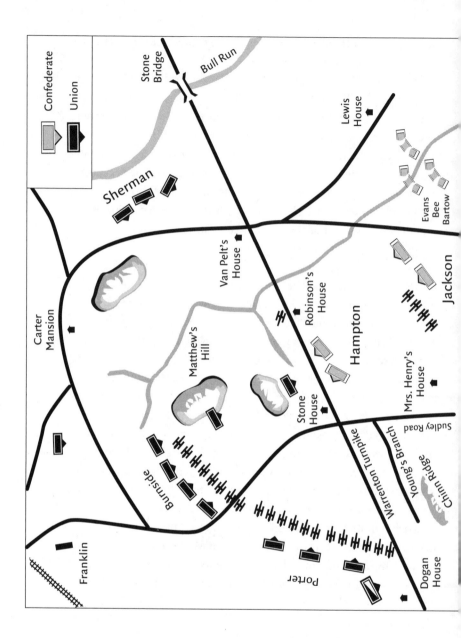

Hampton and his men now received a complete indoctrination in the "hurry-up-and-wait" and bewildering uncertainty of a military campaign. On the morning of July 19, Hampton was ordered to have his legion ready to leave by rail for Manassas by 5:00 P.M. The men did not reach Richmond's Virginia Central depot, where they were to board the boxcars, until sometime between six and nine o'clock. They arrived to find that there were not enough cars for the cavalry and artillery; only the 600-plus infantrymen would board the boxcars. The cavalrymen and artillerymen would have to make a road march, and fretted that they would miss the battle (and they did). The next problem was that there was no engine to pull the boxcars. It finally arrived from Manassas after 10:00 and first had to unload wounded men from the skirmish of the day before. Around midnight the train chugged slowly out of the station, with rain slowing its progress. Less than fifteen miles out of Richmond, it halted to allow the engineer to make repairs and adjustments. It stopped again ten miles farther down the road so the engineer could tinker with the engine some more. By then it was 7:00 A.M. The train reached Trevilian Station around 11:00 A.M. but was sidetracked so another train from Manassas could pass by. By this time, Hampton was running out of patience. The other train did not arrive for hours, and only around 4:00 P.M. did his train begin to move again. Meanwhile, his men had had no rations for nearly twenty-four hours. He telegraphed ahead to Gordonsville to have dinner waiting for them, but all they found there were a few black women on the platforms with pies and cakes for those who had money in their pockets. Sometime before dawn on Sunday, July 21, the engine finally chugged into Manassas Junction, after a hasty foot march and grueling journey of approximately thirty-six hours. At last Hampton could obtain flour, bacon, ham, and coffee for his famished troops.[16]

After stepping off the train, Hampton undoubtedly tried to sort out as much as he could about the developing situation. About two miles north of the station was a stream called Bull Run, running from northwest to southeast. North of it were Yankees. Beauregard, now reinforced by Johnston's army, had made complex, poorly articulated plans to cross Bull Run at three separate fords with eight brigades and turn the Federals' left. As the Union left collapsed, Bonham's, Cocke's, and Evans's brigades would also cross and strike the center in echelon. Before the Confederate attack could begin, however, a Federal division had struck Evans's brigade on the extreme Confederate left around 6:00 A.M., threatening to cross Stone Bridge and overwhelm him. The Fed- 75 erals did not force the crossing, and Evans gamely held his ground, sending word back to Beauregard. Beauregard believed that this was a feint and any larger Union assault would strike farther downstream. He therefore ordered Hampton to take his legion of just over six hundred men to the Lewis House, about half a mile downstream from Evans and the Stone Bridge.[17]

Hampton's men had just gobbled a few bites of breakfast. They set out for the Lewis House and were nearly there by 9:00. They were about half a mile south of the bridge when scouts—and gunfire—informed Hampton that the situation had drastically changed. The enemy had crossed two miles even farther upstream from Evans with an even larger force, and was now bearing down on the left flank and rear of Evans and the entire Confederate army. The Yankees had gained the initiative, and the Confederates now had to react quickly to save themselves.

Beauregard and Johnston did not yet recognize the gravity of the situation, but commanders on the ground, even novices like Hampton, did. Lacking specific guidance, he steered his legion back to the left (northwest) and headed toward the sound of the guns. For awhile he apparently was at a loss where to position the troops, but along the way, he later wrote, he "struck Bee's Brig[ade] going in the same direction."[18] Actually, Brigadier General Barnard Bee's brigade was one of several, including Cocke's, Bartow's, and later Jackson's, that Beauregard had already sent to reinforce the Confederate left. Most of Bee's, Bartow's, and Cocke's troops were already farther north and closer to Evans's beleaguered men than the legion. Bee thought that Hampton should remain behind, align himself with Bee's own artillery battery commanded by Captain John Imboden, and take position at the Robinson House, near the Warrenton Turnpike. Bee probably envisioned Hampton and the battery either forming a reserve or temporarily refusing the Confederate left, for he took the rest of his brigade, along with other Confederate units, slightly farther north to the vicinity of Matthews Hill. Hampton dutifully complied and had his troops lie down just behind the crest of a hill and just in front of the Robinson House. Hampton's choice of ground was tactically sound. His men had some temporary cover, while he could stand a few yards farther forward and observe the developing action. Still, it was not a place of complete safety. Imboden's battery poured fire into the approaching Federal units, which attracted fire in return from Ricketts's Union battery. James Conner remembered grape and canister passing so close over his head that he could feel the air move.

The outnumbered Confederates to Hampton's front took heavy casualties and began to stream to the rear. Hampton moved his legion forward slightly, but quickly, to the turnpike, and provided cover as Bee's, Bartow's, and Evans's shattered units regrouped in his rear. For a time, the Hampton Legion, along with the nearby 7th Georgia regiment, was the only organized Confederate resistance. The Federals, too, were disorganized and weary. In fact, the whole battle up to this point had been utterly chaotic, even as battles go. Regimental and company-sized units charged and countercharged with little coordination. Some Confederate units wore blue, and some Union units gray. This, combined with the smoke of battle, resulted in widespread confusion and numerous incidents of friendly fire.

There were gullies on either side of the turnpike where Hampton had placed his command. In one section, a stone wall with a picket fence ran along the top. A Union unit, which both Conner and Hampton remembered only as "large," appeared within two hundred yards and began pouring a deadly fire into the legion. Hampton's second-in-command, Lieutenant Colonel Johnson, was shot through the head and killed; Hampton's horse was killed beneath him. One veteran remembered that Hampton then grabbed a fallen rifle and began shooting down enemy officers one by one. Another, James Lowndes, wrote his cousin a few days later that Hampton "shot down a man at 500 yards."[19] John Coxe remembered that his buddy Private Story was killed there; in fact, the legion began to suffer heavy losses even in its covered position. According to Conner, Hampton was in the center of the line, "the men in the gully and he and I on top of the bank looking out at the enemy and cautioning the men to keep cool, aim deliberately and take resting shots, and above all to deploy out and not crowd."[20] Meanwhile, a few stragglers from the 4th Alabama and 8th Georgia joined Hampton and the 7th Georgia.

Hampton then noted that an enemy battery was deploying in the turnpike on his left, in a position to enfilade his line. He pulled back about 150 yards, where he was masked from the artillery but not from rifle fire. Then another unit appeared on his right, and Hampton was receiving rifle fire from two directions. Following Bee's and Evans's advice, he fell back again, this time into a wooded hollow that provided good cover.

The Hampton Legion was now in nearly as bad a shape as Bee's, Evans's, and Bartow's brigades had been a few hours before. The men were exhausted and had suffered heavy casualties. Hampton and his surviving company commanders, along with the adjutant, Theodore Barker, tried to reorganize the command. Wounded were gathered and carried to the rear. Probably there was ammunition to redistribute, canteens to fill, and men to place back in their respective companies. Hampton, however, had borne the brunt of the admittedly disorganized Union onslaught for at least an hour, maybe two. So far his performance had been more than adequate for a novice soldier in his first battle. He had the sense and initiative to go without orders to the sound of the firing when he learned that the left was threatened. He had followed, and probably welcomed, Bee's instructions when Bee suggested a general location to deploy his command, but Hampton had the presence of mind to use the terrain to his advantage by deploying his men behind the brow of a hill, where he had both good cover and observation. He later used terrain to even better advantage when deploying along the gullies and wall of the turnpike. Most of all, he had remained cool under heavy fire, ordering neither reckless charges nor precipitate retreats at an hour when much of the army's fate depended on his steadiness.[21]

With the legion licking its wounds, it was fortunate that Brigadier General Thomas J. Jackson's Virginia brigade had now taken up a strong position on Henry House Hill. Beauregard arrived on the scene around noon and began organizing a new defensive line anchored on Jackson, with Hampton ordered to make contact with Jackson's right and form there. While Jackson's brigade fought a confused, fierce, seesaw battle on Henry House Hill, Hampton remained to his right and rear. The legion was still a band of exhausted men, and Hampton himself seems to have been passively waiting for orders rather than pushing his men back into the thick of the fight.

Around 2:00 P.M. Beauregard ordered the right wing of his new line forward. Hampton's men advanced at the double quick, or "as rapidly as their worn-out condition would allow," toward Union units on the other side of Henry House Hill.[22] These included Federal infantry and Ricketts's battery, a unit that had inflicted much damage on the legion and other southern units throughout the day. At one point, Confederates—perhaps Jackson's men—had captured the battery, but some of the guns had again fallen into enemy hands. As Hampton's troops swarmed over Henry House Hill, Hampton saw the battery and changed course slightly to make it his target. Under heavy fire, he briefly halted his men, ordered a full volley, and then charged. As Hampton and his force resumed the charge, the battery fired a volley of canister.

Some of his men went down, and Hampton was shot in the face. He turned command over to Conner, his senior officer still standing, and remained behind. Conner and the remaining officers held the legion together against a Union counterattack and then moved forward, capturing Ricketts's battery and Captain James D. Ricketts himself.

By this time the momentum had swung back to the Confederates, who were continually being reinforced. It was now the Federals who were the most disorganized and exhausted; all along the line they fell back as southerners surged forward. As the Federal retreat became a disorganized rout, Hampton's legion participated in the pursuit until Beauregard halted and regrouped his army.

By the time it was over, Conner counted only 160 men left in the legion's ranks. Hampton's force of 627 had suffered 15 dead, 2 missing, and 100 wounded, 4 of whom would die of their injuries within a week. Hampton keenly felt the loss of the widely respected Lieutenant Colonel Johnson early in the battle, as did his men. Besides the 115 casualties, others had been detailed to carry their wounded comrades to the rear. As in all Civil War units, no doubt there were others who had wandered away to refill canteens or clean rifle barrels fouled by heavy deposits of black powder, some who were simply too exhausted to keep up with the pursuit, and still others languishing in the rear who had witnessed more carnage and terror than they could stand.[23]

Hampton's official report to Beauregard was typical of those he would write throughout the war. He expressed regret over his losses, as well as intense paternal "pride" in his "faithful soldiers" and the "gallantry" of his officers.[24] Unlike many officers on both sides of the conflict, Hampton rarely boasted of gaining a brilliant victory, but only of the performance of his men.

Hampton's own wound frightened him more than he would admit publicly. It turned out to be more serious than initially thought. Certainly it was extremely painful, and he did not resume command of the legion until days after the battle was over. His official report stated that his wound, "though slight," deprived him of the honor of participating in the capture of Ricketts's battery.[25] He also telegraphed his wife and sisters that his wound was minor. Soon after the battle, however, Mary and Mary Fisher visited Hampton near Manassas for a few days and fretted over his wound. Nearly three weeks later Mary Fisher was still at Manassas, worried that her brother's eye was still red and that the ball was still "under the eye. . . . But the doctors say it must be let alone."[26] After three more weeks, he still suffered from it and only belatedly realized how narrowly he had eluded death. "I escaped almost by a miracle," he wrote Mary Fisher. "Had the shot struck me much higher up it would have gone through my head. . . . I fear I shall always suffer from it as I have had fearful neuralgic headaches of late, all the pain coming from the wound."[27]

Ironically, Wade Hampton, the patriarchal knight-defender, would admit his own mortality to the women in his family, but not to his superiors. At first glance, it seems strange that he would admit such frailty to those he was expected to protect. In reality, it was not so strange after all. Hampton's bothersome wound was not simply a reminder of his mortality; it was also a badge of honor. It was demonstrable proof that he had fulfilled society's chivalric expectations of him. He had led ably and fought bravely; most importantly, he had triumphed.

CHAPTER 6

LONG WINTER ON THE OCCOQUAN

Colonel Hampton had indeed performed well in his first battle. Early in the fray, in the absence of complete information or specific instructions, he had shown initiative by modifying the orders he had received from Beauregard and moving toward the exposed left flank. Nor was he too proud to take advice from more experienced officers like General Bee. He had used the available terrain well. After the arrival of Brigadier General Thomas Jackson, he apparently had shown less initiative. But by that time, Beauregard was on the field and Hampton's men had already played a key role in preventing the Confederate retreat from becoming a rout. Finally, he had exhibited a trait that would become a trademark of his combat leadership throughout the war: coolness under pressure. Most importantly for his own confidence and for his reputation among his men, Hampton had shown that he was indeed worthy to bear his grandfather's and father's name.

Hampton's superiors, West Pointers all, noticed. He was one of three colonels in the army whom Beauregard singled out in his official report for "soldierly ability" and for "restor[ing] the fortunes of the day."[1] General Johnston, to whom Hampton's command officially belonged, reported that Hampton "rendered efficient service in maintaining the orderly character of the retreat."[2] On the evening after the battle, Beauregard escorted President Davis around the battlefield. The two of them stopped at Hampton's tent, where they tried to outdo one another in heaping exultant praise on the heavily bandaged colonel. Hampton was profoundly embarrassed, hesitating to repeat their extravagant compliments even to his wife, lest he appear vain. It was not that Hampton minded the praise. Rather, as one historian explains, he was a man "of great natural reserve" and thus "made uneasy by effusion in others."[3] But Hampton was not the only hero—far from it. The press lionized Beauregard, and no unit commander received as much credit for the victory as Brigadier General Jackson, now christened "Stonewall" for his stand on Henry House Hill. Promotions for officers flew thick and fast in Virginia after the battle, but none arrived for Hampton. Colonels Jackson, Jubal Early, J. E. B. Stuart, and several others became brigadier generals many months before him.[4]

Hampton's men certainly held him in high regard after the battle. If earlier he had enjoyed their respect, now he had their adulation. They reported to newspapers and to the folks back home that their leader was a hero. Hampton noticed the change, confiding to a relative that he was "very glad to feel that I now have the confidence of my men & I know that they will follow me anywhere."[5]

Hampton was just as proud of his men as they were of him, which was clear in his official reports and letters home. He was also concerned and grieving for them. Well over a sixth of his command, including his trusted lieutenant colonel, was killed or wounded, though replacements were arriving. Meanwhile, a wave of sickness spread through the camp. Hampton mourned that "my men have suffered greatly of late" and that some had died.[6] He himself was "prostrated by an attack of fever," which Conner called "malarial," and was confined for nearly three weeks.[7] Preston was with his father and was sick as well. Hampton and many of his men were recovering by September 5, but he was still coming to grips with the costs of war. He objected to teenage boys being sent to reinforce the legion, though he knew he could not prevent it. Writing to a female relative, Hampton complained: "It is a great mistake to send boys to this war . . . boys are only in the way. I would not allow anyone under 20 to be with me. . . . This is the most atrocious & unnatural war ever waged, & if it does not soon cease, its horrors will exceed those of any previous war recorded in history. It is fearful. And the sights after a battle are too horrible to think of. I want to see no more of them."[8]

It soon became clear that the great Confederate victory at Manassas would not be enough to make the North concede southern independence. Hampton and his fellow Confederates in northern Virginia spent nearly eight months with little of either the exhilaration of victory or the horror of mutilated corpses. Their main enemies were boredom, homesickness, cold weather, and the anticipation of a Yankee advance—the advance that would hopefully lead to another decisive victory and the chance finally to go home, the advance that never seemed to come.

This period of relative inactivity was trying in its own way for Hampton, but it further revealed the social assumptions and worldview that he brought to the war. First, he brought his version of paternalism to the army, where fortunately it was quite appropriate. In Hampton's paternalism, everyone had a proper role to play. His high social position in South Carolina had translated into high rank in the army; and, though many of his troops were from well-to-do backgrounds, none was a Hampton. In any case, they were now his dependents. Thus Hampton never really doubted that his men would follow him as long as he played his proper role as respectable gentleman, courageous combat leader, and provider for their needs.

There were plenty of needs to meet in the long winter of 1861–62. Hampton strove to get more arms for his legion. As late as September 1861, some of the men still had obsolete muskets rather than the Enfield rifles he had ordered. Meanwhile, more companies were joining the unit, and Hampton wished to convert one of them into another artillery battery. Thanks to the arrival of both rifles and artillery ordered months before, and to his constant wrangling with the War Department, he was relatively successful in meeting his goals for equipment.[9] There was also the challenge of keeping the men warm and healthy during their first winter of the war. The large, taciturn Hampton could be compassionate, particularly to those whom he considered under his charge, whether it be the slave Lizzy, his brother Frank's wife Sally, his children and female dependents, or even his white male soldiers. Hampton stayed busy to see that the sick were in comfortable quarters and near nurses, yet still mourned that "several good men have died."[10] One of the young men felled by illness was the son of Hampton's Mississippi overseer, Mr. Tult, who was in the camp at the time. Hampton grieved deeply, especially for the "broken hearted" father.[11] He worried about the weather's effects on his men and by October had requisitioned new tents and blankets. Hampton informed Mary Fisher that November 16 was "one of the coldest and one of the most windy days I ever saw and we had a little snow. . . . It is very fortunate that I have been able to get good, new tents for my men. They . . . will be, I hope more comfortable. Poor fellows! It makes me feel very sorry to see them exposed to such hardships . . . & I dread the winter for them."[12]

Another of Hampton's traits that carried over into the army was his distrust of democracy, and here again his perspective was appropriate for military life. When President Davis had authorized Hampton to form the legion, it was stipulated that the field-grade officers (majors, lieutenant colonel, and colonel) would receive their commissions from the president. This effectively meant that Hampton had been able to select his own field-grade officers, while the captains and lieutenants in the individual companies were elected by the men. The volunteer companies that reported to Hampton in the spring had elected or would soon elect their own officers, but at least Hampton had the prerogative of choosing which companies he would accept for service, and many of the captains had prewar experience as West Point graduates or militia officers. For both sides in the Civil War, however, it was common to allow the men in the ranks to elect all of their officers up to the rank of colonel, a practice that officers on both sides of the conflict came to see it as a problem. After the losses at Manassas, there were new elections. Hampton was able to get Conner, Stephen D. Lee, and Calbraith Butler elevated to major, and Lieutenant Colonel James B. Griffin briefly replaced the slain Lieutenant Colonel Johnson as second in command. But Hampton was disappointed that he could not get a promotion for his adjutant, Lieutenant Theodore Barker. Also, Lieutenant James Lowndes, who was an effective disciplinarian, did not take Conner's place as commander of Company A. As the men's initial one-year enlistments came up in the spring, and Confederate law required army units to hold new elections and reorganize their commands, the problem arose again. Lieutenant Colonel Griffin was never popular with the men and would later lose his place due to new elections. Hampton, though, believed that he was a good officer. "These elections in military affairs are bad things," he rued. "The best officers are sometimes left out, because they are strict."[13]

By the end of December, Johnston had given Hampton command of an entire brigade, of which his legion, commanded by Griffin, was only a part. When it was time for the troops to reenlist, Hampton feared that the legion would split into separate battalions because the men would not reenlist under Griffin. To complicate matters, Hampton expected to be promoted soon, which would make it impossible for him to command a unit as small as the legion should the men refuse to serve under Griffin. In that case, he considered refusing promotion so that he could continue to head the legion, or perhaps increase it to the size of a brigade. The whole affair, Hampton told his sister Kate, put him "in an embarrassing position."[14] Some men were meant to lead and others to follow. Democracy meant that sometimes the wrong men were put in charge, which in turn meant disorder—not to mention injustice to many upright gentlemen who should be leaders.[15]

Within days of Hampton's recovery from "Malarial" fever in early September, his legion, as part of Brigadier General W. H. C. Whiting's brigade, was deployed in the vicinity of Bull Run where it emptied into Occoquan Creek, which in turn flowed into the Potomac River. Hampton was between ten and twenty miles south of Washington. Sometime in mid-September he received orders to emplace an artillery battery along a bluff at Freestone Point, overlooking the Potomac. He brought cavalry and infantry with him and hid them in a tree line. Observing from their concealed position, the men counted twelve steam-driven craft in the river and over twenty smaller craft, almost all of them armed with howitzers. Working at night and under cover of trees, Hampton and his artillery officer, Stephen Lee, emplaced the battery and waited for several days until he received permission to fire. He jovially wrote Mary Fisher: "We had a warm little brush and drove the whole concern off, luckily without damage to us, though one big shell *scared* me very much." It was a minor affair, but Hampton's superiors considered the work skillfully done.[16]

Minor skirmishing occurred in December and January, including a "smart little skirmish" on New Year's Day with what Hampton estimated to be about one hundred enemy cavalry. Hampton was clearly looking for a fight; he told Mary Fisher that he had twenty men lying in ambush, while he stayed slightly behind with thirty more. "The ambush party fired on the Yankees & as I was cantering down to my men ahead of the party with me, I rode on a bunch of Yanks, who fired on me when I charged running them some distance & firing on them. We broke their squadron & emptied several saddles & if I had only taken more of my men with me, I would have cut the party to pieces. But with 30 men, I did not like to pursue them, fearing an ambush."[17]

Hampton, then, was again eager to fight and had gotten past his earlier desire "to see no more of it." He was not satisfied with only "[emptying] several saddles"; rather, he was itching for a chance to "cut the [Yankees] to pieces." He longed for permission to cross the Occoquan and attack. He grew positively disgusted with the enemy for failing to do so, to the point where he questioned their will to fight. In mid-December he noted that there had been two weeks of dry weather with the roads in fine condition, "so the Yanks have no excuse for not making their long promised attack."[18] Nothing could have prevented their advance, he said, but their "cowardice"—nothing, that is, until January 15, when snow, sleet, and rain arrived. That gave the Yankees their long-desired "excuse."[19]

Northern inactivity, along with plenty of time to fantasize, led Hampton to predict that recognition of southern independence would come by spring. "Indeed I think this will be done as soon as our ministers arrive in Europe. Then will come the raising of the Blockade, & if the Yankees are not sunk so low that nothing *can* arouse them, a [U.S.] war with England will follow. Our affairs are prospering & God seems to bless our efforts. I look for the breaking up of the Yankee government and it will be a blessing to mankind."[20] His predictions failed to note the considerable success Union forces were having in the West at that time.

If there was no fighting to be done in Virginia because of the weather, Hampton hoped for a transfer to his home state. He and his men were embarrassed by the performance of their fellow South Carolinians at Port Royal, South Carolina, which had recently fallen into Union hands. Men raised in a chivalric tradition that gloried home defense were particularly eager to show how they could fight close to home. Hampton claimed that his men were "crazy to go & if they could meet the Yankees *there* [in South Carolina] not many would be spared."[21] Hampton said that he also would "like to show how Carolinians should fight on their own soil."[22] He noted that one company had hoisted a black flag, the symbol that no quarter would be asked for or given.

Hampton also pined for his family. He repeatedly considered applying for a furlough to Columbia and schemed for a way that Mary, Sally, McDuffie, and Mary Fisher could visit him in Virginia. He particularly longed to see McDuffie, the toddler, asking about his height, acquiring a little dog named "Milo" for him, and insisting that Mary bring the boy when she visited. "Tell McDuffie that I will send him a soldiers cap & a gun so he must be good & a man," he wrote in February.[23] After McDuffie turned three, Hampton instructed that he could no longer wear frocks, the usual attire for small children in the antebellum South; he was now to wear "pantaloons."[24]

There is no lonelier feeling for a soldier than being away from home during a traditional family holiday, and Christmas Day 1861 found Hampton especially sentimental. But drawing again on his religious faith, he managed to sound thankful rather than self-pitying in a letter to Mary Fisher:

> Since I left home, six months ago, the hand of our Father in Heaven has protected me from many & great dangers. He has kept me from falling in battle where so many fell, & in the midst of great sickness He has granted to me strength & health. I strive to be thankful for these unmerited mercies & I pray to be made more worthy of them. It would be a great happiness to me, if I could spend this day with all of you at home, but though I cannot be there, I know you will all think of me. I hope we may all be spared to meet again soon in health & happiness. Kiss the children for me & may God bless you all. I have to work today, having rec'd orders . . . though it is Christmas, I have to take the troops up the river ten miles.[25]

Hampton's wife Mary and seventeen-year-old daughter Sally were finally able to visit Richmond in early January 1862. Escorted by a family friend named Tom Taylor, they stayed with their South Carolina friends Mary Boykin Chesnut and her husband James, who was a colonel working in the War Department. But the weather was so bad that Hampton could neither summon the ladies to the Occoquan nor make it to Richmond, and the enemy was near enough that he dared not ask for a furlough. He finally got to Richmond about February 1, where he found Sally sick with measles and then with mumps. He stayed perhaps a week or a little more. By February 19, Hampton, back in camp, found that he had contracted mumps from his daughter, and he was "laid up in his tent" for some time.[26]

Hampton's letters to his sisters at this stage of the war occasionally mentioned business matters, but less frequently than his antebellum correspondence had. He apparently realized that he had to trust Kit and, to a lesser extent, the women back home to handle them. His brother did an admirable job, but disaster befell the Hamptons' 1861 cotton crop in Mississippi. Hampton's lands had finally produced a bumper crop—five thousand bales worth a quarter of a million dollars on the New York market. This was the cotton that was donated to the Confederacy. But before it could be shipped downriver to New Orleans, Union forces captured the port, while Ulysses S. Grant's troops occupied Memphis upstream. To keep the cotton from falling into northern hands, planters in Washington and Issaqueena counties, Mississippi, burned their cotton, including Wade's and Kit's. Hampton's only reference to this calamity was a comment made to Mary Fisher: "I suppose our cotton [his and Kit's] will all be burned. This will ruin us but I would rather see it go to the flames than to the Yankees."[27]

Hampton's superiors placed more and more confidence in him as the winter wore on. During the fall his legion was shifted between various commands, but by Christmas 1861 Johnston had given Hampton command of a full brigade, consisting of the 14th and 19th Georgia Infantry regiments, the 16th North Carolina, and the Hampton Legion. In February Johnston recommended him—along with a handful of other colonels—for promotion to brigadier general, the proper rank for a brigade commander. His brigade came under the command of General Whiting, who now served provisionally as a division commander.[28]

Hampton's brigade covered a twelve-mile front through the second week of March 1862. His was the most exposed position in Johnston's army and where Johnston most expected an attack. Hampton's letters to

Johnston and his immediate superior, Whiting, indicate that he was eager to defend his front, though he knew his lines were thin. Even more difficult was keeping his far-flung command supplied due to a severe shortage of wagons and horses, and miserably muddy roads that became nearly impassable in wet weather. He fortified the position with trenchlines, but he also thoroughly acquainted himself with the terrain to his flanks and rear. He made sure that the roads and fords would suffice in the event of the withdrawal that first Beauregard and then Johnston seemed to anticipate through much of the winter.[29]

In the first week of March, Johnston decided that he could no longer hold the Bull Run–Occoquan line and must withdraw to the Rapidan and Rappahannock rivers. Orders went out to his divisions to prepare to withdraw on the seventh. The operation required careful planning, for Johnston's army had accumulated far more stores and equipment than its animals and wagons could carry. For weeks he and his officers had been warning Richmond that they needed more logistical support. Johnston and Whiting were particularly concerned about Hampton's brigade. In his exposed position, he would have a difficult time getting away quickly before the enemy discovered that he had abandoned his defenses, especially with the terrible roads behind him and the lack of transport.[30]

There was so much baggage to remove that Johnston had to delay the movement of Whiting's division, including Hampton's brigade, until March 9. When the army did move, it destroyed or left behind tons of blankets, clothing, provisions, and ordnance. The losses were bad enough, but reports of the actual quantities were exaggerated by the time they reached Jefferson Davis, who expressed his stern displeasure to Johnston. The Confederate president believed that Whiting's division had been particularly negligent. As a result, Hampton and other officers were required to give an account of the withdrawal explaining why and how much government property was destroyed or abandoned. Hampton's detailed report, according to Douglas Freeman, indicated "candor and independence of mind."[31] Hampton explained that the only public property he had lost was a small amount of ammunition and fifty-nine tents, though to carry off as much as he did with so few resources, he had to abandon the men's private baggage. As he summarized his defense: "With the means at my disposal I moved, literally in the face of the enemy, four regiments of infantry, three batteries, containing 31 guns and gun-carriages, and 120 cavalry . . . over roads that were scarcely passable, a distance of 50 miles. There was no straggling, no confusion, and after the first day's march no loss of any property."[32] Hampton reminded the War Department that he had pointed out the army's lack of transportation capability several times.

Hampton's superiors staunchly supported him. Whiting asserted that Hampton's difficulties "were indeed great." As usual, he wrote, "that distinguished, active, and vigilant officer . . . conducted his brigade with consummate judgment, precision, and skill."[33]

So ended Hampton's long winter of 1861–62 in northern Virginia. Hampton had vigilantly defended his sector and contended with boredom, sickness, harsh weather, and homesickness—only to be told to withdraw and to learn that his president had demanded an unofficial investigation of the conduct of the withdrawal. Fortunately, his reputation did not suffer; in the long run, military and civilian superiors alike were impressed with his potential.

Historians have typically paid little attention to the northern Virginia front in the winter of 1861–62, and understandably so, for little of strategic importance happened. But the long period of drudgery gave Hampton time to mature into a solid brigade commander. He learned how to delegate authority to regimental commanders and staff officers, and to supply and administer a much larger body of troops. The occasional skirmishes only strengthened his confidence in his own and his soldiers' fighting ability. His men, and perhaps even Hampton the outdoorsman, became more hardened to camp life and inclement weather. Finally, Wade Hampton developed a growing bitterness against his former countrymen in blue. He was able to take another step, at least in the abstract, toward dehumanizing the men whose very presence across the river prevented the possibility of him going home. By the time the war in Virginia resumed in earnest, Hampton was eager to empty more Yankee saddles.

AS SOON AS WE WHIP *ALL* THE
YANKEES, I CAN COME HOME

THE PENINSULA, 1862

The coming spring promised Hampton and his men plenty of desperate fighting against their foes, but first they endured more misery simply overcoming the elements. The muddy retreat from the Occoquan to the Fredericksburg area south of the Rappahannock was bad enough, but there were more wet, frigid marches in their future. As a cold, damp March gave way to a soggy April, the focus of the Union's effort in Virginia shifted to The Peninsula east of Richmond. Evidence of a Federal buildup at Fort Monroe under Major General George McClellan continued to reach the Confederates. While Confederate major general John B. Magruder stalled McClellan's advance up The Peninsula with imaginative ruses and bluffs, Joe Johnston began moving the bulk of his army south from Fredericksburg to reinforce Magruder.[1]

The men of Hampton's brigade thus found themselves on the march again. As much as Hampton would have liked to protect them from excessive misery, he could overcome neither nature's caprice nor military necessity on this occasion. From Monday, April 8, to Friday, April 12, the troops made a miserable trek from Fredericksburg to Ashland, fifteen miles north of Richmond. Couriers arrived after midnight on the eighth in a driving rain with orders to sound reveille at 3:00 A.M. and have the brigade ready to move at daylight. The men marched all day in the rain, halted at night, and attempted to sleep with no blankets or tents as the rain turned to sleet, then snow. To speed the march, the troops had loaded their excess gear on wagons, which were fifteen miles behind the main column and unable to rejoin the men because of swollen rivers. Too cold and wet to sleep, many spent the night standing by fires in a desperate attempt to stay warm. From Tuesday morning to Friday night, the only rations were hard biscuits and "fat bacon." James Conner of the Hampton Legion reported that many of the unit's new recruits got sick, and three died from the journey, but those who had been hardened from winter on the Occoquan stood the journey well. Several days later, Hampton's brigade (now a part of Gustavus W. Smith's division) would be just behind the Confederate main line stretching across The Peninsula.[2]

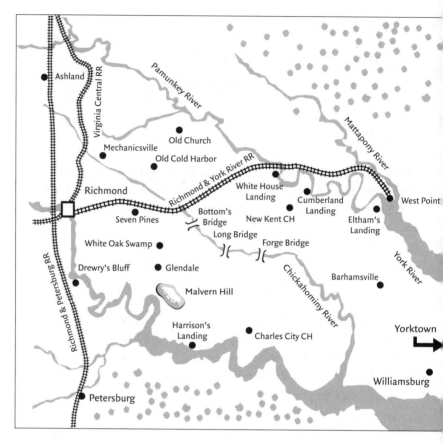

The Peninsula, 1862

By the time Hampton and his brigade arrived in the vicinity of York-town, Johnston had already decided that it was time to retreat again. He could not know the exact odds against him, but McClellan outnumbered his force of 56,000 by roughly two to one. Each of the Confederate flanks rested on broad rivers, which enemy boats could use to land bluecoats in the Confederate rear. On the evening of May 3, the with-drawal from Yorktown began. It was another difficult ordeal, but Con-ner reported that the legion "stood the march . . . splendidly." "One day," he wrote, "we marched from 1 P.M. to 3 A.M. through mud and slush, and only marched seven miles in all that time. The truth is, we are as tough now as lightwood knots, and can live on anything and anyhow."[3]

Johnston's retreat was a "fighting" one. Two of his divisions fought a fierce delaying action at Williamsburg on May 5. The next day, however, Federal brigadier general William B. Franklin was able to land his troops at Eltham's Landing on the south bank of the York River. This move put a Union division on the left flank of Johnston's army, which occupied the area around Barhamsville five miles to the south. The division was not enough to trap or destroy Johnston's army, but he wanted it kept in check until the main body of his force could withdraw farther east. Eltham's Landing was a large cleared area of Eltham's Plantation. Beyond the clearing was a large, thick wood in which Franklin positioned his troops. The guns of five gunboats on the York River protected the northern troops.

Orders went out to Brigadier General John B. Hood—who would emerge as one of the most aggressive commanders in the army—to take his Texas brigade and deal with the threat. Accompanying him on his right would be elements of Hampton's brigade, including the 19th Georgia, the infantry battalion of the Hampton Legion, and the legion artillery commanded by Major Stephen D. Lee. Johnston did not want a major engagement; his orders to Hood were to "feel the enemy gently and fall back."[4] Two other brigades would support him.[5]

Hood, like Hampton, was not a man naturally inclined to "feel the enemy gently." Their respective units marched north toward the landing, with Hood's brigade later deploying into line perpendicular to and on the left side of the road; Hampton's did the same on the right. Hood's men made contact first, sometime after 7:00 A.M. Soon Hampton was engaged as well. A confused melee ensued, with the pines and dense underbrush severely limiting visibility. A North Carolinian supporting Hood's brigade remembered that "untell 12 oclock we was a scurmishing and a running from one place to another hunting the scamps."[6] At one point a few of Hood's Texans accidentally (and harmlessly) fired on elements of the Hampton Legion. By noon, however, the Confederates had managed to drive the enemy through a mile and a half of woods and into the clearing on the other side. Here the Union line was reinforced and resistance stiffened. Hood's men ran into a solid line of Federal infantry at brigade strength, and Hampton's on the right took fire from the gunboats and from an artillery battery in their front. Fearing a counterattack against his right flank, Hampton brought up the 19th Georgia to refuse the flank. Meanwhile, Stephen Lee's battery emplaced and tried to bring fire onto the gunboats.[7]

Around 2:00 P.M. Whiting, the division commander, determined that his forces had accomplished their original objective: preventing Franklin from interfering with Johnston's retreating columns; they had even driven the Federal division back to the landing. Whiting ordered Hood and Hampton to withdraw. Hood began to fall back at 2:30. Before Hampton could get away, however, the Yankees launched a counterattack against the legion, wounding four of Hampton's men. The legion returned fire and Hampton ordered a charge. The Yankees in the legion's front then retreated, and Hampton commenced his withdrawal.

The Confederate attack at Eltham's Landing accomplished its mission at little cost to the southerners. Hampton lost 4 wounded and none missing, and sent back several prisoners. Hood, with a larger force and at times more heavily engaged, lost 8 killed and less than 30 wounded, sending back roughly 40 prisoners and 80 captured weapons. The Federals' losses totaled 186. Whiting praised the "conspicuous gallantry" of both Hampton and Hood.[8] Hampton, in turn, was pleased with the performance of Major Lee, Lieutenant Colonel Griffin, Major Conner, and the officers of the 19th Georgia. For Johnston's part, the success of the operation allowed him to be amused rather than angry with Hood for exceeding his instructions. He asked Hood if this was his interpretation of "feeling gently and falling back." What would Hood's men have done "if I had ordered them to charge and drive back the enemy?" he asked. Hood paused thoughtfully before replying: "I suppose General . . . they would have driven them into the river and tried to swim out and capture the gunboats."[9]

The army's wagons and troops cleared Eltham's Landing, and Johnston continued to withdraw up The Peninsula with McClellan cautiously following. By the end of May, some of Johnston's units had withdrawn to within three miles of Richmond itself. As the position of the armies shifted westward, however, the terrain offered Johnston an opportunity. In this more westerly region, the Chickahominy River bisected The Peninsula, forcing McClellan to straddle the river as he advanced. Johnston noted that the Federal Ninth Corps was south of the river and the rest of McClellan's army on the other side. The rainy weather had swollen the river to the extent that a quick crossing would be impossible. Johnston decided to concentrate twenty-two of his twenty-nine brigades against the Ninth Corps, crushing it before McClellan could cross the river and reinforce it.

Johnston's plan called for his columns to advance along three roads toward the Federal position near the crossroads of Seven Pines and Fair Oaks Station, on the Richmond and York River Railroad. On the morning of May 31, the three columns would simultaneously attack the Union center and left and right flanks. In its execution, the plan

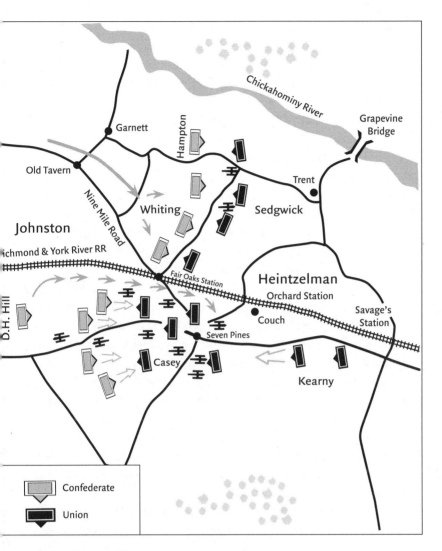

Seven Pines, May 31, 1862

went badly awry. Division commanders misunderstood or never received their instructions, took the wrong roads, and failed to coordinate with each other. Only nine Confederate brigades, instead of twenty-two, ever got into action, and instead of a coordinated attack in three sectors, there were two separate, uncoordinated battles.[10]

Hampton's brigade ended up on the far left of the confused Confederate army. His division commander was still Whiting, who in turn reported to Gustavus Smith, leader of the "Left Wing" of Johnston's army. Due to confusion and delays in Whiting's division and throughout the army, no heavy fighting occurred on the left until after 5:00 P.M., when the brigades of Hampton, Hatton, Pettigrew, and Whiting (commanded by Evander M. Law) swept forward into a wood stubbornly held by northerners of Sedgwick's division. Hampton led his neatly aligned ranks through a patch of woods, across fields, and toward a marshy pond full of fallen timber. All the while the Federal defenders poured withering volleys of rifle fire and artillery into his ranks. The brigade reached the marshy area, but its officers found it virtually impossible to coordinate their units in the dense, swampy terrain. Conner remembered that the Hampton Legion made at least two charges against a Federal battery but was repulsed each time. Smith reported that the gallant attackers made "various attempts . . . to charge the enemy, but without that concert of action almost absolutely necessary to success."[11] Hampton rode up to the legion during the fighting and, with a mixture of pride and fatherly dread, saw that his own beloved Preston had left his horse and run forward to carry the colors and cheer the men. Some of Hampton's troops fled back through the fields, while others held on until dark, when Smith ordered their withdrawal. At some point in the fighting, a Federal minie ball slammed through the sole of Hampton's boot. Hampton informed Mary Fisher that the bullet turned over on impact, "driving the . . . large end [of the bullet] against the bones in my foot."[12] He refused to leave the field, remaining mounted under heavy fire while Surgeon E. S. Gaillard extracted the ball. Moments later, Gaillard received a severe wound in the arm that would require amputation.[13]

Elsewhere the story was similar. The Confederates attacked with great dash and élan, gaining some ground but at a terrible cost. Whiting's division suffered 164 killed. Hampton's legion alone lost 154 killed and wounded out of an original force of 365. The Confederate army's total loss in killed, wounded, and missing, including subsequent action on the morning of June 1, was 6,134. Hampton's fellow brigade commanders Robert Hatton and Johnston Pettigrew were also wounded—

Hatton mortally, while Pettigrew fell unconscious and into the hands of the enemy. Joe Johnston was seriously wounded, and Hampton thanked God that he himself was spared. Four days after the battle, he noted that the bullet that struck him was "mashed up, & the *bones feel pretty much in the same condition.*"[14] One of the bones was broken, and, after leaving the battlefield, Hampton found he could neither walk nor ride for several weeks.[15]

Hampton mourned the losses in his own brigade, especially those of his beloved legion. He was also extremely proud of his men. "Well does the Legion deserve its praise," he wrote, "for it fought as only the best troops can fight. Poor fellows! They are cut down to a handful now. Soon there will be, I fear, none of them left." Paternal feelings of pride and concern for his own sons, Wade IV and Preston, were even more intense. "I feel more dread for [my sons] than I do for myself," Hampton confided. "They both behave nobly & I may well be proud of them. . . . Two braver & nobler boys never lived & I pray God to spare them to me."[16]

Incapacitated and lingering in the hospital, Hampton had more time than usual to long for home. Preston was with him, and Wade IV rode in daily to visit him; wounded men from the legion sought him out to say hello and shake his hand. As gratifying as this attention was, it had been almost a year since he had been in Columbia. As much as Hampton was determined to establish his reputation and that of his legion on the battlefield, he had no greater desire than to return home—back to his wife and children, back to rebuilding his fortune in Mississippi, back to his hunting and fishing. But that could not be as long as the hated Yankees were intent on preventing southern independence. Northern success in abolishing the Confederacy meant extinguishing southern men's right to self-determination; it would make a mockery of southern men's claims to autonomy, manly independence, and honor. There was, then, no honorable way that men like Wade Hampton could go home and enjoy peace and prosperity without first "whipping" the Yankees. Hampton grimly concluded that peace could come only through fighting. Lying in a hospital bed, with thousands of Yankees only a few miles away, he reluctantly decided that he must postpone the visit to Columbia that he had been considering since before Christmas. "As soon as we whip *all* the Yankees, I can come [home]," he wrote Mary Fisher.[17]

The frustrating thing was that the Yankees kept coming. Many white southerners had jubilantly celebrated the glorious victory at Manassas as the manly contest of arms that would convince the cowardly northern race to give up—the triumph that would vindicate southern claims to independence. But the Yankees did not give up. They were, in fact, still pressing on—blockading the coast and occupying southern ports, capturing Forts Henry and Donelson on the Tennessee River, and gradually wresting away more and more southern soil. Southern men fought bravely—Hampton had seen his own troops prove their courage and fighting prowess in half a dozen battles and skirmishes. But the Yankees, whether through arrogance, a perverse ambition to subjugate southerners, or—just maybe—a similar brand of courage, kept coming. Southern soldiers continued to die and civilians continued to suffer. It was maddening, he confessed to Mary Fisher—"When I think how much our people are suffering my heart burns with indignation & I have the most vindictive feelings towards the whole Yankee race."[18] For some people those two emotions—a longing for peace and a burning desire to thrash Yankees—would have been irreconcilable. In the heart of Wade Hampton they reinforced each other. Accomplishing the first had proved to be impossible without the other.

Eight days after his wounding at Seven Pines, Hampton allowed his longing for home to compete with his notions of duty. Maybe he could parlay his injury into an opportunity for a short visit to Columbia. A bone in his foot had been broken, and the foot was still too swollen to wear a slipper, much less a boot. He "suppose[d]," however, that he could still ride a horse. Rather than volunteer immediately, he determined on June 8 to "keep quiet until I am well, if nothing of importance is going on in front."[19] Some days after writing these words, Hampton did indeed go home, crutches and all, where South Carolinians sang his praises and hostesses clamored to entertain him. There were dinner parties and receptions. Conversations in Carolina parlors had turned to Hampton's heroism after Seven Pines, and Mary Boykin Chesnut recorded one of them in her diary:

> Tom Taylor says Wade Hampton did not leave the field on account of his wound.
> "What heroism!"
> "No, what luck. He is the luckiest man alive. He'll never be killed. He was shot in the temple [at Manassas]. That did not kill him! His soldiers believe in his luck."[20]

Though Hampton and Governor Francis Pickens were not friends, Pickens held an elaborate reception in Hampton's honor at the governor's mansion. For Hampton, it was an evening of embarrassment and discomfort. Mrs. Pickens greeted him at the door. Immediately she took his crutch away and put his hand on her shoulder, exclaiming that that was "the way to greet heroes." According to Mary Chesnut, "Poor Wade smiled and smiled until his face hardened into a fixed grin of embarrassment and annoyance. He is a simple-mannered man . . . and does not want to be made much of by women . . . to the last he looked as if he wished they would let him alone."[21]

Despite all the public acclaim, Hampton got more enjoyment from his private time with Mary, Sally, McDuffie, and his sisters. His visit lasted about two weeks; well-wishers saw him off from Columbia's railway station when he returned to Richmond on June 24. Nine months later, Mary would bear him another son, Alfred.[22]

Hampton may have disliked being fawned over at dinner parties, but in his own quiet way he was as eager for promotion and public acclaim as other southern officers. The problem that obsessed him for over six months was that promotion to brigadier general might separate him from his beloved legion. Having brought the legion into existence and nurtured it since its inception, he naturally felt a personal and paternal attachment.

Organizationally, the Hampton Legion was relatively unusual. Its infantry battalion, consisting originally of six companies but later encompassing several more, was roughly the size of a regiment. Unlike most regimental- or brigade-sized units, however, it also included one (later two) artillery batteries and two (later three) cavalry companies. It was an unwieldy arrangement. The three branches rarely fought together, and Civil War armies quickly found it was more efficient to group cavalry units into brigades or divisions rather than detach them piecemeal to infantry regiments, or "legions." Never did all three branches of the Hampton Legion actually fight together. A few other units were similarly organized, but legions like Hampton's were much less common than regiments or brigades.

Hampton's original intent seems to have been to increase his legion to the size of a brigade. At first this did not correspond with any ambition to become a brigadier general. In the fall of 1861, Hampton was as aware of his prior lack of military experience as anyone and did not seem to resent that he was still a colonel after the Battle of Manassas. But after several months on the Occoquan, where he demonstrated that he could handle much greater responsibility, Hampton did desire promotion. Though appointed a brigade commander around the beginning of 1862, he retained the rank of colonel. Joe Johnston recommended him for promotion in January, but in April he was still a colonel. Why?[23]

One reason had to do with Hampton's stubborn pride. There was friction between Hampton and President Davis for a few months. When his commission as brigadier general reached Hampton in May, he initially declined it. He had previously told Mary Fisher that he would refuse a promotion from the president unless it dated back to the day he actually took command of a brigade, which had been in late December or early January. Another sticky issue stemmed from the Confederate policy of grouping regiments from the same state into brigades and Davis's determination to enforce that policy. Because other South Carolina regiments were engaged elsewhere, for the time being Hampton's superiors gave him a brigade consisting of two Georgia regiments, a North Carolina regiment, and his legion. To become a brigade commander on a permanent basis, however, Hampton would have to achieve a dramatic increase in the size of the legion. He strove mightily to do so, eventually receiving authorization to enlarge the legion to brigade strength, but he never reached his goal. In the aftermath of Manassas, eighteen volunteer companies asked state and Confederate authorities for permission to join Hampton's unit, but only a few actually did. By the time he was authorized to put out a call in February 1862 for more troops, the flow of volunteers had slowed to a trickle.[24]

Complicating the issue further was that as much as Hampton wanted to remain with his legion, he was determined to retain the officers of his choosing. Beginning in January, he fretted almost constantly about the expiration of enlistments and the subsequent election of new officers that would take place in June. Hampton was fairly confident that most of his men would reenlist, although he had to consider the fact that they had not had a furlough since leaving home in June 1861. He also had little fear that his men would not reelect him. But he was certain that they would not reelect Lieutenant Colonel Griffin. Some lieutenants and captains were resorting to "electioneering and wire working."[25] Hampton also feared that Major James Conner, whom the men regarded as an excellent combat leader but as too strict in camp, would lose his post as well. The whole idea of electing officers dismayed Hampton, and he objected to not being able to appoint his own lieutenant colonel and majors. He flatly told Mary Fisher that if the troops turned out Griffin and Conner, he preferred to relinquish command of the legion.[26]

100   In the end, Hampton conceded nearly every point. In June, after the

Battle of Seven Pines, he accepted a commission as brigadier general dated May 23, 1862. Conner informed his mother of Hampton's promotion on June 16, reporting that Davis had written Hampton "a handsome letter" after Seven Pines. There "has been a general smoking of the calumet of peace," Conner wrote, "and the Colonel has accepted [his promotion]."[27] The elements of the Hampton Legion splintered for good. Command of the legion's infantry fell to Martin Gary, whom Hampton distrusted. Conner and Griffin both lost their bid for reelection, though Conner managed a promotion to colonel along with an appointment to command the Twenty-second North Carolina. The artillery and cavalry detached permanently from the Hampton Legion and officially took on different designations. Hampton gave a farewell speech to the legion, took temporary command of a Virginia brigade during the Seven Days' battles, and then transferred to the cavalry, taking the legion's cavalrymen with him, as well as one artillery battery redesignated as "horse artillery." Hampton thus got his promotion but failed in his other goals—staying with the bulk of the legion, determining its future officers, or even keeping it together. Sometime in June, Mary Chesnut heard of an acquaintance congratulating Hampton on his promotion. Hampton grumbled in reply that he should never have given up his legion.[28]

The highest-ranking Confederate to become a casualty in the Seven Pines fiasco was the army's commander, Joe Johnston himself. A serious chest wound kept Johnston out of the field for months, allowing President Davis to replace him with an officer in whom he had come to place much more confidence—General Robert E. Lee. Lee immediately began to look for a way to wrest the initiative away from McClellan. He believed that the best way to defend Virginia was to attack—to look for ways to destroy isolated or weakened portions of his opponent's army. Ironically, this was the strategy Johnston had finally resorted to at Seven Pines. The difference was that this "offensive-defensive" strategy was a last resort for Johnston. For Lee, striking aggressively was instinctive.

A remarkable reconnaissance expedition led by cavalry commander J. E. B. Stuart gave Lee the information he needed to formulate a plan. From June 12–16, Stuart's horsemen had ridden in a complete circle around the Union army. On his return he informed Lee that McClellan's right flank north of the Chickahominy was unprotected by natural or man-made barriers or fortifications. If Lee could strike that isolated flank with overwhelming force, the Chickahominy would prevent McClellan from reinforcing it quickly, thus dealing the Federals a smashing blow. Lee's plan was to bring Stonewall Jackson's seasoned Valley Army from the Shenandoah by rail and have it pounce on the right flank and rear of David Porter's 28,000 bluecoats north of the Chickahominy. Meanwhile, the divisions of James Longstreet, D. H. Hill, and A. P. Hill would strike Porter in his front. Nearly 60,000 Confederates would overwhelm nearly 30,000 Federals in front, flank, and rear. The danger was that, on the south side of the Chickahominy, there would only be 27,000 Confederates to defend Richmond against 75,000 Federals. Lee fortified his lines before Richmond and gambled that McClellan would neither recognize nor exploit his advantage.[29]

Hampton, who was away from Richmond until June 24, would have known nothing of these plans at first. Even when he returned, Hampton was a general without a command. While he had been recuperating, his decimated brigade had been split up, with the three regiments and the legion infantry going to different brigades. He certainly heard of the fighting on June 25 and 26. The engagement at Oak Grove on June 25 had nothing directly to do with Lee's plan, but the combat near Mechanicsville on June 26 did. Lee intended for Jackson's army to appear on the right flank of Porter's command behind Beaver Dam Creek early on the morning of the twenty-sixth, precipitating the advance by D. H. Hill, A. P. Hill, and Longstreet on Porter's front. But Jackson did not attack. For once in his career, the ever-aggressive, ever-punctual "Stonewall" was miles away from where he was supposed to be. The other Confederate commanders waited for him, as instructed, until A. P. Hill lost patience and attacked on his own near the village of Mechanicsville.[30]

Hampton was not a man to remain in a hospital bed or comfortable quarters in Richmond when there was fighting nearby. Whether at the request of a superior or on his own initiative, he made his way to the north side of the Chickahominy. Probably he arrived first at the division headquarters of A. P Hill, under whom most of the men of his old brigade now served. Hill's division had absorbed three-fourths of the elements of Hampton's old brigade. Someone undoubtedly updated him on the general situation—the attack was supposed to have started hours ago, Jackson was missing, and now Hill was attacking on his own. It was after 3:00 P.M., six hours after the assault was supposed to begin.

After Hill went forward, Longstreet did also, crossing Mechanicsville Bridge sometime around 6:00 P.M. As the tactical situation changed, Longstreet's artillery was no longer able to provide support. Hampton offered to help. Longstreet later reported that "Brigadier-General Hampton volunteered to give directions and positions to our heavy batteries opposite Mechanicsville, now become useless, and to follow the movements of our army down the river. The battery followed our movements and played up on the enemy lines with good effect."[31] But nothing Hampton or anyone else did that day could prevent the slaughter resulting from Hill's impetuous frontal assault on Porter's fortifications at Mechanicsville. The Confederates lost 1,475 men to Porter's 361. Still, it was McClellan, not Robert E. Lee, who lost his nerve that night. McClellan ordered Porter to withdraw four miles to high ground behind Boatswain's Creek, near Gaines' Mill.[32]

There was another battle the next day at Gaines' Mill, as Lee again tried to strike Porter's front and flank. Again Jackson was slow getting into position and his attack lethargic. The Confederate assault at Gaines' Mill was another bungled bloody affair, but once again McClellan withdrew Porter's corps, this time behind White Oak Swamp. Meanwhile, once more Hampton found himself a general at a battle with nothing to do. No doubt he rode off to find Jackson's command, where his old legion and his son Preston were now serving.

As it happened, the next day an opening appeared in Jackson's army for an underemployed Confederate brigadier. The Third Brigade of Winder's division needed an experienced commander. The Third had originally belonged to William B. Taliaferro, but by the time of this campaign it had come under the temporary command of a fine officer named Colonel S. V. Fulkerson. After Fulkerson received a mortal wound at Gaines' Mill, one of the regimental commanders took over until the following day, June 28, when Hampton assumed command of the brigade, consisting of the 10th, 23rd, and 37th Virginia regiments and an artillery battery led by Captain George Wooding. Hampton had his son Preston with him, but otherwise the officers and troops of his new command were unfamiliar to him.[33]

Porter continued to withdraw, first across the Chickahominy and then below White Oak Swamp. Lee continued to follow, still hoping to deliver a knockout blow. He hoped to smash the invaders on June 30 south of White Oak Swamp near the village of Glendale. While other Confederate divisions were attacking the Federals from the west, Jackson was to strike them on the right flank and rear. He would advance southwest after crossing Grapevine Bridge, then turn south and enter White Oak Swamp—a miserable, tangled, marshy jungle with a stream running through the middle. Once he crossed White Oak Swamp Bridge, his march of eight and a half miles would, it was hoped, put him in Porter's rear. Jackson got off to an early start but moved slowly. Along his line of march were mounds of abandoned Union supplies at Savage's Station on the Richmond and York River Railroad. Delighted Confederate soldiers took time to plunder, one Georgian writing that one could find all manner of abandoned Union booty "from a siege gun to a cigar."[34] Colonel Bryan Grimes of North Carolina was astounded to find a large quantity of metal coffins.[35]

Hampton's brigade and Thomas Munford's 2nd Virginia Cavalry reached White Oak Swamp around noon, only to find the bridge had been burned. Moreover, the ground nearby was too marshy for wagons and artillery to cross the stream. Here Hampton's experience as a woodsman came into play. Hampton took Preston and another aide downstream and found a usable crossing, although there were some Union troops nearby on the other side. He immediately reported to Jackson, who asked him if a makeshift bridge could be built there. Hampton replied that it would be simple to construct a bridge suitable for infantry, but if trees had to be cut down to make a road for artillery, the noise would alert the enemy. Jackson ordered Hampton to build the bridge. Hampton had twenty men cut poles from where his brigade was waiting and then transported downstream to the crossing point. As soon as his troops had constructed a workable footbridge, he rode back to inform Jackson.[36]

Most accounts agree that Stonewall Jackson was so weary during the Seven Days' campaign from weeks of hard marching and inadequate sleep that he had reached the point of mental collapse. Hampton's account of his conversation with Jackson on the afternoon of June 30 supports that interpretation. Jackson pulled his cap over his eyes and listened to Hampton's report. Then, without a word, he simply stood and walked away, leaving Hampton mystified. Later that evening Jackson fell asleep at the supper table with food between his teeth. Again, his veteran troops contributed next to nothing to the Confederate offensive, while their comrades fought and bled two miles away.[37]

McClellan retreated once more after Glendale, this time three miles south to a strong position on Malvern Hill, just north of the James River. Lee was finally able to concentrate his army. The only way to get at McClellan now, however, was in a suicidal, uphill frontal assault against massed artillery. Tactically, it was another bloody repulse. Winder's division, containing Hampton's brigade, was in reserve and saw little action.

104 Despite the problems with coordination, communication, and a

dreadful loss of life, the Seven Days' campaign was a strategic victory for the South. Confederate citizens celebrated Lee's salvation of Richmond. Wade Hampton's participation, on the other hand, was a story of wasted talent. He was an underemployed brigade commander of an underused brigade in an underused division in a mishandled army. He never got into the thick of the fighting, as much as he may have tried. When Mary Fisher asked him why his brigade was "not mentioned in the papers," he replied sardonically that it was because "*we did nothing*."[38] But Hampton had tried to do something. On June 26 he had shown that he had acquired a solid grasp of how to employ artillery while directing fire support for Longstreet's division at Mechanicsville. He had shown enterprise, initiative, and reconnoitering skills in finding a way across White Oak Swamp on the thirtieth. He knew, too, that "the battles here were enough to shock any one" and hoped there was no more hard fighting to be done. But Hampton's shock at the bloodshed did not soften his bitterness toward the enemy. "I wish we had killed about 25000 Yankees," he wrote his sister, "as I could stand *that shock* very well."[39]

RIDING WITH STUART

Hampton had learned much about warfare in his year with the infantry. At Manassas he had shown that he could select key terrain and hold a unit together in a defensive stand. Although there had been no major fighting along the Occoquan, there he had grasped how to overcome the tactical and logistical difficulties of manning an overextended line for several months against a superior, though inactive, foe. He kept an eye on his enemies so as to predict their intentions. He studied terrain with an eye for maximizing the potential for natural and man-made obstacles, predicting possible axes of advance for both the enemy and his own troops, and covering one's flanks and lines of withdrawal if ordered to fall back. At Eltham's Landing, where his task was more difficult than at Manassas, he led two regiment-sized units in attack, not defense, over difficult terrain. He did the same with a full brigade at Seven Pines. Although, there, portions of his brigade had fled in the face of heavy enemy fire, the majority of his command had performed creditably, and he had proved his own courage by remaining in command after being painfully wounded. He had shown on two occasions—at Freestone Point and Gaines' Mill—that he knew how to employ small units of artillery effectively. He had once again demonstrated his knack for evaluating terrain and his woodcraft by constructing an alternate route through White Oak Swamp for Stonewall Jackson's command. Many officers who served with Hampton, in fact, noted that he had "almost an instinctive topographical talent."[1]

After July 26, 1862, Hampton would have to make far more snap judgments about terrain and enemy intentions, as well as on-the-spot decisions on whether to attack or defend, advance or withdraw. He would be required to make them where the pace of action was faster and in the saddle—Hampton was transferring to the cavalry.[2]

After the Seven Days' campaign, William B. Taliaferro resumed command of the Third Brigade of Winder's division, leaving Hampton once again without a command. President Davis suggested that he be given a cavalry brigade under the command of Robert E. Lee's cavalry leader, J. E. B. Stuart. Hampton was reluctant at first and agreed to the change only with the understanding that the appointment was temporary. It was in the infantry that Hampton had learned how to be a soldier; besides, a

General Wade Hampton III
(1818–1902), ca. 1863.
South Caroliniana Library.

transfer to the cavalry would take him farther away from the infantry-men of the Hampton Legion—the men with whom he had shared most of the last year.[3]

In many ways, however, Hampton was well suited for the cavalry. His Columbia neighbors and friends had always known him to be a superb horseman. Even at the age of forty-four, he had the incredible en-durance necessary for long days and weeks in the saddle with little rest; family members laughed at how he could catnap anytime, anywhere—even while sitting astride a horse. His knack for evaluating terrain was also vital to the cavalry's primary mission of reconnaissance and scouting. Moreover, it was the warrior on horseback who epitomized the southern cult of chivalry. Certainly the rifleman, the stoic citizen-soldier, occupied an important post in the realm of American and southern patriotism. But it was the aristocratic knight on horseback who best captured southerners' romantic notions of chivalry, home defense, and manly honor, particularly among those of Hampton's so-cial class. Finally, Hampton could never forget that it was as a Revolu-tionary cavalry officer that his grandfather had distinguished himself.[4]

Hampton's new brigade was a seasoned one. It consisted of the 2nd South Carolina, 1st North Carolina, and 10th Virginia Cavalry regiments, as well as two battalion-sized legions. An important addition to the brigade was Captain James F. Hart's artillery battery, originally part of the Hampton Legion and now converted to horse artillery. The 2nd South Carolina was the new regiment that Hampton had been working for months to build from the nucleus of his four Hampton Legion cavalry companies. Its leader was one of the legion's original cavalry officers, Matthew Calbraith Butler, now a colonel. Butler, called "Matt" by Virginians but "Calbraith" by his fellow South Carolinians, had been a lawyer from Edgefield. Like Hampton, Butler was cool under fire, though his language could become blunt and coarse in combat. He soon became Hampton's most trusted subordinate; Hampton considered him the finest soldier in his command. Rounding out the 2nd South Carolina were several newly arrived companies, including Captain Thomas J. Lipscomb's Bonham Light Dragoons and Captain A. H. Boykin's "Boykin's Rangers." The 1st North Carolina came under the command of a solid officer, Colonel Laurence S. Baker, and later the hard-fighting James B. Gordon. The commander of the 10th Virginia, Colonel J. Lucius Davis, had written a manual on cavalry tactics used by Stuart's officers. Lieutenant Colonel Pierce Manning Butler Young, a fiery twenty-five-year-old, led the Cobb Legion of Georgians. The Jeff Davis Legion, made up of men from Mississippi, Alabama, and Georgia, came under the command of Lieutenant Colonel William Martin. Hampton kept Preston on his staff, and by the end of the year he became a lieutenant and his father's aide-de-camp. The brave and efficient Theodore Barker remained Hampton's adjutant, but now held the rank of major. Most of the men and officers in Hampton's cavalry brigade, including the staff, had already proved themselves in combat.[5]

Finally, there was one member of the staff who served throughout the war but whom Hampton rarely mentioned in letters home: his slave and personal servant, Kit Goodwyn. We do not know the exact nature of their relationship, though after emancipation Goodwyn chose to remain with Hampton as an employee.[6]

Hampton's transfer to the cavalry was part of a thorough reorganization of the Army of Northern Virginia. The Seven Days' campaign had proved the older structure unwieldy and inefficient, so Lee reorganized the infantry into two corps of several divisions each. The corps commanders were Stonewall Jackson and James Longstreet. Stuart's collection of cavalry regiments became a division of two brigades. Fitzhugh

"Fitz" Lee, the nephew of the army's commander and a proven cavalry officer, commanded one brigade; Wade Hampton the other. Within a few days, a third brigade led by Beverly Robertson joined the division. Stuart had little confidence in Robertson's ability, and his former superior, Stonewall Jackson, shared this opinion. On September 5 Robertson lost his post and was reassigned to organize Confederate cavalry in North Carolina. His troops remained with Stuart under the immediate command of Colonel Thomas Munford.[7]

Hampton thus began a professional relationship with "Jeb" Stuart, one of the most colorful and romantic figures in American military history. Stuart was intelligent and bold, and he thrilled at the prospect of danger. For at least two years, he would repeatedly embarrass Union commanders, particularly cavalrymen, while fighting against larger numbers. Stuart the Virginian and Hampton the South Carolina aristocrat could not have been more different. Stuart was a West Point graduate and a product of the regular U.S. Army; Hampton was a citizen-soldier who learned the business of war on the job. Stuart was a youthful, exuberant twenty-nine; his subordinate was a serious, taciturn forty-four. Stuart was charming, outgoing, and charismatic; Hampton had "a certain grave and simple courtesy."[8] Stuart's headquarters was often a place of jollity, singing, and banjo playing; Hampton shunned such frivolity. John Esten Cooke, a relative of Stuart and member of his staff who wrote one of the most complete contemporary sketches of Hampton by a fellow soldier, noted that Hampton "smiled more often than he laughed, never sang at all . . . and had the composed demeanor of a man of middle age."[9] When the pace of action slowed, Stuart enjoyed attending balls at local plantation manors and dancing with ladies. Hampton sought out the local hunters and fishermen, who incidentally were excellent guides for military purposes. While Stuart wore elegant uniforms replete with gold braid and a plumed hat, Hampton's dress was plain, even slovenly, in comparison. War offered Stuart the opportunity for adventure, excitement, glory, and the performance of heroic deeds. Cooke explained that Hampton "fought from a sense of duty, and not from passion, or to win renown. The war was a gala-day, full of attraction and excitement to some; to [Hampton] it was hard work, not sought but accepted."[10] Cooke came to admire Hampton as "an honest gentleman who disdained all pretense or artifice . . . he thought nothing of personal decorations or military show."[11] Hampton and Stuart would eventually come to respect each other's soldierly abilities, but they were never friends.[12]

110   Stuart had already had Fitz Lee under his command. He had high

praise for Lee's ability and genuinely liked his fellow Virginian, who shared his sense of adventure, easy camaraderie, and zest for life. For several reasons, however, Stuart did not receive Hampton as enthusiastically. Hampton carried himself like a soldier but did not dress the part. He showed up at Stuart's headquarters near Richmond wearing a plain gray uniform, a civilian-style sack coat, and a brown felt hat without plume, feather, or star. He had no prior experience as a cavalryman. He had performed respectably in every engagement, but some whispered that most of his legion had fled the field at Seven Pines. Those who had personally served with Hampton or written official reports on him knew him to be a reliable soldier. Nevertheless, most men in the army were more aware of Hampton's reputation for wealth than for his fighting ability.[13]

Hampton and Stuart did not get off to a good start. Stuart appointed Fitz Lee as commander of his "First Brigade," while Hampton's unit became the Second Brigade. This was perhaps an unintentional—but easily avoidable—slight to Hampton, who was two months senior to Lee. Hampton may have made his displeasure known, for Robert E. Lee later instructed Stuart that, in deference to Hampton's seniority, his brigade must be officially known as the First Brigade. Days later, on the new cavalry division's first big mission, Stuart gave Lee the post of honor while Hampton's brigade was to stay behind.[14]

After the Seven Days, Robert E. Lee's forces had George McClellan bottled up on The Peninsula near his base on the James River. It was becoming clear by the end of July that the Yankee general was psychologically whipped and no longer posed an offensive threat, but Robert E. Lee was concerned about another large Union army in northern Virginia under Major General John Pope. Pope's army was moving closer to Richmond and by July 13 threatening the railroad junction at Groveton. Lee began advancing forces under Jackson to counter this threat. Lee additionally feared that, in time, McClellan's forces could steam up the Chesapeake and redeploy where they could reinforce Pope, making Pope too strong for Lee to confront. By early August the bulk of the Army of Northern Virginia, including Stuart with Fitz Lee's—and later Robertson's—cavalry brigades, was sparring with Pope. Meanwhile, a smaller contingent of Confederates, including Hampton's brigade, was left with the less critical mission of keeping an eye on McClellan.[15]

Jackson's divisions fought a fierce battle with the Federals at Cedar Mountain on August 9. Lee ended his brilliant campaign against Pope on August 29–30, bringing both Jackson's and Longstreet's corps to bear and thrashing Pope's army at the Battle of Second Manassas. Hampton was still farther south watching McClellan.[16]

As Pope's defeated Union columns trod miserably back toward Washington, Lee determined to take the war to the north side of the Potomac River. A campaign in Maryland and Pennsylvania during the harvest season would allow his—and his enemy's—army to subsist on the northern countryside for a change, providing more forage for his troops and relief for Virginia farms. A victory on northern soil, moreover, could win foreign recognition of the Confederacy and strengthen the hands of those in the North who wished to end the war and let the South go in peace. Lee therefore called for all available troops still in Richmond to bolster his ranks as he marched into enemy territory.

Even before the great battle at Manassas, Lee sent several messages to Richmond asking that Hampton's cavalry brigade be sent to him. He additionally asked that the 2nd North Carolina regiment be transferred from North Carolina and assigned to Hampton. Davis delayed, desiring some protection for Richmond, but finally informed Lee on August 26 that Hampton as well as the bulk of the requested infantry units were on their way north to rejoin Lee's army.[17]

Hampton joined Stuart on the morning of September 2, too late to participate in the fighting at Manassas, but in time to help harass the enemy's retreat to Washington. Stuart welcomed the reinforcement, and his cavalrymen cheered as Hampton's brigade rode into camp. It must have been a heartening scene for Hampton, whose troops responded buoyantly to the enthusiastic welcome. Stuart was particularly pleased that Hampton had brought Hart's battery with him, bringing the total number of cannon in Stuart's cavalry division to twenty. Before dark, Hampton had that artillery in action. Some of his scouts from the 1st North Carolina had located a large Federal formation near Flint Hill, and Hampton and Stuart were observing the enemy from a knoll in a tree line. Hampton put down his glass and ordered two guns of Hart's battery to unlimber and join some of Stuart's other guns. Within minutes the Union troops fled in confusion, and Hampton's troopers rounded up several prisoners. Hampton himself survived a close call that evening as he scouted the enemy through wooded terrain. An overeager North Carolinian mistook him for an enemy and drew a bead on him before recognizing Hampton's broad hat with the South Carolina palmetto emblem. "Lord, I would a hated it monstrously ef my rifle had tuck down the good old chap," the Tar Heel remarked.[18]

Stuart's first mission in the invasion of Maryland was to screen the

movement of Lee's army north. While the Confederate horsemen kept
Union forces occupied in the vicinity of Fairfax Court House, Lee's
infantry and artillery marched toward Leesburg and then across the
Potomac in the direction of Frederick, Maryland. The cavalry splashed
across the river on the evening of September 5.

Hampton must have had conflicting emotions that evening. Most
troopers crossed the Potomac that night enthusiastically, feeling they
were part of a historic moment. In just over three months, their fighting
and Lee's leadership had shifted the scene of war from the gates of
Richmond to enemy territory. The Army of Northern Virginia was flush
with success, and this could be the campaign that brought victory,
independence, and peace. To be sure there were some Confederates—
already hungry, ragged, and footsore—who used the invasion of enemy
territory as a further justification for falling behind and remaining in
Virginia. They had volunteered to defend their homeland, but now they
were asked to become invaders. Hampton probably had no such second
thoughts. Months earlier he had expressed a desire to take the war to the
North in one of his anti-Yankee diatribes to his sister: "If we whip them
here [near Richmond]—& I have no doubt but that we shall—we will
have every prospect for peace. But I do not like to think of peace until we
have carried the war into Yankeedom. They should be made to feel the
horrors of the war & then perhaps peace would be lasting."[19]

Hampton, on the other hand, had to be aware as he crossed into
Maryland that he did not yet have Stuart's full confidence. Hampton,
of course, was not being relieved of command as Beverly Robertson was
that day. But he was still new to the cavalry, and Stuart had had plenty
of opportunity to observe Fitz Lee's skills. As the cavalry crossed the
Potomac, Stuart assigned Lee's brigade to the vanguard, the post of
honor and responsibility in an advance. Hampton, the senior brigadier,
was next, followed by Robertson's old brigade under Colonel Thomas
Munford.[20]

As elements of Lee's army entered Frederick, the cavalry took a parallel line of march several miles to the east. Stuart's job was to report any
westward pursuit of Lee by McClellan, who was once again leading the
Army of the Potomac. In the unlikely event that McClellan moved rapidly, Stuart and his three brigades were to delay him as long as possible.
This would be vital, because not all of Lee's army would be concentrated
at Frederick. After Jackson reached Frederick, Lee sent him twenty miles
to the west to capture the large Federal garrison and arsenal at Harpers
Ferry, while other Confederate columns were ranging to the northwest

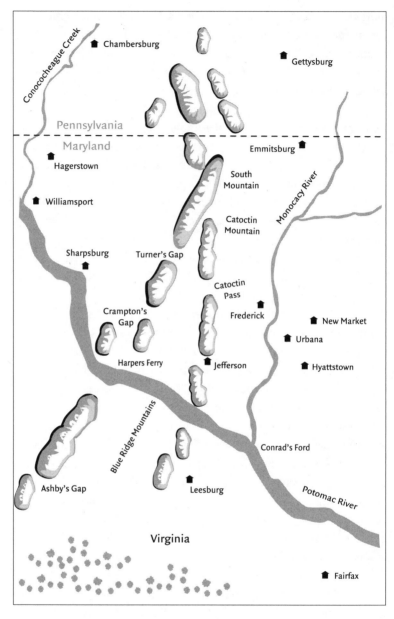

Maryland Campaign and Chambersburg Raid, 1862

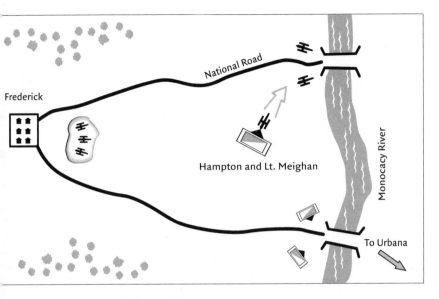

National Road

Frederick

Hampton and Lt. Meighan

Monocacy River

To Urbana

Frederick, Maryland, September 12, 1862

in the direction of Hagerstown, Maryland. A determined, aggressive Union commander—which McClellan was not—could move quickly and smash Lee before he had the chance to reconcentrate his forces.[21]

Stuart made his temporary headquarters at the town of Urbana and established a line facing east. Hampton found himself in the center of the line near Urbana and Hyattstown; Lee's brigade covered the left near New Market and the Baltimore and Ohio Railroad, while Munford was on the right. While detachments throughout the division picketed and scouted, there was time for some of Hampton's men to enjoy getting to know the local inhabitants, especially the ladies. Stuart himself decided to host a ball on the night of the seventh at a female academy in Urbana, inviting his senior officers, staff, and the local gentry. Hampton, of course, did not attend.

The sounds of booming cannon and musketry interrupted the festivities as a force of Union cavalry tried to rush Hampton's outpost pickets. Stuart and other officers hastily left the ball, and part of Hampton's 1st North Carolina charged and scattered the intruders. This allowed the ball to resume temporarily, and Stuart returned to order the band to pick up where it had left off. The gaiety did not last long. Soon some of Hampton's men arrived at the door of the academy carrying their wounded comrades. The music stopped, and Maryland belles in ball gowns became nurses.[22]

Over the next few days, the cavalry's mission of delaying McClellan's westward pursuit became more difficult. The new cavalry division would face its first severe test, and Wade Hampton would have the opportunity to demonstrate whether he had the tactical ability, quick judgment, and endurance to be an effective cavalry leader. As the pressure increased, Stuart pulled his line back on September 12, with Hampton ordered to hold the center in the vicinity of Frederick. In the midst of the withdrawal, Hampton learned around noon that a large Union force was advancing on Frederick via the National Road. Hampton already had two squadrons guarding another road (the one connecting Frederick and Urbana) where it crossed the Monocacy River. If he could not delay the large force on the National Road, his two squadrons at the bridge on the Monocacy would be cut off. Immediately Hampton brought an additional rifled gun to the two that were already on the road. He also ordered up a squadron of the 2nd South Carolina led by Lieutenant John Meighan, a forty-four-year-old Irish shoe salesman from Columbia. Two of Meighan's men were killed while holding this position. Finding that the other two squadrons on the Monocacy were finally on their way into Frederick, Hampton began slowly withdrawing the 2nd South Carolina, simultaneously placing his artillery on some high ground covering the western approaches to the city.[23]

But the danger had not yet passed. The fast-pursuing Federals emplaced a gun on the outskirts of town and, "with unparalleled atrocity," Hampton reported, fired into the "crowded streets" of Frederick.[24] This force, too, was a threat to the brigade's safe retreat. Hampton ordered Meighan's squadron to charge. He also attached to Meighan a provost guard of forty men hastily assembled from the various units of the brigade. The attack, directed by Colonel Calbraith Butler, completely overwhelmed the Federals.[25]

Hampton was proud of the results. Meighan's troops were among the new arrivals from South Carolina and had never before been under fire. "And yet," Hampton reported, "no troops could have behaved better."[26] James K. Munnerlyn of the Jeff Davis Legion wrote that "our men" broke into the enemy's ranks and "did good work with their sabres."[27] The charge scattered the enemy "in every direction, killing and wounding many, [and] taking 10 prisoners," as well as the Union gun.[28] One of the prisoners was Colonel Augustus Moor of the 28th Ohio, who had fallen captive to Lieutenant Meighan. The two officers had sparred with sabers until the Federal expertly twisted Meighan's saber out of his hand. Meighan reacted by riding close alongside, leaning out of his own saddle, and tackling Moor to the ground.[29]

For a few days, Stuart's troopers stubbornly gave ground to the Federals, trying to slow their advance as much as possible, giving Jackson time to reduce the Harpers Ferry garrison and Lee time to gather his army before McClellan's larger force caught up with him. The discovery that McClellan had obtained possession of a lost copy of Lee's orders to his commanders made the cavalry's delaying mission all the more critical. McClellan now knew how scattered Lee's forces were, which explained the increased pressure on the Confederate cavalry screen. McClellan was finally coming after Lee, and Lee needed Stuart not only to hold the line of hills known as South Mountain, but also to ascertain the strength of the columns coming after him.[30]

Hampton soon had more reason to appreciate the abilities of his subordinate commanders and their troopers. Martin's Jeff Davis Legion, with elements of the 1st North Carolina, fought a defiant delaying action guarding Catoctin Pass near Middletown on September 13. For five hours the gray troopers held off a combined attack of cavalry, infantry, and artillery before Hampton pulled them back. The 1st North Carolina then held fast as a rear guard while Hampton withdrew the Jeff Davis Legion to Boonsboro. As Stuart had directed, Hampton took the rest of the brigade south to Burkittsville to help Munford defend Crampton's Gap. Along the way, he came into contact with a Union cavalry column moving in the same direction along a parallel route. Hampton hastily tossed his overcoat to Preston with instructions to hold it for him, then ordered Young's Cobb Legion to charge. Young and his troops charged "in gallant style," wrote Hampton, crossing sabers with the men in blue and chasing them away. Hampton reported that Lieutenant Colonel Young, Captain G. J. Wright, and seven others were wounded; Lieutenant Marshall, Sergeant Barksdale, and two others were killed. The Federals lost thirty killed and wounded. What Hampton did not mention in his official report was his later confrontation with his son. Preston had not held his father's overcoat; he had tossed it into the corner of a fence and ridden off after him to join the fray. After the skirmish, the two Hamptons sat their horses next to the dropped overcoat and stared at each other. Preston turned away and looked around defiantly at the gathering circle of officers. "I came to Maryland to fight Yankees," he announced, "not to carry father's overcoat."[31] Hampton, as well as the other elders present, decided that his son had spoken well.[32]

As Hampton drew nearer Crampton's Gap, Munford mistook his column for one of the enemy and was about to order his artillery to fire. Hampton fortunately recognized the danger and waved a white cloth to alert Munford of his mistake. Munford's gunners had only to pull the lanyard. At the last instant, Munford saw Hampton's signal and withheld the order to fire.[33]

The next day Stuart directed Hampton to the southernmost end of South Mountain, fearing that a large Federal infantry force was marching toward Harpers Ferry to lift Jackson's siege of the garrison. On September 14 Hampton crossed to the Virginia side of the river to protect Major General Lafayette McLaws's infantry division as it entered Harpers Ferry. On the seventeenth he recrossed the Potomac and rejoined Stuart at Sharpsburg, where Lee had finally managed to assemble most of his army. As he arrived, the outnumbered Army of Northern Virginia, with its back to the Potomac River, was in a fight for its life against a Union host that outnumbered it two to one. The Confederate high command looked for an opportunity to use Stuart's cavalry against the Federal right flank, but found none—Hampton's brigade and Stuart's cavalry as a whole played no significant role in the Battle of Sharpsburg.[34]

Strategically, Lee's Maryland invasion was a failure. Able to muster only 39,000 troops against McClellan's 71,500, his army had suffered over 10,000 casualties—more than one-fourth of its strength. The Confederates had managed to inflict 12,410 Federal casualties and had fought heroically, but Lee's army was too bloodied and exhausted to continue its invasion of hostile territory with McClellan's legions so close by.[35] The invasion had not produced the decisive results all had hoped for on that glorious night when the army had crossed the Potomac. Nevertheless, the army's organization—and its confidence—was intact, and Hampton could find no fault whatsoever with the conduct of his own officers and men. Butler's and Baker's regiments and the Cobb and Jeff Davis legions had all performed heroically. Hart's artillery battery, too, had provided yeoman service in helping to break up several Yankee attacks. Even young Preston had sought and passed his own rite of passage. Stuart was pleased as well. His official report did not praise Hampton personally, but he was clearly impressed with the "gallant" behavior of each of Hampton's units, using the word repeatedly to express his appreciation.[36] Hampton had passed his first test as a cavalryman.

His next mission was to create a diversion to help cover Robert E. Lee's withdrawal from Maryland. Lee specified that his nephew's cavalry brigade would form the rearguard as the main body of the Army of

Northern Virginia crossed back into its own territory. Hampton, mean- while, was to make a dangerous night crossing at an obscure ford through deep, fast-moving water. His orders were to move west along the south bank of the Potomac, then recross into Maryland, occupy the town of Williamsport, and distract McClellan from following Lee. Hampton's thoroughly exhausted men occupied Williamsport on the afternoon of September 19 and began spreading rumors among the local population that the rest of Lee's army was close behind. Stuart then ordered Hampton to move north toward Hagerstown and create more havoc and consternation.[37]

Hampton balked. He could be just as bold as Stuart when necessary, but his conservative instincts told him that this was a time to be cau- tious. His scouts had captured prisoners from not one, but several, Federal divisions, indicating that McClellan had more troops coming after him than Stuart realized. Stuart, however, insisted on the move. Some members of Stuart's staff claimed that Hampton complied but said to Major Heros von Borcke, "Good-bye, my dear friend; I don't think you will ever see me or a man of my brave brigade again."[38] This phrasing sounds unusually melodramatic for Hampton, but it captures his sense of foreboding. Hampton's concerns were justified. His col- umns ran into heavy resistance on every road leading from Williamsport to Hagerstown. A large force of cavalry and a division of Federal infantry were blocking every approach, indicating that Hampton's mission of drawing attention to himself had succeeded only too well. Not only could he not reach Hagerstown, he could not even get out of Williams- port. Stuart finally ordered him to return to Virginia.[39]

⭐ During the last week of September and early October, Stuart's cav- alry division enjoyed a respite as the gray troopers occupied a line stretching from Martinsburg to Charlestown, Virginia. Stuart and his headquarters staff spent most of their time at the nearby plantation of the Dandridge family. The Dandridges were gracious hosts, supplying the officers with platters of veal and trays of mint juleps. There were balls, campfire songs, comic skits, and practical jokes. Hampton's only recreation seems to have been hunting on the Dandridge's spacious estates. Several nights later, just before another raid across the Potomac, some cavalrymen noticed him standing alone on the south bank of the Potomac, seemingly deep in thought.[40]

Hampton had good reason to be somber. Sometime after he arrived back in Virginia, he learned that Sally, Frank's wife, had died while

Wade was in Maryland. Wade and Sally had grown close since her marriage to Frank, and her situation had been an extremely sad one. Though she had been happy among her husband's family in South Carolina, after the fall of Fort Sumter she had become despondent with the realization that she was cut off from her parents and siblings in New York. She received no mail from home for over a year. Meanwhile, her tuberculosis grew worse. Wade was concerned about her in the summer of 1862, and about Frank. Frank Hampton had commanded a cavalry company in South Carolina since the beginning of the war but had stayed close to home due to Sally's worsening condition. Beginning in early June 1862, Wade tried to persuade him to take a commission in the newly forming 2nd South Carolina in Virginia, thinking that active service would take his mind off his troubles.[41]

Hampton also tried to help Sally by finding a way for her parents to visit her. He wrote to Confederate secretary of war George Randolph to arrange permission for the Baxters to slip through the Union blockade and travel to Columbia. The Confederate authorities had no objection, but the U.S. authorities seem to have prohibited the visit. For whatever reason, the plan never came to fruition. Twenty-nine-year-old Sally died on September 10, far away from home. She left a grieving husband and four small children.[42]

Hampton grew pensive and sentimental in an October 5 letter to Mary Fisher. He grieved for Frank, knowing firsthand what it was like to lose a wife in her youth. Sally's death also reminded him that his own wife and children, including Wade and Preston, were all well. As he reflected on the past fifteen months of war, a welter of conflicting emotions engulfed him—sadness, thankfulness, longing for peace, submission to God, and bitterness toward the Yankees:

My heart is deeply thankful for that mercy which has spared me & mine. I pray that we may still be spared, but if this is not to be, I pray that I may be able to discharge my duty faithfully, so as to merit the "well-done" not only from my country, but from my God. My heart has grown sick of the war, & I long for peace. If it does not come this winter, there is no saying when we may look for it. As long as the madness of the Yankees continues, so long will this fearful war. . . . Frank has taken his position as Lt. Col. Poor fellow. I feel very sorry for him. He seems calm & I have no doubt but that his duties here, will serve to distract his mind from his sorrow. . . . Kiss the children for me & God bless you all.[43]

Lieutenant Colonel Frank Hampton (1829–63). Youngest brother of Wade Hampton III, killed at Brandy Station. South Caroliniana Library.

When Hampton surmised that if peace did not come "this winter," there was "no saying" when it might come, he was keeping an eye on the political situation in the North. There was significant opposition to the war on the Union side, and some informed Confederates hoped that large Democratic gains in the congressional elections would force the Lincoln administration to negotiate a peace with the South.[44]

Frank Hampton went to Virginia soon after his wife's death and assumed his post as lieutenant colonel of the 2nd South Carolina, making him Calbraith Butler's second in command. Frank was just as tall as his older brother, but contemporaries considered him far more handsome. Those who knew him appreciated his good humor, and Butler became very fond of him. Frank fortunately justified Wade's efforts in finding a field commission for him; Butler spoke of the younger brother's "promptness and gallantry" on the battlefield.[45]

Frank did not go into action immediately. Robert E. Lee, Jeb Stuart, and Wade Hampton were already making plans for a cavalry raid into Pennsylvania, and only a carefully selected 1,800 men would join the expedition. Lee wanted Stuart to cross the Potomac upstream from Williamsport and proceed toward Chambersburg, Pennsylvania, to destroy the railroad bridge over Conocogheague Creek. The Confederates also aimed to collect intelligence on McClellan's dispositions and intentions, and destroy or confiscate any military supplies they found. Horses, in particular, would be valuable prizes for Stuart's command, which by this point in the war was beginning to feel a lack of adequate mounts. Confederate officers were to provide receipts to civilian merchants and families for any shoes, clothing, horses, or provisions seized by their troops. The receipts would state that the goods were taken for the benefit of the Confederate government, so that citizens could apply to the U.S. government for reimbursement. Additionally, Lee authorized Stuart to seize U.S. officials as hostages to be later exchanged for captured Confederate officials. After reaching Chambersburg and stirring up a hornet's nest of pursuing Federals, Stuart was to use his own judgment on how best to make it back to Virginia.[46]

This was just the kind of dangerous, romantic adventure that Stuart relished; it was just the kind of difficult mission that Hampton faced with grim determination. The Confederates selected roughly six hundred sturdy men with sturdy mounts from each of the three cavalry brigades for the raid, along with four pieces of horse artillery, including two of Captain Hart's guns. Hampton appointed Calbraith Butler to lead the six hundred men from his own brigade—selected from among all of Hampton's regiments and legions. W. H. F. "Rooney" Lee, the son of Robert E. Lee and cousin of Fitz Lee, would command the six hundred handpicked men of his cousin's brigade, since Fitz was out of action due to a serious injury. Colonel William E. "Grumble" Jones, the new commander of Munford's brigade, would lead the third contingent. Hampton, as Stuart's second in command, would travel in the vanguard with his own brigade. The Confederates began riding north on October 9 and crossed the Potomac shortly after dawn the next day. Stuart mysteriously informed the men in the ranks that they were about to embark on a dangerous mission but did not tell them where they were going.[47]

Hampton's advance guard scattered a contingent of Federal pickets as it crossed the Potomac on the morning of the tenth. It had hoped to capture the Federals, but a barking dog belonging to the bluecoats gave them away. Hampton immediately sent a detail of twenty men to capture a nearby signal station. The men returned with signal flags and eight or ten prisoners. The prisoners, along with local citizens, told the Confederates that a large force of Federal infantry and artillery under Brigadier General Jacob Cox was in the area. Around midmorning, the northbound Confederate columns crossed the National Turnpike, only one hour after Cox's powerful column had passed that point traveling west on the pike. It was such a near miss that Hampton's men captured ten stragglers from Cox's command.[48]

Around noon, the Confederate raiders rode into Mercersburg, Maryland, where Stuart briefly considered aborting the mission. He was concerned that local telegraph stations had spread word of his location. After conferring with his subordinate commanders, however, Stuart chided himself for his caution and directed the columns to continue toward Chambersburg.

Meanwhile, details of gray-clad troopers fanned out to round up shoes from local merchants and horses from farmers. The "ludicrous" reactions of stunned farmers greatly amused the southerners, as the locals reacted to the sudden arrival of the Confederates with a mixture of alarm and confusion.[49] Even Hampton wrote Mary Fisher that "it was very funny to see the conduct of the Yankees; some took us for Federals; some ran & some gazed at us in total bewilderment."[50]

Hampton's advance guard reached the outskirts of Chambersburg around 7:00 P.M. in a pouring rain. Here Hampton and Stuart paused to consider their next move. There were reports that Union troops were in the town, but it was too dark to reconnoiter to find out. Nor would it be civilized to fire into the town and take it by force without first warning the local citizens and demanding its surrender. Hampton recommended that twenty-five men be sent into the town to demand a surrender. If the citizens refused, there was a good chance that there was indeed a strong Union garrison within, and local leaders would be warned that a Confederate bombardment would begin within minutes. Whether Stuart and Hampton were bluffing or not is uncertain; thankfully, no one had to find out. The town's leaders asked what terms were proposed; Hampton replied "unconditional surrender," with the promise that "private persons" suffer no harm.[51]

In accordance with Stuart's orders, Hampton assumed the role of "military governor" of the city and appointed a "rigid provost guard" to ensure order.[52] He sent a clear message to his troops in one other way as well. Soon after entering Chambersburg, Hampton knocked on the door of a home on Main Street. He then gave the occupants permission to shoot any private who tried to force his way into the house unless accompanied by an officer.

Wade Hampton, and indeed Jeb Stuart and the army commander, anxiously hoped to be regarded as gentlemen, not ruffians. It was a difficult pose to strike. Hampton had assured the citizens that his men would respect their private property, "except such as should be needed for the use of our army."[53] That caveat covered a lot. Stuart's horsemen took more than horses, mules, and wagonloads of forage—they unsuccessfully searched cash drawers in stores and banks. They were generally polite in asking for food and provisions, and the nervous civilians did not refuse them. But the Confederates also sought out local dignitaries and snatched them away from their families. Certainly they assured the families said that no harm would come to them, but that would have only partially assuaged the people's fear and outrage. Still, at least one prominent Yankee was impressed with the ability of Hampton and his officers to strike the gentleman's pose. Pennsylvania editor A. K. McClure recalled that Hampton displayed a "respectful and soldierlike manner" and that his officers offered to pay for the coffee and tobacco McClure gave them.[54]

Stuart's troops may have found little cash, but they hit the jackpot when searching government warehouses on the outskirts of town. There they discovered ammunition, five thousand new rifles, sabers and pistols, and vast quantities of hats, warm blue overcoats, trousers, boots, and shoes. Meanwhile, Stuart sent out Grumble Jones to cut telegraph wires and to destroy the railroad bridge east of town. Jones failed in the important second mission, finding that the bridge was made of iron. The Confederates settled down in their new warm overcoats to spend one more rainy night in Chambersburg.[55]

Stuart decided not to retrace his steps back home. Reasoning that enemy units would be awaiting his return, he instead marched northeast to Cashtown and then turned southeast, crossed the Monocacy, and rode through the towns of Liberty, New Market, and Monrovia. Stuart previously had given Hampton the honor of leading the advance—now he reaffirmed his confidence in him by designating him the rear guard on the return journey. Along the way, the Confederates cut more telegraph lines, captured wagons, and delivered intercepted dispatches to Stuart informing him of Union columns trying to head him off. Stuart's daring band was now between McClellan's army and Washington, and riding hard throughout the night to stay ahead of its pursuers. The exhausted men still pushed on after sunrise, passing through Hyattstown and Barnesville.

The most dangerous part of the mission came at the end, no more than six miles from the Potomac and safety. Stuart received several reports that four to five thousand Union infantry were at Poolesville and guarding the nearby fords; meanwhile, a column of Union cavalry was close behind him. Stuart set out from Barnesville on the road to Poolesville, then veered west. Near the river, he met a column of enemy cavalry and detachments of infantry. With a quick charge, some well-aimed shots, and a bit of bluff and cunning, Rooney Lee overcame those obstacles. The Rebel column then dashed directly for White's Ford. Nearby Union detachments shelled and sniped at the Confederates as they tried to escape through the ford. While Lee's and then Jones's detachments splashed across, Hampton had his South Carolinians and men from a recently joined unit known as Phillips' Legion form a rear guard. He emplaced one rifled gun on some high ground near the ford and provided covering fire as gray troopers continued to cross the Potomac. At the last minute, Hampton, Butler, the gun section, and the last Confederates dashed across under ineffectual enemy fire. The timing was perfect—Rooney Lee's guns were now providing cover from their new position on the Virginia side of the river.

It was expertly done. The entire command had suffered a few slight wounds and lost two men who had fallen behind. Stuart and his gray paladins had ridden completely around McClellan's army and covered a distance of 126 miles, the last eighty of them in a 36-hour sprint with no rest. The effect on morale was greater than the tangible military benefits. Embarrassed Federal officers made excuses and pointed fingers. Confederates, both during and after the war, regarded the feat as further proof of southern dash and chivalric prowess. They had shown the Yankees once again, they believed, that they were the better men.[56]

RAIDING ON THE RAPPAHANNOCK

Jeb Stuart and Wade Hampton had shared much danger and accomplished a great deal, but they were no fonder of each other than before. Stuart continued to make his camp with the Lees' Virginia brigade, where he found the company jollier. Hampton's resentment of Stuart grew but remained just under the surface. The two men never openly quarreled, but Hampton clearly felt he was a victim of favoritism. Hampton was satisfied with Stuart's leadership of the Chambersburg raid itself, as well as with his own men's performance, but felt that Stuart slighted the accomplishments of his men in favor of the Virginians. "My Brigade first crossed the Potomac," he told Mary Fisher, "& protected the others as we came back. But I suppose Stuart, will as usual give all the credit to the Va. Brigades. He praises them on all occasions, but does not often give us any credit."[1]

In his official report, however, Stuart distributed praise fairly equitably. Hampton had another complaint, though. The Virginia troops received easier assignments, less picket duty, and better pasture for their horses, while Hampton's brigade always got "the hardest work to perform & the worst places to camp at."[2] By mid-November Hampton feared that his horses would soon be so broken down that he would be unable to restore their health before spring. The other cavalry brigades were with the main army at Fredericksburg, enjoying, Hampton supposed, comfortable quarters and easily accessible forage. Hampton's brigade was over twenty miles away, where, he groused, it had "to take the hard work, & starve in this poor country."[3]

Hampton's resentment may have been partly justified, but the truth was that worn-out men and horses were a problem throughout Stuart's cavalry in the autumn of 1862. On the other hand, during the same period the Union cavalry seemed more numerous, confident, and aggressive than before—the Confederates could no longer count on the enemy fleeing every time they made a determined charge. Part of the reason went back once again to horseflesh and the Confederacy's inferior system of keeping its cavalry supplied with horses. The Federals' reserve of strong, fresh horses seemed endless by comparison. A new development was the Yankees' tactic of riding to the scene of battle and then dismounting to fight on foot, allowing for more accurate rifle vol- 127 leys and an increased disposition to stand and fight. It served the northern horsemen well, for they typically had never been as comfortable and confident fighting on horseback as their southern counterparts.[4]

Hampton was not willing to concede that his foes' capabilities had improved, and indeed the southern horsemen were still holding their own against superior numbers. On November 22 he wrote home that his troops "always drive the Yankees, & are beating them at their own style of fighting, which is to dismount a large number of men & fight them as Infantry."[5] Actually, though, Hampton had witnessed the Yankees' stiffer resolve firsthand on November 5 at Barbee's Crossroads.

Stuart had brought Hampton's and Tom Rosser's (normally Fitz Lee's) brigades together at the crossroads the night before. Stuart did not intend to hold the position long, but he expected an advance of Federal cavalry the next morning and did not want to leave the place without making a fight. The two understrength Confederate brigades faced north, with Hampton on the left and Rosser on the right.[6]

The Federals came into view around 9:00 A.M. with five regiments of cavalry and a battery of artillery. The two sides exchanged fire until about noon, with the Federals not only refusing to back off but also seeking to get around Stuart's right flank. Stuart, meanwhile, received word that another enemy force had been spotted at Warrenton, in his rear. He ordered a withdrawal. Hampton directed James B. Gordon's 1st North Carolina, which had been his reserve, to move forward and act as a rear guard to cover the withdrawal of the Cobb Legion. Gordon did not get far before he halted, observing that a Union regiment (the 8th New York) had circled around to his left flank. He sent a courier to Hampton, who arrived in minutes. Facing west, Gordon saw a stone wall straight ahead and blue-clad troopers behind it. To his right front was another stone wall, which ran at right angles to the first. Gordon was not sure but thought that he saw dismounted blue soldiers behind that wall also. "Shall I charge them?" Gordon shouted to Hampton. He informed Hampton that he had seen more troops to his right behind another stone fence. Hampton replied that he had been over that ground that morning, and that there was no stone fence there. He ordered Gordon to charge and told him that he would send the 2nd South Carolina to his support. The 1st North Carolina charged ahead, and the Yankees in their front scampered to the rear. Just before coming to the stone wall in their front, however, some Tar Heels tumbled into a broad ditch that had been concealed by thick grass. As they realigned their ranks, the Yankees behind the other stone wall on their right saw their opportunity.

They poured rifle fire into Gordon's right flank, and a nearby artillery piece added to the carnage. Gordon looked around for his promised help, but the 2nd South Carolina's route to his position was blocked by the withdrawal of the Cobb Legion. In an attempt to retire, Gordon wheeled left. As he did so, another body of Union cavalry, previously concealed behind a hill, charged down on his right flank, which now extended to the southwest. That was the final blow. Gordon's men broke ranks and bolted.[7]

Moments later the 1st North Carolina rallied behind the cover of John Pelham's guns, but the affair at Barbee's was disturbing for several reasons. One was that, for once, Hampton's "innate topographical sense" had failed him. The result was that several brave North Carolinians were killed, wounded, or captured. It was also singular that the Yankees had pursued the withdrawing Confederates aggressively—front, flanks, and rear. Finally, it was clear that a spirited charge by gallant southern horsemen had not been enough to drive them away.[8]

Hampton may have been disgusted with Stuart in late November, but he was not idle. The makeup of his brigade had changed several times over the previous several weeks. By December he had three regiments and three legions again. Butler still commanded the 2nd South Carolina, and Gordon led the 1st North Carolina. Hampton had recently been reinforced with the 1st South Carolina, commanded by Lieutenant Colonel J. D. Twiggs. He was happy to have Lieutenant Colonel Will Martin's Jeff Davis Legion back with him, along with the Cobb Legion and Phillips Legion.

By this time Hampton was on the extreme left flank of Robert E. Lee's main army, which occupied a strong defensive position behind the Rappahannock overlooking the river and the city of Fredericksburg. The new Union army leader, Ambrose Burnside, was on the other side of the river and contemplating a difficult—or suicidal—crossing. Burnside's army received supplies via two routes. One was a waterbound course along Aquia Creek, which flowed into the Potomac. The other route was Telegraph Road, which ran from Fredericksburg midway between the courses of the Rappahannock and the Potomac up to Dumfries and Occoquan. Hampton decided, apparently without specific orders from Stuart, to see what mischief he could work in Burnside's rear.

On November 27 Hampton crossed the Rappahannock at Kelly's Ford with just two hundred men. He learned that a body of Union cavalry was encamped near Hartwood Church, or "Yellow Chapel" as Hampton called it, just eight miles northwest of Falmouth. That night

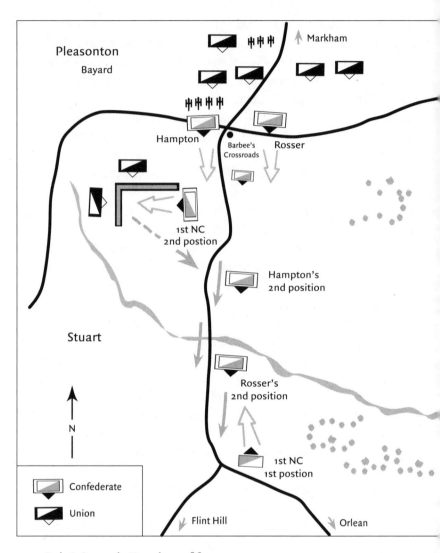

Barbee's Crossroads, November 5, 1862

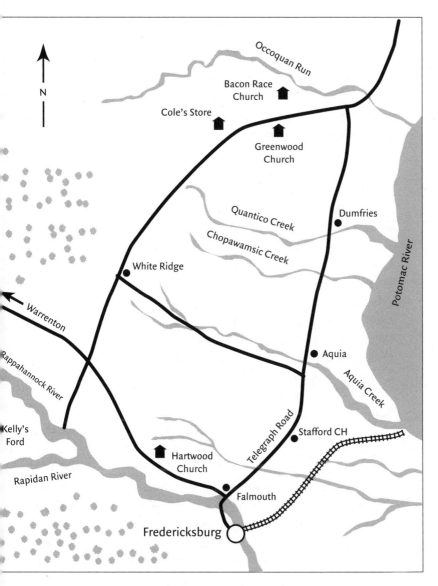

Hampton's Winter Raids, 1862–1863

he halted his small band in some woods two miles from the church. The woods were situated between two roads that led to the church, and both roads had picket guards from the 3rd Pennsylvania Cavalry. He moved out again at 4:00 A.M., staying in the woods and avoiding the roads. His men charged into the camp at dawn and captured all seventy men present. Hampton then sent a detachment from the Cobb Legion to capture the picket guard on one of the roads. He returned to camp with 87 Union enlisted prisoners, 5 officers, 2 stands of enemy colors, 100 horses, and about 100 carbines. His own losses were none.[9]

Jeb Stuart and Robert E. Lee were elated with Hampton's exploit. Lee commended his judgment, skill, energy, and courage, and wrote the secretary of war that Hampton and his men deserved high praise. He also sent the captured colors on to the War Department for display in Richmond. Secretary of War James Seddon in turn applauded Hampton's "dashing exploit" and placed the captured guidons in the War Office with notes attached explaining the details of their capture "to awaken the emulation of his brother officers."[10] In the meantime, the Union high command dismissed Captain George Johnson of the 3rd Pennsylvania from the army for negligence and for allowing most of his command to be captured. Hampton said little to the women at home about the raid, simply joking to Mary Fisher: "You see Burnside has dismissed one of his Capts. caught by me. I wish Burnside had been there and he would have shared the same fate."[11]

Two weeks later Hampton decided to strike again, this time with a larger force and broader goals. The Confederates expected a major assault on their Fredericksburg lines any day, and Hampton hoped to disrupt Federal plans and divert enemy troops. He also wanted to capture much-needed supplies in the Federal depots at Dumfries and Occoquan, nearly thirty miles behind enemy lines. Plans for the raid mirrored those for Chambersburg and the smaller one Hampton had led two weeks earlier—the hardiest 520 men and mounts would be selected from his six subordinate units. The various detachments would fall under two "brigades," one led by Butler and the other by Will Martin of the Jeff Davis Legion; both would report to Hampton.

Hampton and his men splashed across the frigid Rappahannock on the evening of December 10 and took a circuitous, westerly route to Dumfries. His thinly clad men shivered as they traveled throughout the next day across snow-covered ground. On the morning of the twelfth, they rode into Dumfries. A small enemy detachment offered brief resistance before a few shots and a charge by Hampton's men forced all of the Federals to flee or surrender. Hampton intended to march on to Occoquan but learned that a full Union infantry corps under Franz Sigel was marching toward him from that direction. He retraced his route home, bringing with him over fifty prisoners, seventeen wagons, and the apparatus of the local telegraph office. His men had already helped themselves to new boots, gloves, shoes, hats, fine underwear, food, and drink. Again Hampton came in for praise from Stuart and Lee. Stuart summarized the mission succinctly in his official endorsement on Hampton's report: "Respectfully forwarded. Brigadier-General Hampton, with a command thinly clad and scantily fed, displayed, amid the rigors of winter and on the desert track of an invading host, an activity, gallantry, and cheerful endurance worthy of the highest praise and the nation's gratitude."[12]

⭐ On the morning that Hampton returned from Dumfries, the terrible Battle of Fredericksburg began. While Hampton's cavalry remained on the left flank of the Confederate main army, Burnside foolishly hurled thousands of bluecoats against Lee's impregnable position above the town. Stuart's horse artillery under John Pelham meanwhile helped Stonewall Jackson repulse a determined Federal attack on the Confederate right. The most significant result of the whole affair was the useless slaughter or maiming of roughly 12,000 Federal soldiers and 5,000 Confederates.[13]

Burnside regrouped on his side of the Rappahannock, and Hampton struck his rear once again during the week before Christmas. Crossing the Rappahannock on December 17 with 465 men, he made it all the way to Occoquan village this time. A New Jersey cavalry regiment made something of a fight on the eighteenth, but Hampton still rode away with approximately 150 prisoners, 20 wagons, 30 rifles, 300 pairs of boots, a stand of colors, and a rapidly dwindling cache of champagne, claret, and fine cheeses. As on the last two raids, Hampton lost not a single man. Hampton and his brigade were proud of their feats. He told Mary Fisher that although the Yankees swore to stop his raids, he would "teach them, that it is hard to catch me, on the ground I know so well."[14] A homesick Hampton wrote home on Christmas Day to express his sadness at being away; he consoled himself with a glass of "Burnside's champagne [which I] find . . . very good. I must lay in another supply soon."[15] One senses that even the grim Hampton was beginning to enjoy these adventures behind enemy lines.[16]

The last winter raid of Lee's Confederate cavalry was the most ambitious of all, and it was led by Stuart himself. Gathering four guns and 1,800 men from his three brigades—Hampton's, Fitz Lee's, and Rooney Lee's—Stuart set out on December 26. This expedition went far beyond the Occoquan, ranging up to Vienna and Frying Pan. The length of the expedition made it a far more punishing one for the gray troopers than Hampton's had been. After two days and two nights in the saddle, men fell asleep on horseback as the column plodded on through the night. Men dismounted and walked their horses for miles at a time so that the exercise would keep them from freezing. Hampton and most of the division were back in camp by New Year's Day, but many felt that the weeklong journey had not been worth it. Instead of a bloodless romp, the Confederates lost 1 officer killed, 13 men wounded, and 13 missing. They did capture about 200 prisoners, 200 horses, 20 wagons, and over 100 weapons—comparable to the haul taken in Hampton's shorter, smaller expeditions—but many officers and men felt that the mission accomplished more for Stuart's vanity than for the Confederate cause.[17]

Hampton certainly agreed. He ended his official report with the statement that the long march forced him to abandon several "broken down" horses, and that many others were rendered unfit for future service. He reserved his bitterest comments, though, and his boasts, for letters to his family. "The affair was a failure," Hampton wrote his sister, "inasmuch as but little was accomplished & many horses were ruined. My men think Stuart came up here because my expedition had been successful & he was jealous of my Brigade. On the [expedition] he gave my men the hardest work to do, & cut them off from their chance of distinction. The whole Brigade seems disgusted & none are willing to go with him again."[18]

In relating his adventures to Mary Fisher, Hampton's pride in his own martial prowess became evident. He also took satisfaction in the fact that the troops had come to regard him as a heroic leader. He had not deliberately sought fame, as John Esten Cooke noted. But he thrilled to see men of the 10th Virginia, which had previously been under his command, wave their hats wildly in a silent cheer as he passed down their line. In the same letter, Hampton described a charge he had led on an enemy detachment at Occoquan—an action that he mentioned only briefly in his official report and that Stuart did not mention at all. He was leading some regiments that had been under Stuart's direct command early in the war. "Stuart will be placed in some difficulty, for when he praises the charge of his Brigade, he will have to say that I led it," he smirked.[19] Hampton related that he happened to be near the front of the column when the enemy appeared and was the natural choice to lead the charge, being intimately familiar with the ground in the Occoquan area from the previous winter. As he led Stuart's old command forward, "the Yankees stood at first & I rode into the midst of them. They fired on me all around, but the two first blows I struck brought down a man each & the others scattered. The first poor devil had his skull frightfully fractured, the worst case of fracture the Dr. said he ever saw, while the other was badly cut. Another was about to shoot me, but I scared him out of it by demanding his surrender."[20]

As usual, Hampton's memories of his combat experiences ended in a prayer of thanks: "I was not touched, & I am again called on to thank God for his mercy in sparing me. I have been in *forty-three* fights, & yet the hand of God has saved me in all of them. The prayers of those who love me, must have been my shield." Hampton ended the letter with a confession that he was "sick of the horror of war." But with a combination of fierce martial pride, bitterness, thankfulness, and horror, Wade Hampton resigned himself to another year of war.[21]

WINTER OF DISCONTENT 1863

In January 1863 Wade Hampton III of South Carolina was an angry man. As far as he was concerned, he was the victim of favoritism, arrogance, conceit, and professional negligence. One man was the source of all those evils bedeviling Hampton—Major General James Ewell Brown Stuart of Virginia.

Hampton believed that Stuart was destroying his brigade. Throughout his life, Hampton had seen himself as a provider and protector. It was one of his strengths as an officer—he won the confidence of his men partly by doing his best to provide for their welfare. It was a trait of military leadership that came naturally to Hampton the patriarch. All of his life he had played the role of provider for women, children, hundreds of slaves, even livestock. Hampton had served with Stuart for only a few months before he began to suspect that the Virginian was more concerned with glory hunting than providing for the men. As early as November 1862 he had reminded Stuart that "as it [had] commenced snowing," his men would need tents.[1] The warmth of his men was all the more on his mind because of the fact that for much of the late autumn, Stuart had posted his brigade in an area where it was difficult to find firewood. "The country [in the Culpeper–Brandy Station area] is exhausted," he wrote in late November, "& I do not see how we are to live. But Genl Stuart never thinks of that; at least as far as my Brigade is concerned."[2]

In the cavalry, being a provider meant taking care of the horses as well. "Hard service," he claimed, had also exhausted his horses. This was a problem for Stuart's entire division, but while Rooney Lee's and Fitz Lee's brigades enjoyed more abundant forage and fodder in the Fredericksburg area, Hampton felt that his men posted far upstream were not only working harder but also "starv[ing] in this poor country."[3]

Hampton's brigade deteriorated further in December. Part of this was due to his own short raids behind Burnside's lines. Hampton, however, had taken small detachments with him on these raids while the other horses rested and always returned within three or four days. Then Stuart led the extended, far-ranging Dumfries raid of December 26–January 1, which punished the Confederate horses and troopers as much as it did their enemies. In mid-January Hampton complained to his friend, Confederate senator Louis Wigfall, that "Stuart made my Brigade march 54 mils. the other day & we could get but little forage. The consequence was a loss along the road of 25 or 30 of my horses."[4] Stuart was all the more guilty of neglect if, as the Carolinians and Deep South men suspected, his whole purpose of the raid was to see that Hampton did not get all the credit and glory for the raids against Burnside.[5]

Usually when a Confederate cavalry unit lost a horse, it lost a man as well. For the Union army, the U.S. government, or in some cases a unit's home state, supplied the cavalry with horses. But Confederate horsemen brought their own mounts from home. When the animal died from overwork, starvation, or disease, the soldier had to replace his own mount. Occasionally he might be lucky enough to acquire one that his regiment had captured from the enemy. Legally captured horses were supposed to become the property of the Confederate government, though this law was rarely enforced. Nevertheless, a man without a horse usually had to buy one or go home on furlough to get another. If he did not, he would be transferred to the infantry or temporarily placed in "Company Q," the body of dismounted men in his regiment. This archaic system was particularly hard on non-Virginia units, who could not resupply themselves as easily from local sources. Most of the two Lees' brigades were composed of Virginia regiments, as was Grumble Jones's. Hampton's "legions" included troops from Mississippi, Alabama, and Georgia, and regiments from the Carolinas.[6]

These disadvantages only heightened Hampton's feeling that Stuart favored the "Virginia Brigades," who got the easy work while his command scouted and starved itself to death. He claimed that Stuart's favoritism was "as marked, as it is disgusting & it constantly makes me indignant. I do not object to the work, but I do object to seeing my command broken down by positive starvation. We cannot get forage, & in the course of a few weeks, my Brigade will be totally unfit for service. This is a hard case, but unless Genl. Lee, to whom I have appealed, interferes, Stuart will certainly have my Brigade out of the field before very long."[7]

If Hampton was exaggerating, it was only slightly. One of Stuart's own staff officers, Major Heros von Borcke, inspected Hampton's brigade in late January and was appalled. "It was a mournful sight," he wrote later, "to see more than half the horses of this splendid command totally unfit for duty, dead and dying animals lying about the camp in all directions. One regiment had lost thirty-one horses in less than a week."[8] Horses continued to succumb to disease. Hampton's human charges suffered as well. It was another cold, wet Virginia winter, and the men were living on very tough beef and rancid bacon.[9]

Hampton had never allowed his disagreements with superiors to become open and public, but he came close to doing so with Stuart. He had strongly disapproved of the way Governor Francis Pickens had handled the secession crisis but had expressed his disgust only privately, remaining cordial to him in public. Hampton and President Davis clearly had not seen eye to eye over his promotion and future assignments during the previous spring, yet both were so discreet that even today the details of the dispute are not entirely clear. With Stuart, however, Hampton nearly let his rage boil over. He went over his head to Robert E. Lee. He even went outside the chain of command completely when he wrote to Senator Wigfall. His letter to Wigfall of January 1863 criticized a brother officer to a politician, but Hampton couched his barbs in a sincere request that the senator present legislation that would help Confederate soldiers. Hampton wanted the law changed so Confederate cavalrymen could legally keep any horses captured from the enemy. He argued that the current law was unfair to the suffering soldier, particularly if he had lost his horse in public service through no fault of his own (such as enduring a fifty-four-mile march with no rest and little forage while under the command of Jeb Stuart).[10]

In early January, Stuart took Fitz Lee's Virginia brigade out of the line and sent it south where it could find better forage and recover its strength. Hampton was livid. Had not his command been doing "all the hard work," and had he not been the one asking for relief? Nearly a month later, Stuart put Fitz Lee back on the line and gave a respite, not to Hampton but to other Virginians under Rooney Lee. Eventually, news of the plight of Hampton's brigade reached President Davis himself. Someone, probably either Wigfall or Hampton, had gone straight to the president. General Lee intervened in mid-February, ordering Stuart to have Rooney Lee's brigade return so that Hampton's command could recuperate. Lee felt compelled to write Davis on February 24 to explain that Hampton's brigade was now off picket duty and to justify the delay in relieving it. "My Brigade is at last ordered to rest," Hampton informed Wigfall, "after it is so broken down, that it can do nothing more to keep the Va. Brigades off duty."[11]

Hampton took the opportunity to ask for a furlough and to seek a transfer to South Carolina as well as a promotion. He was sick of Virginia, of Stuart, and of the whole situation. The winter inactivity of the

Federals made Hampton suspect that they might shift their focus to expanding their foothold in the Carolinas. If that were the case, Hampton wrote Wigfall, he asked the senator to use his influence to have him transferred there so that he could raise and command a division of "Southern Cavalry," as opposed to the Virginia cavalry under Stuart. If there was to be fighting in his home state, Hampton wanted to be there, and he assured Wigfall, probably correctly, that he could do much to organize the cavalry there. Hampton felt that the size of his brigade would increase significantly if it were serving closer to home, and that an entirely new division would grow out of it. Moreover, as "senior Brigadier," Hampton argued, "[I] think that I have some claim to promotion," an event that would lead to Hampton's command of the division. Besides, he sneered, "the Va. Cavalry being according to the Va. papers the best in the service, should be kept by itself, & Stuart could thus have his Division composed altogether of troops from his own state / which would be a great matter for him, *if he ever runs for Gov. of Va.*"[12]

Wade Hampton was allowing Jeb Stuart to bring out the worst in him. At his core, Hampton was not an ambitious man, but jealousy and bitterness were causing him to intrigue and politic outside the chain of command, and to seek promotion. His pride of reputation was turning into selfish ambition. Likewise, his protective instincts for his own command were leading him into jealousy and even paranoia. His paternalistic, chivalrous desire to defend his own state likewise was being perverted, it seems, into a secret wish that his state would be invaded— that way, he might acquire an independent command far away from the nepotistic, self-serving Virginians.

In all fairness, Hampton was far from being the only officer in Lee's army to complain about the favoritism shown to the Virginians. It was a common grievance among non-Virginia officers. Moreover, many of his concerns flowed understandably from his desire to protect his men from undue suffering and to preserve their strength for campaigns the following spring. Finally, this was not the first time that Hampton had privately expressed the wish that his duties might keep him closer to his loved ones and that he might defend his native soil. This time, however, he was expressing those wishes in an unprofessional, opportunistic way.

Hampton and his men finally got their much-needed break. Hampton took his command into a relatively untouched region of the Shenandoah Valley to rest and recover. He himself took a furlough in Columbia, and the men of his brigade also rotated out on furlough. Such furloughs actually served two purposes. They were a boon to the morale and strength of the cavalrymen, and they allowed them to secure new mounts from home. Hampton was away from Virginia for roughly two months. He was able to be with Mary when she gave birth to Alfred Hampton in mid-March 1863. All four sisters were there, as were his teenage daughter, Sally, and little McDuffie, whom Hampton had missed terribly. ("Tell McDuffie that he must be a man, now that he has pantaloons," he had written in November.)[13]

Hampton was not idle throughout his entire two-month furlough. He had taken 150 South Carolinians home with him to procure horses. In early April Confederates in the state began to fear a Union attempt to seize Charleston. Indeed, the Federals made a determined but unsuccessful naval attack on Fort Sumter on April 7. Here was a chance to punish the Yankees in his own native South Carolina, and it mattered little whether Hampton led a division or a squadron. The barbarians were at the gates—every son of chivalry must rally to defend his home. Hampton published a call for his 150 troops to assemble on April 6 in Columbia. From there he wrote to General Beauregard offering their services. Proudly he informed the War Department that "*every one* of my men" had volunteered to spend the rest of the furlough fighting the Yankees around Charleston, and within a few days he was on the coast helping to organize resistance. He left South Carolina soon after, probably in the third week of April.[14]

Stuart was anxious to have Hampton's brigade back. The Virginia brigades had certainly done their share of work while Hampton's men were gathering and grazing horses. Rooney Lee and two understrength regiments had the lions' share of work in April chasing down and limiting the damage of Union major general George Stoneman's division-sized raid on Richmond. Fitz Lee had emulated Hampton's Hartwood Church raid by making another one on February 24 at the same place and hauling off even more prisoners. A few weeks later, however, Fitz had taken a severe drubbing at Kelly's Ford at the hands of his Hartwood Church victim, William W. Averell. It was there that the cavalry division lost its brilliant artillery chief, the "gallant Pelham."[15]

March turned into April, and still Hampton refused to pronounce his brigade ready to return to the front. Grumble Jones asked Robert E. Lee for Hampton's assistance in the Shenandoah, his district, and Stuart pressed Lee to order Hampton to come back. Lee fended off both requests, but he also must have wondered how long, indeed, would it take

Hampton to be ready to take the field again? Lee had gently chided Stuart in February for being too eager for action when his command was not ready. "Your particular attention must be given to the comfort of your men and horses," he had written, "[maintaining] a due regard to their future usefulness and service."[16] On April 20 Lee wrote that he had urged Hampton to bring his brigade back as soon as it was ready, but he did not see "how you [Stuart] are to keep the cavalry together before the grazing season opens."[17] The same day Lee wrote President Davis that he did not know when Hampton's brigade would be fit for service. "General Fitz. Lee is subsisting his brigade in the region from which it was found necessary to withdraw Hampton, without drawing a pound for man or horse from any other source," Lee wrote.[18] Was Robert E. Lee concerned about the care of Fitz Lee's brigade, or was he having doubts about Hampton's fighting spirit? How could his nephew's brigade subsist in the Culpeper area when Hampton's could not?

Hampton began moving his brigade back toward the action on May 3. Before he reached the main army, it had just dealt a stunning blow to Joseph "Joe" Hooker's Union army at Chancellorsville, several miles west of Fredericksburg. This was the site of Robert E. Lee's most brilliant victory to date, as he outflanked and thrashed an army twice the size of his own. The cost, however, proved too high; it included Stonewall Jackson's wounding and eventual death, from which the army never recovered. Stuart led Jackson's infantry corps for several days after Stonewall received his wounds, but Lee then returned Stuart to his cavalry command.

Hampton's arrival signified that the expansion of Stuart's cavalry division into a full corps was nearly complete. On May 25 Hampton's brigade had more than 2,200 men present, mounted, and ready for duty. Fitz Lee's and Rooney Lee's brigades had over 1,300 and 1,500 respectively. Additionally, Stuart now had part of Robertson's North Carolina brigade back under his command, and he would soon have Grumble Jones's Laurel Brigade and Albert Jenkins's brigade as well. By June Stuart would have over 10,000 officers and men present for duty, the largest force he would ever command. Hampton noted how many of the regiments joining Stuart's cavalry were from North Carolina. He still hoped that the army would form a division of "Southern cavalry," and that he would lead it.[19]

Once Hampton's brigade finally returned, it was apparent that not only its men but also its commander were eager and ready to fight. It lifted Hampton's spirits when local residents around Orange and Culpeper welcomed him back, and expressed regret that his brigade had not been there "when the Yankees came." He chuckled to hear residents say, "If old Hampton had been there, the Yankees never would have got across the river." Hampton underlined the word "old" as if he found it humorous. His men, he said, seemed delighted to see him and were eager to "get at the Yankees again."[20] One of his first orders to the entire brigade was to have all the sabers sharpened.

Hampton was looking for action. On June 1 he recommended that an aggressive raid be made across the Rappahannock to capture an entire infantry division. Hampton had reconnoitered Union lines and thought he saw one such division that was so unsupported that, with Stuart's cavalry division and one infantry division, it might be cut off and captured. (The details of Hampton's plan are not extant.) Stuart forwarded the idea to Lee. The army commander doubted that the division was as isolated from the rest of its corps as Hampton suggested; furthermore, he wanted to concentrate and rebuild the cavalry for a fuller invasion of the North itself. But it seemed to relieve Lee to see evidence of Hampton's old fighting spirit once again. He told Stuart that "the gallantry of [Hampton's] proposition" pleased him, that it was "what I should expect of an officer of his boldness and daring."[21] The "Old" Hampton was back.

Hampton's rising spirits were typical of most of Stuart's cavalrymen in the spring of 1863. The cavalry of the Army of Northern Virginia was numerically stronger than it had ever been. The winter had been a hard one, but men and mounts were now as fit and refreshed as they had been for nearly a year. Stuart celebrated at Culpeper on May 22 with a grand review of the brigades of Hampton and the two Lees, and of the horse artillery, now commanded by Robert Beckham. More units continued to pour in to strengthen the division, including Robertson's two regiments from North Carolina and Jones's Laurel Brigade. Two more grand reviews followed, the last attended by Robert E. Lee himself. By this point the grandstanding was beginning to irk some of Stuart's participants in the ranks, but morale was high. No one, civilian or military, doubted that the mounted paladins in gray were on the verge of performing more heroic deeds. Surely southern valor would again prove the foolishness of northern ambitions to direct the destiny of the South.[22]

BRANDY STATION TO GETTYSBURG

On the night of June 8, 1863, Stuart, Hampton, and the Confederate cavalry slept confidently following their grand review performed in the presence of Robert E. Lee. Unknown to any gray troopers, their side of the Rappahannock had been under observation by Union scouts. Stuart had three brigades bivouacked north of Brandy Station, a few miles south of the Rappahannock. Grumble Jones's was at St. James Church. On Jones's right as one faces the Rappahannock was Rooney Lee's brigade and to Jones's left was Fitz Lee's, temporarily led by Thomas Munford. Behind this line and overlooking Brandy Station to the south was Fleetwood Hill, on which Stuart had placed his headquarters. Hampton's brigade and Beverly Robertson's demi-brigade were camped south of the railroad between Brandy Station and Stevensburg. The brigades were situated in a way that indicates that Stuart anticipated soon beginning his march north to screen and support Lee's invasion of Maryland. The dispositions also suggest that Stuart did not expect a large-scale enemy attack.[1]

The scenario was ready-made for an especially chaotic battle and a frustrating one for the Confederates. Union cavalry leader Alfred Pleasonton had known for some time that Stuart's division was concentrated around Culpeper, though he did not realize that it had recently moved about five miles northwest to Brandy Station. He convinced his superiors that the time was ripe to strike an offensive blow against the Rebels. On June 8 Pleasonton divided his command into two columns. In the predawn hours of the ninth, one division led by John Buford crossed Beverly Ford while David Gregg's division crossed Kelly's Ford. Pleasonton's original plan was for the two columns to link up at Brandy Station and slam into the Confederates near Culpeper. While the Federals did not know that Stuart had moved to Brandy Station, the Confederates did not know that the Federals were coming at all. The result was that the Federals had an unexpected opportunity to strike the unsuspecting Stuart from two directions at once—the planned linkup at Brandy Station became a pincer movement with the Rebels trapped in between and taken by surprise.[2]

Neither Hampton nor any other Confederate knew this on hearing gunfire to the north shortly before 6:00 A.M. Over an hour before, Jones

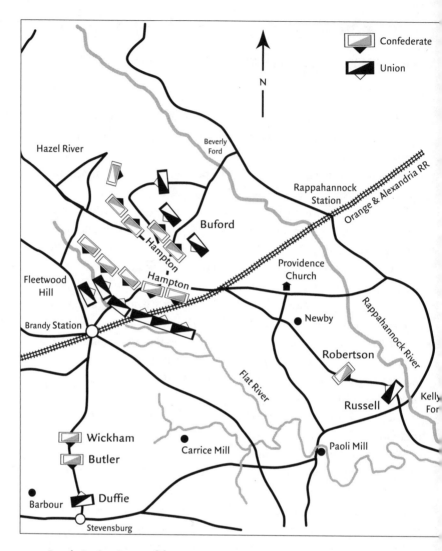

Brandy Station, June 9, 1863

had reported to Stuart that Union columns were driving in his pickets at
Beverly Ford. Stuart had already ordered Hampton's 1st South Carolina
to ride northeast and take up a blocking position astride the road from
Kelly's Ford. But no one on Stuart's staff had bothered to tell Hampton that one of his regiments had been detached from him. Thus, on
hearing the sounds of battle to his north, Hampton, on his own initiative, quickly mounted up his brigade without knowing where one
of his regiments was. He rushed his brigade—minus the one missing regiment—to Brandy Station and reported to Stuart's headquarters.
There a staff officer relayed Stuart's instructions to rush to Jones's
support on the Beverly Ford Road, while leaving one regiment behind at
Brandy Station to picket the roads leading to Kelly's Ford and Carrico
Mills to the east and south. Hampton detached the 2nd South Carolina
led by Calbraith Butler and Wade's brother Frank; this was the last he
would see of that regiment until the battle was over.[3]

As Rooney Lee maneuvered to support Jones's left, Hampton came to
the support of Jones's right just below St. James Church. Here Hampton
found some enemy troops in a wood and determined to drive them
back, hoping to turn the Federal left flank. Hampton had been one of
the first Confederate cavalrymen to overcome the southern distaste for
dismounting cavalrymen at the scene of battle and deploying them as
infantry. Now he ordered one hundred men of the Cobb Legion to
dismount and advance as sharpshooters. The Federals fled until they
reached their reserve line. About this time Hampton located his long-
lost 1st South Carolina and ordered its commander, Colonel John Black,
to have more men turn over their mounts to their comrades and advance
into the woods. Buford then ordered a mounted charge against Hampton, whose line of two hundred or three hundred sharpshooters wavered. Hampton further bolstered his line by committing the Jeff Davis
Legion, dismounted. Hampton's brigade then swept forward, driving
the enemy before it.

Hampton was pleased, as victory seemed within his grasp. By this
time Buford had already decided to withdraw and remain on the defensive, at least until Gregg arrived in the Confederate rear. But Hampton
could not have known that; all he knew was that his men were driving
the Yankees into the woods along the Rappahannock and taking prisoners as they went.[4]

Suddenly disaster struck. Hampton was shocked to see enemy units
attacking Fleetwood Hill in his rear! How had this happened? Wasn't
Beverly Robertson picketing the road to Kelly's Ford near the ford? 147

Wasn't Butler covering the southern and eastern approaches to Brandy Station? It turned out that Robertson had seen Gregg's Union division marching from Kelly's Ford but had done nothing to delay its advance. Calbraith Butler—whether on his own initiative or in response to instructions from Stuart's adjutant Major Henry B. McClellan—had advanced south toward Stevensburg to respond to reports of enemy cavalry there. Gregg had marched right past Robertson and then turned northwest toward Brandy Station and Fleetwood Hill without going within miles of Butler and Frank Hampton's 2nd South Carolina.[5]

Hampton knew nothing of these developments at the time; he only knew that he was being surrounded. A large Union force with artillery was about to occupy a commanding position in the rear of his, Jones's, and the two Lees' brigades. He immediately began pulling his regiments back one by one, wheeling them about, and sending them off in a furious gallop toward Fleetwood Hill. It was a complex operation. Hampton ordered the men who were still mounted to head directly for Fleetwood, while his dismounted sharpshooters were to disengage and follow as rapidly as they could on foot. Jones was executing a similar maneuver. As Hampton turned his command around, a member of Stuart's staff belatedly rode up with orders for Hampton to send one regiment up the hill at a gallop. This may have been the same officer who, observing that Hampton was already disengaging from Buford and turning back to Fleetwood Hill, said, "All things considered, it was the speediest all round movement I ever remember."[6]

Jones had left one of his regiments, the 6th Virginia, under Hampton's command as Jones went to retrieve the rest of his brigade. Hampton ordered it forward, while other regiments, battalions, and gun sections were also racing to the rear to stop the Yankee attack on Fleetwood. There was a race for the crest. Jones's 12th Virginia got there just fifty yards ahead of the Yankees but could not hold the crest when it collided with Gregg's larger, better organized force in blue. Other Confederate units, including the 6th Virginia, arrived in piecemeal fashion, breathless but fighting desperately to save themselves from encirclement and annihilation. For well over an hour, blue and gray charged and countercharged over the crest of Fleetwood Hill. The fighting was savage and hand-to-hand. Soon Hampton's brigade arrived in fairly good order and slammed into the Federals' front and right flank. The Cobb Legion and the 1st South Carolina charged up the hill, while Hampton personally led the 1st North Carolina and the Jeff Davis Legion around the flank. After a few more minutes of the most desperate cavalry fighting of the war, the

attack of the South Carolinians and the Cobb Legion swept the bluecoats
off the hill, capturing many prisoners as well as the Yankee artillery. As
the Federals streamed down the hill and along the railroad to the west,
Hampton's flanking force of Tar Heels and Deep South troopers cut
several blue units apart and captured the regimental colors of the 10th
New York. Hampton's son Preston eagerly rode at the front of one of the
companies of the 1st North Carolina.[7]

Hampton now believed that he was close to capturing the entire
routed Yankee command. But as he tried to finish the job, artillery
rounds began exploding near the head of his pursuing columns. As he
reported: "Our own artillery, which had again been posted on the hill we
had recovered, opened a heavy and well-directed fire at the head of the
column."[8] The Confederate pursuit was delayed. While Hampton's staff
corrected the friendly fire problem, Gregg's shattered units escaped into
some woods. Hampton, however, was still eager to deliver a coup de
grace. He ordered the 1st South Carolina and the Cobb Legion to descend the hill and help his flanking force destroy the retreating foe. He
then found to his dismay that, for at least the second time that day,
Stuart had undermined his control of his brigade. The division commander had directed Hampton's 1st South Carolina and Cobb Legion to
stay on the hill, once again without informing Hampton. Hampton
was extremely proud of the performance of his brigade, but this latest
bombshell was almost too much. For the second time, it seemed to him,
someone else's incompetence had deprived his gallant command of
total victory. Stuart's troopers then faced north once again and eventually forced Buford to withdraw back across the Rappahannock.[9]

It had been quite a day. Hampton and his men had faced near-
disaster twice, and they had rallied to the occasion both times. They had
captured more than 200 enemy soldiers, 60 horses, 82 carbines, 64
pistols, 35 sabers, and a stand of colors, and they had inflicted heavy
casualties. But their own losses were heavy as well; the eventual tally
came to 15 killed, 55 wounded, and 50 missing. Hampton seethed at
how Stuart had handled his brigade. Of course, the division commander
had the authority to issue orders to Hampton's individual regiments.
And Stuart's decision to consolidate his line of exhausted companies
and regiments on Fleetwood Hill was logical, considering the surprises
of the day and the fact that Buford was still a threat to the north. By not
informing Hampton, though, he had undermined Hampton's authority
and control of his brigade. Hampton felt that Stuart's orders more than
once had left him fighting with one hand tied behind his back. Then

there was Robertson's bewildering failure to protect the rest of the division's flank, not to mention Hampton having to watch the horse artillery shell his own men.[10]

There was plenty to seethe over, but that was not all. Couriers arrived from the 2nd South Carolina with worse news still—very bad news, indeed. Frank Hampton had been severely wounded, and an artillery round had irreparably shattered Calbraith Butler's leg, soon to be amputated. Bit by bit Wade Hampton pieced the story together. Butler had moved rapidly to Stevensburg to investigate the presence of Colonel Alfred Duffié's six Union regiments and two batteries moving in that direction. Whether he had done so on his own initiative or in response to an order from Stuart's staff, once again bypassing Hampton in the chain of command, was not immediately clear. Just short of the junction at Stevensburg, Butler had deployed his regiment in a line facing south and protecting the approach to Brandy Station, with Frank Hampton holding the right flank where it ended on the road itself. Meanwhile, Colonel William Wickham's 4th Virginia had been instructed to move down the same road to support Butler. Wickham halted a quarter to a half mile in Butler's rear and sent his lieutenant colonel to ask Butler how he might support him.[11]

Here the historian confronts the difficult problem of determining the actual course of events from conflicting reports. Butler requested that several of Wickham's squadrons be sent to reinforce Frank Hampton, who had only two small squadrons with him. He may also have asked for one dismounted squadron on his left. While Wickham was in the process of deploying his troops, the Federals charged up the road "in masses" at Frank and his handful of men.[12] In accordance with the standard procedure within his brother's brigade, the handsome young Carolinian had had most of the men dismounted. Frank held his position for at least half an hour, and no help came from Wickham.[13]

The South Carolinians and the Virginians bitterly disagreed over what happened next. Wickham claimed that the 2nd South Carolina broke in confusion, "without meeting the charge," and that its rout "utterly demoralized" his own men, who, he humbly admitted, also fled.[14] Only Frank's contingent, however, had come into contact with the enemy, and Butler scoffed bitterly at the idea that Frank's small force could have "run over" an entire mounted regiment of friends.[15] It is clear that some of Frank Hampton's men finally broke under the weight of the Federal assault. Frank himself rallied the thirty-six men who were still mounted and still near him—and charged. He was exchanging saber slashes with a mounted Yankee when another Federal shot a pistol ball into his abdomen. Shortly before or after, a Yankee saber also slashed his head and face. Frank's men carried him off as they abandoned their position and took him to a nearby house.

Preston Hampton was able to go to his uncle's bedside. He grasped Frank's hands in his own as the badly wounded man repeatedly called out for his older brother. But Wade did not come. Captain William Bachman, a veteran officer in Hampton's horse artillery, went to Frank, who smiled when he was told that another courier had been dispatched to find his brother. Frank knew he was dying but assured everyone that his brother "would soon come when duty permitted."[16]

Wade never made it in time. Frank died around dusk. William Bachman was overcome with emotion and left the house. When he reached the gate to the yard, he saw Hampton ride up, "his horse covered with foam." "Am I in time?" asked Hampton. "No General," replied Bachman. "You are too late." Hampton's face "twitched with emotion," and he eventually spoke in a choked voice. "Bachman, you know that nothing but the sternest duty could have detained me. Our position is so critical that I felt called upon to see personally to the posting of every picket." With tears streaming down his cheeks, Hampton strode into the room where his dying brother had spent his last hours waiting for him.[17]

Wade Hampton had seen many friends and neighbors die already, but how was he to deal with this loss? Though Frank was eleven years younger than Wade, they had been close; there was no one who knew Frank who was not fond of him. The two brothers had enjoyed hunting together the previous winter after Frank's arrival in Virginia. Handsome, cheerful, and possessing a gentle, kind manner, the younger man charmed women and men alike. Wade had grieved for Frank when Sally died and took him under his protection when he secured him a commission in the 2nd South Carolina. He had hoped that service at the front would help Frank avoid dwelling on the loss of Sally. He reported on Frank's health and well-being in most of his letters home. Now it was obvious that Wade's protective wing had not been wide enough to save Frank.

Hampton worked hard to restrain any public expression of grief. He had to keep his emotions from spilling over, or he would be incapable of minding his duties. A commander must be in command, not only of his men and the situation around him, but of his own emotions. So also must a southern patriarch display mastery—not only over slaves and dependents, but also over his own conduct and feelings. Even Hampton's letters home, or at least the ones that are extant, did not discuss the tragedy—indicating that the Hampton family destroyed some letters, that they were lost, or that he simply did not trust himself to write about it. Hampton tended to business, completing the necessary tasks at hand, just as he had done after the death of his first wife Margaret. He made arrangements to ship Frank's body home. It was to be buried next to Sally in the graveyard of Trinity Episcopal Church, where all the other Hamptons were buried. Preston would accompany his uncle's remains back to Columbia. Wade also had to consider the four children who had lost their mother, Sally, and now their father within a period of nine months. Once again Hampton's sisters would become surrogate mothers.[18]

Then there was the official report to write, including the part where the commander traditionally summarized his casualties and noted the deaths of brave officers. Hampton buried the terrible information by making it one clause of a larger sentence: "Among the killed I regret to announce the name of Lieut. Col. Frank Hampton, Second South Carolina Regiment, a brave and gallant officer."[19]

⭐ Technically, the Confederates could claim Brandy Station as a victory. Facing odds that were roughly even, they had held the field and inflicted more losses than they themselves suffered. Jeb Stuart tried to present it as a glorious victory, but the men in the ranks knew better. They had been taken off guard, had come within an ace of being crushed, and had lost good men. Newspapers, politicians, and other officers criticized Stuart for being surprised and for allegedly being too addicted to pomp and show. Hampton believed that Stuart had handled the cavalry badly, but this time he did not participate in the gossip. He seems to have made a conscious decision not to undercut the public's faith in the high command, restricting his criticism to his official report that he submitted directly to Stuart's headquarters. Hampton frankly and matter-of-factly reported that Stuart "sent off" the 1st South Carolina without informing him; and that by Stuart's orders to his men on Fleetwood Hill, "I found myself deprived of two of my regiments at the very moment they could have reaped the fruits of the victory they had so brilliantly won."[20]

It could have meant little to Hampton that Stuart was desperately reacting to an emergency situation, or that possibly Stuart's couriers had tried but failed to reach him to inform him of recent orders. Nor did Hampton draw consolation from Wickham's awkward attempt to apologize for his regiment's behavior while simultaneously blaming the 2nd South Carolina for its supposed flight "without meeting the charge." Wickham and his men had performed well in the past and would do so again. That mattered little to Hampton when he thought of his brother's death. Wickham's report, in fact, implied that Frank must have died as a coward, or at the very least as an incompetent leader. To a man, the officers of the 2nd South Carolina agreed that if Wickham had supported Frank, they could have held the position—there would have been no flight at all, no desperate charge by Frank Hampton. Frank and several other beloved comrades would still be alive. Wade Hampton could not allow himself to become unhinged by the tragedy or by what the South Carolinians considered to be the shameful behavior of the Virginians. If he did, the rage would consume him, make him an ineffective leader, and prove him incapable of mastering his emotions. Only years later did Hampton trust his emotions enough to pronounce a verdict on the affair. Speaking to one of his former soldiers, he said that but for "the fact that the Fourth Virginia Cavalry, under the command of Colonel Wickham, broke and ran . . . my brother, Lieutenant Colonel Frank Hampton, would not have been killed that day."[21]

⭐ Brandy Station had been a severe test of Robert E. Lee's cavalry division. The gray troopers had been taken off guard, but the men in the ranks and most of the officers had responded with incredible courage and resolve. Hampton himself had fought well, and his brigade's performance had been a key factor in fending off a disaster. Most importantly, the Confederate troopers' confidence in themselves was very much intact. That was fortunate, because more severe tests and bitter fighting lay ahead for Hampton and his men.

Even before Brandy Station, Robert E. Lee had plans for Stuart's cavalry. Lee had decided to gamble once more on an invasion of the North. More aware than ever that the South could not expect to win a long war of attrition against the North, he hoped that a decisive victory on northern soil would finally convince the government in Washington to let the South go in peace. Failing that, a southern victory in Maryland or Pennsylvania might persuade Britain and France to recognize the independence and legitimacy of the Confederate nation and secure their help in lifting the Federal naval blockade, which was already beginning to strangle the southern economy. Even if a signal victory accomplished none of those goals, a campaign in the North would at least give Virginia farmers and citizens relief from the foraging of both armies.

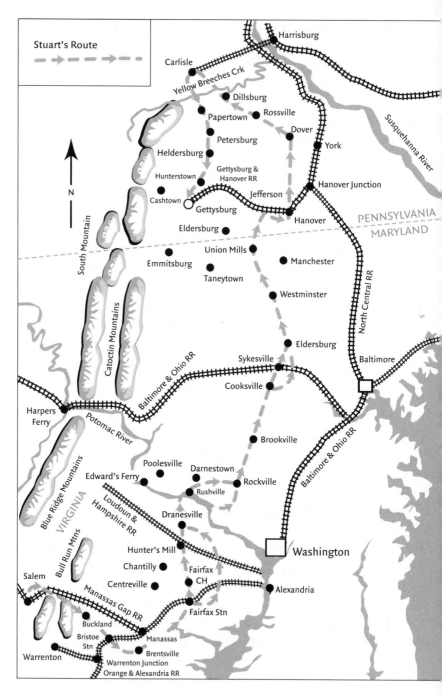

Legend:
Stuart's Route

Harrisburg
Carlisle
Yellow Breeches Crk
Dillsburg
Papertown
Rossville
Dover
Petersburg
York
Heldersburg
Gettysburg & Hanover RR
Hunterstown
Hanover Junction
Cashtown
Gettysburg
Jefferson
Hanover
Eldersburg
PENNSYLVANIA
MARYLAND
South Mountain
Union Mills
Emmitsburg
Manchester
Taneytown
Westminster
North Central RR
Catoctin Mountains
Eldersburg
Baltimore & Ohio RR
Sykesville
Baltimore
Cooksville
Harpers Ferry
Potomac River
Brookville
Baltimore & Ohio RR
Blue Ridge Mountains
Poolesville
Darnestown
Edward's Ferry
Rockville
Rushville
VIRGINIA
Loudoun & Hampshire RR
Dranesville
Washington
Bull Run Mtns
Hunter's Mill
Chantilly
Fairfax CH
Salem
Centreville
Alexandria
Manassas Gap RR
Fairfax Stn
Buckland
Bristoe Stn
Manassas
Warrenton
Brentsville
Warrenton Junction
Orange & Alexandria RR

N

Cavalry's Route to Gettysburg, June–July 1863

The cavalry's first mission would be to screen the advance of Lee's army from the prying eyes of Federal scouts and cavalrymen. As a result of Brandy Station, however, Lee delayed Stuart's march for a week, telling him that his command must refit and recuperate so it would be ready to take on the Federal cavalry when the time came. On June 10 Lee ordered Lieutenant General Richard S. Ewell's infantry corps toward the Shenandoah Valley corridor and the Potomac without Stuart's screen. A few days later he sent A. P. Hill's and then Longstreet's corps. Stuart was to begin his march on June 16, and screen Hill's and Longstreet's right flank as they advanced through the valley. Stuart would thus be marching by a parallel and more easterly route on the east side of the Blue Ridge.[22]

Fitz's and Rooney Lee's brigades (temporarily led by Thomas Munford and John R. Chambliss, respectively) and Robertson's brigade led the way north. Hampton's and Jones's brigades, which had suffered the heaviest losses at Brandy Station, would bring up the rear a few days later. As Hampton led his brigade across the Rappahannock in trace of the first three cavalry brigades, word reached him of heavy fighting ahead. On June 17 and 19 there was fierce combat at Aldie and Middleburg as the Confederate cavalry halted determined Yankee attempts to drive west and penetrate its cavalry screen. Hampton himself stopped and skirmished with Alfred Pleasonton's cavalry on the eighteenth at Warrenton. The enemy withdrew under cover of a heavy evening thunderstorm, leaving Hampton and his men to attempt to sleep on the battlefield in the pouring rain.[23]

Hampton joined Stuart's main force south and east of Upperville in the late afternoon of June 20. Stuart needed him badly. His other brigades had been fighting and stubbornly withdrawing in the face of superior numbers during the previous days; now Stuart had been driven west of Middleburg, and Pleasonton was still threatening. Stuart formed a line that covered two roads leading into Upperville, near which he placed his own headquarters. Hampton occupied the right flank, covering the rightmost, or southern, road. To his left were the brigades of Robertson, Jones, and Chambliss. North of this road, the Upperville Pike, Hampton placed the Cobb Legion on his extreme left, with the 2nd South Carolina to its right. South of the road, Laurence Baker commanded the Jeff Davis Legion and his own 1st North Carolina, which held the extreme right.[24]

On the morning of June 21 Hampton's men realized that they were in for a tough fight. Pleasonton sent three brigades of cavalry to turn the

Confederate left under Chambliss and Jones. When this attempt failed, the Federals concentrated on the Confederate center and right held by Robertson and Hampton. Hampton could see a full brigade of infantry attempting to move around his right while a large force of cavalry moved against his front. He knew that the Confederates did not have to hold this line indefinitely—only delay the Federal advance for a day or so to permit Longstreet's corps just west of the mountains behind them to clear the area unobserved. With the odds facing the Confederate cavalry, however, this task would be difficult enough.[25]

His men and fellow officers recalled this day as yet another in which Wade Hampton demonstrated extraordinary coolness under fire. To his front, Federal cavalrymen armed with Spencer repeating rifles applied constant pressure, while the Confederates replied with their old muzzle-loading single shooters. On the right, the pressure from the Federal infantry was becoming too much for the troopers of the 1st North Carolina. Stuart ordered Hampton and Robertson to fall back to a line of wooded heights behind Goose Creek. The Jeff Davis Legion was to act as a rear guard as the other regiments fell back one by one. During the withdrawal, Pierce Young, who was leading the Cobb Legion and the 2nd South Carolina, did not see anyone on his right and did not yet know that he was to withdraw. He sent the regimental adjutant of the 2nd, James Moore, to Hampton for instructions. Moore found Hampton on a ridge in the rear overlooking the battle, "as calm and composed as if no battle was in progress." Hampton asked, "Well, Moore, what is it?" Moore relayed Young's message, to which Hampton coolly replied, "Tell Colonel Young to fall back to the next crest, I am going to make a stand there."[26]

At that instant, a Federal round struck one of Captain James Hart's guns, exploding the limber chest and knocking the gun off its carriage. For a moment, a cloud of smoke obscured the scene and the gun's four terrified horses bolted. Hampton's sturdy artillery officer had been in tight spots before and had never lost a gun, but it was clear that he would be unable to save this one from capture. It was one of the two Blakely guns that Hampton had imported from England with his own money and, as Moore explained, "highly prized by the men." Moore reported that Hampton remarked quietly, "Well, I am afraid Hart has lost a gun this time."[27]

The Confederates made another stand for several hours along Goose Creek, then withdrew once again toward Upperville. More Union units were being thrown into the fight, and as the Federals advanced, they were able to separate Chambliss's and Jones's brigades from the rest of the Confederate force and push them back toward Ashby's Gap and away from Upperville. Stuart ordered Robertson and Hampton to withdraw through the town and hold the road junction on the other side. The vastly superior Union forces were following closely and swarming into any gaps left as the southerners attempted to fall back regiment by regiment. As Hampton managed the retreat, he saw that a powerful Yankee attack had thrown Robertson's 5th North Carolina into confusion. The 5th was breaking apart. Hampton immediately recognized the danger—the loss of an entire regiment as an effective fighting force could cause the whole Confederate line to collapse and bring utter disaster. The way would then be clear for the Union forces to enter the Shenandoah, observe the movement of Lee's army, and strike Longstreet's corps as it marched down the valley.[28]

Hampton immediately ordered his Jeff Davis Legion to hurry to the support of the 5th North Carolina. The legion, in turn, found itself flanked by more enemy horsemen. The time for calm reserve had passed; now was the moment for the commander to lead from the front. Hampton found the right wing of his 1st North Carolina—five companies led by Lieutenant Colonel James B. Gordon—and turned his horse to face the Tar Heels. He drew his saber, held it over his head, rose in his stirrups, and shouted "First North Carolina, follow me!"[29] Hampton and the Tar Heels charged into the flank of the Yankees who were driving into the flank of the Jeff Davis Legion and were, in turn, struck in the flank by more bluecoats. Hampton committed the Cobb Legion and then the remaining half of the 1st North Carolina, each of which was struck in turn by Yankee units.[30]

The fighting had become a general melee. Men were killing each other with sabers, pistols, and carbines, but the Confederates were gradually getting the better of the fight. Only the man in charge could have perceived any order at all in the action, which, to the troops, must have appeared chaotic. Hampton remembered that the series of charges and countercharges went on "until all of my regiments named had charged three times, and I had gained ground to the right and front of more than half a mile."[31] Finally, the 2nd South Carolina, which had been withdrawn first from the Goose Creek line, returned to the front to hold the line while the rest of the brigade re-formed. Hampton's line was now stabilized, but Robertson had already withdrawn through Upperville to the west side of town, leaving Hampton's left flank unsecured. Hampton therefore gave up the ground he had won and continued his withdrawal until reestablishing contact with Robertson's brigade west of the town. Amazingly, his hard-pressed men managed to take eighty prisoners with them.[32]

Stuart then slowly withdrew Hampton and Robertson to the mountain passes, unmolested by the Federals. That part of the cavalry division had accomplished its mission. Northward toward Ashby's Gap, however, a few Union scouts were able to peer over the Blue Ridge in the last rays of sunlight and observe Longstreet's camps in the valley below. Pleasonton relayed the information to Union army commander Joe Hooker, who did nothing about it.[33]

Just eleven days after Brandy Station, Hampton's clear thinking and decisive action had again helped salvage another desperate situation. He had lost 102 men and still kept his brigade together in a fighting withdrawal in the face of a superior force. Stuart had personally witnessed enough of Hampton's fight at Upperville to know that the Carolina aristocrat had performed well, but not enough to know exactly what had transpired. He filed his own report before receiving Hampton's and could say only: "In [the rearguard action near the town] Hampton's brigade participated largely and in a brilliant manner."[34] Stuart's adjutant, Henry McClellan, gave a far more detailed account after the war and clearly believed that it was Hampton who had saved the day: "If victory [at Upperville] is to be claimed by either side, it must belong to Hampton's brigade, which at the close of the day relieved the pressure on Robertson's two regiments, drove back the forces opposed to it, regained more than half a mile of ground, and retired from the battle at a walk, and unmolested. This success was mainly due to that personal influence which . . . has marked Hampton as a leader of men."[35]

Stuart allowed his bloodied division to rest for a few days before saddling up again. He had completed the first part of his mission in the Confederate invasion, that of screening the advance of two of the three infantry corps. Now he hoped that Lee would approve a more offensive role for his command. Stuart hoped to make another long-distance raid deep into enemy territory, the kind of raid that had made him and his men famous. He proposed to march east and south, get between the Army of the Potomac and Washington, and while marching north disrupt the enemy's communications, gather intelligence and supplies, advance into Pennsylvania, and finally join with Ewell's infantry corps somewhere on the Susquehanna River. Lee approved the general outline of the plan but specified that if the cavalry chief found his way blocked, or if he found the Union army to be on the move, he must return at once to Lee. Lee also ordered Stuart to leave two brigades behind to guard the mountain passes leading to the Confederate army's rear. Once those two brigades determined that the enemy had left their front, they were to notify Longstreet and march north to rejoin the main army in Maryland. To ensure that Lee was not left "blind" without a cavalry force for reconnaissance purposes, Stuart left some five thousand men of his division with the main army.[36]

On June 25 at 1:00 A.M. Stuart set out with what he considered his three most reliable brigades—Hampton's, Fitz Lee's, and Rooney Lee's (temporarily commanded by Chambliss because of Rooney Lee's capture). The expedition got off to a slow start due to a long detour made necessary by the appearance of Winfield S. Hancock's Second Corps. Stuart finally sidestepped Hancock and eventually turned north toward the Potomac, with Hampton in the lead. There were more delays on the way, as the troopers paused to plunder enemy supply depots. A regiment belonging to the Defenses of Washington command, the 11th New York Cavalry, used up another few hours when it waylaid Hampton's lead regiment, the 1st North Carolina, on the twenty-seventh at Fairfax Station, Virginia. Hampton counterattacked, killing, capturing, or scattering the bulk of the rash New Yorkers, but the "Bloody First" lost several good men, including Major John H. Whitaker.[37]

Other events slowed the march after the Confederates crossed the Potomac. There were more stores to capture, the locks of the Chesapeake and Ohio Canal to destroy, and enemy resistance to overcome at Rockville and Westminster, Maryland, and Hanover, Pennsylvania. Another impediment was the large train of 125 supply-laden wagons captured by Hampton's and Chambliss's men near Rockville.[38]

Stuart was aware that he was behind schedule and might not find Ewell soon enough to help Lee in any ensuing large battle. He was frustrated that he could not seem to get good information on where Ewell might be. He pushed his troopers harder and harder. Early in the expedition, the men and horses had suffered from hunger. On the second day of the march, one man in the 4th Virginia wrote in his diary: "Rations out. Nothing to eat for man or beast."[39] Others remembered that the route through northeastern Virginia took them through "a miserably poor country" that had been ravaged by both armies for over two years.[40] The capture of enemy supplies relieved the men's hunger for a day or two, but after Stuart began marching through the night to make up for lost time, fatigue became a dire problem. Stuart, perhaps exaggerating slightly, reported that "whole regiments" of men slept in the saddle while their beasts plodded along in column.[41] Some dozing men fell from their horses.[42]

On July 1 Stuart headed northeast from Hanover, Pennsylvania, toward Carlisle, still looking for Ewell. He did not know it, but a battle had already started twenty miles to the east near the town of Gettysburg, as elements of A. P. Hill's and then Ewell's Corps collided with Federal cavalry and elements of John Reynolds's First Corps. At 1:00 A.M. on the morning of the second, a courier from Lee found Stuart and informed him that the army had been battling Federals and relayed orders to bring his three long-lost brigades to his support. Within an hour, Stuart's exhausted men were in the saddle and hurrying toward Gettysburg via Papertown, Heidlersburg, and Hunterstown—in all, another twenty-five or thirty grueling miles. A Virginia lieutenant wrote that the constant exertion, excitement, and lack of food and sleep had left the men "overcome and so tired and stupid as almost to be ignorant of what was taking place around them."[43]

By this point in the expedition, Hampton was no longer leading the vanguard but was bringing up the rear. He was still at Dillsburg, ten miles behind the main column, when Stuart received word to march south to Gettysburg. Stuart therefore ordered Hampton to halt his march toward Carlisle and instead move directly to Gettysburg to take a position on the left flank of Ewell's infantry corps. Hampton reached Hunterstown, five miles east of Gettysburg, on the morning of July 2. He passed through the town, then stopped on the road southwest of it when Stuart halted the entire column and rode off to report to Lee in person. Soon Hampton received reports of Federal cavalry units entering Hunterstown itself. These units later turned out to be elements of the 6th Michigan, a regiment belonging to George Armstrong Custer's brigade. Custer's men had routed a rear guard of Hampton's brigade out of Huntersville and could threaten to roll up the Confederate flank. Hampton immediately informed Stuart. Sometime later Hampton received Stuart's orders to return to Hunterstown and, in Hampton's words, "hold the enemy in check."[44] Meanwhile, Hampton was supposedly involved in one of the more bizarre incidents to occur in the Gettysburg campaign.[45]

As the story goes, Hampton was sitting astride his horse several hundred yards away from his brigade or from any other Confederates when a bullet whizzed past him, fired from a copse of woods 200 or 300 hundred yards away. With a "knightly spirit of adventure," according to an unlikely source, Hampton rode forward to investigate.[46] After riding nearly 200 yards, he stopped at a high stake-and-rider fence and looked into the woods, where he saw a Union private standing on a tall stump at the edge of the woods holding a carbine rifle. At a range of 125 yards, Hampton fired his pistol at the same time that his opponent fired his carbine. Both shots were near misses. Hampton raised his pistol to shoot again when he saw that his adversary was not ready. Hampton "courteously waited"; then both men fired again.[47] When Hampton lowered his pistol for his third shot, he saw that his opponent had raised his hand "as if to say 'Wait a bit, I'll soon be with you.' "[48] The base of the Union man's barrel was fouled, and he cleaned it so that he could fully insert the next cartridge. It was said that "the delay sorely taxed the patience of Hampton, as it would that of any gentleman who was kept waiting to be shot at. But he was . . . incapable of taking unfair advantage of his enemy."[49] Finally the Union man fired. Hampton's return shot struck above the wrist of "the high-roosting cock of the woods," who dropped his carbine, then picked it up with his left hand and fled.

Seconds after Hampton's last pistol shot, the story continues, a Yankee lieutenant dashed up behind him (the soft, marshy ground muffling the sound of his horse's hooves), and before Hampton knew it, a saber had slashed into his skull. Hampton's hat and hair helped cushion the blow; it also helped that the giant Hampton sat taller in the saddle than his assailant, making it more difficult for the lieutenant to land a crushing blow. Hampton turned and drew his pistol. He pulled the trigger only five feet from the man's head, but the pistol would not fire. The Michiganer was already turning his horse to flee from the large, enraged Confederate. Hampton's horse sprinted after him. The two men raced across the field toward the Union lines, with Hampton still trying to fire his faulty pistol and—uncharacteristically—yelling profanities. After the last round in his chamber failed to fire, the exasperated South Carolinian hurled his pistol after his fleeing foe. He was already close to the Union lines by now and therefore turned back. Safe within his own lines, the still angry Hampton had a surgeon close the gash in his head with plaster.[50] This story almost certainly is purely fictional (as is explained in the Appendix).[51]

What is certain is that Hampton turned back toward Hunterstown in compliance with Stuart's order and established a line astride the road between Hunterstown and Gettysburg. The Cobb Legion was on the road itself, with the Phillips Legion and the 2nd South Carolina on the flanks. Here the Yankees made a foolish attack. A squadron of no more than a hundred men of the 6th Michigan Cavalry advanced in a column down the narrow road directly toward the Cobb Legion. There were fences running along either side of the road, so the enemy column was channeled into a narrow front. Other bluecoats dismounted on the sides of the road and took cover farther back. Custer also had a few artillery pieces placed on the right side (Hampton's left) of the road. Hampton let the doomed column of Yankee horsemen get within range of his carbines. Then the column spurred into a gallop. The Confederates opened fire, and several blue horsemen went down. Some of them made it to the lines of the Cobb Legion and traded saber blows in an unequal fight. It became more unequal still when Hampton had the 2nd South Carolina and Phillips Legion converge on the enemy squadron's flanks. The Yankee survivors fled in confusion, with a loss of thirty-two killed, wounded, or missing. One of the wounded was General Custer himself.[52]

Then the Confederates made a foolish decision of their own. Hampton either allowed or ordered (the record is unclear) the Cobb Legion to charge down the same road in pursuit. The results were equally disastrous. Small arms and artillery fire ripped into the Georgians' ranks. Some of Custer's men galloped up to engage the survivors with sabers until the Phillips Legion and the 2nd South Carolina moved up to extricate the Cobb Legion and convince the Yankees to withdraw. This rash decision cost the Cobb Legion sixty-four killed and wounded. Among the wounded was Lieutenant Colonel William Deloney and four other officers. It was not like "Old Hampton" to order—or allow—such impetuous, fruitless charges.[53]

Hampton held his blocking position until the next morning, when he found that the enemy in his front was gone. Stuart ordered him to move through Hunterstown and attempt to get around the far right of the Union cavalrymen, who were themselves holding the right of the Union line. This was part of a larger movement. Lee envisioned Stuart putting himself on the right rear of the Union army. Ewell's corps would renew its attack on the Union right, while the divisions of George Pickett and Johnston Pettigrew would make a determined frontal assault on the Union center at Cemetery Ridge. If the infantry achieved a breakthrough, Stuart would try to exploit it and harass the retreating Federals from his position behind the Union center. Sometime after 10 o'clock, Stuart had moved his command about three miles west of Gettysburg and posted it along some wooded heights known as Cress's Ridge, facing east and south. Gregg's division of Federal cavalry was one-half to three-quarters of a mile away. Hampton occupied the center of the ridge, with Fitz Lee on his left and Chambliss on his right. To the right of Chambliss were two regiments from Albert Jenkins's brigade that had recently rejoined Stuart's command.[54]

For several hours dismounted skirmishers from the two cavalry commands sparred back and forth on the ground south and east of Cress's Ridge. In the afternoon, Stuart apparently decided that it was time to make a determined attack. The Confederate cavalry chieftain hoped to fix the enemy in place with a determined advance of dismounted sharpshooters while simultaneously sweeping around the enemy left with mounted troops. He sent word for his two senior brigadiers, Hampton and Fitz Lee, to ride back to report to him for a conference. The order did not reach the two men until 4:30 P.M. Hampton thought it would be imprudent for both himself and Fitz Lee to leave the front lines at the same time, so he told Fitz that he would go to Stuart and then return so Fitz could go. Hampton rode off to meet with Stuart but could not find him. Meanwhile, the situation had changed. Jenkins's men on the right were low on ammunition and falling back from a determined Union advance. Stuart ordered one of Chambliss's regiments to charge to their support. This set off a chain reaction by impetuous southern officers. Fitz Lee ordered a mounted assault by his whole brigade and someone, probably Fitz, also ordered Hampton's brigade forward.[55]

When Hampton returned to his position, he was astonished to see his brigade charging down the hill toward the Yankees. Once again, someone else had issued orders to his command without his knowledge. While Fitz's 1st Virginia tangled with some of Custer's men, an annoyed Hampton countermanded the order to his own brigade and brought it back to its concealed position in the wood line. Hampton's description of the event in his official report barely concealed his disgust: "This order I countermanded, as I did not think it a judicious one, and the brigade resumed its former position; not, however, without loss, as the movement had disclosed its position to the enemy."[56]

Shortly afterward, a courier arrived from Chambliss asking for help. Hampton sent the 1st North Carolina and the Jeff Davis Legion. The Tar Heels and Deep South men drove the Yankees back in confusion but pursued them so far that they, in turn, were in danger. They soon found themselves entangled in hand-to-hand combat with the main line of the enemy.[57] Hampton saw their predicament and dashed after them to take charge of the situation. Glancing back, he saw to his chagrin that most of the rest of his brigade had begun to follow him. Yet again someone else was trying to direct Hampton's brigade. This time it turned out to be his own trusted adjutant, Captain Theodore Barker. Hampton was much more forgiving of Barker than Fitz Lee in his report, conceding that Barker's "mistake . . . was very naturally brought about by the appearance of affairs on the field."[58] Fitz Lee's brigade was advancing as well.

In concise, unromantic prose, Hampton described the climax of the battle for him. "In the hand to hand fight which ensued," he wrote in his official report, "as I was endeavoring to extricate the First North Carolina and the Jeff. Davis Legion, I was wounded, and had to leave the field, after turning over the command to Colonel Baker."[59]

The truth was much more dramatic. Union observers recalled the Confederate advance as a grand but terrifying spectacle. "Their polished saber blades dazzled in the sun," recalled Captain William E. Miller of the 3rd Pennsylvania. "All eyes turned upon them."[60] Union cavalry leaders recognized the new Confederate advance as a threat to the rear of their main line of infantry and counterattacked against the front and flanks of the Confederate columns. Hampton arrived at the head of the 1st North Carolina and Jeff Davis Legion and saw that scattered fragments of Yankee units as well as organized reinforcements were rallying and converging on his columns. The best way to "extricate" his command was to continue its momentum and sweep through. "Charge them, my brave boys, charge them!" he yelled.[61] A Virginian from Fitz's brigade saw Hampton at the front of the column carrying the unit colors, then handing them to a man beside him. A vicious melee ensued.[62]

As Hampton's brigade collided with the Union units around it, the Confederates initially had the better of it, gradually pushing the Yankees back in a saber-and-pistol fight. Then Union reinforcements arrived, and the Confederate troopers began to give way. Soon it was Hampton himself who needed to be extricated. Two Yankee horsemen rushed him, though he was able to fend them off with his saber. As he fired his pistol at others coming toward him, Privates Moore and Dunlap of the Jeff Davis Legion attempted to ride to his rescue. They wielded hard saber blows against Yankees around Hampton until they too went down. Another bluecoat attacked Hampton with his saber while Hampton was trying to shoot him with his pistol. The pistol, which had been exposed to wet weather the night before, misfired several times, and Hampton's enemy was able to inflict a saber cut on the side of his head and forehead. At the same instant, Hampton pulled the trigger again, tumbling his assailant out of the saddle. Hampton reeled from the saber blow, then rode to the support of another trooper. With blood coursing over his face and partially obscuring his vision, he found himself crossing swords with another foe. This Yankee horseman brought a forceful saber blow down on Hampton's head, leaving another gash in his scalp and fracturing his skull. Hampton then raised his heavy sword overhead and swept it downward, cleaving his enemy's skull to the chin. (One of Hampton's men who described this incident conceded that such a feat was rare and often attributed to mythical heroes, but he swore that in this instance it was true.) Hampton, nearly alone, now gave ground until he was backed up to a fence. Sergeant Nat Price of the 1st North Carolina and a Private Jackson of Georgia rode to his rescue. As another Federal took a swipe at Hampton's head, Sergeant Price shot him dead. Jackson and Price fended off the Federal pursuit while Price shouted: "General, general, they are too many for us. For God's sake, leap your horse over the fence; I'll die before they have you!"[63] Obediently, the semi-dazed general managed to leap his horse over the fence. While in midair, a piece of shrapnel entered his thigh or hip, and his two rescuers followed close behind. Finally Hampton turned over the command to Baker with orders to stand fast if possible. Other men helped their bleeding commander to the rear.[64]

The Confederate high command regarded Hampton's serious injuries as one of many tragic setbacks to the army at Gettysburg. Stuart referred to the wound of the "brave and distinguished" Hampton in his report, as did Lee, who also mentioned Hampton's "gallantry" in his report to President Davis.[65] Pickett's and Pettigrew's heroic infantry assault on the Union center had failed, and Lee was compelled to take his army back to Virginia. Lee appreciated the magnitude of the disaster and told some of his men that "all good men must rally."[66] The problem was that so many "good men," including general officers, were dead on the field or, like Hampton, seriously wounded and likely to be out of action for a long time. The army needed those good men. The cavalry, in particular, would face some grim fighting in the days ahead as it protected the main army's retreat. Hampton's brigade would find itself in desperate straits as it held off a Federal division on July 31 near the Rappahannock. Hampton's replacement, Laurence Baker, was wounded so badly that it seemed he would never return to the front. The same day three regimental commanders—Pierce Young, John Black, and Thomas Lipscomb—were also wounded as each in turn assumed temporary command of Hampton's brigade. The 2nd South Carolina alone lost 37 men and 50 horses and could hardly be called a regiment any longer. Even harder fighting lay ahead. For the time being, though, Wade Hampton was going home.[67]

CHAPTER 12

THE HOME FRONT

On July 4, 1863, Brigadier General Wade Hampton was only one of hundreds of miserable, wounded Confederate soldiers trekking south in a bumpy convoy of ambulance wagons. At one point he assumed that he was dying. He spent several days in a Confederate military hospital at Charlottesville, Virginia, where a surgeon declared that his injury was serious enough that he would have to be sent home for at least fifty days to recuperate. One of the two saber cuts, he informed Louis Wigfall, "cut through both tables of my skull."[1]

Judging from his correspondence, he must have brooded over his fate for several days. His wounds were hauntingly similar to the ones that had killed Frank, but for some reason the Almighty had spared him. There was also the difficult matter of being nearly killed by Yankee swordsmen on horseback. Hampton was a physically powerful man, a splendid horseman, and a fine swordsman, and he was proud of all those traits. Each of them was important to his self-image as an example of chivalry and southern manhood. How, then, had those despised Yankees, whom he had once considered cowards, nearly managed to best him? They had, of course, enjoyed the advantage of numbers, but his closest brush yet with death was still unsettling. Nearly two weeks later, he wrote about the event to Mary Fisher. By that time, his relief at being a survivor had enabled him to laugh about his misfortune: "Don't you feel mortified that any Yankee should be able, on *horseback*, to split my head open? It shows how old I am growing, and how worthless."[2] Even the joke betrayed Hampton's reluctance to accept that a warrior in the chivalric Hampton tradition could be bested by Yankees.

By the time of this letter Hampton was also able to laugh about the wounds themselves, especially when it was clear that he would be sent home for a while. "My head is well, *externally*," he joked, "but seems tender inside; perhaps it is only *weak*. The penitentiary style, in which my hair is cut, half the head being shaven, is striking, if not beautiful. It suits all kinds of weather, as one side of my head, is sure to be just right, whether for cool, or for hot weather. But the flies play the mischief, as they wander over the bald side. When I get home, I will shave my whole head, to be uniform at least."[3]

Hampton headed home from Charlottesville in late July in good spir- 167 its, despite the feeling that the army had fought a "terrible and use-less battle" at Gettysburg.[4] He received permission for Preston and his young neighbor, Captain Rawlins Lowndes, to accompany him. He certainly looked forward to seeing his wife Mary, the baby Alfred, little McDuffie, Daisy, and Sally, who was nearly grown. Before his return to Virginia, he would also get to see young Wade, who was on leave from his position on Joe Johnston's staff. Mary Boykin Chesnut wrote in her diary that she saw Hampton's oldest son in late October and described him as a delightful young man: "Wade, without being the beauty or the athlete that his brother Preston is, is such a nice boy."[5]

This homecoming, however, was not as joyful as the one during the previous winter. The women, children, and remaining men at home were struggling with tragedy and hardship nearly as much as the men at the front. The first reminder was Frank Hampton's four orphaned children. They were now under the care of Wade's thirty-three-year-old sister Caroline, undoubtedly assisted by Mauma Nelly. Frank's body had been lying beneath the sod of Trinity Churchyard for less than two months, and his death had made a deep impression on the folks at home. The Hamptons' family friend Mary Chesnut had gone with a Hampton relative, Mrs. Singleton, to view the open coffin. The ghastly wound and disfigurement of the once-handsome face haunted her for days. Mrs. Singleton was convulsed with grief, and Chesnut's memory flashed back to the day she saw Frank and his beautiful new bride Sally step off the steamer in Charleston soon after their wedding, full of life. Now they were both gone, she mourned, and "our world, the only world we cared for [is] literally kicked to pieces."[6] Besides, Frank's resting place was not the only freshly turned soil in Trinity Churchyard. Hampton's stepgrandmother, Mary Cantey Hampton, had also died in June.[7]

Unfortunately, the extant letters provide little insight into how the Hampton women managed to cope on the home front. Wade Hampton wrote to his wife Mary even more than he wrote to Mary Fisher, but none of Mary's letters to him survive, and only one or two of his sisters' have been found. In many southern families, women had to take over the traditionally male roles of planter, slave overseer, and businessman. The burden fell particularly hard on poorer women whose men could not avoid conscription. The Hampton women, at first, seem to have largely maintained their customary roles as nurturers of their men and children. Especially in the early stages of the war, they knitted socks and other clothing for the Hampton Legion. Before the legion ever left Columbia for Virginia, they hosted picnics, feasts, and balls for the unit.

They nursed their dying sister-in-law Sally Hampton and cared for her four children. Occasionally Mary, daughter Sally, and Mary Fisher spent time in Richmond with friends or even visited Hampton's headquarters in the field. Mary Fisher, especially, seems to have taken great pride in her beloved brother's exploits. Visiting the wounded Hampton in his camp several weeks after the Battle of Manassas, she praised him in a letter to a female relative: "The President has given my Brother four more Companies so his Command will be very large. His men are perfectly devoted to him & well they may be, for oh how [illegible] he is, so noble, so good, such a brave & stout heart & yet so gentle & precious. The Legion has already made a glorious name, & it is delightful to me to hear all the compliments paid to it by the President, & Genl Beauregard & Johnston."[8]

Hampton's little sister clearly basked in the honor bestowed on her closest male relative. Besides praising him to others, she collected newspaper articles on his exploits for a scrapbook. Hampton pretended to be embarrassed by this, but in reality he was flattered. "You are very foolish about your Book, as well as about me," he told her. "I only do my duty & thousands do as much."[9] Despite this admonishment, Hampton assisted Mary Fisher on at least one occasion by sending her an article from a Richmond paper that mentioned his name.[10]

The Hampton women were certainly wracked by the tragic deaths of neighbors, friends, and relatives. By the middle of the conflict, even their wealth did not protect them from wartime inflation and shortages. Nevertheless, they were more fortunate than women in nonelite households because the twenty-slave exemption in the Confederate conscription law allowed their brother Kit to stay home, as well as Mr. Tult, the overseer. Kit performed some government service but was able to spend much of the war in Columbia performing traditional male roles for the family.

Despite Kit's extensive business experience, he was able to keep only the slimmest portion of the Hampton estate intact. The loss of the 1861 cotton crop that Wade Hampton had donated to the Confederacy was a heavy psychological blow. Wade's adjutant Theodore Barker was riding with Hampton on the afternoon of the day that the news of the loss of the crop reached camp; he was stunned at the "equanimity with which [Hampton] bore the loss."[11] Barker concluded that Hampton was actually more concerned that losing the cotton interfered with his plan to procure additional arms for his troops than with his own financial loss. He remembered Hampton reciting poetry as they rode along:

Ah, well! For us all some sweet hope lies,
Deeply buried from human eyes.[12]

A year and a half later, however, Hampton attempted to receive compensation for his cotton burned by order of the Confederate government. Either he now realized how desperate his financial situation had become, or he had decided that it was not unpatriotic to ask for reimbursement. As he explained to his friend Senator Wigfall in December 1863, "It seems just, that the planters who have suffered first, by the absence of the protection of their own Government & then by the destruction of their property by direct orders from that Government, should not be made to bear the whole loss." By this time, Hampton knew that the destruction of his Mississippi holdings was all but complete: "I have had 800 bales & three of the finest steam ginhouses in Miss. Burned. The Yankees are now pulling down all the houses on my largest plantation, to make shelters for themselves & I expect every thing which can be destroyed out there, to be ruined. Two Regiments of negroes are camped at Skipwith's Landing & they will destroy the country."[13]

The simultaneous loss of Kit's cotton was an even greater financial blow to the entire Hampton family. Wade was already headed for postwar bankruptcy, and Kit was barely hanging on. Fortunately Kit was present to handle Frank's estate when his brother died. He sold most of the assets, including slaves, to a creditor of Wade's, Confederate treasury secretary George Trenholm. He then invested the money wisely for Frank's children. For many years his sister Caroline would make annual reports to the courts on her expenditures for the children.[14]

Kit also spent a good deal of time in Mississippi trying to keep his and Wade's plantations intact as much as possible. Though he was a civilian with no position in the Confederate or state government, Ulysses Grant's forces arrested him in April 1863 while he was riding over the Hampton lands. Released a few weeks later, he immediately returned to Columbia and acquired an appointment as Governor Milledge Bonham's aide-de-camp, with the rank of colonel.[15]

A large part of Kit's duties would have included trying to hold the slave labor force together in Mississippi. It is unclear how long he managed to do so. Many Hampton slaves may have escaped to Union lines as early as April 1863, when Grant's forces moved through the area. As late as December 1864, Hampton obtained a "passport" from the War Department giving Kit permission to travel to Mississippi, explaining that "it is very important to us that he should go to look after our negroes."[16] Wade's letters make almost no other mention of this issue, though his early postwar letters indicate his gratification when most of his old hands returned to work as tenants.[17]

Kit could not handle everything, however, and he was not always around. One letter indicates that when he was absent, Kate Hampton, the oldest surviving sister, was quite capable of taking charge. This letter strongly suggests that, although the Hampton women had no deep desire to challenge traditional gender roles, they could and did assume male roles when necessary. In January 1864 Kate wrote her "Dear Uncle Manning" (former governor John L. Manning) to take advantage of his "offer to assist us in any way." Kit had gone to Mississippi, and Kate and her sisters had been "constantly employed since he left." With Kit away, Kate was completely on top of what needed to be done to feed and care for the large Hampton household and workforce. She informed Manning that her overseer, Mr. Tult, would be sending a boat with empty sacks for five hundred bushels of corn. But the five hundred bushels would not be enough, so Kate asked Manning to inquire in his area about good prices on bacon, peas, hay, fodder, or "any thing in the feeding line for 'man or beast.'" She knew exactly how many of her brother Wade's "negroes" had died from sickness and reported on Tult's efforts to remove them from Mississippi to a healthier location near Columbia. She also explained why it might be easier if Manning shipped the corn to her by rail rather than transporting it by boat. These were matters that Kit handled when he was in Columbia, but one must assume that since he was often in Mississippi, this was not the only time that Kate had to take charge.[18]

Even with Kit's and Kate's presence, Wade still tried to conduct his business from afar as much as possible. He frequently relied on Mary Fisher's help, but she assisted only in a limited way. Occasionally he directed her to forward correspondence to one of his cotton factors. At least twice he relayed instructions through her to Mr. Tult. It is significant that in these cases Tult was overseeing the Millwood estate that Wade Hampton II had willed to his four daughters, not Wade III's own plantations in Mississippi. Hampton in effect was helping, through Tult, to run his sisters' estate, even while he was off fighting in Virginia. In one letter, he wondered why Mary Fisher had not sent her "Bills" to him.[19]

The reality was that no matter what Kit or Wade did, the Hampton fortune was disintegrating, and the Hampton women knew it. Publicly, at least, they faced the fact with the same stoic resolve of the oldest

Hampton. As Mary Chesnut noted in her diary, a relative asked "the Hamptons" in late April 1862 "how they relished the idea of being paupers." "If the country is saved, none of us will care for that sort of thing," was the reply. "Philosophical and patriotic," Chesnut remarked.[20] Chesnut noted the same stoic attention to duty among the Hampton women in a conversation she had with Kate in 1863. Chesnut was upset. She wished to visit her ailing mother in Alabama, but her husband forbade her to go, citing the risks to her health from traveling by train in hot weather. Should she disobey her husband, she wondered, or neglect her mother? "Miss Kate Hampton, in her soft voice, said: 'The only trouble in life is when one can't decide in which way their duty leads. Once know your duty—then it is all easy.' I do not know whether she thought it my duty to obey my husband."[21]

For several reasons, then, the Hamptons only temporarily altered the strictly defined gender roles of their antebellum world. The men continued, as much as possible, to command, protect, provide, and handle business matters. The women nurtured and stepped up to take over male roles when necessary, but only when necessary. The Hamptons were wealthy enough at the beginning of the war that wartime inflation and the absence of male breadwinners did not threaten the women and children with starvation. The structure of the family itself, moreover, tended to reinforce antebellum gender roles. It was unusual for four sisters to remain without husbands so late in life. The war found them still naturally relying on their father's fortune and their brothers' provision rather than making do with the absence of husbands gone to the front. Additionally, the deaths of their brothers' wives and of Frank had thrown the Hampton sisters again and again into the customary, mothering roles. They had helped care for Hampton's first brood of children after the death of Margaret, Kit's daughter Annie after her mother's death, and now Frank's children. Hampton, for one, was grateful for what his sisters had done, but the situation tended to reinforce their traditional feminine role as nurturers, not only to Hampton's children but also in an indirect way to Hampton himself.

The women's individual personalities also came into play. Kate Hampton had a reputation for independence and force of character, but always remained a "lady." She took charge when necessary but never seriously challenged gender norms. We know little of Ann's personality, except that the Hamptons joked that she was idle or "un-restless." We know even less of Caroline. Letters indicate that Mary Fisher was often sick, suffering from ill-defined "attacks." Mary McDuffie, Hampton's

Catherine "Kate" Hampton
(1824–1916). Second sister
of Wade Hampton III.
Historic Columbia
Foundation.

second wife, had the reputation of being shy and bookish, and perhaps more frail even than Mary Fisher. Mary McDuffie Hampton belied this image when she joined her husband at the front in the winter of 1864–65 during a time of profound emotional crisis for Wade. Normally, though, both women were likely to defer to male competence, particularly in light of Wade's great energy, confidence, and physical strength, and Kit's business sense.

It seems that Hampton tried to retain the role of provider even while off fighting in Virginia. The results were often comical, if not pathetic. In December 1863 his letters to Mary Fisher revealed that he was trying to find a pony for McDuffie and a doll for Daisy. By the following August he was still on the same quest. He had hoped to get Daisy's doll in Fredericksburg but had no luck, prompting him to joke that he would send to "Yankee land" for one.[22] Another letter indicates that wartime shortages in Columbia induced Hampton to seek basic provisions for his family from the front. He wrote in September 1864 that he had "sent for the cloth & shoes for the children." If Robert E. Lee directed Hampton's command to Maryland, he would "try to lay in a good supply."[23] Hampton meant to buy rather than steal those goods, as the next sentence in his letter condemned the thefts and depredations that had occurred in a recent Confederate raid in Maryland.[24]

Obviously the war brought difficult adjustments to the entire Hampton clan, and the women at home had to bear up bravely under shortages, fearful rumors, and crushing tragedy, not to mention the burden

173

of once again becoming foster mothers after Frank's death. Wade himself, despite his heavy responsibilities as a leader of soldiers and despite Kate's competence, still felt it his duty to substitute as a patriarchal figure for his sisters. Writing from the Virginia front five years after their father's death, he reiterated that concern to Mary Fisher: "I have done all I could to take the place of our father, & all my efforts have been to save [my sisters] from trouble & suffering. I need not tell you how much I have loved you & how deeply I feel all that you have done for me & mine. God will bless you for it & I will always love you."[25]

DIVISION COMMANDER
NOVEMBER 1863–MAY 1864

Hampton had been out of action for a full four months before returning to the front on November 8. While he was gone, Stuart's cavalry division had been reorganized into a corps of two divisions. Hampton and Fitz Lee both received promotions to major general, and each took command of a division. Lee's division consisted of three brigades composed entirely of Virginia regiments, except for the 1st South Carolina, which had once served under Hampton. Hampton's division consisted, first, of Grumble Jones's Virginia brigade, soon to be commanded by Tom Rosser; Calbraith Butler's brigade, consisting of the Cobb, Jeff Davis, and Phillips legions and the 2nd South Carolina; and Laurence Baker's brigade of four North Carolina regiments. Baker and Butler, however, were both recuperating from wounds. Baker would never return, but the brigade was lucky to have Colonel James B. Gordon to take his place. And until the now one-legged Butler arrived the following May, the experienced, hard-fighting Pierce M. B. Young would lead his brigade.[1]

Stuart had personally directed Hampton's division in his absence. If Hampton hoped for a gentle transition back to army life after his long hiatus, he was not to get it. Not only would he step right into division command on his first day back, he would do so in the midst of a battle. Robert E. Lee was withdrawing the Army of Northern Virginia to the south side of the Rapidan when Hampton reached the front. Elements of his division were fighting a rearguard action against Union general George Meade's advancing infantry in the area of Stevensburg, within a few hundred yards of where Frank had died. Hampton rode up to his battle lines in the midst of the fight, as the wild, hearty cheers of his men greeted him. The battle continued until dark, allowing the Confederate infantry to withdraw unmolested; Hampton pulled back at 10:00 the next morning. The "first day's work made me very tired," he admitted to Mary Fisher, "but since then I have improved every day."[2]

Lee's Confederates expected that the withdrawal behind the Rapidan would mean the end of active campaigning for the season and the beginning of picketing and reconnaissance duty for the cavalry. Hampton, though, was thinking of raids as well as picketing. On the night of November 17–18, he crossed the Rapidan with Gordon's (formerly

Baker's) North Carolina brigade and pounced on the 18th Pennsylvania Cavalry. His force captured all of the regiment's wagons and forty of its men. "I never saw such a complete rout as we gave the Yankees," Hampton wrote. "The officers, some of them ran off in their drawers & barefooted, leaving all their clothes behind. The men were scattered all over the woods, & my men were chasing them about like rabbits. It will be a long time before that unfortunate Regt. can get organized again."[3]

The fact that Hampton himself accompanied one of his brigades on a small-scale raid was only one sign that he was still making the transition from brigade to division command. At the next big fight, Mine Run, he would remain mostly with his old brigade. He considered the administrative duties of a division commander "irksome." "Sometimes I have to sign one hundred papers & that is the most tiresome kind of writing," he complained.[4] Hampton enjoyed field duty much more, although that was the very work that gave him the most pain and fatigue after his long convalescence. The expedition of November 18 included a seventy-mile ride with only five hours' rest; Hampton admitted to his sister that "it was too much for me. . . . But a good night's rest has made me feel better & as I captured a very nice iron bedstead, I can sleep well."[5] After several weeks Hampton felt stronger, but as late as December 8 he said privately that the shrapnel wound in his hip still caused him pain. Long rides were agonizing, and he found it difficult even to mount his horse. Undoubtedly he concealed these weaknesses from his men as much as possible. Acknowledging his own force of will in overcoming the pain probably made Hampton even prouder of what his division accomplished in his first month back. He reckoned on December 8 that over the last thirty days, his division had captured five hundred prisoners and waged "several sharp fights."[6]

In one of those fights, Stuart proved that he was having just as much trouble adjusting to being, in effect, a corps commander as Hampton was having in adjusting to divisional command. Cavalry scouts reported in late November that General Meade was crossing large bodies of infantry over the lower fords of the Rapidan. Lee advanced Ewell's and Hill's corps to meet this threat. The cavalry was to support the operation by guarding the eastern and western flanks of the army and providing reconnaissance to the front. The two armies faced off along a north-south stream called Mine Run on November 28. That night, Lee ordered Stuart to move around Meade's left and rear to reconnoiter and assess his intentions. Stuart picked Hampton's division, which was spread out along several miles of the Catharpin Road, as the logical choice for this mission.[7]

Stuart did not leave room for Hampton to lead his division in the fulfillment of this mission; indeed, Hampton may have never learned what the mission was until the battle was over. On the night of the twenty-eighth, Stuart sent orders to Hampton; the dispatch itself does not survive. In Stuart's version of the message, he directed Hampton to have his brigades "in readiness at an early hour" and communicated his intention to reconnoiter the Union left and rear.[8] Hampton, who received the dispatch at 4:00 A.M. on the twenty-ninth, later remembered that it instructed him only "to have my command supplied with ammunition as soon as possible after daylight." Hampton immediately complied with the directive,[9] then stayed at his headquarters, expecting couriers to arrive soon with further instructions. Stuart seems to have expected Hampton to meet him personally on the road, though it is not clear why he did. Stuart reported that he rode "to Hampton's command on the Carpathian Road. . . . Not finding Gen. Hampton on the ground, I sent to his headquarters, which were some distance off, and waited for some time for his arrival."[10]

Despite Hampton's headquarters being "some distance off," Stuart did not wait long. He clearly was intent on personally leading Hampton's division on its reconnaissance. His courier finally arrived at Hampton's headquarters with instructions to find Stuart, who would be located with either Rosser's or Baker's brigade, the latter now commanded by James B. Gordon. At this point, Hampton still had no idea what Stuart contemplated for his division. He departed immediately to locate his superior, finding Gordon's brigade "a few minutes" after receiving the message.[11] To his surprise, Gordon's brigade was already in motion in accordance with Stuart's orders. Stuart himself was not there, having already departed with Rosser's brigade. Slightly mystified by this point, Hampton found messengers from Stuart, who directed him only to follow Rosser's route with the other two brigades.[12]

When Hampton arrived at Parker's Store, he found Rosser engaged in a seesaw fight with Union cavalry. Hampton deployed the other two brigades, which helped Rosser drive off the enemy, capture around one hundred Federals, and discover information on the location of Union general Gouverneur K. Warren's Second Corps. No serious damage resulted from Stuart's micromanagement, but it took the corps commander out of contact with the rest of his cavalry. Moreover, it was only one of at least two occasions during the Mine Run campaign on which Stuart assumed direct control of one or more of Hampton's brigades. The two commanders, on filing their reports on the Parker's Store fight months later, interpreted the events differently. In Stuart's telling, Hampton was unaccountably late, because he was not where Stuart expected him to be. Hampton understandably maintained that Stuart never told him where to be and almost certainly resented the corps commander's failure to allow him to lead his own division. Stuart partially mollified him with praise. Hampton wrote his sister that although the fight "was not a very grand affair," it was successful and his men behaved splendidly. "Stuart, who saw it, said he had seen nothing finer" than the way Hampton's men fell into line "and drove the enemy from the field."[13]

⭐ The end of the 1863 campaign found Hampton in an optimistic mood. His men had performed well and, he believed, so had he. He was gratified that the Virginia regiments he now led seemed to respect him, and, unlike Fitz Lee, he had a good relationship with Tom Rosser, who was now a brigadier and under his command.

There had been one setback. Preston was wounded in November and furloughed for several weeks. When a bullet struck his arm, the twenty-year-old had lost so much blood that he was unable to sign his own furlough papers on November 17.[14]

Hampton looked forward to visitors from home. Among them was his daughter Sally, now nineteen, who remained for some time around Christmas, staying near Guinea Station with one of her father's hunting companions. Other Confederate officers were also glad to see Sally. One of them was a twenty-three-year-old lieutenant colonel named John Cheves Haskell of Abbeville. Haskell and Sally had previously met at a party at the Prestons' mansion in Columbia. By this point in the war, young Haskell was proving himself a capable and gallant artillery officer. But his first attempt to impress Sally's father had ended disastrously. Back during the winter of 1861–62, when Haskell was a major on General Joe Johnston's staff and Hampton was a colonel in charge of an infantry brigade along the Occoquan, the two officers were riding together from Johnston's headquarters toward Manassas Junction and had to cross Bull Run. When they came to Mitchell's Ford, they found that recent rains had turned the stream into a torrent flowing far beyond its banks. Haskell thought the logical thing to do was to ride several miles upstream to cross at a nearby bridge. To his chagrin,

Hampton disagreed, suggesting that they swim their horses across the frigid stream. Haskell had little experience in swimming his horse and the current was raging, but he was "ashamed" to object. As Hampton expertly swam his horse across, the current swept Haskell and his horse downstream. He finally made it to shore after a "hard struggle, . . . utterly exhausted and soaking wet from head to foot, with the weather far below freezing."[15] Doctors later said that the hot drinks and warm blankets provided by another officer probably saved his life. They did not save him from a severe case of pneumonia and high fever. The frightful experience, however, did not dissuade Haskell from courting Sally Hampton. By the time she returned to Columbia in January 1864, Sally and Haskell were engaged to be married. Still, Haskell must have considered that it would take a certain amount of grit to be a son-in-law to Wade Hampton.[16]

During the third winter of war, Hampton concentrated most of his efforts on working desperately to keep his division from falling apart from malnutrition and sickness. Hampton had never been one of those officers who felt that his duties were over once the guns stopped firing. He had always taken an active role in recruiting, outfitting, and maintaining his units. His valiant attempt to ensure that his division would be a credible combat force in the spring resulted in just that—a division that was ready to take on the Yankees by April. Those efforts also led him to jump the chain of command and arouse the ire of Robert E. Lee.

In December 1863 the Confederate cavalry suffered from lack of forage more than ever before. While Federal cavalry units enjoyed regular rations of ten pounds of corn per horse per day, Confederate units typically had five pounds or less. Often their horses survived by gnawing the bark from trees. Veterans remembered that it was easy to locate a Confederate cavalry camp because the bark on trees was gnawed away from the root to the height of a horse's head. The officers of the Jeff Davis Legion informed their superiors that their entire command had only eighty horses, many of which could not survive "a march of ordinary length."[17] Hampton's men, too, were hungry and lacked clothing. Colonel John Black of the 1st South Carolina noted that in the coldest part of winter nearly three hundred men lacked blankets.[18]

Recalling the brutal effects of the last winter on his brigade, Hampton wasted no time in making plans for the recuperation of his division this time around. In early December he suggested that his North Carolina brigade (Gordon's) and his Deep South brigade (Butler's, temporarily commanded by Young) be allowed to winter in North Carolina, where forage was more abundant and where they could help protect against further enemy incursions in the eastern part of that state. He recommended that Rosser's brigade be sent to the Shenandoah Valley, where it also could be of valuable service and take better care of its horses. Meanwhile, he listed several regiments and companies then serving in Georgia and South Carolina that had little to do, and urged that they be ordered to join his division. Hampton believed that this plan would help all three of his brigades recover. In the meantime he hoped that President Davis would direct him to join Joe Johnston for temporary service in Mississippi. Johnston had specifically requested Hampton's services in late November to lead his cavalry. Hampton relished the thought of evicting Yankee and black trespassers from his lands and the surrounding territory in Mississippi. He wrote Mary Fisher that "If Genl. Johnston will give me a few good cavalry, I think I could break up the party at Skipwiths [Skipwith's Landing, near Hampton's plantation on the Mississippi]."[19] Hampton formally requested that he be sent to Mississippi, assuring Senator Louis Wigfall that, with his knowledge of the terrain, he could "break up these pestilent nests of robbers."[20]

Over a month later, Stuart still had not replied to Hampton's suggestions. Rosser was busy in the valley, but Hampton's other two under-strength, underfed brigades manned the picket lines from the Rapidan in the army's front all the way to the lower Rappahannock on its far right flank. By February 28 his two brigades were down to 718 men present for duty with serviceable horses. Two of Fitz Lee's Virginia brigades, meanwhile, got the rest that Hampton was seeking for his units. Most of Colonel William Wickham's and Colonel Lunsford L. Lomax's regiments had been furloughed for two months or more. Because they temporarily ceased to exist, the men could go home, procure new mounts, or find good forage for the ones they had. Hampton's soldiers labored on. Lee finally allowed him to send two North Carolina regiments to the Old North State to recruit, but their absence only increased the workload on Hampton's remaining troopers. The seeming unfairness of it drove Hampton to distraction. In a letter to Mary Fisher, he predicted that if it continued, "My command will be unfit for duty next spring & in this event, I shall ask to be transferred to some other army, or I will resign. I am thoroughly disgusted with the way things are managed here, & I have no doubt but that the Yankee cavalry will be better next spring, than ours. No care is taken of ours & they are made to perform very hard, & very useless work."[21]

180   Hampton did not give up. Failing in his attempts to get furloughs for

his men, he tried to ease their burdens. He pointed out that some river fords they had to picket were forty miles away from their camps and from where they could find adequate forage for their horses. The long ride to those locations exhausted the forage they could take with them before they even got there. The infantry, he suggested, could man some of those picket lines instead. Stuart favored the plan, but Lee shot it down. Though he sympathized with Hampton's predicament, he explained that it would put the infantrymen too far from their bases; they could be cut off and surroundeded in the event of a determined enemy attack.[22]

Hampton continued to bombard higher headquarters with complaints about the condition and workload of his command, usually with concrete suggestions on how to remedy them. In February he proposed a scheme to replace some of his units altogether, at least temporarily. Young's brigade of South Carolinians and Deep South legions (Hampton's former command) could no longer mount five hundred men and had seen hard service since the beginning of the war. It had captured two thousand horses over the last year, in addition to those acquired from home, but was still in woeful condition. Couldn't the army send this brigade to South Carolina or Georgia and replace it with four full-sized regiments in that department that had had relatively light duty since their organization? Young's brigade could then acquire horses, recall its dismounted men who had been sent home to find horses, and simultaneously perform the easier picket duties in that quieter theater of the war. This exchange of cavalry would benefit the Army of Northern Virginia in the short run and the service as a whole in the long run.[23]

Stuart rejected this plan out of hand. His endorsement on Hampton's letter, sent to the War Department, strongly favored sending the idle regiments and companies in South Carolina to Virginia. But under no circumstances would he sanction the assignment of units stationed in Virginia elsewhere. As Stuart wrote, "The enemy has kept his largest and best forces of cavalry in the Army of the Potomac, while our largest opposing has been six brigades."[24] Theaters of war outside Virginia had less of an enemy threat to meet, he argued—with more Confederate cavalry to meet it with. Lee was initially cool to Hampton's plan, but he later gave it a cautious endorsement provided that he was informed beforehand which regiments were to be sent to Virginia.[25]

Up to this time, Lee had responded patiently and sympathetically to Hampton's requests. He also defended Hampton when Hampton objected to sending his men on a useless mission. During the first week of

February 1864, Major General Arnold Elzey, commander of the Department of Richmond, learned of Federal plans to raid the Confederate capital. Specifically, he had word that Union brigadier general Isaac Wistar left the Federal base at Yorktown on February 6 intending to sack Confederate depots, prisons, and ordnance facilities around Richmond, forty miles in Lee's rear. Elzey managed to stop the assault with the miscellaneous forces at hand, but before he did he sent an emergency call to Lee for help. Hampton's dilapidated two brigades rushed south on a freezing winter ride only to find that they were not needed. Hampton complained about the unnecessary damage done to his command. Four days later, Elzey issued another alarm. This time Hampton informed Lee that he would delay sending help until he received direct orders from Lee himself. Lee agreed with Hampton's course and chided Elzey for overreacting to unreliable reports, citing "the injury done to the troops morally and physically by movements at this season."[26]

Hampton's main goal obviously was to preserve his division, but it would have been understandable if the army leader were beginning to lose patience with his constant lobbying. The possibility of Hampton's transfer was still on the table, and Lee tired of discussing the issue. During the previous winter, Lee had fended off several requests from other theaters for Hampton's transfer, and Hampton knew that Lee valued his services in Virginia. Now not only was Johnston asking that Hampton be given command of his cavalry, but also James Longstreet was making the same request for the Army of Tennessee. Twice Longstreet insisted that Hampton be sent west, praising his "experience," "confidence," and "dash."[27] Hampton's fellow officers were making no similar calls for Fitz Lee, the other cavalry division commander in Virginia.[28]

It is likely that Hampton used the threat of his transfer as a bargaining chip. The past had proved that he was not averse to lobbying in Richmond outside his chain of command. He was close to Jefferson Davis and Senator Louis Wigfall of Texas, and his relative John Preston was an official in the War Department, as was his friend John Chesnut. President Davis had written to Johnston on December 13, 1863, that Hampton could not be spared for service in Mississippi. But Hampton continued to discuss the transfer in January as if it were a possibility. Finally Lee called his bluff. "If you desire to take a command in the Army of the Mississippi," he wrote on January 23, "I will not interpose any objection, though I should be sorry to lose your services in this army."[29] Hampton backed down. Evicting trespassers from Hampton

lands on the Mississippi was a fantasy, and he knew it. He was committed to carrying on the fight in Virginia as long as he still had a
command with which to fight.[30]

Hampton passed another test of his determination to fight on at
the beginning of March. Earlier in the winter high-ranking officers in
Meade's army had grossly overestimated the number of men available to
Hampton—one report put his command at 8,000 troopers, another at
4,000, and still another at 6,000. By the end of February, however,
they had a sense of how weak he really was. Moreover, Hampton's
few hundred cavalrymen were the only forces on the right flank of Lee's
army—the only forces available to stop a southward cavalry dash directly
toward Richmond. Union brigadier general Judson Kilpatrick, therefore, hatched a plan for a powerful, extended raid on the Confederate
capital.[31]

Around midnight on the morning of February 29, 1864, Kilpatrick
captured Hampton's 19-man picket on the Rapidan and raced for Richmond with over 3,500 troopers. The Union column divided near Mt.
Pleasant behind Confederate lines. The plan was for a detachment of
500 troopers under young, handsome Union colonel Ulric Dahlgren to
swing wide to the west while Kilpatrick advanced directly on the city.
The two forces would converge on Richmond from different directions
and launch a two-pronged assault. They would free Union prisoners at
the infamous Libby Prison and Belle Isle and return—either the way they
had come or by traveling east to the safety of General Benjamin Butler's
lines near West Point. Because his pickets had been captured, Hampton
did not learn of Kilpatrick's move for several hours. He then tried to
alert his immediate superior, but Stuart was preoccupied with a diver-
sionary raid against the army's left flank led by Custer. When he got no
response, Hampton realized it was up to him to try to catch Kilpatrick,
who by now had roughly a twelve-hour head start. He could not reach
Richmond first but hoped at least to make life more difficult for the
Yankees once he got there. Hampton led 306 troopers of the 1st and 2nd
North Carolina regiments on a hell-for-leather, freezing ride after the
Yankee raiders. Along the way he picked up two guns from James F.
Hart's battery and a few dozen mounted men from Colonel Bradley T.
Johnson's Maryland line. Hampton's force, now roughly 500 strong,
was trying to catch up to an enemy army seven times its size.[32]

Kilpatrick lost his nerve when he got to Richmond's outskirts on the
morning of March 1, and Dahlgren's attack on the south side also
failed. Kilpatrick moved his thoroughly exhausted and frozen men sev-

eral miles eastward down The Peninsula toward Mechanicsburg. That night he halted a few miles east of the city and bivouacked at Atlee's Station, hoping to get a few hours' rest despite the driving rain, sleet, and snow. Hampton's troopers had been following at a distance and were only a few miles away. When Hampton spotted campfires near Atlee's, he believed that he had found his prey. Though he had been hesitant to take on such a larger force in daylight, Hampton decided that the cover of darkness would protect his smaller force in a nighttime attack if he could achieve surprise. He dismounted one hundred men so they could approach silently on foot while the rest of his band waited on horseback to exploit whatever situation developed. It was a prudent plan. If Kilpatrick was alert and ready to fight, Hampton's much smaller command would be in serious trouble. Having most of the command still mounted would facilitate a rapid withdrawal. If, on the other hand, the Yankees were surprised and fled in confusion, men on horseback could more easily exploit the confusion, cut off escape routes, and round up prisoners. Hampton also seems to have reasoned that if the Federals knew that he was nearby, they could be ready and waiting, and his 100-man detachment could be walking into a trap. This is almost certainly the reason that he decided not to send the dismounted men into the camp until Hart had fired fourteen cannon shots. Those fourteen explosions would be enough to disorganize, disrupt, and distract the Federals before Hampton's men charged in.

The plan worked. As Hampton's dismounted men crept up to the exhausted Federals, a few Yankee pickets fired in the direction of the suspicious noises. Hampton had ordered his men not to return fire until they were on the verge of the Union camp itself. He waited several minutes after the Yankee pickets' shots, so that the shooting would seem to be a false alarm. At 1:00 A.M. Hart's guns shattered the silence. After the fourteenth round crashed into the Yankee position, whooping Confederates charged out of the darkness and into the camp. Kilpatrick's stunned command put up a brief resistance and then fled in panic, leaving Hampton with roughly one hundred prisoners, some horses, arms, a wagon and ammunition caisson, and scattered clothing and rations.[33]

Kilpatrick kept running until dawn; he eventually escaped to the safety of Benjamin Butler's lines farther down the James Peninsula, while Dahlgren wandered over the countryside seeking to rejoin him. Local militia and home guards began tracking Dahlgren and, with the help of some of Fitz Lee's troopers who were on leave, finally cornered and shot him at Mantapike near King and Queen Court House. Allegedly found on his body were papers that outraged Confederate citizens. Dahlgren had apparently ordered his men not only to open the prisons, but also to assassinate President Davis and his cabinet and "burn the hateful city."[34]

Hampton had done his part to punish Kilpatrick and Dahlgren for their alleged dastardly intentions, but the hard riding without rations was not what his command needed. Relief was, however, finally on the way. Hampton's influence in Richmond had finally borne fruit with his plan for the exchange of cavalry units. Despite Stuart's objections and Lee's misgivings, the bureaucratic machine in the War Department started moving in mid-February in the general direction of Hampton's recommended course. On March 17 the orders went out from the War Department. Butler's (Young's) brigade would go to South Carolina to "recruit" or remount. The 4th, 5th, and 6th South Carolina, the 7th Georgia, Colonel Millen's mounted Georgia battalion, and five separate cavalry companies in South Carolina would transfer to Virginia. The 4th, 5th, and 6th regiments would become a brigade in Hampton's division under the immediate command of Calbraith Butler, who was expected to return soon minus his right foot. The last unit mentioned in these orders was the Hampton Legion infantry under Colonel Martin Gary, which had been serving in Tennessee. That unit would receive a twenty-day furlough for the purpose of acquiring horses, re-form as a "mounted infantry" regiment, and move to Richmond for service on The Peninsula. Finally, Richmond ordered Hampton himself to go to Charleston and then Columbia to oversee the movement. By the nineteenth he was already in Charleston.[35]

Unknown to Hampton and maybe even Lee, the War Department had already settled on the details of the cavalry exchange by March 14—the very day that Hampton finally lost his cool and penned insubordinate letters to both Stuart and Lee.[36] On March 9 Hampton, in a letter to Stuart, had requested that Butler's (Young's) brigade be allowed to spend some time manning the Richmond defenses, where its horses could find forage. He promised that the brigade's effective strength would recover rapidly after only a few days. Besides, he pointed out, Fitz Lee's regiments were now returning at full strength and could easily relieve Young's duties on the Rappahannock. Stuart refused, citing the objections of Lee himself. Additionally, he gave specific instructions on the organization of Hampton's division if Butler returned and if fresh units arrived soon from South Carolina. His orders would give Butler only two South Carolina regiments for the time being, while the legions from Georgia, Alabama, and Mississippi would form another brigade under Young.

Hampton exploded. Not only did no one seem to care about the condition of his command, but also Stuart was again micromanaging his affairs and depriving Hampton's finest brigadier, Calbraith Butler, of the full responsibility Hampton wished to give him. On March 14 he addressed a letter to Robert E. Lee to be forwarded through Stuart. In it Hampton protested Lee's decision that Young's (Butler's) "broken-down brigade" must be stationed on the lower Rappahannock rather than in the vicinity of Richmond as Hampton suggested. Hampton angrily reminded Lee that on the Rappahannock, the brigade would "have to be constantly on the alert to guard against attacks of the enemy, and where their only supply of forage will have to be obtained from the Northern Neck. . . . As I regard the location selected by General [Lee?] unsuitable and dangerous, it is due to myself to declare that I cannot hold myself responsible either for the condition or safety of the brigade if it is placed there." In the same letter Hampton informed Lee of Stuart's order to break up Butler's brigade. In bold defiance, Hampton announced: "I have received no orders from competent authority to break up one of my brigades, and until such orders come I shall not divide Butler's brigade. I respectfully request the commanding general not to authorize any change in my command without at least consulting my wishes on the subject."[37]

Hampton's concerns were legitimate, but he had now clearly crossed the line into insubordination. Ideally, no commander should have to tolerate such interference with the internal organization of his command without at least being consulted, but Hampton had just disobeyed a direct order from Stuart. Then he had written an angry letter to the commanding general, the tone of which constituted a challenge to Lee's authority.

Now Lee's temper snapped. Within a day or two of Hampton's impudent letter, the two men had a personal meeting. At some point in the conversation, Lee declared: "I would not care if you went back to South Carolina with your whole division."[38]

Hampton was mortified. He had a deep respect for Lee, who had always given him a sympathetic hearing even when the army commander had supported Stuart's position in the Hampton-Stuart squabbles. The wounded Hampton went straight to President Davis. Sometime between

186

the fifteenth and the eighteenth—immediately after his conversation with Lee—Hampton was already in Richmond. Probably the War Department had summoned him at that point to discuss the cavalry exchange, but Hampton undoubtedly also sought reassurance from Davis. Hampton was so hurt that he even forgot his customary reserve and first unburdened himself to his friend Mary Chesnut. According to Chesnut, "Wade said [Lee's] manner made this speech *immensely* mortifying." "While General Hampton was talking to me," Chesnut continued, "the president sent for him. It seems General Lee has no patience with any personal complaints or grievances. He is all for the cause and cannot bear officers to come to him with any such matters as Wade Hampton came."[39]

Davis's explanation to Hampton could have given him little comfort. It suggested that Lee suspected Hampton of being motivated by petty personal concerns rather than patriotism. It was generally unfair—Hampton's contributions to the cause were undeniable, even if he could be prickly. But now a man whom Hampton admired for his courage, patriotism, judgment, and ability seemingly had questioned the purity of his motives. Besides, Hampton must have realized, it was uncharacteristic of Lee to show his temper in such a way, to rebuke an officer to his face. Lee had been so angry that he had said something that he could not have meant; surely he did not want to lose Hampton's division.

Wade Hampton was a proud man and often just as overprotective of his reputation and personal prerogatives as any other southern officer. And that was saying a lot. It was Robert E. Lee's misfortune to be constantly defusing personal quarrels, soothing sensitive egos, and occasionally shelving otherwise talented officers who could not get along with their superiors because of their excessive concern with personal honor. Hampton could be utterly unselfish at times, but he occasionally fell into that larger category of southern officers, specifically when battling Stuart over interference with his command. Hampton's other problem, though, stemmed from one of his virtues—he was fiercely protective of his men and devoted to the welfare of his command. The same protective, paternalist instinct that governed his behavior toward his domestic dependents also influenced his conduct in the army. When superiors disregarded his men's welfare and safety, he did not hesitate to challenge them. This time, however, his protectiveness had overwhelmed his sense of decorum and self-control. He had stepped over the line.

Hampton smarted over Lee's rebuke for months. For the time being, though, there was no time for further intrigue. He had to rush to South Carolina to oversee the transfer of new cavalry units. He did not resign, and he did not demand a transfer to another army. He soldiered on, determined to rebuild his division and prove to other men once again that his character, his patriotism, and his claims to being an examplar of southern chivalry were beyond question.[40]

IF WE ARE SUCCESSFUL NOW
MAY 1864

Despite his frustrations and insults in the winter and spring of 1864, Hampton managed to keep his eyes on the bigger picture. He was able to think about issues larger than those concerning his own division. Though unhappy with the condition of his command, he was glad that Fitz Lee's regiments were returning in greater numbers than they had fielded in the fall, and he still had hopes of getting rest and more horses for his own men. And despite the shortages and hard work, Hampton insisted all winter that his men were nevertheless in "good spirits."[1]

One reason that he did not let snubs and hardships drive him from the army was his sense that the critical, decisive campaign of the war was about to occur. Civil War students have long insisted that the southern losses at Gettysburg and Vicksburg in 1863 spelled long-term defeat for the Confederacy. Some find the beginning of the end even earlier, noting that Robert E. Lee's defeat at Sharpsburg and the failure of General Braxton Bragg's invasion of Kentucky in the spring of 1862 precluded the possibility of foreign recognition of the Confederacy and the lifting of the Federal blockade. The ultimate outcome was not nearly so obvious, however, to southern men at the front in early 1864. Confederate soldiers in Virginia especially were conscious that they had "never been whipped." They had been forced to abandon their invasions of Maryland and Pennsylvania, but no Yankee general had been able to beat their beloved "Marse Robert" on his own turf, even with larger armies. They looked forward to the imminent fighting ahead with a combination of dread, confidence, and hope for success.[2]

Wade Hampton himself sensed that another terrible bloodletting was about to occur, one that would bring either ultimate victory or defeat for the Confederate cause. Eighteen sixty-four was an election year in the North, where many Democrats opposed the Federal conscription law and Abraham Lincoln's conduct of the war generally. Many were even ready to call a truce with the South. Southerners were well aware of these facts. Wouldn't another great victory—another Chancellorsville or Second Manassas or Seven Days—finally convince the Yankees that they would never capture Richmond? Wouldn't victories by both Joe Johnston in the West and Robert E. Lee in Virginia make the North finally tire of the war and let the South go its own way? Hampton expressed these hopes in a letter to Mary Fisher in late February, just before he took off after Kilpatrick and Dahlgren. "If we can only win the first great battle of the campaign, I hope that we can see the 'beginning of the end.' If Johnston & Lee can each defeat the enemy I do not think there will be another great Battle during the war."[3] "If we are successful now, in Va.," he wrote his relative Mrs. Singleton, "I hope & think that we shall have seen our 'darkest day.' " Hampton wrote this several weeks after his rebuke from Lee. He was still in South Carolina trying to effect the cavalry transfer and about to rush to Virginia amid signs that the Federals were about to embark on a new campaign. Instead of considering resignation or transfer in response to Lee's snub, he wanted to be where the action was at this critical time—"Succeed or fail, it becomes every soldier to hurry to his post."[4]

But Hampton's sense that great events were about to occur combined optimism with foreboding. The stakes were so high that he "shudder[ed] to think what failure would bring."[5] They might fail, and even if they succeeded, good men would die. On the eve of the terrible fighting in the Wilderness of May 7–8, Hampton confided to Mary Fisher: "I hope confidently for success, but at the same time I can not but feel anxious . . . how many thousand of the brave hearts, now eager for the strife, will have ceased to beat, when [this] great fight is over!" Success, on the other hand, would make "our cause . . . safe, & . . . we shall have fair prospects for peace."[6]

On May 2 Hampton returned to his division headquarters at Milford, Virginia. But his command was hardly a division at all. Tom Rosser's brigade was still detached for duty on the western wing of the army, and Hampton requested its immediate return. Most of Pierce Young's brigade had already departed for South Carolina as part of the cavalry exchange, but the new regiments—the 4th, 5th, and 6th South Carolina —had still not arrived. All Hampton had at hand were the three legions and the 1st and 2nd North Carolina of James B. Gordon's brigade—673 men in all. Then he received orders to relinquish Gordon's brigade. Rooney Lee, son of Robert E. Lee, had returned from a Union prison, and Stuart wished to promote him and create a third division for him to lead. That would require Fitz Lee giving up one brigade and Hampton giving up Gordon's North Carolina brigade. Fitz readily complied, but Hampton objected. Gordon's brigade, which had served with Hampton since he had joined the cavalry, was a tough, proven outfit, led by an extremely able brigadier, James Gordon. Hampton grieved at being separated from these men and made that clear to them in a farewell message. For the time being, his division would consist of one under-strength brigade while the junior division commander, Rooney Lee, would have two brigades. Hampton was careful this time to make his objections respectfully and to stress the military reasons for them rather than what was due him as the senior division commander. Gordon's loss would leave him, he reminded Stuart and Lee, for the time being with between two hundred and three hundred men—his "division" was smaller than a full-sized regiment until the arrival of Rosser's brigade from western Virginia and the new men from South Carolina.[7]

Hampton promised to comply with the transfer order, but before he did the Army of the Potomac began to move. Technically the enemy force was still under the immediate command of George Meade, but Meade's newly arrived superior, Ulysses Grant, would direct its destiny. Grant had repeatedly proved his ability in the West, and now Lincoln had brought him East to take on Robert E. Lee. Meade's boss brought a new determination to the ill-starred Yankee force. Unlike former Union commanding generals, Grant would not withdraw and lick his wounds after every Confederate repulse. He steadfastly resolved to force Lee's smaller army into open battle and destroy it, no matter how long it took. Grant brought with him a new cavalry commander, Philip Sheridan. Sheridan was young, cocky, and bombastic. His official reports exaggerated his successes and disguised his failures with dubious claims about his own and Confederate losses and panicky flights by the graybacks. There was no doubt, though, that he had ability and that he would not be intimidated by southern dash and élan.[8]

Hampton's predictions about the upcoming campaign would prove partially true. The fighting would be terrible, and many "brave hearts" would "cease to beat." Instead of the great Battle of the Wilderness being a decisive winner-take-all contest, however, it would lead to weeks of further bloodletting on a daily basis and other horrific battles on an equally large scale.

The Army of the Potomac began crossing the Rapidan and trying to slip around Lee's right on May 4. Grant hoped to march through and out of the Wilderness, getting around Lee's right and rear. This would force the Confederate commander to come out of his entrenchments and confront Grant in open terrain, where Grant's legions of 115,000 men could smash Lee's 64,000. The mission of Stuart's cavalry would be to guard Lee's flanks, warn Lee of large-scale enemy movements, and attempt to delay those movements in time for Lee to counter them with his infantry divisions. Stuart's reconnaissance informed Lee of Grant's move through the Wilderness, and Lee determined to strike his opponent there, where the dense terrain would negate Grant's numerical advantage. The two armies collided and blazed away at each other for two days in the scrub oak and pine, with Lee inflicting 17,500 casualties on Grant's side to just over 10,000 on his own.

Grant decided to keep moving, trying to get around Lee's right and beat him to the key road junction at Spotsylvania Court House. Once again it was the Confederate cavalry's job to identify this movement, report it to Lee, and delay it so Lee could get there first. Grant gave Sheridan's cavalry the mission of clearing the Brock Road, especially at Todd's Tavern, where it intersected the Catharpin Road on the way from the Wilderness to Spotsylvania. But when Sheridan's men approached Todd's Tavern, they found Fitz Lee's division waiting for them behind hastily constructed log barriers. After sharp fighting, Fitz withdrew to another, stronger position about a mile in his rear. Sheridan meanwhile managed to get another of his divisions to Todd's Tavern, but before he could finish Fitz, Hampton arrived from the west, threatening the Union right as he advanced up the Catharpin Road. With Hampton was Young's brigade as well as Gordon's, which he was delivering as promised to Stuart for reassignment to Rooney Lee. Hampton and Fitz were pleased with the day's results. Sheridan crowed to Meade that he had driven Fitz Lee three miles down the Brock Road. The fact was, however, that Fitz had regained much of the lost ground and that Sheridan had failed to open the Brock Road for travel by the Federal infantry to Spotsylvania. The next day found Hampton fighting Union infantry in the same vicinity, as both armies raced to get their infantry columns to Spotsylvania first.[9]

Meanwhile, Sheridan was about to embark on May 9 on an expedition designed to draw Stuart's cavalry off toward Richmond, where it would be of less use to Robert E. Lee. Sheridan swept around the far right of the Confederate line with his entire cavalry corps. His pace was deliberate, because his purpose differed from most cavalry raids. Rather than avoid a fight until he could threaten Richmond or destroy Rebel supplies, Sheridan hoped to draw Stuart's cavalry into an open fight and crush him. Stuart had to respond to this threat to Lee's rear, but he dared not take his entire corps. Lee still needed cavalry for reconnaissance and intelligence. Hampton was skirmishing with infantry north of the Po River on the army's left, and Fitz Lee was engaged in similar work on the army's right, while the infantry was slugging it out with

Grant at Spotsylvania. Stuart decided to chase Sheridan with Fitz's division and Gordon's brigade from Rooney Lee's division, leaving Hampton and Rooney's other brigade with the main army. He finally met Sheridan on May 11 at Yellow Tavern. Outnumbered two to one, the southern cavalrymen got the worst of the fight. Even worse was the fact that in the course of the fighting, a Federal trooper fired a pistol ball into Stuart's lower abdomen. Stuart immediately knew the wound was mortal. As he was carried to the rear, he shouted to his retreating troopers: "Go back! Go back! and do your duty, as I have done mine. . . . Go back! I had rather die than be whipped." Jeb Stuart died the next night.[10]

Everyone in Lee's army was so busy marching and riding and fighting during those bloody days of May that there was hardly time to digest the awful news. But it hit hard. A Confederate staff officer recalled that the officers in the camp of Robert E. Lee openly wept when Lee read the news, and Lee himself said, "I can scarcely think of him without weeping."[11] Every man in Lee's ranks knew that the army had sustained a terrible loss. Stuart's rivals agreed. One of them was Grumble Jones, whose relationship with Stuart was even worse than Hampton's. Unlike Hampton, Jones had proved totally unable to work with Stuart and had been transferred to his own department in western Virginia. On hearing of his former chief's death, Jones told another officer: "You know I had no love for Stuart, and he just as little for me. But that is the greatest loss the army has ever sustained except the death of Jackson."[12]

Despite his past animosity, Hampton, too, praised Stuart after his death. As the senior surviving cavalry officer in the army, Hampton disseminated a general order to the corps on May 16 eulogizing Stuart. "In the death of Maj. Genl. J. E. B. Stuart the A. N. V. has lost one of its most brilliant, enthusiastic, & zealous military leaders; the Southern cause, one of its earliest[,] most untiring & devoted supporters & the Cavalry arm of the service a chieftain who first gave it prominence & value."[13] Then followed several more sentences celebrating Stuart's heroism and his legacy to his children and the nation. The last sentence of Hampton's order made clear what he thought was the duty of the living: "It becomes the men he has so often led, while they mourn his fall, to emulate his courage, to imitate his heroic devotion to duty, & to avenge his death."[14] As far as Hampton was concerned, the fight must go on. The death of brave men made it impossible for those who were spared to give up the fight; in fact, they had to fight even harder so as not to dishonor the fallen.

Hampton's general order was more than just a politic move or a bid to sustain his troopers' morale. Hampton had never doubted Stuart's courage or patriotism, nor his capacity to lead. Though their personalities off the battlefield could not have been more different, Hampton recognized in Stuart a fellow subscriber to the chivalric code—death before dishonor and commitment to defense of home and country. Stuart likewise appreciated Hampton's courage and ability; it was just that they did not like each other personally. After the war Hampton privately wrote words about Stuart that were as complimentary as his official orders, such as the assertion that "in his fall, the South lost as true a soldier & patriot as any who drew a sword in her defense."[15]

With Stuart gone, Lee had to make a decision about his replacement. Hampton was the senior cavalry officer, and Lee knew him to be a capable commander. Since the death of Stonewall Jackson, however, Lee had seen more than one example of an excellent division commander proving that handling a corps was too much for him. Hampton could be depended on to hold a position, and often he showed, as Longstreet said, "dash." But did he have the brilliance, the vision, and the boldness of Stuart? He was certainly good at conducting reconnaissance, and he responded well in times of crisis, but how would he react to the increased responsibility of managing a cavalry corps with dwindling resources? Would he complain about shortages of mounts, fodder, and food for his men rather than fight? Well into middle age and suffering the effects of several wounds in his body, did he have Stuart's endurance? And could he and Fitz Lee get along well enough to get the job done? Finally, wasn't it just a little unrealistic to expect a man with no formal military education and no prewar experience to handle an entire corps?

Lee decided that for the time being, all three cavalry divisions would report directly to him. Only when Fitz's or Rooney Lee's divisions operated in conjunction with Hampton's would the South Carolinian's authority extend to them. For the moment, then, Hampton controlled only his own division. Fitz was many miles away trying to deal with Sheridan, while Rooney Lee was guarding the opposite flank of the Army of Northern Virginia from Hampton. If Hampton felt slighted by Lee's decision, he said nothing at the time.[16]

For the next three weeks, the two armies fought a running, bruising battle, with Grant continually seeking to get around Lee's right and Lee moving to head him off. The scene of the fighting shifted south, from Spotsylvania to the North Anna, to the Pamunkey, to Cold Harbor. The cavalry's mission remained the same—to anticipate and delay enemy movements, to get information to Lee, and to screen its own army's movements. Hampton's division continued to move and fight, often against infantry, sometimes against larger numbers of cavalry, and sometimes against both. Every day from May 6 to June 3 the division or parts of it were in action near rural Virginia crossroads—at Shady Grove Church, Todd's Tavern, Wright's Tavern, Atlee's Station, Pole Cat Creek, Haw's Shop, and others in between. As Private Edward Wells recalled, it was a test of Confederate morale. Every day found the Rebel horsemen attempting to delay the advance of heavy Federal columns "and always forced to fall back gradually before their larger numbers. This is a sort of service that is the hardest that can be put upon troops, for they know full well each morning that the struggle is, for them a hopeless one, and yet that they must encounter it day after day, forced back always, but disputing every inch. Troops that can dispute this, undemoralized, are veterans tried and true."[17]

On May 27 Lee's three cavalry divisions were reunited at Atlee's Station. For the past twenty-four hours, the Confederate chieftain had been unsure of Grant's intentions. Grant had vacated his lines on the North Anna River, but Lee had no idea where he was going. It would be Wade Hampton's job to find out. Lee ordered Hampton to move toward the Pamunkey to see if Grant had crossed the river. Hampton decided to take elements of the entire cavalry corps. It would be the first major expedition of the cavalry corps since Stuart's death and the first time that Hampton would lead more than just his own division. He took Wickham's brigade from Fitz's division and John Chambliss's brigade from Rooney Lee's, as well as elements of the North Carolina brigade under Colonel John A. Baker and a few sections of horse artillery. Representing his own division was Rosser's brigade and parts of the brigade that were arriving in bits and pieces from South Carolina. Hampton still planned to have Calbraith Butler command this brigade, but Butler's return to the army was still several days away. The 5th South Carolina was present, having arrived several days before and fighting a losing engagement at Wilson's Wharf while under the temporary command of Fitz Lee. Part of the 4th South Carolina had also just arrived and was even more inexperienced. In Butler's absence, these two regiments would come under the temporary command of Colonel Benjamin Huger Rutledge of the 4th South Carolina.[18]

The new contingent from South Carolina was a curiosity and an object of ridicule to the ragged survivors of the Confederate cavalry corps. The veterans called the new units "bandbox regiments," as they

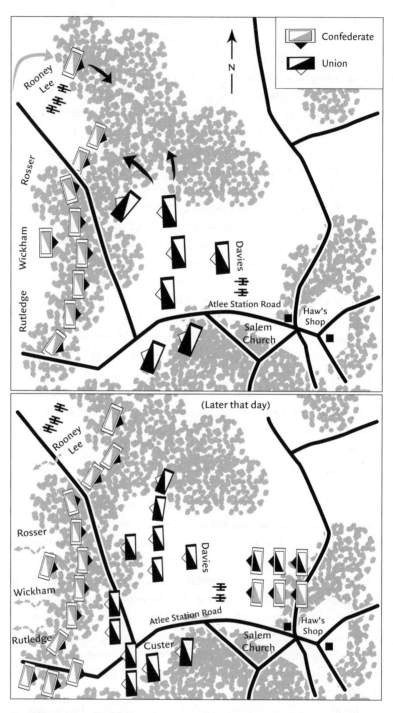

Haw's Shop, May 28, 1864

sported a full complement of officers and men. While the old-timers wore gray jackets and wielded breech-loading carbines captured from the Yankees, the new men wore coarse, brown homespun and carried long-barreled, muzzle-loading infantry-style Enfields. The thought of the rookies trying to adapt the "Long Toms" to fighting on horseback amused the veterans. To top off the startling contrast, the Charleston Light Dragoons of the 4th wore natty white gloves.[19]

At 8:00 A.M. on May 28 Hampton set out from Atlee's Station, riding down Atlee's Station Road toward Enon Church. He diplomatically gave Fitz Lee's division the honor of leading the advance, with Wickham's brigade taking the vanguard. At about ten o'clock the column collided with the advance pickets of Sheridan's cavalry headed in the opposite direction, near Enon Church and about two miles west of a dilapidated machine shop formerly operated by an elderly farmer named John Haws III. Ironically, the Union cavalrymen were on the same mission as their Confederate counterparts, advancing up Atlee's Station Road to look for the main body of the enemy's infantry. Wickham's lead regiment drove the enemy pickets until they reached the main Union line. Hampton went to the front and placed Wickham's brigade in a north-south line straddling Atlee Station Road. Rosser moved to Wickham's left, and Fitz Lee received permission from Hampton to place Butler's (Rutledge's) new men on Wickham's right.[20]

Hampton's position was a strong one. It was protected on both flanks by bodies of water or marsh, making a Federal flanking attack virtually impossible. At this early stage of the fight, in fact, Hampton's lines were longer than those of his opponent, Union brigadier general Henry Davies. All along the front, he had his men dig shallow rifle pits and gather logs and fallen trees to construct crude breastworks. Hampton intended for his men to fight like infantry.[21]

A fierce and bloody engagement developed in the woods on either side of the road, both sides fighting on foot. As the hours dragged on, the battle disintegrated into an unorganized Indian-style brawl, with small bodies of partially concealed soldiers maneuvering through the trees and underbrush and pouring musketry and artillery fire into each other. The Federals' repeating carbines allowed them to fire roughly seven shots to every one Confederate round. The Confederates' Enfields, though, especially in Rutledge's brigade on the right, had greater range and accuracy, giving the Southerners an advantage when the terrain was open enough to fire at longer ranges.[22]

Hampton was able to bring up Chambliss's brigade under Rooney

Lee and place it on his left. The Yankees, however, were receiving many more reinforcements, including the brigades of Generals George Custer, Thomas Devin, and Wesley Merritt. Eventually they outnumbered the Confederates and began pressing Hampton's center and right. Hampton ordered Rooney Lee to turn the Federal right if possible, but Lee balked, claiming incorrectly that his own flank was endangered. Rooney probably could at least have applied strong pressure on the Federal right.[23]

Hampton also sent a message to Jubal Early, whose Second Corps of the Army of Northern Virginia was only two miles away on the south side of Totopotomoy Creek. He thought that Early could easily cross the creek and strike the rear of the Union force at Haw's Shop. Early declined. Such a blow might have disrupted Grant's army as it attempted to complete its crossing of the Pamunkey, but Early apparently considered it too risky to put his corps on the same side of the creek as the Federals. If he ran into a force stronger than his, it would be difficult to withdraw and difficult to be reinforced. Hampton's message suggests that while he was content to fight a defensive battle to his front, his mind was still seeking a way to deal an offensive blow and find out what was behind Sheridan's cavalry screen.[24]

After several hours of a deadly volley exchange at close range, Hampton decided to withdraw. The reason was twofold. Rooney Lee claimed that he was fighting Federal infantry and asked permission to withdraw. He actually faced dismounted cavalry, but Hampton probably considered that the pressure he was withstanding was strong enough without trying to hold off infantry on his far left flank. More importantly, though, Rooney's report suggested that Hampton had accomplished his mission—he had found the Federal infantry. Hampton also believed that he had captured "some Infantry prisoners . . . from whence was obtained the information desired by General Commanding."[25] It is hard to see how Hampton could have captured Federal infantrymen, as none are known to have been directly engaged in the fight. It is possible, though, that his prisoners knew that Federal infantry were close behind Sheridan. In Hampton's words, "Finding that in addition to the whole of Sheridan's Cavalry, a large force of Infantry was in my front & the object of the reconnaissance having been accomplished, I ordered my command to withdraw."[26] Sheridan's entire cavalry corps was in the vicinity of Haw's Shop, and just east of him Grant's army was in the process of crossing the Pamunkey. Thus, while it appears that all the evidence indicating the presence of Union infantrymen was bogus, Hampton's conclusion that they were near was correct.[27]

Hampton pulled back Rosser's brigade, then Wickham's. Rosser withdrew in good order, but Wickham was under such pressure that his departure was precipitate and disorganized. Hampton later attributed Wickham's rapid retreat to the subsequent predicament of the South Carolina regiments on the right, who had fought fiercely all day and proved themselves to friends and foes alike. The better explanation was that the couriers delivering the order to withdraw never reached some of the new men. Smoke, dense terrain, and unseasoned officers and couriers made communication difficult. At least one squadron of the 4th, the Charleston Light Dragoons, never got the word at all. Then again, one inexperienced officer, a Captain Pinckney, ignored an order from Rosser to withdraw, thinking that he should wait for word from Hampton himself and probably reasoning that Rosser was outside his chain of command. Moreover, when Wickham pulled back, Rutledge and his green officers were slow to recognize their danger. Federals poured into the gap left by Wickham's retreat, and the new men of the 4th and 5th South Carolina soon found themselves in a crossfire from front and flank. The 4th suffered especially heavy losses. Hampton quickly realized that something was wrong. He rode forward and, with what one South Carolina trooper called a "calm, cool, and reassuring" presence, personally extricated the two regiments.[28] Finally locating William Stokes, the acting commander of the 4th, Hampton assured the inexperienced officer that he had done all that was expected. He ordered Stokes to remount his men as quickly as possible and re-form behind the second line of defense. The Charleston Light Dragoons of the 4th was nearly wrecked as an effective unit, but, overall, the pride of the new men was salvaged. Referring to the "seven or eight engagements" the 5th had encountered since its recent arrival in Virginia, one private wrote, "We have won a name as fighting stock."[29]

Both sides claimed success, though both Hampton and Sheridan recognized that they had been in a severe fight and taken heavy losses. The Confederates suffered 378 casualties. By far the heaviest losses were in the 4th South Carolina, due to the new men's reckless style of fighting and belated withdrawal. Sheridan's losses were roughly equal—about 365. As one historian points out, though, Hampton had succeeded in his mission of locating the main body of the enemy army, whereas Sheridan had not.[30]

Hampton's first performance leading more than one division had been respectable but not brilliant. He had made mistakes. At the tactical level, he probably should have pushed harder on the Federal flanks early in the battle when he briefly had the advantage of numbers and a longer line. No doubt it was also a bad idea to make Rutledge's green brigade the last unit to withdraw, in effect assigning it the rearguard position. Such a task should have been left to a veteran brigade with experienced officers. Somehow the coordination had broken down between Hampton and that brigade, and the answer probably lay partially in the fact that Hampton had not ensured that command relationships were clearly defined. Since Hampton was acting as corps commander, he had left temporary command of his division to his senior brigadier, Tom Rosser. Rosser therefore thought that he should control Rutledge's brigade, though Fitz Lee somehow got the impression that Rutledge was under his authority. Rutledge himself was unsure to whom he reported. It was a confusing situation in a fluid, ad hoc chain of command, and this probably contributed to the brigade's near-encirclement at the end of the battle. At least Hampton had the presence of mind to take charge himself when he sensed that Rutledge's brigade was in danger of being cut off.[31]

Despite Hampton's mistakes, he did the most important things well. First, his chosen method of fighting was the right one for the situation. Fighting on foot was the best course in wooded terrain and allowed the Confederates to take better advantage of their marksmanship, particularly those with the infantry-style Enfield rifles. More importantly, Hampton never lost sight of his larger mission—finding and reporting the location of Grant's main army. For this reason, he can be forgiven for settling down into a strong defensive position rather than aggressively seeking to turn the enemy's flanks. Temporary success in driving the lead brigades of Yankee cavalry would have been just that and would have meant nothing but heavier Confederate casualties unless Hampton could help Lee discern the intentions and location of Grant's infantry. Hampton had made mistakes, but he could report to Lee that he had accomplished the mission.

After Haw's Shop, the fighting continued as before. The cavalry divisions often fought in different sectors again, with Fitz on the right and Hampton either in the center or helping Rooney Lee on the left. Every day there was more reconnoitering and more fighting—at Matadequin Creek, Hanover Court House, Ashland, and again at Atlee's Station and Haw's Shop. On May 30 Hampton was glad to see that the rest of the new brigade had finally arrived from South Carolina and that Calbraith Butler was finally back in the saddle, as crusty as ever. With his cork leg tucked into a high-topped boot, he told those who welcomed him back, "I am not much of a pedestrian, but in the saddle, I am as good as ever."[32]

At dawn on June 3, Grant resorted to a frontal assault on Robert E. Lee's fortifications at Cold Harbor. It went down as one of the most disastrous, useless assaults of the war. By early afternoon, Grant's men had needlessly suffered 6,000 casualties, with nothing to show for their bloody sacrifice. Lee's losses were less than 1,500.[33]

For a few days, the two armies paused from their constant maneuvers to glower at each other over no-man's-land. A month's worth of constant fighting had cost the Army of the Potomac over 50,000 casualties, while Lee had suffered just over 31,000.[34] Grant was geographically closer to Richmond, but at the time he seemed no closer to defeating Lee's army. Thanks to hard marching, constant entrenching and intelligent use of terrain, shorter lines of march, and the unceasing work of the cavalry, Lee had thwarted every flanking maneuver and every Union assault. The cavalry had done its job.

⭐ The question of whether Wade Hampton could ever replace Jeb Stuart had lost some of its urgency. The cavalry was performing well. The answer, of course, was that no one could replace Stuart. Much of Lee's success from the Wilderness to Cold Harbor was due to J. E. B. Stuart and his legacy even after his death, for Stuart had no peer in reconnaissance and intelligence gathering. He had passed those skills down to Fitz and Rooney Lee, Wade Hampton, and many others. Moreover, no one could ride circles around an entire Federal army or conduct audacious raids behind enemy lines like Stuart.

Hampton's strengths in other areas, though, may have excelled those of both Stuart and Fitz Lee. At Yellow Tavern, Sheridan had proved that Stuart could be beaten in a stand-up fight, if earlier contests had not sent the same message. In the days after Yellow Tavern, Fitz Lee had suffered further reverses at Meadow Bridge on May 12 and Wilson's Wharf on May 24. Under Hampton's command, however, the outmanned and outgunned Confederate troopers seemed once again to give as good as they got in a stand-up fight. The Yankees knew that they had been in a fight at Haw's Shop. Three days later, Hampton had led Rooney Lee and Rosser in a thorough rout of Brevet Major General James Wilson's division of Union cavalry at Hanover Court House.[35]

Renewed confidence began to bolster Hampton's troopers. Robert E. Lee still had not officially recognized Hampton as the commander of the cavalry corps, but Hampton had already put his stamp on it. Hampton's style of fighting—taking every available man to the fight, fighting with the entire command dismounted, holding ground as stubbornly as infantry—had already made its mark. An officer in Fitz Lee's division who had never before served under Hampton gloated that Sheridan had crossed the Pamunkey on May 27 expecting to clear Grant's path to Richmond, only to be stopped cold by "Hampton's half fed, half armed half mounted, ill-disciplined yet ubiquitous and resolute cavalry."[36] Hampton could not claim all the credit for the cavalry's recent successes. But he had made his mark. What was significant about Robert T. Hubard's comment on the "resolute cavalry" was that he called it not "Stuart's," "Lee's," or "Fitz's" cavalry, but "Hampton's."[37]

THE TEST AT TREVILIAN

The gory results of Cold Harbor convinced Grant that he would never capture Richmond using the direct approach. Over the next few days, he hatched another scheme. He would continue south around Lee's right flank, cross the James River, and capture the more southerly city of Petersburg. By doing so, he could cut the railroad between Petersburg and Richmond, stop the vital flow of supplies to Lee's army, and thus leave the Confederate capital virtually indefensible. For Lee's army to survive, he would have to withdraw to the west, leaving Richmond open to capture.[1]

Neither Lee nor Hampton, of course, could know immediately that Grant had changed his operational objectives. Hampton, however, did suspect that the Federal cavalry was up to something. His scouts reported Sheridan's cavalry units marching north and crossing the Pamunkey River. Later reports indicated that most or all of Sheridan's troopers were moving west along the south side of the Mattapony toward Gordonsville.[2]

Hampton supposed that Sheridan intended to cut the Virginia Central Railroad near the key junction of Gordonsville and link up with Union general David Hunter's force near Charlottesville, which was rapidly rolling up Confederate resistance in the Shenandoah Valley. He guessed correctly. Grant wanted Sheridan to accomplish both of these tasks. He hoped that Sheridan could cut the railroad in several places— at Gordonsville, Charlottesville, and Lynchburg. After joining with Hunter, the two commands were to return east to rejoin Grant's army, destroying the James River Canal and more of the railroad as they went. By that time, Grant hoped, his main army would be south of the James threatening Petersburg. After the war, Sheridan claimed that Grant had an additional objective for the raid. As the Confederate cavalry followed Sheridan, it would leave Robert E. Lee without the intelligence, reconnaissance, and mobile firepower he needed to slow Grant's crossing of the James, allowing Grant to get around Lee's right and capture Petersburg. Grant was probably thinking along those lines, as he had used similar tactics before, but there is little evidence that he communicated those thoughts to Sheridan.[3]

Hampton intended to counter Sheridan's move with the largest 203

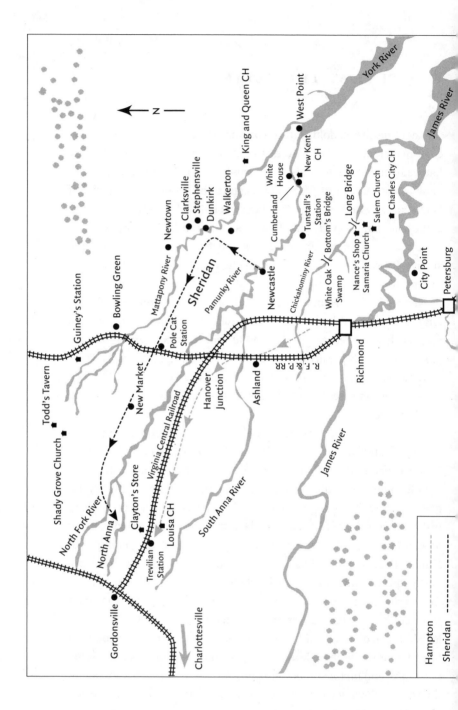

possible force. Stuart's style would have been to take a brigade or two, discover and thwart Sheridan's intentions, and discomfit and humiliate him with surprise attacks and predawn raids. But Hampton thought in terms of mass concentration, not economy of force. He wanted to take at least two full divisions and several batteries of horse artillery in order to defeat Sheridan in a knock-down, drag-out fight. Hampton consulted with Lee, who ultimately approved the outline of his plan. Hampton would proceed west and interpose himself between Sheridan and Gordonsville. He would have not only his division, but Fitz Lee's as well—the first time that Robert E. Lee issued explicit orders that put his nephew under Hampton's control. The army commander insisted, however, that Hampton leave Rooney Lee's division with the main army.[4]

Hampton set out at 3:00 A.M. on the morning of June 9 in a driving rain with Fitz Lee's division several miles behind him. He also had fifteen artillery pieces from various elements of the cavalry's horse artillery—in all, a force of roughly 6,400 men. Sheridan, marching along a roughly parallel route north of the North Anna River, had about 9,300. The Confederates were aiming for Trevilian Station, where the Gordonsville Road intersected with the Virginia Central Railroad a few miles south of the North Anna. If Sheridan intended to cut the Virginia Central on his way to Gordonsville, that would be the first place he was likely to do it. Sheridan had a two-day head start. But Hampton had a shorter route. If he pushed hard, he could get to Trevilian first. His men had been issued three days' scant rations consisting mainly of musty cornmeal and fat bacon, some of which was rancid. They could only guess at their destination. Lieutenant Colonel J. Fred Waring, commander of the Jeff Davis Legion, wondered in his diary, "Can Hampton be intending to make a raid?"[5] Horse artilleryman Sergeant George Neese observed: "General Hampton . . . is after the raiders in hot pursuit, and when he strikes a warm trail there is usually some blood left in the track and some game bagged."[6]

The column of thin horses and hungry men moved at a steady walk throughout the day. Hampton scheduled a two-hour break around noon so the horses could graze. Then the march would resume and continue until midnight, when it paused for another two-hour break. Hampton covered nearly thirty miles the first day, then rested his command as planned. He marched again at 2:00 A.M. the next morning, and by 3:00 P.M. his division had reached Trevilian, where he found to his relief that he had won the race. That night he telegraphed Robert E. Lee: "I am getting between him and Gordonsville. Everything going well."[7] Hampton immediately posted Rosser's brigade on his far left, astride the Virginia Central and the Gordonsville Road. Gilbert J. Wright's brigade was at Trevilian Station. Butler would camp just to the east near the Netherland's family dwelling, where Hampton made his headquarters. Fitz Lee's division was three or four miles to the east at Louisa Court House. Despite having just completed a grueling two-day march, Hampton stayed awake all night collecting information on Sheridan's whereabouts. His enemy, he learned, had crossed the North Anna at Carpenter's Ford and moved south to the vicinity of Clayton's Store.[8]

Hampton hoped to deal Sheridan a crushing blow. He ordered Fitz Lee to move up the road from Louisa to Clayton's Store. Wright's and Butler's brigades, he reasoned, could advance up the Fredericksburg Road, link up with Fitz's left, and converge with him on the Clayton's Store crossroads. With Butler and Wright hammering Sheridan's front, Fitz could slip around the enemy's left. Rosser would remain slightly to the rear on Hampton's own left to foil any maneuver by Sheridan in that direction, and to prevent the possibility of Hunter advancing from the west. As had become Hampton's custom, most of the troopers would fight dismounted. Approximately every fourth man would become a horse handler, keeping the mounts in the rear while his comrades on the front lines fought on foot. If all went well, Hampton would drive Sheridan into the North Anna River.[9]

Hampton sent his instructions to Fitz, but one story suggests that neither Butler nor Rosser knew what Hampton's plans were. The commander had an excellent relationship with both Butler and Rosser, but perhaps felt no need to give them their orders until the moment they were to move out. Instead, the first hints of daylight revealed that Hampton had finally laid down to take a nap. At about sunrise, the story goes, Tom Rosser rode to the headquarters of his friend Calbraith Butler and asked what Hampton's intentions were. "Damned if I know," replied the salty-tongued Butler. "We have been up mounted since daylight and my men and horses are being worsted by non-action." Rosser replied, "Let's ride down and enquire what Hampton's plans are." Butler ordered his men to dismount and rode with Rosser to find Hampton at the Netherland House. The general was lying on a carpenter's bench outside. He greeted them warmly, and Rosser politely asked, "General, what do you propose to do here today, if I may enquire?" Hampton replied, "I intend to fight." Butler pointed out that the thickly wooded terrain seemed unsuitable for maneuvering cavalry, to which Hampton answered, "Well, let's ride out and reconnoitre a little." Rosser rejoined his command while Hampton and Butler rode north. They encountered some of Butler's pickets, who said that they had been driven in by a strong force of Yankee cavalry. Only after hearing this news, according to the story, did Hampton form and communicate his plan.[10]

The dialogue in this account fits all three characters, but it seems impossible that Hampton had made no plans before dawn. It is clear from the story that his brigades were up, mounted, and prepared for action by daylight, and Hampton's report and a postwar account by Butler support that fact. Fitz Lee apparently was aware of the plan. He had already dispatched one of his brigades north to Clayton's Store at 3:00 A.M. to reconnoiter and sent Hampton a message shortly after daylight that he was moving out to attack. In his own report, Hampton stated that "dispositions were made" and "at daylight my division was ready to attack at Trevilian."[11] It is possible that although Hampton had his units ready for action, he still had not adequately briefed his brigade commanders on the specific plan of attack, perhaps not even until elements of Merritt's Union brigade ran into Butler's outlying pickets. At that point Butler's brigade moved north, followed by Wright's. Hampton's plan had already miscarried, however, because Sheridan, unintentionally, had struck first.[12]

Sheridan had been unaware that Hampton was in his front in force. He planned for two brigades from Brigadier General Alfred A. Torbert's division—Merritt's and Devin's—to march on Trevilian Station via the Fredericksburg Road. Torbert's other brigade under George Custer would also converge on the station via Nunn's Creek Road. David Gregg's division would move with the wagon train toward Louisa Court House and guard Sheridan's left flank.[13]

The fighting began in earnest around 6:00 A.M. Butler's brigade dismounted and pushed back the 2nd U.S. Cavalry for up to three-quarters of a mile until the 2nd was reinforced and Merritt's entire brigade counterattacked and retook most of the lost ground. Butler expected to get support from Fitz Lee on his right at any moment, but that help never materialized. As long as Butler was driving the Yankees or holding his own, Hampton, who was also expecting Fitz, delayed in committing Wright until his whole line was ready for a general advance. Finally the pressure on Butler became so intense that Hampton had no choice. Colonel B. Huger Rutledge, commanding Butler's leftmost regiment, sent an urgent message to Butler that he was being flanked. His line was stretched to the limit, and he could no longer refuse his left. 207

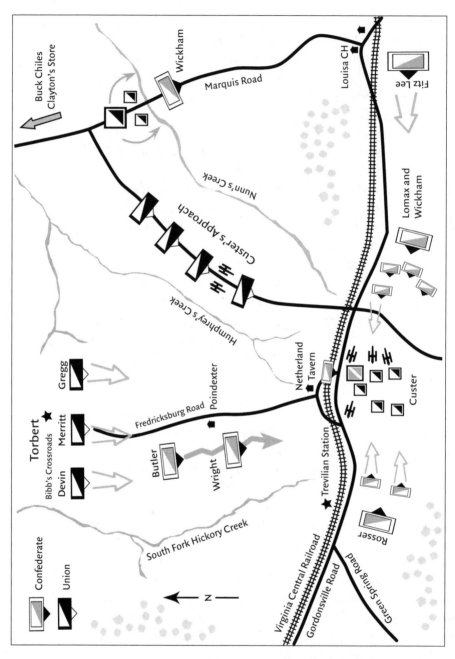

Situation at Trevilian, Midmorning, June 11, 1864

Butler turned to the courier and coolly replied, "Give my compliments to Colonel Rutledge and tell him to flank back." The two men laughed about the incident later, with Rutledge remarking that it was the "cheekiest" order he ever received. "Didn't you know," Butler replied, "pressed as I was in front and on both flanks, I had no reinforcements to send you."[14] Butler did, however, send to Hampton for reinforcements. Hampton ordered Wright's brigade to reinforce Butler's left, while he also brought up Hart's artillery. Rosser was still in reserve to the left rear, while Sheridan had not yet committed Gregg's division.[15]

Still there was no sign of Fitz. Hampton had received a message from him hours earlier that he was advancing to the attack. Where was he? It turned out that Wickham's brigade had sortied up the Marquis Road cautiously around 3:00 A.M. Not until daylight did it cover the three miles or so that brought it into contact with Custer's brigade. Wickham skirmished with Custer for about an hour and then withdrew. This left Custer free to follow his orders, which were to advance southwest down Nunn's Creek Road, a march that took him between Hampton's and Fitz Lee's divisions and into the rear of Hampton's. Fitz apparently never took his division up the Marquis Road as directed. If he had, he would have either struck the rear of Custer's column or appeared on the Federal left and rear. Instead, he seems to have moved—extremely slowly—westward toward Trevilian along the Gordonsville Road.[16]

Custer found himself in the rear of Hampton's entire division. He could have turned north and slammed into Butler or Wright from the rear while Torbert's division pounded them in front. He saw instead an even greater prize—Hampton's wagon train and led horses just east of Trevilian Station and south of the railroad.[17]

Around midmorning couriers dashed up to Hampton to tell him that Federal cavalry were in his rear. It must have been a hair-raising moment. Here was Hampton's first battle as acting corps commander of Lee's cavalry, and he was about to be surrounded and humiliated. How did this happen, and . . . where was Fitz? Hampton hurried toward the rear to investigate the shocking reports. There were the Yankees—they had not only moved behind Hampton but were now making off with his wagons and led horses. Hampton's division was about to become a cavalry command with no horses.

Once again, just as at Manassas, Brandy Station, and Upperville, Hampton would need every ounce of his self-possession, calm nerves, and gritty determination. And he would have to act quickly. His actions and words would have to inspire confidence in men whose first instinct at this point would be to panic. He ordered Rosser to attack Custer from the west. Butler and Wright would have to send elements of their brigades to the rear to help as well. Hampton therefore sent orders for the Jeff Davis Legion of Wright's brigade and the 6th South Carolina of Butler's to turn around and attack Custer from the north. He sent word for Fitz to join him at Trevilian; the Virginian finally appeared, just in time to block Custer's escape to the east. Hampton seemed to be everywhere at once, here giving instructions to the Jeff Davis Legion, there countermanding an order to the 35th Virginia battalion of "Comanches" to charge directly into a Federal battery. He took time to speak to individual soldiers as well. At one point Willie Hayes, a feisty young private of the 20th Georgia battalion, strode up to the commanding general and demanded treatment for his shattered arm. Hampton asked a nearby surgeon to tend to the lad, whose arm was soon amputated.[18]

Now it was Custer who was trapped. The charge of Rosser's men sliced through Custer's Michigan brigade, isolating regiments and companies from each other. On the other side, the nearly encircled Wolverines suffered from the attacks of Lomax's brigade of Lee's division. To the north they had to contend with Butler's 6th South Carolina and the Phillips Legion of Wright's brigade. The wagon train and captured Confederate horses quickly fell back into the hands of their owners. Custer's brigade, in fact, was fighting for its life. The 7th Michigan lost the horses of its dismounted men, its rations and cooking equipment, and its black servants. Custer's personal wagon fell into Confederate hands, along with his bedding, desk, and underclothing; his recently arrived brigadier general's commission; a dress uniform; and—most embarrassing—intimate love letters from his wife that were subsequently published in Richmond newspapers. With Confederates firing into Custer from three sides, with guns, wagons, and prisoners being captured and recaptured, one Michigan private said that it was "the most mixed up fight I ever saw."[19] In what Eric J. Wittenberg has called "Custer's First Last Stand," the "Boy General" fought heroically to hold his decimated brigade together.[20] In the process he suffered 11 killed, 51 wounded, and 299 captured—for total losses of 361. One of his regiments, the 5th Michigan, lost nearly half of its strength.[21]

Hampton had recaptured his wagons and horses and narrowly averted disaster, but he had been unable to destroy Custer. Worse, signs of activity to the north indicated that Torbert was preparing to renew his assault in an attempt to rescue Custer. Hampton issued orders for his brigades to withdraw to the south and west and set up a new, consolidated line on a low ridge west of the railroad. This move would ensure that Custer was no longer in his rear. The Federals did not let him get away that easily. Rosser's men, who had been fighting Custer, now found Torbert's troopers coming at them from the other direction. Swarming Federals cut Rosser's brigade off from Wright's. Rosser was wounded leading a charge, while his disorganized command fought to extricate itself and take its place on the left of the new line that Hampton was trying to establish.[22]

Butler was having a difficult time as well. He was losing contact with Wright's brigade on the left and still had no contact with Fitz's division on the right. When receiving his orders to fall back, he exclaimed: "Say to General Hampton that it is hell to hold on and hell to let go! If I withdraw my entire line at once the blue coats will run over us, and that the best I can do is to mount one regiment at a time and gradually retire."[23] Butler would have to execute the same maneuver that a former brigade commander, Wade Hampton, had carried out at Brandy Station and Upperville. Butler maintained good order in his brigade, but he was pushed all the way back to the railroad. At one point, his supporting battery, Hart's, was isolated and close to being captured. Hampton himself rode up to the 5th South Carolina and ordered it to dismount and protect the battery. Then he rode to the 6th South Carolina nearby and ordered a charge on the Federals moving toward the battery. The only company available was Company F, the "Cadet Rangers," some of whom were recent graduates of The Citadel in Charleston. Most, however, were former cadets who had disobeyed orders and gone AWOL from their institution to enlist. They had seen little action until transferred to Virginia only months before. Hampton led the young troopers in a fierce saber charge and pitched himself into the fray, personally emptying two Yankee saddles with his revolver. Throughout this desperate phase of the battle, Fitz Lee's entire division was out of the fight and providing no help at all.[24]

Hampton finally succeeded in establishing his new line west of the Gordonsville Road. Throughout the afternoon he had ridden among his brigades exerting a steadying influence through his cool courage, confident demeanor, and timely orders.[25] His withdrawal left Trevilian Station to Sheridan, which he promptly destroyed, along with several miles of track around Trevilian and Louisa. Hampton had suffered 530 casualties out of 6,512 men engaged. He was still in a perfect position to block Sheridan's march to Gordonsville. Sheridan's force of 9,300 troopers lost 699, including 372 captured. It was clear to both sides, though, that this was no Confederate victory. At the tactical level, it was a defeat. Calbraith Butler called it a disaster. Union troopers realized that they had driven the Rebels back and that at times their foes seemed to be fleeing in confusion. For about twenty-four hours, many Virginians in the ranks of the Comanches battalion blamed Hampton "for allowing his men to be beaten in that way, by brigades." By the end of the next day, though, they would conclude that "he was working out his problem and baiting his trap for tomorrow."[26]

The truth was that in Hampton's first day as an acting corps commander, he had been beaten. Hoping to drive Sheridan's command into the North Anna, he had instead been compelled to fall back, with his division gallantly fighting for its survival. There had been plenty of events in the day's fight to celebrate—inspired leadership by Hampton, Butler, Rosser, and countless other officers, not to mention the fierce courage of the men. Most of those gallant feats, however, were part of a desperate attempt to turn a complete disaster into a mild setback. Hampton might have shared some of the blame, but not much. It is possible that he did not adequately brief his own brigade commanders before the fight began. It also would have been better if he had started the advance of his three brigades before first light, despite their exhausted condition. But even if he had, Fitz's failure to carry out his part of the plan would have produced the same result—Custer's brigade in his rear. Fitz's absence was difficult to excuse and harder to explain. In a report written after the war, Fitz cited the distance that he had had to travel—three or four miles with mounted troops—as the cause of his delay. Surely he must have thought of a better excuse than that when he met with Hampton the next day. Hampton's officers suspected Fitz not so much of incompetence as of deliberately refusing to obey the orders of any cavalryman other than Jeb Stuart.[27]

Hampton himself never publicly criticized Fitz's performance. Perhaps he sensed that somehow part of the test of his leadership would be how well he could handle and work with Fitz Lee, his peer and rival. Fitz's uncle, Robert E. Lee, had seen Hampton when he was at his pettiest, and he had been at his pettiest when he had criticized Stuart and revealed his jealousy of Fitz. As a corps commander, Hampton would either have to take responsibility for Fitz Lee's failure or court-martial him. He was not prepared to do the latter. Besides, Hampton had great respect and affection for Fitz's uncle. He omitted any reference to Fitz's failure in his official report to Robert E. Lee, stating only that "Maj. Gen. Fitzhugh Lee co-operated with me heartily and rendered

valuable assistance."[28] Hampton could not have truthfully been referring to the events of June 11. Instead, he was writing about the next day,
when Fitz's presence finally gave Hampton the success he was looking
for. Many years later Hampton confided to his former trooper Edward
Wells: "[Fitz] Lee returned to Louisa C.H. just after Rosser's charge, &
he did not join me until 2 P.M. the next day!" He added, "Of course I
shall not say anything about it unless forced to do so."[29] He also explained: "I really did not know at first how greatly he had failed on the
first day, & my regard for Genl. R. E. Lee induced me to omit all mention
of [Fitz's] misconduct."[30]

Despite the frustrations of the day, Hampton was still full of fight. As
darkness and rain fell over the forests around Trevilian, he strengthened
his line along the Gordonsville Road and probably wondered whether
Fitz Lee was carrying out his latest orders. He had instructed his un-
cooperative peer/subordinate to march south, swing around the Federal
left and Hampton's right, and take up a new position on Hampton's
left. After receiving these orders, Lee covered little more than two miles
on the evening of June 11 before bedding down for the night near Lastly
Church. He did not break camp the next morning until 9:30. He continued his leisurely pace until noon, when he halted and allowed the animals to graze "for some time after which we drew rations and corn."[31]
Fitz finally joined Hampton around 2:00 P.M. One wonders what was
said between the two generals.[32]

Morning found Hampton's division occupying a strong position
along the Gordonsville Road. Butler's brigade was in an L-shaped position near the Ogg family's house; his men were lying in a line of brush
that they had fortified with fence rails and a few hastily dug trenches. In
front of them lay a wide, open field across which the bluecoats would
have to advance to drive them off the road. Rosser's and Wright's brigades occupied Butler's right, and the whole line was studded with
artillery.[33]

Hampton waited for Sheridan to attack his strong position. Sheridan
did not oblige him until at least noon, when Torbert's division began
trying to dislodge the Confederates. Not until 3:00 P.M. did the fighting
become heavy and fierce. Once again Butler's brigade bore the brunt of
the assault. Butler counted seven assaults on his line between noon and
sunset, most of them toward the end of the day. At times it appeared that
sections of his line might break, if for no other reason than a shortage
of ammunition. At one point Butler's men were scrounging cartridges
from the dead and wounded. The bluecoats had the advantage of larger

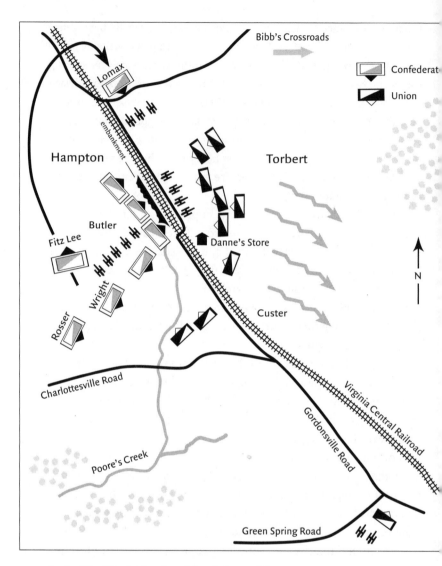

Battle of Trevilian Station, Second Day, June 12, 1864
Torbert's division makes piecemeal attacks on Butler during the day. Fitz Lee, who began the day miles south of Hampton's position, marches west and north and finally takes his place on the far left of Hampton's line, making the attack on Torbert's right flank possible.

numbers and a rapid rate of fire from their Spencer repeating carbines. In this situation, though, the Union advantage was offset by the
long barrels of the Confederates' Enfields, which provided greater range
and accuracy as the Yankees attempted to advance over relatively open
ground. Shooting dismounted from a partially fortified position provided even greater accuracy. The fire from the Confederate Enfields was
so steady and accurate that Torbert's men thought that they were fighting infantry and that they were up against superior numbers, when the
opposite was true. Despite the losses suffered by Torbert's men, Sheridan never committed his other division under Gregg to the action.[34]

Unlike Sheridan, Hampton was still hoping to get his other division
into the fight. Once Fitz Lee finally arrived, Hampton directed him to
reinforce Butler's left with Wickham's brigade, while sending Lomax's
brigade and a battery of horse artillery to the far left "so as to strike the
enemy on his right flank."[35] Unfortunately, Lomax was not in position
until shortly before dark. Hampton waited. Finally all was ready, and the
entire Confederate line moved forward. Merritt had no idea that Lomax
was on his right, and the sudden din of Rebel artillery and the Rebel yell
to his front and flank unnerved the Federals. The blue line broke under
the sudden onslaught, with the Yankees fleeing in pandemonium.[36]

For Hampton's troopers, it was an unforgettable moment—the stuff
of which mythology was born. According to Sergeant W. H. Dowling of
the 5th South Carolina, "The moment was awful, the scene sublime, the
rebel yell and exultant shouts of victory all along our line, lasting ten to
twenty minutes, will never be forgotten while one of those brave men
stay this side of the Jordan."[37] A trooper in Fitz Lee's division still had
the energy that night to write in his diary that the final charge "was one
of those sublime spectacles sometimes witnessed on a battlefield. Amid
the surrounding gloom could be seen a constant stream of fire from our
lines as we advanced with victorious shouts upon the bewildered foe."[38]

Sheridan's men also knew that they had been whipped. A diary found
on a captured Federal cavalryman read: "Saturday, June 11th. Fight at
Trevilian station. Captured and killed 600 rebs. . . . Sunday, June 12th.
Fought on same ground. Got whipped like the devil. Lost more men
than the rebs did the day previous."[39] Sheridan began his retreat back
across the North Anna around midnight. Firing had continued until
around 10:00 P.M., but Hampton's men were too exhausted to pursue
the Yankees, which would have been doubly difficult in the dark and
over wooded terrain. Sheridan would later claim Trevilian as a victory,
but he did not regard it as one at the time. He had failed to break

through to Charlottesville, find Hunter, or help Hunter join the Army of the Potomac, and his damage to the Virginia Central was not extensive enough to put it out of commission for long. It must have been difficult for the hard-fighting "Little Phil" to swallow his pride and confess to Grant, "I regret my inability to carry out your instructions."[40]

Fighting against odds of three to two, Hampton had inflicted more losses than he had suffered and accomplished his mission of stopping Sheridan's raid. He had managed to snatch victory from the jaws of defeat, and he had done it fighting his way. Like Stuart before him, Hampton benefited from good intelligence from his "Iron Scouts" led by Sergeant George Shadburne, who provided him early warnings of Sheridan's movements. Then he intercepted Sheridan along his route with hard marching of his own. Unlike Jeb Stuart, he brought with him not just a few crack regiments or brigades, but as much combat power as he could find—and as soon as he could find it. In the words of Nathan Bedford Forrest, a Confederate cavalry commander of more plebeian speech and origins, the key was to "get there first with the most."[41]

Another Hampton trademark was the way his men fought the battle almost entirely on foot. Stuart had eventually adopted the tactic of dismounting a few men and sending them forward as skirmishers, while the "main" or "reserve" line remained mounted. Even at Trevilian, there were a few romantic holdouts, like Tom Rosser, who still preferred to fight on horseback. But as a whole, Hampton's force fought nearly the entire battle dismounted. For Hampton, and now for most of his men, the mounted charge was a last resort rather than a preferred method. Ironically, it was the mounted cavalry charge that was so much a symbol of southern chivalry both before and after the war, and Hampton was a part of that chivalric tradition. As the grandson of a Revolutionary cavalry officer and an expert horseman all of his life, Hampton could lead a cavalry charge as effectively as anyone, but he chose to do so only in emergencies. Lost Cause mythology preferred to remember Hampton leading mounted charges and vanquishing his adversaries on horseback with saber and pistol. Today, a huge mural in the campus library at The Citadel features Hampton leading the charge of the Cadet Rangers at Trevilian. Confederate troopers at the time, however, noted how often they fought on foot now that Hampton was their chief.

Hampton's preference for fighting on foot was not only tactically sound at this stage of the war, but also matched his personality. He won the Battle of Trevilian through patient, steady application, not precipitate charges. His first attempt to take the offensive on the morning of

Hampton leading the charge of Citadel cadets at Trevilian Station, 1864 (mural).
South Caroliniana Library.

June 11 failed due to poor execution on Fitz's part and perhaps poor communication on his own. Then Custer's men appeared behind him. The original plan had failed and he was hard pressed; now Hampton would have to work out his own salvation with hard work and determination. He reacted decisively and appropriately to the threat in his rear. He was at his best during the long afternoon and evening he spent stubbornly withdrawing and establishing a new line. His defensive stand along the Gordonsville Road on the twelfth resulted in severe losses to Torbert. Before he finally resumed the offensive late on that day, he patiently waited until Wickham and Lomax were in place, the numbers were in his favor, and he was able to hit Torbert in both front and flank. Unluckily for the Confederates, the lateness of the attack prevented the Union rout from being more complete than it was. Without Hampton's patience, though, it probably would not have succeeded at all. It was the same patience and determination that characterized so many struggles in Hampton's life.

The flight of the Federals across the North Anna gave Confederate cavalrymen a chance to reflect on the merits of their new cavalry chief. All of them recognized that Hampton was a very different sort of commander; most, including Fitz Lee's men who had never before served under him, appreciated the change. The most negative assessment came from Colonel Richard Dulaney, acting commander of Rosser's brigade after Rosser's wounding: "Hampton I think is superior to Stuart in prudence, good judgment and in military [affairs, but] not the extreme dash . . . and perseverance for which Gen. Stuart was remarkable."[42] The junior officers and men in the ranks decided they liked the new style of fighting, in which they dug in and fought on foot. One did not have to be a general to see that charging Yankee seven-shooters on horseback through wooded terrain was clearly the wrong approach. They left the field at both Haw's Shop and Trevilian not only proud of the fight they had made, but also with an appreciation for their new commander. Men of Wickham's brigade, noting how often they now went into battle and won on foot, began calling themselves "Riding Infantry," proudly comparing themselves to Stonewall Jackson's famous "Foot Cavalry" and asserting that they were "able to hold a line as well as our veteran infantry."[43]

One of the most thorough assessments of Hampton's fighting style came from Captain Frank Myers of the 35th Virginia Battalion's Comanches: "The Cavalry Corps . . . discovered a vast difference between the old and the new, for while General Stuart would attempt his work with whatever force he had at hand, and often seemed to try to accomplish a given result with the smallest possible number of men, Gen. Hampton always endeavored to carry every available man to his point of operation, and the larger the force the better he liked it. The advantage of this style of generalship was soon apparent, for whereas under Stuart stampedes were frequent, with Hampton they were unknown, and his corps soon had the same unwavering confidence in him that the 'Stonewall Brigade' entertained for their General."[44]

HAMPTON'S CAVALRY
JUNE–JULY 1864

It was the tradition of the Army of Northern Virginia to pursue a beaten foe if at all possible. Hampton's worn-out men did not begin their pursuit of Sheridan, however, until late in the day after the battle. Sheridan stayed on the north side of the North Anna and then the Mattapony and Pamunkey, marching east and seeking to comply with his instructions to rejoin Grant's army. Hampton followed on a parallel course that allowed him to protect the Virginia Central Railroad and prevent Sheridan's union with Grant. Hampton seemed to want to force Sheridan to fight, but to do so he would have had to push his men even harder. Without actually cutting off Sheridan's eastward course, he stayed close enough for Sheridan to give battle and hoped that he would. The Union commander, whose forces were also worn out, was in no condition to do so.[1]

Both sides suffered from heat, exhaustion, and thin provisions during their respective marches. The night after the battle at Trevilian Station, Hampton's troopers drew three double handfuls of corn per horse, the first grain that the horses had eaten since the beginning of the campaign on June 8. They would get little more over the course of the next week. The men themselves, including Hampton, were filthy, unwashed, and lousy. By the time they reached Garrett's Store on the fourteenth, Hampton's troopers had been completely without rations for forty-eight hours. He paused to procure and issue them, explaining in telegrams to Robert E. Lee that he would continue the pursuit as soon he could feed his men. Hampton had sometimes thought that Jeb Stuart had not enough concern for his men, that he allowed the condition of his cavalry to deteriorate by pushing them too hard for no good reason. Now that he was in command, he was not going to drive his men and horses into the ground unless there was a life-or-death reason for doing so.[2]

On June 19 Hampton reached the perimeter of the Federal landing place and logistics base at White House on the Pamunkey River. Instead of assaulting the position right away, he positioned artillery on heights above it and made plans for an assault the next morning. He shelled the Federal garrison there for several hours, but his artillerymen were fight- 219 ing an unequal duel against the Union's artillery and powerful gunboats in the river. By the morning of June 20, Hampton had changed his mind. There was a full brigade of enemy infantry there. Cavalry were not meant to assault fortifications, nor fight toe-to-toe with infantry. Besides, Sheridan was on the way to reinforce the infantry from the other side of the river, and the entire Union force was protected by heavy shells from the gunboats. Fitz Lee concurred. The situation reminded him too much of an ill-advised attack he had made on a fortified Federal base at Wilson's Wharf a few weeks before that had resulted in a useless sacrifice of Confederate lives.[3]

But Hampton still hoped that he could acquire a brigade of infantry and take White House. He wrote to General Braxton Bragg, President Davis's military adviser, to suggest that Bragg send him an infantry brigade. If the infantry could drive the gunboats down the river toward Cumberland's Landing, firmly held by Hampton, he reasoned that he could capture the gunboats. His combined force of infantry and cavalry would then be strong enough to capture White House along with a huge haul of wagons, horses, and prisoners. Without this supply base, Sheridan would be forced to retreat again. If he did not and attempted to march overland to join Grant, Hampton felt that his own cavalry supported by the infantry had a grand "opportunity to crush this cavalry."[4]

The brigade from Richmond never appeared, of course, and Lee needed every regiment just then to counter Grant's threat to Petersburg. It is curious, too, that Hampton appealed to Bragg rather than to Lee, his immediate superior, for reinforcements. Perhaps he did not know how to reach Lee, as he requested that Bragg inform Lee of his letter to Bragg. It was unlikely that such a plan would ever come together, and Hampton expressed it vaguely. It does indicate two things about Hampton's thinking at this point. First, he was leery of wasting his command in a fruitless assault against superior firepower. Second, he was looking for a way not only to neutralize, but also to "crush" Sheridan.

While Hampton and Sheridan had spent the last two weeks marching and fighting with each other, the rest of the war had moved away from them. Grant had begun his massive movement to the south of the James. Initially the absence of most of the Confederate cavalry had enabled him to get a head start on Lee, who did not know about the move for several days. Bungling and missed opportunities by Federal officers, however, as well as the advantage of marching along interior lines, enabled Lee to meet the threat in time—Petersburg remained in Confederate hands.[5]

Lee's instructions to Hampton indicated that he wanted Hampton to continue to keep tabs on Sheridan and destroy him if possible. If Sheridan boarded transports and floated down the James, Lee directed Hampton to rejoin his army south of the James, taking up a position on his right flank. On the other hand, if Sheridan continued marching overland, Hampton was to look for an opportunity to "crush him."[6] That was Hampton's intention as well, but he was not sanguine about the opportunity unless he was reinforced. His June 20 letter to Bragg stated that if he did not receive the requested infantry support, he would "watch Sheridan, striking if I can."[7] Lee reinforced Hampton in the next few days not with infantry, but with more cavalry. Hampton eventually received Chambliss's brigade from Rooney Lee's division as well as an independent brigade. The commander of the independent brigade was an old protégé of Hampton's—Martin Gary. Gary's brigade consisted of the remnants of the old Hampton Legion infantry, now mounted, along with the 7th South Carolina and 24th Virginia.[8]

For Grant, there remained the task of getting Sheridan and retrieving the bulk of his cavalry. The Union plan was for Sheridan to march south from White House while escorting a supply train of nine hundred wagons, cross the Chickahominy, reach Deep Bottom on the James, and then allow his command to be ferried downstream to the Federal-held landing at City Point. At that point Sheridan would finally be safe within the lines of the Army of the Potomac.

Hampton very much wanted those nine hundred wagons, and Sheridan knew it. To get them, the South Carolinian would have to fight for them, resuming the tactical offensive against an enemy that still outnumbered him. His troops and mounts were more exhausted and emaciated than ever. He determined, however, not to allow Sheridan an easy march to the James. Hampton's troopers thus shadowed alongside and withdrew before Sheridan's southward march, harassing and skirmishing with the bluecoats along the way.[9]

Sheridan was never able to cross the James as far west as Deep Bottom, but he did manage to get his wagons and one of his divisions intact to Harrison's Landing, near Charles City Court House. Fearing that Sheridan might be able to march westward along the James toward Richmond, Hampton interposed himself in a blocking position about six miles from Charles City Court House. He was able to gather his full division, most of Fitz's, and Chambliss's and Gary's brigades at Samaria Church. Gregg's division, posted in that vicinity, was directed to face westward and fend off Hampton while the rest of the Union

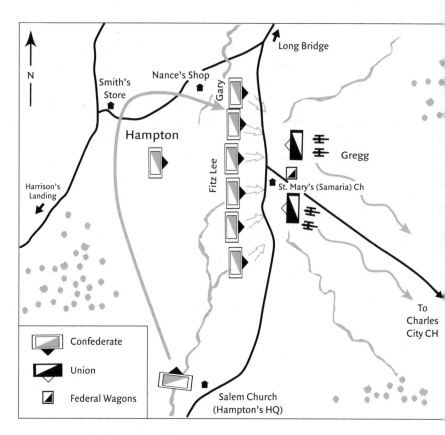

Samaria Church, June 24, 1864

cavalry continued on to Harrison's Landing. David Gregg, then, would be the unfortunate recipient of Hampton's last blow of the Trevilian campaign.[10]

Gregg established a blocking position east of Hampton and threw up strong breastworks along his front. But Hampton's six brigades, which outnumbered him, were able to strike him not only in front but also on both flanks. The bluecoats held for about two hours, but eventually the whole line gave way in utter confusion. The Federals fled the entire six miles to Charles City Court House. Hampton committed his reserve—the Jeff Davis and Phillips Legions and the 12th and 24th Virginia—to pursue them on horseback. Other units tried to follow suit, but the feeble condition of their mounts slowed them down. As darkness fell, Gregg cobbled together a new line around the courthouse, but his units were hopelessly intermingled and confused. As one Yankee recalled, "It

was the most disorderly retreat I have ever seen since I have been in the
service."[11] Another wrote, "We realized for the first time how it felt to
get a good thrashing & then be chased for our lives."[12] Hampton reported that he captured 157 Yankees, including a colonel. Gregg's total
loss was 357, while Hampton's may have been as much as 200. The next
morning, Hampton managed to get a brief dispatch through to his
commander: "We routed Gregg's division thoroughly last evening,
charging them for 5 or 6 miles. Their loss was heavy."[13]

Sheridan's long Trevilian expedition and return to Grant were over.
The most thorough and able study of the Trevilian operation claims that
Hampton conducted the campaign superbly and that the strategic result
was to extend the length of the war for at least six months, maybe ten.
The Virginia Central, that vital lifeline to the supplies of the Shenandoah
Valley, was still largely intact; and Hunter and Sheridan were unable to
join forces and close in on Lee from the north and west while Grant
pressured him from the east. Sheridan had accomplished little, other
than giving Grant a head start on Lee in Grant's move across the James;
even that advantage was squandered, enabling Lee counter the move in
time.[14]

Hampton had proved that he was ready for corps command. He had
turned what Sheridan hoped would be a successful raid into a miserable
ordeal for the Yankee troopers. His own men also had suffered from
heat, fatigue, and hunger, but they were in good spirits and proud
of what they had accomplished under their new commander. Some
regretted that they had failed at least twice to press their advantage and
wreck Sheridan's command. Most, however, admitted that at both Trevilian Station and Samaria Church, they and their horses were too exhausted to accomplish more than they did. Moreover, while they still
venerated the memory of Jeb Stuart, they now considered themselves
Hampton's cavalry and had complete confidence in him. One trooper
wrote: "Gen. Hampton has won the admiration and esteem of all his
men; they are in fine spirits—ready and willing to meet the enemy, by
day or by night, and at any point."[15] Lieutenant James B. Ligon of the
Hampton Legion cavalry jubilantly wrote his mother about the victory at
Samaria Church and crowed that Hampton was now crossing the James
after Sheridan to give him "a little lackin [licking] if he wanted it."[16]
Robert E. Lee was pleased with Hampton's performance as well. Lee's
note to Hampton the day after the victory at Samaria Church must have
gratified him greatly. "I am rejoiced at your success," Lee wrote. "I   223

thank you and the officers and men of your command for the gallantry and determination with which they have assaulted Sheridan's forces and caused his expedition to end in defeat."[17]

⭐ After two solid weeks of hard marching and fighting, Hampton's troopers were exhausted. But before they could rest, they would have one more chance to prove that a new, brighter day had dawned for the Army of Northern Virginia's cavalry. While Hampton had been tormenting Sheridan north of the James, Grant had sent a large cavalry raiding expedition around Lee's right south of the James. James Wilson's division of cavalry plus Brigadier General August Kautz's division of Benjamin Butler's army—roughly 5,500 cavalry and artillery in all—launched their raid on June 21, intending to destroy the Southside Railroad and burn the railroad bridge over the Staunton River. Against this large force, the Confederates could only commit two brigades under Rooney Lee. The Federals reasoned that Sheridan's presence north of the James would prevent Hampton from interfering with Wilson; indeed, they based their hopes for success on that assumption.[18]

Rooney Lee harassed Wilson and Kautz as much as he could. Wilson did serious damage to the Southside Railroad, but Rooney and some local militia managed to repulse him at the Staunton River bridge on the twenty-fifth and save the structure. Wilson began withdrawing eastward in the direction of Grant's lines, with Rooney chasing him. By that time, Hampton had just dealt his parting blow to Sheridan at Samaria Church, and Lee now wanted him to cross south of the James and cut Wilson off as he tried to return to his own lines.[19]

Hampton received Lee's orders on June 27 and by noon the next day had advanced Chambliss's brigade and his own division to Stony Creek Depot near Sappony Church, along the Petersburg and Weldon Railroad. Fitz Lee's division was following, and Hampton asked Robert E. Lee to place Fitz's division and two infantry brigades at Ream's Station, about seven miles north of his own position. Hampton hoped that at least one of these positions would block Wilson's eastward withdrawal, with Rooney Lee snapping at Wilson's heels.[20]

On reaching Stony Creek Depot, Hampton received word from his scouts that Wilson was marching east toward Sappony Church. He sent Chambliss westward to stop him and followed with the rest of his command. A general engagement ensued near the church, with both sides dismounted and the Federals occupying a naturally strong defensive position. Fighting continued into the night of June 28. At dawn on the twenty-ninth, Hampton sent Butler and some of Rosser's men around the Yankee left, while Chambliss assaulted in front. The result was a Federal rout. Wilson's men abandoned their position, fleeing in several directions. The bulk of them headed northward toward Ream's Station, where Hampton knew that Fitz Lee and part of William Mahone's infantry division would be lying in wait. Wilson arrived at Reams Station later that day, expecting to find Federal infantry but colliding with Fitz and Mahone instead. Wilson was surrounded on three sides. After several hours of severe pressure, he ordered his men to flee for their lives, making their escape as best they could. For the second time in one day, Wilson's command was routed, abandoning most of its artillery and wagons. Individual detachments tried to escape the closing ring. Hampton rounded up some prisoners himself. Leading a small body of his staff, Hampton rode up to one Union detachment and ordered it to halt. Approaching the captain in charge, he leveled his pistol and ordered the Union officer to surrender. When the man made a move as if to draw his weapon, Hampton warned that he would shoot him dead if he did. The Federal captain surrendered his men, who numbered 103. Overall, though, an ineffectual Confederate pursuit allowed many stranded units to make their way back to Federal lines.[21]

Despite the day's successes, Hampton, Butler, and Rosser were incensed at Fitz Lee. Fitz had made little effort to communicate or coordinate with Hampton until he belatedly sent him a note on June 30 rather impudently addressed to "commanding officer, Stony Creek Depot."[22] Rosser and Butler advised Hampton to seek Fitz's court-martial. Hampton believed that had Fitz made a serious effort to coordinate with him, their success would have been even more overwhelming. Too many Yankees had escaped.[23]

As it was, the Confederate cavalry had still had another fine day. They had taken twelve of Wilson's artillery pieces, thirty wagons, five hundred prisoners, hundreds of their own previously captured men, small arms, horses, provisions, and several hundred slaves recently freed from local plantations. Hampton's division had lost two killed, eighteen wounded, and two missing. The losses of Chambliss, Fitz Lee, and Mahone would swell those numbers, but the Confederate casualties were miniscule compared to Wilson's.[24]

★ Hampton's continued success again raised the unspoken question of what was to be done about a permanent commander for the cavalry corps. For over six weeks, Hampton had silently accepted Lee's decision to continue to direct the three cavalry divisions personally. For the time being, he was pleased enough with his own performance and with that of his men since Stuart's death not to dwell on what could have been perceived as a slight. The victory at Trevilian and subsequent successes, despite the accompanying losses, lifted a burden from Hampton's shoulders. He was extremely proud of his men, writing to Mary Fisher at the end of the Trevilian–to–Sappony Church campaign: "For twenty-five days, my men were in constant pursuit of the Yankees, fighting six days often without food & continuing marching all night. But they have behaved magnificently & they have done better service than ever before. In those 25 days, we killed, wounded, or captured nearly if not quite 2000 Yankees, whipping them in every fight. They have left their dead all over the country, as well as their wounded. My own loss was about 900."[25]

Modern historians may dispute Hampton's estimates, but he was right to be proud of what he and his troopers had accomplished. Equally gratifying was the fact that he had won the admiration of the men who had never served under him before, men from Fitz's and Rooney's divisions. "The cavalry Corps has received me very warmly," he wrote. "The Regts from the other divisions greet me as kindly as those of my own."[26] The soldiers of the 9th Virginia expressed their esteem in gestures more concrete than cheers and greetings. The 9th—Rooney Lee's old command—had always served under him or Fitz Lee, but never under Hampton. After Sappony Church, however, the men of this veteran regiment honored Hampton by presenting him with two enemy battleflags that they had captured. Hampton was deeply touched and remembered the incident long after the war.[27]

Finally, Hampton was relieved that he had passed several tests of his ability to command more than one division. God had granted his men success, he wrote Mary Fisher, and he was thankful, "for I was greatly concerned at the responsibility of my position."[28] Hampton could never adequately exercise that responsibility, however, unless given unequivocal command of the cavalry.

Robert E. Lee had never intimated that he might promote his nephew over Hampton, and Hampton's place as the senior division commander was secure. Whenever other officers in the corps fought with Hampton, his authority over them, in theory, was unchallenged. But events had driven home the fact that such an arrangement was not ideal and could only be temporary. Hampton's dissatisfaction with it grew after the near-debacle at Trevilian when he found that, in practice, he could not make Fitz do what he wanted him to do.

This frustration was evident in a letter to Mary Fisher just a few days after Trevilian. Amid expressions of relief, gratitude, and pride in his men, Hampton nevertheless asserted: "But I do not seek the command of the corps, & I will not have it unless I can have full command of it."[29] Lee, too, recognized the awkwardness of the situation, and Hampton probably spoke of it with him when the two generals conferred at the end of June. Hampton, of course, would have had to employ his customary tact when explaining to Lee that, while all concerned had performed gallantly, cooperation between Hampton and Lee's nephew had been less than perfect. Hampton knew that he had overstepped his bounds with the army commander back in March and that Lee respected self-control and carefully worded arguments rather than hotheaded outbursts and unseemly criticism of brother officers.[30]

Finally, Lee was convinced. On July 2 he sought Jefferson Davis's permission to give Hampton command of the cavalry corps. His letter to the president indicated that although he had always thought Hampton a fine officer, he had not been immediately convinced that Hampton was ready for corps command. Part of the problem was that Lee still had difficulty imagining anyone besides Jeb Stuart leading the entire cavalry. "You know the high opinion I entertain of Genl Hampton, and my appreciation of his character and services . . . although I have feared that he might not have that activity and endurance so necessary in a cavalry commander, and so eminently possessed by Genl Stuart." But Hampton's repulse and pursuit of Sheridan had persuaded Lee otherwise—"In his late expedition he has displayed both energy and good conduct." Lee pointed out that as affairs stood, Hampton could "neither feel nor exercise the authority which is required by the responsibility of his position. . . . I request authority to place him in command."[31]

On August 11 it was official. Lee's Special Order No. 189 announced Hampton's appointment as commander of the army's cavalry, asserting that division commanders would "report to him accordingly."[32] The former members of Stuart's staff would now be part of Hampton's staff. Calbraith Butler would take over Hampton's division, and Colonel John Dunovant would lead Butler's brigade of South Carolina regiments. On Hampton's recommendation, Dunovant received a promotion to brigadier general. All of this was only official confirmation of what the troops had begun to feel at least since Trevilian two months before and probably since Haw's Shop—they were now "Hampton's Cavalry."[33]

THE CAVALRY ALWAYS FIGHT WELL
NOW JULY−SEPTEMBER 1864

The months of July, August, and September 1864 brought more successes to the Confederate cavalry serving under Wade Hampton. The
only exceptions were the embarrassments suffered by portions of the
command temporarily sent to aid Jubal Early's army in the Shenandoah
Valley. Around Petersburg and Richmond, however, the confidence of
Hampton's men was sky-high.

Historians of the war in Virginia have rightly seen the arrival of siege
warfare in the trenchlines around Petersburg as the beginning of the
end for the Army of Northern Virginia; they have emphasized Lee's
narrowing field of options as he dug fortifications in preparation for
slugging it out with the blue behemoth threatening his front and lapping around his flanks. Yet the perspective of Hampton and his men was
very different. Rather than living a tedious life in the trenches, they were
constantly sallying forth to turn back Federal raids and flanking maneuvers, and, as far they could tell, whipping their foes in every fight. As
Hampton saw it, "My men drive them off whenever they choose."[1]
Confederate cavalrymen writing home commented, to a man, that they
had seen "harder service" over the last several weeks than at any other
time during the war. The constant marching and fighting in response to
Grant's offensives had taken a heavy toll on men and horses, but officers in Hampton's command insisted that, overall, the cavalry was
better, not worse, off than before. J. Fred Waring, whose Jeff Davis
Legion had virtually ceased to exist after surviving the previous winter,
noted on July 19, "I have twice as many effective men as I had at the
beginning of the campaign." A month before he had written in his diary
that "the army, if the Yankees only knew it, is better fed & better clothed
than ever. We get not only enough, but can actually help with our rations
the poor creatures whom the Yankees have robbed."[2]

It was not just a matter of better management and provisions. Hampton's victories had revived the morale of the Confederate cavalry. Writing in late July, Major Christian D. Owens of the 1st Virginia Cavalry
informed his cousin that "the whole state of our affairs [in the] cavalry,
has been entirely altered by this campaign, for the better. When Gen
Hampton took command of the cavalry forces, he had to handle men   229

spiritless and partially demoralized by bad management and continual defeat. Surmounting every difficulty, he successfully combated the prejudice of the Virginia State Troops, inspired confidence in his ability and led them on from Victory to Victory."[3]

The lack of forage and strong horses was serious, but that had been evident for at least two years. The difference now was that Hampton had proved that even with those problems, the gray riders could still win. After two months of constant fighting—and, in Confederate eyes, winning—the defeats at Yellow Tavern, Meadow Bridge, and Wilson's Wharf seemed like ancient history.

Things were going so well that Hampton, too, suspected that the beginning of the end had arrived—for the Yankees. In August he noted "some signs of peace" and predicted that "if we can only avert any disaster this summer[,] we shall I trust soon force a cessation of the war. God grant that it may soon come!"[4] Hampton's hopes had some basis in reality. As he wrote, Confederate forces still stubbornly held Petersburg, Richmond, and Atlanta, and the North had suffered around ninety thousand casualties during May and June alone. Late June and early July saw Jubal Early's fifteen thousand Confederates drive David Hunter out of the Shenandoah Valley, then march north down the valley into Maryland and threaten Washington. On July 17 and 18 there had been peace talks in Richmond and Niagara Falls, Canada. These talks had gotten nowhere, but many northerners condemned President Lincoln for their failure. One northern paper, for example, blasted him for being so caught up in his "mania" for black emancipation that "tens of thousands of white men must yet bite the dust."[5] Lincoln's popularity plummeted so severely in mid-1864 that he began to wonder whether he could win reelection in November. There were, then, several reasons for southern soldiers to hope for victory and peace.

During most of July, the three cavalry divisions of the Army of Northern Virginia got a much-needed rest. They had had precious little sleep or food since Grant had crossed the Rapidan at the beginning of May. As it performed routine picket duty and recuperated in camps south of Petersburg (on the right flank of Lee's army), Sheridan's cavalry command licked its wounds. There was finally some fighting near Malvern Hill on the north shore of the James on July 28 and more at Lee's Mill on July 30. For six weeks, though, the Federal cavalry made no serious threats. Hampton himself had sustained over seven hundred casualties since the beginning of the Trevilian campaign, but as usual his effectiveness suffered even more from the loss of horses, causing hundreds of his men either to serve dismounted or be furloughed home to obtain a mount. He noted that his cavalry was recuperating, "& if we only had horses, we should be all right."[6] Hampton chose his usual mode for relaxation when in camp—hunting and fishing. He rejoiced that since he and his staff had killed three deer, they were "living finely."[7]

Even a ten-day bout with stomach sickness in late July and early August did not seriously dampen Hampton's spirits. While he improved on a diet of milk, rice, and tomatoes, he played a practical joke on his staff by sharing some "portable soup" with them that he had received in a package from home. He told his messmates that the lumps of soup mixture were "new styles of cake, but [they] did not think the cakes good eating. I advised them to drink some warm water after eating them, so as to make soup."[8]

The pace gradually picked up in August. Near the beginning of the month, Robert E. Lee sent Fitz Lee's division with an infantry division to the Shenandoah Valley to assist Jubal Early. The valley cavalry serving with Early were notoriously undisciplined and unreliable, and Lee hoped that his nephew could provide a steadying hand. Moreover, the valley was becoming a major theater of the war, and Early needed help, especially as it became clear that Grant was strengthening his forces there. A few days after dispatching Fitz's division, Lee learned that more enemy units were being sent to the valley and that Grant was placing all Union forces in the Shenandoah under the command of Philip Sheridan. That news convinced Lee to order Hampton to northern Virginia with Calbraith Butler's division on August 11. Before Hampton could get near enough to cross sabers once again with Sheridan, though, a new threat developed on the James. With new orders from Lee, Hampton turned his troopers around on the morning of August 15 and raced back toward Richmond.[9]

Hampton's mission was to fly to the support of Rooney Lee, who had been rushed north of the James to help thwart a combined cavalry and infantry force then marching up the Charles City Road toward Richmond. On the fourteenth the Federals attacked Rooney in force near White Tavern, just eight miles from Richmond. His outnumbered men gave ground, while one of the best brigade commanders in Hampton's cavalry, John R. Chambliss, was shot dead. Hampton had been moving toward the sound of the firing and arrived at the scene moments after Chambliss's fall, around 10:00 A.M. He then placed Butler's division and Martin Gary's brigade on Rooney's right. The Confederates counterattacked and, according to Hampton, "drove the enemy in confusion

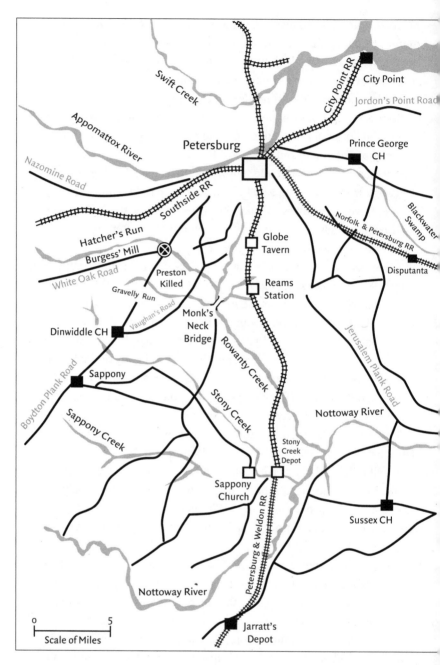

Hampton's Battles around Petersburg, 1864

across the White Oak Swamp." Hampton graciously gave Rooney credit for the victory, saying, "I found [him] quite able to maintain himself."[10] On August 18 Lee ordered the cavalry and the First Corps infantry under Major General Charles W. Field to attack again. Hampton struck the enemy in its front and got around the Yankee left flank with Butler's division. The Federals were in no mood to continue their half-hearted thrust toward Richmond, or even to hold their ground. Hampton drove the infantry in his front for two miles and captured 167 prisoners. The next day Lee formally thanked him for the cavalry's "gallant and valuable services" north of the James.[11]

After White Tavern and White Oak Swamp, Hampton concentrated Butler's and Rooney Lee's divisions once again south of the James, keeping watch for another Yankee attack on Lee's right. Within a week there was another fight and another victory for Hampton's horsemen.

Since Hampton had crossed to the north side of the James on August 14, the Union's Second Corps had broken the Confederate picket lines south of Petersburg and advanced beyond Reams Station. When Hampton went south to reestablish the picket line on August 23, Butler's division struck the enemy at Monk's Neck bridge on Rowanty Creek, two miles west of the station. It was a bloody fight. In several lines of works around the station, the Federals had positioned Winfield S. Hancock's Second Corps and Gregg's division of cavalry—about six thousand men in all. Despite the numbers and the breastworks, Hampton believed that, with infantry support, he could retake Reams's Station. Lee approved his proposal and ordered him to coordinate with Henry Heth's division of A. P. Hill's Third Corps, Hill commanding.[12]

Hampton's troopers led the infantry to Monk's Neck bridge on August 24, and Hampton and Hill made plans for an attack first thing the next morning. In the ensuing battle, it was difficult to tell the difference between Hill's veteran infantry and Hampton's cavalry. Hampton dismounted most of his men and advanced on foot through the thickly wooded terrain against the Yankee breastworks. Hill did the same on Hampton's right. The enemy position was a strong one, and numerically the odds were no better than one to one. The wooded terrain, however, gave the advancing Confederates cover. At least one dismounted Rebel horseman remembered that the Yankees were shooting high and wild. Some of the Federals were still in the process of completing their breastworks when Butler's division suddenly emerged from the thickets. Advancing side by side, Hampton's and Hill's men captured the works after twelve hours of fighting, driving the bluecoats away from Reams Station. It was a rare moment of camaraderie between infantry and cavalry, whom the foot soldiers traditionally had loved to hate. As Hill poetically put it, "Sabre and bayonet have shaken hands on the enemy's captured breastworks."[13]

The Confederates' complete success in this battle was barely short of astonishing. Out of the 6,000 Union troops engaged, Hancock admitted to losing over 2,300. He reported 87 killed, but Hampton's cavalry alone, who buried their bodies, interred 143 dead Federals. Hancock reported over 1,700 men missing, whereas the Confederates captured 2,150 prisoners, 9 artillery pieces, 7 stands of colors, and 3,150 small arms. Hampton's cavalry suffered only 16 killed, 75 wounded, and 3 missing. Total Confederate losses were about 800. In short, the Federals' losses exceeded the Confederates' by roughly three to one.[14]

The rout of the Federals at Reams Station produced jubilation throughout Lee's army. Hill's veteran infantrymen who fought alongside Hampton's troopers had nothing but praise for those "damned cavalrymen" who now stormed breastworks manned by Yankee infantry. Soldiers from the enlisted ranks up to General Robert E. Lee himself commented on the unusual feat of cavalrymen storming breastworks and doing it successfully. "That old fellow Hampton is a rusher," said one foot soldier. "He helped us mightily."[15] Hill, too, lauded Hampton's cavalry. What probably mattered most to Hampton was the esteem of Lee himself. The old tension between the two southern aristocrats had disappeared. Hampton wrote his sister, "Gen. Lee says 'the cavalry always fight well now' & he is very civil to me."[16]

Lee's remark that "the cavalry always fight well now" was just another indicator of the feeling that the cavalry of the Army of Northern Virginia was experiencing another golden age, or "rebirth." Oblivious that their final demise was only seven months away, it seemed to some that since the passing of the beloved Jeb Stuart and the rise of Wade Hampton, a new style of fighting and a new type of commander had brought a string of victories. In case anyone thought that the horsemen's only mode of operation was slugging it out with infantry and dismounted cavalry, however, Hampton reminded everyone that the gray riders were still capable of lightning raids behind enemy lines.

On September 5 Hampton's elusive and reliable scout Sergeant George Shadburne dispatched a note informing his commander of a vulnerable and available target—about three thousand Yankee cattle grazing near Coggins Point on the James River. A herd of that size could supply Lee's hungry army with meat for weeks. Shadburne reported that the drovers numbered no more than 150, and some were unarmed. The largest enemy force in the near vicinity was a cavalry regiment, the 1st District of Columbia Cavalry, bivouacked at Sycamore Church about two miles away. Shadburne also gave Hampton detailed information on other nearby Federal units, roads, and bridges. Hampton passed this information to his commander, and Lee gave him permission on the ninth to go cattle rustling.[17]

On the morning of the fourteenth, Hampton slipped around the Union right flank via the Boydton Plank Road and marched to Wilkinson's Bridge on Rowanty Creek, about eleven miles away. With him were Rooney Lee's division, Henry Dearing's and Tom Rosser's brigades, a small detachment from Young's and Dunovant's brigades led by Lieutenant Colonel Lovick Miller, and several artillery sections. The pace had been stealthy and deliberate.[18]

Very early on the fifteenth, Hampton led the command to Cook's Bridge over the Blackwater. Now the pace was faster. Knowing that Cook's Bridge had been burned, Hampton chose it as a crossing site, guessing correctly that the Yankees would leave it undefended. That evening, while men and horses rested and fed, engineers took only a few hours to repair the bridge. No fires were allowed, which made for culinary experimentation. Hampton's hungry troopers went into the nearby fields and dug up sweet potatoes. Since they could not cook them, many of the men ate them raw.[19]

At midnight Hampton continued the march. The column moved swiftly but stealthily. The artillerymen had inserted grain sacks between the elevating screws and the cannons to muffle the noise. This time, unlike at Trevilian, Hampton made sure that each commander thoroughly understood his mission ahead of time. To Rosser, the officer Hampton trusted most on this expedition, he gave the primary job of scattering the 1st D.C. Cavalry at Sycamore Church and pushing on to Coggins Point to corral the herd. Hampton would personally accompany this column. Rooney Lee's division would seal off the left, blocking roads leading from the main body of the Union army to the west to Sycamore Church. Dearing's brigade would seal off the right.[20]

At 5:00 A.M. on September 16, Rosser's men rushed out of the woods screaming the "Rebel Yell." The 1st D.C. made a valiant stand for several minutes but then fled, leaving its dead and wounded behind. Rooney Lee and Dearing overwhelmed nearby detachments as Rosser's men made off with the cattle and most of the drovers. By 8:00 A.M. Hampton was retracing his steps and had reunited the entire force by

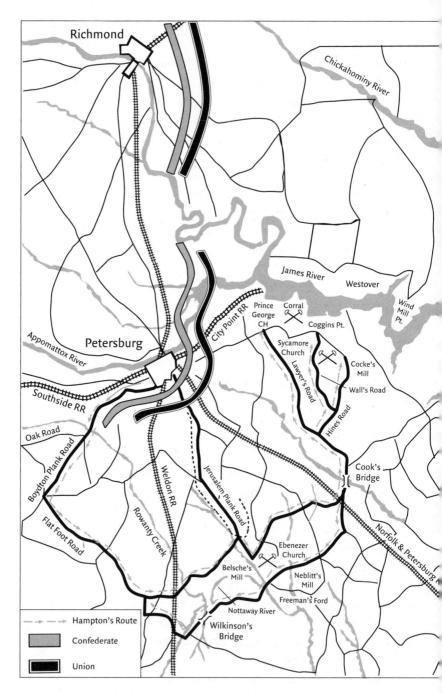

Hampton's Beefsteak Raid, September 16–19, 1864

the time he reached the Blackwater. One of his concerns was to intercept any pursuing column advancing southward from the rear of the Union lines down the Jerusalem Plank Road. He sent Rosser's brigade ahead to picket that road. Sure enough, Rosser soon reported that a large enemy force was advancing south down the road. Hampton ordered Rosser to make his stand at Ebenezer Church, while Hampton diverted the cattle by a slightly more southerly route. Rooney Lee took the rear guard.[21]

The Federal high command reacted with consternation and confusion. Telegraph lines crackled with urgent messages, demands for information, and orders to intercept Hampton. But where was he? Did he have 6,000 men or 14,000? (Hampton in reality had fewer than 3,000.) Was the raid a diversion to disguise a general Confederate offensive? Did he get *all* of the cattle? While Brigadier General Henry Davies's Second Division tangled with Rosser at Ebenezer Church, Kautz followed Hampton's column with, he wrote, only five hundred men from his division. Hampton had several hours' head start on him, but it was impossible to move cattle as quickly as horses. Near the Blackwater, elements of Kautz's column came into contact with Rooney Lee's men at the rear of the Confederate column but retrieved no cattle. What they got instead were the sounds of Rooney Lee's men bellowing like cattle and taunting the Yankees to come over and get their bulls.[22]

On the nineteenth Hampton returned to his own lines, leaving an embarrassed Federal cavalry corps and Union general George Meade behind him. Confederate citizens and soldiers cheered the South Carolinian's audacity and élan. At one level, it was a stupendous feat. Hampton had marched one hundred miles, fought behind enemy lines, and brought back 2,468 cattle, 304 prisoners, 3 guidons, 11 wagons, and a good number of blankets. In addition to steak, Confederate soldiers would feast on sardines, pickles, and other canned delicacies. There was a cost for filling Confederate bellies: 10 men killed, 47 wounded, and 4 missing.[23]

Hampton's famous "Beefsteak Raid," on the other hand, was another reminder of how desperate the Confederate cause was becoming. The Rebels had to steal food to get a decent meal. And although their gallantry and feats of derring-do did much for morale, they could not save the Confederacy or greatly prolong its life. Nevertheless, the Beefsteak Raid was a favorite story of ex-Confederates after the war. No other anecdote could more brilliantly illustrate the claims of Lost Cause mythology—the prideful boast that the "better men" had lost the war, that they had succumbed only to superior numbers of men and re-

Sarah "Sally" Buchanan
Hampton (1845–86).
Oldest daughter of Wade
Hampton III. South
Caroliniana Library.

sources. Hampton's troopers could ride circles around the Yankee cavalry and even steal their cattle herds from beneath their noses, but the
very fact that they bothered to do so illustrated the scarcity of their own
resources.

⭐ Hampton's battlefield successes and growing fame had not changed
his attitude toward war; it still represented a grim duty to be fulfilled,
not a romantic adventure. He grieved for the close friends and comrades
he continued to lose day after day. Many of the fallen were friends of his
family, and Hampton wrote home to report each tragedy, often expressing sorrow for the young men's kin. One-armed John Haskell, the
fiancé of his daughter Sally, would be slightly wounded on October 7;
about the same time Haskell's older brother Alex would be seriously
wounded, losing an eye. Hampton also missed fellow senior officers
who had faced death and hardship with him. He mourned the loss of
his longtime subordinate, Brigadier General James B. Gordon, leader of
Hampton's former North Carolina troops, who was shot the day after
Yellow Tavern and died several days later. Gordon's replacement, Pierce
Young, another long-serving and proven officer, was badly wounded
shortly afterward. At White House Landing, the gallant John Chambliss
238   was shot dead moments before Hampton arrived on the scene. All of

Colonel John C. Haskell
(1842–1906). Confederate
officer and husband of
Hampton's daughter Sally.
South Caroliniana Library.

these men had served alongside or under Hampton since he had joined the cavalry corps, and he had come to respect each of them. Brigadier General John Dunovant, meanwhile, had come to Virginia as commander of one of the new South Carolina regiments that summer. He had been cashiered for drunkenness but had redeemed himself many times over in several fights since then. Hampton had been the one who had secured his promotion from colonel. Dunovant was wounded at least once, but on October 1 he received a bullet in the brain at the Boydton Plank Road. When Hampton heard that Dunovant had been shot, he ordered his medical director, Dr. Fontaine, to go to his assistance. "He cantered off & the next minute he too was struck down," Hampton lamented. Fontaine was, Hampton wrote Mary Fisher, "a very nice young fellow who leaves a poor young wife & child."[24] Amid the thrill of victory and the pride in his men's achievements, Hampton declared: "It is a grievous thing to see our best young men falling daily before these vile wretches who are desolating our country. . . . We gain successes, but after every fight there comes to me an ominous paper, marked 'Casualties' & in this I often find long lists of 'killed' & 'wounded.' Sad, sad words, which carry anguish to so many hearts. And we have scarcely time to bury the dead, ere we press on in the same deadly strife. I pray for peace."[25]

Hampton eulogized or praised each of these men. Rather than let the losses discourage him from continuing the fight, however, the opposite occurred. Each death required a statement, either publicly or privately, of the dead man's gallantry, courage, and patriotism. Those words, in turn, made it impossible to give up the struggle. To quit would make their sacrifices useless and make a mockery of their virtues, as if those virtues really were not so important after all. That was a possibility Hampton refused to—indeed, could not—accept. Thus, a grim equation helped determine why he and so many others fought on: the more that good men died, the more that quitting was a moral impossibility—an impossibility, that is, until they killed enough Yankees that the North finally decided to quit. Unfortunately for Hampton, many northerners found that option as intolerable as he did.

MY SON, MY SON!

Despite the losses, Hampton continued to fight with confidence during September and October 1864. Throughout the fall, he and the bulk of his command continued to assist the infantry of A. P. Hill's corps in maintaining the right (southern) flank of the lines around Petersburg. Martin Gary's brigade was still on the opposite flank keeping an eye on Grant's movements north of the James River, and Fitz Lee's division was aiding Jubal Early in the Shenandoah Valley. After Confederate disasters at Cedar Creek and Fisher's Hill, however, Robert E. Lee detached more men from Hampton's immediate command to help Early restore the situation in the valley. Tom Rosser's brigade was detached from Hampton on September 27.[1]

Hampton's cavalry, minus Rosser's brigade and Fitz Lee's division, helped man the lines in front of the Boydton Plank Road, one of the few remaining lifelines into Petersburg. Even the stunning victory of Hampton's and Hill's men at Reams Station had not been enough to reopen the Petersburg and Weldon Railroad, which brought vital supplies from the port at Wilmington, North Carolina. Instead, those supplies had to make the final leg of the journey to Lee's army by wagon via the Boydton Plank Road. Fierce fighting occurred on almost a daily basis, especially from September 27 to October 1, as Grant tried to cut the road as well as the Southside Railroad from Petersburg to Charlottesville. During one Federal maneuver, Henry Dearing's cavalry brigade of Beauregard's army—temporarily attached to Calbraith Butler's division—was caught off guard and driven from its trenches. After initial gains by the Federals, Hampton directed a counterattack by Rooney Lee and personally led another one himself, in which the Confederates drove in the Union left flank and restored the gap in the lines left by the retreat of Dearing's brigade. Hampton reported taking more than one thousand prisoners.[2]

On the tactical level, Hampton had succeeded once again and was proud of his troops' performance. He particularly praised Butler and Rooney Lee, but as usual made a point of saying that the men in the ranks deserved "the highest credit."[3] Shortly after the war, Hampton wrote proudly to Robert E. Lee of a private in the horse artillery who had saved his gun by fending off a squad of Yankees with a tree limb.[4]

The tactical and personal successes of his own troops made it difficult for Hampton to admit to himself that final defeat was near. Instead, he felt that one more big victory would be enough to ensure Lincoln's electoral defeat on November 8. On October 11, Hampton mistakenly predicted that "Grant will make desperate efforts in the next few days to gain some success, for unless he is successful, before Nov. Lincoln will be defeated & we shall be safe. If Hood gains a great success in Geo. & we can defeat Grant here, we may hope for peace. But until we do whip them, there will be no peace-party in the North. We are watching the Yankees very closely & I hope that they will always find us ready."[5] Five days later Hampton wrote: "My men here, think that they can whip anybody now, & they are in the finest possible spirits. If a great battle comes off, I think that they will make their mark."[6] Nearly six weeks before Hampton's October 11 prediction, Atlanta had fallen to William T. Sherman's forces. Hampton was holding on to the unrealistic hope that Confederate general John B. Hood could turn the tide there, as well as the sense that events in Virginia were ultimately more important.

Even as Hampton wrote, more events were occurring that, unknown to Hampton, would ensure Lincoln's reelection and the demise of the Confederacy. The tide had turned against Jubal Early in the Shenandoah Valley, largely due to the dismal performance of his cavalry forces first under Fitz Lee, then William Wickham, and finally Tom Rosser. On October 16 Hampton admitted that the "news from the cavalry in the Valley is not good" but still hoped that the Rebels would "whip the Yankees."[7] Three days later, Early suffered the stunning defeat at Cedar Creek that would lead to Sheridan's control of the Shenandoah Valley and celebrations in the North.

Apparently what this news meant to Hampton was that it was all the more critical for the Confederates to win a big victory against Grant on the Petersburg-Richmond line. Shortly after writing that the Yankees must be "whipped" before the election, and hearing news of Early's disaster at Cedar Creek, Hampton made plans to deliver that "whipping" on his front. He went to great efforts to strengthen his lines and provide for a combined infantry-cavalry reserve that could launch an immediate, powerful counterattack should Grant once again strike the Confederate right. He showed Third Corps commander A. P. Hill the dispositions he had made, and the two agreed that if Lee could strengthen that reserve by 1,000 to 1,500 infantrymen, their counterattack would do tremendous damage to the Union left. Hampton informed Robert E. Lee of his actions and plans on October 24. Lee replied on the twenty-sixth, pleased that Hampton had strengthened his position. He wished that he could provide 1,500 troops but explained that "the difficulty is to get the men."[8]

The Federal attack that Hampton was preparing for came the next day, October 27. It was much stronger than even Hampton had anticipated. On a cold, rainy morning, Grant threw three entire infantry corps—the Second, Fifth, and Ninth—as well as a cavalry division against Hill's and Hampton's troops. The assault came at dawn as the Confederates were cooking breakfast. Their pickets were driven in, and along most of the line the Confederates drew back. Disrupted communications between Hill and Hampton made the situation worse, and Hampton's original plans for a counterstroke fell apart. The Federals broke through in at least one sector. As Hampton and Butler worked to restabilize the line in Butler's sector at Monk's Neck Bridge, Hancock's Second Corps, along with Gregg's cavalry, slipped around Hampton's extreme right and advanced to Hatcher's Run in his rear. The danger was clear—the Southside Railroad and Lee's entire position at Petersburg were in jeopardy.

It was about 1:00 P.M., and a cold rain was still falling. Hampton reacted decisively to the threat in his rear, pulling Butler out of the line and establishing a new line with Rooney Lee's and Butler's divisions along the Boydton Plank Road. Coordinating with Heth's infantry division of Hill's corps, Hampton dismounted his own men and counterattacked, hitting Hancock from several directions at once in the vicinity of Burgess Mill on the Boydton Plank Road.[9]

As his men swept forward, Wade Hampton and his staff were riding with Butler's division just a few yards behind the front line. Twenty-year-old Preston Hampton, however, was in the front line itself, shouting encouragement to the troops and conversing with Nat Butler, the younger brother of Calbraith Butler. As the two staff officers parted, Preston waved his hat and shouted "Hurrah, Nat!"[10] Hampton had spotted Preston in his exposed position and sent his older son Wade forward to retrieve him. Before Wade reached Preston, the younger brother turned as if to return to his father's entourage. Just as he did, he reeled and fell from the saddle. As the troops rushed on, Wade dismounted and bent over to lift his brother when another bullet struck him in the back. Hampton spurred forward. He saw immediately that Preston was the worse off—he was shot in the groin. A crowd of staff officers was already gathering as the general dismounted.

Cradling Preston's head in his arms, Hampton knew immediately that he was dying. "My son, my son!" he cried. He kissed Preston, then whispered something in his ear that no one else heard. There was a look 243

of recognition in Preston's eyes; then they began to roll backward. Calbraith Butler rode up and asked who was wounded. With tears running down his face, Hampton replied in an agonized voice, "Poor Preston has been mortally wounded."[11]

Young Wade staggered to his feet and to his horse with the help of Captain Zimmerman Davis of Butler's staff. Meanwhile, at Butler's order, a few men brought a small wagon for Preston. A miserable father handed the body of his son to his surgeon, Dr. Tom Taylor. As the wagon bumped along, Preston's head sagged against Taylor's shoulder. Clearly the young man was dead. Hampton rode alongside the wagon for a moment. Then, in an excruciating act of self-denial, he announced, "Too late, doctor."[12] The general rode away from his son's body and returned to direct the battle. His men were driving the enemy.[13]

Hampton's ability to shut out his own crushing grief left a profound impression on his contemporaries. Every one of the many eyewitnesses to this poignant scene commented on the commander's act of turning away from his son and back to the battle. Each one also mentioned his profound grief. One veteran later remarked that he had learned "here my first great lesson of life from General Hampton, which is self-control." Hampton, he remembered, "dismounted and kissed his brave boy, wiped a tear from his eye, remounted and went on giving orders as

though nothing had happened. How can we control others if we do not control ourselves?"[14] Zimmerman Davis reported that Hampton spent the next few hours until dark directing the fire of one of Hart's artillery batteries. The battery was dueling against a Federal battery, and Hampton gave specific orders on fuse length and tube elevation with each round. The artillerymen were impressed the next morning when they saw how well their grieving commander had performed the task. At the former site of the Federal battery there were twenty dead horses and several exploded caissons. After dark, the brokenhearted Hampton relinquished command to a subordinate so he could spend the night beside the body of his dead son.[15]

Back in Columbia, Mary Chesnut marveled: "The agony of that day—and the anxiety and the duties of the battlefield—it is all more than a mere man can bear. . . . Until night he did not know young Wade's fate. He might be dead, too."[16] Varina Davis, wife of the Confederate president, wrote: "I know nothing in history more touching than Wade Hampton's situation at the supremest moment of his misery—when he sent one son to save the other and saw them both fall."[17]

Chesnut's assessment implied what everyone who heard the story thought—Hampton's behavior came close to transcending the limits of mortal ability; it approached the superhuman. Actually what was remarkable about his response was that it came close to matching the strived-for ideal of the chivalrous knight on horseback. Hampton loved, suffered, and wept over his beloved child, just as a benevolent patriarch should. Yet he never lost his self-control, nor yielded to the enemy. He continued to fight no matter what the cost. His tenderness as a father and his vulnerability to pain only made his incredible self-control as a warrior more admirable to his contemporaries.[18]

Though the folks at home learned of Preston's death shortly afterward, Hampton did not write to them about it for nearly three weeks. The silence from his pen, once again, was startling. On November 14, he finally wrote Mary Fisher that all the letters from home had been a "great comfort." "God only knows," he confessed, "how much I need comfort, for my heart is sorely bruised. It cries out for my beautiful boy, all the time, & I cannot become resigned to his loss."[19]

Even when Hampton finally allowed himself this expression of grief, it was not a cry of rage but an agonized effort to maintain self-control, at least outwardly. He did not speak of Preston's death to fellow officers other than to note in his official report to Lee on November 21: "In this charge, whilst leading the men & cheering them by his words & example, Lieut. Thomas Preston Hampton A.D.C fell mortally wounded, & Lt. Wade Hampton who was acting on my staff received a severe wound."[20] While outwardly he remained the stoic, privately he labored to submit to God's will. On the fourteenth he told his sister that "it is very, very hard to lose him, but I pray that God has taken him to His eternal rest."[21] A week later, though still admitting his profound grief, he wrote, "It must be all for the best."[22]

Hampton's friends and relatives did what they could to comfort him. His sisters all wrote to console him, as did Braxton Bragg, Robert E. Lee, and Jefferson Davis. He sent his son's body home with his slave Kit Goodwyn and instructed that Preston be buried in the Trinity Episcopal Churchyard next to his mother Margaret, Hampton's first wife. Here others gave what support they could. Dr. Robert Wilson Gibbes of Columbia pronounced that there was not enough space to bury Preston next to his mother, so another grave was dug nearby. Jacob Motte Alston, a wealthy planter and neighbor, intervened at the last moment, asserting that there was enough room after all. As Preston's coffin was lowered next to that of his mother, the other grave several yards away yawned open, haunting those attending the burial. "It was sad enough, God knows, without that evil augury—or omen," Mary Chesnut wrote in her diary.[23] Hampton told Mary Fisher to thank Jacob Alston "for his great and thoughtful kindness. I will not forget any kind acts performed for my boy."[24]

The most welcome support that Hampton received, however, came in visits from family members. Sally Hampton immediately went to her father, and Hampton's wife Mary followed a few days later. Wade IV, too, spent a week recuperating at the general's headquarters, conveniently located in a house loaned to Hampton by a local family during the November lull in fighting.

What followed was a curious period of over two months in which Hampton pretended to be the supporter and protector of those who were, in fact, supporting him. Hard times often provide a window through layers of social convention and myth to view human relationships. They reveal what is at the core of those relationships and of individual personalities. With the death of Preston, the Hampton family underwent such a time of crisis, one more difficult for Preston's father than for his stepmother Mary. Hampton men were supposed to comfort fragile females physically and emotionally. Often, though, it was the other way around. Mary Chesnut commented on how Sally Hampton, grieving the loss of her brother, nevertheless did her best to keep herself together for her father's sake. But the most startling performance was that of Mary McDuffie Hampton.[25]

The Hampton family's antebellum and wartime correspondence is filled with letters (mostly in Hampton's hand) mentioning his wife's fragility. Hampton continually commented on her ill health and repeatedly urged her to spend more time riding outdoors. According to family lore, Mary preferred to stay indoors reading. As Drew Gilpin Faust observes, "white ladies" were "socialized to believe in their own weakness."[26] Yet in the greatest emotional crisis of her husband's life, Mary seemingly transformed into a tower of strength and physical hardiness. On her arrival in the Petersburg lines, Hampton was amazed that she had completed the journey from Columbia "without very great fatigue."[27] A few days later the couple drove a wagon five miles to church in bitterly cold weather, but Mary "stood the trip well."[28] For years, Hampton had wished that his wife would spend more time exercising and riding with him. Now she did. Nearly three weeks into her visit, Hampton still thought that he was helping her, forgetting that the reason she was there was to comfort him. In several letters Hampton hopefully predicted that his wife's visit to the miserable front lines of Virginia would be of "great benefit to her."[29] Mary was "remarkably" well, he marveled.[30]

Mary herself did not seriously challenge gender conventions, other than by proving far more durable than her earlier persona indicated. When the fighting resumed, she accepted Robert E. Lee's offer to leave the front lines and stay at his headquarters, and Lee kept her informed of Hampton's movements with the cavalry. Hampton may have expected his supposedly delicate wife to return home in a matter of days or weeks. On January 10, however, she was still there, and Hampton observed, "Mary drives out when it is *freezing* in an open buggy and she grows fat on the life she leads here."[31] In fact, Mary did not return home until her husband was transferred to South Carolina to help stop the advance of General William T. Sherman.[32]

The crisis revealed that, at heart, Mary McDuffie Hampton was not the dainty creature that antebellum gender norms allowed, or expected, her to be. Supposedly passive and nearly helpless, she left her two smaller children, traveled without a male escort over several hundred miles, and spent two and a half winter months at the front lines with her husband without complaining of her usual aches, pains, or illnesses. While Hampton continued to believe that he was nurturing his wife through the experience, the truth was that she comforted him at least as much as he protected her. She could play that role of comforter, though, only by expanding the boundaries usually placed on the passive, retiring plantation mistress.[33]

⭐ Eulogization of the handsome, popular Preston Hampton began almost immediately. One element of the Lost Cause mythology that was so influential in the postwar South was the glorification of valorous Confederate soldiers. Much recent literature on the legend of the Lost Cause has tended to treat it as a deliberate, conscious attempt to rewrite the past in order to reestablish white supremacy. David Blight, for example, has called it a "quest for thought control," and Catherine Clinton has described it as conscious "reconfiguring facts to conform to political agendas."[34]

For Wade Hampton, the eulogization of the Confederate dead was initially, at least, a grieving father attempting to come to grips with his son's death. His first epitaph of Preston was properly restrained and suitable for an official military report, but in 1867 he told Robert E. Lee far more, privately. Lee was attempting to write a history of the Army of Northern Virginia and had sent out a circular to his former officers asking for their reminiscences and records. Appearing immediately after Hampton's copy of his 1864 report of the Boydton Road–Burgess Mill action was a passage in which he elaborated at length on his son's death. One cannot help suspecting that politics and race were the last things on Hampton's mind when he wrote Lee that Preston deserved more than "the mere mention of his death" in an official military record. "But even after the lapse of three years," he acknowledged, "I fear to trust myself to speak of that brave boy, who had stood [by] my side in more than seventy fights . . . lest my words of praise should be attributed more to the fond partiality of the parent, than to the just commendation of the commander."[35] After several more sentences of praise, Hampton got to the point: Preston's military record provided "not only his noblest eulogy, but my only consolation for his loss."[36]

This one phrase by Hampton explains much of the postwar rhetoric that aimed to immortalize Confederate valor. Hundreds of thousands of southerners still deeply grieved the loss of loved ones. Reflecting on such themes as wasted sacrifices and misguided causes could bring no comfort. To most, denying that the cause had been noble or asserting that the sacrifice of life had no moral value would be akin to spitting on their loved ones' graves. Only praise for the virtues of the dead and their cause could bring "consolation."[37]

Hampton described his son in the language of nineteenth-century chivalry. Preston was gentle and kind to others except when he was fiercely courageous in combat. He had "an almost womanly tenderness . . . with his friends," but his courage on the battlefield was conspicuous even among an army of men for which courage was "the rule."[38] "He fell at last," Hampton concluded, "as he was leading his way to Victory, dying as he had lived—brave, true, and thank God, free."[39]

Another reason for the South's glorification of its dead was the romantic bent of the age itself. Nineteenth-century Americans looked for heroes, particularly tragic ones who blended the virtues of duty, courage, and tenderness. They tended to honor those heroes with poetry and flowery prose. As a South Carolina newspaper wrote of Preston Hampton, his short life was "crowned with deeds of chivalry," and he "died as a hero would wish to die—on the field of glory, with the Christian's God for his friend and the last sound in his ear the triumphant sound of victory." The article continued:

And how can man die better
Than facing fearful odds
For the ashes of his fathers
[A]nd the temples of his God?"[40]

These sentimental lines appeared not at the height of the Reconstruction or Redeemer periods, but in an 1864 obituary within weeks of
Preston's death.[41]

The twelfth day after Preston's death was election day in the North.
Abraham Lincoln won reelection, dashing the hopes of southerners
who, like Hampton, had predicted that the North would soon give up
the fight. In one sense, however, it no longer mattered to Wade Hampton. He allowed the event to pass without comment. For the rest of the
war, his letters contained no more talk of a "peace party" in the North.
There were fewer confident predictions of victory, only grim expressions
of satisfaction at the number of Yankees killed in this or that fight. For
Hampton, the war had become more personal than ever. Preston was
gone and would not come back. The only solution was to continue the
struggle, to salvage whatever honor and security was left, to make Preston's death worthwhile by avenging it, and to convince himself that his
"beautiful boy" had not died in vain.

CHAPTER 19

DISASTER

Hampton continued through the end of 1864 to pour himself into his duties as he saw them—improving the condition of his cavalry and killing his country's foes. Preston's death made his personal situation grimmer, but it did not change his obligation to be a valiant warrior and defender, as well as a patriarchal provider for his men. Hampton had often felt that Jeb Stuart had mismanaged the cavalry by neglecting its basic needs, and he was determined that the same could not be said of him. In the autumn and winter of 1864–65 Hampton attempted a "reorganization" of the cavalry to address its needs and shortages. One of the first things he had done after assuming command of Robert E. Lee's cavalry in August was to recommend that a "bureau of cavalry be established" as part of the Adjutant and Inspectors General Office to deal with issues of supply and armament pertaining to the cavalry. Lee agreed and suggested Lieutenant General Richard S. Ewell for the position. When Ewell declined it, Hampton proposed Major Heros von Borcke, the volunteer from the Prussian army who had served on Stuart's staff until suffering a severe wound in the neck in June 1863. Von Borcke had been popular among cavalry officers and had sympathetically reported on Hampton's shortage of fodder and horses in the difficult winter of 1863.[1]

The paucity of fighting in November and December allowed Hampton's command to recoup some of its horseflesh and thus increase the number of mounted cavalrymen. Hampton took pride in the fact that the effective strength of the units under his direct command had actually *increased* from 5,907 at the end of August to roughly 7,000 by December 31, despite the natural attrition resulting from constant riding and fighting.[2] Meanwhile, his troops around Richmond and Petersburg, he reckoned, had captured 7,800 prisoners. In Hampton's eyes, his men had won every battle they had fought, while his own attention to duty had kept their numbers steady. As if to punctuate the previous five months of success, in the cavalry's last fight of 1864, Hampton and his men decisively repulsed an enemy attack in the Bellefied–Stoney Creek Depot area.[3]

Still, material shortages impaired the corps' efficiency. Besides the usual lack of food for both horses and men and a chronic scarcity of 251 horseshoes, Hampton's troopers also suffered from a want of clothing as bitterly cold December winds returned to Virginia. Hampton took a personal interest in their comfort. On November 17 Captain Zimmerman Davis, who commanded a company in the 5th South Carolina, had sent a request to Hampton's adjutant complaining that his men had "neither overcoat nor blanket, and . . . are obliged to stand picket duty clad in tattered remnants of jackets and pantalones."[4] The memorandum wound its way up the successive levels of command, with perfunctory endorsements and explanations by the regimental commander, brigade quartermaster, brigade commander, division quartermaster, division commander (Butler), and then Hampton. Hampton used the memo to strengthen his pleas for his whole command. He wrote the longest endorsement by any commander in the chain and forwarded it to Robert E. Lee himself, urging that "extraordinary exertions may be made to supply the necessities of the men" and asserting that "the sufferings of my men were great" on a recent march. The harried quartermaster of the Army of Northern Virginia soon read the captain's dispatch and promised that, due to recent shipments, he would soon be able to deliver "at least 1500 suits" and sufficient blankets to the cavalry. The memo, if not the promised clothing, made it all the way down the chain of command back to Captain Davis.[5]

Hampton's men were also inadequately armed, certainly in comparison with their mounted northern counterparts. Hampton addressed this issue with equal determination but less success. His troopers carried a hodgepodge of pistols, infantry-style Enfield rifles, sabers, carbines, and Spencer repeating rifles captured from the enemy. Each type of weapon required different ammunition, some of which was unavailable. Besides, there was a shortage of all these weapons. As of December 15, 1,100 men in Hampton's regiments, representing one-fifth of the men in the ranks, had no arms at all. Hampton devised a plan in December to achieve uniformity within regiments, and simplify the distribution of ammunition, by collecting and reissuing arms. Lee approved the plan in January; he also suggested that Hampton not allow men going home on furlough or horse detail to take issued or captured arms with them, which often were "deposited" in citizens' homes. Hampton was already aware of that problem. Back in November his adjutant, Henry B. McClellan, had requested partisan leader John S. Mosby's assistance in rounding up cavalry carbines found in private homes, explaining that the increase in Hampton's numbers left many men "without proper cavalry arms, and some have no guns at all."[6] In addition, Hampton and

Lee elicited promises from Confederate ordnance bureau chief Josiah Gorgas to try to import repeating carbines from abroad. Meanwhile, Hampton had von Borcke sent to Europe to acquire arms, but the Confederacy collapsed before he could complete his mission.[7]

⭐ As eager as Hampton was to strengthen his forces in Virginia, his heart was divided. He had one eye on events in Georgia, where General William T. Sherman was wreaking devastation. After completing the destruction of Atlanta in mid-November, Sherman blazed a trail of desolation twenty-five to sixty miles wide between Atlanta and Savannah in an attempt to cripple the South's ability to continue the war. By Christmas he was in Savannah, just across the border from Hampton's home state. South Carolinians guessed—correctly—that they were next. Sherman promised that "vengeance" would be wreaked on South Carolina, dramatically claiming that he "almost tremble[d] at her fate."[8] With South Carolinians bracing for the worst, Hampton's sisters contemplated sending the family's valuables to Nassau for safekeeping. Hampton told Mary Fisher in early January that there was no need "to do more than pack up at present," assuring her that Columbia would be safe if Lee agreed to send some troops from Virginia there. He hoped that those troops would be his own.[9]

Though Hampton claimed that Sherman could be stopped, he had no illusions about the Union general's intentions. Sherman's actions in Georgia, in fact, corresponded exactly to the fiendish image that Hampton had formed of Yankees. As early as the spring of 1862, Hampton had expressed a desire to kill more Yankees and carry the war to the North so the enemy would get a firsthand taste of the pillaging inflicted on Virginia. That was when it was still official Federal policy to respect the property of southern civilians. While the looting of Federal troops during McClellan's Peninsula campaign, for example, had angered Hampton and other Confederates, McClellan and his officers had sincerely tried to limit the damage. Since then, however, the war had only gotten meaner, and Hampton had been close enough to Union depredations—real and imagined—to have his fierce hatred of his foes only deepened. After he had chased down Union general Judson Kilpatrick in his winter 1864 raid on Richmond, rumors had spread throughout the South that Kilpatrick's subordinate, Ulrich Dahlgren, had been ordered to burn Richmond and hang Jefferson Davis and the members of his cabinet. Confederate citizens and soldiers were outraged. Hampton wrote that he hoped to capture Kilpatrick and angrily promised his sister that if

Kilpatrick had directed Dahlgren to carry out these vile actions, "I shall give orders that my men shall never take any of his officers alive."[10] While following Philip Sheridan's retreat from Trevilian Station, Hampton's men had been infuriated at the brutal and senseless pillaging of some of Sheridan's men along their route. Comparatively well-fed Yankee troops destroyed or took everything they could find from scores of unprotected southern families, leaving women and children without the means to feed themselves. "What manly sport, to starve women & children," sneered one of Hampton's officers. " 'Pile it on' Mr. Yankee, the higher we pay for Independence, the more we shall prize it."[11] Some of Hampton's men summarily shot some of the plunderers who fell into their hands, and Hampton surely would not have disapproved. During the fighting around the Stoney Creek Depot six months later, stragglers from Yankee regiments burned and looted private homes. Enraged Confederate pursuers caught some of the culprits and slit their throats, and Hampton wrote Lee that he was glad to learn of the vandals' fate.[12]

Chivalry demanded home defense, and Hampton's own family and home were now in danger. And while chivalry required magnanimity in some circumstances, those who failed to abide by its code of behavior toward women, children, and defenseless citizens deserved a fate worse than death. Paul Anderson has shown how war could bring out the harsher, even bloodthirsty side of chivalry—the part of the code that called for blood vengeance. Hampton himself, in fact, had already become a victim of the hard hand of war. While Mary was visiting him in Virginia shortly after Preston's death, his home had been robbed and vandalized. Unknown culprits stole all of Mary's jewelry and scrawled curses on the walls, including "Damn Hampton," "Rebel," and "Cattle Stealer."[13] Neighbors like Mary Chesnut surmised that the perpetrators were Yankee fugitives from the military prison in Columbia, from which prisoners supposedly escaped every night. Far worse could be in store for the Hamptons. The same Kilpatrick who was suspected of ordering the burning of Richmond and the murder of Jeff Davis was now in command of Sherman's cavalry. Rumors circulated that he had issued matches to his troopers with orders to apply them liberally to South Carolina homes.[14]

More than ever, Hampton longed to return home. "I wish I could be there," he wrote in December, "for I should like to strike one blow on the soil of my own State."[15] Not only his home but also his sisters and children were in danger. The thirst for vengeance merged with longing for his children. While Sherman's army was approaching, so was Daisy

Hampton's fourth birthday. "My dear little daughter," he wrote, "As I cannot see you to give you a kiss on your birthday, I write a letter to tell you how much I love you & how I hope that you will be a good girl. You will soon be a young lady so you must learn to write. Then you can write to me when I am away & tell me all the news." Hampton promised to send her a doll from Richmond; when it arrived she "must name her Virginia, because she was born here. . . . Kiss your brothers for me, & God bless all of my dear little children."[16] Daisy must have had only a vague idea who this letter was from when her aunts read it to her. The last time she had seen her father was the preceding spring, when she was barely three.

At the time Hampton wrote to Daisy, he had already requested that Calbraith Butler's division be sent to South Carolina to remount and to help stop Sherman. He had also asked—or was soon to ask—Lee to send him as well, even though there was no command for him. Lee cautiously agreed, with the understanding that Butler and Hampton would both return to him in time for the spring campaign. Furthermore, if South Carolina governor Andrew Magrath could not provide horses or forage for Butler's command, it must return to Virginia immediately. By January 19 Butler and Hampton got their wish. Butler's command received orders to South Carolina, with Hampton directed to follow a few days later, as Lee thought that Hampton's presence would arouse "the spirit & strength of the State & otherwise do good."[17] Hampton wrote Mary Fisher that he was "going out to see if I can do anything for my State."[18] As he left for home, Preston's death was on his mind again. To his confidant Louis T. Wigfall, he wrote: "My spirit has been crushed. . . . But I bate not one jot or tittle of our claims & I shall fight as long as I can wield my sabre." Preston's loss would not make him give up the fight. "I have given far more than all my property to this cause & I am ready to give all."[19]

Hampton arrived in South Carolina near the end of January 1865.[20] General P. G. T. Beauregard had recently assumed command of Confederate plans for the state's defense, and those plans were in disarray. While Sherman had around 60,000 men poised along the Georgia–South Carolina border, the Confederate forces facing him were scattered and disorganized. Lieutenant General William J. Hardee, who led the Department of South Carolina, Georgia, and Florida until Beauregard's return, counted 13,700 effectives, most of whom were in Charleston. Other elements included small bodies of state militia, newly arriving remnants of the shattered Army of Tennessee previously under the command of John B. Hood, and 6,700 cavalrymen under Major General Joseph B. "Fighting Joe" Wheeler. Butler's division of 1,500 cavalrymen had just entered South Carolina but was short of horses and equipment. Altogether, the Confederates had some 30,000 men (a careful historian has recently put the number of effectives closer to 17,000), but these were scattered across the state, serving under separate commands and generals who were trying to sort out ad hoc command relationships. As Hampton lamented years later, "It would scarcely have been possible to disperse a force more effectually than was done in our case."[21] Many were inexperienced second-line troopers or, like the Army of Tennessee veterans, exhausted and demoralized from recent defeats and a grueling journey to reach South Carolina ahead of Sherman.[22]

As the Confederate high command sorted out new command relationships, one question was what to do with Hampton. Wheeler was senior to Hampton by date of rank, though he was eighteen years younger. A West Point graduate, Wheeler was known for his hard fighting. He was also considered a lax disciplinarian, and his men had achieved a reputation for lawlessness and plundering southern civilians exceeded only by Sherman's. Many citizens of Georgia and South Carolina, in fact, complained that Wheeler's men were as bad or worse than Sherman's. Two months later, civilians in Fayetteville, North Carolina, marked the contrast between Wheeler's men and those who had served under Hampton and Butler in Virginia. As Josephine Bryan Worth remembered: [Hampton's] cavalry passed by, the horses in ranks and every man with his saber held up over his shoulder. . . . After these well-ordered ranks came a more disorderly body of cavalry—Wheeler's I presume—many of them ragged, some of them hatless, and most of them with two or more horses."[23] Used to commanding his own corps, Hampton had no desire to serve under another West Pointer who was even younger than Jeb Stuart had been. He proudly asserted that he would request a transfer to the infantry before he would report to Wheeler. On February 7, 1865, Beauregard officially placed Hampton in command of Butler's division and his old brigade led by Pierce Young, recently recalled from Georgia. On the tenth he gave Hampton command of all Confederate troops in the vicinity of Columbia, including those cavalry units and a small command of infantry from the Army of Tennessee.[24]

Beauregard also sought to give Hampton full authority over Wheeler's command, even though Wheeler was senior in rank. For that to happen, Hampton would have to be elevated to lieutenant general over

Wheeler. There was plenty of support for this promotion in the Confederate high command. (A military inspector, Colonel Alfred Roman, had recently reported to the War Department on the appalling state of discipline in Wheeler's command.) On February 12 Beauregard wrote to Robert E. Lee, who was by then "General-in-Chief" of all Confederate forces, recommending that very course "for the good of the service and cause." "Wheeler," he wrote "is a modest, zealous, gallant, and indefatigable officer, but he cannot properly control and direct successfully so large a corps of cavalry."[25] Hampton, on the other hand, was universally respected. Lee had come to value him more highly than ever. President Davis had already been at work on the Hampton-Wheeler issue before Beauregard made his request. The Confederate Congress confirmed Hampton's promotion to lieutenant general on the fifteenth, and officers in South Carolina were aware of it by the next day.[26]

Long before Hampton was given military cognizance over Columbia, he was already thinking in terms of his usual strategy—the concentration of all available forces. After the war he wrote that he thought that he had convinced Beauregard in a February 7 meeting to abandon Charleston and effect a concentration at Branchville, south of Columbia and along the railroad route from Charleston. Beauregard, though, was not thinking along those lines at all. Not knowing whether Sherman's target was Charleston, Columbia, or Augusta, he decided that he must hold all three cities as long as possible. With Hardee at Charleston, Hampton gathering a makeshift force (after February 10) around Columbia, and D. H. Hill in command at Augusta, all three fragments of Beauregard's army sat impotently while Sherman advanced through the southern South Carolina. Sherman's three columns were dispersed enough to mask his intentions from Beauregard, but close enough to converge quickly on his next target, Columbia. Beauregard hesitated making a move until the fourteenth, the day before Sherman reached a point four miles south of Columbia.[27]

While the Confederates sorted out command relationships, found horses for Butler, and helplessly pondered their strategic options, Sherman's legions were already literally blazing a trail through the southern portion of South Carolina. Refugees were pouring into Hampton's Columbia with horrific tales of destruction. Yankee soldiers had burned nearly every building in the town of Barnwell, which they jokingly renamed "Burnwell." Blackville, Camden, McPhersonville, Hickory Hill, Brighton, Purdysburg, Lawtonville, Hardeeville, Robertsville, and other towns suffered a similar fate. The Federals stole valuables, slaughtered livestock they did not plan to eat, desecrated churches, and insulted ladies. There were numerous accounts of rape, and a few of them, especially of black women, were true. Even some of Sherman's men were stunned by the devastation they could inflict. A few were appalled. A Michigan lieutenant swore that if any army did the same to Michigan, he would "bushwhack until every man was either dead or I was. . . . I do not blame the South and shall not if they go to Guerilla warfare."[28] What made a further impression on Columbians were stories of other enemy soldiers thoroughly enjoying themselves, like those who competed to see who could break the most dishes with one stroke of a rifle butt, or who could make the loudest noise when pounding piano keys with an axe. What is clear is that most of Sherman's men took grim satisfaction in punishing arrogant South Carolina, the home of secession. One Union army chaplain boasted to his wife that, like Moses's Israelites, Sherman's columns were literally led by a "*pillar of* cloud by day and fire by night."[29]

Wade Hampton found himself in the ultimate position of the warrior driven by a visceral instinct to defend his own home—he stood between the hated invader and the humiliation, if not destruction, of his hometown. And yet he must have found the situation thoroughly depressing. Outnumbered six to one, commanding many demoralized and undisciplined troops, and serving in an overall atmosphere of defeatism, confusion, and dread, Hampton no doubt felt that he had no good options. Should he make a determined military defense, which might result in the shelling of Columbia and fighting in its streets? Or should he withdraw in the hopes that the city might be spared and that Sherman could be defeated in the open country? To stand and fight invited disaster; to retreat without a fight would bring personal disgrace and belie his reputation among his neighbors as a chivalrous protector and defender. Besides, he was unsure of the limits of his own authority. Though he commanded all the troops in the vicinity of the capital as early as February 10, this initially included only Butler's 1,500 men and Major General Carter L. Stevenson's small infantry division. Not until the sixteenth, after Sherman's arrival at the city's gates, was it clear that Hampton had authority over Wheeler's 5,000-man corps. This brought him up to 7,600 soldiers on paper, but he probably had around 6,000 effectives. Sherman's entire force outnumbered his troops by almost ten to one.

If Hampton worried over whether to make a do-or-die stand for Columbia, he probably was relieved when it became clear that Beauregard had made the decision for him. The Confederates would seek to delay Sherman and then retreat. The day after Sherman's forces were reported only a few miles below Columbia, Beauregard withdrew the Charleston garrison toward North Carolina, not toward Columbia. He ordered Hampton to delay Sherman along the Saluda and Congaree rivers as long as possible. Then, he wrote, "[Columbia] must . . . be held as long as circumstances will permit to give time to our re-enforcements to arrive. When forced back retire [northward] toward Winsborough [sic]."[30] A withdrawal from Columbia, then, was already written into the plan. The reinforcements Beauregard spoke of were Wheeler's men, whom Beauregard ordered on February 14 to join Hampton, as well as Frank Cheatham's and A. P. Stewart's infantry formations from the Army of Tennessee, then in the vicinity of Augusta. The infantrymen had little hope of reaching Columbia in time to help Hampton, and for two more days it would still be unclear whether Hampton had direct authority over Wheeler.[31]

The Confederate defense and evacuation of Columbia was a disaster, and Hampton was not without blame. For some time he continued to assure prominent Columbians that the city could be held—historians have charged that neither Hampton nor Beauregard made it clear to civilian officials that they could not stop Sherman before he reached the city. It does seem that, for several days or at least until February 13, Hampton still expected a Confederate concentration and stubborn defense. Yet he sent his own family away under the care of his brother Kit. The four Hampton sisters took down the heavy drapes at Millwood and wrapped the family silver, china, and crystal in them. These, as well as some paintings, were placed in wagons under the charge of slaves, who took them northward to the town of York. Then the sisters gathered the children and joined the mob of civilians hoping to find space on crowded northbound trains.[32]

By the fifteenth, even Hampton knew that Columbia could not be held, and the city was in chaos. War Department, state, and city officials were all trying to determine when and how to evacuate ordnance, ammunition, supplies, official records, and Union prisoners, not to mention thousands of terrified civilians. Transportation was inadequate and there was no overall evacuation plan. Though Hampton had never been directed to assume the role of military governor of the city (his authority extended only to military units in the vicinity), he was probably the only one in a position to provide order and direction to the chaos. He did not. Whether due to uncertainty about his authority over civilians, his concentration on purely operational decisions, or his inexperience in 259

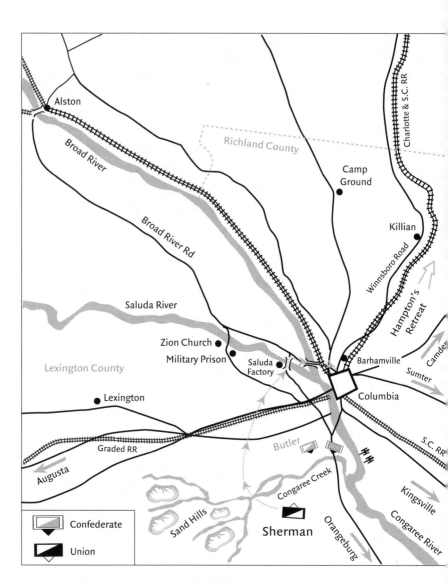

Columbia, South Carolina, February 1865

handling such matters, Hampton was ineffectual in untangling the logistical nightmare.[33]

Instead, he concentrated on Columbia's military defense. Late on the night of February 13, Hampton ordered Stevenson to attempt to hold a line along Congaree Creek, a few miles south of the city. Butler's cavalry was to protect Stevenson's right. Meanwhile, Hampton placed guns near the mouth of the creek where it emptied into Congaree River to guard Stevenson's left in case he was forced back. If it came to a fight, Butler and Stevenson would be outnumbered by as much as seven to one. Hampton then ordered that the thousands of bales of cotton in Columbia's storehouses be piled in the streets and outlying roads to block access to key parts of the city. As one historian has noted, this action impeded evacuation efforts more than it did Yankees.[34]

On the night of February 15, the Union army was within four miles of Columbia. That afternoon, Hampton had relayed Beauregard's instructions to Wheeler, Cheatham, and Stewart to join him for the defense of the city. In the same message, he had further suggested—all he had clear authority to do at the time—that, if possible, those forces should strike Sherman's columns in the flank and rear after they crossed Congaree Creek, "enabl[ing] us to hold the line of the Congaree [River]."[35] But it was too late for such counterstrokes, and that night Beauregard ordered all forces to fall back behind the Congaree River. During the night Hampton's guns on the north side of the river shelled some of Sherman's troops that were nearby.[36]

On the sixteenth Sherman decided not to attempt a crossing of the swollen Congaree with its burned bridge, lightly held by Butler. Instead his troops moved northwest, crossed the Saluda, and prepared to push their way across the Broad River and into Columbia from the west. That night Hampton learned that he had been promoted and placed in charge of all Confederate cavalry forces in the state. He also met with Beauregard and asked him to rescind a previously published order to burn the cotton, which now lay piled on streets and roads throughout Columbia. By now a stiff northwesterly breeze was blowing, and the flames could spread and destroy the city. Besides, Hampton argued, Sherman could not take the cotton with him and it might be spared. Beauregard agreed. Thus Hampton's first order as a lieutenant general, at 7:00 A.M. on February 17, was not to burn the cotton.

On the Confederate side, Hampton's directive that morning represented one of the last vestiges of military order in Columbia. Wheeler's men were then withdrawing through the city, pausing occasionally to

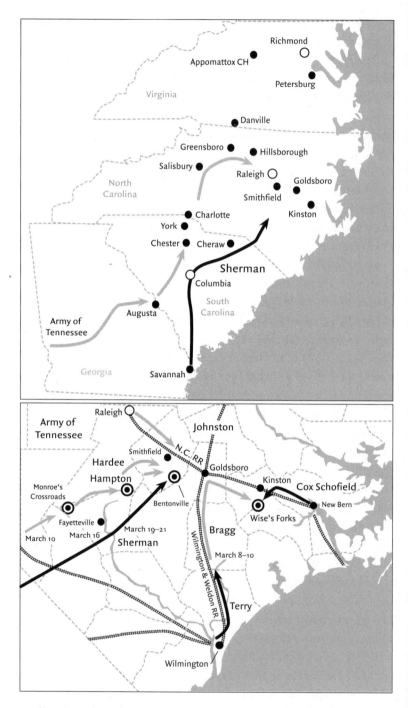

Carolinas Campaign

Sherman's and Johnston's forces converge on Bentonville, Mid-March 1865

fire a few shots or to plunder and to drink the liquor they were stealing. With all traces of normal daily life at an end, Hampton's order not to burn the cotton could not be published in the newspapers, which days before had printed Beauregard's order to burn the cotton. A detailed study of the affair suggests that the Confederate chain of command in the city was breaking down and that many of the soldiers concerned probably never received Hampton's order. Hampton himself failed to post guards over the cotton on the night of the sixteenth or morning of the seventeenth. Columbia descended into chaos as drunken white citizens, soldiers, and blacks plundered shops and stores. City leaders had earlier asked Hampton to order that all alcohol be eradicated, but Hampton had refused, claiming that he did not have the authority to destroy private property. But he did ride up to a drunken band of twenty cavalrymen in Wheeler's command to stop their plundering. In a stunning act of insubordination, several of them drew their pistols on Hampton, who acted in the only way he could to save face. Mary Chesnut's husband, General James Chesnut, was nearby. Hampton called out, "Chesnut, these fellows have drawn their pistols on me." In her diary Mary reported: "He is a cool hand, our Wade. General Chesnut galloped up—'Fall in there, fall in'—and by instinct the half-drunken creatures obeyed. Then Chesnut saw a squad of infantry and brought them up swiftly. The drunken cavalry rode off. Wade was quite tranquil about it all. He insisted that they did not know him, and besides they were too much intoxicated to know anything. He did not order any arrests."[37]

A terrific explosion at the South Carolina Railroad depot rocked the city at 6:00 A.M. on the seventeenth. Mayor Thomas J. Goodwyn rushed to the town hall to raise a white flag over the city, but Hampton arrived before he could do so. The plan had been to evacuate all Confederate troops before Goodwyn and the aldermen surrendered the city. Because Stevenson's men were still defending its western approaches, Hampton ordered Goodwyn not to raise the white flag until he gave the word. One Columbian stated that the general threatened to shoot anyone who tried to raise the flag prematurely. Hampton then rode out to Stevenson's command, where he found that Stevenson's position was no longer tenable. He ordered him to retreat toward Winnsboro with Wheeler covering his withdrawal. He then directed Butler, posted south of the city near Granby, to withdraw as well. With the final retreat set in motion, Hampton returned to Goodwyn and told him to hoist the white flag. Butler's men burned the depot of the Charlotte Railroad on the east side of the city around 10:00 A.M. They and Hampton were among the last Confederate soldiers to leave Columbia.[38]

Between the time of the withdrawal of the last Confederate soldiers on the seventeenth and late that same night, the city of Columbia became a blazing inferno. The question of who was responsible for the fire has raged ever since, though South Carolinians almost unanimously blamed Sherman and his men, who, after all, had deliberately burned almost everything else in their path on the way to Columbia. It is clear, however, that smaller fires were already smoldering at the railroad depots—and, in some cases, bales of cotton were burning—when the Yankees arrived. Union troops did deliberately burn Hampton's Sandhills and Millwood residences, as well as those of other prominent citizens. But Sherman's officers extinguished other blazes and initially tried to maintain a semblance of order. Later, though, the situation—and the flames—raged out of control. As more Union troops entered the city that afternoon "drunkenness mounted," and Columbia descended, if possible, into even deeper chaos than the night of the sixteenth.[39] Drunken Federal soldiers looted and vandalized property; some were observed setting fires, though officers tried to stop them. A strong wind continued to blow through the city and fan the flames. According to eyewitness accounts, while some troops battled to extinguish the flames, others slashed fire hoses with axes. By the next morning, about one-third of Columbia had been destroyed.[40]

Hampton's attempts to defend his hometown had been a disaster in every way. Expected to command, the patriarch had been forced to tolerate Confederate troops who defied his authority. Depended on by his fellow Columbians to be a savior, he had been unable to prevent catastrophe. His own home as well as the ancestral mansion of Millwood was burned to the ground. An invading enemy had imposed its will on Hampton and his neighbors in the most brutal, terrifying way. For a man who had gone to war to preserve the stability of his society and the sanctity of his home, it was the ultimate nightmare.

PART III ★ VINDICATION

THE SEARCH FOR VINDICATION

With the destruction of Columbia and his own home, Wade Hampton had lost the core of what he had originally set out to defend in 1861. Along with safeguarding slavery, white southerners had hoped to maintain control over their own destiny, their own property, and their own homes. Hampton personally had hoped the war would preserve some semblance of the social order, tranquility, and wealth of his antebellum world. Now most of that was gone.

The loss of Preston was a key event, marking a gradual change in why Hampton fought. After the death of his son, Wade Hampton's war had become a struggle not only to preserve what lived, but also to salvage vindication for what had already been lost. Then came the disaster at Columbia. With his hometown in ruins and his father's estate in ashes, there was little left to fight for other than vengeance, duty, and honor, and the memory of lost loved ones. Of course, it was still theoretically possible that Sherman could be whipped and Columbia redeemed; Hampton had seen his side triumph against overwhelming odds before. And yet, with Preston, Millwood, and Diamond Hill all gone, in some ways it was already too late. Hampton still entertained hopes of Confederate independence after the burning of Columbia, but personal vindication now competed with victory for the reasons that he fought.

Hampton deeply mourned the destruction of Millwood and of his own property. Six weeks later, with almost all communication with family members cut off, he still had no idea what his sisters had been able to save. For comfort he turned once again to his God and urged Mary Fisher to do so as well. "You know that God orders all things for the best," he reminded her. "Let this hope sustain you: place your whole confidence in God, & having asked Him to answer your prayers, leave the issue to Him."[1] Yet although Hampton's faith provided him with reassurance and comfort in mourning, he was unable to draw Christian forgiveness from it. In the same paragraph in which he preached trust in God's provision, he confided to Mary Fisher, "I hate to see my men take these devils who have done all these evil deeds, prisoners."[2]

Hampton spent the last two weeks of February 1865 trying to ensure that Sherman would not get through the rest of South Carolina without taking some punishment. The day after the burning of Colum-   267 bia, Hampton wrote Beauregard urging him to strike back. The Union army's Seventeenth Corps, he thought, was sufficiently isolated from the Fifteenth Corps and other forces to allow the Confederates to effect a quick concentration, pounce on the Seventeenth before it could be supported, and thus "cripple Sherman greatly." Hampton's detailed plan would require outstanding coordination and fast marching, but Confederate forces in the Carolinas still seemed capable of neither. Instead, Beauregard intended to withdraw his troops from South Carolina and unite them somewhere in North Carolina, depending on where Sherman was headed.[3]

Soon after February 22, Hampton was encouraged to learn that Joe Johnston, his former superior in Virginia in 1861–62, had been placed in command of the department over Beauregard. Though Hampton got along well with Beauregard, he had always considered Johnston an outstanding commander, equal to or perhaps even better than Robert E. Lee. Lee ordered Johnston "to concentrate all available forces and drive Sherman back."[4] Those "available forces" consisted of no more than 25,000 men, scattered from Wilmington, North Carolina, to Georgia. Johnston openly doubted in a letter to Lee whether "driving Sherman back" was possible. After the war, Johnston reiterated his opinion that the South no longer had a chance to win in March 1865; he claimed that his goal had been to put up enough of a vigorous fight to enable the South "to obtain fair terms of peace."[5]

What that meant in operational terms was that Johnston needed time and space to concentrate his scattered forces so he could strike Sherman and make a stand. He did have one effective tool at hand—Hampton's cavalry. In the spring of 1865 Butler's single division and Wheeler's three divisions still constituted a tough, credible force. Despite the lax discipline in Wheeler's ranks, his men, like Butler's, were hard fighters and veterans of literally hundreds of battles and skirmishes. Johnston planned to use Hampton's cavalry "to retard the enemy's progress, and as much as possible to protect the people of the country from exactions of Federal foraging-parties, and robbery by stragglers."[6] In the more revealing language of trooper Edward Wells, Hampton's men were "to hover by turns around his front, his flanks and his rear; to pounce upon his foraging parties, who were burning and harrying; to dash between his marching columns and cut off marauders; to save the lives and property, as far as practicable, of women and children."[7]

Hampton was constantly on the go, trying to coordinate the movements of Butler and Wheeler and to keep Beauregard, or Johnston, informed. There was frequent skirmishing, often involving the capture of Union pickets or foragers.[8] But the larger story was that the Confederate army was retreating. Nearly every town that Hampton eventually had to evacuate, including Camden and Cheraw, faced a fate similar to Columbia's. Citizens were robbed at gunpoint, and food and homes were destroyed. Hampton could do little to prevent the mayhem, or to stop Sherman's advance. Yet over the next several weeks Hampton would relish a few small but precious moments of vindication. The first was an angry exchange of letters between him and Sherman; the second, a surprise predawn raid on Judson Kilpatrick's camp at Monroe's Crossroads; and finally, a thrilling act of derring-do in the streets of Fayetteville, North Carolina.[9]

The first of these incidents was, in Hampton's eyes, a moral victory. In at least two cases, Union troops found comrades who had been murdered after being captured by Hampton's men, often with signs around their necks reading "Death to all Foragers." Kilpatrick wrote forcefully to Wheeler on February 22 about one instance, threatening to kill Confederate prisoners and burn every dwelling within his reach if it happened again. Wheeler replied rather tamely to the threat of house burning but promised that he would regard the execution of Confederate prisoners as murder "and act accordingly."[10] Then, in a letter to Hampton of February 24, Sherman specifically mentioned the execution of a lieutenant and seven men near Chester and another twenty about three miles from Feasterville—twenty-eight in all. In retaliation, Sherman wrote Hampton, he had ordered "a similar number of prisoners in our hands to be disposed of in like manner. I hold about 1,000 prisoners captured in various ways, and can stand it as long as you; but I hardly think these murders are committed with your knowledge." He therefore advised Hampton to tell "the people at large" that every murder of a Federal prisoner would result in the death of a Confederate. Sherman admitted that his need to forage for provisions was "the occasion of much misbehavior" by his men, but that Hampton could not question his "right to 'forage on the country.' It is a right as old as history." Above all, he would not permit foraging to be punished with murder and resolved "to protect my foragers to the extent of life for life."[11]

If Sherman thought his letter would elicit any apology or contrition from Wade Hampton, he could not have made a worse calculation. Not a week had passed since the Columbia fire, which Confederates attributed to Sherman, and the Columbia native was not about to tolerate northern claims to moral superiority. Hampton responded with barely controlled rage; if anything, Sherman's letter gave him the chance to say what had probably been on his mind for some time. But it also offered Hampton an opportunity for vindication, by enabling him to claim the moral high ground in this increasingly barbaric war. In his reply, Hampton eventually got around to confirming that he neither knew of nor authorized the killing of Federal prisoners; but first and foremost he assured the Union general that for every one of his captured men killed by Sherman, he would kill two of Sherman's. Then, however, Hampton clarified his statement that his men had not murdered any of Sherman's. They had done so, it turns out, but only "under circumstances in which it was perfectly legitimate and proper that they should kill them. It is a part of the system of the thieves whom you designate as your foragers to fire the dwellings of those citizens whom they have robbed. To check this inhuman system, which is justly execrated by every civilized nation, I have directed my men to shoot down all of your men who are caught burning houses. This order shall remain in force so long as you disgrace the profession of arms by allowing your men to destroy private dwellings."[12]

It is important to emphasize that when Hampton vowed that Yankee house burners would be shot, he believed that he was claiming—not forfeiting—the moral high ground. Chivalry, the code that he had striven to uphold his whole life, demanded blood vengeance, not magnanimity, when it was violated; burning private homes and insulting women were the ultimate violations of the code. Hampton was swearing fealty to chivalry's highest demand. But he was only warming to his task:

> I do not, sir, question this right [of foraging on the country]. But there is a right older, even, than this, and one more inalienable—the right that every man has to defend his home and to protect those who are dependent on him; and from my heart I wish that every old man and boy in my country who can fire a gun would shoot down, as he would a wild beast, the men who are desolating their land, burning their homes, and insulting their women.
>
> You are particular in defending and claming "war rights." May I ask if you enumerate among these the right to fire upon a defenseless city without notice; to burn that city to the ground after it had been surrendered by the inhabitants who claimed . . . that protection . . . always accorded in civilized warfare to non-

combatants; to fire the dwelling houses of citizens after robbing them; and to perpetrate even darker crimes than these—crimes too black to be mentioned?

You . . . laid . . . [Columbia] in ashes, leaving amidst its ruins thousands of old men and helpless women and children, who are likely to perish of starvation or exposure. Your line of march can be traced by the lurid light of burning houses, and in more than one household there is now an agony more bitter than that of death. The Indian scalped his victim regardless of age or sex, but with all his barbarity he always respected the persons of his female captives. Your soldiers, more savage than the Indian, insult those whose natural protectors are absent.

In conclusion, I have only to request that whenever you have any of my men "murdered" or "disposed of," for the terms appear to be synonymous with you, you will let me hear of it, that I may know what action to take in the matter. In the meantime I shall hold fifty-six of your men as hostages for those whom you have ordered to be executed.

I am, yours, &c.,
Wade Hampton
Lieutenant-General[13]

When hearing of Hampton's letter to "that vandal Sherman," Beauregard wholeheartedly endorsed it, agreeing that his compatriot's "system of retaliation must be carried out at any cost."[14] Meanwhile, Hampton received no response from Sherman, and Sherman executed no captured Confederates, further convincing Hampton that he had won the argument. After the war, southerners reprinted the Sherman-Hampton exchange several times. They did so not to illustrate bloodthirstiness on the part of Hampton; the objective, rather, was the moral vindication that Hampton had sought in writing the letter. Often they claimed the same vindication for themselves when they proudly admitted to shooting Sherman's "bummers" when they caught them. One member of Calbraith Butler's division boasted, "We would shoot these brutes down like so many mad dogs."[15] The clear implication was that while Sherman and his Yankees violated the most sacred claims of chivalry, Hampton and his men fiercely and loyally defended them. Sherman attacked the home, the family, and women and children; Hampton killed in retaliation.

Hampton's next opportunity for vindication came in a surprise attack against his nemesis Judson Kilpatrick, leader of Sherman's cavalry. No Union officer could have provided a more convenient model for southerners seeking to contrast southern chivalry with Yankee villainy. Kilpatrick was, admittedly, an officer of great energy and ambition, who occasionally showed tactical skill. But most soldiers who knew him, North and South, described him as a scoundrel. Fellow Union officers also considered him a braggart who consistently exaggerated or lied about his accomplishments. Earlier in the war he had been charged with bribery and selling confiscated southern horses and tobacco for his own profit rather than turning them over to the government. He spent three months in prison before the remarkable decision to restore him to command. Though his troopers in Virginia often had bested their Confederate counterparts, his own men called him "Kill-Cavalry" for sacrificing their lives in needless charges. Moreover, Kilpatrick openly kept mistresses and prostitutes, black and white, in his headquarters—even before his wife's death in late 1863. It was a scandal even among his troops. Since leaving Columbia, he had been accompanied by a beautiful, young, unmarried woman named Mary Boozer of a South Carolina Unionist family. To her neighbors' disgust, Mary shared Kilpatrick's carriage and sleeping quarters for several weeks as Sherman's army completed the conquest of the state. There was also a woman known to history only as "Alice" and several others. Southerners also remembered Kilpatrick as the blackguard who allegedly ordered Ulric Dahlgren to burn Richmond and hang Jeff Davis before Hampton's exhausted command tracked him down and routed him in a night attack. In Barnwell, South Carolina, he had held a grand ball in his hotel headquarters while his troops deliberately burned the town. To Hampton, then, Kilpatrick was no chivalrous cavalier—he lacked integrity; magnanimity; respect for women, homes, and property; and the respect of his own men. Perhaps just as important, Kilpatrick did not look the part. He was 5 feet 5 inches tall, scrawny, and not blessed with handsome or graceful features. Nevertheless, Hampton had had to swallow the humiliation of giving up more and more soil of his native state to Kilpatrick's troopers.[16]

During the retreat from South Carolina, Hampton had been traveling mostly with Wheeler's corps, which was shadowing the Left Wing of Sherman's army, including Kilpatrick's cavalry. Butler's division was monitoring and skirmishing with the Right Wing farther east. Eventually, Sherman changed the general course of march in a more easterly direction, aiming for Fayetteville, North Carolina. This move had the

effect of temporarily cutting Butler off from Wheeler and of putting
Kilpatrick's cavalry between Hampton and the main body of Johnston's
army near Fayetteville. For the time being, Hampton's cavalry was divided and cut off. Meanwhile, without Hampton's force as a buffer
between the Federals and William Hardee's infantry, the Federals had an
opportunity to strike the rear of Hardee's retreating column. They could
also beat Hardee in the race to the strategic town of Fayetteville, situated on the Cape Fear River. This would force Hardee to retreat in a
more westerly direction to Raleigh and prevent Johnston from having
the option of defending either Fayetteville or the equally vital town of
Goldsboro, situated at a critical railhead. Hampton determined to re-
unite his forces quickly, which he was able to do on March 8 just north
of Rockingham, North Carolina; then he planned to move around Kilpatrick's left to get in his front.[17]

Realizing that he was now between Hampton and Fayetteville, Kilpatrick hoped to set a trap. He placed forces astride the three east-
west roads leading to the town, intending to cut Hampton off from
infantry support and from rejoining the main Confederate army. In the
process, though, Kilpatrick divided his 4,300-man force into three,
leaving each detachment vulnerable to a determined attack by Hampton's 4,000 troops.[18]

On March 9 the largest of Kilpatrick's three detachments led by
Kilpatrick himself was slogging eastward through a driving rain on the
Morganton Road, just west of Monroe's Crossroads. Hampton's soaked
troopers were only a few miles behind them, advancing along a parallel,
more northerly route on the Yadkin Road. For most of the day, Hampton
rode alone far ahead of the column, no doubt pondering his strategic
dilemma. He had to find a way to get around Kilpatrick and block his
approach to Fayetteville and Hardee's rear. "Look out boys," some of
Hampton's troopers surmised, "Old Wade is fixing a trap for them; we
will be into it tonight."[19]

The men understood their commander's instincts but overestimated
his knowledge of the situation. Hampton did not have enough of a fix
on Kilpatrick's location to spring a trap, at least not until nearly sundown. That was when, at the junction of the Morganton and Yadkin
roads, Butler's advance guard captured a thirty-man detachment that
constituted Kilpatrick's escort. The advance guard did not realize that it
had come within an ace of capturing Kilpatrick himself, who hid in the
woods when he realized the approaching horsemen were Confederates.
Hampton and Butler concluded that they had captured a small portion

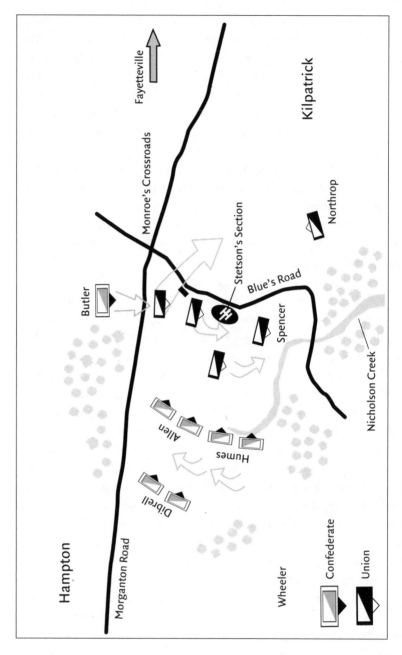

Monroe's Crossroads, March 10, 1865—Hampton's Attack

of a Union column that had already passed the road junction and that that column was isolated from the others. Additionally, it was evident that Kilpatrick intended to camp for the night only a few miles east at Monroe's Crossroads. Here was Hampton's chance—he decided on a dawn attack.[20]

Despite Kilpatrick's earlier narrow escape and the knowledge that Hampton's troopers were just a few miles away, the tired, wet Federals were lax in their security. The Yankee camp was bound on the south and partially on the west by a swamp, perhaps assuring Kilpatrick that few pickets were necessary on the west. On the north side of the camp, there were no pickets at all. Hampton and Wheeler, along with a few of their scouts, reconnoitered the bivouac closely enough to observe the enemy's campfires. Under cover of darkness and thick mists from the recent heavy rains, Confederate scouts slipped into the sleeping Federal camp and captured several dozen pickets on the west side. They located the cabin where Kilpatrick was sleeping with his female companion, who the Confederates mistakenly assumed was the beautiful Mary Boozer. Both Wheeler and Butler had detailed handpicked men to capture Kilpatrick. The scouts also located a pen in which over 150 Confederate prisoners were incarcerated. Meanwhile, orders went out that the Confederates were to have no fires—no cooking, no tobacco, no warmth against the damp chill. Hampton was counting on achieving total surprise.[21]

Hampton planned to have Wheeler's three divisions crash into the camp from the west, while Butler's division charged from the north. With the marsh blocking an escape to the south, Kilpatrick would have only one route out, and there was an opportunity to destroy his command. The Confederates hoped to achieve partial vindication for the humiliation of South Carolina by bagging Kilpatrick himself. Hampton placed himself at the head of one of his old regiments, the Cobb Legion. This was the unit of one Captain Bostick, the man specifically charged by Butler to lead his squadron in the capture of Kilpatrick. The fact that Hampton rode into camp with this regiment suggests not only his attachment to his former command but also his desire for a personal meeting with Kilpatrick. Around 5:20 A.M., Wheeler reported to Hampton that his men were ready and asked permission to have them dismount, "making the capture of the entire camp sure."[22] Hampton quietly replied, "General Wheeler, as a cavalryman I prefer making this capture mounted."[23] This time, Hampton would eschew his pragmatic dismounted tactics. He would humiliate Kilpatrick as a chivalric avenger should, on horseback. Hampton's voice rang out, "Follow me, men! Charge!"[24] Butler repeated the order, and his men stormed into the camp "yelling like devils."[25] Sleeping Federal soldiers awoke in panic and surrendered or fled into the misty gloom, though most had the presence of mind to take their carbines with them. Others were sabered or trampled as they emerged wide-eyed from their blankets or tent-flies. The Confederates soon found themselves with hundreds of Union prisoners, as well as overjoyed comrades just released from the prison pen. Kilpatrick himself dashed out of his cabin barefoot and in his nightshirt, stunned to see "the most formidable cavalry charge I have ever witnessed."[26] Years later he confided to Calbraith Butler that his first thought was, "Here is four years' hard fighting for a major-general's commission gone up with an infernal surprise."[27]

Almost as soon as a total Confederate victory seemed assured, however, things began to unravel. Wheeler's men found that they could not advance through the marshy ground in their front, and Wheeler had to maneuver them around to the left in order to enter the camp from the side that Butler had. By that time, Butler's men had ridden all the way through the dimly lit camp and were, in Butler's words, "scattered like the devil."[28] Under the inspired leadership of a few officers, knots of northern soldiers gathered and offered resistance. A Federal lieutenant gallantly recaptured his two artillery pieces and began pouring canister into the Rebels until he was shot down. In the woods surrounding the large clearing that had been their camp, other Yankees poured a withering fire into Butler's men with their Spencer repeating rifles. Butler would remember that he lost sixty-eight men in five minutes. Hampton and others later claimed that once Wheeler's undisciplined men entered the camp, they stopped to plunder rather than press the advantage. Also, the glorious release of Confederate prisoners turned to tragedy. Butler's men, believing the overjoyed former prisoners rushing toward them were Yankees, mistakenly shot down a few of their own comrades. One man found to his horror that he had killed a boyhood friend. Finally, the Confederates failed to capture the arrogant little Kilpatrick. Captain Bostick rushed up to the cabin where Kilpatrick had been sleeping. Seeing a man dressed only in a nightshirt, long underwear, and slippers, he demanded to know where Kilpatrick was, not realizing that he was speaking to him. The wily general pointed to one of his men dashing by, exclaiming, "There he goes on that black horse!"[29] Bostick rode after him, while Kilpatrick mounted a horse and rode off in his nightclothes. After his narrow escape, Kilpatrick turned energetically to rallying and reorganizing his men. In time—due to Wheeler's ineffectiveness, the confusion in Butler's ranks, superior Yankee firepower, and solid leadership—the Federals rallied and recaptured the campsite. Meanwhile, when informed by his scouts that a large body of Federal infantry was marching rapidly to Kilpatrick's support, Hampton ordered a withdrawal.[30]

Hampton had certainly humiliated Kilpatrick, but the moral vindication the Confederates had achieved at Monroe's Crossroads was only partial and ultimately unsatisfying. Hampton's men took Kilpatrick's hat, coat, pants, sword, pistols, and three of his private mounts, but the villain himself had escaped. Moreover, the surprise attack was just barely a victory in purely military terms. Hampton's troops had captured roughly 500 of Kilpatrick's men and rescued 173 of their own. They had made off with a few wagons and disabled a few others. But Hampton had failed to take Kilpatrick's wagon train and artillery as he had hoped, and he had suffered losses as well. Kilpatrick reported burying 80 Confederates and capturing 30, and with the arrival of a Federal infantry division from the Fourteenth Corps, he was able to force Hampton's withdrawal. The most important outcome in the long run was that Hampton was now able to get around Kilpatrick and protect Hardee's rear, enabling Hardee to win the race to Fayetteville.[31]

After the war, some ex-Confederates tried to use the plight of Kilpatrick's female companion (probably "Alice") to put a chivalric spin on the story. In one version, the woman was the beautiful and infamous Mary Boozer, who emerged from the doorway of the cabin scantily dressed. An eager Confederate officer approached her, removed his hat, and offered to find her a safe place. The confused and frightened woman went with the southerner, who escorted her to a ditch where she would be protected from stray bullets. In another version of the story, Confederate troops were dismayed to see that the lady standing in the doorway was not Mary Boozer, but an old, ugly " 'school-marm' from Vermont." The behavior of the Confederate trooper was the same, but, as Edward Wells wrote, "It was all a sad disappointment to those expectant boys."[32]

Those words probably described Wade Hampton's thoughts as he contemplated the morning's outcome. He had embarrassed Kilpatrick but could have achieved much more. At least his superiors were pleased. Robert E. Lee gladly reported on the affair to the secretary of war, and the Confederate government, desperate for any good news by this point, published a broadside announcing "Glorious Confederate Victory! Hampton Whips Kilpatrick!"[33]

The next day, another incident reassured Hampton and his troops that they were the "better men," and allowed them to exact a small but precious measure of revenge. Hardee's infantry corps was completing a withdrawal through Fayetteville with the intention of crossing the Cape Fear River, which ran east and north of the town. Hampton's cavalry was to act as a rear guard and cover the retreat. Already a few cavalry detachments were in the town, and Hampton had found breakfast at a downtown hotel. But either Hampton's or Hardee's men failed in their duty to picket one of the roads leading into town, and a 68-man scout company of Union cavalry under Captain William Duncan rode in, surprising and scattering knots of Wheeler's cavalry. Duncan then rode ahead with about 18 men toward the Cape Fear River bridge, intending to secure it and block any further Confederate withdrawal.

Hampton heard the commotion, left the hotel, and rode toward the bridge, unsuccessfully seeking to rally some of Wheeler's men. An eighteen-year-old scout, Private Hugh Scott, galloped up to Hampton, told him where the Yankees were, and asked to be placed in charge. Scott had already exchanged hurried pistol shots with some of them and knew their exact location. "General, there are not over ten or fifteen Yankees here. Give me four or five men, and I will whip them out of town." (Obviously Scott had seen only part of the Union contingent.) Inspired by the youngster's pluck, Hampton turned to a handful of other headquarters scouts nearby and said, "You scouts follow me." Before long they were joined by three privates from Company K, 4th South Carolina Cavalry, Butler's division, and one man from Wheeler's corps. The tiny band turned a corner and spotted the bluecoats. Hampton turned toward the men around him and yelled "Charge them!" General Wade Hampton and seven privates from various commands dashed down the street toward the body of Federal cavalry that had just appeared.[34]

The ferocity of the Rebels' attack, combined with their pistol shots, powder smoke, and wild yells, stunned the Yankees, apparently making them think the gray host charging them was much larger. After firing a few random shots, they turned and fled for about one hundred yards, then attempted to turn a right angle down another street to retrace the way they had entered the town. While trying to turn the corner, they crowded each other, making themselves easy targets. Private Scott saw Hampton cut down two Yankees with his gigantic saber; Private Edward

Wells boasted to his aunt of "the pleasure of cleaving one fellow's head with my saber."[35] Altogether the Confederates killed eleven (or thirteen, according to one eyewitness) and captured twelve Yankees, at the loss of one Confederate horse.[36]

One of the prisoners was a spy disguised in a Confederate uniform whom Hampton promised to hang as soon as he crossed the river. The Yankee spy, David Day, managed to escape before Hampton could carry out his threat. Captain Duncan also was taken prisoner, then escaped; he later complained that his captors had stripped him of his valuables while Hampton and Butler looked on. If the story was true, Hampton felt no remorse at the enemy officer's treatment. He was now fighting with the gloves off. Besides, Confederate troops were convinced that any watches or other valuables found on the persons of Union soldiers were stolen property.[37]

The young men who accompanied Hampton on this charge were extremely pleased with themselves and undoubtedly elated to ride side by side with "Old Wade" himself on a heroic adventure. In a letter to the company commander of three of the men, Hampton commended their "conspicuous gallantry"; Wells and Scott fondly recounted the story in letters home and later in life. Hampton publicly spoke of the incident years later, but for the time being he informed his family members neither of the surprise raid on Kilpatrick nor the charge in Fayetteville. His only comment to Mary Fisher was that he had killed and captured many of Sherman's "rascals."[38] Though such feats obviously were not enough to stop Sherman, they must have given Hampton some satisfaction. As young Edward Wells wrote to his aunt: "Charleston is gone, Savannah is gone, Wilmington is gone, but rest assured we will redeem them in the blood of our enemies."[39]

As satisfying as these knightly adventures may have been, Hampton had not given up on his goal to defeat Sherman and redeem South Carolina through a large, pitched battle. He had been urging Beauregard to concentrate Confederate forces and deliver a counterblow since before the burning of Columbia. Now that Johnston was in charge, he continued to press his argument. On March 3 he implored his commander: "Can you not get the troops from Charlotte over to join Hardee? . . . If all this Infty can be put together we can punish Sherman greatly, for his troops are much scattered."[40]

Johnston certainly wanted to concentrate his forces, but for the moment he was not thinking of striking Sherman. Johnston was still unsure whether Sherman's next objective was Raleigh, the state capital, 279 or Goldsboro, which lay along the Wilmington and Weldon Railroad. Sherman's capture of Goldsboro would allow him to join Grant's army in Virginia and break the siege by Lee's lines around Petersburg. During the second week of March, Johnston worked to concentrate his forces at Smithfield, which was equidistant between Raleigh and Goldsboro. He was now able to count four previously distinct forces under his direct control—William Hardee's corps, the reliable division of Major General Robert Hoke formerly under Braxton Bragg, the Army of Tennessee contingent now led by Lieutenant General A. P. Stewart, and Wade Hampton's cavalry of about 4,000 mounted troopers. Altogether, Johnston could muster about 21,000 men, while Sherman had about three times as many.[41]

By this time the westernmost position of Johnston's infantry formations was held by Hardee's corps, whose withdrawal Hampton was trying to cover. On March 16 Hardee had gamely fought Major General Henry W. Slocum's Left Wing as it advanced on Averasboro, North Carolina. Hampton's cavalry had provided some support, but during the nights of the sixteenth and seventeenth, its twofold mission was to cover Hardee's withdrawal to Smithfield, ordered by Johnston, and keep tabs on and delay Slocum's Left Wing and Major General Oliver O. Howard's Right Wing. While performing the latter task on the seventeenth, Hampton became increasingly convinced that Sherman's real aim was to turn east and capture Goldsboro. He informed Hardee that he intended to slow that eastward drive, though reassuring him that he would continue to cover Hardee's withdrawal to Smithfield as long as possible. From Fayetteville, two roads—an "upper" and a "lower"—led to Goldsboro. It appeared that Slocum's Left Wing was on the upper road, while the Right Wing was on the lower. This meant, Hampton surmised, that the two enemy forces could be a dozen or more miles apart, about a day's march, and that an opportunity existed to punish one severely before the other could go to its support.[42]

Johnston, too, was beginning to think offensively. He wrote to Hardee on the night of March 16 asking for information on Sherman's forces. Receiving little or none, he wrote to Hampton, who received the dispatch just before midnight on the seventeenth. Where was the enemy, Johnston asked? Did Hampton think it feasible to attack him? When and where could an attack be made? Was it feasible to advance from Smithfield and strike some of Sherman's corps before the Union army reached Goldsboro? Hampton replied immediately, informing him of Sherman's dispersion and vulnerability. The place to attack him, the cavalry leader said, was right where Hampton himself was camped— at the Cole plantation two miles south of the hamlet of Bentonville, where the road from Smithfield intersected the upper road between Averasboro and Goldsboro. Near the junction of the roads was a large field, just south and west of some wooded high ground. He promised to delay the enemy's approach to Goldsboro long enough for Johnston to march the infantrymen from Smithfield and place them around the Cole plantation to spring a trap for Slocum.[43]

Hampton sent one of the two couriers who had delivered Johnston's questions back to Johnston. The one remaining was Lieutenant Wade Hampton IV, who had recovered from his wound and returned to Johnston's staff. Young Wade spent the night at his father's camp, then wrote to Johnston that he had relayed to his father Johnston's reminder to provide "frequent and full dispatches."[44] Hampton had sent plenty of dispatches on the seventeenth, but mostly to Hardee, whose retreat he was charged with covering, and Hardee had forwarded some of them to Johnston. Johnston, in turn, had sought information on Sherman's intentions from Hardee. Now the proper relationship between army commander and cavalry chief was reestablished. Johnston received his intelligence directly from Hampton. The commander also clearly had adopted Hampton as his chief tactical adviser. He responded immediately to Hampton's recommendations by ordering Bragg's, Stewart's, and Hardee's infantry to Bentonville as suggested, and also by riding to Bentonville to confer with Hampton personally.[45]

On March 18 Johnston arrived at Bentonville to find Hampton using one division of cavalry (Brigadier General George Dibrell's division of Wheeler's corps) to contest and delay the advance of Slocum's entire Left Wing, consisting of the Fourteenth Corps and most of the Twentieth Corps behind it. The rest of Wheeler's corps was off to the north and west, protecting the army's right from Kilpatrick and small portions of the Twentieth Corps. Butler's division was sparring with the Federal Right Wing farther south and east. By the end of the day, Hampton wrote, he and Dibrell's division had retired to the wooded hill overlooking the large field "that I had selected as the proper place for the battle, which was to take place as soon as our infantry reached the ground."[46] As it was vital for Hampton to hold this position until the infantry arrived, he resorted to his tried-and-true tactic of dismounting Dibrell's men. He also employed his two available batteries of horse artillery. "At great risk of losing my guns," he later explained, "I put my artillery some distance to the right of the road, where, though exposed,

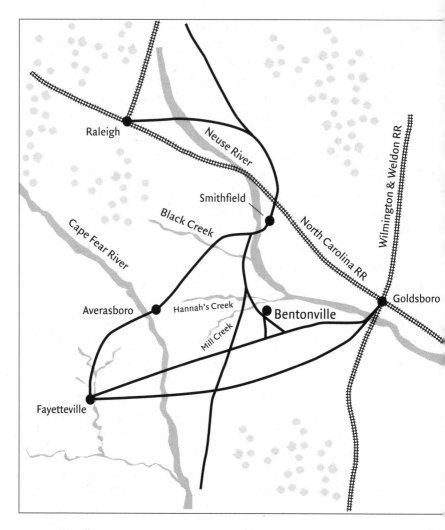

Bentonville Vicinity

it had a commanding position. I knew that if a serious attack was made on me the guns would be lost, but I determined to run this risk in the hope of checking the Federal advance."[47]

One of these exposed batteries was Hampton's beloved "Hart's Battery," which had just rejoined him from the Army of Northern Virginia the day before. This band of cannoneers had served with him since the early days of the Hampton Legion. When Hampton had transferred to the cavalry in 1862, he had taken Hart's men with him as horse artillery, and they had served "Old Wade" faithfully and dependably. Hampton had frequently commended their service, and they responded with letters and gifts to their beloved chief. Captain James F. Hart, their long-time commander, had had his leg blown off the very day that Preston had been killed. When Hampton left Virginia for South Carolina in January 1865, the battery had asked to be sent with him. Hampton had originally expected to return to Lee's army by spring, but now Hart's Battery had joined him instead. The artillerymen were aware of Hampton's boldness as he placed them in their opportunistic, but exposed, position. One soldier jokingly commented to his comrades, "Old Hampton is playing a bluff game, and if he don't mind Sherman will call him." Hampton fondly observed that the soldier "evidently understood the game of war as well as that of poker!" and noted the "quick perception of our private soldiers."[48]

On March 19 Slocum's unsuspecting lead elements collided with Johnston's concealed army near Bentonville. After repulsing the initial Union advance, the Confederates charged, punishing the Federals badly and driving them back for three-quarters of a mile. As the day went on, Slocum was able to bring up more forces and stop the Rebels' advance, thanks in part to nervousness on the part of Braxton Bragg and some bungling by the Confederate leadership. Hampton himself spent most of the day with his horse artillery, which he had placed in a wide gap that he found in the lines between Stewart's and Bragg's forces. Dibrell's division was worn out from the last several days of skirmishing and held in reserve, while Wheeler was still too far away to help out. Despite the early, hard blows delivered against Slocum's Fourteenth Corps, Confederate mistakes prevented the victory from being more complete, and by the end of the day more of Slocum's Twentieth Corps had arrived. It was Johnston who was now outnumbered.[49]

Johnston and Sherman's Left Wing continued to spar throughout Monday, the twentieth. Hampton spent the first part of the day ensuring that Wheeler's cavalrymen were posted on the Confederate right to thwart a flanking maneuver by Slocum's Left Wing. Johnston would soon have to contend with Sherman's Right Wing as well. Several miles to the east, Calbraith Butler's cavalry, temporarily commanded by South Carolinian Evander Law due to Butler's illness, was trying to buy time for Johnston's left flank. The bulk of the Union's Fifteenth Corps of Howard's Right Wing was marching west from Cox's Crossroads toward the right and rear of Johnston's army at Bentonville. Law used skirmish-and-delay tactics to slow them as much as possible, but soon the Confederates became aware that the real danger was now on their left flank. Johnston shifted Major General Lafayette McLaws's infantry division from his right to the newly endangered left, while Hampton extended the line farther with Wheeler's and Butler's cavalry.[50]

At first glance, Johnston's line was a strong one. By the end of the day, the Confederates had prepared breastworks and rifle pits all along the line. Part of the left overlooked a marshy ravine through which Union attackers would have to maneuver under fire. In reality, Johnston's line—now horseshoe-shaped and bent back on itself—was thin and weak; the left was especially vulnerable. The left extended to Mill Creek, where Hampton's thin line of lightly armed cavalrymen was posted. By midafternoon on Monday, Sherman's Left and Right wings were reunited and in position to pound their southern foes, who they now outnumbered by three to one. A determined Union assault on Hampton's cavalry on the left could easily enable the bluecoats to capture Mill Creek Bridge in the Confederate rear, cutting off Johnston's only escape. As Hampton later wrote, "Our line was a very weak one, and our position was extremely perilous."[51] Johnston, however, stayed in place overnight, endeavoring to evacuate more wounded and perhaps hoping that he could punish any frontal assault on his breastworks. For a general always known for his caution, it was a risky decision.[52]

On March 21 Sherman did indeed strike the Confederate left. Amid active skirmishing, Hampton's pickets warned him that the enemy was moving on them in force. Hampton immediately galloped off to tell Johnston that he did not have the strength to repel a determined attack on the left, and that such an attack could easily block the Confederates' only route of retreat. Johnston sent Hampton back "to ascertain the exact condition of affairs."[53] On the way back, Hampton found that it was almost too late; a courier informed him that the enemy had nearly reached the main road leading to Mill Creek Bridge. It turned out that the Federal attackers comprised the division of Joseph A. Mower, who had received orders simply to reconnoiter the Confederate left. On finding that it was held by only a thin line of dismounted cavalry, however, he had launched an all-out assault. Mower's soldiers had driven back many of Wheeler's units and captured Johnston's headquarters. They were now only a few hundred yards from the all-important Mill Creek Bridge and in a position to ensure the destruction of Johnston's army.[54]

The situation was as desperate as the most dangerous moments at Manassas, Brandy Station, or Trevilian. Hampton would have to act fast. Just before he met the courier, Hampton had passed Brigadier General Alfred Cumming's Georgia brigade in reserve, which numbered only about two hundred veterans. He ordered this unit to "the point threatened," as well as an artillery battery that he had passed.[55] Hampton also sent a courier to round up "any mounted men he could find," and the remnants of Wheeler's 8th Texas Cavalry and 4th Tennessee Cavalry arrived within minutes.[56] He then conferred with Hardee, apprising him of the situation. Hardee proceeded to gather more units; Joe Wheeler, on his own initiative, prepared more cavalry for a counterattack; and Hampton's own staff jumped down from their horses to help man the guns of the battery Hampton had corralled. It was an ad hoc, seat-of-the-pants affair, in which the prompt action of Hampton, Hardee, and Wheeler, as well as the desperate courage of a few thousand Confederate troops, saved the day. During or just after the initial charge of the 8th Texas and Cumming's Georgians, Mower's reeling Federals were also struck by large elements of Wheeler's cavalry and Hampton's beloved old commands in Butler's division, the Cobb Legion and Young's brigade. Screaming the high-pitched Rebel yell, the Confederates drove Mower's division back in confusion. It was the last great Confederate charge in the Carolinas campaign, and one of the last of the war. As happens so often after the confusion and stress of battle, it was hard for the participants to recall exactly what happened, except that the Yankees were soundly repulsed.[57]

Writing thirty-two years later, Hampton modestly omitted any reference to his participation in the charge, noting only that Hardee "led this charge with his usual conspicuous gallantry."[58] According to some accounts, Hampton personally led Young's brigade into action alongside the Cobb Legion; Hampton's own narrative says nothing of this but leaves the impression that he was with the 8th Texas and Cumming's brigade. It may be that Hampton was located with various units as the counterattack progressed.[59]

In any event it was a thrilling moment, recalling the dash and élan of Confederate charges earlier in the war. Hardee's face was beaming as he rode back from the front lines, turned to Hampton, and exclaimed, "That was Nip and Tuck, and for a time I thought Tuck had it."[60] Within moments, however, Hardee's glee turned to misery. As Hampton tells it, Hardee learned that "his only son, a gallant boy of sixteen, who had joined the 8th Texas Cavalry two hours before," had been mortally wounded in the charge.[61] Like Hampton five months before, Hardee kissed his dying son and then rode away to perform his duties. Surely no one could empathize with Hardee more than Wade Hampton.

Johnston got his army across Mill Creek that evening, ending the Battle of Bentonville. In one sense, the fight was a useless sacrifice.

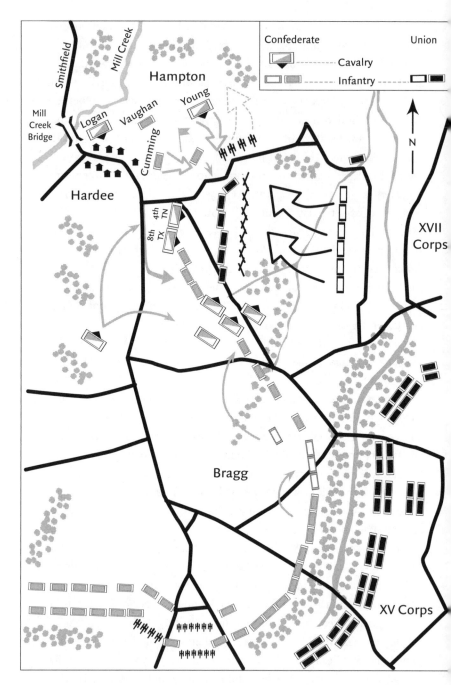

Bentonville, March 21, 1865. Hardee and Hampton counterattack to prevent Federal
seizure of the Mill Creek Bridge in the rear of Johnston's army. This map shows only the
eastern side of the "horseshoe-"shaped lines.

With the end of the war only a month away, the Confederates had lost 2,343 men to Sherman's 1,595.[62] Within two days Sherman would control Goldsboro and be in position either to join Grant in Virginia or march on Raleigh, as he chose. Essentially the Carolinas campaign was over. Hampton, though, was proud of what the Confederates had accomplished. He praised Johnston's boldness in throwing his force upon the Left Wing of Sherman's army, which "offered the only hope of success left to us."[63] In fact, according to Hampton, the whole affair reflected the gallantry of Joe Johnston and his army. After Johnston's initial blow, "no more gallant defense was ever made . . . when he confronted and baffled this force, holding a weak line for three days against nearly five times his number."[64] Johnston's boldness was matched by his chivalrous concern for the wounded, both his own and Sherman's: "For the last two days of this fight he only held his position to secure the removal of his wounded, and when he had accomplished that he withdrew leisurely, moving in his first march only about four miles. All the Federal wounded who fell into his hands were cared for in his field-hospitals."[65]

Hampton knew that he personally had contributed much. It was he who had provided the intelligence, selected the ground, conceived the plan for the first day's attack, and helped prevent the collapse of the left flank on the third day. What he did not know was that it was the last time he would lead lines of yelling southern soldiers in a charge. At Monroe's Crossroads and Bentonville, though, the Confederates had proved that they could still strike Sherman a blow. The day after Bentonville a slightly vindicated Hampton wrote his sister, "We have injured Sherman a good deal, so that he cannot boast of getting through free."[66]

CONSIDER THE POSITION
IN WHICH I FIND MYSELF

Modern historians recognize the Battle of Bentonville as the Confederates' last-ditch effort to defeat Sherman in the Carolinas campaign. By
the end of March 1865, many contemporaries also suspected that the
Confederacy could not hold out much longer. But Wade Hampton was
either unable or unwilling to accept the inevitable. Even if he had,
honor, duty, memories of the dead, and the need for vindication would
not yet allow him to quit fighting.

The retreat from Bentonville, North Carolina, was hardly in progress
before Hampton began looking for another opportunity to strike a blow
against Sherman. As Johnston withdrew the main body of the army
toward Smithfield, he ordered Hampton to place Wheeler and Butler "in
close observation of the enemy" around Goldsboro, covering the northern and western approaches from the town.[1] Hampton did more than
observe the enemy. On the morning of March 24, he withstood an attack
by elements of the Union Twenty-fifth Corps south of Moccasin Creek,
midway between Bentonville and Goldsboro. He then counterattacked
the Federals, driving them, he reported, "two miles to their works close
to Cox's Bridge." He concluded this account to Johnston by urging him
once again to resume the offensive. "If the troops at Cox's Bridge remain there to-morrow you could strike them to great advantage, and
could partially destroy their pontoons [over the Neuse River]."[2] Over the
next three weeks Hampton's cavalry skirmished with the enemy along
Moccasin Creek, on the Stage Road between Goldsboro and Smithfield,
and on the outskirts of Raleigh. On March 27 Hampton asked Johnston
to send him explosives so he could destroy the "Bridge at Kinston" and
cut the Wilmington and Weldon Railroad in the event that Sherman
tried to use it to join Grant in Virginia.[3] As late as April 16, a week after
Lee's surrender in Virginia, he urged Wheeler to "strike [the enemy]
where you can" in the vicinity of Hillsborough, North Carolina.[4]

In the most startling example of the search for vindication against
his nemesis Sherman, Hampton sent out a scouting party to capture the
Yankee commander himself. Shortly after the Battle of Bentonville, he
ordered his most trusted scout, Sergeant George Shadburne, to take as
many men as he needed on a special mission. He said that "he wanted   289

Sherman"; Shadburne "must get him for him." Showing Shadburne his route on the map, Hampton said that he was to "cross the Cape Fear [River] to the east, break through the division of cavalry guarding that flank of Sherman, pass to the rear, recross the Cape Fear—swimming that river this time—ride into Goldsboro, grab Sherman & bring him out. Sherman was to come any how!!" Clearly, Hampton wanted Sherman dead or alive. Shadburne took thirty men behind Union lines. He was able to break through the Union cavalry, destroy some wagons, and ride into Goldsboro, only to find that Sherman had already left. The sergeant did return, however, with eighteen captured wagons and one hundred mules.[5]

Despite Hampton's pugnaciousness, the overall situation was less encouraging than ever. Elements of his own command were widely scattered performing numerous missions, and much of his correspondence in late March involved his efforts to reconcentrate Confederate cavalry units under his immediate command. Desertion within Hampton's units had never been as severe a problem as it was in other parts of Lee's and Johnston's armies, but anecdotal evidence suggests that it was getting worse, especially in Wheeler's corps. Hampton's overall numbers remained steady, but there were hints that morale was slipping. After the stubborn fight near Smithfield on April 11, Confederate cavalry detachments performing rearguard duties seemed to put up very little fight before melting away.[6]

Most discouraging of all was the rumor that Lee's army in Virginia had surrendered to Grant on April 9.[7] Confederates and even many northerners had long considered Lee's famed army to be invincible. As the war dragged on through 1863 and 1864, both Lee and his hardy band had become the most prominent symbols of Confederate nationhood. Their demise was the main event signifying to most Americans that the war was over. For the time being, though, many men in Johnston's army, as well as Confederate citizens, angrily rejected the rumors as vicious lies. Hampton was one of the nonbelievers.[8]

President Jefferson Davis himself had already fled Richmond and was in Greensboro, North Carolina. From there he summoned Johnston for a meeting. Davis, Johnston, Beauregard, Secretary of War John C. Breckenridge, and other members of the Confederate cabinet met on April 12 to discuss the deteriorating situation. After receiving confirmation of Lee's surrender, both generals and nearly the entire cabinet urged their president to initiate peace negotiations. Davis, however, insisted that the fight continue.[9]

Meanwhile, rumors of Lee's surrender added momentum to a movement among a few prominent North Carolinians in Raleigh to seek a
separate peace between their state and the federal government. Leading this movement were Governor Zebulon B. Vance, former governor
and current senator William Graham, and University of North Carolina
president David Swain. Graham and Swain met with Vance and persuaded him to arrange a deal with Sherman whereby Vance would take
North Carolina out of the war. In return, Vance would be allowed to
remain in office to restore civil order. Graham and Swain, now styled
"peace commissioners," meant to take Vance's offer to Sherman. The
two commissioners boarded a train in Raleigh at 10:00 A.M. on April 12
bound for Sherman's headquarters several miles away. To get there, they
would have to pass through Hampton's lines east of the city and then
through Kilpatrick's.[10]

Vance later claimed that he fully intended to inform President Davis
of his action; instead, Davis learned of it through other channels. The
source was Duncan McRae, editor of the *Raleigh Confederate*. McRae had
heard about Graham and Swain's mission almost immediately and angrily reported it to Johnston's headquarters, where Hardee was temporarily in command. Before sending Graham and Swain on their assignment, the governor had obtained written permission from Hardee to
forward a flag of truce through the army's lines. Hardee probably did
not know the exact content of Vance's letter to Sherman; he may have
simply assumed that he was attempting to arrange the peaceful surrender of Raleigh. In any event, Hardee seems to have been the only
Confederate officer who knew that he had granted Graham and Swain
permission to pass through the army's lines. When McRae stormed into
army headquarters, only the assistant adjutant general, Colonel Archer
Anderson, was there to meet him. Shocked at McRae's story, Anderson
telegraphed Hampton on his own initiative and directed him to stop the
peace commissioners' train.[11]

Hampton intercepted and boarded the train several miles southeast
of Raleigh. Graham and Swain promptly showed him Vance's letter as
well as Hardee's safe-conduct pass. At this point Hampton was confused, for Hardee's staff officer, Archer Anderson, had directed Hampton to stop a mission that Hardee himself had authorized. Moreover,
Hardee seemingly had authorized a state governor, not a military officer, to negotiate with Sherman. Did a state government have authority
to arrange a separate peace, and did a Confederate military officer have
the authority to facilitate it? Did Johnston or Davis know about the

mission? Expressing his doubts on its "propriety," Hampton confiscated the letters, wrote his own dispatch to Sherman, and sent all of the messages to Sherman by a mounted courier. He also included a note from Graham and Swain requesting a conference with Sherman. Then Hampton let the train proceed slowly pending Sherman's reply.[12]

The train had advanced only a mile when one of Hampton's staff officers rode up and again ordered it to halt. By this time, Colonel Anderson had wired Johnston and Davis in Greensboro. Johnston replied with Davis's order to cancel Hardee's pass and return the train to Raleigh. When Graham heard this news, he indignantly told Hampton's messenger that such an order must come from Hampton himself, refusing to allow the train's return until Hampton's arrival. Hampton proceeded to the train and relayed Davis's instructions. He also read them his latest dispatch to Sherman informing him that Graham and Swain were returning to Raleigh. The engine reversed course. Before it got far it was stopped again, this time by advancing Union cavalry. Troopers of the 9th Michigan Cavalry and the 92nd Illinois Mounted Infantry fired on the train, ransacked the coach, robbed the commissioners, and passed them on to Kilpatrick, who insulted them further before sending them to Sherman. Hampton felt no sympathy when he learned of the commissioners' fate.[13]

Throughout the rest of the day Kilpatrick's troopers rapidly closed on Raleigh. "Little Kil," still smarting over his humiliation at Monroe's Crossroads, was anxious to capture Hampton himself. That night Hampton barely escaped into Raleigh as Kilpatrick's men closed off the southern approach to the city. Wheeler's men entered the town from the east and withdrew through it that night. Unfortunately they sustained their reputation for loose discipline and lawlessness, looting and robbing their countrymen just as they had done in Columbia. The next day Hampton communicated with Kilpatrick and helped arrange the peaceful surrender of Raleigh by civilian authorities. On the same day, he ordered Wheeler to assist him in setting up an ambush for the Federals after they emerged from the western side of the city in order to "whip the enemy's cavalry."[14]

Hampton may have thought that the bizarre Vance-Graham-Swain affair was over, but he was mistaken. While in Sherman's custody, the two commissioners had chatted amiably with the Union general and his officers, then were allowed to return to Raleigh on April 13. They carried a message from Sherman to Governor Vance, who had fled to Hillsborough. Hampton knew nothing of their return until the evening of the fourteenth, while at Strayhorn's Farm nine miles east of Hillsborough. Butler's cavalry, still led by Evander Law, was with him; Wheeler's corps was nearby at Chapel Hill. The cavalry chief was sitting on the veranda of the farmhouse with a staff officer, Major William J. Saunders, when a horse-drawn carriage pulled up at the front gate. The two officers were startled to see that it carried Graham and Swain. While in Sherman's camp, the commissioners had learned from Sherman's special order to his troops that Lee had indeed surrendered the Army of Northern Virginia. Though these rumors had been rife on the Confederate side for days, they were still unconfirmed, and even the peace-seeking commissioners had found the news difficult to digest. When they relayed the report to Hampton, he said he did not believe it.

The report rattled him, though. Hampton had immense confidence in Robert E. Lee and the men with whom he had served for three and a half years. No other army so perfectly represented the defiance and the hopes of the Confederate nation. Hampton was so preoccupied with the news that he neglected to quiz the commissioners on their meeting with Sherman. As Graham and Swain drove off, Hampton and Saunders returned to their seats on the veranda. With a puzzled expression, Hampton turned to Saunders and asked, "What do you think of all this?" Saunders said that he had expected Hampton to "ask them in." "What do you mean?" asked Hampton. Saunders had been carefully eyeing Graham, who had his hand thrust deep into his coat as if he were hiding something. He told Hampton that he suspected Graham was concealing a letter from Sherman to Vance.[15]

Hampton sprang from his chair. As long as he had anything to do with it, no private citizen would sell out the remainder of the Confederacy while brave soldiers were still in the field. "Go and get your horse, sir," he ordered Saunders, as he hastily scribbled two dispatches.[16] Saunders was to deliver one of them to Graham, demanding that Graham hand over Sherman's letter to Vance. If Graham succeeded in delivering the letter to Vance before Saunders could catch him, Saunders was to arrest Graham immediately. The other dispatch was for Johnston. Traveling in a driving rainstorm, Saunders found Graham that night at his home in Hillsborough. The elderly senator kindly informed the crestfallen major that he had already delivered the letter to Vance but did not tell him that Vance was staying at Graham's own house that very night.[17]

Over the next several days, Wade Hampton and Judson Kilpatrick became the intermediaries between Johnston and Sherman as the two army commanders attempted to arrange an end to the fighting. This was ironic, for no Confederate officer opposed the idea of surrender more than Hampton. As the men in the ranks heard rumors of surrender and observed flags of truce passing between their lines and the Yankees', morale began to falter. But Hampton still spoke in a defiant tone. While a truce went into effect on Sunday, April 16, he visited Pierce Young's brigade and spoke to the troops. J. Fred Waring of the Jeff Davis Legion recorded that "the men cheered [Hampton] heartily. No surrender in him."[18] For his part, Kilpatrick repeatedly tried to convince Sherman that Johnston was lying—only trying to buy time so that the Confederates could escape Sherman's pursuing columns. "Little Kil" had also publicly sworn to pursue Hampton to the death. Soon, however, it was all arranged—Johnston and Sherman would meet on April 17 at Bennett Place, a farmhouse several miles east of Hillsborough on the road to Raleigh.[19]

The meeting between the bitter foes took place at noon, as scheduled. Johnston and Hampton set out from Hampton's headquarters at ten o'clock with a retinue of staff officers and a cavalry escort. Hampton was accompanyied by Major McClellan, Major Saunders, Captain Rawlins Lowndes, and his young kinsman Wade Hampton Manning. Johnston's staff included Major John Johnson and Lieutenant Wade Hampton IV. Sherman brought similar staff, along with Judson Kilpatrick. Johnston and Sherman saluted each other when they came into view. Introductions and handshakes followed, though neither Sherman nor Hampton wished to shake the other's hand. Major Johnson remembered that Hampton's horse suddenly became "fractious" and that Hampton did not bring it under control until the two army commanders had gone off alone. As every Confederate present knew Hampton to be a superb horseman, Johnson implied that Hampton feigned his difficulty to avoid shaking hands with Sherman.[20]

While Johnston and Sherman met privately inside the Bennett House, Hampton and his son spent most of the time sitting on a carpenter's bench outside. If the northern officers expected the elder Hampton to be courtly and polite, they were disappointed. Mostly they had no such expectations. Hampton was the Confederate Sherman's officers loved to hate. Sherman, Kilpatrick, and others viewed him as arrogant and bloodthirsty, a caricature of northerners' worst stereotypes of rich southern planters. Union major George W. Nichols described Hampton as "a large and powerful man" whose face was "bold beyond arrogance."[21] Major Henry Hitchcock's portrayal of the Carolina aristocrat could have come straight from an abolitionist tract. Hampton's "whole demeanor," he wrote, "was marked with the easy 'well-bred' essentially vulgar insolence which is characteristic of that type of 'gentleman'; a man of polished manners, scarcely veiling the utter arrogance and selfishness which marks his class, and which I hate with a perfect hatred."[22]

To be sure, Hampton was not on his best behavior. He was an angry and reluctant participant who wanted no part of surrender. He dressed for the occasion in his best uniform, including a black felt hat, gold braid, and brightly polished boots. In a carefully calculated insult, he showed up at the meeting carrying not a sword, but a freshly cut switch—a weapon designed for use on children, slaves, or impudent Yankees, not honorable warriors. On the other side, according to Colonel J. Fred Waring, "Sherman is hard-featured and ill favoured. What shall I say of Kilpatrick? His looks and his deeds favour each other."[23]

Kilpatrick, who was present, made a sarcastic comment to Hampton. Hampton stood up, towering over Kilpatrick; one eyewitness remembered that the South Carolinian "looked savage enough to eat 'little Kil.' "[24] The two exchanged taunts. Hampton reminded Kilpatrick of his promise to pursue Hampton "to the death," then of his humiliation of Kilpatrick at Monroe's Crossroads as well as at Atlee's Station over a year before, concluding: "You never ran *me* out of Headquarters in my stocking feet!"[25] Kilpatrick replied that Hampton had had to retreat from the Monroe's Crossroads clearing faster than he had entered it, though one Union cavalryman thought that Hampton's jab was "a thrust home and too true to be funny."[26] Hampton made it clear to all within earshot that if he were responsible for writing the terms of the armistice they would remain unwritten, "for I could never bring myself to live again with a people who have waged war as you have done."[27] As tempers approached the boiling point, Sherman and Johnston emerged from their negotiations, ending the confrontation.

Inside the Bennett House, the discussion had been amiable. Johnston suggested that he and Sherman arrange the surrender of all the remaining Confederate armies, not just Johnston's. He also hoped that the cessation of hostilities would allow the "civil authorities" of the two governments to reach an agreement. Sherman sincerely wished to end the fighting, but he doubted whether either general had the authority to arrange the surrender of the other Confederate armies. He also doubted whether his government would negotiate with Davis's, since the Federals did not officially recognize it. The two generals agreed to consult their superiors and to meet the next day.[28]

Johnston returned to Hampton's headquarters at a house in Hillsborough. Though President Davis had already left for Charlotte, there were plenty of civilian authorities nearby for Johnston to consult. After midnight, Confederate Secretary of War Breckenridge, Postmaster General John Reagan, and Governor Vance arrived by train and sat down to a late supper with Johnston and Hampton. When the meal was over, Hampton made it clear that he was bitterly opposed to any negotiations with the Yankees. He angrily confronted Vance in front of the other officers, accusing him of improperly treating with the enemy. He also denounced the Graham-Swain mission—he did not care that "*such men*" had suffered the indignity of being fired on by Union cavalry.[29]

Johnston and Sherman met again the following day. By the time Johnston returned to Hampton's headquarters that night, he and Sherman had agreed to end the fighting. The remaining Confederate armies —not just Johnston's—were to disband, while the people of the southern states were to retain their property and "political rights and franchises" as defined by the U.S. Constitution *and* as defined by the current state constitutions. Former Confederate soldiers were to be left undisturbed as long as they took up peaceful pursuits. Federal courts would be reestablished in the southern states. Finally, while the generals acknowledged that they lacked the full authority to carry out those terms, they agreed that their armies would remain in place and suspend hostilities until their civilian superiors approved them.[30]

Sherman's terms were more generous than the Confederates could have hoped for—no military rule, no hanging of Confederate officers, no disenfranchisement of Confederate soldiers, no confiscation of property. The only assurance Johnston had failed to secure was amnesty for President Davis and his cabinet. Despite the leniency of the terms, Hampton was not impressed. He told Johnston not to include him in any surrender.[31] The next day he wrote to Jefferson Davis, vowing to continue the fight if Davis would only give the word.

Hampton's April 19 letter to Davis is one of the most desperate expressions of southern defiance written during the American Civil War. It marks Hampton's temporary metamorphosis from home defender into desperado. Hampton began by assuring his president that the military situation was not hopeless. Many of his own officers "are not subdued, nor do they despair."[32] He estimated that there were still 40,000 to 50,000 armed Confederate soldiers east of the Mississippi and a like number west of it. He suggested that the Confederacy could disband the infantry, call upon it for volunteers for the cavalry, and send the entire mounted force toward the Mississippi River. "When we cross that river," he wrote, "we can get large accessions to the cavalry, and we can hold Texas. As soon as forces can be organized and equipped, send this heavy cavalry force into the country of the enemy, and they will soon show that we are not conquered. If I had 20,000 mounted men here I could force Sherman to retreat in twenty days. Give me a good force of cavalry and I will take them safely across the Mississippi, and if you desire to go in that direction it will give me great pleasure to escort you."[33]

Hampton's determination was leading him close to madness. He had struggled for months to keep 4,000 to 5,000 men mounted, and now he casually tossed out the figure of 20,000. His proposal to take such a force to the Mississippi, a journey of eight hundred miles through enemy-held territory, ignored logistical and strategic realities. His claim that he could defeat Sherman facing odds of four to one reflected more bravado than common sense and was out of character for a commander who had always carefully weighed the odds before committing his troops to action.

What could have led Hampton to make such rash claims? One reason for his unclear thinking may have been that he was physically and emotionally exhausted. Postmidnight conferences and predawn messages along with surrenders and rumors of surrenders had taken their toll. But also Hampton strongly believed that restoration of the Union would result in more, not less, suffering for the southern people, as well as utter degradation:

> No suffering which can be inflicted by the passage over our country of the Yankee armies can equal what would fall on us if we return to the Union. In this latter event I look for a war between the United States and England and France, when we of the South, under a more rigorous conscription than has yet obtained here, shall be forced to fight by the side of our own negroes and under Yankee officers. We shall have to pay the debts incurred by the United States in this war, and we shall live under a base and vulgar tyranny. No sacrifice would too great to escape this train of horrors.[34]

The final passage in his letter to Davis suggests that, at least momentarily, Hampton was ready to forsake his home and the assurance of ever seeing his family again: "My own mind is made up as to my course. I shall fight as long as my Government remains in existence; when that ceases to live I shall seek some other country, for I shall never take the 'oath of allegiance.' . . . I can bring to your support many strong arms and brave hearts—men who will fight to Texas, and who, if forced from that State, will seek refuge in Mexico rather than in the Union."[35]

While Johnston and Sherman waited for their governments' approval of the terms, rumors of surrender spread through the camps of the Confederate army. Thousands of infantrymen and artillerymen deserted in droves. Most believed that they would be sent to prison camps and were determined to avoid that fate. Some wished to join other Confederate commands in the West and continue fighting, while still others simply wanted to go home. Desertions also decimated the cavalry ranks.[36]

Hampton tried to bolster morale through more personal appearances and by approving equestrian tournaments. He also wrote again to his fleeing president near Charlotte. Having received no reply to his April 19 letter, he wrote a shorter one on the twenty-second, repeating his offer to escort Davis to Texas but omitting most of his other grandiose schemes. He simply promised "to collect all the men who will stick to their colors, and to get to Texas. I can carry with me quite a number, and I can get there."[37] Once there, Hampton hoped that Texas would "hold out, or seek the protection of [Emperor] Maximilian."[38] As it happened, Sherman's government was not about to approve the sweeping benefits that he had offered the Rebels, a fact that gave Hampton time to plan his and Davis's escape. Washington rejected the terms of the surrender on April 21, though Johnston was not aware of this until April 24.[39]

On the twenty-fourth, Davis wired Johnston from Charlotte with instructions to accept Sherman's terms—the same ones that Hampton had urged Davis to reject. An hour later, Johnston learned that the Federal authorities had dismissed them and instructed Sherman to arrange new terms that only affected Sherman's and Johnston's armies. Johnston immediately informed Davis and recommended that Davis allow him to disband his army to prevent the war from inflicting any more "devastation to the country."[40] Now Davis stiffened his backbone. He and Secretary of War Breckenridge wanted Johnston to continue the fight, or at least bring out the cavalry and as many other troops as could be mounted. The remaining infantrymen could be disbanded and rendezvous later at an appointed place. Then the entire force could "march away from Sherman and be strong enough to encounter anything between us and the Southwest."[41] Clearly, Breckenridge and Davis had now adopted the outlines of the plan Hampton proposed in his April 19 letter to Davis.[42]

298   Johnston rejected this desperate plan and instead sought to make

new terms with Sherman. Rather than promise Davis a large mounted army, he offered only a mounted escort to "save the high civil functionaries."[43] To that end he sent Hampton to confer with Davis in Charlotte. Hampton left his headquarters in Hillsborough (Johnston's headquarters was in Greensboro) by train that very day and conferred with Davis on April 25. Davis and Hampton agreed that Hampton would escape with as many mounted men as possible before Johnston could surrender them. Obediently, Hampton rushed back to Hillsborough on the twenty-sixth. He arrived at 11:00 P.M., only to find that it was too late to implement his and Davis's plan; Johnston had surrendered the army. But that was not all. A large portion of his old command, consisting of much of Butler's division and Hart's Battery, had refused to surrender and abandoned their camps, marching south for Charlotte.[44]

Now Hampton had two choices to make. First, should he stay and surrender or flee to Charlotte and help his president? The easiest course would be to sign his parole and go home. Failure to do so would make him a fugitive in Union eyes, and he could be sure that Sherman, his personal enemy, would brand him an outlaw. The thought of surrender, however, still revolted him. Besides, he felt personally, if not formally, obligated to Davis. This first decision was easy for him, but explaining his position was paramount. He immediately wrote Johnston to say that while under direct orders from the secretary of war he had learned of Johnston's surrender. Additionally, he noted that he had not been with the army during the latest round of negotiations. "I beg most respectfully to say that I do not regard myself as embraced in the capitulation. It is due to you, as well as myself, that this explanation should be made. I will add that if the Secretary of War regards me as embraced in your terms, or desires me to accept them, I shall at once disband my men."[45]

This last phrase represented the second choice Hampton had to make. The success of his mission might depend on those renegade Confederate veterans who had violated orders and refused to surrender. Should Hampton lead them on to Charlotte and then to Texas, or should he discourage them from becoming outlaws?

By midnight, just one hour after arriving in Hillsborough, Hampton was in the saddle, with several of his staff and seventeen scouts and couriers riding alongside. Writing to Johnston again, he asked "most respectfully" for permission to go over his head and submit his case to Secretary Breckenridge. To Breckenridge, he wrote: "You gave me orders to move on the 25th. On return I find army surrendered. I think I am free. What is your decision?"[46]

At sunrise Hampton overtook his men who had bolted rather than surrender. He explained to them that while he was under orders from President Davis, "and therefore free to join him," they were included in the surrender. He knew "they were willing to share [his] fate," but if they disobeyed Johnston now they would be considered outlaws. Hampton then bade his men farewell. He remembered the meeting as "a most painful interview" and admitted years later to shedding tears.[47] The men of Hart's Battery, he said, "threw themselves upon their . . . guns" and "wept like children."[48] J. Fred Waring wrote in his diary that Hampton's speech "was the most affecting I ever listened to. There was not a dry eye in the Brigade."[49] Afterward Hampton and his entourage of two dozen men rode on toward Charlotte.[50]

At some point during his journey on April 27, Hampton received a reply from Johnston, who objected to Hampton's use of the word "surrender" in his letter. Johnston preferred the word "convention." Hampton wrote again, first apologizing for his mistake in terminology. Then he explained his position more fully. Hampton wanted no one, especially his friend Johnston, to consider his actions dishonorable or illegal:

> I wish solely to have my own record right, and if you will consider the position in which I find myself placed, you will see how great is my embarrassment. By your advice I went to consult with the President, the armistice having been annulled. After full conference with him, a plan was agreed on to enable him to leave the country. He charged me with the execution of this plan. . . . On my return here I find myself not only powerless to assist him, but placed myself in a position of great delicacy. I must either leave him to his fate, without an effort to avert it, or subject myself to possible censure by not accepting the terms of the convention you have made. If I do not accompany him I shall never cease to reproach myself, and if I go with him I may go under the ban of outlawry. I choose the latter, because I believe it to be my duty to do so. . . . I shall not ask a man to go with me. Should any join me, they will be stragglers like myself and, like myself, willing to sacrifice everything for the cause and for our Government.[51]

Hampton also received a reply from Breckenridge, endorsing the course he had already taken. In the opinion of the Confederate government, Hampton was free to join Jefferson Davis, but his men fell under the terms of the surrender. Meanwhile, Joe Wheeler was in a similar position. He too had been absent when the surrender terms were signed, and he and a body of several hundred men were also on their way to link up with Davis and move southwest. Starting from Greensboro, however, Wheeler had a significant head start on Hampton.[52]

Hampton, his exhausted staff, and two dozen broken-down horses arrived in Charlotte on the afternoon of May 1 after a grueling, 130-mile, five-day journey. There they learned that the remnants of Davis's government had already fled farther in the direction of Yorkville, South Carolina. This was the up-country town where Mary Hampton, the Hampton sisters, and the children had been staying since becoming refugees. Hampton ordered his men to rest and to rejoin him the next day, while he rode on to Yorkville, thirty-five miles away. Not knowing that Davis had already left Yorkville for Abbeville, the fugitive general rode alone through the night. He swam his horse across the Catawba River in the dark. At 2:00 A.M. he appeared at the door of the house where his wife was staying.[53]

Mary Hampton was shocked at her husband's "broken appearance." Hungry, wet, tired, and discouraged, he must have been the picture of exhaustion. Mary pleaded with him not to go on. In desperation she sent an urgent message to Wheeler, who had arrived in town the day before, asking him to call on her in the morning and intercede with her husband. Wheeler chivalrously complied. During their meeting, Mary insisted that her husband was in no condition to continue riding after Davis. Seeing Hampton, Wheeler agreed that his superior was "harassed in mind, and worn in body"; he finally convinced him to stay in Yorkville while Wheeler rode on in search of the president. As Wheeler recalled, "He had a family, and his vast business interests, which had been left to others for four years, demanded his attention. I explained that it was very different with me, as I had no such obligations. He finally yielded."[54]

In a very real sense, it was Mary Hampton who brought an end to her husband's Civil War. Had she insisted, or even suggested, that Hampton fight on, chivalry's code would have left him no choice but to continue the search for Davis and to fight on to Texas. Although no one recorded the exact words of the late-night conversation between husband and wife, it is clear that she wished him not to continue. Chivalry gave her the right to demand male protection and to imply, at least, that Hampton's leaving her and the children and fighting on to Texas would be a dereliction of duty, not a fulfillment of it. Going away to fight to protect all that was dear made sense to Hampton in 1861, but now he would be leaving his wife and children as refugees in enemy-held territory. Besides Kit, their only armed protectors would be the men of Sherman's army, men who considered Hampton a fugitive from justice, if not a war criminal. Would they use Hampton's family members as hostages? Just because we know it did not happen does not mean that the Hamptons would not have to consider it a possibility.

Mary Hampton was also astute enough to know that, to her husband, the verdict of other warriors would be just as important as hers. Her appeal to Wheeler allowed the younger man to demonstrate his chivalry by acceding to her opinions and her wishes, to demonstrate his superior vigor and stamina, and to assume the role of Davis's senior military commander. With both his wife and a fellow officer assuring him that there was no dishonor, Hampton agreed to stay in Yorkville, perhaps telling himself that the delay was only temporary. He sent a letter with Wheeler for Davis and asked Wheeler to tell the Confederate president that if there were any way in the future "in which he could serve him, he would do so to the last."[55] Hampton's men rejoined him that day, May 2, and he sent two couriers after Davis. They, too, failed to find him.[56]

The truth was that Hampton's Confederate service was over. That probably became obvious to him over the course of the day, as he regained strength and cleared the cobwebs from his exhausted mind. Now that Mary Hampton and Joe Wheeler had absolved him of the shame of laying down his sword, he would have to absolve himself. The Hamptons of another generation had never given up, even when South Carolina was overrun by the enemy. They had been the ultimate victors, securing their nation's independence. Their legacy—and the code of honor ingrained in Hampton since he was a boy—called for death before dishonor, for sacrificing one's life before submitting to tyranny. And what about Preston, Frank, and all the others who had paid the ultimate price, who had given their lives—only for the survivors to surrender to the likes of William T. Sherman?

On the other hand, Hampton had originally gone to war to protect and preserve all that he could of his antebellum life. Most of it was in shambles, but he still had Mary, Wade, Sally, little McDuffie, Daisy, and Alfred. If he fought on to Texas and Mexico, he probably would never see them again; he would be cut off from the joys of domestic life forever. Mary convinced him that there was no shame, that surrender could be reconciled with the demands of chivalry and paternalism. Chivalry demanded valor, but it also demanded that men be protectors and providers. Mary persuaded her husband that he was now obligated to stay in South Carolina, rather than fight to the death or live as an outlaw in another land. She needed his protection; so did the children and his sisters. They had no home and no money, and, as far as Hampton could tell, could count on no legal protection in the wake of wartime anarchy. Wade IV would need his father's help to get a decent start in life and carry on the Hampton name. The patriarch would have to salvage what was left of his estate, find free black laborers for his cotton fields, build a new house, somehow redeem his promissory notes, and save himself from bankruptcy. Based on the terms Grant and Sherman had given Lee and Johnston, he could at least hope to avoid the hangman's noose. Maybe he could even regain his citizenship.

It was time to repair, restore, and redeem what could be salvaged of the Hamptons' life—but this time through peace, not war.

HIS SOLEMN OBLIGATION
1865–1866

Hampton's former subordinate, Matthew Calbraith Butler, said that he returned home after the surrender to Sherman "with one leg gone, a wife and three children to support, seventy emancipated slaves, a debt of $15,000, and in [my] pocket $1.75."[1] As disheartening as Butler's prospects were, the situation of his old commander was, if anything, more desperate. With a wife, five children, and four unmarried sisters to support, Hampton had lost his home as well as the ancestral mansion of his grandfather to arsonists. His vast estate in Mississippi had been obliterated. Though he still had title to his land, his debts now far exceeded the value of his ruined plantations, and his slave property, formerly his collateral, was gone. Paying off his debts would prove an insurmountable task. The hometown to which he returned was largely in ashes as a result of the terrible February fire. He had even lost his citizenship. Added to these disasters were the empty places in the family circle left by brother Frank, sister-in-law Sally, and most of all his "beautiful boy," Preston. One resident who saw him soon after his return to Columbia said that "General Hampton . . . looks crushed."[2] Hampton's world had fallen apart.

The years 1865 and 1866 were a bewildering, chaotic time for all southerners—black and white. Hampton himself had many urgent personal, financial, and political issues to tackle simultaneously, and at first he vacillated on how to handle them. Would he seek a "pardon" from his enemies and pursue a role in rebuilding his home state, or would he join other ex-Confederates in making a new start in Brazil, free from "Yankee tyranny?" How would he rebuild his fortune or even pay his debts? What type of relationship would he strive for with freed African Americans, particularly his own former slaves? Would he attempt reconciliation with the North? Was reconciliation even possible? How could it occur and still leave room for vindication for his dead comrades, his dead son, and the cause for which they died?

Amid the confusing course of events in 1865 and 1866, several themes emerged that would shape the rest of Hampton's postwar life. First, he would attempt to guide his own behavior by the chivalric gentlemanly code that he had learned as a young man. He would conscientiously try to fulfill his promises and to abide by the agreements made with other white men and with ex-slaves, and he would demand that the North do the same. The chivalric code also demanded that he strive manfully to provide for and protect his own, whether it be his family or home state. Second, Hampton consistently sought a partial restoration of the political and social system that South Carolina had known since his youth. Though he accepted emancipation and was one of the first white men in the South to advocate limited suffrage for black men, Hampton still envisioned a system in which educated and propertied elites governed, while protecting the basic rights of lesser citizens, white and black. In regard to black men, Hampton's paternalism was tied up with his racism. He wished to reestablish patron-client relationships between white elites and ex-slaves, relationships that rested unabashedly on the assumption of black inferiority but nevertheless placed moral obligations on men like himself as gentleman-patrons.

A third emerging theme was Hampton's deep bitterness and distrust of "Yankees," the arrogant white men of the North who had played such an important part in the unraveling of his antebellum life. In Hampton's mind, Yankees stole, Yankees burned houses, and Yankees lied. Yankees would make false promises to black men if it would help them further humiliate their ex-Confederate foes.

Finally, Hampton continued a long search for redemption and vindication—an unending determination to vindicate the honor of his state, the Confederate cause, and his dead comrades, and to refute his enemies' portrayal of him as a "moral and financial bankrupt."[3] The sacred message of the Lost Cause would find no more militant prophet than Wade Hampton of South Carolina.

On May 2, 1865, Hampton had acceded to his wife's urgings to recuperate in Yorkville, while Joe Wheeler and some of Hampton's own men rode on in search of Jefferson Davis. For over a week, he pondered his next move and awaited events. In a May 10 letter to his aide, Captain Rawlins Lowndes, he urged the young officer to lie low. "Nothing can be done at the present . . . so I advise quiet for a time. . . . If I determine on any course, you shall hear from me."[4] Davis, however, was captured that very day, ending the possibility that the fight for independence might continue. On hearing the news, Hampton returned briefly to Columbia. He surveyed the ruins of Millwood, Woodlands, and his own home on Diamond Hill, where he resided temporarily in the overseer's cottage with his former slave Kit Goodwyn. His family, he decided, would have to stay at the lodge in Cashiers Valley, North Carolina, while he contracted with carpenters and ex-slaves to build a new structure on the Millwood site and a simple cottage on Diamond Hill.[5]

While in Columbia, Hampton took advantage of the opportunity to apply for parole. On May 15 he wrote Major General Mansfield Lovell, the Confederate officer detailed by Union authorities to receive and transmit parole applications. "Having been absent when the Military Convention between Generals Johnston and Sherman was held, engaged on special duty by the Hon Sec. of War," Hampton explained, "I did not sign the obligation given by the other officers of Genl. Johnston's Army." Hampton was now ready to sign the parole previously offered by Sherman. It is necessary to read the terms of Hampton's parole agreement, for he considered them all-important. These were the terms by which he laid down his arms and sought protection against charges of treason:

Lieutenant General Wade Hampton, P.A.C.S.

has given his solemn obligation not to take up arms against the Government of the United States until properly released from his obligation; & is permitted to return to his home, not to be disturbed by the United States Authorities so long as he observes this obligation and obeys the laws in force where he may reside.[6]

Hampton suspected that more specific conditions were forthcoming, but for now he had only to lay down his arms and obey the laws of Columbia and South Carolina as they were then written. Six years later he would cite the wording of his parole as the basis of the peace between North and South.[7] As early as September 1866, he strongly urged other Confederate veterans to strictly comply with their parole agreements, including the "laws of the land." Despite his conviction that the South had been right to defend its interpretation of the U.S. Constitution in 1861, Hampton said that "we should fulfil [sic] all the obligations we have entered into, to the letter, keeping our faith so clear that no shadow of dishonor can fall on us."[8]

Two weeks after Hampton signed his parole agreement, President Andrew Johnson modified the simple arrangement with his amnesty proclamation of May 29, 1866. The terms were still relatively generous, but they represented a change from the original terms of Hampton's parole. Hampton was no longer cleared of wrongdoing. Johnson extended amnesty for the charges of "conspiracy" and "rebellion" to most ex-Confederates, exempting fourteen classes of citizens. Hampton was ineligible for amnesty on two counts: he had held a Confederate rank above that of colonel, and he owned over $20,000 worth of property. Men who fell into this category would have to apply personally to the president for pardon. If he did apply, and President Johnson approved his application, he would be bound to "support and defend the Constitution of the United States, and the Union of the States thereunder," and "faithfully support all laws and proclamations which have been made during the existing rebellion with reference to the Emancipation of slaves—SO HELP ME GOD."[9] In return, he would be immune from charges of treason and from confiscation of his property. Hampton hesitated before bowing to this new mandate from his conquerors.

Rather than immediately authorize new elections for South Carolina, Johnson appointed provisional governors for the ex-Confederate states. These governors were to call constitutional conventions to draft new state constitutions. As long as the new constitutions met Johnson's requirements—repudiating secession, repudiating all Confederate debts, and abolishing slavery—the states would presumably be readmitted to the Union. Johnson's plan said nothing about whether the freedmen would be allowed to vote; this question was still unresolved. Northern Republicans, in fact, had not made clear demands for black suffrage and would not do so for several years. Yet some white southerners insisted that the federal executive had no constitutional authority to force states to hold constitutional conventions. Hampton agreed with them on legal grounds, but asserted that, as a "conqueror," Johnson did have that right. In mid-November he lectured his fellow South Carolinians that they had accepted Washington's "terms" and were "bound, by every dictate of honor and manliness, to abide by them honestly and to keep, in good faith, the pledges you have given."[10]

Hampton approved, at any rate, of Johnson's choice for governor, Benjamin Perry. Perry, a member of the antebellum elite, had once been Hampton's ally in attempting to prevent or delay the state's secession. Like Hampton, Perry had eventually come around to supporting the Confederate war effort and was certainly no traitor in the eyes of white Carolinians.

Still, it seems that earlier Hampton had briefly entertained the idea of fleeing federal authority and rebuilding elsewhere. A movement developed among southern ex-slaveholders to establish a colony in Brazil, and many expected Hampton to lead it. There is in Hampton's papers a July 25 letter from an agent in New York offering to arrange the emigration of southerners for a fee. The detailed letter reads as if the writer assumed that Hampton was very interested in the idea. Only two days after this letter was written, however, Hampton wrote to the *Columbia Phoenix* urging his neighbors to reject the idea of emigration. Citing the lack of "all mail facilities," Hampton used the *Phoenix* to answer the "numerous communications" that had been addressed to him on the subject. "The very fact that our State is passing through so terrible an ordeal as the present," he asserted, "should cause her sons to cling the more closely to her." Hampton advised that "all . . . who can do so" should swear allegiance to the United States, for if "the best men of our country" refused to accept amnesty or pardon, the future of the state would rest in the hands of those "who would gladly pull her down to irretrievable ruin." Instead, all "true patriots" must work to restore law, peace, and "whatever liberty may be saved from the general wreck." Hampton urged the voters to elect delegates to the upcoming constitutional convention who had fought for their state, not skulkers or "politicians, who after urging war dared not encounter its hardships." (Here Hampton took a swipe at men who had questioned his patriotism when he opposed secession, but who had failed to fight during the war.) He promised that he would continue to gather information that would be useful "should we be ultimately forced to leave this country." But for the time being, he had obligations to his state, as well "personal" ones, that would not allow him "to leave the country at present."[11] These personal obligations included massive debts to be redeemed in Mississippi. Nearly two years later, he told his friend Louis T. Wigfall that those debts were the only obligations that kept him from moving away from "our poor country."[12] A conversation that Hampton had with his six-year-old niece, Lucy Hampton, summed up his attitude. Aware of the rumors swirling around her, the little girl asked her uncle if he were going to move to another country. "No my child," he gently replied. "Only rats leave a sinking ship."[13]

Hampton, then, had decided to stay in South Carolina. His daughter Sally had just married John Haskell, her longtime suitor who had lost his arm in battle, and Hampton wished to provide the couple a respectable dowry. Additionally, he had decided to support the writing of a new state constitution. Or had he? A month after urging his neighbors to send their "best men" to the convention, Hampton changed his mind. In an open letter to Columbia mayor James G. Gibbes, he asserted that the state should not abase itself by submitting a new constitution to Washington in hopes of being readmitted to the Union. "The State is either a member of the Federal Union, or it is not," he declared. If it was a member, it did not need to ask for readmission and had the right to determine its own laws and constitution. If it was not a member of the Union, then it was a conquered province or territory and should be under military law. The state should not destroy the constitution bequeathed by its fathers and adopt one "representing not the views and interests of the people of South Carolina, but those of Massachusetts." It would be better to be ruled by the bayonet than "to give your State a constitution which misrepresents . . . humiliates . . . degrades." Besides, Hampton claimed, President Johnson had mandated what sort of constitution the state must write, but he had not explicitly promised that such a constitution would allow the state to return to the Union. The North had not invited South Carolina's return to the Union, nor had the authorities in Washington "manifested great zeal in the restoration of that Union for which they have professedly been fighting for the last four years." In Hampton's mind, the North sought the South's subjugation, not its reconciliation, and the South should not respond by licking the conqueror's boots. Hampton's letter clearly demonstrated his bitterness toward the North and his determination to see "home rule" for South Carolina.[14]

South Carolina held the constitutional convention anyway, and Hampton did not attend. Yet the mood of the delegates was as defiant as Hampton's. The new constitution contained a few liberal reforms, such as providing for the popular election of the governor and eliminating all property qualifications for office holding. Hampton most likely opposed those reforms. The new constitution did not, however, repudiate the state's debts accumulated while a member of the Confederacy, as Johnson demanded. And rather than repudiate the doctrine of secession, the convention only reasserted the state's autonomy by repealing its own ordinance of secession. Instead of abolishing slavery, the convention simply noted that since the federal government had emancipated the slaves, slavery no longer existed in South Carolina.

Shortly afterward, the reconstituted state legislature did ratify the Thirteenth Amendment outlawing slavery, but it also acted to restrict the freedom of black South Carolinians. In laws called "Black Codes," the state attempted to regulate the relations between landlords, or "masters," and tenants, or "servants." The laws mandated humane treatment by masters and allowed blacks to buy and sell property, sue and be sued, and enjoy legal protections of their persons and property. They did not, however, confer voting rights on blacks. They forbade servants from leaving their master's premises without permission, and they made "vagrancy" a crime punishable by imprisonment and twelve months' hard labor. Magistrates were to bind orphans over as "apprentices" to white masters, to be released on reaching adulthood. Now that black people could no longer be property, South Carolina whites attempted to create a new system that would retain much control over their labor. African Americans, supposedly simpleminded and childlike, were to be neither slaves nor full citizens, but the legal wards of white landowners.[15]

The state's other task was to elect a new governor to replace provisional governor Perry. A state convention had met over the summer to nominate candidates. Showing that Hampton was already first in the hearts of his fellow white South Carolinians, convention delegates put up his name for governor. Hampton declined the nomination, saying that the northern prejudice against ex-Confederate generals would hamper his usefulness. Instead, he urged the election of former conditional Unionist James L. Orr. On October 18, however, white South Carolinians went to the polls and tried to elect Hampton anyway, as a write-in candidate. Hampton went to the polling sites in Columbia, the seat of Richland District, and personally begged his fellow townsmen not to vote for him; as a result, Richland was the only district that went heavily for Orr. The initial returns indicated that, despite his wishes, he had won the election.[16]

Hampton was extremely upset. Not only did he want no part of overseeing South Carolina's groveling return to the Union, he was still not even a citizen. He had finally applied for a presidential pardon, with Perry's endorsement, on August 4, but the U.S. president still had not responded. On seeing the election returns, Perry urgently pressed Andrew Johnson on the matter of Hampton's pardon, citing obvious reasons. Perry recalled that Hampton, "very much annoyed," went to him for advice. Perry told Hampton that "he would have to serve if elected, no matter what the sacrifice to him or how repugnant to his feelings." The state's welfare depended on its speedy reconstruction, and this "was an appeal to his honor and patriotism which he could not resist," Perry recalled. "Most reluctantly he consented to follow my advice."[17]

Johnson telegraphed Perry that Hampton's pardon was on the way. Soon, however, it turned out that Orr had defeated Hampton after all, by only a few hundred votes. Mortified that he had nearly lost to a man who was not running, Orr thought of declining the office until Perry convinced him that he must take it. For his part, Hampton would allow no one to say that he had wrangled a pardon from Washington by a sneaky trick. He asked Perry to inform the president that "as his pardon had been issued under a wrong impression [that Hampton had been elected governor], he should decline to accept it." Perry refused to write this letter but thought that "this was certainly punctiliously honorable on the part of General Hampton."[18]

The whole affair revealed the obstinate attitude of white South Carolina, as well as Wade Hampton's "punctilious" sense of honor. As James DeCaradeuc boasted, "Our little State is still defiant. Our Convention . . . has said nothing about the repudiation of all debts. . . . The Convention has not declared the act of Secession null & void . . . and lastly, our people in the late election for Governor have shown their spirit in the vote for Gen. Wade Hampton."[19] Believing that Hampton had won the governorship, the New York Times editorialized on October 30 that his election did "not encourage confidence in the loyalty and fidelity" of South Carolina to the Union.[20] Later in his career, Hampton would be known for his moderate and conciliatory views. For now, however, he was a symbol of white defiance.

Another vital, unsettled issue in the summer of 1865 was the future place of freedmen in the South. Abraham Lincoln's Emancipation Proclamation and military events had secured their freedom, but key questions remained. Would they be full citizens? Would they be allowed to vote? (The Civil Rights Act of 1866 and the Fourteenth and Fifteenth amendments were still in the future, and as yet no one knew what role the national government would play in securing their full citizenship.) Were illiterate men of African descent, many whites wondered, even capable of responsible citizenship?

Hampton and other white men were skeptical. Hampton himself was willing to agree that a small, educated minority of African American men could play a limited leadership role. He accepted the reality of emancipation and would soon be one of the first and most outspoken advocates of granting suffrage to literate or land-owning blacks. By no means, though, should that limited suffrage be allowed to challenge traditional elite white control. It would, he hoped, only strengthen it. In the summer of 1865, however, Hampton was interested mainly in stability and racial harmony. Speaking to a gathering of black men just after the war, he advised them "that we both [have] to live here, and we ought to try to get along well together."[21] Speaking to Confederate veterans in the upstate village of Walhalla, Hampton preached that white men had an obligation to the freedman. "As a slave, he was faithful to us; as a freeman, let us treat him as a friend," Hampton urged. "Deal with him frankly, justly, kindly, and my word for it he will reciprocate your kindness, clinging to his old home, his own country and his former masters. If you wish to see him contented, industrious, and useful, aid him in his effort to elevate himself in the scale of civilization, and thus fit him not only to enjoy the blessings of freedom, but to appreciate its duties."[22]

The role of African Americans as a source of labor was as crucial to the South's future as their role as citizens. To make an 1866 crop, Hampton turned naturally to blacks; he was especially hopeful that his former slaves would work for him. In December 1865 he and his son Wade traveled to Mississippi to "collect the fragments of my property" and resume planting operations.[23] They had to stop at New Orleans to arrange credit with Hampton's factors, Conner & Seixas, and to purchase tools, seed, and supplies. All along the railroad, at Augusta, Montgomery, and New Orleans, crowds of people cheered Hampton, demonstrating that he was a hero to many white southerners, not just South Carolinians. While traveling upriver from New Orleans to Vicksburg, he informed Mary Fisher that the "boat is full of Yankees but William Blanton & his mother are on board, so that we have some decent people."[24]

Hampton intended to use ex-slaves from his Mississippi lands and from Columbia to plant crops at Wild Woods. Many freedpeople in Columbia had relatives among Hampton's former slaves in Mississippi. It is unclear how many slaves the Hamptons had separated from their Mississippi kin during the antebellum period and how many Wade's brother Kit had brought back East in the confusion of the Union invasion of Mississippi. Regardless, Hampton was determined that for both his benefit and theirs, he would find a way to send them out West. He asked Mary Fisher to help arrange the hiring and transportation of one hundred black laborers for himself and fifty for Wade IV. "There are a good many here," he wrote, "who have relatives in S.C. & they are very anxious that they should come out. I wish that you would see Tom Taylor & ask him to tell the negroes that their families here want them to come out & I will pay the passage of all who will come."[25]

Hampton's laborers were, in his eyes, just as inferior to white men and yet just as naturally docile as they had ever been in slavery. To a congressional subcommittee investigating conditions in the South in 1871, Hampton explained:

You gentlemen do not know the negro at all, and there is the great difficulty. You all think the negroes are actuated by the same feeling as the white men, but that is a mistake. I do not pretend to know

313

why it is, but they are not. They have been dependent for a long time; they have no provision; they have no forethought at all; they are content to live from hand to mouth . . . they are very credulous. . . . I am not speaking of the more intelligent ones, but of the great mass of laborers. I have had a great deal to do with the negroes. I have spoken kindly to them always, and all the negroes that I have living with me now, or the larger number of them, are my old slaves. I talk very freely with them. I give them the best advice I can. They talk very freely to me; and either they tell very wonderful lies or have been badly informed.[26]

Hampton very much wanted—needed, in fact—to establish good relations with his former labor force. For a brief time after his return to Wild Woods, it seemed that wish might be in danger. Hampton found that, immediately after the war, a "hanger-on" from the Union army had taken advantage of his absence and squatted on his Mississippi lands, hiring Hampton's ex-slaves to work for him.[27] As Hampton attempted to negotiate labor contracts with these workers for the coming year, they asked to know his intentions. As he later related: "They came up to see me. They went down to see this [squatter], who had moved away, and came back and asked me for the truth. They said this man . . . had told them that if they hired to me they would all be branded and be put back into slavery for five years. I said, 'Are you fools enough to believe that?' A man answered, 'I don't know; this man told us so.' I asked them, 'Did I ever tell you a lie in my life?' They said, 'No, sir; you never did.' I assured them that it was not so."[28]

Undoubtedly, long experience with white masters had taught Hampton's slaves not to question a white man's word to his face. Perhaps the story of their conversation with the white squatter was indeed a "wonderful lie" designed by Hampton's old hands to confirm whether he intended to honor their new status. Still, his labor force initially went to work for him willingly enough. Hampton was pleased. After his return to Wild Woods in December 1865, he had noted that "the negroes all seem delighted to see me."[29] In June 1866, he wrote: "The negroes are working well & my crop is very good. The only hands in the country who work, are Kit's & mine. They give no trouble & behave well."[30]

Hampton, in fact, was less concerned about his black labor force than he was about "interference" from "Yankees." One interloper, of course, had already tried to farm Hampton's lands as his own. At the end of January, Hampton wrote his sister that he hoped "to make something this year, if the Yankees do not interfere with me. They seem disposed to give me some trouble & my places & that of Mr. Davis, are the only ones in the State not given up. But as I am in possession, I hope that I can get on." It is unclear exactly who Hampton was referring to as "the Yankees," but they were probably either U.S. military authorities or agents of the Freedmen's Bureau whom Hampton suspected of seeking to appropriate his land and redistribute it to the freedmen.[31]

Reorganizing his labor force was only one part, and perhaps the simplest part, of Hampton's attempt to restore some semblance of his prewar fortunes. He had emerged from the war saddled with huge debts. Before the conflict Hampton had unwisely extended himself, buying land and borrowing too fast. He had trouble paying all the notes due on his mortgages; bad weather and flooding on the Mississippi in the late 1850s had only made the situation worse. Then he had inherited $400,000 of his father's debt in 1858. Donating his entire cotton crop to the Confederacy in 1861 had hurt as well, with the result that when more notes came due during the war years, he was unable to pay them.

His largest creditor was Stephen Duncan, a native Pennsylvanian who had become one of the leading slaveholders in Mississippi. Duncan and Hampton were neighbors and friends, and Duncan had helped finance Hampton's prewar expansion. During the war Duncan had remained loyal to the Union and, whether deliberately or not, profited from the misfortune of his Confederate neighbors. At one point Hampton considered him "a contemptible traitor."[32] By the end of the war, Duncan held notes worth over $1.3 million from other planters in the region, Wade Hampton among them. He then pressed his debtors and obtained vast landholdings from them.[33]

After the war, Hampton and Duncan reconciled. When Duncan died in 1867, his son Stephen Duncan Jr. took over his father's debts. Hampton still had to borrow money from others to keep the Duncans at bay until he could produce some good crops. His lands were his only remaining asset, and he hoped to make them profitable again so he could sell some of them and satisfy his creditors. Hampton's explanation to his friend and legal counselor, Armistead Burt, summarized the plight of many planters: "The unsettled aspect of affairs, has made land here, valueless, for the present, & some of my creditors have brought suit against me. . . . I am only solicitous to serve the interests of my creditors & to protect my name from any stain."[34] Hampton found it "repugnant . . . to take advantage of the Bankrupt Act," but by late 1868 he had no choice.[35] Over one million dollars in debt, he could afford to pay neither the principal nor the interest on his loans. He declared bankruptcy in December in U.S. District Court in Mississippi. At this point, Stephen Duncan Jr. saved Hampton from total ruin, as he did several of his other debtors. Duncan assumed over $113,000 of Hampton's notes to the bank. He then paid Hampton $500 for all of his Mississippi lands and forgave the notes he had assumed. This arrangement kept Hampton's properties off the auction block and allowed him to work and live on them in the hope of gradually buying them back.[36]

Back in Columbia, much of Hampton's furniture and household effects were auctioned on the courthouse steps, bringing $118.85. His 108-acre Diamond Hill estate also landed on the auction block. Apparently out of respect for Hampton, none of his neighbors made a bid. Hampton, the lone bidder, was able to buy it back for $100.00. At least he, Mary, and the children still had a place to live.[37]

While many of Hampton's friends sympathized with him in his distress and humiliation, political enemies used them for their advantage. Details of his bankruptcy proceedings in Mississippi soon appeared in the *Washington National Republican* under the headline, "Wade Hampton's Financial Intrigues: A Specimen of the Transactions of a Chivalric Southron—Maids, Wives, and Widows Mourn Because of His Villainy, and Refuse to be Comforted—A Moral and Financial Bankrupt." The paper sneered that "[Southerners] know that Hampton systematically entered into various schemes of plunder after the War; that he robbed widows and distressed orphans; but forgetting all else save his inordinate disloyalty, they simply worship him."[38]

Hampton attempted to bear his financial troubles stoically. He almost never complained of his poverty until the 1890s, when it became clear that even after two decades he had not recovered enough to provide well for his children. He did nourish, however, a passionate desire to pay his creditors and salvage his good name. It was, he confided to a former army subordinate, the "hope of my life."[39] Paying his debts and protecting his name from any "stain" was just one crucial part of his search for vindication in the postwar years.

CHAPTER 23

HAMPTON, SHERMAN, AND THE YANKEES

Another part of Hampton's quest for vindication was defending himself against an accusation made by William T. Sherman. Here Hampton's quest for personal vindication, instinct for chivalric home defense, and hatred of Yankees reinforced one another. After much of Columbia had burned to the ground the night that Sherman's men arrived in the city, most southerners, including Columbians, assumed that Sherman either ordered the destruction or refused to take steps to control it. A modern historian has since concluded that the burning of Columbia was an accident due to high winds, drunken soldiers and civilians, the breakdown of Confederate command and control in the city, and overall confusion. Sherman, however, blamed Hampton, citing the February 16, 1865, order from P. G. T. Beauregard, transmitted over Hampton's signature, to burn the cotton in the city. Hampton, of course, had later convinced Beauregard that the order was unwise and had countermanded it. Sherman seems to have been aware of this fact but ignored it in his April 4 official report on the South Carolina campaign. Sherman's report appeared in northern newspapers in early June 1865. "And without hesitation," Sherman declared, "I charge Gen Wade Hampton with having burned his own city of Columbia, not with malicious intent, or as the manifestation of a silly 'Roman stoicism,' but from folly and want of sense, in filling it with lint cotton and tinder."[1]

Sherman's accusation enraged Hampton more than any other event in his life. Probably he was already sensitive to the humiliation of being unable to save his hometown when he was in command of its defenses. The highest duty of the chivalric knight was home defense. Sherman's charge was not just that he had failed to defend his community, but that he had in fact destroyed it. It was the ultimate slander. Hampton responded immediately in a long letter to the *New York Day Book*. The letter was at once a point-by-point refutation of Sherman's charge and a furious counterattack on Sherman's actions and character. Hampton, of course, pointed out that he had countermanded Beauregard's order to burn the cotton in Columbia's streets and then given explicit orders that it not be burned. Then, citing the testimony of other residents and a recently published pamphlet by one Columbia citizen, Hampton charged   317 (and most Columbia citizens agreed) that (1) Sherman had violated his personal pledge to Mayor Goodwyn to protect the city from destruction by deliberately setting fires, (2) Sherman's men had pillaged and plundered the city, and violated the persons of women, (3) Sherman's men had burned churches, (4) while firemen had struggled to extinguish the fires, some of Sherman's men had deliberately cut the fire hoses with axes, and (5) Sherman had done nothing to stop or punish these atrocities. Hampton and his neighbors considered it outrageous that Sherman would deny setting fire to Columbia when he clearly was responsible for the burning of "Barnwell, Blackville, Graham, Bamberg, Buford's Bridge, Orangeburg, Lexington, Allston, Pomaria, Winnsboro, Blackstock, Society Hill, Camden and Cheraw. . . . Along the line of march, followed by him there is scarcely one house left standing . . . and yet he dares to declare solemnly, that he did not burn Columbia."[2] In words that would have incited a duel in the South, Hampton explicitly called Sherman a liar and a violator of ladies.[3]

Hampton's zeal to expose "Sherman's lies" occupied him for over three more decades, and the controversy raged nearly as long. In the spring of 1866 the city of Columbia formed a commission to investigate the fire. Hampton acquired a statement from Beauregard reinforcing his version of events and submitted it to the commission. With other newspapers fanning the controversy, Hampton even strove to have his case made on the floor of the U.S. Senate. Because South Carolina still had no senator, Hampton asked Democratic senator Reverdy Johnson of Maryland to read his letter to the lawmakers. Bitterly noting the South's lack of representation in the Senate, Hampton's letter explained that he had countermanded the order to burn the cotton and asked Congress to appoint a committee to investigate the truth. Johnson read the letter and moved that it be referred to the Committee on Military Affairs.[4]

Sherman's brother, Senator John Sherman of Ohio, angrily denounced "the charge of this most impudent rebel."[5] Defending his brother, he read letters from other Union officers indicating that the Confederates were to blame for the fire. Senator William Pitt Fessenden of Maine argued that the reading of private letters regarding a private dispute had no place in the Senate. Senator John Conness then remarked that a man [Hampton] who would destroy the U.S. government would certainly destroy a city. In the face of this firestorm, Reverdy Johnson withdrew his motion and the matter was dropped. Outside the South, then, Hampton's cry for vindication would not even be heard.

Union veterans continued to defend their old chief and blame Hampton for the fire, while asserting that Columbia deserved to burn anyway. Similar comments by Sherman did nothing to lessen his guilt in the eyes of South Carolinians. The Union general declared that if he "had made up my mind to burn Columbia, I would have burnt it with no more feeling than I would a common prairie dog village, but I did not do it!"[6] In reference to the burning of the town of Blackville, South Carolina, Sherman admitted that his troops may have been responsible, but that Blackville "was a dirty little hole anyway."[7] In an August 1866 issue of *Harper's New Monthly Magazine*, former Union officer George W. Nichols cited Sherman's official report and a few Union soldiers' accounts as proof that Hampton was responsible for the fire. Nichols asserted that Hampton's attempt to pin the blame on Sherman added "a deeper shame to a dishonored name."[8]

South Carolinians who lived through the fire found the northern attempts to excuse Sherman and blame Hampton both unconvincing and outrageous.[9] Columbia resident James McCarter responded to Nichols's *Harper's* article in the October 1866 issue. Striving for a conciliatory tone, McCarter accepted the possibility that Sherman did not intend to burn the city, but that his troops and the high winds were responsible. McCarter went on to defend Hampton, asking what was so dishonorable in Hampton's attempt to relieve himself of the false charge and "deep disgrace" of having burned his own city. Indeed, McCarter demanded: "When and where was General Hampton's name ever dishonored? . . . Here in Columbia he is known as a quiet, unpretending gentleman, the good master, the good citizen, the good man—courteous, kind, considerate, and brave. His escutcheon is untarnished, his good name a household word, his reputation the common property of our citizens."[10] Others were less diplomatic than McCarter. The final report of the investigative commission in Columbia featured many accounts by Columbians indignantly accusing Sherman and his men. In 1866 D. H. Trezevant of Columbia published a thirty-three-page pamphlet entitled "The Burning of Columbia, S.C.: A Review of Northern Assertions and Southern Facts."[11] Another angry Columbian was seventy-two-year-old Agnes Law, whose three-story brick house was deliberately set afire by four Union soldiers whom she had fed earlier and allowed to nap on her sofa. Law told investigators: "I have been for over fifty years a member of the Presbyterian Church. I cannot live long. I shall meet General Sherman and his soldiers at the bar of God, and I give this testimony against them in full view of that dread tribunal."[12] Clearly, Wade Hampton was not the only Columbian who shared a deep sense of violation and a thirst for ultimate vindication.

In 1873 a joint U.S.-British investigation of the Columbia fire concluded that the U.S. government was not responsible for the destruction of Columbia and resulting property damage, though neither did it blame Confederate forces. Hampton and Sherman both testified, as did numerous other officers and eyewitnesses—white and black. As far as Hampton was concerned, the hearings were further proof of Yankee dishonesty. Sherman stuck to his original story, though in his subsequently published memoirs he retreated somewhat from his charge against Hampton. He admitted that in his report he had "distinctly charged [the fire to Hampton] and confess that I did so pointedly, to shake the faith of his people in him, for he was in my opinion boastful and professed to be the special champion of South Carolina."[13] Hampton pointed out another statement in Sherman's account: "Having utterly ruined Columbia, the [Federal] right wing began its march northward, toward Winnsboro."[14] Hampton read the sentence as an unintended but revealing admission of guilt.

Then there was the testimony of Union general Oliver O. Howard, one of Sherman's key subordinates and an eyewitness to the fire. In 1865 Howard, in immediate command of the Union troops in Columbia, had endorsed Sherman's charge that Confederate forces started the fire. On January 9, 1867, however, Howard was in the office of Governor James Orr, along with Mayor Gibbes, John S. Preston, and a reporter named F. DeFontaine, when Hampton entered the room. On seeing Howard, Hampton immediately asked, "General Howard, who burned Columbia?"[15] Howard stood up, took his hand, and admitted that he was "fully mistaken" in the matter of the Columbia fire—that he had seen Federal troops starting fires.[16] Years later, every man present remembered this conversation in virtually the same way, except Howard. While on the stand during the Joint Commission's hearings, Howard's memory suddenly became fuzzy when reminded of the meeting. After further questioning, he finally concluded, "I think I stated that the Confederate troops set it on fire." Noting the discrepancy, Hampton bitterly remarked to the *Baltimore Enquirer*, "Strange things do happen when any United States officer who was present is questioned about the burning of Columbia."[17]

In Hampton's eyes, Yankees did more than lie, steal, and burn. They also broke agreements. After South Carolina rewrote its constitution in the fall of 1865 and formed a new state government, many citizens felt that they had met President Andrew Johnson's requirements in the spirit of the U.S. Constitution. If the constitutional model used were the agreement of 1789, they had. That 1789 arrangement had granted far more room for state sovereignty and had allowed the states, not the national government, to determine the limits of citizenship for the people within its borders. The new South Carolina constitution, however, did not reflect the results of the war and certainly not the unwritten, new constitutional understanding prevalent in the North in 1865. Nor did the Black Codes. No one, in fact, was quite sure yet of what that new constitutional understanding was, except that it would prohibit slavery and secession.[18] All Hampton had known in May was that he had to swear "not to take up arms" against the United States and obey "the laws in force where he may reside."[19] Still, he believed that his state had now met not only the terms laid down by Generals Grant and Sherman, but also the ones dictated by President Johnson. In November 1865 he wrote: "It is our duty to support the President of the United States so long as he manifests a disposition to restore all our rights as a sovereign State."[20] A deal was a deal.

While other Carolinians exulted over their defiant stand and Hampton lectured on "sovereign States," Republicans in the North fumed. Congress refused to seat South Carolina's delegates. Political observer Sidney Andrews interpreted Hampton's statement as "cool arrogance" and Hampton himself as "the very exemplar of [South Carolinians'] spirit—of their proud and narrow and domineering spirit." In the South, Andrews claimed, there was scarcely even a "pretence of loyalty."[21]

Determined that the blood of 360,000 Union soldiers would finally bring real political and social change to the South, Congress took the initiative away from President Johnson when it overrode his veto and passed the Civil Rights Bill in April 1866. Designed to nullify the Black Codes of the southern states, the bill clearly defined blacks as citizens with the right to buy, sell, enter into contracts, and give evidence in court just as any white person; it also gave federal officers, deputies, and agents of the Freedmen's Bureau broad enforcement authorities. Even before Congress acted, the U.S. military commander in South Carolina, General Daniel Sickles, had declared South Carolina's Black Codes null and void on January 1. Federal authority trumped state authority, and Congress, not the states, now defined who were citizens.[22]

Congress made the point even more forcefully by passing a Fourteenth Amendment to the Constitution on June 13, which it then submitted to the states for ratification. Saying that "No State shall" deprive any person of life, liberty, or property without due process of law, it was the first federal amendment to instruct the states in what they could or could not do. The amendment also prohibited any former state or federal officeholder who had sworn to uphold the U.S. Constitution and then participated in the rebellion from holding any future state or national office. This affected Hampton. Having been paroled once and then pardoned once, he was again barred from holding public office.

Clearly the insult, humiliation, and wrong that Hampton believed he was suffering were both personal and political. To Hampton, Sherman's accusations against him about the burning of Columbia, for instance, were one in a piece with what he considered the North's tyrannical treatment of the white South. Sherman's "lies" came ultimately from the same source as the North's broken agreements: Yankee treachery toward an honorable, defeated foe. In August 1866 Hampton wrote a long open letter to President Andrew Johnson complaining of what he regarded as the North's political oppression of the South thus far. But the letter also dealt with matters that were not purely political. These matters—the honor, virtue, and courage of white southerners—did have implications for politics and were sometimes expressed in political terms. Hampton lectured Johnson, for example, that native white Republicans, often ex-Confederates who now sided with their conquerors, could not be trusted by anyone. He claimed that the past valor of Confederate veterans proved that they were the ones who Johnson must entrust with honest leadership. They had demonstrated their character on the battlefield. The majority of the white South, he claimed,

> is loyal. By this I mean that she intends to abide by the laws of the land honestly; to fullfil [sic] all her obligations faithfully, and to keep her word sacredly. And I assert that the North has no right to demand more of her. You have no right to ask or to expect that she will at once profess unbounded love for the Union, from which for four years she tried to escape at the cost of her best blood and all of her treasure. Nor can you believe her to be so unnaturally hypocritical, so base as to declare that the "Flag of the Union" has already usurped in her heart the place which has so long been sacred to the "Southern Cross." The men at the South who make such professions are renegades or traitors, and they will surely betray you if you trust them.
>
> But the brave men who fought to the last in a cause which they believed, and still believe, to have been a just one, who clung to their

colors as long as they waved, and who, when their cause was lost, acknowledged their defeat and accepted the terms offered to them— as they were true to their convictions in the one case, they will prove true to their obligations [to the North] in the other. . . .

[The South] regards herself as fully the peer in honor, in reputation, in character and in glory of any other portion of the Republic, and she will never . . . tarnish her name by inscribing on her escutcheon, with her own hand, that she has been guilty.

"I'll not disown
A single pulse-throb, nor a single breath."[23]

Hampton's political viewpoint was obviously based on his own understanding of the war. The argument above was in fact an early statement of the legend of the Lost Cause—the body of facts, myths, and legends by which southerners attempted to understand and explain their Confederate experience. Clearly, the Lost Cause could be part of a political argument, but it was also a statement by which Hampton sought personal and collective vindication for himself and those who had fought alongside him. As Hampton's misfortunes were both political and personal, so was his response. Standing literally in the ashes of Columbia and among the graves of loved ones and former comrades, Hampton and others sought to give their experiences meaning and moral relevance.

Modern historians have been increasingly aware of how the mythology of the Lost Cause could serve to justify the restoration of white supremacy in the postwar South. There has been a growing tendency, in fact, to assume that white southerners invented and promulgated the Lost Cause in a conscious, deliberate attempt to rewrite the history of the war, the Old South, and slavery. Catherine Clinton, for example, has charged that white southerners consciously participated in a "conspiracy" to "conjure up a dream world" that obscured the misery lived by their slaves.[24] This was only one part of white southerners' attempts after the war to "rebuild their region . . . by laying a foundation for historical revisionism. To many, this involved reconfiguring facts to conform to political agendas."[25] Similarly, David Blight has argued that the Lost Cause was a deliberate, cynical attempt to reinterpret the real meaning of the war—that is, emancipation—and replace it with legends of valor and calls for white supremacy. It was a conscious effort toward "thought control."[26]

The biographical perspective, especially when used with Hampton, provides other explanations. One is that the struggle over the way that the Confederacy would be remembered was related to the rapid transformation in Americans' understanding of constitutional government. Hampton saw that if the northern Republican understanding of citizenship and republican government was the original, true, and correct one, he and his former comrades were indeed traitors. If secession and slavery had been illegal, if states did not have the right to determine their destiny or determine which of their people were citizens, Hampton and his valiant followers were guilty of treason and worse. Hampton would not and could not accept that argument.[27]

Instead, he asserted that the South had been right. It was, of course, willing to accept limited, "legitimate" results of the war—emancipation and the death of the doctrine of secession. Those results also included his vow to lay down his arms and accept any federal laws or proclamations made during the war itself, as his parole agreement stated, but little more. Guided by his own understanding of honor and obligation, Hampton knew that he himself would never have signed his parole without the agreement that he could now return home with his basic citizenship rights intact, and with the South's ability to rebuild its society roughly along the lines it determined. The "legitimate" results of the war could never include the South's requirement to "abase herself," as he wrote Johnson, or admit that it had been wrong in the first place.

The biographical perspective also helps us realize that the Lost Cause was rooted in severe emotional pain—intense grief and a dire sense of loss. Memories of holding his dying son in his arms would never allow Hampton to admit that he had fought for an evil, or even morally ambivalent, cause. He implored his fellow southerners not to "cover ourselves with eternal infamy by branding as traitors those who died for us."[28]

Hampton's focus on dead heroes and Confederate valor leads to another point. Historians recently have paid much attention to Lost Cause rhetoric that attempted to sentimentalize slavery. Some of Hampton's speeches did stress supposed mutual understandings and amicable feelings between slaves and aristocratic planters. While Hampton's racism made it possible for him to overlook the suffering and degradation of his slaves, he sincerely believed that there had been sentimental master-slave ties—ties that he attempted to build on to construct a conservative, paternalistic New South. The vast majority of the nostalgia in Hampton's speeches and private letters dwelled, however, on the valor of Confederate soldiers. In this sense, the attention that Blight and others pay to the southern immortalization of valor as a defining element of wartime memory is appropriate. But these historians are wrong to assume that this focus on valor was deliberate fabrication or dishonest reinterpretation. For men like Hampton who had seen the mud and the blood, the desperate charges and mangled corpses, the hardy few who refused to desert even when they could, valor and sacrifice would always be at the heart of their Civil War experience. They had experienced enough of southern valor and Yankee cruelty to assert the existence of both without engaging in deliberate "thought control." And even if they ignored other verses in America's Civil War saga, it was the image of burning homes, pillaging foragers, and dying loved ones that would remain seared in their memories and that would define the entire conflict for them.[29]

Hampton began his postwar efforts to preserve tales of Confederate valor after receiving a copy of a July 31, 1865, circular from Robert E. Lee to his former officers. Lee intended to write a history of the Army of Northern Virginia in order to transmit the record of the "bravery and devotion" of his men to posterity, and asked his former officers to send campaign narratives and copies of old reports. Hampton was taken with the idea and set to work, compiling over a year and a half a 125-page narrative covering the period after he assumed command of Lee's cavalry. He sent it to Lee in July 1867. Hampton was responding not only to Lee, but also to northern officers. He was fighting Sherman's charges about the Columbia fire. He had also read reports by Philip Sheridan, who claimed to have defeated Hampton at Trevilian Station. Throughout the postwar period, ex-Confederates attacked the published reports and memoirs of northern officers, offended by alleged inaccuracies and an ungentlemanly failure to adequately recognize the virtues of a brave but defeated foe. A more detached viewpoint, of course, would recognize that Confederate officers were also guilty of bias in their official reports and postwar reminiscences. In Hampton's mind, though, virtually every Yankee report he read minimized Confederate successes, concealed Yankee failures, and, in short, lied. As Hampton assured Lee, "Thank God, the Yankees, though they write History, can not make the world believe it, & Time will prove that you have not fought in vain."[30]

From Hampton's point of view, memoir writing was not an exercise in manipulating history, but in rescuing it from oblivion. It was literally an attempt to preserve southern honor from Yankee depredations. As he explained to Lee, Sherman's rapacity was hindering his efforts to make a complete report. "When my house was robbed & burned by Sherman's troops, all my papers which were in it shared the same fate. From . . . [original torn] however of my reports which fortunately escaped the hands of these robbers & incendiaries, & from reports of subordinate officers," Hampton had endeavored to write as complete a report as possible.[31] He was quite literally trying to rescue southern honor from the flames.

By 1869 Hampton was president of the newly formed Survivors' Association of the State of South Carolina. Led by former Confederate officers, the organization attempted to compile a roll of every South Carolinian who had served in the Confederate military, to provide aid for disabled veterans and the widows and orphans of soldiers who had died in the service, and to achieve "the vindication of the cause and [preserve] the memory of their comrades."[32] At the same time, he took an active role in the organization of the Southern Historical Society, which aimed to produce a southern version of the war through publication of veterans' reminiscences. It was an organization that could do much to record "our struggle for freedom, and thus preserve untarnished our glorious position and our heroic deeds," he wrote James Conner. "If we let the Yankees manufacture a history, as they do wooden nut-megs, we shall have of the former about as good an article as they gave us of the latter."[33]

On June 16, 1870, Hampton was the main speaker at a monument dedication to the dead of the Washington Light Infantry, a volunteer unit from Charleston that had been Company A of the original Hampton Legion. Like much Lost Cause rhetoric, his speech combined Christian motifs, political advice, and personal and collective mourning. The cause that is right, he asserted, does not always triumph: "The religion of the Savior does not promise that virtue will always triumph on this earth, but does promise trials and afflictions for His followers."[34] In other words, Hampton asserted, the bad guys had won. Just as the sword had "turned over Spain and Portugal to the tender mercies of the Saracens," in this case it had, "directed by unscrupulous power against prostrate States, reeking with fratricidal blood, [enforced] the laws which it alone has made."[35]

Hampton offered political advice: his audience must carefully observe the terms dictated by the sword and accepted by the South. But never, never, must they fail to honor the sacrifice of those who had died to defend "those inalienable rights established by our fathers."[36]

326   Hampton then looked over his audience of veterans, widows, and be-

reaved parents—and got to the heart of the matter. The speaker and his audience knew that they shared a common bond, their personal grief:

I know that many a parent in our mourning land, as he looks through eyes blinded by tears . . . at some loved name, perhaps on that tomb, or on some stone that covers all that was mortal of one who was his pride, his hope, his darling, cries out in the pathetic language wrung from a bereaved father's heart: "Oh my son Absalom! My son, my son Absalom! Would God I had died for thee! O Absalom, my son, my son!" I understand, I can feel—I have felt all this. But still . . . knowing how and for what our sons died, cannot . . . the father . . . say proudly, as he stands by the grave of his son:

Why then, God's soldier be he!
Had I as many sons as I have hairs,
I would not wish for them a fairer death.[37]

The sacrifice would not—could not—be in vain. For Hampton and his people, the Lost Cause message transcended politics and even race— it was personal.

⭐ The next chapter will show how the Republican Party's attempt to remold southern society and provide meaningful citizenship for blacks could further enrage Wade Hampton—a man who shared many of the racist assumptions of his contemporaries, but who had no particular fear of African Americans unless they were under the spell of "lying" Yankees. To accomplish these reforms in the South, Congress had to rewrite the U.S. Constitution and violate the terms under which Hampton had, or thought he had, laid down his arms. Having abided by the terms of his parole and his pardon, he would soon have fewer rights than his former slaves. He believed that his state had met the requirements of Johnson's Reconstruction plan, refusing to see that the South Carolina Constitution of 1865 met neither the strict letter nor the spirit of the president's terms, and certainly not what northerners considered the terms by which the South had surrendered.

There were glimpses of hope in Hampton's life. His Diamond Hill residence was now rebuilt, albeit on a very modest scale. Sally was married to a fine young man, and Hampton had been able to resume planting operations. He seemed to have amicable relations with his ex- 327 slaves and labor force. On March 21, 1866, Sally gave birth to Hampton's first grandchild, Ann Hampton Haskell. The child was nursed by Mauma Nelly, the faithful black servant who had nursed Hampton himself. Hampton's own wife Mary was expecting and would soon deliver another daughter, Catherine Fisher Hampton.

Yet as Hampton examined his fortunes in early 1867, he must have felt despair. He was about to lose his full citizenship status once again. He was a favorite target of abuse in the northern press and, he thought, of Sherman's slanders. His creditors were closing in. Mauma Nelly, beloved by all the Hamptons, passed away near the end of 1866. "A long farewell to Marse Wade," she said, just before she died.[38] Mary Fisher Hampton, Hampton's favorite little sister, became ill while tending to Mauma Nelly on her deathbed. Within a few weeks she too was gone, leaving Hampton without one of his most faithful friends, confidants, and admirers. It was a heavy blow. Then the baby died. She was, Hampton confided to Robert E. Lee, "my youngest child, a little girl, who only lived long enough to make us love her."[39] Sometimes it still seemed as if Hampton's world were falling apart. For the next year and a half, he would continue to fight back.[40]

CONQUERED PROVINCES

By the spring of 1867, the political situation in the South had grown even worse from the white southern perspective. It was so depressing that Hampton told a friend he wished that he had never surrendered. Writing to former Confederate senator Louis T. Wigfall, Hampton bewailed that he saw "nothing but anarchy and ruin" for "our poor country." He continued:

It would have been far better for us had our whole people been exterminated, fighting to the last for their rights. Now we see that we were deliberately cheated by the North, who laughs to scorn all her pledges to the South. Disarmed, bankrupt, heartbroken, our people realize too late the *fatal mistake* they made in not devoting *every* thing to the success of their cause. . . . I often envy those who fell, when our arms were triumphant. For they died in the blessed hope that their country would be free, while we live to see that we fought in vain.[1]

Hampton would have never said these things in public, and he tended to lean toward melodrama in his letters to Wigfall, but these comments captured his deep sense of humiliation and grievance. It resulted from the fact that Republicans in Congress that spring rewrote the terms under which the South was to be restored to full membership in the Union, beginning the period known as "Congressional" or "Radical" Reconstruction. Hampton began the spring with a growing sense of injustice over broken agreements, a fear of greater political and social change, and a determination to defend the Confederate legacy.

In the period 1866–76 Hampton was a leading symbol of white unity and defiance in South Carolina, as well as in the South as a whole. But he also became one of the leading white spokesmen for moderation, peace, and reaching out to the South's new black citizens. The two roles frequently overlapped and obviously could be contradictory. They sometimes made Hampton appear hypocritical or deceitful and have led to wildly differing interpretations of Hampton's role, even in modern scholarship. And indeed they are confusing—unless we are truly able to understand Hampton's most deeply held concerns and beliefs. Those concerns and beliefs included home rule for native whites, a paternalis-   329 tic relationship between white patrons and black clients, and the vindication of southern honor.

Hampton's open letter to President Johnson in August 1866 began and ended with a tone of gratitude to Johnson for doing what he could to save the South from the "malignant spirit of fanaticism" arrayed against it. Mostly, though, his message was an extremely angry one. Hampton claimed that he and his people had laid down their arms in good faith, abiding first by the terms of surrender, then by the terms of their amnesties and pardons. In return, Washington had refused to readmit the southern states, appointed military governors, and humiliated the South.

Hampton complained of the Thirteenth Amendment being rammed down the South's throat. Elsewhere he lectured white southerners that they must not long to reverse emancipation, but in his letter to the president he complained that his comrades had found that not only did they have to surrender, but now they also were "required to change the time-honored Constitutions of our States—to declare the abolition of slavery legal—and to repudiate the Confederate debt." Whether or not Hampton considered slavery to be a "time-honored" institution, he attempted to convince Johnson that his real objection to emancipation was that it had been forced on the South in an unconstitutional way. The amendment would have a drastic effect only on the states that had no role in drafting it. "We are States," Hampton protested, "whenever our votes are needed to ratify a constitutional amendment, but in all other respects we are only *conquered provinces*." Besides, the Thirteenth Amendment was allegedly another mechanism by which the paternalistic control of blacks by white southerners was delivered into the hands of unscrupulous northerners.[2]

Northern leadership of the black man incited Hampton's hatred of the Freedmen's Bureau as well. Just before writing to the president, Hampton had returned to South Carolina from Mississippi, where he believed he had established mutually beneficial relations, based on paternalism, with his black laborers. White southerners had "honestly endeavored" to accommodate themselves to emancipation, he told Johnson, and had no desire to reinstitute slavery even if they could. But the "Southern people, among whom the negro had lived for generations, naturally imagined that they were fully competent to direct, to instruct and to protect him. Humanity and interest, which so seldom point in the same direction, in this case impelled the South to do all in its power to fit the negro for his new condition." Congratulating himself on his benign paternalism, Hampton was dismayed that Congress had put the South on notice that the southern white man would no longer have the right to discipline and "instruct" the black man in "not only the blessings, but the duties of freedom."[3] The racism inherent in Hampton's paternalism did not allow him to see how unacceptable South Carolina's Black Codes had to be to blacks and to northern Republicans. Convinced of the supposed improvidence, lack of ambition, and natural docility of African Americans, he believed that the limited protections given to black civil rights would be not only satisfactory to blacks, but also generous on the part of white paternalists.

Instead, Hampton railed that "that most vicious institution, the Freedmen's Bureau," had interfered, with "the basest men . . . swindling the negro, plundering the white man, and defrauding the Government."[4] The Freedmen's Bureau had grown out of the War Department during the war and had taken on the urgent task of feeding, sheltering, and educating millions of destitute freed slaves. It also assumed responsibility for approving all labor contracts between white landowners and black laborers to ensure that illiterate freedmen were not cheated. Hampton's opposition to the Freedmen's Bureau was common among southern whites. His private letters suggest that he distrusted the bureau's "interference" in Mississippi as well as South Carolina. In some cases, at harvest time Freedmen's Bureau agents set aside contracts that they deemed unfair to the workers, even though they had approved them earlier. Also, agents were authorized to charge landowners a fee of fifty cents per laborer for each labor contract they approved, allowing a few dishonest agents to enrich themselves. Though the bureau grew out of philanthropic motives and played an indispensable humanitarian role, there was enough dishonesty in it to make that organization another symbol of Yankee corruption to southern whites. The Freedmen's Bureau evolved into an arm of the southern Republican Party, urging black voters to reject the leadership of white elites for that of northern men. Finally, the assistant commissioner of the Freedmen's Bureau in South Carolina, Rufus Saxton, encouraged black people in the hope that they would receive lands confiscated from ex-Confederates—"forty acres and a mule." Such hopes went largely unfulfilled, but they promised to make northerners more gracious paternalist providers than southerners could hope to be, or would be if they could. Overall, the Freedmen's Bureau was a threat to southern-led white supremacy.[5]

Finally, Hampton shared the rage of other white southerners on hearing accounts of the treatment of his friend Jefferson Davis. It was reported that the former Confederate leader was still a prisoner locked in an inner cell, shackled in chains, and ill, and that after a year of captivity, no trial date had been set.[6]

Besides these political grievances, Hampton objected to white southerners being placed under the authority of black troops and northern officers. He charged that the North had responded to the South's gestures of good faith by subjecting whites to "a horde of barbarians, your brutal negro troops, under their no less brutal and more degraded Yankee officers." Hampton's political grievances were specific enough, but his charges of brutality by black troops were mainly abstract ones. They reflected a broad sense of injustice more than specific offenses by black soldiers. He did cite the story of a returning Confederate veteran being bayoneted in a hospital bed, but his most documented complaint involved cases of black soldiers seizing Confederate soldiers returning home and "roughly and ignominiously" ripping the buttons off their gray uniform jackets. "No armed foe being in the field, the great armies of the North waged active and honorable warfare against Confederate grey and its brass buttons! Noble occupation for brave soldiers." Obviously, Hampton's biggest problem with black troops was neither with specific atrocities nor with their skin color—black men were only dangerous when armed and led by "degraded Yankee officers."[7]

★ Every southern state but one (Tennessee) refused to ratify the Fourteenth Amendment drafted by Congress in 1866. In retaliation, Congress passed the Reconstruction acts and "Military Bill" in March and April 1867. These laws dismantled the state governments the ex-Confederate states had set up after the war, divided the South into military districts, provided for an army of occupation, and disbanded the white militia units the states had organized in the fall of 1865. Ex-Confederates were barred from holding office, meaning that future officeholders could only be white "traitors" to the South, or "scalawags"; new immigrants from the North, or "carpetbaggers"; and blacks. Additionally, each state was once again to hold a new constitutional convention. All adult males, black or white, would be able to register and vote for delegates to this convention. This one provision wiped out Hampton's and other whites' hope of denying suffrage to the majority of blacks until they had acquired property or education, not to mention his desire to preserve South Carolina's tradition of rule by native, wealthy, educated elites. The exceptions to this universal suffrage were prominent white men, like Hampton, who had at any time been disenfranchised due to their support of the Confederacy. Now they were disenfranchised once again and would be unable to vote for delegates to the upcoming convention. If the state's voters decided not to hold such a convention, they would remain under military rule. If the state did produce a new constitution, it would have to be submitted to Congress for approval. Hampton believed that the Military Bill, as he sometimes collectively called the Reconstruction acts, would "bring destruction to every vestige of republican freedom."[8] The legislation was unconstitutional in that it allowed black men to vote on a constitutional amendment before they had become citizens, it took the right of granting citizenship away from the states and gave it to the federal government, and it simultaneously disenfranchised thousands of white men. Hampton, having submitted his request for a pardon and receiving it, had once again lost his citizenship.[9]

By passing this legislation, Congress reopened questions about black men's role in the South's new political order. Since the end of the war, Hampton had accepted the emancipation of African Americans as an accomplished fact. Although he believed that sudden, total emancipation had been a mistake, Hampton had never been a pro-slavery ideologue, nor one who, like other southern men, considered slavery the cornerstone of the Confederacy. In the latter days of the war, he and Robert E. Lee had discussed the policy of emancipating slaves and agreed that it was a good idea, no matter how the conflict ended.[10]

Emancipation, however, did not necessarily imply the right to vote. Hampton thought that it would be madness to enfranchise all of the South's black men before educating them and ensuring they understood that their old masters were still their "natural" leaders. For that matter, he did not think that illiterate or landless white men should vote, either. This was not so reactionary given the historical political culture of his state. South Carolina had instituted universal white manhood suffrage in 1810, but the decision was the result of political compromise, not shared ideology. Many elites like Hampton continued to doubt the wisdom of granting the franchise to the riffraff and had at least preserved officeholding in the house of representatives for men who owned over 150 pounds sterling, or a minimum of 500 acres and 10 slaves. The property-holding requirements for senators and governors were higher still. Traditionally, state legislators and governors had far exceeded those minimum requirements, and the understanding was that while all white men would be allowed the franchise, elites would rule. Now the prospect emerged of an electorate that was 60 percent black and 40 percent white. Such an electorate could transform the entire political culture of the state.[11]

Instead of universal suffrage, Hampton pragmatically proposed a modest property or educational qualification for men of both races. In his 1871 testimony to a congressional subcommittee, he implied that he had "always" (since the end of the war) supported granting the franchise to black men "under proper qualifications" and that he had said so to the group of black men he addressed in the summer of 1865. Hampton often claimed (based on the 1865 meeting) that he was the first white man in the South, or in America, to advocate black suffrage. There is no other record of this informal event, and Hampton certainly had not objected when the 1865 state constitution failed to enfranchise any African Americans at all. Still, Hampton's version of events is plausible in light of his other comments then and later. Few other ex-Confederates made appeals for black suffrage in 1865. A few, like Hampton, did so in 1867, but only for pragmatic political reasons. In South Carolina, though, Hampton was still in the minority on that issue among his fellow white leaders. Throughout his political career, no one North or South publicly challenged Hampton's frequent claim to being among the earliest proponents of black suffrage. Indeed, most northern states still did not allow black voting during the early years of Congressional Reconstruction, and several would not until after it had come to the ex-Confederate states. The point is that Hampton's real concern was neither suffrage nor nonsuffrage for qualified black men, but continued elite control and black and white men trying "to get along well together."[12]

In March 1867 several black leaders from Columbia called on Hampton and asked him to speak at a political meeting. Hampton warned that they might not agree with his views, but they asked him to speak anyway. On the day of the meeting, Hampton told his black listeners that, in his view, they were undoubtedly free. He reiterated, though, that he favored "impartial" suffrage rather than universal suffrage; in other words, all black or white men who could read or who owned a certain amount of property should be allowed to vote.[13]

Hampton's advocacy of limited black suffrage reflected both pragmatism and instinct. It was not that he supported racial equality—such a concept was unthinkable to him. He did think that blacks, if educated and intelligent, would see the wisdom of bestowing the mantle of leadership on traditional elites like himself. Besides, if the southern states did not take some action on black suffrage, the federal government would, establishing the new precedent that Washington, not the states, had the right to define the citizenship rights of a state's residents. This pragmatism fit comfortably with Hampton's paternalism; or, as he put it, "humanity and interest" for once pointed "in the same direction."[14] Extending limited suffrage allowed Hampton and other white gentlemen to be patrons and benefactors rather than tyrants as they bestowed the gift of suffrage on their social inferiors. Finally, Hampton himself had relatively little fear of black people as long as they were led by responsible and moral whites. As explained before, the Hamptons had never feared or loathed their slaves, though they certainly considered them inferior.

The beginning of Congressional Reconstruction was a potential disaster to white southern hopes. Hampton rose to the challenge. The key to conservative control of the South Carolina constitutional convention and the future would lie in limiting or controlling the all-important black vote. Hampton thus renewed his overtures to the state's black men, this time with much more urgency than before and probably more sincerity. He envisioned a political partnership between native white elites and their ex-slaves, and particularly with educated black leaders. The whites, of course, would be the senior partners, but he hoped that white and black leaders could cooperate to limit universal suffrage and radical change. Maybe they could influence ordinary black voters to trust their old masters rather than carpetbaggers and northern Republicans. Obviously the Reconstruction acts would allow universal suffrage to elect delegates to the convention, but Hampton naively thought he might persuade black leaders that universal suffrage should not be written into the new constitution. The key was to make them allies, not enemies. To General James Conner in Charleston, Hampton wrote:

We can control and direct the negroes if we act discreetly, and in my judgment the highest duty of every Southern man is to secure the good will and confidence of the negro. Our future depends on this. . . . Say to the negroes, we are your friends, and even if the Supreme Court pronounces this Military Bill unconstitutional, we are willing to let the educated and tax-paying among them vote. Of course, we should put on the record our strong protest against this Bill and should do nothing to bring it with all its humiliations upon our devoted country, but that should not prevent our trying to give

335

direction to the wave that would otherwise surely overwhelm us. Like you, I am only solicitous about our State government, and if we can protect that from destruction, I am willing to send negroes to Congress . . . and I should rather trust them than renegades or Yankees.[15]

The real enemies, then, were not uneducated blacks, but scalawags and Yankee Republicans. Hampton had more confidence in the goodness of "inferior" blacks than that of educated Yankees. He tried to explain his point of view to other native whites who opposed any black suffrage at all, and to Democratic leaders at the national level, such as John Mullaly, who objected to his stance. Mullaly, an Irish-born Catholic sympathetic to the South, was the editor of the *Metropolitan Record and New York Vindicator*, which the U.S. government had shut down temporarily when Mullaly opposed conscription during the war. Hampton gently explained to Mullaly that until northern Democrats had the courage to make a stand against the Reconstruction acts on constitutional grounds, the South, "struggling for bare life," would have to make alliances with blacks:

If we can not direct the wave it will overwhelm us. Now how shall we do this? Simply by making the Negro a Southern Man, & if you will, a democrat, anything but a Radical. Beyond these motives for my action, I have another. We are appealing to the enlightened sense & the justice of mankind. We come forward & say, we accept the decision rendered against us, we acknowledge the freedom of the negro & we are willing to have our love for him stir us. We are making up our record for posterity & we wish no blemish or flaw to be found there.[16]

Mullaly replied quickly. Though his letter is not extant, Hampton's response indicates that Mullaly still could not see the wisdom of Democrats accepting black suffrage, and Hampton struggled to be patient with him. In a subsequent letter, Hampton wrote that he "could not have made [his points] plainer . . . our condition is simply this: the negroes will certainly vote: *how* they vote depends greatly on us. If you can show us how to prevent this voting, we will adopt the plan [Hampton made this point rhetorically]. You see then why I tell the negroes, that we *are* willing to let *some* of them vote. A limited suffrage would do us good, for universal suffrage is a curse."[17] Once a "Constitutional" party regained control of the state, Hampton assured Mullaly, the

Brigadier General James Conner (1829–83). Charleston attorney, former Hampton Legion officer, and state attorney general under Governor Hampton. South Carolina Historical Society.

national Democratic Party would be strengthened and could eventually overthrow the Radicals (Republicans).[18]

Hampton frankly conveyed his beliefs to black audiences, especially the one in Columbia to which he advocated "impartial" suffrage for literate and property-owning blacks and whites. A black minister, Reverend Pickett, endorsed Hampton's views, predicting that literacy and property would surely come to those who strove for them. Another black leader, Beverley Nash, said that the black men of South Carolina would not rest until all the voting rights of white men were restored, but Nash went on to advocate universal male suffrage, which Hampton and other conservatives deplored. Nevertheless, Nash's apparent willingness to seek an alliance between blacks and southern whites encouraged Hampton, and he commended Nash to other white conservatives as "respectable" and "true."[19] Thus, Hampton and other elites held out hope of a partnership between white and black elites, one that would control the black vote and preserve elite white leadership. "Why should we not be friends?" Hampton asked his black audience. "Are you not Southern men, as we are? Is this not your home as well as ours? Does not the glorious Southern sun above us shine alike for both of us? Did not this soil give birth to all of us?"[20]

Some local whites deplored Hampton's efforts to win over black voters. His friend Benjamin Perry warned that "General Hampton and

337

his friends had just as well try to control a herd of wild buffaloes as the Negro vote."[21] Ex-Confederate officer Thomas W. Woodward of Fairfield used a far more insulting tone: "Why, oh why, my Southern nigger worshippers, will you grope your way through this worse than Egyptian darkness? Will you not cease crawling on your bellies and assume the upright form of men. . . . Stop, I pray you, your efforts at harmony . . . or you will goad these people by flattery to destruction, before they have a chance to pick out the cotton crop."[22]

Though some black leaders like Pickett and Nash accepted Hampton's olive branch, other Republican leaders rejected it outright. Republican newspapers ridiculed Hampton's comment about blacks not being responsible for the "present state of affairs." What was so bad about the "present state of affairs?" asked the *Charleston Advocate*. What was so terrible about universal suffrage or all black men finally having the right to vote? The *Advocate* scorned Hampton's plea for black men to trust their old masters with leadership:

Wade Hampton is one of those deep-dyed rebels who staked his all . . . in an attempt to fasten the chains of slavery upon the neck of the colored man. But he now advises those same men to "try those whom they have known." They have already been tried and are known—weighed in the balance and found wanting. They held the colored man in brutal slavery, and sold him as a dumb brute in the shambles, and dare they to refer to slavery, and set themselves up as the colored man's best friends. . . . It is too late in the day for Wade Hampton, or any other Southern man, to attempt to make believe that slavery was a good institution, and the old masters have always been, and are still, the freedmen's best friends.[23]

It soon became clear that most black voters had rejected Hampton's overtures. Published accounts of black political meetings made it clear that most blacks would vote for northern and home-grown Republicans, or "Radicals." As late as May 19, Hampton desperately hoped to make blacks "*Southern men*," thinking that blacks might elect conservative delegates to the constitutional convention who would roll back the "curse" of universal suffrage.[24] By July those hopes were dead. To James Conner, Hampton confided: "The indications are that the negroes will not listen to reason & they will therefore have to learn in the only school that teaches fools. But while they are getting wisdom, we shall be ruined. The '*platform*' adopted by them here, precludes any union with

Cartoon (1868) of Hampton shining a black man's boots. Cartoonist Thomas Nast mocked southern leaders for allegedly hating blacks but courting their votes after the passage of the Fourteenth Amendment. At left rear (seated) is former Confederate general Nathan Bedford Forrest, and on the right is Henry Wise, governor of Virginia during the hanging of John Brown. Harper's Weekly.

them & the wide disfranchisement now ruled, denies all hope to us of moulding [sic] the course of the State."[25]

Hampton therefore called for a change in strategy. If a majority of those who registered failed to vote yes on holding a constitutional convention, the state would remain under military rule and perhaps ride out the tide of rapid constitutional change without adopting a new state constitution. Instead of trying to control the course of the constitutional convention, whites should register to vote on the question of whether or not the state would hold a constitutional convention. Then they should vote no, or boycott the vote, which amounted to the same thing, and remain under military rule. In late July a group of citizens asked Hampton to make a public statement of his views. Hampton wrote a letter that was later printed in the Columbia Phoenix and the Charleston Mercury. "None of the Radicals pretend that the military bills [Reconstruction Acts] are constitutional," he asserted. It would be better to

339

live under military rule than to sanction measures that were "illegal, constitutional, and ruinous."[26] Besides, writing a new constitution would mean approving the Fourteenth Amendment, which would bar ex-Confederates from holding office. The only men who could represent South Carolina in Congress would be those who had refused to defend South Carolina in its hour of need (1861–65) while its other sons fought and died, or those who were dishonest enough to swear falsely that they had never supported the Confederacy. Representation in Congress was not worth trusting men who could or would take that oath.[27]

Hampton maintained that the 1865 constitutional conventions in the southern states had been mistakes as well, held as they were under duress from the Johnson administration. The greatest error of those conventions was in ratifying the Thirteenth Amendment, as it too had been forced on the states without their consent. "I am well aware," he conceded, "that the action of the Southern people, at that time, was dictated by an honest desire to secure the blessings of peace, and by a high sense of honor . . . to show that they were sincere in their wish to do everything that would tend to the restoration of the Union on honorable terms."[28]

Hampton still refused to direct his bitterness toward African Americans, however. He reminded the members of his audience that Yankees were the real enemy, not blacks, and warned them not to direct their anger against the latter:

> All classes should cultivate harmony and exercise forbearance. Let our people remember that the negroes have, as a general rule, behaved admirably, and that they are in no manner responsible for the present condition of affairs. Should they, in the future, be misled by wicked or designing men, let us consider how ignorant they necessarily are, and let us, all the more, try to convince them that we are their best friends. Deal with them with perfect justice, and thus show that you wish to promote their advancement and enlightenment. Do this, and the negroes will not only learn to trust you, but they will soon appreciate the fact so evident to us, that we can do without them far better than they can do without us. . . .
>
> We have recognized the freedom of the blacks, and have placed this fact beyond all probability of doubt, denial, or recall. Let us recognize in the same frank manner, and as fully, their political rights also. I am perfectly willing to see a constitution adopted by our State, conferring the elective franchise on the negro, on precisely the same terms as it is to be exercised by the white man, guarding

against the abuse of this privilege by establishing a slight educational and property qualification.[29]

Hampton was sincere in his lack of enmity toward blacks. He expressed the same sentiments in his private letters. To Conner he wrote that he was "willing to give the negro all his rights, but I cannot deny all to the whites at the same time."[30] But his private letters also said something that his public statements did not. Agreeing with Benjamin Perry and other native white leaders, Hampton wrote Armistead Burt that "it would be better for the State to be remanded to Military Government rather than that which places the negro permanently in power."[31] Hampton's paternalism was as racist as it was benevolent. Southern black men were no threat until placed in power, especially when placed in power by "unconstitutional" methods and Yankee conquerors.

On November 19 and 20, 1867, whites stuck to Hampton's plan. Having previously registered, they now refused to vote for the constitutional convention. Registered black voters, however, outvoted them. The convention met in January 1868, and its 124 delegates consisted of 73 black men, 36 southern whites (virtually all Republicans), and 15 carpetbaggers. The presence of black delegates in the chambers of government, of course, was the most novel feature of the convention. White conservatives railed against the imposition of "negro rule" and shouted that "intelligence, virtue and patriotism are to give way . . . to ignorance, stupidity and vice. The superior race is to be made subservient to the inferior."[32]

Soon the new constitution was ready. It contained several beneficial reforms. It provided women more legal protections. It established the basis for free public schools that would be open to all the state's children. Owners of homesteads received some protections against overzealous creditors. Other reforms gave more autonomy to local courts and county governments. None of these changes were particularly objectionable to most conservatives. On the other hand, the free public schools were to be racially integrated, as was the university. The constitution mandated universal male suffrage, one of the conservatives' greatest fears. It prohibited any property or literacy requirements for voting, while disenfranchising prominent men like Hampton who had supported the Confederacy. It also eliminated minimum residency requirements for the first state election, so that recent immigrants to the state—carpetbaggers—could be elected. To white conservatives, the new constitution was less a reform than it was an illegal power grab. 341

As predicted, the state's black majority approved the new constitution when voters went to the polls on April 14, 15, and 16, 1868. New state officers were also elected, nearly all of them blacks, carpetbaggers, or scalawags.[33]

★ One immediate concern for the conservative white population was the fact that the white militia was legally disbanded in the presence of a potentially larger and hostile force. The federal Reconstruction Act of March 2, 1867, had disbanded all volunteer military organizations in the ex-Confederate states, including the official state militia. By the time of the April 1868 state elections, however, there was already talk of forming a new state militia. When Congress readmitted South Carolina to the Union after the April elections, it removed the restrictions on the state having its own militia; thus the way was now open for a state military force consisting of black men and controlled by the Republican authorities. White hostility and fear against the very idea of black men carrying guns, especially when led by northern whites and scalawags, made the situation only more volatile. White Carolinians in the low-country towns of Charleston, Beaufort, and Georgetown, where large black majorities existed, were especially fearful of blacks being incited to violence when removed from the control of native whites. Theoretically, the South Carolinian white minority was vulnerable to greater despotism and even massacre. Federal and state officers had no such intentions, of course, but Hampton's opinion of them would not allow him to assume that.[34]

With South Carolina reentering the Union under Republican terms and a Republican government in June 1868, a movement developed to organize an underground, statewide military force composed of white men. Because of their racist fears of armed blacks and distrust of Republican authorities, whites jumped the gun. The Republican government in Columbia did not authorize its large black militia until 1869, after a massive wave of Ku Klux Klan violence the previous year. And as whites were arming and organizing in June 1868, plans were already in place to withdraw federal troops from the state once it was officially readmitted to the Union in July.[35]

The rise of the Ku Klux Klan in South Carolina in 1868 has inspired several excellent studies. As Richard Zuczek has pointed out, the Klan "lacked statewide organization, being based instead on local . . . membership and jurisdiction."[36] It was never centrally controlled. Also, Republicans often applied the term "Ku Klux" to local terrorist organizations that did not consider themselves part of the Klan. Many never wore disguises or Klan insignia and tried to organize as volunteer militia companies rather than night riders. Much of the violence was spontaneous rather than carefully planned. Whatever form it took, however, white violence had a chilling effect on the development of democracy in South Carolina and among its black and white Republican victims.[37]

Though Wade Hampton was a leading symbol of white unity and defiance, no historians have connected him directly with organizing the Klan; not even his Republican opponents suspected him of organizing or ordering the violence, either of Klansmen or other white militants. On the whole, this interpretation is correct. Yet no one has mentioned Hampton's extraordinary letter to James Conner written on June 12. To his old subordinate in black-majority Charleston, Hampton sounded a call to arms. The letter indicates that Hampton participated in the effort to organize an underground white militia. A Mr. Salley and a Mr. Legare of Orangeburg wrote to Hampton in June and asked him to lead the movement to form an "organization" throughout the state. "To this," Hampton informed Conner, "I replied that the object they had in view met my approval." He told Salley and Legare that he would lead the movement on two conditions. First, "That the sole object of the organization was to be self-protection." And second, that he could appoint his own subordinates in each district. For Charleston, Hampton wanted Conner.

The next step, Hampton explained, was to procure arms. A "General Alexander" had told Hampton that he could obtain a large quantity of Winchester rifles (Alexander's source or means is not clear). Hampton informed Conner that the Winchesters were "*the most effective yet invented.*" He continued:

Now my idea is to get as many of these guns as possible in each Dist. Let the men thus armed be under the direction of a Com. or Council stationed at each Court House, or central town, & have the chief authority vested in one person, to reside here [Columbia] or in Charleston. Each Dist. Having a sufficient number of men to protect it, they could be called out in case of any sudden mob, or other outbreak. The whole organization could be wielded by these means easily & rapidly, & could thus secure the safety of our whole people. The details will suggest themselves to you, at once, as well as the advantages of such an organization. Now what do you think of it? If you agree with me, as to its importance, go to work at once.[38]

Conner had his marching orders.

Several observations are in order. First, this is the only document linking Hampton to the formation of extramilitary organizations. Additionally, Hampton apparently intended these organizations to be strictly concerned with "self-protection," guarding against black mobs or abuses by black militia companies. He did not want them to seek out Republicans or "insolent" black men for abuse or murder—the type of activity for which the Klan and white paramilitary groups would become most notorious. Finally, after the election of 1868, Hampton essentially withdrew from the state and was largely absent during the worst of the Klan violence, especially in 1870–71.

Hampton's letter to Conner, however, is remarkable. Having rejected any armed activity and scrupulously adhering to federal law and the terms of his parole, Hampton now flouted them, at least temporarily. The white Democrat who, both before and after writing this letter, was a leading spokesman for moderation toward blacks, calm, and order, was briefly involved in trying to organize an underground, statewide military organization.

Why had the "punctiliously honorable" Hampton finally violated the terms of his parole? It was not because he sought a race war; far from it. The best answer is that, first, he and other conservatives felt by 1868 that they had nothing more to lose. The Reconstruction acts and the 1868 constitution had fulfilled every conservative nightmare—black political dominance rather than white paternalism, foreign rule, and the loss of state sovereignty. If whites could not protect their interests in the legislature and the courts, at least they could be armed and organized. Second, Hampton felt released from his obligations because of bad faith on the part of the North. Two years before, in his 1866 letter to President Andrew Johnson, Hampton had argued that the entire course of events since May 1865 consisted of broken promises on the part of the North and the honorable intentions of a beaten but proud South. Back then he had reiterated his promise to Johnson to abide by the laws, saying that the South intended "to abide by the laws of the land honestly; to fullfil [sic] all her obligations faithfully, and to keep her word sacredly." The "brave men" who were true to their convictions from 1861 to 1865 would also "prove true to their obligations" to the North.[39] After making this assertion that the white South had been faithful in fulfilling its obligations, Hampton concluded nearly two years later that the North had continued to ignore its side of the bargain.

Clearly, 1866 and 1867 were years in which Hampton and other white conservatives saw increasing evidence, and finally proof, that they could neither preserve their model of order for South Carolina nor protect their leadership positions. They would be unable to rebuild along the lines they wished and would have to salvage what they could. Hampton later lectured Conner that it would take "steady, patient, and persevering work. . . . We must," he concluded, "work out our own political salvation."[40]

ANOTHER BATTLE AND A RETREAT

Between June and November of the election year 1868, Hampton helped lead one more battle in the war to "redeem" his state from what white southerners called "negro rule" and Yankee tyranny. The fight did bring him a touch of personal vindication, as Democrats and Republicans alike acknowledged his importance and influence. But once again the year ended in defeat, and for the next several years Hampton staged a tactical retreat from public affairs. Scholarly assessment of his role in the election occasionally has appeared as partisan as the views of Republicans and Democrats in 1868. Hampton's admirers have portrayed him as a much-needed voice of moderation and conciliation. Others, such as Richard N. Current, have condemned his "rabble-rousing" and hypocrisy.[1] The truth is that he simultaneously symbolized North-South reconciliation, moderation toward blacks, and angry resistance to Radical rule.[2]

As South Carolina descended into violence in 1868, Hampton sympathized with the goals of white vigilantes. As for their methods, however, he vacillated between ignoring and condemning them. Rumors and reports of secret societies called the Ku Klux Klan began to surface in communities across the state as early as April, about the time of the constitutional referendum and state elections. Several Republican leaders were assassinated or received threatening notes, and coffins were mysteriously deposited on front porches. The violence escalated through the late summer and early fall as the November elections drew nearer.[3]

Conservative newspapers across the state cautiously condemned the violence, while blaming Republican corruption or black insolence as its root causes. As Lou Falkner Williams explains, "Conservative whites who would have personally disdained the violence and refused to participate in the Ku Klux Klan overlooked the atrocities and contributed to [legal] defense efforts because they shared the [Klan's] racism and constitutional principles."[4] This statement roughly describes Hampton's attitude.

It was easy for white conservatives to convince themselves that violence was a two-way street. Democratic newspapers, of course, were likely to downplay or ignore white violence while trumpeting cases of 347 black violence on whites. On two occasions during the 1868 campaign, Hampton personally witnessed black Democrats being physically attacked by black Republicans for speaking on the Democratic stand. Still, Hampton's sense of helpless rage during Reconstruction blinded him to the horror of what his basic decency and paternalism should have sooner condemned.[5]

Hampton was chairman of the Executive Committee of the state Democratic Party in 1868. As violence escalated in late summer, he played a dual role that would become familiar for him. While fanning the flames of Democratic anger by denouncing the illegitimacy and corruption of the Republican regime, he also tried to pull the state's rougher elements from the brink of all-out race war. On August 29 Hampton sent a letter to be read at the September 2 rally in Edgefield that used metaphors for peace and violence interchangeably. He called on his old "devoted soldiers . . . to enlist again with me in this great fight for Constitutional Liberty, which is now going on, and adjure them to be as good soldiers in the cause of peace as they were in that of war."[6] On October 18 he and other leading Democrats published another address that mixed propaganda with calls for peace. Hampton's Executive Committee denounced the "despotism" and "subversion of the Constitution" by the Republican regime. Still it called for peaceful methods in opposing that regime. Acknowledging the "criminality of a few, and perhaps, the indiscretions of many," the committee asked the white population to prevent and restrain from violence, and to treat "with great kindness and forbearance the colored population of the State," which "you have ever done."[7]

By that time, the state's Republican leadership recognized the Klan and similar organizations as dire threats to lawful order and to their own party. Republican governor Robert K. Scott felt nearly helpless. Black men began to organize locally to fight back, but Scott dared not encourage the development of a race war, knowing that unarmed and inexperienced blacks had no chance "against organized and disciplined ex-Confederate soldiers."[8] Few Union soldiers remained in the state, and Congress still had not lifted its ban on state militias. Scott's cabinet members made a variety of suggestions—he could declare martial law, or he could recruit two-hundred-man companies of thugs in New York and send them on sweeps through the most lawless counties. In a belated effort to follow a third course, building up the state constabulary, Scott ordered rifles from a gun manufacturer in Massachusetts in

September. By the time he did, the company was temporarily out of stock and unable to send any.[9]

Finally, Scott appealed to the one man he thought would have enough influence to stop the violence—Wade Hampton. Scott initially spoke to two of Hampton's friends whom he chanced to meet at a bank in Columbia, Colonel L. D. Childs and a Colonel "Gibbs."[10] He warned them that if Hampton did not openly condemn the violence, a race war was inevitable. Childs and "Gibbs" made Scott promise that he would publicly recognize such an action. If Hampton was the only man in the state who could preserve law and order, his friends wanted everyone to know it. Hampton received the message and called on Scott not long afterward. This time Scott made the request directly to Hampton, who told him that he had already written an address for the *Columbia Phoenix* and that it would appear the next day, October 23. "We feel it our duty to invoke your earnest efforts in the cause of peace and preservation of order," the address read. Hampton and the other members of the Democratic Executive Committee asked white citizens to condemn "these recent acts of violence . . . by which a few lawless and reckless men have brought discredit on the character of our people. . . . No cause can prosper which calls murder to its assistance, or which looks to assassination for success."[11]

Almost immediately the violence declined sharply. Some disturbances occurred on election day, but not enough to prevent a solid Republican victory. The state remained relatively quiet, by South Carolina standards, for the next eighteen months. A week after Hampton's appeal, Governor Scott published a proclamation congratulating the people "upon the beneficial results that have ensued from the admirable and well-timed address of General Hampton."[12] Hampton had not planned or directed the violence, but only he had the prestige to stop it. It would not be the last time that Republicans would have to recognize who really held the reins of power in the state.[13]

While Hampton guided the course of the state Democratic Party, he also fought in the national political arena. In July, he was one of the most prominent members of the Democratic National Convention in New York. Here, also, he was a symbol of both southern defiance and reconciliation—reconciliation, that is, with northern Democrats. Recognized as the leading spokesman for the southern delegates, Hampton received cheers from southern, northern, and western men every time he rose to speak. At his suggestion, the Democratic Party adopted the statement that the Reconstruction acts were "unconstitutional, revolutionary, and void" as part of its platform.[14] Meanwhile, the southern delegates, including Hampton, readily accepted another plank stating that the issues of slavery and secession were permanently settled. After the party nominated Horatio Seymour of New York for president, Hampton and the other southern delegates warmly endorsed Missouri's Francis P. Blair, a former Union general, for vice president. Hampton said that he had met Blair "on more than one field" and that it was "due to the Federal soldiers that they should have the second place on the ticket."[15]

Hampton continued reaching out to northern Democrats after his return from New York. In an open letter to a correspondent from Wisconsin, G. L. Park, he assured voters from the Badger State of his desire to guarantee basic rights for blacks, of his recognition that slavery and secession were "settled forever," and of his promise that the South would meet northern magnanimity and generosity with "a cordial and heartfelt response."[16] Hampton also invited John Quincy Adams II, of Massachusetts, known for his opposition to the Reconstruction acts, to speak at a political meeting in Columbia.[17]

Despite these overtures, Wade Hampton became the Democrat that Republicans loved to hate. From the end of the Democratic convention until the November elections, Harper's Weekly attacked him nearly every week as the epitome of Democratic treachery and treason. Another part of Hampton's speech at the convention had urged his fellow Democrats to ensure that all white votes from the South were fairly counted, and "if there is a majority of white votes, that will place Seymour and Blair in the White House, in spite of all the bayonets that shall be brought against them. I only want to see the election fair, and if they do that, even with the incubus of black rule, we can carry the Southern States. [Applause.]"[18]

Unfortunately, Hampton's words were easily interpreted to suggest that black votes would or should be ignored or suppressed. Harper's claimed that Hampton's insistence on the rightful winner taking his office despite military coercion meant that he recommended putting Seymour and Blair in the White House "at the point of the bayonet."[19] After The Nation began repeating this charge against Hampton, Harper's moved on to accusing him of being a "ringleader" in the Ku Klux Klan disorders.[20] The New York Times accused Hampton of fomenting violent revolution. Soon after the convention, Republicans printed a pamphlet condemning the "Democratic rebel Convention," entitled "25 Rebel

Generals, 30 Rebel Colonels, 10 Rebel Majors, 20 Rebel Captains. . . . 105 Rebel Members, Nearly One Fifth of the Whole Number, of the Late Democratic National Convention . . . Together with a Brief History of Their Lives, Sayings, and Doings." At the top of the rogue's gallery of Democrats in this publication was Wade Hampton, followed by Nathan Bedford Forrest, whom the pamphlet misnamed "Napoleon Bradford Forrest." In its mini-biography of Hampton, Republicans identified Hampton as "one of the most vindictive cavalry generals of the rebel army . . . who caused seventy-five of our Union prisoners to be put to death . . . under circumstances of atrocity almost without parallel in the history of civilized or savage nations. He was thoroughly chivalric in the Southern sense of that word, thinking no more of 'nailing a nigger's ears to a pine-board fence and then shooting at him,' than in partaking of the hospitalities of the Convention."[21]

These latter charges ranged from simply false to ridiculous, but it is true that Hampton could still sound angry and defiant to northern ears. He made Lost Cause speeches in Baltimore and Charleston on his way home from New York. In Baltimore, Hampton praised the devotion of Marylanders who had fought for the South. In Charleston, he explained to his fellow South Carolinians that northern Democrats were extending "the right hand of conciliation and friendship, and I for one am willing to accept the hand of a man who fought for his cause and State as I fought for mine. . . . I yield to no one in devotion to the lost cause. I would never be the traitor to ignore my past acts. . . . But I am willing always to welcome those who, having fought only for honor and the Constitution, now meet us as friends and brothers."[22] Whereas Hampton thought he was being conciliatory in these speeches, Republicans saw only cussed defiance and treason.[23]

⭐ For nearly a century, a pro-southern, anti-Republican interpretation dominated the historiography of Congressional Reconstruction in the South. Historians took the accounts of racist white southerners and disillusioned northerners at face value when they portrayed a helpless white South suffering under the rule of greedy carpetbaggers, unprincipled scalawags, and ignorant blacks. Since the 1960s, historians have overturned that traditional interpretation, recognizing the inherent racism and bias in white southern accounts, as well as the good intentions and abilities of many Republican leaders in the South. These revisionist works have tended to place more faith in accounts of Republican state officials, African Americans, and official state and federal records than the traditional white sources. The more recent literature has shown that black southerners suffered far more injustices than whites in the long run, and that the traditional interpretation, for the most part, unfairly maligned black and white Republicans.[24] It takes little imagination, however, to see why white southerners, biased as they were, felt a profound sense of grievance and humiliation. And in the particular case of South Carolina, the original interpretation (stripped of its racist assumptions) of a corrupt Republican state regime remains firmly intact in scholarly writing. For several reasons, white South Carolinians at the time regarded the state's leaders from 1868 to 1876 as illegitimate usurpers who were dragging the state's proud name through the filth of degradation and disgrace.

The first reason has to do with the makeup of the Republican leadership itself. Over half of the legislators in the 1868 General Assembly were black. Most of the white men were Republicans—either carpetbaggers from the North or native scalawags. Even without the presence of outsiders, the racism of white conservatives would have not allowed them to accept the legitimacy of such a government. Hampton was one of the few South Carolinians who were actually willing to cooperate with educated black leaders and "send some of them to Congress," but most whites, from former conditional Unionists like Benjamin Perry to fire-eaters like Ellison Keitt and Martin Gary, furiously rejected black political participation altogether. Gary, for instance, preached that white men must determine "that the negro shall not become a part of the body politic, or from any qualification either as to education or property, be allowed to vote in this country."[25]

Recently, historians have pointed out the unfairness of charges that the black leadership was mostly illiterate and inherently incapable of good government. As Thomas Holt, William Hines, and others have noted, as many as 80 percent of black state legislators during Reconstruction were, in fact, literate. Many had been free before the war, and others represented the most respectable elements of the black community. Some were lawyers, doctors, and small landowners, while others were independent craftsmen such as carpenters, masons, wheelwrights, and wagon makers.[26]

The question of the abilities of black lawmakers during Reconstruction is akin to the question of whether the glass was half empty or half full. Certainly most black lawmakers were not the venal, illiterate bumpkins portrayed in contemporary white accounts, but they were also a far cry from what South Carolinians traditionally expected to see in their state's political leadership. The fact that any state legislators at all were illiterate, or possessing only a rudimentary education, was a revolutionary change. And the notion of carpenters, brick masons, tailors, and recently freed ex-slaves debating the fine points of law and parliamentary rules of order naturally seemed ludicrous to whites. As Benjamin Perry raged, "Is it not infamous that such an assemblage of negroes and yankees should be forming a constitution for the once proud, honored, and glorious state of South Carolina. . . . There is not a single member of this infamous convention which would even have dared, before the war, to enter the house of a gentleman except on a message or matter of business."[27]

White conservatives were also outraged that the vast majority of their new "rulers" who levied taxes and passed appropriations were not even taxpayers. Even before the new Republican regime went into operation, Hampton led a meeting of "the Conservative People of South Carolina" that petitioned the U.S. Senate not to approve the proposed constitution of 1868. In a detailed study of the composition of the newly elected legislature and the tax books, Hampton and his allies showed that the 74 "Colored" members of the constitutional convention paid a total of only $117.93 in state taxes, with 59 paying no taxes at all. Even the 47 whites paid only $761.62, with one white conservative member paying $508.85 of that amount. The newly elected governor, secretary of state, comptroller general, treasurer, attorney general, and superintendent of education all paid no taxes. This constitutional convention of nonproperty owners had written property taxes of 3 percent into the state constitution, six times higher than the rate before the war. Clearly, Hampton's committee argued, the new legislators and fathers of the constitution represented "not the wealth of the State, neither its commercial, nor its agricultural, nor its mechanical interests. . . . They do not represent its intelligence, its tone, its sentiments. . . . It is shown, also, how little interested in the matter of excessive taxation they will be who shall levy the taxes."[28] It was not only a case of taxation without representation for native whites, but also of "representation without taxation" for the state's Republicans.[29]

The Republican government continued its policy of levying high taxes on real estate. It was part of an effort to redistribute land from white landowners to the Republican Party's poor black constituents. The high taxes would, as Governor Scott explained, "compel [the owner] to cut up his ancestral possessions into small farms, and sell them to those who can and will make them productive; and thus the masses of the people will become property owners."[30] The tax program did force the forfeiture of huge acreage to the state for nonpayment of taxes. To Republicans, this was social justice for landless blacks; to conservatives, it was outright robbery. As Lou Williams writes, "Resentment of the high taxes they had never had to pay before bound the white yeoman to the planters and undermined the authority of the Republican government as surely as did the racism that bound the whites together."[31]

Rife corruption in state and local government proved to be the "Achilles heel" of the Republican Party in South Carolina, notes Walter Edgar.[32] Those leaders whom white conservatives already considered illegitimate soon amassed "a sordid record unmatched by any other Southern state during Reconstruction."[33] Between June 1868 and December 1872, the Radicals managed to swell the state debt from $5.4 million to nearly $15.8 million. Some of this was due was to educational initiatives and internal improvements, but much of it resulted from lawmakers, judges, and governors lining their pockets. In one legislative session alone, the General Assembly spent $125,000 (roughly $1.54 million today) on wine and whiskey for its members. Because the Republican Printing Company bribed members of the legislature to award the company bloated contracts, the state's printing bill increased from $21,000 in 1868 to $450,000 in 1873. Over a four-year period, the legislature paid $200,000 for furniture for the statehouse. An 1877 appraisal indicated that only $17,775 worth of furnishings remained, the rest making its way into private residences. The "most gigantic steals," says Joel Williamson, were bond frauds in which officials issued state bonds in excess of amounts that the legislature had authorized.[34] There was also the "Railroad Ring," in which state officials obtained shares in the Blue Ridge Railroad and the Greenville and Columbia Railroad at devalued prices, the phosphate "job," and other scandals.[35]

One of the most unfortunate results of the regime's corruption was that it established a firm link in white Americans' minds, North and South, between "negro rule" and corruption. Beverly Nash (who Hampton had once trusted), Everidge Cain, H. H. Hunter, W. C. Glover, Prince Rivers, and probably Robert Brown Elliott, Robert Smalls, Francis Cardozo, and a number of other black officials and legislators received bribes or participated in the frauds. Clearly, though, it was white leaders who reaped the greatest profits and concocted the most nefarious schemes. Comptroller General J. L. Neagle (southern white Republican) played a key role in organizing the railroad and bond frauds, as did

354 Governor Scott (white carpetbagger), his successor Governor Frank-

lin J. Moses Jr. (from a prominent Charleston Jewish family), and John J. "Honest John" Patterson (white carpetbagger), who was the most successful thief of all. One of Patterson's most notorious acts was literally buying a U.S. Senate seat in 1872 for forty thousand dollars by bribing the state legislators who elected him. Even white conservatives occasionally dipped their hands in the till when they could. It would eventually became clear that Hampton's former officers, Martin Gary and Calbraith Butler, attempted to profit from the railroad and bond schemes. Still, the most startling features of the new Republican regime were the pigments of its members and its sordidness, and these features became fused in white imaginations.[36]

Even South Carolina's Republicans were disgusted by the behavior of their leaders and understood the damage the corruption was doing to the cause of black civil rights. Republican newspapers like the *Beaufort Republican*, *Missionary Record*, and *Beaufort Tribune* rebuked the government regularly. As the *Missionary Record* lamented, "We know that the colored men of this State will have to bear the odium of all the crimes or misdoings of the whites who manipulate the finances of the State."[37] According to the *Beaufort Republican*, the most evil result of the frauds had been "the loss of confidence of the great body of the people of the United States in the capacity and willingness of the colored race to select suitable rulers and produce a commendable local government. . . . The feeling that this experiment [universal suffrage] has failed is spreading with such rapidity that . . . it will create a reaction *fatal* to the rights and privileges of the colored race."[38] Hampton and other conservatives who had warned against universal suffrage, of course, had already been convinced that the black masses were incapable of selecting "suitable rulers." Eventually northern newspapers—mouthpieces of both parties—came to condemn the Republican governments in the South, particularly in South Carolina. The *New York Times*, for example, claimed in 1874 that "ignorant negroes [in South Carolina] transplanted from the cotton fields to the halls of the Capitol, where they have been drilled by unscrupulous white adventurers, have naturally made a mockery of government and bankrupted the State."[39]

Like so many political events of the day, Republican rascality directly impacted Hampton's personal life. In 1872 Franklin Moses Jr., the notorious scalawag, became the state's second Republican governor. Instead of moving into the executive mansion, he purchased the famous Hampton-Preston mansion from Hampton's aunt, Caroline Hampton Preston, and her husband John Smith Preston, whose financial straits were little better than Hampton's. Hampton's grandfather had bought the magnificent downtown mansion in 1823, and the family had held the funerals of both Hampton's grandfather and father in its halls. With its beautiful gardens and fountain, it was the showplace residence of Columbia, a symbol of the Hamptons' prominence in the history of the state, and an ancestral homestead. Moses, or rather his wife Emma, bought the house for the princely sum of $42,000, and Columbians gossiped that the money for the down payment came from Moses's take in the printing scandal. This symbol of white elite pride soon became the site of drunken and mixed-race social entertainments. When a Republican judge issued a warrant for Governor Moses's arrest in 1874 on charges of breach of trust and grand larceny, Moses posted four companies of black militia around the house to protect himself from arrest. The grand house had been defiled. It was yet another mortifying episode that demanded vindication.[40]

⭐ With the 1868 elections ending in failure, Hampton largely withdrew from the public stage, or at least from electoral politics. For the next six years, he spent far less time in Columbia, dividing most of his time between Mississippi and the center of his new business interests in Baltimore, Maryland. His children McDuffie and Daisy attended schools in Virginia. He was far from idle, however, and he never lost interest in "redeeming" South Carolina. He advised James Conner that conservatives "must, by steady, patient, and persevering work, get possession of the State government."[41] For the time being, though, someone else would have to lead the fight at home. Hampton had his own battles that took him outside the state, and several of them were related to the ongoing fight for personal redemption.

December 1868 was the month that Hampton declared bankruptcy and began making a new financial start. By February 1869 he was writing letters from Mississippi to friends who had helped him get back on his feet, sounding optimistic about his prospects and expressing satisfaction with his black labor force. He was confident enough to bring out even more workers from South Carolina. To Colonel L. D. Childs, Hampton wrote: "Say to [Sibley], that Abraham Ladsen & three women, are, or soon will be at my house, wishing to come out. They have signed a contract & I wish that he would send them at once. I should like to get two or three more men or boys to work with Ladsen on the same contract—½ of the crop. Some of my hands last year, made upwards of 200 dllrs. on this contract."[42]

The days of quick profits in southern cotton planting, however, were over. After two more seasons, Hampton was dissatisfied with his black labor force, perhaps for the first time in his life. He believed that the idleness of his workers was making the sharecropping system unprofitable. On January 2, 1871, he complained to Armistead Burt that his last few crops had been good ones, "but much of the cotton is wasting because the negro is too idle to pick it." Long after the cotton should have been harvested, he had "400 bales still in the field, where every rain & wind is [picking] it out." This year, Hampton vowed, he would avoid sharecropping and rent his land, "so that the negroes may waste their own cotton."[43]

Hampton did not abandon cotton planting in his postbankruptcy career, but he did look for other ways to redeem his debts and rebuild his fortune. In 1869 he joined with Jefferson Davis and Georgia politician Benjamin Hill to form the Southern Life Insurance Company; later he, Davis, and others formed the Carolina Life Insurance Company. Hampton manned the branch office in Baltimore. In 1872 he became president of the Baltimore Fire Extinguisher Works, an enterprise that he believed "promise[d] great results, from very small investments." All too familiar with the destructiveness of fires, Hampton predicted to Abbeville lawyer Armistead Burt that "all villages & country houses, will adopt these machines. Perhaps Abbeville will get one of the Engines & I wish that you would bring the matter to the attention of the authorities."[44]

Hampton also engaged agents to sell subscriptions to the *Southern Magazine*, which published southern accounts of the war and Lost Cause rhetoric in the form of the *Southern Historical Society Papers*. Hampton wholeheartedly believed in this method of publishing the "truth" about the war, but he also hoped to make money. Explaining to Conner why he had seemingly left the state and become a magazine salesman, Hampton pleaded that he was accomplishing much good, and "Owing to the condition of Mrs. Hampton, I can not go to Miss & I must engage in something, which while not taking me away from her, will give us the means to live."[45] None of these schemes made Hampton a wealthy man again or even lifted him out of debt, though he was able to buy back some of his Mississippi land in the 1870s. They provide an insight, though, into the question of whether the old planter elites were instinctively tied to cotton or reborn after the war as New South capitalists. For Hampton, at least, the answer was that they did whatever they could to get by.[46]

Hampton was also keenly interested in the joint U.S.-British "Mixed Commission" that was investigating the Columbia fire in late 1872 and early 1873. Before testifying, Hampton spent months enlisting the aid of friends in gathering evidence against William T. Sherman. His reputation was at stake not only locally, but also internationally. Hampton wrote one friend that "I don't know how wide a range this examination of mine will take, but as all testimony will go before England as well as this country, I want to nail Sherman's lies to the counter."[47]

The strongest force dragging Hampton away from active political participation may have been the failing health of his wife. Mary had rarely exhibited a vigorous constitution, and her health declined noticeably after the death of the Hamptons' baby in 1867. She was ailing off and on for most of the period between 1867 and 1874, and much of Hampton's correspondence from these years, including insurance company business and angry political statements to newspapers, was written as he sat at her bedside.[48] Her symptoms varied.[49] Though Hampton consulted several doctors (even summoning a Dr. Josiah Nott from New York to Baltimore), it appears that no one was able to make a proper diagnosis. Hampton sometimes worried over her "distressing nervousness."[50] One Hampton biographer has surmised that she suffered from profound depression. Hampton wrote to Dr. D. H. Trezevant that Dr. Nott essentially agreed with Trezevant, "that there is no organic disease, & that hysteria is the disease under which she suffers. He also pronounced that there is no serious displacement of the uterus, but simply an engorgement of it."[51]

This diagnosis temporarily relieved Hampton, but Mary grew no better. By the following spring, he had decided that the city noise in Baltimore around their boardinghouse was not good for Mary and that she needed to be moved to the country. He arranged to rent rooms from the brother and sister-in-law of his first wife, Margaret Preston, in the Virginia mountains near Charlottesville. He and Mary finally made the move in early summer. Mary never left. In February 1874, as the leading conservative citizens of South Carolina held a "Taxpayers' Convention" to protest the abuses of the Republican regime, Hampton did not attend. He was with Mary. She died on March 1.[52]

Mary Hampton had never challenged her prescribed role as the loyal, submissive wife. Intelligent, bookish, and introverted, she had played the part of the southern lady while her husband buried his father, resisted secession, fought Yankees, struggled against debt and bankruptcy, made speeches, and organized political resistance. But she had always been there for him at his lowest points, and her loyalty produced the greatest proof of her courage. In the weeks after Preston's death, she had braved the Virginia winter at the front, amazing even Hampton with her fortitude and endurance. During that long miserable night in York-ville when Hampton realized that the Confederate cause was lost, it was she who gently forced him to see it. It was she who convinced him that defeat was not dishonor—that he had not failed her nor proved himself unworthy. Her reassurance had contributed as much to Hampton's Lost Cause doctrine as any battlefield feat by his troopers.

Hampton received condolences from his friends, including his old comrade Calbraith Butler. As usual after the death of a loved one, his own pen fell silent and provided little insight into his personal grief. His first extant letter was written six weeks later, in which he confided to Armistead Burt that he was "still not strong and suffering much from pain in my old wounds."[53]

HAMPTON AND THE KU KLUX

In October 1871, disturbed at "the frightful condition of this state," Wade Hampton wrote a letter to his close political confidant, Armistead Burt of Abbeville. "It is very desirable that there should be some concert in action among us in relation to political affairs," Hampton pleaded. "When some course of action can be settled on, it is very desirable too, that we should engage the services of some Northern Lawyers to defend our Ku Klux cases. . . . Suppose you try to make up some contributions for a few? We will do the same here."[1] Historians have generally overlooked the ironic fact that one of the least negrophobic white men in South Carolina helped raise legal defense funds for Klansmen. One scholar who has noticed has concluded that there was really no difference between "moderates" like Hampton and super-racists like Martin Gary, since all white conservatives were fundamentally committed to white supremacy.[2] But while Hampton was certainly a racist and believed that whites were superior, the term "white supremacy" carries modern connotations that conceal as much as they reveal. What we must remember is that the program of "white supremacy" in late nineteenth-century America was broad enough to include wide differences in ideology and behavior. Two or more white supremacists, even in the same state, could have fundamental disagreements on the proper future role of African Americans. After helping to raise legal funds for the defense of Klansmen, Hampton as governor appointed scores of black men to office, authorized black militia companies, ensured that blacks received equal funding for public schools, and strived to protect black suffrage. Contemporary South Carolinians, white and black, recognized the differences between the racial programs of white leaders, and those differences would one day become a central issue in the state's politics.

During Hampton's semiwithdrawal from South Carolina after 1868, the battle to redeem the state continued. In their efforts to regain control of the government, white conservatives tried several electoral strategies. One of them was "fusion" with disgruntled Republicans; another was continued violence. In 1870 white conservatives tried to engineer a return to state government by allying themselves with breakaway Republicans. The "Union Reform" ticket featured Richard B. Carpenter, a Republican judge from Kentucky, as the gubernatorial candidate and Matthew Calbraith Butler, who was running for lieutenant governor. In their challenge to the corrupt regime of Governor Robert Scott, conservatives promised to preserve the franchise for black voters and tried to convince them that the Republicans were only using them for their own purposes.[3]

Meanwhile, the state was becoming an armed camp. Concerned about a rising tide of white violence and intimidation, Governor Scott began raising a "colored" militia—"colored" because native whites predictably refused to serve alongside blacks. Republicans, of course, recognized that such a move would enflame white opinion and risk stirring more violence, but Scott also felt pressure from within his party to provide armed protection for his constituents. Twice he asked Hampton's opinion on how best to preserve the peace, and both times Hampton warned him that building up the state militia would be dangerous. Scott proceeded nevertheless. The state government organized a large black militia, acquiring 88,000 rifles from the War Department and making contracts with three private firearms companies worth over $126,000. Whites also acquired thousands of modern firearms and organized themselves into companies. In response to the formation of black militia companies, the white companies patrolled and garrisoned up-country towns and demanded that blacks hand over their weapons. As the tension built, Hampton left the state, preoccupied by business concerns in Baltimore, the education of his children in Virginia, and his wife's health.[4]

As the campaign proceeded, both sides resorted to fraud and intimidation, though the whites were still better armed and organized. The overall result, however, was a humiliating and infuriating defeat for the Union Reform Party on October 19, 1870. Carpenter lost to Scott by a vote of 85,071 to 51,357. As Lou Falkner Williams explains: "The Reform party had humiliated white citizens by 'pandering' to the black vote and then failed to produce a white majority. . . . Never again, upcountry whites vowed, would they be so humiliated."[5]

The South Carolina up-country exploded in violence after the election. The Klan initiated a new wave of terror in November and December, and the violence raged at fever pitch through September 1871. Between March and June 1871, President Ulysses S. Grant sent four hundred additional troops to the South Carolina up-country, bringing the total number of federal troops in the state to nine hundred. In April Congress passed the Third Enforcement Act, or "Ku Klux Act," authorizing the president to suspend the writ of habeas corpus whenever widespread violence deprived citizens of their constitutional rights. Grant took that step in October and ordered all "persons composing the unlawful combinations and conspiracies" to hand in their weapons and disguises.[6]

Democrats once again deemed Congress' legislation high-handed and unconstitutional. Besides the suspension of the writ of habeas corpus, the Ku Klux Act disqualified anyone from sitting on a jury in a Ku Klux case unless he swore an oath that he had never supported rebellion against the United States. Theoretically, then, jurors would all be "good Union men," not former Confederate soldiers. The First Enforcement Act, passed in the spring of 1870, had another controversial provision. As Lou Williams observes, the 1870 law

> extended federal power to ordinary crimes committed by Klansmen in the process of violating other sections of the law. A Klansman who committed murder on a Ku Klux Klan raid, for example, could be prosecuted in federal court. Technically, the federal offense was the civil rights violation, not the murder. But the state penalty for the crime determined the punishment of the civil rights violation. Thus the federal courts could possibly prescribe the death penalty— the state penalty for murder—for a civil rights violation.[7]

Hampton was one of those who considered the combination of federal troops, the packing of juries, and the increased possibility of the death penalty as yet another travesty against constitutional government. The presence of an armed black militia and an angry white population only made the situation more explosive. In October 1871 he lamented to Burt: "I apprehend for our unfortunate people greater trials and wrongs than they have yet suffered, from the Ku Klux laws. God only knows what the end will be, but I can only see sorrow & suffering ahead for them."[8]

Congress also formed a joint committee to "Inquire into the Condition of Affairs in the Late Insurrectionary States." Hampton and Butler were among those called to testify in July.[9] Both former generals were aware of the violence, but they attributed it to Republican misrule and claimed to be unaware of the Klan's existence. Hampton testified that in his view the rage and disorder in the South were due to the North not fulfilling the magnanimous terms it originally offered to the South in 1865, and to the corruption of the Republican regime combined with the gullibility of black voters. He said that since he had been out of the state for some time (most of the past twelve months), he could not be sure of the existence of an organization called the Ku Klux Klan. Hampton "deplored" the fact that outrages "no doubt" had been committed but said he knew nothing of them other than what he read in the newspapers.[10] In any event, he did not believe there was an organized effort "to intimidate the colored vote."[11]

At first glance, Hampton's July 1871 congressional testimony that he was unsure of the existence of the Ku Klux Klan seems incredible. How could the symbolic leader of white unity and defiance know nothing of the Klan's existence? It is true that Hampton had been out of the state for most of the past twelve months. He was probably in Mississippi when the violence escalated after the election, at the time of year when he usually traveled west to oversee the cotton harvest and its sale. His first extant letter after the election—dated January 2, 1871—was written to his friend and political confidant Armistead Burt from Hampton's plantation in Mississippi. Though Hampton frankly discussed political issues with Burt, he mentioned nothing about the Klan. As blacks and local Republican officials were being whipped, murdered, and lynched, both in broad daylight and at night by hooded night riders, Hampton naively asked Burt: "What has been done since the defeat of the Reform Party? What are we to do?"[12]

By late 1871 Hampton used the term "Ku Klux," as did everyone else, when referring to the upcoming trials of white terrorists.[13] These references suggest that he now recognized that there had been a serious wave of violence, but they also reflect Hampton's belief that Republicans were manipulating the "Ku Klux" situation for political purposes. Contemporaries as well as many historians have recognized that Reconstruction violence was about politics as well as race. Richard Zuczek, for example, argues that Reconstruction violence in South Carolina was part of an ongoing political-military struggle beginning in 1861. Hampton and other contemporaries agreed that the Klan issue was fundamentally political, though with a twist—it was political despotism by Republicans that inspired white crime, which Republicans in turn exploited for political gain.[14]

To the Klan's victims and their families, especially in the upstate where white violence was concentrated, the Ku Klux Klan was only too real. But to those who were farther away from the violence, the Klan was often a shadowy and nebulous thing. Even the *Beaufort Republican* was not quite sure what to make of the reports from the up-country. "Ku Kluxism manifestly exists," asserted the editor, "but the extent of it is hard to know."[15] The paper actually criticized Governor Scott for suspending habeas corpus and calling for federal troops, claiming that such intervention was unnecessary. And like Hampton, the *Republican* attributed the violence as much to corruption and the "criminality of a few" as to white racism or to an organized conspiracy.[16] Some of the crimes committed, said the paper, are "Ku Kluxism and the others are riotous individuals which exist in every community."[17] And like many conservatives, the *Republican* was willing to lay much of the blame at the feet of the current regime. "We see no prospect for a change under the present political administration—strike the axe at the root of that evil, and you deal a blow to Ku-Kluxism from which it cannot and would not rally."[18] Four days later, the paper retreated from this stance by saying that "the infamous rule of the thieves at Columbia, may give a colorable occasion for [the violence] but no real cause." The blame lay with Democrats, Republicans, sympathy with the "lost cause," and "habits of tyranny" engendered by slavery—"in a word, society itself."[19]

Convinced that the "Ku Klux laws" were unconstitutional and that the Klan cases were "political affairs" as much as criminal cases, Hampton helped raise legal defense funds for the accused.[20] By the end of the year, with habeas corpus suspended and federal troops in the up-country, authorities had arrested six hundred accused Klansmen, while many more had fled the state. Tragically, Hampton's rage and humiliation had led him to the defense of acts that he never would have committed or normally even condoned. He was on the wrong side of justice.[21]

At the 1874 Taxpayers' Convention in South Carolina, Martin Gary would echo the sentiments of many whites when he said that the political struggle in the state was "entirely a question of race." Gary shouted that "the negro [is] arrayed against us [not] as Democrats, but as against the white man."[22] Though other white leaders shared that outlook, Hampton never agreed. He clearly believed that the real enemy was the Yankee-led Republican Party, not blacks. That is one reason why he supported the defense of vigilantes in what he called the "political cases" but never directed any actual violence. At one level, the goal of Martin Gary, Benjamin Perry, and Wade Hampton was the same—the overthrow of the Republicans and the restoration of native white leadership. At another, there were important differences. Whereas Perry and Gary wanted absolutely no political role for blacks, Hampton envisioned white leaders cooperating with black elites, and paternalistically protecting the basic civil rights and educational opportunities for the black masses. Hampton saw the racial issue as part of a larger struggle to restore "good" government, a measure of state sovereignty, the proper role of traditional elites, and redemption of the state's honor.

Wade Hampton III, ca.
1876. South Caroliniana
Library.

Limiting the political power of blacks was one part of that project, not the project itself. The differences in the two programs may seem irrelevant today, but they were not in Hampton's time.

The battle for the state continued, though conservatives played little active role in the 1872 election. The Republican Party divided again, and this time conservatives let Republicans fight it out among themselves. The 1872 Republican convention in August dissolved into shouting recriminations, charges and countercharges of corruption, and drawn pistols. The Reform Republicans, whom the conservatives preferred, lost decisively. Hampton, meanwhile, was in Baltimore with his ailing wife.[23]

Conservatives failed again in 1874. They endorsed the "Independent Republicans," with John T. Green and black leader Martin Delany at the top of the ticket, but lost to the mainline Republican candidate, New Englander Daniel H. Chamberlain. Hampton, still preoccupied with business and personal affairs, again played almost no role in the campaign, though he personally opposed any attempts at fusion with South Carolina Republicans.[24]

Momentum was building, however, for an all-out challenge by white conservatives to regain control of the state in 1876. Republicans nationwide were on the defensive like never before. Democrats had already

366

regained control of several southern states; in 1875 they were able to re-capture the state government even in black-majority Mississippi. South Carolina's Republican regime was discredited even in the national media and the national Republican Party. During that year Governor Chamberlain attempted, with moderate success, to win native white support and to reform many of the abuses in Columbia. Chamberlain, a native of Massachusetts and former Union officer, had served as state attorney general from 1868 to 1872. Democrats accused him of being a member of the corrupt "bond ring" of that period, though he denied it and won the governor's seat in 1874, promising to weed out corruption. He strived earnestly to do so, but his fragile alliance with conservatives collapsed in December 1875, when Republicans in the General Assembly, against Chamberlain's wishes, nominated William J. Whipper and Franklin J. Moses Jr. as circuit court judges. Whipper was a northern black man whom whites suspected of corruption, while ex-governor Moses was undoubtedly one of the most debauched politicians in the state. Chamberlain boldly refused to sign Whipper's and Moses's commissions, and received praise for this stand among some conservatives.[25] But the damage was done and only got worse when "Honest John" Patterson's response to the crisis became public. Urging Moses's and Whipper's supporters to stand fast against Chamberlain's moralistic stand, Patterson assured his Republican compatriots that there were "five years of good stealing in South Carolina yet."[26] White conservatives exploded in rage, reorganized the state Democratic Party, and swore that cooperation with Republicans, even Chamberlain, was no longer possible.[27]

Hampton was personally ready to reenter the fray. He had given up on the insurance business in Baltimore. By unloading some of his lands in Mississippi, he was able to redeem others, and his son Wade could oversee them. Widowed for the second time, he no longer had an ailing wife to nurse. The youngest of his children were nearly grown. Moreover, despite his frequent absences, Hampton was cementing his place as the leading Lost Cause figure in the state—the symbol for white suffering, for southern honor, and for vindication. He was, of course, the first choice for speaker whenever the Hampton Legion held a reunion. And on June 28, 1876, Charlestonians and other white South Carolinians organized a centennial celebration of the defense of Fort Moultrie against a British attack in 1776. It was an occasion to celebrate South Carolina patriotism, white heroism, and revolutionary defiance against debauched tyrants. The man chosen to lead the parade was Wade Hampton.[28]

HURRAH FOR HAMPTON

On November 28, 1876, Wade Hampton prevented a bloodbath in Columbia, South Carolina. Standing on the steps of the statehouse, the fifty-eight-year-old Hampton still cut a powerful figure. He was six feet tall with gray in his sideburns and mustache, barrel-chested, and with a few more pounds around the middle than during his days in the cavalry. As a symbol of the Lost Cause among South Carolinians, no one overshadowed him except perhaps Robert E. Lee, who had been dead five years.

In the square and streets below him stood five thousand angry white men who had descended on the capital from all over the state. Many of them had followed Hampton into combat over a decade before and now believed that carpetbaggers and black men intended, through fraud and armed force, to deprive him of the governor's seat. Armed and enraged, they intended to overwhelm the handful of federal troops guarding the statehouse, install a Democratic government, and terrorize anyone who opposed them. Hampton told the troops to stand down. In an even, measured tone he assured his followers that his cause would prevail and that violence would not help it. Amazingly, the crowd dispersed. Within minutes, the streets were calm.[1]

The old gray hero had appeared on the statehouse steps that day to show that he could prevent violence. His supporters, conversely, had come to show that they were willing to use violence to accomplish their will. Hampton hoped that Washington and the nation would see that he would and could protect the rule of law and the constitutional rights of African Americans. The angry men in the mob gathered outside the statehouse had intended to show that they would violate both if necessary to reinstate white supremacy. On a superficial level, Hampton and the mob had the same goal: Hampton in the governor's seat and the restoration of native white political leadership. Yet deep differences divided Hampton and other conservatives from some of his most angry and extremist supporters. These differences were not only tactical, they were also philosophical. They were wide enough for many black South Carolinians to recognize and important enough to threaten white unity in later years.

This chapter aims to clarify three issues surrounding the infamous 369

1876 electoral campaign in South Carolina. First, the "Red Shirt" campaign reveals the fundamental differences that divided southern Redeemers, despite their superficial agreement on the need to restore white Democratic control of the state. In 1876 Hampton offered conciliation and constitutional protections to South Carolina's black voters, while many of his Democratic supporters, inspired by arch-racists like Martin Gary, simultaneously waged a campaign of violence and intimidation. Hampton sought to build a biracial, but white-led Democratic Party. Gary, on the other hand, sought not to woo black voters but to intimidate them from voting. Rather than see them become Democrats, he would see them excluded from the political process altogether.

Second, this chapter addresses Hampton's role in the Democrats' campaign strategy of 1876. Beginning with George Brown Tindall in 1952, historians have often described the Democratic crusade in 1876 as a "dual campaign" or "dual strategy."[2] This characterization has often made the charge, either explicitly or implicitly, that Hampton consciously and cynically profited from the violence and fraud of his supporters that he publicly condemned. It is undeniable that Hampton's campaign profited from the nefarious tactics of violent men, but there is no evidence that he approved or encouraged those methods. This chapter suggests, though, that once the violence became nearly uncontrollable, Hampton made shrewd calculations on how to minimize the damage it might bring his campaign, and even how to profit from it by suggesting that only he could restore peace and order. Hampton perceived that as the violence escalated, so did the danger that Governor Chamberlain could convince President Ulysses S. Grant to send more federal troops to South Carolina and impose martial law, suggesting that the Republicans did indeed have the will and ability to govern. Hampton hoped, however, that the violence on both sides might play into his hands if he could persuade black voters that he was the one who could protect them—Chamberlain could not and the federal government would not. Even if U.S. troops returned to the state in force, Hampton might be able to convince federal authorities that, in the long run, only he could maintain peace, order, and civil government. As at other times in his public career, Hampton strived to reconcile principle with pragmatism, or as he put it "humanity" with "interest."[3]

Finally, it is important to recognize the role that Hampton's personality and character played in influencing white tactics and white memory of the Red Shirt campaign. His virtues helped white South Carolinians celebrate the victory they won in 1876 largely through violence and electoral fraud. His war record, principled stands, and magnanimous promises helped South Carolinians convince themselves that they were still a noble, heroic people even as they violated the rule of law, stuffed ballot boxes, and gave the lie to their claims of being paternalistic, charitable protectors of African Americans. While some white men threatened and shot black Republicans, Hampton, the symbolic leader of the white conservative cause, played the role of brave protector and sincere friend to his would-be black charges. As one newspaper editor reflected twenty-six years later, just after Hampton's death, "The people loved him because he represented them as they knew they should have been, rather than as they knew they were."[4]

Hampton appeared not only as a protector to blacks, but also as a savior and suffering Redeemer to whites. Scott Poole's perceptive study of "Confederate memory" and "Confederate religion" in South Carolina explains how often South Carolinians expressed their deepest yearnings for a return to an older social and moral order in religious terms.[5] The Lost Cause was fused with white southern religion, and this relationship was particularly evident during Hampton's 1876 campaign—indeed, Wade Hampton was the most prominent living symbol of the Lost Cause in South Carolina.

As the election year 1876 began, conservatives were already considering an all-out fight for control of the state government. In the past three elections, they had attempted to combine forces with breakaway Republicans by splitting the ticket or had sat back and hoped that the less objectionable Republican faction would win. This was called the "fusionist" or "cooperationist" approach. Hampton had never favored such a passive approach, nor did he now. Now, for the first time since 1868, conservatives reorganized the Democratic Party and contemplated a "Straightout" strategy, nominating only Democrats for state offices.[6]

The first South Carolina event pushing conservatives toward the straightout approach was the legislature's election of William Whipper and Franklin Moses to judgeships in December 1875. Despite Governor Chamberlain's sincere attempts to control the damage, the scandal convinced many, though not all, whites that reform was impossible under a Republican regime. The second decisive event was the riot-turned-massacre at Hamburg on July 8, 1876. The sordid affair began with a hostile verbal exchange on July 4 between two young white men attempting to drive their buggy through a Hamburg street and the local black militia company that was drilling and blocking the way. Led by

Calbraith Butler, Hampton's old comrade, local whites demanded that the black company surrender its weapons and apologize to the white men. Black militia officers, of course, refused to meet these outrageous demands. On the eighth, Butler led several white rifle clubs from all over Aiken County as they besieged the black company fortified inside its arsenal. A nineteen-year-old white youth was killed early in the shootout. Before the day ended, however, the whites had acquired a cannon from Augusta, shelled and then stormed the arsenal, killed two black officers, and captured twenty-nine black prisoners. A detail of white men then shot some of the prisoners in cold blood while marching them to the county jail.

The conservative press condemned the outrage, while also asserting the dubious claim that it was brought about by the blacks' misbehavior. Hampton was vacationing with his family in the North Carolina mountains and declined to criticize his old friend Butler, though it was an atrocity he never would have led himself. It was difficult to turn on the comrade who had fought beside him throughout the war, the man who had ordered up the ambulance for the dying Preston Hampton. Few men had shared more danger and hardship with Hampton than Calbraith Butler. Regardless of Hampton's feelings about the Hamburg massacre, the tragedy led indirectly to his nomination for governor. It destroyed the possibility of either side reaching across party lines for the upcoming election. Republicans took it as a sign that Democrats had already decided on a "campaign of blood and violence," such as that recently waged in Mississippi.[7] Meanwhile, white conservatives who had advocated the cooperationist approach came over to the straightout policy favored by Hampton, especially since Governor Chamberlain had responded to the massacre by asking the Grant administration to send more federal troops to South Carolina. As cooperationist Joseph B. Kershaw conceded, "I think the unhappy affair at Hamburg will be made such use of in the canvass that no alternative would probably have been left us than to 'take it straight.' . . . At all events it is a luxury once more to be able to put forward the men we like best."[8] Thus, the decision to run a straightout campaign stemmed partly from the desire for good government, which Hampton shared, and partly from racial hatred, which he did not.[9]

But the straightout campaign also fed off genuine white anger that had been growing for over a decade against Republican corruption and alleged black crime.[10] Since emancipation, white South Carolinians had regularly complained of black theft and arson, and they sincerely believed that the Republican government in power had no interest in prosecuting these alleged offenses. Letters, newspapers, and memoirs from the period strongly suggest that white fears, though probably exaggerated, were genuine. The Ku Klux Klan uprising of a few years before, many felt, had been justified, but had only brought federal retaliation. What was needed, thought many whites, was a leader who could restore order, and he had to be powerful, virtuous, Democratic, and white.

On August 15 the Democratic Convention met and voted 88–64 to nominate a straightout ticket. Once that difficult decision had been reached, the next one—who to nominate for governor—was much easier. Former general Martin Gary of Edgefield County had already planned for that scenario. Gary had been one of the original company commanders in the Hampton Legion. A thirty-year-old lawyer in 1861, he had been an avid secessionist before the war began. He was bold, extremely ambitious, incredibly profane, and infamously outspoken. Men who admired him did so for his frankness, not his tact. His personality clashed with that of the more reserved, mild-mannered Hampton. After the Battle of Manassas, Gary believed that Hampton had slighted him by not properly recognizing his part in the fight. In later years he would claim that he, not James Conner, had taken over the legion at Manassas after Hampton's wounding and led the final charge, and that Hampton had unfairly slighted him while recommending others for promotion. When Hampton had to give up command of the infantry portion of the legion in 1862, it passed to Gary, who eventually achieved the rank of brigadier general. At Appomattox, he had refused to surrender, turning over his command to a subordinate and announcing "South Carolinians never surrender!" before riding away. Ever after he boasted of having never surrendered, to the annoyance of other equally proud South Carolinians who had.[11]

During Reconstruction, while Hampton had repeatedly tried to forge a white-led coalition of white and black Democrats, Gary had consistently argued for a hard line against African Americans. Gary believed that it was useless to try to persuade or cajole black men. They must be threatened, intimidated, and physically abused if necessary—they must be driven, not led. "It is a *question of race*, and not of politics," he asserted in 1874. Later Gary would assert that the 1876 election was "a struggle for supremacy between the races and not a mere contest for honest

Brigadier General Martin
Gary (1831–81). Planter,
lawyer, former Hampton
Legion officer, and finally
political rival to Hampton.
South Carolina Historical
Society.

government as has been alleged."[12] While Hampton and other conservatives tried to convince black voters that they would be better off with
the lower taxes and honest government promised by the Democrats,
Gary and others scoffed that such reasoned appeals to black men were
akin to "singing Psalms to a dead mule."[13] Hampton regarded Gary's
views as "narrow, dangerous, and unwise."[14]

In the summer of 1876, however, Gary and Hampton found themselves temporary allies. Both desired a Democratic victory, and Gary
recognized Hampton as the one man who could unite and reinvigorate
the party. Gary and Butler favored a straightout campaign for the coming fall. Hampton, though more moderate in his racial and political
views, agreed. Conner, whom Hampton personally trusted more than
Gary, nevertheless favored a fusionist policy, supporting Chamberlain
in exchange for a few Democratic places on Chamberlain's ticket. Sharing Conner's opinion were General Joseph B. Kershaw and the influential editor of the Charleston News and Courier, Francis W. Dawson.

After the June 28 centennial celebration in Charleston, Hampton
found himself leaving Charleston on the same train as Gary. Also on
the train was Kershaw and General Johnson Hagood, another ex-
Confederate officer who favored the fusionist approach. Gary approached his old commander, Hampton, and first confirmed that he
was in the straightout camp. Gary later recalled:

I discovered that [Hampton] was in sympathy with the movement General Butler and myself were trying to inaugurate. He told me that he did not expect to return to Mississippi. I then said to him that I intended to try and have him . . . nominated for governor on the straightout ticket; that with Butler and myself on his flanks we could win this battle as we had won others in the war. He replied that he was poor, and come back to get the odds and ends of his former estate together; that he did not desire to run for the office, but that he had made so many sacrifices for South Carolina that if he was the choice of the convention he would run. I was delighted at his acceptance, for I believed that he could harmonize all of the differences of the Democratic party. . . . Governor Hampton had commanded Butler, Conner, and myself. We entered the war as Captains under him as colonel in the Hampton Legion. He came out of the war a lieutenant-general and continued to rank all of us. I did not believe that Kershaw and Connor [sic] could all agree upon any one man, but I believed that we all could rally under Hampton.

After their conversation, Gary and Hampton spoke with Hagood and Kershaw. Gary announced his success in persuading Hampton to run, and on a straightout ticket. Hagood was taken off guard but agreed to support Hampton. Kershaw simply replied: "Well, if the general is nominated I will fall into line and support him. I always obey orders from headquarters."[15]

Hampton left Columbia the next day, as planned, to vacation with his family in Cashiers. While he was gone, Gary communicated with other Democratic leaders, especially Butler, who enthusiastically supported the plan to nominate Hampton. Meanwhile, news of the Hamburg massacre rocked the state.[16]

The proceedings of the Democratic Convention that met in the statehouse on August 17 to nominate Wade Hampton for governor resembled a coronation. Lesser nobles dutifully renounced their claims and hailed Hampton as the rightful heir and standard bearer. Butler, for one, had recently made it clear that he would not run. When the floor opened for nominations, Gary urged him to be the one to nominate Hampton. Butler stood on his one good leg and did so. The nomination was seconded. Hampton then made a short speech. He warned the delegates that there were two good reasons not to nominate him. First, many good Democrats believed that his name would hurt the chances of the Democratic Party at the national level. There was also his war record as a die-hard Confederate, which many voters (presumably Republicans) would consider a "disqualification." Hampton added: "That is the record of fifty thousand South Carolina soldiers, and if I am to forfeit that, and say that I am ashamed to have been one of them, all the offices in the world might perish before I would accept them."[17]

In a sad voice, Hampton confided to the convention that he had believed that "my day was past, and that in returning to my native State I was like him who said, 'An old man whose heart is broken is come to lay his weary bones among you. Give me a little earth for charity."

This was high oratory for Hampton, but it was from the heart of a man who had suffered much. As he spoke, he turned to face toward the graveyard of Trinity Church, just across the street from where he stood. Gesturing toward the graves of his ancestors, where his siblings, two wives, and three of his children lay, he declared, "I have claimed nothing from South Carolina, but a grave in yonder churchyard."

"I implore you," Hampton concluded, "to look over the whole field and not let any kindness for me lead you astray. I will now retire, so that you may discuss [these topics] freely. If you decide to nominate some other as true and sincere as I, and I know there are thousands of them, I will devote myself to secure his election. Come weal or woe, I am with you to the last."

Hampton bowed and exited to the outer corridor. In his absence two other men, General John Bratton and ex-governor John L. Manning, received nominations. Both immediately and emphatically declined, and in a matter of minutes Hampton was invited to return to make his acceptance speech. Gary, Butler, and the other straightouts were elated, but there were lines in his short address which indicated that he would not campaign on their platform of racial proscription. "I shall be Governor of the whole people, knowing no party, making no vindictive discriminations . . . seeing, as far as in me lies, that the laws are enforced in justice tempered with mercy, protecting all classes alike."[18]

The champion had accepted the guidon. It remained to be seen how faithfully his lieutenants would follow his course. Martin Gary immediately set one at odds with Hampton's. Gary was the foremost advocate for what was variously called the "Mississippi Plan," the "shotgun policy," or the "Edgefield Plan," modeled on the campaign of violence and intimidation by which white men had overcome a black majority in Mississippi and restored white rule in 1875. White South Carolinians were naturally interested in how conservatives in another black-majority state had managed to achieve this feat and eagerly read reports from

Mississippians on the methods employed. One of these reports was a letter from a General S. W. Ferguson of Washington County, Mississippi, to Theodore G. Barker, of Charleston, Hampton's former wartime adjutant and close friend. The letter came into Gary's hands and evidently helped the latter formulate his ideas on how the present campaign should be run. Ferguson boasted that in a county of less than 1,200 white voters and over 6,000 black voters, the whites had managed to obtain victory through superior determination and the willingness to use violence. "We determined to carry the election at all hazards, and, in the event of any blood being shed in the Campaign, *to kill every white Radical in the Country; we made no threats*, but we let this be known as a fixed and settled thing." Ferguson reported that although white Republicans actually welcomed disturbances that might prompt Washington to send federal troops, none of them were personally willing "to sacrifice themselves on the altar of rascality." Thus, out of cowardice they counseled peace. Ferguson further claimed that black men did not bother to vote on election day after seeing their party's leaders "cower and finally retire from the contest."[19]

Ferguson prescribed detailed methods. Democrats must be organized on a military basis and armed. They must send out competent speakers to stump the state and attend Republican meetings in order to abuse Republican candidates "to their faces." White men must go to the polls when they opened and stay until they closed. Finally, he wrote, "never threaten a man individually; if he deserves to be threatened, the necessity of the times require that he should die. A dead Radical is very harmless—a threatened Radical . . . is often very troublesome, sometimes dangerous, always vindictive."

Inspired by this approach, Gary attempted to have Hampton adopt it. He spelled out his strategy in his "No. 1 Plan of Campaign." The first several paragraphs insisted that Democrats in each township were to organize into "Democratic Military Clubs," elect officers, and arm themselves with rifles, thirty rounds of ammunition, and three days' rations. These men would go to the polls at 5:00 A.M. on election day and remain all day to ensure that underage black men did not vote, to prevent squads of black men voting at one precinct and then going to another, and to guard the ballot boxes. Some of the recommendations were lawful. Gary emphasized that the Democrats must endeavor to have as many Democrats as possible appointed as election managers and have at least one Democrat on the three-man state Election Commission. The Democrats would not ask the people for campaign contributions until the sale of the cotton crop in October. Other suggestions were more aggressive. In the event that the Republicans refused to seat Democratic members, for example, two hundred "select men" must be sent to Columbia to "compel and enforce" the Democratic members' right to be seated. Democrats must attend all Republican meetings and, when Radical leaders made false statements, "tell them *then* and *there* to their faces, that they are liars, thieves and Rascals . . . and if you get a chance get upon the Platform and address the negroes." Finally, some recommendations were downright chilling. White men must treat blacks "so as to show them, you are the superior race, and that their natural position is that of subordination to the white man." If there were any bloodshed, burned houses, or fraud, Republican leaders must understand clearly that white Democrats would hold them "*personally Responsible*," whether the leaders were present or not, "*beginning first* with the white men, second the Mulatto men and third and last with the Black leaders." Underscoring this point was paragraph sixteen, which quoted a passage from the Ferguson letter word for word: "Never threaten a man individually, if he deserves to be threatened, the necessity of the times require that he *should die.*"[20]

The Ferguson letter, or at least the recommendations in it, made the rounds among South Carolina's conservative leaders. It was definitely in Gary's hands, and a copy of it remains in his personal papers. Hampton almost certainly knew of it. He owned land in Washington County, Mississippi, and probably knew Ferguson personally; and, of course, he was close to the letter's addressee, Theodore Barker. On the day after Hampton's nomination, however, the *Columbia Daily Register* tried to redefine the "Mississippi Plan." This newspaper had been a mouthpiece for Hampton's views in the past, and it reported that "Colonel Ferguson" of Washington County, Mississippi, had spoken in Columbia on Wednesday, August 16. According to the article, Ferguson said that the Mississippi Plan was really about winning over the black vote through persuasion "without one drop of blood being shed or a single case of intimidation being heard of."[21]

This claim, either by Ferguson or the *Daily Register*, was false. White men had reclaimed Mississippi through the shotgun policy, not "milk and cider" and "flattery of negroes," as Gary contemptuously described Hampton's appeals.[22] Someone was misrepresenting the Mississippi Plan, and it was probably Hampton's allies. The fact that the *Daily Register's* editorial appeared in Columbia the day after Hampton's nomination may have implicated Hampton itself.

What is clear is that Hampton and his campaign manager, Alexander Haskell, rejected Gary's plan. The Executive Committee of the state Democratic Party, from which Gary was excluded, consistently called for conciliation toward black voters and made earnest appeals for their support. The official party platform and Hampton's acceptance speech at the convention promised to protect the black vote, sustain the rule of law regardless of race, and provide better public education for both races. Hampton avoided speaking on the stand with the more extremist party leaders in Edgefield, Butler excepted, and Gary was never a part of his campaign entourage. In nearly every speech he made, Hampton condemned violence. At Newberry, in the heart of the more violence-prone up-country, Hampton frankly told his audience that he "didn't care" to have the votes of Democrats who "think that because they are Democrats they can violate the law, and look to him to protect them."[23] Yet while Hampton condemned violence, he did advocate peaceful shows of force. At virtually every campaign appearance, Hampton rode at the head of uniformed formations of supporters called "Red Shirts." These paramilitary units committed no violence in Hampton's presence, but they effectively communicated Democratic strength and will. Hampton used the phrases "force without violence" or "peaceful coercion" to describe the effect he wished the Red Shirts to have.[24]

His campaign began in the up-country—in Anderson, Greenville, Spartanburg, Union, Laurens, Newberry, and Abbeville—where Hampton had a solid base of white support. From the beginning, it resembled the triumphal march of a returning, conquering king more than a political canvass. Everywhere Hampton went, bands played and throngs of men, women, and children shouted "Hurrah for Hampton!" In every town, large contingents of mounted and dismounted Democratic "clubs" greeted him or else marched in ranks before and behind him. Most of them were uniformed in red shirts, creating the most colorful spectacle that many rural South Carolinians had ever seen. In Union, 2,000 mounted Red Shirts followed Hampton's carriage as he rode into town. In Abbeville, the carriage carrying him and his running mate, William D. Simpson, arrived at night. Waiting for him was a large group of ladies who "literally loaded him down" with flowers. With him were 1,000 mounted men and 600 dismounted men, 250 of whom the *News and Courier* claimed were black; a company of the old Hampton Legion; three brass bands; and banners with the names of Democratic candidates and the slogan "Home Rule and Reform." The whole entourage formed a torchlight procession that wound its way through town "like a huge fiery serpent." It was, reported an awed newspaper correspondent, the "grandest affair ever witnessed in the upcountry."[25] Between September 2 and November 4, Hampton spoke at fifty-seven rallies containing crowds of 3,000 to 10,000 each. Some locations could be reached only by horseback. By the end of September, the old cavalryman Hampton boasted of his endurance by teasing his staff, claiming that he had "broken down all the gentlemen who had started with him."[26] The campaign culminated in Charleston. Leading a parade of thousands into the city of his birth, Hampton heard the band play "Hail the Conquering Hero."[27]

Hampton's own personality enhanced his popularity, a point that modern accounts often neglect. It was not just that he was a war hero—South Carolina was full of men with honorable war records. Politicos and ordinary voters sensed a warmth and sincerity beneath Hampton's aristocratic, calm demeanor. No one described him as "aloof" anymore. Hampton had developed, or at least had become known for, a "common touch" while leading men in the army. He had a knack for remembering the faces and names of junior officers and enlisted men who expected no such recognition from someone of his status. One private wrote of him: "A born aristocrat, his breeding showed itself in every feature, word, and look. Yet his manners and bearing with the troops were so thoroughly democratic . . . that no man ever excited more enthusiasm."[28] Alfred Williams, a reporter who traveled with Hampton through most of the 1876 campaign, remembered an unplanned train stop between Columbia and Graniteville. Hampton and his party amused themselves with target shooting while repairs were made. Eventually, wrote Williams, "a farmer living nearby recognized the General and after looking him over, spoke—'Say, Gin'ral, they tell me you're a kind of dog man. I wisht you'd come over here an' look at somethin' I've got.'" Yeoman farmer and born aristocrat "tramped together to where there was a litter of new hound puppies." For an hour, the two men discussed the breeds of hounds and how to train a young dog to hunt possums effectively instead of getting distracted and "going off after rabbit trails." Williams concluded: "That was characteristic of Hampton. He never posed, never tried to look or do like somebody else—always and everywhere just plain Wade Hampton, simple, unaffected gentleman, dauntless warrior of South Carolina, loving and reverencing his God, his cause and his commonwealth to the last recess of his clean soul."[29] Williams's prose was sentimental, but it did not exaggerate the affection Hampton's people had for him.[30]

Hampton campaigned on a platform of "Home Rule" and good government. He pledged to reduce the bloated state government, slash taxes, and root out corruption. Like all Democrats, he blasted the Republican regime as composed of a lot of foreign adventurers and plunderers who had robbed citizens and misled their black supporters. To the state's black citizens, Hampton pledged to support the Thirteenth, Fourteenth, and Fifteenth amendments. "Not one single right enjoyed by the colored people shall be taken from them," he promised.[31] True, these pledges were only promises not to do harm, but they were a retreat from Hampton's original stand against universal male suffrage. Moreover, Hampton promised that his administration would provide "better facilities for education" than black South Carolinians had ever enjoyed.[32] He reminded black voters that he had been the first South Carolinian publicly to support the black franchise, though he neglected to mention that he only approved it for educated and property-holding blacks.

His promises were paternalistic ones of protection and provision. Hampton gave assurances to African Americans like those a powerful patron might make to his clients. Though he promised equality before the law, he did not yield on the right of men like himself to dominate the state's political offices. He pledged to allow "no bullying" of black citizens, to enforce the laws equally "or die in the attempt."[33] He boasted of his good relations with his ex-slaves in Mississippi who now worked for him and trusted him. In his Abbeville speech, Hampton read a letter he had received from an ex-slave named Francis Davie:

> Dear Marse Wade:
> Seeing you are nominated for governor by the white people and hearing you have promised the black man all the rights he now has, and knowing you were always a good and kind man to me when your slave and knowing you are a good and kind man who will do what he promises I write to say that I will vote for you and will get all the black men I can to do the same. I have bought a piece of land in York county and am trying to make a support for my family, which I can do if we had good laws and taxes. My wife, Flora, is still living and we have but one child whom we wish to educate. Please write to me, care of Dr. T. C. Robertson, Rock Hill, S.C.
> Your friend and former slave,
> Rev. Francis Davie[34]

Black South Carolinians were not unused to hearing Hampton boast of his friendship with African Americans. Back in 1867, in a speech to a black audience, he had referred to his relationship with Kit Goodwyn: "From many of you I have met not only kindness, but affection. I cannot forget how faithfully some of your people clung to me through all the perils and privations of the war. I cannot forget that it was one of you, who was always amongst the first at my side when I was wounded, and the last to leave me. Such affection is not often met with, nor is it easily forgotten, and while I have a crust of bread it shall be shared with this well-tried, this true, this trusty friend."[35]

Hampton was probably sincere in these sentiments and no doubt appreciated the loyalty of Goodwyn, who lived with or worked for Hampton for the rest of Hampton's life. As one modern historian has written, "There is little reason to doubt the genuineness and depth of his feelings toward [African Americans]. What is important is that this feeling had been expressed within very clear societal boundaries."[36] When Hampton called someone a "friend," he did not necessarily imply that he was an equal.

Often Hampton tried to evoke fraternal feelings between blacks and other white Carolinians as well. In Kingstree, for example, he claimed that there was "room for all honest Carolinians to gather around the family altar," extending an "earnest appeal to all Carolinians, white and black, to rally around their old mother and unite in one, last pull to drag her out of the mire."[37] Such hints at black-white family ties and social equality doubtless made many white listeners uneasy, but in other passages Hampton frankly indicated that blacks would be the subordinate brethren around the "family altar." In Marion, he repeated his frequent refrain that more corruption in Columbia would mean more economic suffering, both for whites and the black people who worked for them— "If you allow the white people of South Carolina to go down this time, you will go down so deep that no plummet can ever reach you."[38] But if blacks helped bring about a Democratic victory, "the men who own the land, the men who pay the taxes, the men who have the title-deeds from the Almighty, will take you by the hand as their friends."[39]

It is easy to charge Hampton with hypocrisy for his claims of friendship with blacks. Anytime he advertised his friendly relations with African Americans, he was referring to his ex-slaves or current laborers, men who were supposedly grateful to him for his kindness to inferiors and his honesty. Yet one could just as easily emphasize his frankness. For Hampton to pretend that he had ever related to black men as social equals would have been dishonest and transparently false to his black listeners. He and his audiences came from a racially divided and hierarchical social structure; he was seeking common ground and exploiting any goodwill that could be found within that system. He could not suddenly pretend to be an egalitarian.

Hampton served almost as a messianic figure to some, and Democratic political rallies captured this emotion. When Hampton and his Red Shirts rode into Sumter on October 7, a girl awaited him at the speaker's platform. She was bowed and draped with black mourning garb and chains. As soon as Hampton mounted the platform, "the chains were cast aside with a clang, the mourning robes were thrown off and a radiant young woman in pure white stood tall and stately, head uplifted and eyes shining like stars . . . a golden coronet on her hair— 'South Carolina.' " An eyewitness remembered that "big men were not ashamed to let tears come."[40] The performance was repeated or slightly altered in other towns along the way, with young white women representing "Liberty" and "Justice" coming forth as soon as Hampton rode into view and rescued a suffering maiden lying in the dust. The "prostrate state" had been redeemed, and crowds responded with cheers, Rebel yells, and tears of emotion.[41]

Of course these scenes were, in part, typical grandstanding in an election year. But they also captured the deepest hopes of white South Carolinians and revealed what they had come to believe about themselves, or what they hoped to see in themselves. They were a chosen people, chastised by God for their sins, but not rejected. One day, one day soon, they would be redeemed by God's chosen instrument— one of their own kindred who would restore them to their proper place through his courage, his virtue, and his own suffering. Wade Hampton, they began to hope, was that instrument. South Carolina historian Walter Edgar has noted that Hampton "had even suffered the indignity of having his possessions sold at public auction to meet his creditors' demands. That, however, was unimportant. He was Wade Hampton."[42] Actually it did matter that Hampton had suffered indignity, loss, and pain. He had suffered as much as any South Carolinian over the past fifteen years. Without quite crossing the line into heresy, white South Carolinians often regarded Hampton as a suffering savior, poised to deliver his people from shame and degradation. As one matron remembered, "Wade Hampton was the Moses of his people, the God-given instrument to help them free themselves from their enemies."[43]

A savior must be not only one who has suffered, but also one who represents virtue. As Joel Williamson has observed, Hampton represented the best of the antebellum world that had reared him, personify- 383 ing the "inflexible rectitude, the sober courage which all South Carolinians idolized but few possessed."[44] One might also add magnanimity and self-control to this list of rare but sought-after traits. There was no doubt about his courage. Every Carolinian knew something of Hampton's war record, which was already morphing into legend. No one questioned his integrity—he was a man who stood by his word. He would never deliberately humiliate a peer or social inferior, but neither would he tolerate an insult to his honor or to his state. He did not believe in social equality, particularly of the races, but he was willing to promise protection, peace, and honest leadership to his subjects. He would keep his promises, even to black men. He lectured white audiences that "any candidate that would sink so low as to deceive a colored man is unworthy of the name of 'man.' "[45] Finally, he was able to make those promises because he was powerful—socially, politically, and physically. A prerequisite for a Christian knight and protector was that he had the power to preserve the peace as well as punish his enemies. He could unleash destruction but preferred forbearance. As white men in South Carolina threatened and shot black men, stuffed ballot boxes, and exploded in rage in the fall of 1876, Hampton's righteous appeals for calm restraint and honorable dealing convinced his supporters that their campaign was a "religious struggle between good and evil," and their enemies represented evil.[46]

Hampton did receive some black support, though never as much as he hoped or believed. African Americans turned out to watch Hampton's rallies, some out of curiosity and a few who openly claimed to support him. As in Abbeville, some black men marched in the Democratic parade, either in their own clubs or alongside whites. The News and Courier often reported on the growing membership of black Democratic clubs or "Hampton Clubs" and on the number of black Red Shirts at Hampton rallies. Usually the paper inflated the numbers of both. Still, not all of the anecdotal evidence of black support for Hampton was invented, and there was enough of it to encourage Democrats that his paternalistic appeals were working. Martin Delany, a prominent black Charleston leader and former "Reform" candidate for lieutenant governor, stumped for Hampton. Richland County's Merriman Washington, who said that he had been "raised" by Hampton, named his son "Wade Hampton"; he also organized a Red Shirt club of sixteen young black men after being defrauded by Republican trial justices.[47] One of the club's members was Jonas Weeks, who had belonged to Hampton's father; he remembered the son as a good man who treated his slaves kindly. Weeks would later testify to a congressional committee that when black Republicans threatened and abused him for supporting Hampton, he told them that he did not fear them and that "if I died I would die for General Hampton."[48] In Little Rock, South Carolina, near Marion, two black men spoke in favor of Hampton at a Democratic meeting. Black Red Shirts rode or marched in Hampton's processions in Greenville, Abbeville, Clover, Marion, Laurens, Kingstree, Sumter, and even the heavily Republican low-country towns of Charleston and Beaufort. At St. George's, one of the speakers was John Overton, a "colored Democrat" who had once chaired the Republican Party in that precinct. Overton said that he would vote for Hampton because he believed that Hampton would "work on a Republican platform" and because Overton had been unable to get honest Republicans elected.[49] In the Kingstree parade, a black Democrat led one of the cavalry companies. He carried a banner that pictured a black man kicking a white man who carried a carpetbag on his shoulders.[50] In Mount Pleasant, a pro-Hampton black man endured verbal abuse from some black Republicans before turning on them and invoking the name of Hampton— "You may curse me but I won't curse you back again, 'cause I'm a Hampton man. Gen. Hampton is *a gentleman, and he don't curse, and I won't curse neither, but just let one of you put his hand on me, and you'll see!!*"[51]

As the Democratic campaign gained momentum, the Republicans struggled to get theirs off the ground. The Republican convention did not meet until September 14. The delegates were at least able to prevent another bolt by Republican independents, partially by keeping Chamberlain as the gubernatorial candidate but placating his enemies by nominating Robert Elliott for attorney general. Elliott was an able black leader who nevertheless had a widespread reputation for corruption, and he and Chamberlain despised each other. Elliott's nomination drove many remaining moderates into Hampton's camp, including several white Republican leaders, such as Judges Thomas J. Mackey, Thompson H. Cooke, and Solomon Northrup.[52]

While Hampton lectured to enthusiastic but peaceful crowds along his campaign trail, other Democrats were conducting a very different type of fight. Hampton's popularity, his promises to blacks, and Republican weakness were not the only themes of the 1876 campaign. One Democratic tactic was economic proscription, refusing to buy goods from or do business with Republicans. Landlords refused to rent land to

Republicans, and physicians denied them medical care. Other Democrats tried to bribe blacks to vote Democratic, a tactic that had become endemic to Reconstruction South Carolina within both parties.[53]

Violence, however, was perhaps the most prominent theme of the campaign in the long run, and it is certainly the most remembered one. The violent arm of the Democratic Party consisted of the rifle and saber clubs. There were close to 300 of them throughout the state, with a total membership of some 15,000 men. At official Democratic rallies where Hampton spoke, the clubs were on their best behavior, and no violence occurred along Hampton's campaign trail. Elsewhere they could be murderous. At Republican rallies, club members, or Red Shirts, would show up in force, surrounding the meeting, shouting threats, and firing pistols in the air. Armed men would escort a Democratic speaker to the stand, who would denounce the "lies" of the Republican speaker and demand a chance to take the platform. These tactics often demoralized or broke up Republican meetings, and many intimidated Republicans submitted to threats and declined to speak. Armed white men singled out white and black Republicans and threatened them personally. A new wave of political murders washed across the state. The violence was not all on one side. There were numerous incidents of black men—and women—attacking other blacks who dared to "hurrah for Hampton." But Democrats were undoubtedly extracting more blood and were more organized and deliberate in doing so. The more out of hand the situation became, the greater likelihood that Chamberlain could convince Washington to send federal troops.[54]

The violence exploded into all-out warfare in Aiken County the week after Chamberlain's nomination. Between September 15 and 21, fighting raged around the town of Ellenton in the southern corner of the county. To this day, the facts of the "Ellenton riots" are unclear, and contemporaries were confused as well. Republican and Democratic witnesses and newspapers printed wildly contradictory accounts. What is now certain is that whites were generally the aggressors and inflicted much heavier casualties. Somewhere between twenty-five and one hundred black people were killed, in contrast to one white man killed and five or six wounded. The violence abated in Ellenton only to spill over into neighboring Barnwell County in late September and early October. While Hampton preached peace, the Red Shirt campaign was becoming one of the bloodiest electoral campaigns in American history.[55]

Hampton understood that violence on such a large scale invited federal intervention. He and James Conner, his close confidant and Democratic candidate for state attorney general, believed that Chamberlain's strategy was to try to arrest key men in Aiken and Barnwell, including Calbraith Butler. If those men resisted arrest or were rescued by Red Shirts, Chamberlain could persuade President Grant that the insurrection was too formidable for state authorities to suppress it and then "cover the whole State" with federal troops. "But we see the game," Conner told his wife, "and don't mean to play into his hands."[56]

Hampton responded to the crisis in three ways. First, he appealed to his supporters to end the violence. He sent telegrams to local Democratic leaders across the state, including Butler, instructing them to use their influence to prevent further turbulence. Speaking in Marion on September 30, Hampton tried to calm the situation by asserting his right to command—"You have placed me in command, and I have the right to ask your attention to what I shall say. . . . All bloodshed must be avoided, and I will say to you that the people of Charleston in the late riot in that city behaved magnificently."[57] (Here Hampton referred to a black-instigated riot on September 6 in which Theodore Barker, leader of the Charleston rifle clubs, refused to allow his men to retaliate and faced heavy criticism as a result.)[58]

A second, parallel approach was to suggest that Chamberlain had lost control of the state. Hampton repeated reports in the *News and Courier* and *New York Herald* that Chamberlain had left South Carolina during the Ellenton riots, either to secure military aid from Washington or to visit sick relatives in New York. Either way, charged Hampton, the governor had abandoned his post. Besides, if Chamberlain could not control white violence without help from Washington, it was manifest that he did not have enough of the people's goodwill to rule and should therefore resign. He was equally unfit to rule if he could not control black-on-black violence. In Hampton's September 30 speech, he chose to dwell not on white violence around Ellenton, but on the situation in Combahee, Beaufort County. In late August and early September, at the usual time for the rice harvest, black laborers struck for a 50 percent wage increase. Strikers beat or whipped their fellow hands who refused to go along with the strike or imprisoned them in outhouses. Later they overpowered a sheriff and a posse before order was finally restored. Hampton charged that the black men who had been abused for going to work had written time and again to Chamberlain for protection, but to no avail. "He dares not go there and [instead] runs to Washington. *I say here that if Governor Chamberlain will call on me and give me the authority for three days, I pledge myself to go amongst those Combahee rioters, not armed with* even a pen knife, and I further pledge myself that they will listen to me and order will be restored in twenty-four hours."[59] Thus Hampton hoped to persuade black listeners and a northern audience that the real problem was Chamberlain's lack of will and courage—only Hampton had the power, prestige, and courage to protect white and black citizens and preserve peace.[60]

The third official response of the Hampton campaign to the violence was to pretend that there was no real problem. Although this logically contradicted the other two responses, it was intended to prevent intervention by the Grant administration. In early October Alexander Haskell sent letters to leading Republican jurists asking them to state their opinion publicly on whether conditions in South Carolina merited martial law or the use of federal troops. Democratic newspapers printed the responses of Chief Justice Moses, Republican ex-governor Scott, Associate Justice Willard, and circuit court judges Mackey, Cooke, A. J. Shaw, and Northrup. All said that general quiet pervaded in their circuits and that they were unaware of the need for troops. The only real threat to public order, Democratic newspapers claimed, was Chamberlain's minions.[61]

On October 7 Chamberlain ordered the disbandment of all rifle clubs. Hampton urged local leaders to comply, hoping to avoid giving the governor more evidence of the need for federal troops. On October 15, however, there was more violence, this time in Cainhoy, near Charleston. And this time black men were at least partially responsible, and inflicted a heavier casualty toll on the whites, but the event was enough to persuade President Grant to get involved. On the seventeenth he ordered the disbandment of all rifle clubs and commanded all those involved in violent insurrection to return to their homes. The next day the Democratic Executive Committee promised to comply in "perfect submission," while simultaneously denying any responsibility for the violence.[62] Over the next few days, sixteen companies of federal troops were stationed in ten major South Carolina towns.[63]

Hampton again sent word for the rifle clubs to disperse. "Some of the younger men," reported Conner, "are very much dissatisfied. . . . But it was necessary and was urged by the State Executive Committee and General Hampton."[64] But most of the rifle clubs honored the commands of Chamberlain, Grant, and Hampton only in the breech. Some disarmed but retained their organization and remained on the alert. Others reported that they had disbanded but had really only changed their names. The Columbia Flying Artillery became the Columbia Musical Club with Four Twelve Pounder Flutes; the Allendale Rifle Club became the Allendale Mounted Baseball Club, with 150 baseball players on the team. Others reorganized as the Mother's Little Helpers or the First Baptist Church Sewing Circle.[65]

Hampton had several reasons for opposing the growth of violence. He had long keenly felt that he and other white southerners were "making up our record for posterity."[66] Ever since his opposition to resuming the slave trade in 1858, Hampton had publicly projected himself as a defender of constitutional government and law and order. He did not want anyone to be able to say that he had won the election through terror and lawlessness.

There were pragmatic reasons that were just as compelling. Because Hampton's references to them are scattered, fragmented, and propagandist in nature, it is revealing to read the frank, unguarded comments of one of Hampton's inner circle. James Conner traveled with Hampton through much of the campaign, and his letters to his wife in October explained the official thinking of the Hampton campaign on the issue of Democratic force and federal intervention. On October 18 Conner expressed the opinion that Chamberlain's and Grant's proclamations would "damage our election very much. We are getting the darkey splendidly in hand, and now he will go back to the United States power, and Chamberlain."[67]

Within two days, however, Conner's thinking had shifted. "People differ as to the effects of troops on our election," he wrote on the twentieth. "I don't think they will do us any hurt. But for them, we have the election, but I hardly think they will drive off [pro-Hampton] negroes enough to defeat us, but we can't tell yet." Over the next few days, U.S. troops arrived in the state and were politely received by the white population. Violence subsided and the white rifle clubs at least pretended to disband. On the twenty-fourth, Conner developed his thinking on the use of force more fully. Conner believed that Hampton had added greatly to his own prestige and "influence over the people" through his "judgment, tact, and good sense." He now worried, though, that the employment of federal troops might turn out to be the Republicans' ace in the hole:

How the election will go is hard to say. The troops will undoubtedly lose us votes in the upper and middle counties. Our chance to carry the negro was not by argument or reason, but by letting him see that we were the stronger—and to impress him with a sense of our power and determination. Hence the demonstration we made—for the darkey is impressionable—and the spectacular takes him every pop. We were winning on that line and had the election sure. To check the tide of the darkies to us—and to show him that we were not the stronger, Chamberlain brought in the United States troops, and showed to the negro that there was a power stronger than ours, and the negro ceased to come to us. . . .

But if we can get troops at the precincts in Beaufort and Colleton we can more than counter balance what we lose in the upper sections. We have sent a Committee to Columbia to ask for them. The fear is, that even if we win, they will count us out. The Board of Canvassers is six—and four is a quorum, and four of them are candidates.[68]

Hampton's strategy, then, rested on several assumptions. Knowing that eligible black voters in the state outnumbered white ones by roughly 35,000, Hampton and his advisers still believed that black men were overawed by pomp, ceremony, "demonstration," and the white man's "power and determination." Since the days of slavery, white men had been conditioned, even socialized, to make a show of "power and determination" to keep black laborers under control and were apt to resort to the same tactic still. Hence the Democrats feared that the use of federal troops by state and federal administrations would reveal that it was really the Republicans who had the most power. Hampton's inner circle also feared that while the presence of troops would encourage harassed black voters to go to the polls and vote Republican in the "whiter" counties, military force would also give reassurance to anti-Hampton blacks in low-country precincts around Beaufort and Colleton. They were convinced, in fact, that this was Chamberlain's strategy. Judge Thompson Cooke, a Republican who went over to Hampton midway through the campaign, testified to Congress that he had heard white Republican leaders say "time and again" that they needed to find a way to bring federal troops to the state to "induce the negro to vote the republican ticket."[69] Cooke cited these words from a private conversation with Chamberlain (which Chamberlain denied); he also asserted that Senator "Honest John" Patterson said that the Republicans "would have to kick up hell and get the troops down here."[70] Cooke may have exaggerated in his testimony, but he probably shared Patterson's and Chamberlain's alleged comments with his new Democratic allies, for Haskell, Conner, Hampton, and Democrats in general shared the suspicion that Chamberlain would use violence as an excuse to bring federal troops to the state to ensure a Republican victory.

Publicly, Hampton assured his supporters that federal troops would ensure law and order and would act impartially. He made it known that he had spoken personally with General Thomas Ruger, commanding the South Carolina garrisons, and that the general had satisfied Hampton that he would "not be made the tool of Governor Chamberlain."[71] This was yet another attempt by Hampton to show his power. If he did not have ultimate military power in the state, he had an amicable understanding, he claimed, with Ruger. Privately, though, as Conner's letters reveal, the Democrats were aware that a U.S. military presence would suggest that black South Carolinians must ultimately turn to Chamberlain and Grant for security and protection, not southern patriarchs like Hampton.

Finally, Conner's letter indicates that the Democrats assumed that the Republicans would cheat if they could. The latter controlled the Board of Canvassers and, considering South Carolina Republicans' history of corruption and cheating, they might be expected to "count out" votes for Hampton. But as election day approached, advocates of the Mississippi Plan in the counties of Edgefield, Laurens, Spartanburg, and elsewhere determined that, with or without the presence of federal troops, they would outdo the "Radicals" at "counting out."

CHAPTER 28

INTERREGNUM

The campaign of 1876–77 was full of ironies and contradictions. One involved the fact that Hampton symbolized to his followers their hope of restoring white supremacy. Yet no Democrat, or "conservative," in the South reached out more to blacks or made more promises to respect their civil rights. Sternly warning his own supporters not to make a liar out of him, Hampton won admiration for his magnanimity and political courage, sometimes even among white men who had no intention of honoring his promises in their name. Hampton appeared as the symbol of honor, courage, and nobility that the white South imagined itself to be.[1]

Another irony hinged on the evolution of popular democracy in South Carolina. Elites like Hampton and his allies saw the election as an attempt to vindicate the antebellum political system in which they had ruled. To win, however, they had to conduct the election in a political context radically different from before the war. South Carolina governors were now popularly elected, rather than chosen by the legislature. Rather than win the assent of other gentlemen of his claims to leadership, Hampton had to appeal to the masses—black as well as white. Yet his appeal to them rested on noblesse oblige as well as popular democracy. Hampton campaigned in the style of a modern democratic politician, but he couched his claims to rule in older notions of aristocratic virtue and paternalism.[2]

Finally, as much as he wished to show that he could preserve peace, Hampton was largely unable to control the excesses of his own supporters occurring outside his immediate gaze, at least until after the election. Though he eventually convinced northern political leaders of his ability to maintain order, the election campaign went down as one of the most violent in American history. And while the election was also one of the most fraudulent in American history, Hampton's search for vindication at the polls depended, in his mind at least, on proving that he and men of his class were worthy of leadership—that only they had the prestige, intelligence, and moral virtue to govern.

As the Red Shirt campaign of 1876 had become wilder and bloodier, Hampton had tried to position himself as a force for law and order. The days after the election did not bring an end to the uncertainty and deadly   393 tension in the state. At the national level, it was unclear who had won the presidential race. Democrat Samuel J. Tilden won the popular vote, but the electoral count was disputed because of charges of fraud in Louisiana, Florida, and South Carolina. White South Carolinians desired a Tilden victory, but they were far more concerned with the outcome of the state election, particularly with whether Hampton or Chamberlain would be their next governor. The initial returns gave Hampton a slightly larger vote than Chamberlain, but the Republicans charged fraud and attempted to throw out the returns for some Democratic counties. For five months, both Hampton and Chamberlain claimed to be the governor of South Carolina, and two rival assemblies claimed to be the legal state house of representatives.

In this chaotic situation, Hampton found it more useful than ever to position himself as the master of both peace and war, as the only man in the state who could preserve lawful order. Again and again he was able to demonstrate that he had such power—and in far greater measure than he had possessed during the campaign. Despite the fact that the U.S. troops in Columbia came under the orders of a Republican president, Hampton showed that he was the real master of the state. He was also able to present himself, rightly or not, as the true representative of constitutional government and Chamberlain's government as illegal and illegitimate.

This was more than crafty political maneuvering on Hampton's part, although it did illustrate a shrewd understanding of northern concerns, Republican fears, and white longings. South Carolinians understood mastery over violence, and forbearance in the use of it, as clear indicators of a white man's right to rule—an understanding with roots in the antebellum, slaveowning world of Hampton's youth. They expected men of Hampton's class to be powerful. They were even more powerful if they could be forbearing in the use of power and still accomplish their will. Patriarchs like Hampton had to be able not only to punish their enemies, but also to protect their people—and even to restrain their people in the use of violence. Mastery, then, implied not simply bloodthirstiness, but power tempered by restraint and principle. One is reminded of Harry Hampton, a great-nephew, scoffing at the claim that "Uncle Wade" killed eighty bears in the Mississippi forests with nothing but a hunting knife. The mighty Hampton sliced the throat of only one bear, Harry boasted, and then only because he felt obligated to protect loyal, lesser mortals—his hunting dogs.[3]

Election day, November 8, saw less violence than many feared. Another race riot in Charleston left a handful of casualties on both sides, and there were isolated incidents of shots fired and scuffles elsewhere. Though there was little bloodshed overall, there was plenty of fraud and intimidation. Illiterate black voters received ballots showing pictures of Rutherford B. Hayes and William A. Wheeler (the Republican presidential and vice presidential candidates) but with Hampton's name printed on it. White men crossed over the borders from North Carolina and Georgia to vote for Hampton. Some white South Carolinians boasted of having voted for Hampton eighteen or twenty times. At some precincts, Red Shirts turned black men away from the polls and threatened others. Democrats charged the Republicans with using similar tactics in the low-country counties of Charleston, Beaufort, and Colleton, and complained when congressional subcommittees investigated charges of Democratic abuses while ignoring Republican ones. Nevertheless, the Democrats were far more effective at cheating. Martin Gary and other Red Shirt leaders were actually too successful in Edgefield and Laurens counties, where Hampton received more votes than there were adult males in the 1875 census. When the votes were tallied, Hampton had 92,261 votes to 91,127 for Chamberlain. There is little doubt that Hampton actually received more votes, whether legally or illegally. It is equally clear that had his fraudulent votes been thrown out, Chamberlain would have won.[4]

Early in the campaign, Hampton predicted that he would get 10,000 black votes. Immediately after the election, he appears to have believed that he actually received 17,000, though he later revised that estimate downward. A careful study of black Red Shirts surmises that those black men who voted for Hampton had several motivations besides the economic proscription and threats from Hampton's more ruthless followers. Many of them, says Edmund Drago, confronting "economic hard times increasing turbulence, and Republican corruption . . . sought a way out."[5] "Voting for Hampton," Drago concludes, "seemed the safest way to restore peace."[6] Many also responded to Hampton's paternalistic appeals and shared the anti-Yankee bias of Democratic leaders. Another fact that allowed Hampton to think that he had won black support was that he got more votes than the Democratic candidate for president, Samuel J. Tilden. During the campaign, a good number of blacks claimed that they would vote a "Hayes and Hampton" ticket, voting Republican at the national level but for Hampton as governor. When the ballots were counted, it seemed clear that many had done just that. Hampton, in fact, would always contend that black votes had been crucial to his victory.[7]

Most black South Carolinians, however, did not trust white Democrats enough to be moved by Hampton's promises, or else they considered his promises to be not enough. The *Charleston Republican* questioned Hampton's sincerity in pledges to protect the black vote. Both that paper and the *Port Royal Standard* interpreted his promises of protection for black supporters as veiled threats to those who opposed him. Often these publications regarded Hampton as more moderate than other Democrats around him but asserted that if his promises were sincere, he would do more to control the excesses of his followers. James Conner, who helped direct Democratic efforts in Charleston, realized that anticipated support for Hampton in his city had not materialized. "The negroes went back on us fearfully," Conner admitted to his wife. "They fooled us to death. Thousands who had promised Hayes and Hampton voted the solid Republican ticket."[8]

The Board of Canvassers, composed of five Republicans, acknowledged that Hampton had received 1,134 more votes than Chamberlain. But it also ruled that it would throw out the votes from Edgefield and Laurens counties because of fraud. This gave Chamberlain an advantage of 3,145 votes over Hampton. The board was certainly correct on the matter of fraud, but its constitutional authority to make such a decision was weak. The Democrats appealed to the state supreme court, also controlled by Republicans. The supreme court ruled that, according to the state constitution, only the legislature could legally certify who won the governor's race—the only function of the Board of Canvassers was to count the votes. But even if Chamberlain had recognized this decision by the supreme court, it did not solve the problem. The initial vote count indicated that Democrats from Edgefield and Laurens had won seats in the house of representatives. The Board of Canvassers, however, gave the seats to Republicans. If the Democratic candidates were the true victors, the Democrats would control the General Assembly and would certify Hampton's victory; if they were not, there would be a Republican-controlled General Assembly and undoubtedly a Republican governor. Those candidates declared victors by the Board of Canvassers received certificates of election from the secretary of state; the Democratic candidates from Edgefield and Laurens lacked such certificates but held certificates from the state supreme court. The Board of Canvassers abruptly adjourned on November 22 to avoid being served with the order of the state supreme court. In response, the court held the board in contempt and ordered the arrest of its five members.[9]

Hampton thought that his victory was legitimate. He expressed this view not only in public pronouncements and letters to officials in Washington, but also to intimate friends like Armistead Burt, to whom he wrote, "The State went democratic by a heavy majority which has been cut down by radical frauds."[10] Hampton was aware of Democratic cheating at the polls but claimed that, regrettably, his followers had only mimicked the tactics of Republicans.[11]

Richard Zuczek has observed that, at this point, South Carolina whites could feel victory just within their grasp, a victory they had been striving for since Appomattox or, more accurately, since Fort Sumter. They were close to winning the long struggle over who had the right and authority to govern their state, and to determine the racial and social order of their society. "A victory years in the making was almost theirs," writes Zuczek, "and it was up to the chosen savior, Wade Hampton, to reach out and take it."[12] Such a victory would be the ultimate vindication—it would mean that Hampton and native whites were once again the legitimate, constitutional rulers of the state. Chamberlain and his minions had to be shown as pretenders whose reign could not survive without federal bayonets. As the representative of the master class in South Carolina, Hampton hoped to demonstrate that it was in his power to unleash violence or to preserve peace; he could unleash the dogs of war or rein them in. Most importantly, he was able, without federal military force, to preserve law and order, the most laudable goal of statesmanship.

Zuczek's observations are undoubtedly correct, but it should be added that the electoral crisis was also the climax of a long struggle for personal vindication, for redeeming the personal loss and tragedy that tore at the soul of virtually every South Carolinian. When Hampton and his lieutenants spoke of "redemption," it was not mere political propaganda. The term had not only political but also intensely personal meanings. Hampton himself had suffered much, and personal tragedy continued to stalk him during the campaign. Only days before the election, he endured the death of his three-year-old grandson, Wade Hampton Haskell. Days after the election, the cottage occupied by Hampton's sisters and brother Frank's orphaned children burned to the ground. The Hamptons had built this residence in 1866 after the destruction of Millwood by Sherman's men. Contemporaries agreed that the fire was a result of arson by Radicals who mistook the house for Hampton's own residence. Such an event, a direct attack on the beloved Democratic leader, could have been the catalyst for another wave of violence. Hampton declined to use it for that purpose. No doubt he was enraged and embittered. But publicizing the event could set off another white rampage and endanger his electoral victory with a return to martial law. Hampton would have to control his own anger as well as that of others. Incredibly, newspapers across the state gave the incident almost no coverage.[13]

The next test of Hampton's power—and self-control—came on November 28. The legislature was scheduled to meet that day, and the Democrats expected to be able to control the organization of the house of representatives. Chamberlain, however, had stolen a march on his opponents. He managed to have two companies of General Thomas Ruger's troops posted inside the statehouse to preserve order and gave instructions that no one would be allowed to enter without a certificate of election from the secretary of state; one from the state supreme court would not suffice. This would allow the Republican candidates from Edgefield and Laurens to enter, but not the Democratic ones, ensuring a Republican majority in the house to augment its control of the senate. With control of the General Assembly, Republicans could then decide who was governor and inaugurate Chamberlain.[14]

At the appointed hour of noon, the Democratic members of the house walked en masse from Carolina Hall to the statehouse to find sentries guarding the entrance. The representatives from Edgefield and Laurens were in the lead and were refused admission. At this point Hampton was inside the statehouse, as were Chamberlain and General Ruger. Hampton asked Ruger to change the orders to the guards to admit representatives with certificates from the supreme court as well as the secretary of state. After some discussion and delay, the guards allowed the Democrats to enter. Once inside the building, however, they were not allowed to enter the hall of representatives itself. By the time that one of them slipped in, he discovered that the Republican members of the house had already organized and elected a speaker.[15]

For a moment, it looked to the Democrats as if all were lost. An immense, angry crowd of roughly five thousand was already swarming over the statehouse grounds, and the tension was high. Anger ran deep. The *Edgefield Advertiser*'s editor, James T. Bacon, an eyewitness assuming the role of a reporter, wrote: "We have committed murder, in thought, a thousand times. And, so help us God, we do not believe that the end of all this trouble will come until we—South Carolinians—arise and shoot the last carpetbagger in our State. If we kill out this crop, no more will come! We see no other solution."[16]

In his office, a nervous Chamberlain spoke with Ruger and reluctantly agreed that the one man who could defuse the situation was Wade Hampton. A messenger sent to look for him quickly found him in one of the corridors. It was then that Hampton, six feet tall and two hundred forty pounds, assumed his stance on the front steps, facing the crowd with the solid edifice of the state capitol behind him. His words were not overly dramatic, but those who were there never forgot the scene. "My friends," he began,

> I am truly doing what I have done earnestly during this whole exciting contest, pouring oil on the troubled waters. It is of the greatest importance to us all, as citizens of South Carolina, that peace should be preserved. I appeal to you all, white men and colored, to use every effort to keep down violence or disturbance. One act of violence may precipitate bloodshed and desolation. I implore you then to preserve the peace. I beg all of my friends to disperse, to leave the grounds of the Capitol; and I advise all colored men to do the same, keep perfectly quiet, leave the streets and do nothing to provoke a riot. We trust to the law and the constitution, and we have perfect faith in the justice of our cause.[17]

Instantly the crowd began to melt away, some of its members sullen that Hampton had not ordered a charge. Yet even the *Advertiser*'s James T. Bacon, who wanted to "kill out this crop" of carpetbaggers, conceded that "General Hampton is calm, dignified, self-possessed, and continues to counsel peace, moderation, and strict abiding by the law."[18]

The significance of the event was obvious to everyone who witnessed it. Chamberlain, the sitting governor, had to appeal to Hampton to preserve law and order, and Hampton did so with apparent ease. Some southern newspapers recited the facts of the story and simply asserted that "Comment is as impossible as it is unnecessary."[19] Other eyewitnesses did comment, however. Hampton's friend Bradley T. Johnson, now a Virginia legislator, wrote Hampton: "You had only to raise your hand, and Ruger's garrison would have been swept off the face of the earth. But you held them back, and I know of no more remarkable demonstration of moral force than your control and their obedience."[20] Ohio politician Samuel Shellabarger concluded that without Hampton's restraint, the rifle clubs would have assassinated Republican leaders and

Drawing from Frank Leslie's Illustrated Newspaper. Original caption reads: "General Wade Hampton on the Steps of the Capitol at Columbia, November 28th, Advising the Citizens to Avoid All Acts of Violence." South Caroliniana Library.

taken over the state. The *New York Herald* asserted: "The credit of preserving the peace at Columbia is due to General Wade Hampton, Democratic candidate for governor. He had only to lift his finger," and thousands of armed Democrats would have "annihilated" the federal force of three hundred. "It is fortunate that they have a leader so strong, so sagacious, so self-possessed and so thoroughly trusted as Wade Hampton."[21] The *Herald* obviously had a Democratic bias, but years later Chamberlain said much the same thing. Assessing the character of the man whom he called a usurper in 1876–77, Chamberlain wrote in 1901 that Hampton was "unselfish, resolute, level-headed, and determined. He was for the hour a true 'natural leader'; and he led with consummate mingled prudence and aggressiveness."[22]

The event seemed to bolster Hampton's own belief that he was indeed all that stood between lawful government and mayhem; therefore, he should be governor. Hampton tried to impress this logic on black Republican leader Robert Elliott, whom he hoped would convey it to Chamberlain. Two days after dispersing the crowd at the statehouse, Hampton approached Elliott, the Republican candidate for attorney general. According to Elliott, Hampton expressed his hope for a peaceful solution and recited his efforts to preserve order. Elliott expressed the same desire. Then Hampton explained that he considered Chamberlain responsible for the current confusion, and that he thought it was the duty of "leading colored men" like Elliott to withdraw their support. Hampton told Elliott: "I can protect the people of the State, black and white alike, while Chamberlain cannot protect either. . . . Governor Chamberlain cannot protect his own life. I have had to protect him from the just indignation of the people, and if I were now to take my hands off the brakes for an hour, his life would not be safe."[23]

Hampton was arguing that his power to prevent violence legitimized his authority. Chamberlain and Elliott, however, interpreted his comments as a threat, not a claim to moral authority. In his inaugural address, Chamberlain said that Hampton claimed to hold "not only the peace of this city and State, but my life, in his hands. I do not doubt the truth of his statement. Neither the public peace, nor the life of any man who now opposes the consummation of this policy of fraud and violence, is safe from the assaults of those who have enforced that policy."[24] While Hampton hoped to appear a peacemaker, Chamberlain portrayed him as an assassin.

Hampton reacted angrily. In his own public statement, Hampton called Chamberlain's charges "infamously false." He did not dispute the words imputed to him but hotly denied that he "countenance[d] the hand of the assassin. . . . I have, by my unwearied exertions, endeavored to preserve the peace of the State, and I have thus contributed to shield from popular indignation one who has proved himself a disgrace to his rank and a traitor to his trust."[25] To bolster his case against Hampton, Chamberlain printed a statement from Republican judge Thomas Settle. Chamberlain's defenders have cited Settle's letter as a confirmation of Chamberlain's and Elliott's portrayal of Hampton as a blackmailer, but it actually gave more support to Hampton's claim that he intended to prevent violence. Settle wrote that he and Chamberlain supporter John B. Dennis had called on Hampton and expressed concern that Chamberlain's life was not safe. According to Settle, Hampton responded "that his efforts to preserve the peace had been incessant; that he had constantly advised moderation, and that by doing so he had doubtless protected [Chamberlain's] life."[26]

After the Republican takeover of the statehouse, Hampton boldly made the case that he represented legitimate government; that Chamberlain was a usurper. On hearing that General Ruger intended to prevent the Democratic representatives from Edgefield from taking their seats, Hampton, Haskell, and Georgia senator John B. Gordon protested to Ruger. They charged that not only had the general reneged on previous verbal assurances to Hampton, but also that he had conspired in a military coup—"Let the American people behold the spectacle of a Brigadier General of the Army seated by the side of Governor Chamberlain in a room in the Statehouse, and issuing his orders to a legislative body peacefully assembled in one of the original thirteen commonwealths of this Union."[27]

Hampton had made his appeal to Elliott on November 30, a day in which the tension was mounting in Columbia. The Democratic members of the house, including the Edgefield and Laurens delegations, had once again marched up to the statehouse. This time federal troops let them in, and they were able to force their way past the Republicans' sergeant-at-arms into the hall of representatives. A bizarre scene ensued in which Democrat William Wallace and Republican E. W. M. Mackey both claimed to be the lawful speaker of the house. Eventually two chairs were provided, and the "Wallace House" and the "Mackey House" sat side by side in the same hall and conducted business simultaneously. Rumors circulated that Ruger had issued orders to remove the Democratic Edgefield delegation, though his troops took no such action. Meanwhile, Hampton attempted to enter the hall of representatives as well. By this point, a Democratic sergeant-at-arms stood beside the Republican sergeant-at-arms. The Republican refused to allow Hampton to enter, and the two guards proceeded to scuffle. The *Charleston News and Courier* reported that "trouble again appeared inevitable, but before the issue came Gen. Hampton declined to enter and withdrew."[28] For five days, the Mackey and Wallace houses occupied the statehouse simultaneously.

Over the next several days and weeks, Hampton fired off telegrams and letters to President Grant, Secretary of State Hamilton Fish, Democratic allies in Washington, and each of the new claimants to the White House, Rutherford B. Hayes and Samuel J. Tilden. In each communication, Hampton delineated the Democratic position and tried to appear as the representative of constitutional government. The Republicans were defying the state supreme court; the house of representatives had the sole right to judge the qualifications of its members; there was no justification for federal force; and, he pointed out correctly, even Republican representatives were disgusted by the course of events and were defecting to the Wallace House. Most of all, Hampton wished to

402

show that the Republican position could be sustained only by military force, "but we earnestly desire a peaceful solution."[29]

Tension rose even higher on the afternoon of December 3, when Hampton received an anonymous letter signed by "A Hayes Republican." The writer claimed that fifty to sixty ruffians of both races would descend on the capital the next day, some of them from the Charleston Hunkidori Club, and receive state constable badges by Chamberlain's authority. They would enter the hall of representatives, after which Speaker Mackey would order the removal of all unauthorized persons from the hall, including the Edgefield and Laurens members of the Wallace House. When the Democrats resisted, the "constables" would spring into action, federal troops would be called in, and the Republicans would once again control the house, clearing the way for the Republicans to declare Chamberlain the next governor. The letter, whether it was genuine or not, created consternation among Hampton's supporters in Columbia. Calls went out once again for Democrats to surround the statehouse to thwart the alleged plan, and Red Shirts began swarming into Columbia by train and horseback. Hampton immediately informed federal secretary of state Fish, enclosing a copy of the letter and asking that Ruger be ordered not to interfere. Democrats would not resist U.S. troops, Hampton pledged, but if murder occurred in Columbia, the blood would be on Chamberlain's hands.[30]

It is hard to tell whether the Hunkidori Club plot reflected Republican desperation, Democratic fantasy, or both. The scheme did not materialize, either because the Democrats were ready or because it never existed in the first place. Still, the Democratic leadership decided once again (and again one detects Hampton's influence) to avoid conflict. The next day, Speaker Wallace had the Democrats withdraw voluntarily from the statehouse and reconvene in nearby Carolina Hall. Hard-liners protested bitterly, but Democrats surrendered possession of the capitol to the Mackey House. They did so noting that the state constitution required only that the house meet in the city of Columbia, not in the statehouse itself, and that they had enough members to constitute a quorum without the members of the Mackey House.[31]

On December 6, predictably, the Mackey House declared Chamberlain governor and, also predictably, angry white men gathered in downtown Columbia. By noon, there were between 2,500 and 5,000 Red Shirts in town, having poured in from the surrounding counties throughout the night and following morning. They crowded around the

Democratic headquarters, eagerly awaiting an order to storm the state-house nearby. Once again, it was up to Hampton to calm them. But the general would have to do so in a way that did not compromise his position as one who could enforce his will when he chose—he must not appear to be a coward, since many were already irritated by Hampton's and other Democrats' outwardly passive stance. As Hampton stepped on a box to speak, one man yelled, "We'll leave everything we've got with you and tear down the State House with our hands if you'll just give us the word, General!"[32] A roar of approval erupted from the crowd. Hampton replied, "When the time comes to take the State House, I'll lead you there."[33] He then assured the crowd that the only thing that could rob it of victory was an act of violence. He had just hinted, however, that a time might come when force would be appropriate. Hampton asserted that he had received the most votes despite "all the powers of the State government and the bayonets of President Grant. I have been by, 75,000 white men and 17,000 colored men, chosen to be the Governor of the State of South Carolina and Governor I will be. The ballot-box has announced the verdict of the people, and I will be their Governor or they shall have a military government."[34] Once again, the crowd drifted away. Years later newspaper reporter Alfred Williams wrote that Hampton's "manner, his intense earnestness but avoidance of excitement and gesture, his fatherly friendly tone, carried conviction that he was master of the situation and to be trusted and followed, even when leading in apparent retreat men eager to advance."[35]

One could interpret Hampton's "military government" comment as a simple observation that only federal bayonets could sustain Chamberlain's power. It also could have been another promise to hotheads in the crowd that he would lead them into battle when the time was right. What is even more likely is that Hampton envisioned a policy of civil disobedience that would cripple Chamberlain's government unless the U.S. Army intervened in a massive way. Only seconds before, Hampton had pointed out that Chamberlain's regime had no support from the "property owners of the State," was bankrupt, and had not even the funds to keep the gaslights on in the statehouse. "Such a government," he explained "would starve to death. The people will refuse to pay it any taxes."[36] This tactic would, in fact, prove to be the next weapon in the Democratic arsenal. Over the next several months, the Democrats would execute the "starve them out" policy, in which property owners refused to pay taxes to Chamberlain's tax collectors and voluntarily paid them to

Hampton instead.[37]

Chamberlain was inaugurated on December 7, but Hampton's momentum was building. Whereas the Democrats could bring thousands of Red Shirts to Columbia in less than twenty-four hours, the Republicans could not manage even a hundred "hunkidories," even in the wildest imaginations of their opponents. Chamberlain's inauguration was a subdued affair in which the governor complained that his life was in danger. The Democrats, in contrast, staged an inauguration for Hampton a week later that was a joyous celebration with a confident speech by Hampton. It concluded with members of the crowd placing Hampton on a chair and carrying him on their shoulders up Main Street with shouts and cheers. Already, Republican presidential candidate Rutherford B. Hayes had expressed support for Hampton and his opinion that Grant's military actions had been ill-advised. He promised that he would speak with Hampton once the count of the electoral vote had confirmed his [Hayes's] victory. The northern press increasingly expressed admiration for Hampton and dismay at the actions of Chamberlain and federal troops. Even the *Republican* of Springfield, Massachusetts, Chamberlain's native state, condemned the soldiers' seizure of the statehouse. "Either Hampton or Ruger is governor," the paper asserted, "for Chamberlain certainly is not."[38]

Not only was Hampton convincing outsiders of the legality of his government, but also he was the only South Carolina governor who could collect taxes. The Wallace House passed a joint resolution requesting all taxpayers to volunteer one-fourth of the previous year's assessment to Hampton's agents. Democratic newspapers urged citizens to "starve out" Chamberlain's government but to "render unto Hampton what is Hampton's."[39] Most of Chamberlain's supporters—overwhelmingly black and poor—owed no taxes and could pay none, while donations poured in for Hampton's government. On January 10 Hampton announced that he had enough funds to meet the humanitarian needs of the penitentiary and the state lunatic asylum. By March 1 he had collected over $119,000, while Chamberlain's government could muster less than $1,000. Even Grant admitted as early as February that Chamberlain's position was hopeless. "Unless Governor Chamberlain can compel the collection of taxes," he told a *New York Tribune* reporter, "it will be utterly useless for him to expect to maintain his authority. In South Carolina the contest has assumed such a phase that the whole army of the United States would be inadequate to enforce the authority of Governor Chamberlain."[40]

A congressional house subcommittee completed its investigation in

Drawing from Frank Leslie's Illustrated Newspaper. Original caption reads: "The Inauguration of General Wade Hampton as Governor, December 14th." South Caroliniana Library.

Drawing from Frank Leslie's Illustrated Newspaper. Original caption reads: "South Carolina—The Disputed November Election—The Democratic Citizens in Columbia Carrying Wade Hampton in Triumph, After His Inauguration as Governor, December 14th." South Caroliniana Library.

Columbia on December 28, and concluded that Hayes had won the presidential race in South Carolina, but that Hampton had won the governorship. Hampton began appointing local officeholders and judges, including Republicans and black men. He commissioned militia units. The state supreme court acknowledged his executive pardons of a man named Amzi Rosborough and a woman named Tilda Norris.[41]

Clearly, the momentum of events was flowing Hampton's way. Chamberlain's regime was a paper tiger, unable to control any part of the state outside the ring of bayonets surrounding the statehouse in Columbia. The state supreme court had ruled against it, it could not collect revenue, banks would not loan it money, the authorities in Washington were growing less sympathetic to its plight, and Republican representatives were defecting to the Wallace House. Republican U.S. senator T. J. Robertson openly urged Hampton's claims in Washington, as did a growing number of northern newspapers, Democratic and Republican. All that was needed was for a new president to be inaugurated, formally recognize Hampton's authority, and withdraw federal troops. Just as complete vindication for Hampton was around the corner, however, a new threat emerged from an unexpected quarter. Someone within Hampton's own party accused him of treason.[42]

VICTORY

A close examination of the 1876–77 election campaign in South Carolina, particularly one written from Hampton's point of view, reveals how
problematic it is to assume that Hampton was complicit in white violence and certainly how simplistic it is to lump all conservatives, including Hampton, together as white supremacists. Hampton was a racist,
but painting him in the same image as Martin Gary or Benjamin R.
Tillman is possible only when using broad strokes. Such a picture ig-
nores the details of the campaign—the opposition Hampton faced from
within his own ranks, the ambivalence of his feelings toward blacks,
and the tricky political course that he had to steer from the summer of
1876 until the following spring. He had to portray himself as a man of
"inflexible rectitude" as well as one of magnanimity while his own
supporters attempted to cheat and cow their opponents—as the foe of
dishonest government who simultaneously reached out to white and
black supporters, or members, of the tainted regime. These were men
Democrats considered hopelessly corrupt or even unfit for citizenship.[1]

Hampton earnestly strove to position himself—and be—a force for
law and order even as his supporters conducted a ruthless campaign of
terror and fraud. That he succeeded at all was testimony to his sagacity
as well as his character. It was proof of how many white South Carolinians lauded him, and white and black Republicans acknowledged
him, as a genuine example of what he claimed to be—a representative
of the virtues that popular lore claimed for the elite leadership of the
Old South.

★ Even during the confusing interregnum, when Democrats were
striving to assert Hampton's authority over Daniel Chamberlain, Hampton's conciliatory gestures toward Republicans made some Democrats
seethe. Hampton associated with fence-sitting Republicans both during
and after the campaign. In late December, for example, he appointed
Martin Delany, a talented black Republican, as a trial judge. Shortly after
Chamberlain's nomination, Hampton had welcomed into the fold Republican judges Thompson H. Cooke and Thomas J. Mackey, the uncle
of E. W. M. Mackey, speaker of the Republican "Mackey House." These
two former scalawags campaigned with Hampton, urging blacks to vote 409

for "Hampton and Hayes." Men like Martin Gary felt that the state Democratic Executive Committee gave such turncoats more prominence in the statewide canvas than fire-eaters like themselves. After the election, while Gary exhorted angry Red Shirts in the streets of Columbia into an angry frenzy, some of the latter were dismayed to see Hampton negotiating with General Thomas Ruger, cautioning Democrats against violence, and writing letters to Ulysses S. Grant and Rutherford B. Hayes. And while Gary and other straightouts felt that they deserved more recognition in securing Hampton's victory in places like Edgefield, Laurens, Barnwell, and Spartanburg, Hampton began appointing former Republicans and even blacks to judgeships and minor offices.[2]

Some straightouts harbored a (mostly unspoken) suspicion that Hampton was selling out the national Democratic ticket to secure his own success at the state level. He had made it clear throughout the campaign that while South Carolina Democrats hoped for a Tilden victory in the presidential race, he was most concerned with "saving" South Carolina. Near the end of the year, Hampton wrote letters to Hayes and Samuel J. Tilden defending his position as the rightfully elected governor. He allowed Mackey to hand-deliver the letter to Hayes, as Mackey claimed that he already had business in Columbus, Ohio, anyway. Democratic newspapers both in South Carolina and elsewhere had criticized Hampton's communication with Hayes, as well as his choice of an "ambassador," fearing that it gave legitimacy to Hayes's claims at a time when the question of whether he had defeated Tilden was still unresolved. At worst, some claimed, Hampton's move was treachery; at best, it was an "error of judgment."[3] People who suspected Hampton of selling out Tilden understood that Tilden's campaign had kept Hampton at arm's length, thinking that his reputation as a Confederate leader and symbol of the Lost Cause would damage the national ticket. Many northern Democrats had opposed Hampton's nomination, citing his prominence as a Confederate general and fearing that his views were not "conservative" enough, meaning that he was too well known for opposing the Fourteenth Amendment and Reconstruction acts. Democrats across the nation did not blame Hampton if he was miffed at Tilden but condemned his actions that might endanger the national party as a whole.[4]

These suspicions and resentments of straightout Democrats found full expression in a letter to the *Augusta Chronicle and Sentinel* on January 10, signed by "A Tilden Democrat." The new charge, essentially, was that Hampton had betrayed the national Democratic ticket by seeking a bargain with the Republicans. According to the writer, Mackey and Cooke met with the state's Democratic leaders a day or two after Chamberlain's nomination in mid-September. Democrats present included Hampton, Georgia senator and ex-Confederate general Robert Toombs, Democratic presidential elector General Samuel McGowan, Colonel J. S. Cothran, William D. Simpson, and Colonel James A. Hoyt. Mackey and Cooke promised that if the state Democratic Party withdrew its presidential electors (conceding the state's electoral vote to Hayes), national Republicans could ensure the success of Hampton's campaign at the state level; Mackey and Cooke even promised a gift of ten thousand dollars from the national Republican Party. Though McGowan thought the scheme dishonorable, Hampton supposedly favored it. Since "Hampton's word was law," the writer surmised, the only factor preventing the move was that the plan was suggested too late to be approved by the party as a whole at the state level. And even though the state's Democrats reached no explicit understanding with the national Republican Party, Hampton allegedly adhered to the "spirit" of the plan by virtually ignoring the national ticket in his own campaigning and by privately urging Democratic presidential electors not to cast their vote for Tilden.[5]

For a few weeks the "Tilden Democrat" letter made for explosive headlines. Alexander Haskell, in refuting the charges, angrily interpreted them as saying that "General Hampton has deliberately betrayed his party and the honor of his people."[6] Many contemporaries believed that the author of "A Tilden Democrat" was Martin Gary. Though Gary denied writing the letter, he never denied that he inspired it or that he believed its substance to be true. And it was Gary who publicly repeated the charges in 1878 and 1880 as he attempted to use them for his own political gain.[7]

Hampton made a brief and forceful denial of the charges, but it was his loyal lieutenant and campaign manager, Alexander Haskell, who mainly took up the cudgels. Haskell wrote a scathing rebuttal on January 12, refuting the substance as well as most of the alleged facts of "A Tilden Democrat." In Haskell's telling, Hampton did not bitterly turn on the national Democrats who shunned him, but selflessly offered to distance himself from them if they wished. Before accepting his nomination, he had warned South Carolina Democrats that national Democrats did not favor it. According to Haskell, Mackey and Cooke did meet with members of the state Democratic Executive Committee and declared that they had abandoned Chamberlain and would support Hampton. They did urge the "abandonment of the national contest" by the 411

Democrats but made no secret promises of national Republican support.[8] Hampton, who was in Abbeville campaigning, was not present at this meeting. The next day Judge Cooke and Colonel Hoyt of the Democratic Executive Committee broached the idea with Hampton in Abbeville. Both Hampton and the Executive Committee, said Haskell, agreed that no action should be taken until conferring with Tilden and the National Executive Committee. Hampton wrote Tilden the next day through Tilden campaign staffer Manton Marble, and Haskell now reprinted Hampton's entire letter to Marble:

> . . . Our Executive Committee seems to apprehend that our friends at the North are embarrassed by our alliance with them. . . . If these apprehensions are well founded, how can we best relieve our friends at the North of their embarrassment? Before our convention met I wrote fully to Mr. Tilden, telling him what would probably be its action, and asking his advice so that we could promote the interests of the Democratic party. He did not reply to my letter, and I was forced, by irresistible public opinion, to accept the nomination for Governor. I have made the canvass thoroughly conservative, and it has been a perfect success so far. With aid from abroad the State can be carried for Tilden. There is no doubt of its being carried for our State ticket, for our opponents would gladly agree to let us elect our men if we withdraw from the Presidential contest. Of course we are most anxious to aid in the general election, but you can understand our solicitude to find out how we can best do this. If our alliance is a load, we will unload. If our friends desire us to carry on the contest as begun, we shall do so. If you will give me your views on these points I shall be indebted to you. The enclosed extracts will show you the line I take in the canvass.[9]

Ten days after the date of this letter, Marble replied in a telegram addressed to Haskell advising Hampton to stay the course he was already on—"It is agreed here that your friend's persistence and his present efforts and plans are wise and advantageous."[10] Before receiving this reply, however, Haskell said that Hampton had already "on reflection, come to the conclusion that the proposition (withdrawing the Democratic electors) was not wise or proper."[11] Hampton did not abandon Tilden.

Internal evidence in "A Tilden Democrat" bolsters the case that Gary wrote or at least inspired it. Certain statements in it precisely captured the frustrated ambition of Gary, as well as the resentments of the minority of white Democrats who were disillusioned with Hampton. First, they believed that Hampton and the clique surrounding him gave a cold shoulder to the courageous straightout men who had secured Hampton's nomination. Hampton excluded those stalwarts by denying them choice appointments or even a prominent place in the campaign. Second, Hampton's conciliatory policy toward African Americans and moderate Republicans was unwise, bordered on treason, and nearly cost Hampton the victory that the "shotgun policy" won for him. In the words of the "Tilden Democrat":

> There was a milk and cider, "peace and prosperity," conciliation of Radicals and flattery of negroes policy instead of the bold and aggressive policy inaugurated by the straight-out leaders, and thus a majority of ten or fifteen thousand votes was lost to Tilden in South Carolina, while the State ticket was only elected by a bare majority. Though the straight-outs brought about his nomination in the face of a tremendous opposition from within the Democratic party, and though their courage and skill had so much to do with redeeming the State, they claim to have been practically ignored by General Hampton when he selected the State Executive Committee. . . . Five out of six of these gentlemen failed to carry their own counties in the election, while the straight-outs carried Edgefield, Laurens, Abbeville, Barnwell, Aiken and Colleton by storm. Richland, General Hampton's own county, went heavily against him. It is safe to say that but for the fatal mistakes made in this campaign—the desertion of Tilden and the surrender to Cooke and Mackey—the majority for the State and National ticket would have been too large to admit of investigation or question.[12]

This was a classic statement of Gary's understanding of the campaign, held by many racial radicals in the state and a large number of Gary's followers in Edgefield, including twenty-nine-year-old Ben Tillman, who later became Hampton's nemesis. Haskell's response, likewise, was a classic statement of the conservatives' interpretation— that of Hampton and his strongest supporters. First, Haskell asserted, Hampton "owed" his nomination to no one. He had not sought the nomination and did not desire it; his agreement to accept it was a selfless act of patriotism for his state. Moreover, Hampton "did not select the State Executive Committee." All the nominees of the state ticket, along with the president of the Democratic convention, selected the committee's members. Several of the latter, including Haskell him- 413 self, were "straightouts" in the original meaning of the term in that they had advocated a straight Democratic ticket in August instead of a fused one that included Republicans.[13]

Most of all, though, Haskell argued that it was Hampton's "conservative" policy that won the state, not the "shotgun" policy, which actually threatened to bring disaster. According to Haskell, when Cooke and Mackey met with the Democrats, they "stated that the plan of the Radical leaders was to be passive for a time; allege that they were restrained from canvassing from fear of violence; meanwhile to excite riot and violence among the colored race, cause bloodshed, and then invoke military interference. . . . Judge Cooke confirmed the views above stated, saying he knew of contemplated riot and bloodshedding from conversation with leading Republicans with whom he was allied up to that time."[14] Hampton had countered this nefarious plot by calling for peace and making promises of protection and good government for both races.

There is other evidence that Democrats close to Hampton actually believed that the Republicans planned to create an excuse for federal intervention. James Conner, as has been noted, expressed those fears in private letters to his wife during the campaign. Such fears would also help explain the Democrats' reaction to the alleged "Hunkidori" plot in early December—both the summoning of Red Shirts to prevent infiltration of the statehouse by Republican "constables" and the voluntary surrender of the statehouse the next day by the Wallace House. Hampton himself did not make such charges against the Republicans in public speeches, but he repeatedly and earnestly urged his supporters to prevent violence, which he seemed to think might play into Chamberlain's hands. Years later Hampton's first biographer, Edward Wells, expressed the same suspicions of Republican hopes to obtain military intervention by inciting riots. Wells, if not a Hampton sycophant, was nearly always a faithful mouthpiece for Hampton's recollection of events.[15]

Such fears also fit neatly into Hampton's enduring belief that he succeeded in 1876 by winning over "honest men" who were Republicans, including African Americans, and by discouraging violence, not promoting it. Gary's strategy, he thought, if taken too far, actually endangered his success by playing into the Radicals' hands. It is virtually certain, in retrospect, that Gary was correct as to how Hampton got his majority of votes. Some Republicans were disgusted with their own party, and some black men did voluntarily vote for Hampton, but his electoral majority over Chamberlain was mostly due to Red Shirt intimidation, the stuffing of ballot boxes, and other Democratic frauds, particularly in the counties where Gary's tactics were most prevalent. But Hampton's interpretation did have merit for the period after the election. In the confusing, tense period in which Republican officials at the state and federal levels judged between the claims of Hampton and Chamberlain, Hampton's ability to present himself as a force for law and order was critical to his ultimate success.[16]

For the time being, few South Carolina Democrats were willing to listen to the "Tilden Democrat" story. Now was no time for mutiny in the ranks. Not only Hampton and Haskell but also Samuel McGowan flatly denied the charges, as did J. S. Cothran and Robert Toombs when the story resurfaced in later years. The Democratic papers in Charleston, Columbia, Spartanburg, Abbeville, and indeed across the state rallied behind Hampton. The *Spartanburg Herald*, for example, denounced the "sore head" who, "with more ambition than patriotism," dared impugn the motives of "the noble Hampton."[17] The *Columbia Daily Register* called the writer of the letter a "Judas" and maintained that Haskell's publication of Hampton's offer to sacrifice himself if it would help the national Democratic Party only increased the people's respect for Hampton throughout the state and the nation. The "people," said the *Register*, "were not mistaken. They knew their man—a truly representative man of the honor, the character, the integrity, the self-sacrificing spirit of South Carolina."[18]

★ While the political fires set by "A Tilden Democrat" subsided, Hampton continued the fight for recognition from Washington and solidification of his own rule. First, he reaffirmed his campaign promises to blacks. Second, he reassured Washington that he would protect black civil rights and ensure constitutional government. And third, now that he had shown outsiders and white South Carolinians that he could preserve order, he took care to protect his reputation as a peacemaker in his own right, not as a humble supplicant to Washington.

Hampton's inaugural address proved that although black voters might suspect the sincerity of his promises to them, they could not charge that his rhetoric, at least, was inconsistent. Hampton continued to reach out to black voters even while speaking to this all-white audience and while still relying on the enthusiastic support of the rifle clubs. He reaffirmed his pledges to build up the state's public education and to provide equal protection of the law for both races. He warned the Wallace House that "we should be not vindictive, but magnanimous" to black voters "who, misled by their fears, their ignorance, or by evil counselling [sic], turned a deaf ear to our appeals." In a comment that must have set Martin Gary's teeth on edge, he claimed that Democrats "owe much of our late success to those colored voters who were brave enough to rise above the prejudice of race, and honest enough to throw off the shackles of party in their determination to save the State." "It is due, not only to ourselves, but to the colored people of the State, that wise, just, and liberal measures should prevail in our legislation." Hampton declared that he would hold himself "bound by every dictate of honor and of good faith, to use every effort to have these pledges redeemed fully and honestly."[19] On January 10 Hampton issued an official proclamation in which he called on white landowners to end the policy of economic proscription against black Republicans:

> Great suffering will be inflicted on the colored people if they are left without employment, and the material interests of the State will be seriously affected. . . . Humanity and sound policy concur in this case to urge us to find work for all those who honestly seek it. Many of those who opposed us in the late canvass now acknowledge the lawful government of the State and are willing to support it. Our efforts should now be directed to the establishment of law and order and to the promotion of good will and harmony among all classes of our citizens.[20]

Besides white and black South Carolinians, of course, the third intended audience of these statements consisted of officials in Washington, especially Grant and presidential claimants Hayes and Tilden. Hampton assured Hayes and Tilden in late December that his government was respecting the persons, property, and rights of all the state's inhabitants. After Hayes's inauguration in March 1877, Hampton again promised to respect African American rights. These pledges echoed the claim in his own inaugural speech that his party had accepted the recent amendments to the Constitution "in good faith."[21] Again and again he emphasized that federal troops and federal authority, not his government, were the major obstacles to constitutional government and normalcy in South Carolina.[22]

President Grant had inadvertently helped Hampton make that point in early 1877. As February 22 approached, many white militia units hoped to stage traditional parades in Charleston and Columbia in honor of George Washington's Birthday. In the current political context, such plans were also meant to display white power, organization, and determination. These companies were the ones also known as Red Shirts, the ones Grant had ordered disbanded in October and that Hampton was now commissioning. Probably fearing an armed clash, Grant issued an order forbidding the rifle clubs from participating in Washington's Birthday celebrations that they had planned. Hampton did not want violence either, of course, and certainly did not want trouble to develop between his former Red Shirts and Ruger's troops.[23]

Hampton played the card Grant had given him to the hilt. In his own proclamation of February 20, Hampton, out of "deference to the office" held by Grant, called upon the militia companies to delay their celebration:

> If the arbitrary commands of a Chief Executive who has not sought
> to emulate the virtues of Washington deprive the citizens of this
> state of the privilege of joining publicly in paying reverence to that
> day, so sacred to every American patriot, we can at least show by our
> [emphasis added] obedience to constituted authority however arbi-
> trarily exercised that we are not unworthy to be the countrymen of
> Washington.
>
> We must therefore postpone to some more auspicious period . . .
> the exercise of our right to commemorate the civic virtues of that
> unsullied character who wielded his sword only to found and per-
> petuate that American Constitutional liberty which is now denied to
> the citizens of South Carolina.
> Wade Hampton
> Governor[24]

Grant's proclamation helped Hampton in several ways. If Hampton could make his supporters obey it, he could prevent the disorder he feared and simultaneously make Grant appear as the suppressor of civil liberties and even of national patriotism. There was virtually no danger of hothead militia captains, or straightouts, ignoring Hampton's or- ders, for doing so would be to challenge his authority as governor and thus their units' right to exist. Finally, he could appeal once again to his followers' pride in their own supposed virtues. Cloaking submission to Grant with patriotism, he allowed violent men to see themselves as virtuous and law-abiding. Men who had stuffed ballot boxes and threat- ened poor black men could style themselves "not unworthy to be the countrymen of Washington." Once again, Hampton secured the high ground in the battle of public opinion.

Hampton's assumption of a righteous, indignant tone in the Washington's Birthday proclamation was part of yet another pose he was attempting to strike. It was critically important for Hampton's standing among his white followers, as well as his own pride, that he not be seen as submissive. He would not meekly accept Grant's alleged tyranny but would postpone the exercise of his people's "right" to a better time. In his December 23 letter to Hayes (which, of course, was published in newspapers), Hampton proudly stated that his people were "not wanting either in the spirit or the means to maintain their rights" but were leaving their "vindication to the proper tribunals."[25] After Hayes's inauguration, the new president wished to confer with both Chamberlain and Hampton. When Hampton's spokesmen in Washington suggested that he make his case to Hayes personally, Hampton telegraphed Thomas J. Mackey that he would not go "unless specifically requested by the president."[26] When the invitation arrived, Hampton stiffly responded to Hayes that he would comply with the request out of "proper courtesy," but he doubted whether he could throw more light on a question whose solution was "so obvious and simple."[27] As Hampton departed for the nation's capital, he denied that he was seeking "recognition" from Hayes; his "recognition" came from the people's votes. "I am going there to demand our rights—nothing more—and, so help me God, nothing less."[28] After his return, Hampton insisted that "I did not go to Washington . . . to offer, or to hear, terms of compromise, or to lay my case before the tribunal. I told them I held my title from the people of South Carolina. . . . I went on from motives of personal courtesy to the President."[29]

In response to Hayes's invitation, Chamberlain arrived in Washington on March 27. Hampton arrived on the twenty-ninth. Both men met with Hayes individually, and on the thirty-first both wrote letters outlining their position. Chamberlain predicted oppression of blacks and Republicans should federal troops be withdrawn from the state; Hampton promised that if the troops were removed, he would use his authority to provide "full and equal protection" of "both parties and both races."[30]

On April 3 the order went out from Hayes's office. The federal garrison was to leave Columbia on April 10. From Washington, Hampton had just telegraphed W. D. Simpson, his lieutenant governor: "Everything is satisfactorily and honorably settled. *I expect our people to preserve absolute peace and quiet. My word is pledged for them. I rely on them.* W. HAMPTON."[31] The news electrified the Democratic press. Citizens in

Columbia planned a huge reception for his arrival on April 6, only to hear rumors that Hampton did not approve. Instead, a group of seventy-five citizens from Columbia met him with handshakes and bouquets when his train arrived in Charlotte on April 5. Then the *News and Courier* announced that Hampton would not object to a public reception in Columbia after all. On Friday, the sixth, Hampton arrived in his hometown to address an exuberant crowd. He took satisfaction in praising his followers' restraint as well as his own leadership—"I felt I was safe in trusting to your forbearance, in relying upon you to respect the laws, and in telling you that victory would surely come, if you would be patient and forbearing."[32] Chamberlain's private secretary surrendered the keys to the statehouse to Hampton's young secretary, Wade Hampton Manning, on April 11.

Hampton had achieved the most glorious victory of his life—greater than Trevilian Station, Samaria Church, the raid on Kilpatrick, or even the Beefsteak Raid. His greatest contribution as a statesman had been to disperse the crowds in front of the statehouse in Columbia. His most triumphant moment as a man came, however, when he could announce to white South Carolinians that final vindication was theirs. Out of the heartbreak and humiliation of Sherman's burning, Appomattox, Bennett Place, and a hundred battlefields and twenty thousand graves; of living with black magistrates, "robber" governors, and their former slaves wielding bayonets—finally there was news to celebrate.

With Chamberlain and the federal troops gone, the white population of the state continued to celebrate for weeks, while black South Carolinians noted with relief that Hampton did not change his moderate tone, and there was no swift tide of violent retribution. Hampton himself must have felt that the ultimate vindication had finally been achieved. He and his allies were recognized, finally, as the legitimate rulers of the state. The vindication was made even more complete as the Republican Party turned in on itself and confessed to past crimes. The *Beaufort Tribune* suddenly sounded like a Democratic paper, celebrating "the end of misrule" and ironically noting, "It is astonishing how many have just remembered that they voted for Hampton."[33] The *Union Herald*, formerly a mouthpiece for Chamberlain and the dominant Republican faction in Columbia, mused: "When an earnest and thoughtful republican considers what his party might have done in this state, and is brought face to face with what it has done, he is forced to admit that its fate though sadly bitter to him and his immediate hopes, is not altogether unjust. . . . Had our organization been reasonably honest in its character, and in the character of its leaders, our desertion by the president would have been an impossibility."[34]

Throughout April the celebrations continued, and not the least of them was the "Grand Military Parade" in Charleston on April 18, a "Review of the Troops by the Commander-in-Chief." Exuberant South Carolinians called the event "Jane Washington Day," in mockery of Grant's prohibition of military parades on Washington's Birthday, and treated it as a belated celebration not just of Washington's Birthday, but of Hampton's victory.[35] Hampton, on horseback, acknowledged wave upon wave of shouts and applause, the playing of bands, and bouquets of flowers from white, and even black, women. At least fourteen companies of troops awaited him in formation.[36]

Hampton's deification in the minds of white South Carolinians was as complete as it would ever be. The headline in the News and Courier reporting the event called Hampton "THE DELIVERER OF SOUTH CAROLINA." A reporter called him "hero," "chieftain," and "Liberator of the People."[37] Captain William A. Courtenay, who gave the introductory address, addressed Hampton in messianic terms—"Our honored Chief Magistrate: Wise as he is brave. Hero, statesman, patriot, deliverer! Our Hampton! With uncomplaining fortitude, he has shared the broken fortunes of his people these long years of ignorant and corrupt misrule, has with them drained the bitter cup of poverty and wrong! But he 'kept the whiteness of his soul,' and behold he comes, our chief man, bringing with him the dawning of that brighter day."[38]

An earthly savior had wrought redemption, and that redeemer-king was Wade Hampton. And he did it by taking the high road, which was, after all, what made him a redeemer. In the eyes of many Democrats, in fact, Hampton's course in the election campaign covered the sins of those who had taken the low road. In reality, of course, Hampton's platitudes could not atone for others' crimes. And Hampton himself was not such a principled martyr that he could not think and act practically and shrewdly in politics. But his official course in the campaign helped convince white South Carolinians that their cause was just, that they were still a virtuous, honorable people. Whether the redeemer-king could now keep his party on the high road was another question, for it would entail him countering not only his people's prejudices, but also his own.

PROMISES TO KEEP

In April 1877 Wade Hampton was at the pinnacle of his political career. Federal recognition of his victory over Chamberlain was the culmination of a long struggle by the white South to reassert control over southern state governments and of an even longer struggle with the North over the nature of the Constitution, over race and the proper place of African Americans, and of the very meaning of democracy itself. Southern whites had finally won much of that struggle, though they had sacrificed much in the way of lives, property, and pride in the process.

Whether it was fair to do so or not, the majority of southern whites during Reconstruction had considered the Republican governments forced upon them by Washington as travesties of republican government. To the majority of white southerners, the very fact that they were led largely by northerners and blacks made those governments not only illegitimate, but also corrupt. Southern Democratic leaders promised to "redeem" this situation by restoring the South to white rule, by returning it to its "natural," traditional, and supposedly virtuous leadership. The Redeemers, of course, were not necessarily more virtuous than the carpetbaggers they replaced and often performed or sanctioned criminal acts in their quest to restore native white rule. And, in some states, they were not always the traditional rulers—the men who led the South in 1877 were not necessarily those who did so in 1860, even if they claimed to be.

In South Carolina, though, they were. Hampton's chief lieutenants— John Bratton, Matthew Calbraith Butler, James Conner, Johnson Hagood, Alexander C. Haskell, William. D. Simpson, Joseph B. Kershaw, John D. Kennedy, and Samuel McGowan—had all been Confederate generals or colonels. They, or their families at least, had all been prominent before the war. They represented the traditional planter elite, though a few were now more involved with banking and railroading than they had been before the war. As Walter Edgar has explained, men with this much leadership experience and social prestige "did not expect to be questioned or challenged."[1]

The fact was, however, that they had been challenged, and this reality makes the term "redemption" all the more useful in explaining the motives of men like Wade Hampton. Hampton deeply felt the need to "redeem" what he had already sacrificed since the shells began exploding over Fort Sumter. He had lost a son, a brother, and a family fortune. There was more—Yankee officers and Republican politicians had challenged Hampton's right to lead. They had done so by ridiculing his convictions about himself, convictions that served as the foundation of his claims to leadership. Hampton was, according to his opponents, "a moral and financial bankrupt," a man who defrauded his creditors and made false promises to blacks.[2] Instead of being a valiant defender of his home, some Union officers had said that he was arrogant, vengeful, and bloodthirsty. Rather than being chivalrous and magnanimous, he thought nothing of nailing a "nigger's ears to a pine board fence and then shooting at him."[3] Such accusations stung, as they struck at the heart of who Hampton believed he was supposed to be. Antebellum southern elites had rested their claims to rule on their wealth and their character as honorable men. Hampton no longer had great wealth. As a man who already took pride in his courage and his reputation for honesty, then, it was even more important after the war that he be seen as one who deserved his high social rank. He must be honorable and chivalrous, as southern aristocrats had long claimed to be—a man of courage, a man who stood by his word, a man who was magnanimous to social inferiors and forgiving to defeated foes.

Redeem, restore, and reconcile—these were Hampton's aspirations in his two years as governor. He longed to show, and needed to show, that he was indeed magnanimous and that he was a man of his word. Despite his earlier opposition to the Fourteenth Amendment and the Reconstruction acts, he determined to keep his political promises to blacks, despite his belief that most were generally unfit for full citizenship. He would be a protector, just as a southern aristocrat was supposed to be, protecting blacks even from his own more extremist followers. He would seek reconciliation with Republicans whom he considered honorable men and leniency in punishing many who were not. He would redeem past wrongs, especially those allegedly committed against whites during Reconstruction, but also against blacks. His moderation had nothing to do with seeking racial equality. Such a concept was nonsense to Hampton. It was not about the character and virtues of black people at all, but rather about his own.

It was now time for Hampton to deliver on his promise to be "Governor of the whole people," protecting the rights of white and black alike. Fortunately, he was able to fulfill many of his promises to African Americans. In all of his opening messages to sessions of the General Assembly, Hampton stressed the importance of the Democratic-controlled legislature meeting those pledges. There were tangible results. During Hampton's tenure as governor, for example, the state spent an equal amount per student for white and black public education, which meant that it actually spent more overall for black schools than for white. He appointed over 116 black men to office, mostly at the county or municipal level. Republican ex-governor Robert K. Scott admitted that within a few months Hampton had "already appointed more colored men to office than were appointed during the first two years that I was Governor."[4] In the first days of his administration, Hampton met with the First Regiment National Guards, a black militia company in Charleston, and promised to do all he could to have the unit recognized as a legal organization. He swore to appoint the officers the black soldiers elected, not those chosen by him. "I recognize your equality, and I intend to uphold it," he asserted.[5] Hampton followed through with this promise as well. A quarter of a century later, black officeholders as well as black militia companies were virtually nonexistent in the Deep South, and state support for black education was far behind that for whites.[6]

As a candidate, Hampton had sworn to uphold equality under the law. To his credit, his government apparently expended as much effort in apprehending white murderers of black men as it did black murderers of whites. The "Proclamation Books" from his governorship, for instance, reveal that Hampton offered a two-hundred-dollar reward for the apprehension of W. Butler Putnam, a white man suspected of murdering "Willis Todd, colored, in Laurens County." Two months later he announced a fifty-dollar reward for the arrest of Stephen Wood, a black man suspected of murdering W. T. Hill (no race given) in Darlington County.[7]

If Hampton tried to respect the principle of equality before the law, he was even more faithful to individual black leaders. One was Martin Delany, the Republican who had supported Hampton in the election and whom Hampton had appointed a trial justice in Charleston. In March 1878 twenty-six Charleston Democrats petitioned Hampton to have Delany removed on the vague charge that he had conducted his duties in a "discreditable" manner.[8] Clearly, the main motivation was racial prejudice. Hampton stood by Delany, who kept his job until 1879, when, according to Delany, "I lost as soon as they got rid of [Hampton] by sending him to the U.S. Senate, as he was too liberal for the rank and file of the party leaders."[9]

Actually, it was not that Hampton was "liberal" so much as he was 423 determined that he, his party, and his state would meet their respective obligations. Some of these obligations were financial, and in delivering on his promise to make state government less expensive, he unwittingly contributed to the growth of social injustice in the state. In his first message to the legislature, Hampton insisted that while "every dictate of enlightened humanity" mandated that the penitentiary be "well regulated," this must be done economically.[10] He suggested that the General Assembly use convict labor to make the penitentiary self-supporting. (The Republicans had briefly hired out convict labor in 1873, and Governor Chamberlain, in his last year in office, had suggested use of the convict lease system on a regular basis. Other southern states already did.) The result of Hampton's suggestion was the convict lease bill, passed on June 8, 1877. With reasonable assurances to the state that prisoners would be humanely treated and adequately fed, the board of directors of the penitentiary could hire out the labor of the state's convicts to companies and individuals.[11]

Despite the bill's passage, Hampton was still urging the legislature in November to utilize the state's convicts for labor.[12] During the following February, the lawmakers passed the "chain gang bill," which would authorize the use of convict labor on roads and streets.[13] This time Hampton's paternalism conflicted with his desire for strict economy. A delegation of black leaders called on Hampton to express their concern that the bill was especially aimed against their race. They certainly had a point, as a great majority of the state's convicts were black, and white citizens clearly saw the measure as one that would put black criminals to work. Hampton's veto message informed the General Assembly "with great deference" that the bill "violates the Constitution of the State, by being *ex post facto* in its provisions" because it applied not only to those convicted of crimes in the future, but also to current prisoners. Hampton also charged that the bill placed "dangerous power in the hands of Trial Justices" and would produce "great wrong and injury to our people."[14] The legislature sustained his veto by a vote of 102–10. By the time Hampton left office, however, the convict lease system set up by the 1877 statute had already resulted in scandals, shameful abuses, investigations, and an appalling death rate (nearly 50 percent) among the prisoners. The convict lease system, though not as brutal in later decades in South Carolina as in other states, was atrocious enough, and Hampton had had a hand in introducing it.[15]

The most critical financial issue facing the state was its own debt. During Reconstruction, the Republicans in Columbia, realizing that they had led the state into a fiscal crisis, passed the 1873 Consolidation Act. This law repudiated many of the state debts that were deemed fraudulent and provided funding for those believed valid. Democrats considered this a positive step but still complained about the bloated, fraudulent state debt. The debt was still an issue three years later, and Republicans in 1876 denounced their opponents as "repudiators" who would defraud the state's northern creditors. With an eye on northern public opinion, Hampton and his inner circle denied the charge during the 1876 campaign. In October 1876 Hampton's state Democratic Executive Committee announced its position that the 1873 Consolidation Act was the final settlement and promised to abide by it. After Hampton's election, the Wallace House did the same.[16]

Hampton thus assumed the governor's office in April 1877 saddled by promises that the state would honor its debt of $5.6 million. The situation was complicated by the widespread view that most of the debt was fraudulent and that therefore the state should refuse to honor it. Aware of this sentiment, Hampton asked the General Assembly to form a joint commission to research the money owed by the state and to make a report on which bonds were fraudulent or suspicious and which were valid. Meanwhile, a movement was afoot to repudiate nearly the entire state debt, which was much further than Hampton wanted to go. Led by Martin Gary, the state senate blocked the house's attempt to appropriate $270,000 for the state's interest payments.[17]

The debt issue had now reached the crisis level. Joint senate-house committees reached tentative, ad hoc agreements on interest payments that were due, but failed to resolve the larger impasse. Hampton and other conservatives worried about the effect this news would have on northern creditors and investors. If Hampton's South Carolina repudiated its debts, the result would be profoundly humiliating for Hampton, the former bankrupt. Northern Republican newspapers that had attacked his personal honesty would have a field day. Hampton's reputation for integrity and gentlemanly character was, in his own eyes, his most valuable political possession, and yet it was also his most vulnerable point. As a man who preached peace but was elected by terrorists, and who preached good government and honesty but had defaulted on his own debts, he had to prove that his word was good.[18]

First he rushed to reassure northern investors. In a speech in Auburn, New York, Hampton assured his hearers that "South Carolina has her honor at stake, and will protect her honest creditors."[19] In an interview with the New York Herald, he downplayed the possibility of repudiation. Back home, Hampton lectured South Carolinians that "we have the honor of the state in our hands, and her just debts must be paid. *We mean to put the credit of the State where it was before the war.*"[20] He warned the legislature in November that "repudiation would bring inevitable disaster and would entail indelible disgrace." It was vital, he argued, to see the state's credit "restored to, and maintained at, its ancient high character."[21]

While Hampton spoke of "honor," "disgrace," and "restoration," most of the state's newspapers came to his defense. Paraphrasing Hampton, the *News and Courier* declared that "everything must be made right, made whole, and redeemed."[22] Other Democrats, however, called the 1873 Consolidation Act a "cheat and a fraud" and said that previous Democratic pledges to honor it were matters of expediency, not honor.[23] When the bond commission's report came out in February 1878, it recommended repudiating a whopping $3.6 million of the debt that the 1873 Consolidation Act had previously declared valid. Hampton was able to marshal enough support to defeat the General Assembly's adoption of this report, and state leaders continued throughout the remainder of the year to work out a compromise. The state did not resolve the issue until 1879, after Hampton had left the governor's office. In the end, the state repudiated $1.1 million of its debt and honored the other $4.5 million. Hampton had narrowly averted another deep humiliation.[24]

⭐ Besides keeping his promises, a southern gentleman was supposed to be magnanimous and forgiving to his foes. During and after the war, northern politicians and editors had attacked Hampton's claims to chivalry by describing him as bitter and vindictive toward the North and toward blacks. During the campaign of 1876, however, Hampton had promised a policy of reconciliation. This was not only good politics, but also an attempt to prove his enemies wrong and vindicate his own reputation. Hampton, for example, appointed not only black but also white Republicans to office. In March 1877 Republican state chief justice Franklin J. Moses Sr. died. While ensuring that Moses's heirs received payments of back salary owed to him, Hampton moved to replace him with white carpetbagger Amiel Willard. Willard was already a member of the court and had supported rulings in favor of the Democrats after the recent election. Hampton explained to federal secretary of state W. W. Evarts that "we do not intend to be proscriptive, & . . . our fight here has not been against northern men but against a band of plunderers."[25] He chided South Carolina Democrats that "there ought to be no hesitation in acting with magnanimity and justice" toward an honest gentleman.[26] But Hampton's nomination of Willard angered some Democratic straightouts. Even the pro-Hampton *News and Courier* warned that while the governor's promises of equality before the law were right and proper, it was time to "draw tight the party line" and not allow Republican appointments to office.[27] Despite the murmurings of leading Democrats, Hampton's prestige was still great enough to bulldoze his choice through the General Assembly, with only Gary and one other representative voting against it.[28]

There were other efforts to conciliate the North. During Hampton's June 1877 trip to Auburn, New York, he found an enthusiastic reception from former Union general James Shields and hundreds of Union veterans. Hampton spoke on the theme of party and sectional reconciliation. As his former enemies crowded around him one after another to shake his hand, Hampton repeatedly said, "We are all on the same side now."[29] Hampton also made an interstate goodwill tour with President Hayes, other Republican leaders, and a group of state governors. Hayes intended for the trip to defuse sectional and partisan tensions, and Hampton played his proper role. *Harper's Weekly* praised him as one of those "whose words breathed the same sentiment of union and good-will."[30]

Hampton sought a close relationship with Hayes. He wrote him frequently, promising to visit Washington and sending his best wishes to Mrs. Hayes. When Calbraith Butler, now a U.S. senator, criticized the president, Hampton tried to intervene and minimize the friction. He warned Hayes early in 1878 of rumors of a new legal challenge by Democrats to Hayes's electoral victory. He informed Hayes of his cooperation with federal revenue agents in apprehending moonshiners and outlaws in the South Carolina mountains.[31]

Most of all, Hampton cooperated with Hayes on how to deal with what both of them referred to as "political cases" or "political offenses" —federal charges against white South Carolinians charged under the Ku Klux acts and for participation in the Ellenton riots and state charges against Republicans accused of corruption. In this effort, Hampton sought to be magnanimous while simultaneously obtaining vindication for past "wrongs." The federal government had found it impossible, or deemed it not worth the effort, to prosecute the scores of "Ku-Klux" cases from the crackdown of 1870–71. Since then, more white South Carolinians had been charged with similar offenses surrounding the Hamburg and Ellenton riots in 1876. South Carolina attorney general

James Conner and the Democratic legislature, likewise, had dozens of corruption cases to investigate from the Republican regime. Republicans in the state considered the investigation of members of the previous government to be political persecution and a violation of Hampton's conciliatory promises. By Hampton's recommendation, the legislature appointed a joint committee headed by state senator John R. Cochran, a respected white Republican, to investigate alleged corruption.[32]

Eventually, the South Carolina delegation in Congress, the federal attorney general's office, and Hampton and Hayes colluded to have most of the "political cases" on both sides dropped. Hampton's government indicted fewer than twenty-five members of the former "Radical" regime. Out of the twenty-five indictments, there were three trials and three convictions, though Hampton assured Hayes that there was "sufficient evidence for two hundred." (One problem was that so many who were indicted had fled the state.) The convicted scapegoats were white carpetbagger judge L. Cass Carpenter; former secretary of state and state treasurer Francis Cardozo, a mulatto; and Robert Smalls, an African American state legislator and a onetime congressman. Hampton later pardoned Carpenter, and his successor, Governor William D. Simpson, pardoned Cardozo and Smalls. Hampton informed Hayes that in the other cases, he had convinced the General Assembly to give him the authority "to direct the Atty Genl. to '*nol pros*' any of the cases which are political." Going easy on vanquished Republicans angered many in Hampton's party. In return, however, Hampton was able to secure a proclamation from Hayes that all those charged under the Ku Klux laws were free to return to their homes without fear of prosecution. Hampton also asked Hayes to grant pardon or amnesty to three convicted Ku Kluxers who had already served several years' time in federal prison, citing reports that they were very ill, that they had been well-behaved prisoners, and that justice had already been served. Hampton gave two reasons for these requests. First, it was "very desirable that all agitation should cease in the State & to this end I desire as full amnesty (for the Republicans) as can be granted." Hayes's pardon of those convicted under federal conspiracy charges would also bring reconciliation and peace to the state. Second, if Hayes would do this for Hampton, "public opinion would then sustain me, in the course I wish to pursue here. . . . My position here has been a very difficult one, for besides the opposition to me from political opponents, I have had to meet & control that of the extreme men of my own party. . . . I can crush out all opposition if you can grant amnesty to our citizens."[33]

A vindicator and redeemer can only go so far, however, in overlook-ing evil. Hampton made it clear to Hayes that there were a few scoun-drels whom he would seek to prosecute. One was U.S. senator "Honest John" Patterson, the most notorious thief of the Republican regime. Patterson was still in office and hoped to benefit from the general spirit of amnesty. Hampton's government charged him with bribery, fraud, and conspiracy. When Patterson offered to resign his Senate seat if Hampton's government would drop the case, Hampton made it clear that he would make no deals with "Honest John." Hampton also took a hard line with Howard H. Kimpton. Kimpton had been the state's finan-cial agent in New York during the Moses administration. He had per-sonally pocketed over $700,000 in commissions on bond sales alone. According to Victor Ullman, "No one could even begin to estimate his totals on over-sale of bond issues, receipt of interest of monies guaran-teed by him, or his profits from participation in the two railroad frauds that made dozens rich."[34] Kimpton was a fugitive from justice during Hampton's term, and Hampton tried to lure him to the state by promis-ing not to prosecute him if he would provide information concerning the state's finances. When Kimpton failed to return voluntarily, but was arrested instead, Hampton changed course and sought to have him extradited from Massachusetts. He failed in his attempt, and Kimpton again disappeared from public view.[35]

Vindicating past wrongs was a relatively difficult matter in the "polit-ical cases," requiring compromise, conciliation, and tact. Other efforts at vindication were more straightforward. Hampton urged the legisla-ture to provide tax relief and redress for citizens whose land had been confiscated for nonpayment of taxes during Reconstruction. As noted earlier, the Republicans had raised taxes on real estate partly in an effort to redistribute land to landless freedmen. The government in Columbia had confiscated a total of 770,000 acres in 1873 and 1874. Native whites considered this robbery, and Hampton sought redress for them. There was also the issue of black citizens who had paid taxes to Chamberlain's tax collectors during the period in which the governorship was dis-puted, only to have Hampton's government demand payments as well. Hampton sympathized with the "colored population" misled by "igno-rance and credulity" into paying their accustomed, but now illegitimate tax collectors. He urged the General Assembly to adopt "a liberal and magnanimous policy," whereby such citizens would receive credit for their payments to Chamberlain.[36] Another wrong the Hampton regime attempted to right was the continued occupation by federal troops of

The Citadel, the state's military academy in Charleston. Federal troops had occupied the campus in 1865 and never left. The school's alumni petitioned Columbia to demand the return of the property to the state, as well as rent payments from the federal government for the years that its troops had used the college as a barracks. Hampton endorsed this petition.[37]

A final "wrong" that the Hampton regime addressed was the situation of the state university. The Republican government had begun integrating the University of South Carolina in 1869. In response, white parents angrily withdrew their sons and most of the faculty resigned, as did many trustees, including Hampton. Early in 1877 the Democratic legislature closed the integrated university. But later that year Hampton urged the lawmakers to reopen it for white students only and to establish another state college for blacks.[38]

In economic matters, Hampton sided with the owners of property, especially of land. Hampton disliked the legislature's new anti-usury law that limited interest rates to 7 percent. Hampton considered such laws unconstitutional and believed that, in the past, they had actually hurt borrowers' attempts to get loans. He wrote a veto message on the usury bill, but apparently never sent it to the legislature, and ultimately signed the bill. Other actions by the General Assembly reflected Hampton's concerns with protecting the rights of property. The lawmakers passed "deadfall laws," which prohibited the sale of crops after dark. These laws targeted the practice of sharecroppers selling part of the crop secretly without giving the landowner his prearranged share of the profit. The legislature also reformed the state's crop lien laws to benefit landowners rather than merchants or tenants.[39]

Hampton's agenda to restore, redeem, and reconcile, then, was decidedly conservative. The rights to be vindicated were largely those of property and of the white population that had felt oppressed under Republican rule. That which was to be restored was the good name of the state, as well as white supremacy. Even as Hampton fulfilled his promises to blacks, he bolstered his class' own paternalistic claims to be protectors, providers, and men of their word, and also reinstated much of the antebellum order. Yet Hampton's version of white supremacy left ample room for black political participation and certainly for protection of black civil rights.

Despite Hampton's achievements in following through on his promises, all did not go well for black South Carolinians in 1877 and 1878. The gradual disenfranchisement of African American voters, in fact, had its beginnings during Hampton's administration. The first legislation designed to limit the black vote in the post–Reconstruction era passed while Hampton was governor. The General Assembly acted in 1878 to reduce the number of polling places in several Republican-dominated districts. The result was that large numbers of black citizens had to travel twenty miles or more, a full day's journey, to vote. And not all past wrongs were to be redeemed under Hampton. Shortly after Hayes recognized Hampton's control of the state, the General Assembly repealed a law that the Republicans had passed to give relief to the widows and orphans of Republicans killed by Klan violence. And of course, the abusive convict lease system began its notorious career.[40]

Racial conciliation and black progress did not define South Carolina in 1877 and 1878. Yet both black and white voters recognized a clear difference between Hampton and other leaders of his party. Hampton's personal prestige was great, but some Democrats angrily resented his racial policy. So far white South Carolinians had not eliminated blacks from the political life of the state, and Hampton was a major reason for that. The main issue facing South Carolina in the 1878 elections was whether the Democratic Party would do more than pay lip service to Hampton's promises to the state's black citizens. Hampton was in another fight to make good on his word.

★ ★ ★ ★ ★ ★ ★ ★ ★ ★ ★ CHAPTER 31

AND NOW WOULD YOU TURN YOUR BACKS ON THEM? 1878

If any other race places itself in opposition [to the white race] it must give way before the advancing tide and die out as the Indians have done . . . [Hampton to black supporters in Charleston, October 2, 1878].
  Charleston News and Courier, October 3, 1878

And now would you turn your backs on [the colored people?] If this be the policy of South Carolina, then I am sadly mistaken in the people of South Carolina, and they are mistaken in me, for I can carry out no such policy as that. . . . I would give my life for South Carolina, but I cannot sacrifice my honor, no not even for her [Hampton to white supporters in Blackville, July 4, 1878].
  Charleston News and Courier, July 6, 1878

The first quotation above is taken from Hampton's campaign speech in Charleston. Besides thousands of ecstatic white supporters, the crowd included hundreds of black supporters—men, women, and children. Hampton hoped to retain the support of these African Americans, while yet delivering some of the most bombastic, spread-eagle white supremacist rhetoric of the nineteenth century. Hampton predicted that while other races either accommodated or submitted to white leadership,

> the white man will go on bearing the flag of civilization and Christianity until the last trump shall sound from Heaven. [Cheers.] It is the law of God; it is as fixed as the law which fixed that sin in the firmament. It will not be changed, and I say to the colored people of South Carolina that if they array themselves against the white men as a race, if they draw the color line which I have been trying to obliterate—if they say, because we are black, we intend to be Republicans always . . . I tell you here to-day, that if you place yourselves in this attitude towards the white race . . . never will you have control over South Carolina."[1]

Hampton's promises to protect black Carolinians in 1878 were, if anything, more emphatic than those of 1876. Yet they were always couched in the assumptions of white supremacy. Hampton's brand of white supremacy was a peculiar one, though—one that modern readers often find puzzling if not dishonest. In Hampton's very next sentence to

433

his Charleston audience, for example, he offered the "other race" good-will and even the hope of partnership with the "superior" race: "You can, my colored friends, have your share of South Carolina—you can have all the share that any citizen has—you can aid in choosing its rulers, and if you show yourselves worthy, honest and capable, you can become office-holders yourselves. But you can do it only in one way, and that is by joining this strong, grand old Democratic party. [Cheers.] We hold out the hand of fellowship to you. . . . We will try to aid you, my colored friends, in every way." Hampton then went on to boast of his efforts in behalf of black education.[2]

It was also a version of white supremacy that not only boasted of, but demanded, honesty and generosity from the stronger race. Hampton stressed this point every time he spoke in public in 1878:

If it is thought that we can be successful in this election by fraud (and I have heard rumors floating throughout the State occasionally, intimating that we had the machinery of the elections in our own hands and that we could count in anybody we pleased), I tell you people of Barnwell and the people of South Carolina, that if you once countenance fraud, before many years pass over your heads you will not be worth saving, and you will not be worthy of the State you live in. . . .

If you are to go back upon all the pledges I have made to the people—if you are to say that the colored men who sustained us are no longer to be citizens of South Carolina, earnestly as I would desire to spend or be spent in her service, willing as I am to give even my life for my State, I should have to decline. I would give my life for South Carolina, but I cannot sacrifice my honor, no not even for her.[3]

Hampton threw down this gauntlet to the extremists of his own party on July 4, 1878, during a speech in Blackville. Blackville was in Barnwell County, one of the hotbeds for fraud and Red Shirt violence in 1876. He was giving his own forceful answer to the dilemma that faced the state's white Democrats in 1878. It was the same one they had faced in 1876: How were they to overcome the black majority in the state, almost all of whom voted Republican? Democrats could either try to win over the black vote with paternalistic appeals or neutralize it with frauds and shotguns. Hampton's approach was to stand upon his reputation for integrity, as a paternalistic protector to the inferior race, and to shame other whites into doing the same:

You went to the colored people and told them their rights would be protected. . . . You appealed to them to come out and help you work out the redemption of the State. They came by hundreds and did help you. . . . And now would you turn your backs on them, and after trying for ten years to convince the colored man that his true interests lay with the Democratic party, would you say, "Now we have no use for you. You shall not vote even at the primary election?" If this be the policy of South Carolina, then I am sadly mistaken in the people of South Carolina, and the people are mistaken in me, because *I can carry out no such policy as that.*"[4]

Hampton lectured his white listeners that they must not only be kind to "colored people," but also provide for their education. He did so by appealing to race pride, by reminding them of their status as the former master race, and of the supposed loyalty and kind feeling existing between the races. "We are to be their guardians and protectors," he exhorted white men in Greenville. Hampton claimed that most African Americans had kindly feelings toward their old masters, "and in nine cases out of ten he will go to his old master for assistance and not to one of his Republican leaders." Blacks, Hampton said, had been misled in 1876 by the Republicans, who told them that the Democrats would reenslave them if they regained power. Now the Republicans had been proved wrong, and whites must continue to honor his pledges, even allowing blacks to compete for office if they were qualified. And "the white man who is afraid to enter the race upon such terms does not deserve to be called a white man."[5]

Hampton told both blacks and whites that their actions would determine whether or not their descendants lived in peace and prosperity. While Gary and his supporters listened, presumably with cynical ears, Hampton spoke dreamily of the future:

I have thought that in that far future, in the day when you and I and all of us shall have been gathered to our God, I could see a great and happy State and people. Our children's children—wise by the errors we have committed, chastened by our sorrows we vicariously have borne for them, instructed by the experiences we have gained— shall build up South Carolina and place her where God intended her to stand—with a united, free and happy people, walking on the great road to National prosperity and peace. I have seen that future, I have worked for it; I have prayed for it. . . . I trust in God it may come.[6]

Hampton's words at Blackville, Greenville, and throughout the campaign did have a limited shaming effect on white attitudes, at least in official circles. The official Democratic platform mirrored that of 1876, reaffirming the party's commitment to equality before the law, just treatment of blacks, public education, and honest government. The press generally supported Hampton's tack, including the *News and Courier*, which stated that to win, the Democrats "must be just and generous to the colored people."[7]

But the very fact that Hampton had to make such strident appeals shows that he felt the real danger of other Democrats undermining his reputation for honesty. The white voters of Blackville cheered the words of their gallant general, but the more thoughtful and knowledgeable among them certainly remembered that it was fraud, not gentle appeals, that had ultimately carried Barnwell County for the Democrats in 1876. As Hampton spoke, the Democrats in neighboring Edgefield County, Gary's bailiwick, had already banned black voters from their party convention and prohibited African Americans from voting in their primary, just as Hampton now warned Barnwell not to do. Most newspapers in the state denounced this move by the Edgefield Democrats, but Hampton was not exaggerating the challenge to his racial program. As much as he, the state Democratic Executive Committee, and the Democratic press may have decried them in 1878, fraud and violence would occur at polling sites throughout the state on election day.[8]

Predictably, it was Martin Gary who led the challenge to Hampton's program. Both personal ambition and conviction inspired him. Gary knew he could not challenge Hampton's nomination for governor, but he hoped to build his own popularity and make a run for the U.S. Senate seat that was coming open. Infuriated by Hampton's appointments of Republican officials, his own failure to obtain a position higher than that of state senator, and Hampton's insistence that whites assume the tax burden for supporting black public schools, Gary gave voice to thousands of whites who admired Hampton personally but hated his attempts to create a biracial Democratic Party. Gary first hoped to weaken Hampton by endeavoring to replace the moderates on Hampton's ticket with men whose racial views were closer to his own.[9]

In his home territory of Edgefield, Gary openly challenged Hampton's racial philosophy. "Our leaders," he said, misunderstood the issue. It was not an issue of politics, but one of race. "As far back as 1874, I announced . . . that whenever the Caucasian united upon this issue the negro had to go to the wall, as the Ruler of the Universe had made the white race the dominant race of all the races."[10] In Greenville, he argued that it was the Edgefield Plan, not Hampton's, that had brought success in 1876. He complained that, under Hampton's proposed constitutional amendment to provide a two-mill tax to support education for both races, "nine-tenths of this tax would be paid by white people, and three-fourths of it would be spent in educating piccaninnies."[11]

The Gary-Hampton feud became public in August. Gary was scheduled to speak at a Democratic rally in Greenville on the seventeenth, shortly after General J. W. Gray. Gray had just marched white militia companies in a military review side by side with the Negro Mountain City Guards. He then boasted that such displays of interracial harmony were the natural result of "Hampton Democracy." The sight of white and black men marching together in the ranks deeply offended Gary. When it was his turn to speak, he denounced it. In front of a mixed-race audience, Gary sneered, "I suppose we will next hear of '*dining*' or *dancing* with the colored brothers and sisters as events the natural result of Hampton Democracy."[12]

Gary's comment was a sarcastic reference to a rumor that was raging across the state during the summer of 1878: Wade Hampton had dined at the same table with two black men. Sometime during the summer, Edward Cooke, the northern white president of Claflin University, had invited Hampton and his superintendent of education, Hugh Thompson, to dinner at Cooke's home in Orangeburg. Hampton and Thompson took a seat in the parlor. When they were invited into the dining room, however, they were shocked to see that there were two other guests present—a black Claflin faculty member named Sasportas and the black ex-state supreme court judge Jonathan J. Wright. Treating black men with paternal condescension came naturally to Hampton; sitting down to dine with them certainly did not, nor to other white Carolinians in 1878. Thompson recalled that "Wade looked at me and I looked at him," each wondering how to respond.[13] After a brief moment of awkwardness, Hampton and Thompson sat down and all began to eat.[14]

News of the incident spread quickly by word of mouth and private letters. Either out of sympathy for Hampton or concern for his reputation and party unity, the state's larger papers refused to report the story, and smaller papers referred to it only indirectly. Gary's friends did what they could to spread the rumors privately. Gary sent letters to state newspapers warning that "dining" with blacks would lead to "dancing," "miscegenation, Mexicanization," and "general damnation."[15]

While they spread the rumors privately, Gary's friends begged him not to let the newspapers identify Gary as their author. Hugh S. Farley, editor of the Columbia Phoenix, warned Gary that if he insisted on Farley publishing the "dining" article, it would only create sympathy for Hampton and hurt Gary's chances for winning the Senate seat. The rumor, said Farley, was "flying like wild fire over the State . . . but if the charge is directly made it will afford Hampton the opportunity to explain, and the blame will be thrown on Cooke who is ready to shoulder it so as to let Hampton out."[16]

Gary did fight a war of words with General Gray over the Greenville fiasco but publicly denied that his "dining and dancing" comment was directed at Hampton. It was too late—Hampton was angry. Hampton wrote James Conner that Gary had previously given Hampton "no ground to attack him, but he has done so since in his card replying to Gray of Greenville. . . . I shall denounce his allusions to the results of Hampton democracy as a piece of impertinence. I am tired of his pretended support and his covert insolence."[17] With slightly more reserve, he wrote ex-governor Milledge Luke Bonham that "[Gary] has been praising me in public and trying to fly-blow me in private so I have grown tired of this proceeding."[18]

Hampton struck back. For the rest of the campaign, he refused to speak on the same platform as Gary. The next time he saw Gary, he did not speak to him. The state Executive Committee informed Gary that he would not be needed as a speaker at future political meetings. Leading newspapers such as the News and Courier, Charleston Journal of Commerce, and Columbia Daily Register declined to print Gary's speeches on the public debt. An enraged Gary concluded correctly that he was being "gagged." Speaking in Greenville on September 18, Hampton denounced Gary by name. If Gary's comments about "Hampton Democracy," Hampton retorted, meant that "the proud banner of our party has been lowered in my hands; if he intended to reflect upon myself personally or officially, I pronounce the imputation as unfounded as it is impertinent."[19] Hampton told his audience that Gary had no right to speak for the party, that "in the name of our State and of our God, I protest against any . . . adoption of the 'shotgun policy!' We cannot do evil that good may come of it." In an obvious allusion to Gary, he warned that there was no room for "Independent" Democrats who opposed the official platform of the party and chafed under party discipline—"an Independent at this crisis in our affairs is worse than a Radical."[20]

Once again, Hampton's prestige protected him from serious damage from Gary's attack, even from the "dining" incident; it also prevented the party and the Democratic press from officially renouncing his politics. Enthusiastic crowds continued to greet the "gallant, noble Hampton" wherever he spoke.[21] A few local papers tended to support Gary's position, or the "Edgefield" policy, but most of the press supported Hampton. The Columbia Daily Register noted Hampton's boast that he had fulfilled his promises of 1876, which "naturally attracts attention to the enunciation of principles by the Democracy in 1876. The old platform is good for second use."[22] The News and Courier agreed that Gary must be treated as a renegade from the party until he modified his views on race.[23] Even straightouts who hated Hampton's moderation found it difficult to turn against Hampton himself. Major Tom Woodward, for example, had castigated "Southern nigger-worshipers" like Hampton in 1868 for not leaving blacks alone to "[pick] out the cotton crop."[24] In a speech in April 1878, Woodward listed his grievances against Governor Hampton's policies, especially the appointment of blacks and other Republicans to office, but ended with: "Despite all this, and more that can be alleged, I honor and love this man. I know . . . that he possesses those magnetic attributes of head and heart which will endear him to this people, and will keep the honor of the old Palmetto State . . . uppermost in his mind."[25]

Hampton had black support as well, much more than he had enjoyed in 1876. Of course, he enjoyed the support of black leaders whom he had assisted, like Delany and Jonathan J. Wright. Wright said that Hampton had "kept every pledge he has made. . . . There is not a decent Negro in the state will vote against him." Black legislator Robert Smalls of Beaufort praised Hampton's "just and liberal course," and Charleston postmaster Benjamin A. Boseman expressed "absolute confidence in Gov. Hampton and entire satisfaction with his course. We have no complaint whatever to make. He has kept all his pledges." A northern reporter quoted Boseman and another black postmaster, C. M. Wilder, as saying that it was "Providential" that Hampton had become governor. "God only knows what would have become of us if things had kept on the way they were going." Half a century later, black legislator Thomas E. Miller wrote that it was impossible "to express in words the great worth of that very distinguished, faithful, patriotic, self-sacrificing humanitarian, Governor Wade Hampton."[26]

Hampton enjoyed support from the Republican rank and file, not just the black leadership. When he spoke in Charleston on October 2, the *News and Courier* reported that a few hundred "colored Democrats" greeted him, many of them wearing red shirts. Hundreds of black women and children carried sticks with pieces of red flannel attached to the ends. In a more well-known story, Hampton received the impromptu endorsement of a black woman in the small up-country village of Helena. On March 26 he had traveled by train from Columbia to Anderson, stopping to make short speeches along the way. At Helena, Hampton did not leave the train, but "a small crowd of colored people" gathered under his window out of curiosity. A white reporter who was present said that Hampton nodded politely to them and "addressed a few kind words" to one who spoke to him. As the train began to move off, "a middle aged colored woman who had been standing near and regarding him intently for some moments, suddenly strode to the front, and directing her hand at him with outstretched arm, almost shouted in his face through the open window: 'Governor Hampton! You *stay*, Governor! *We's* had a better time since *you* was made Governor than we's had *since the war!*' " Others in the crowd shouted their approval.[27]

Hampton's black support in 1878, unlike the situation in 1876, was significant—so much so that the Republican Party found it impossible to challenge his reelection bid. Instead, the party tried to appropriate Hampton's prestige for its own benefit rather than the Democrats'. On July 31 the Aiken County Republican Party adopted resolutions in which it approved of Hampton's administration. Republicans on Edisto Island cheered a speech pointing out that Hampton's "school amendment" would not have passed without Republican support. Though the Democrats "boasted of Hampton as their leader, . . . the Republicans had to come up to his support on all occasions."[28] At the Republicans' state convention in August, some delegates sought their party's official endorsement of Hampton. The convention chairman, former Charleston sheriff C. C. Bowen, narrowly managed to defeat that resolution, but the Republicans did not nominate anyone to oppose Hampton in the gubernatorial race. Instead, they tried to win back seats in the General Assembly, attacked the Democrats for the new unfair election laws, and argued that only the presence of Republicans in the legislature had made it possible for Hampton to keep his promises.[29]

On election day, November 6, 1878, Hampton won reelection by a vote of 119,550 to 213. The lopsided count should have been the ultimate vindication of his policies; instead, members of the Democratic rank and file showed that they had no intention of helping Hampton keep his promises. Republicans called the election "a farce," charging that Democratic poll managers in Charleston's First District stuffed in 2,500 false ballots. On Edisto Island, inhabited by 1,000 Republicans and 50 Democrats, the polls never opened. Armed Red Shirts patrolled elsewhere, often forcing hundreds of black voters away from the polls over the course of the day. Northern observers hinted that Hampton and his party had been insincere all along. Hampton, wrote Edward Hogan, promised political equality. But when it was time for an election, "the negro is bulldozed and intimidated, and his vote is thrown out of the ballot box. . . . This done and the object attained, the Butlers and Garys retire, and all is once more moderation and conciliation."[30] Even Hampton's ally President Hayes expressed his disappointment, though taking care not to attack Hampton himself. Hayes admitted that his own attempts to win over southern leaders had failed, and that those leaders had been unable to ensure free and fair elections—"Governor Hampton, for example, has tried repeatedly to repress the violence which has characterized the campaign in South Carolina and failed."[31]

The truth of Hayes's statement tarnished Hampton's victory even in his own eyes. Even before the election, Hampton admitted that "disturbances" had occurred.[32] This time, unlike in 1876, there was no national electoral crisis to deflect northern attention; no similar abuses by the Republicans, or strong-arm tactics by Chamberlain in the statehouse, that would allow Hampton's men even to make a claim to moral superiority. The fantastic landslide, along with the fact that Hampton received more black votes than he did in 1876, should have provided him the ultimate vindication as a patriarch who could lead both black and white South Carolinians, and restore honor and virtue to the politics of the state. Instead, it was an embarrassment. There was nothing left for a high-toned patriarch to do but to admit that abuses had occurred and express his disapproval. Hampton would soon concede to a reporter for the *Columbia Daily Register* that fraud had occurred and invite a federal investigation. "No one," he insisted, "can regret this more than I do, and no one could have striven harder to impress its wrongfulness and absolute impolicy [sic] upon our people."[33] Later he would have to stand before colleagues in the U.S. Senate and make the same admission. Hampton initially charged, though, that Republicans were more guilty of intimidation than Democrats. He told the *Register* reporter that two black servants of his son-in-law, John Haskell, had been beaten for voting Democratic.[34]

For several weeks, however, personal criticism of Hampton, whether from racial extremists or northern Republicans, was muted.[35] The reason was that Hampton was feared to be dying. On the day after the election, Hampton celebrated by engaging in his favorite activity: hunting. He was looking for deer in lower Richland County, along the Wateree River. No proper horse was available for the aging huntsman, so he mounted a mule and headed into the woods. He was far out of sight from the rest of his party when he spotted a deer. Firing from the saddle, Hampton felled the deer, then threw his reins over the mule's head and began to dismount. The mule, startled by the gunfire and the lash of the reins on his muzzle, began to buck. With his feet out of the stirrups and with no reins in his hands, Hampton threw himself away from the mule, landing heavily on his right ankle. He recovered from a semidaze to see that the mule had run away, that both bones between his knee and ankle were broken, and that the jagged ends were protruding from his flesh.

Resting against a tree, Hampton fired his gun repeatedly and blew his hunter's horn, but the day was nearly gone by the time a black servant found him and fetched a rescue party. Over the following days, doctors set his broken bones but soon discovered that the wounds in his flesh had become badly infected. On November 18, suffering from excruciating pain and fever, Hampton officially authorized Lieutenant Governor William D. Simpson to take over his duties. At the age of sixty, Hampton's wounds and infections were life-threatening and more serious even than the ones he had sustained at Gettysburg. Churches across the state offered prayers for his recovery and even held special prayer services for him. Citizens across the state anxiously read daily news reports from Columbia on his condition. Hampton was aware of the concern and later stated his firm conviction that the prayers of other South Carolinians had saved his life.[36]

On December 10 the South Carolina General Assembly voted to appoint Hampton the state's next U.S. senator. This event, too, on the surface, could have symbolized victory and vindication. This was the Senate seat that Gary had craved and schemed for, and it was the seat being vacated by "Honest John" Patterson, one of the most hated holdovers from the corrupt Republican regime. Previously there had been talk of electing Hampton to replace Patterson; Hampton had simply stated that it was up to the people to decide whether he should serve as governor or senator. As the doctors prepared that very day to amputate Hampton's leg, the General Assembly honored him, nearly unanimously, with the title of senator.[37]

And yet it was also a day of defeat. It was not just that Hampton would never quite regain the physical vigor in which he had always taken great pride. (For the rest of his life he would ride and hunt less, and fish more, and his wooden leg would always cause him pain.) More significantly, Hampton's election to federal office was the beginning of the end of his mild version of white supremacy in South Carolina. From then on, his influence in the state gradually diminished. There would be no biracial Democratic Party in the state or in the South. South Carolina would not be a land of racial harmony, in which ex-slaves and their former masters grew in prosperity and goodwill toward one another. White Carolinians would not generously extend ever-growing opportunities in education, equality, and land ownership to their black neighbors. Maybe Hampton's words promising such a society had been a pipe dream all along.

Why did South Carolina's leaders send Hampton to Washington in 1879, and why did Hampton accept the senatorship? The first question is easier to answer—it was a combination of affection and political convenience. Samuel McGowan's voice choked with emotion when he stood in the General Assembly and nominated South Carolina's hero for the vacant Senate seat. Not a single Democrat, including Gary, wished to be put on record as having voted against him. Most historians have suspected, though, that many negrophobic Democrats were glad to have Hampton's great influence removed from the state. Many black citizens certainly thought so. One of them was Martin Delany, who finally lost his Charleston County judgeship only weeks after Hampton reported to Washington.[38]

But why did Hampton accept? This question is more difficult to answer. Hampton Jarrell has theorized that Hampton was tired of the fight against the extremists and worn down by mental fatigue and physical pain. That may be part of the answer. Hampton had now led the fight for his vision of South Carolina for many years, and he could hope for less arduous duty on Capitol Hill. He may have convinced himself, besides, that he had left the situation in Columbia well in hand—Simpson, the new governor, was a "conservative," or moderate, like himself, as were the rest of the state cabinet and most of his appointees. The Garyites were a threat, but still a minority faction within the Democratic Party.[39]

The best explanation, however, is that vindication, not black progress or even racial harmony, was Hampton's deepest desire. In Washington, he could take the fight for the South's vindication, its rehabilitation in northern eyes, to the national stage. He could achieve the goal he had sought since his angry letter to Andrew Johnson in 1866.

Hampton did desire racial harmony. But the only racial harmony he knew was the kind existing between masters like himself and black servants or loyal followers—Daddy Carolina, Mauma Nelly, Francis Davie, and his bodyservant Kit Goodwyn. It was a racial harmony that validated, he believed, his kindness as a superior. He had made his promises to protect black civil rights and provide education and prosperity not for the sake of racial equality, but to restore social harmony and validate the leadership of his own class. Without a doubt, he had taken those promises seriously and had taken political risks to fulfill them. He had done so mainly out of a sense of obligation and for the sake of his own reputation. As long as he was in Washington, however, he could no longer be blamed if the promises were broken.

On April 15, 1879, five months after his hunting accident, Wade Hampton finally boarded a train for the nation's capital. South Carolina's hero had left his home state to win renown on other fields. By the time he departed, the words of his promises had already grown fainter.

YOU CANNOT EXPECT US
TO APOLOGIZE

In December 1879 Wade Hampton lost yet another child. While tending to business during an unusually warm autumn in Mississippi,
thirty-eight-year-old Wade Hampton IV contracted malaria. Hampton
rushed westward to be with him, but his oldest son died on December
22, before Hampton could reach his bedside. It was a tremendous blow,
coming after many others. The younger Wade had just married during
the previous summer and left no children. Though never as charismatic or as handsome as his younger brother Preston, Wade had been
a dutiful son and a good soldier. He had shied away from the limelight
as his father became South Carolina's hero and tended the family's
planting interests. His father grieved deeply. Writing over three months
later, Hampton confessed: "Life seems closed to me, and I have nothing but duty to live for. It is very hard, but I try to say, God's will
be done."[1]

It was not entirely true that Hampton had nothing left but duty to live
for, though he must have felt so at the time. Hampton still got immense
pleasure from hunting and fishing. He cherished time with his remaining children—sons Alfred and McDuffie, daughters Daisy and Sally, and
his surviving grandchildren, though the rambunctiousness of the latter
taxed his energy. He also thoroughly enjoyed socializing with Confederate veterans, both privately and at official reunions, where he was usually a speaker or the guest of honor.[2]

But the specters of tragedy and loss continued to define much of his
life. The cemetery beside the church where he worshipped was filled
with the graves of his children and two wives. His friends were nearly all
former comrades—survivors of a disastrous, lost war. Pain from his
wounds and the joint of his artificial leg plagued him constantly, and
served as a constant reminder of lost youth and vigor. His younger
brother Kit died in June 1886, only two months after the devastating loss
of Hampton's forty-one-year-old daughter, Sally. At that point, Hampton had buried two wives, six children, and four grandchildren, not to
mention three younger siblings. Sally had been the last surviving child
of Hampton's marriage to Margaret Preston, of the generation that had
come of age during the war and that Hampton had led (Preston and

Wade) into battle. There was nothing left by which to remember Margaret but the grandchildren she never knew.[3]

"I have nothing but duty to live for"—but what did duty require? Hampton identified with the southern sense of tragedy and loss because it was his own; he was living it in his personal life. He believed it his duty to vindicate and redeem as much as possible—to see that all the excruciating loss was not without some meaning, the dead without some honor. In political terms, this meant that he would continue to defend the honor of the southern cause, the legitimacy of his political victories in 1876 and 1878, and the good name of his home state, whether such a defense was wholly deserved or not. When Hampton began his service in the U.S. Senate in 1879, he took the battle for personal and southern vindication to the national stage.

Meanwhile, Hampton sought reconciliation with the North, much as he once had with black Republicans in South Carolina. He pursued both goals—vindication and reconciliation—at the same time and in the same speeches. While publicly admitting the goodwill and honest motives of northerners who were former foes, he demanded that they respond in kind. While pleading for national unity and peace, he insisted that white southerners had fought for what they thought was right, that Reconstruction had been a travesty, and that the North could and should entrust leadership of the South to the South's "natural" leaders. As other historians have recognized, Hampton and other Redeemers sought "reconciliation so long as it came about on southern terms."[4] They would not return to the Union cringing and begging for forgiveness.

While Hampton fought this war for vindication and reconciliation, the Republican press and a few Republican politicians continued to attack him. And, for a time at least, Democrat Martin Gary ensured that the battle for vindication was a two-front war. Speaking to a *New York Herald* reporter in December 1879, Gary repeated the charge that Hampton had betrayed presidential candidate Samuel J. Tilden in 1876 in return for Republican support in his own race for governor. This time it was clear that Gary was taking the lead role in spreading the story. Gary now had his eyes on the governor's seat and the 1880 election; he hoped to discredit Hampton and his "clique" who then dominated the state government. And this time Gary said that Hampton approached Gary himself on the advisability of carrying out the scheme.[5]

The revamped charge created a stir in the nation's newspapers, especially in South Carolina. Hampton replied in a newspaper interview of his own. He stated that he only deigned to notice the charge because it was being published outside his state and thus reflected badly on South Carolina's Democratic victory in 1876. He further asserted that once the 1876 campaign commenced, he had not sought Gary's advice on any matter whatsoever, finding his views "narrow, unwise, and dangerous."[6] The controversy continued, though Hampton withdrew from it for over a week as he traveled west to visit the malaria-stricken Wade. Others took up his defense. Hampton's son-in-law John C. Haskell wrote editors that Gary, "in his usual good taste," had launched the latest attack on Hampton while the old hero was "at the deathbed of his son."[7] Alexander Haskell reprinted the correspondence between Hampton and Tilden's campaign manager Manton Marble to disprove Gary's story, and most of the state's newspapers rallied around Hampton again. By February 1880 the story played itself out, but not before Gary lost his composure in a newspaper interview and exploded that he would meet Hampton "on any field he might select."[8] Hampton and his old subordinate Gary never reconciled, unlike Hampton and many of his former foes in blue. The "Bald Eagle" of Edgefield and his old commander remained enemies until Gary's death in 1881.[9]

Hampton had been unable to ignore Gary's "Tilden Democrat" charges because they reflected on the legitimacy of his victory in 1876–77. Hampton was proud of that victory, the culmination of his vindicatory triumph over Yankee rule. He would later claim that the proudest moment of his life did not come on any battlefield, but on the day he returned to Columbia from his meeting with President Hayes to announce to "our people" that victory was theirs, and his.[10] If Gary's version of events were allowed to stand, Hampton's victory was a sellout and Hampton was a traitor.

While Gary sought to rob Hampton of his political victories by accusing him of collaborating with Republicans, those Republicans linked him to the murder of other Republicans. While Gary called him a traitor, Republicans called him a cheater. When Hampton arrived in Washington to take his Senate seat, northern newspapers, at least Republican ones, considered him a man of fraud and bloodshed, who was all the more dangerous because he often beguiled others with hypocritical calls for peace. The distrust of Hampton was so intense that, after his hunting accident, the *New York Times* printed a report under the headline "Wade Hampton's Mule-Fraud." According to the story, Hampton's broken leg was a hoax concocted so he would not have to sign election

447

results that he knew to be fraudulent; he could excuse himself from his duties long enough for the lieutenant governor to commit the deed, so his "fingers were [not] soiled."[11]

The amputation of Hampton's leg destroyed that hypothesis, but the *Times* continued a barrage of articles accusing him of winking at, or even ordering, fraud and violence. This was nothing new. Democratic papers in the North frequently praised Hampton, but Republicans were the dominant party there, and Hampton had been a favorite target of the northern Republican press ever since the end of the war. Occasionally, even Republican papers such as the *Times* and *Harper's Weekly* praised Hampton for his moderation, promises to blacks, and apparent willingness to compromise with Republicans. More often, they attempted to connect him with the Ku Klux Klan, the bloodshed of 1876, and the cheating of 1878. Northern Republican praise for Hampton never appeared close to election time, when the abuse picked up considerably, especially in the months just before and after election day. The dominant Hampton image in the mind of the North was of a die-hard Rebel breathing moderation one day of the week and angry defiance the other six, always with a dagger hidden behind his back. He seemed the epitome of the "Bourbon" Democrats—haughty southern aristocrats, former slave moguls, who refused to admit that they had lost, that times had changed.[12]

In 1880, for example, Hampton lectured South Carolina Democrats that they must not resort to fraud. When they did, and won, the *New York Times* sneered in a headline, "Wade Hampton's Advice Taken." The story charged that "Hampton's advice to his men was that the State and country must be saved at all hazards, by fair means or foul."[13] The article was a slander, but it reflected much of the North's suspicions about Hampton, at least at times when politics were heated.

Hampton's admission in early 1879 that there had been unfortunate fraud and irregularities brought a brief respite from criticism when he arrived for Senate duty in April, and the sight of his cork leg may have generated some sympathy. By June he had enough political space that he ventured to give his first Senate speech. Standing on his one good leg and resting the stump of the other on his desk, the aging ex-Confederate delivered an hour-long address that was full of stubborn pride and conciliation all at once.

A minute into his speech, the president of the Senate invited Hampton to sit while speaking if it "would be more convenient."[14] The old soldier, of course, politely refused. Hampton spoke in favor of an army appropriations bill and against a federal law passed in 1862 that forbade ex-Confederates from serving on federal juries. Now that war and Reconstruction had passed, Democrats argued that the law should be repealed. Hampton considered the law an insult not only to the loyal citizens of the South but also to constitutional principles.[15]

Hampton's speech, though, covered far more than the law itself; in fact, its themes set the tone for his political course over the next twelve years in the Senate. Mixing courtesy with firm conviction, Hampton emphasized the South's loyalty, its right to participate fully in the political life of the nation, its respect for its former foes who had actually fought against it during the Civil War, and the alleged injustices inflicted on the South by Republican tyrants during Reconstruction. He quoted prominent Republican leaders who had denounced military despotism and the use of federal power to determine the makeup of state legislatures and control elections at the state level. He then asked why southern leaders should be denounced for making the same arguments. In fact, he asserted, the "whole discussion" was permeated by "the strong and steady insinuation that the South is not true to the Union. . . . We are tauntingly told that proof of these charges is found in the presence on this floor of twenty-two members who served in the confederate army, and the South is reproached, nay, denounced, for sending such men to represent her here."[16]

Hampton thus prepared to defend his own right to serve in the Senate. Who could blame the South, he demanded, "for trusting . . . in peace the men who risked their fortunes and lives for her in war [?]"[17] It was the northern states that deserved reproach for sending so few of their own veterans to Congress. Had they sent more, the nation would have avoided much of the upheaval of Reconstruction and the South much of its misery, because northern veterans, men with whom Hampton had crossed swords, would have been more disposed than politicians to treat a defeated foe with honor: "The men who served in the opposing armies are now the strongest advocates of a true reconciliation. We learned in a common school how to respect our enemies; we learned that personal courage and honor and truth were better guarantees of patriotism than constitutional learning or eloquent speech . . . were our antagonists of the late war here to-day, in the contests on this floor as in fiercer battles of yore, whoever might be the victor, we should be assured of a fair field and an honest surrender."[18]

These sentiments, of course, contradicted the way Hampton had felt about Union army officers during the war, particularly those, like William T. Sherman and Judson Kilpatrick, whom he considered war criminals. But his words were a compelling attempt to define patriotism as valor in battle, not as adherence to the platform of the Republican Party. After he uttered them, applause exploded from the galleries, and the president pro tem had to demand order.

Besides, he reminded the North, there was another reason why ex-Confederates, the South's traditional leaders, were back in Washington —the North, in the name of "Union," had not allowed them to leave. "What we were you knew when you insisted that we should still be part and parcel of this Union. . . . When you insisted

> that the States should return to the Union; when you called upon them to send back their Representatives, did you mean what you said or did you mean the Southern States to be rotten boroughs to be filled by nominations of the republican party? Indeed, did you not for fifteen years make them so? And I will leave it to the candor of republican Senators to say whether they are satisfied with the result of the experiment they made at such a frightful cost to us and the whole country. [Here Hampton reminded the North of the general feeling then prevailing that Reconstruction had been a failure—that blacks had not taken proper advantage of their newfound rights and that many carpetbag governments in the South had been embarrassments.] We are here because we do represent the popular majority, the character, the intelligence, and the property of the States which have sent us. We are here because left to themselves the instincts of the recently enfranchised voters have taught them that their interests are identical with ours. We are here because, belonging to your own race, trained in the same political experience as your own, taught by years of rule how to govern, we could not be subordinated, to such a mass of ignorant voters as you had rashly and suddenly created. We are here, we trust, for the good of the whole country.[19]

Hampton mixed stubbornness with reconciliation. "For the past you cannot expect us to apologize," he declared. "To do so would be to sacrifice our own self-respect and to forfeit the respect of all honorable men. In the heat of conflict we struck hard blows, and doubtless we spoke hard words." A few sentences later, though, he insisted: "We [of the South] wish to promote the best interest of the whole country; we wish to restore harmony and good-will; we hope to see permanent peace and widespread prosperity among all classes of our people; we desire to see the painful memories of the late unhappy war buried in our own hearts, not rising to the lips in bitter words which can only provoke sectional animosity." Despite denunciations from the North, the South would stand by the Constitution, pray that "our children" would be bound together by "true fraternity," living in freedom, prosperity, and "all the glories which God in his infinite mercy can bestow." Again the galleries erupted with applause.[20]

The New York Times gave favorable coverage to Hampton's speech. For several months he was out of the national headlines, until a crowd in Abbeville booed and hissed him for his comments on the treatment of blacks. As a Times reporter wrote, Hampton advised his audience "to treat negroes better in the future, and to pay them more wages." Men in the audience swore, "gesticulated wildly," and departed in disgust, expressing "their displeasure in a manner that could not be misunderstood."[21] The Times later editorialized that the event was proof not only of new divisions within "Bourbonism," but also of the racial extremism of southern Democrats. And rather than portraying Hampton as a man of brave words, the Times argued that his conciliatory statements "have always been equivocal. His preaching has been better than his practice. He has winked at occurrences which . . . he could have sternly repressed."[22] Still, 1879 was not an election year, and Hampton appeared not as a chief villain as he had in 1868, 1876, or 1878, but merely as an appeaser of criminals.

The coverage was different in 1880, when Hampton played a prominent role in the Democratic National Convention. On June 24, in response to calls that he speak, he advanced to the platform. There he said that the South would not push its own candidate for nomination; instead, a "solid South" would loyally support the "gallant soldier" Winfield Scott Hancock, its former foe on the battlefield.[23] Republican papers feigned shock that Hampton would dare make such a pledge—the only way he could guarantee a "solid" southern vote for the Democrats, they said, was by controlling the election machinery and cheating Republican voters. Besides, they charged, Hampton's comments only perpetuated sectional divisions.[24]

Hampton counterattacked in his typical style, offering reconciliation in one breath and demanding in another that the other side recognize southern virtue and Republican villainy. He charged that it was Republicans who had turned the phrase "Solid South" into a device "to array one part of the country against another." The South, he assured a New York audience, was not "solid" against the North or the U.S. Constitution. "Admitting, however, for the sake of argument, that the South is solid, why did not the Republican Party point out the danger when the South was solidly Republican?" or "when the South was full of carpet-baggers, political bummers, and thieves[?]"[25]

Hampton thus refused to yield the moral high ground to his foes. His defense was even more determined when the attacks were personal. In the heat of the campaign, personal insults came from a familiar quarter—a Sherman. Treasury Secretary John Sherman, the brother of Hampton's most hated enemy, had once contemptuously dismissed Hampton's attempt to get his side of the Columbia fire story told in the Senate. In a September 1880 address to a New York audience, John Sherman said: "And now you are asked to surrender all you have done into the hands of Wade Hampton, and the Kuklux, and the little segment in the North that is called the Democratic Party."[26]

Hampton would not tolerate such an attack on the legitimacy of his political victories, particularly from a Sherman. He had come to Washington to defend the honor of his own name and that of his state. He was not about to let a Yankee politician, the brother of the arsonist and slanderer William T. Sherman, call him a "Kukluxer." From a vacation lodge in the Virginia mountains, he wrote Sherman, demanding to know whether the secretary meant to "connect me, directly or indirectly, with what was known as the Kuklux Klan?" He asked Sherman to mail his reply to a friend's address in New York, then hurried to New York, where he soon delivered the speech quoted above. Hampton had not received a reply by the time of his arrival in New York, and so did not mention Sherman in his speech on the "Solid South" controversy. By the time he returned to Virginia, however, he had Sherman's reply in hand. In the letter, Sherman denied saying that Hampton was directly connected with the Klan and admitted that Hampton had "in one or two important instances resisted and defeated its worst impulses." Still, Sherman understandably asserted that Hampton and other Democrats owed their power to crimes of murder and ballot-box stuffing committed in their behalf. What was more, Sherman charged, "you may, in logic and morals, be classed as I classed you, as joint copartners with the Kuklux Klan."[27]

Hampton recognized that Sherman's retraction was no retraction at all, but rather a deeper insult. In a terse note he informed Sherman that "you uttered what is absolutely false, and what you knew to be false. My address will be Columbia, S.C."[28]

This was the traditional language of a duel. In calling Sherman a liar and telling him where he could be found, Hampton's words read like those of an offended gentleman seeking redress with pistols. Sherman turned the correspondence over to the media, which printed it under the headlines "Wade Hampton in a Rage," "Wade Hampton Wants a Fight," and, mockingly, " 'Chivalry.' " The story fit well with northern stereotypes of hotheaded Rebels, and the Republican press ridiculed Hampton as a "bully" and a "swaggerer."[29] When Hampton denied that he was seeking a duel, the New York Times scoffed:

> When the Honorable Elijah Pogram, of South Carolina, has a dis-
> agreement with the Honorable Decimus Sniffles, of Georgia, he
> sends to Sniffles a note informing him as to the manner in which
> he can address the writer. Or the Honorable Pogram addresses to
> the Honorable Sniffles a note to this effect: "Sir: You are a liar and a
> thief, and your clothes don't fit. My address is Euchre FourCorners,
> Sumter County, S.C." . . . This is the Southern manner; it is the
> manner in which Wade Hampton has been reared. And when he
> said, in substance, to Secretary Sherman, "You are a liar, and my
> address is Columbia, S.C.," he knew perfectly well that he could
> say to his South Carolina barbarians that he had challenged Secre-
> tary Sherman to send a challenge, and that Mr. Sherman had failed
> to respond.[30]

Hampton's letter did sound like a formal challenge to exchange shots at dawn, but it was probably so in a rhetorical sense only. If he were really eager for such a fight, he could have gone to Washington to meet Sherman or exchange more notes, not back to Columbia. South Carolinians in aristocratic circles knew Hampton to be a firm opponent of dueling. He had acted more than once among his acquaintances to prevent arguments from leading to pistol shots, and he had followed the example of his father when his own sisters had been violated by James Henry Hammond. Rather than starting a fight, the elder Hamp-ton had counseled his sons that he would make Hammond pay by dogged opposition at every turn, over a period of years.[31]

Still, even Hampton must have been tempted to shoot a rival like Sher-man, and South Carolinians opposed to dueling worried that Hampton had set a bad example. The Episcopal bishop of South Carolina, W. B. W. Howe, politely asked Hampton to clarify his position, "knowing you to be a communicant of our Church." Bishop Howe hopefully assumed that Hampton, in his address, only meant to let Sherman know where he would be if Sherman wished to explain himself further. Hampton thanked the bishop for his letter and assured him, probably disingenuously, that it "never occurred to him for a moment that any one would construe my language as giving or inviting a challenge." Thanking him for his kindness, Hampton jokingly told Howe that he hoped he would not misinterpret his meaning "when I tell you that 'my address' will be Washington after the 10th. With my best wishes, I am, very respectfully and truly, yours, Wade Hampton."[32]

Hampton did not really want to be seen as a duelist, but the *New York Times* was right about one thing: Hampton felt that he had to show his fellow South Carolinians that he would not tolerate John Sherman's insults to him or to his state. He explained to Bishop Howe that Sherman had not only abused his official position, but also vilified Hampton's constituents and the whole South. Hampton had to know there was truth to the charge that violence had played a role in the Democrats' return to power in the South. That did not matter—it was his duty to defend the honor of his people. In doing so, he defended his own honor as well. The Klan may have been an unfortunate reaction; there may have been too much ballot-box stuffing and too little kindness to "ignorant negroes." But Wade Hampton and his people believed that they had suffered and sacrificed too much at the hands of Yankees to tolerate further insult. "You cannot expect us," he warned, "to apologize."[33]

SENATOR HAMPTON

Back home in South Carolina, Hampton played a decreasing role in state politics, retreating from the stage on his own accord. His old lieutenants occupied the governor's mansion for over a decade, but an aging and ailing Hampton showed little desire to dominate the state, other than to refute Martin Gary's attacks. When Hampton did get involved in other South Carolina issues, it was to promote two goals: ensuring some measure of justice for African Americans and preserving white Democratic unity. Tragically, the second goal became far more important to him than the first.

Hampton advised white citizens not to resort to fraud to carry the 1880 election. Once again he urged them to overcome the majority of 15,000 "colored voters" by winning their votes, not by cheating. The latter course would not only be wrong, but it would also make "our elections a mockery" and invite federal prosecution. Nevertheless, Democrats carried the state elections in South Carolina in 1880 much as they had in 1878—through fraud.[1]

Increasingly, though, the white leadership of the state grew dissatisfied with resorting to illegal means to win elections. On the other hand, nearly all recognized that Hampton's strategy of honestly appealing for black votes was unreliable. Democrats discussed finding legal ways to manipulate elections. Hampton's 1881 comments in the Senate on South Carolina balloting asserted that there were many honest men working on a solution to the problem. And the problem, thought Democrats, was that too many black men were not intelligent enough to vote for honest Democrats rather than corrupt carpetbaggers or black candidates. Reporting on Hampton's Senate speech, the Charleston News and Courier stated that "what was done in 1876, in 1878, and in 1880 was necessary. Similar work is indispensable no longer, and the people will not put up with it. The Democratic masses cannot be whipped or spurred up to the point of taking the chances of Albany Penitentiary."[2] (The News and Courier thus finally admitted that Democrats had been cheating.)

The 1882 election clearly illustrated that Hampton was more concerned with party unity than black suffrage. With Gary dead, the threat to white elite rule now came not from shotgun-wielding Red Shirts, but from the emerging Greenback-Labor Party, or "Greenbackers." The Greenbackers strove to create an alliance between poor white farmers and blacks. When they fused with the Republicans in 1882, they seemed a real threat to Democratic unity and thus to white rule.[3]

Meanwhile, the legislature was working to limit black suffrage with a complicated measure that came to be known as the "Eight-Box Law." Years before, Hampton had hoped to apply a literacy test for voting. The problem, others recognized, was that while such a measure would disenfranchise a majority of black voters, it would also affect a great number of whites. The Eight-Box Law created incredibly complex registration procedures designed to confuse uneducated voters and disqualify those who changed residences often, such as tenants or sharecroppers. Additionally, polling sites would contain not one or two but eight ballot boxes corresponding to local, state, and national contests. If a voter placed a ballot in the wrong box, his vote was disqualified. Election managers, who by this time were all Democrats, could assist illiterate voters in selecting the right box, or easily mislead them.[4]

Hampton opposed the Eight-Box Law, but not nearly as much as he did threats to Democratic unity. His main concern with the Eight-Box Law and with a stock fencing law, in fact, was that they were unpopular with lower-class whites and threatened that unity. "Without reflecting in the slightest degree upon either the wisdom or the patriotism" of the legislature, he called the two laws "unfortunate." But that was no reason "to desert the only party that has given honest and good government to the State since the war." The legislature could repeal those laws in the next session if the people desired, but "an Independent is, if possible, worse than a Radical." Dividing the white vote among Democrats and "Independents," or Greenbackers, would bring the "restoration of Radical rule."[5]

The Eight-Box Law worked for white Democrats throughout the 1880s; there was no longer any need for shotguns and tissue ballots on election day. Hampton continued to promise black voters that Democrats would respect their lawful rights and continued to receive their applause, but those promises were becoming more empty and irrelevant than ever. The vast majority of blacks could no longer vote at all, and black representation in the General Assembly was virtually nil. Unlike the former Hampton administration, the state's Democratic Party now made little pretense of being a biracial party. Yet Hampton said little. Peace had finally returned to South Carolina politics for the first time in 456 a quarter of a century. Now that white supremacy and stability had returned, Hampton was little more than a cheerleader for the conservative faction—his protégés—who controlled the state.[6]

★ As Hampton's Senate career progressed from 1879 to 1891, his public comments on racial matters gradually became less magnanimous and more negrophobic. His 1879 essay in a public forum published in the *North American Review* sounded little different from what he had said in 1867 or 1876. The forum—entitled "Ought the Negro to Be Disenfranchised? Ought He to Have Been Enfranchised?"—was in part a response to a growing belief in the North that enfranchisement of blacks had been a mistake. Hampton's answer was the same as it had been in 1867—blacks had to be given the franchise; the only mistake had been granting it in an unconstitutional way and without a literacy test or slight property qualification. That is why "they were easily misled by the wicked and designing men who flocked to the South when she was prostrate. But, in spite of the evil advice they have so constantly received, they have on the whole behaved better than any other people similarly situated would have done, and the whites of the South have no reason to cherish any ill will toward the blacks."[7] In 1879 Hampton still believed that, with education, "the Negro" would become a responsible voter and citizen, appreciating good government and home rule. "As the negro becomes more intelligent, he naturally allies himself with the more conservative of the whites," for then blacks would see that the interests of white and black southerners were similar.[8] Hampton claimed that the South would not pursue black disenfranchisement if it could, for that would diminish the South's representation in Congress.

Hampton's writings a decade later read differently. In 1888, *The Forum* published his essay entitled "What Negro Supremacy Means." His views on the Constitution and the franchise had not changed, but his tone had. For one thing, Hampton had never even used the phrase "negro supremacy" in years past; he had always tried to convince other whites like Gary that the conflict was one of politics and principle, not race. The essay as a whole was another reminder of the dangers of universal suffrage when a majority of the population was uneducated. Hampton once again told his tale of dishonest Republican government in Reconstruction South Carolina. What was new in his 1888 telling was that he assigned nearly as much blame for the situation to black South Carolinians as he did to northern carpetbaggers. He repeatedly cited James S. Pike's *The Prostrate State*, a book by a former abolitionist that blasted the Republican regime of Reconstruction-era South Carolina. In several places, Hampton quoted some of Pike's most racist language—"[In the Reconstruction legislature] the speaker is black, the clerk is black, the door-keepers are black, the little pages are black, the chairman of the Ways and Means is black, and the chaplain is coal black. At some of the desks sit colored men whose types it would be hard to find outside of Congo; whose costumes, visages, attitudes, and expression only befit the forecastle of a buccaneer."[9]

These were words that Hampton had never used back home in South Carolina. They are intolerable today and should have been offensive in 1888. Yet they should be seen, not as an example of growing race hatred on his part, but as another attempt to justify and vindicate the movement he had led in 1876, as well as continued white elite rule in the South.

Hampton had not developed a dislike for black people, but he was retreating from his earlier views that whites and blacks could live side by side with peace and prosperity for both. Black people, he seemed to think, had shown they could advance little as long as they lived alongside whites. In 1889 and 1890 he supported a black emigration scheme proposed by Calbraith Butler and endorsed by Henry McNeal Turner, bishop of the African Methodist Episcopal Church. The plan was for the federal government to assist African Americans who wished to emigrate to the West, to Canada, back to Africa, or anywhere else. Citing a "deep-seated, ineradicable race antagonism" in America, Hampton argued that the presence of Africans in America had created strife and bloodshed among whites, and the presence of the more advanced Caucasian race now checked black "aspirations for equality and independence."[10] He stressed, however, that any "forcible expulsion" would be a violation of black citizens' rights, not to mention "impolitic, unjust, and cruel."[11] Nor did he think they should be allowed to leave "empty-handed," without "comfortable transportation," "pleasant homes," and "ample means of support for one year at least."[12] Hampton's optimism for a peaceful, biracial society had waned; his paternalism had not.[13]

On the surface, then, it might seem that Hampton's racial views had changed, that he had retreated on the issue of racial equality. He had not. As governor, his real goal had never been racial equality at all, but rather proving that his word was good. He had done that in 1877 and 1878. Governor Hampton had been determined to fulfill the political promises he had made to black South Carolinians. Now that he had no direct role within the state itself, he was less concerned with the way his successors treated the black population. He protested little as fellow

Democrats increasingly restricted black political participation. As a U.S. senator, he could move on to the larger project of vindicating the honor of his state on the national stage. Involved in politics only on the national level, he spent his time ensuring that Radical Reconstruction was discredited, that white supremacy in the South was safe, and that the actions of the white South in war and Reconstruction were defended, even honored. It was a tragic failure of statesmanship.

Part of the reason for Hampton's bad press in the North was not just that he epitomized the defiant Rebel; he also seemed to be an intensely partisan Democrat. He had played prominent roles in the Democratic National Conventions of 1868 and 1880, and of course had led the Democratic resurgence in South Carolina. As the 1880s progressed, however, Hampton acquired a growing reputation for moderation and conciliation on the national stage, much as he already had in South Carolina. He took the first step in April 1881, when he again admitted— this time on the floor of the U.S. Senate—that there had been "irregularities and frauds" in South Carolina elections.[14] Hampton's admission included what Republicans considered lame excuses, pleading "the cruel wrongs inflicted on our people" and the presence of a large illiterate population.[15] Hampton asked northerners to consider the hypothetical situation of a Massachusetts suddenly overwhelmed by a mass of Chinese immigrants, "even as intelligent people as they." Suppose the suddenly enfranchised Chinese majority monopolized government offices, paid no taxes, and yet taxed the taxpaying citizens "to practical confiscation." It would not be forty-eight hours, Hampton predicted, "before those Chinamen would be hung to the nearest lamp-post in Massachusetts."[16] And yet, Hampton reminded his colleagues of his own efforts to do everything in his power to protect the "colored people of South Carolina" and show both races that "their interests were identical."[17] Hampton was still trying to justify his own victory and vindicate the name of his own state on the national stage. Sadly, in doing so, he partially excused crimes that he had never endorsed. His admission was not the mea culpa that Republicans wanted, but his opponents considered it significant.[18]

Hampton seemed moderate on other issues as well. Though he called any bolter from the Democratic Party in South Carolina "a traitor to his State," Hampton showed that he could break party ranks in the Senate if matters of conscience were involved.[19] At that time, there was a lingering dispute over who lawfully held one of the Senate seats from Louisiana: Democrat Henry M. Spofford or Republican William Pitt Kellogg. After 459 the disputed 1876 election, the Republican-dominated Senate had finally voted in November 1877 to seat Kellogg rather than Spofford. In 1879 Democrats regained control of the chamber and raised the issue again. In an address the next year Hampton said that, although all his sympathies were with Spofford in the case, he had to admit that the Senate had had the right to seat its own members in 1877.[20]

Later, Hampton supported a Republican proposal to provide federal funding for public schools. Many southern congressmen, including Hampton's colleague Calbraith Butler, opposed the "Blair Bill" as an unconstitutional threat to states' rights. Hampton's opinion was that his own state of South Carolina needed and deserved all the help it could get in education. In saying so, he not only demonstrated his paternalism, but also defended the state's honor and denounced Reconstruction all at once. Those who had "unfortunately been denied" the blessings of education were "potent for evil," he said, and the state had a duty to them. But hadn't the federal government, he asked, arbitrarily created hundreds of thousands of illiterate citizens at one stroke? Hadn't Republican plunderers left the state hopelessly in debt and with illiterate school officials? (Hampton, as governor, had once displayed a teacher's pay certificate to the state legislature; the certificate had been signed by a Republican state school superintendent with an X. Hampton had presented it as a "literary curiosity" and proof that the school system needed reform.)[21] Hampton quoted statistics to show that his state now spent over two-thirds of its total budget on education and that Charleston, though recently ravaged by fire, sword, and plunder, contributed more per capita to the education of its children than Boston, Massachusetts. Though whites paid over 90 percent of the state's taxes, "the whole fund collected is applied to public education without discrimination as to race or color, and I would not have it otherwise. But surely in the face of these facts we are authorized to ask aid of the General Government in behalf of these people who were made citizens and adopted as wards by it."[22]

Hampton supported a bill to reimburse black southerners who had been swindled during Reconstruction by the Freedmen's Bank. Unofficially connected with the Freedmen's Bureau and chartered by Congress in 1865, the Freedmen's Bank had encouraged freed slaves to save and invest. It collapsed in 1874, largely due to mismanagement and fraud by its directors, and thousands of African Americans lost everything they had invested. Hampton argued that reimbursing the victims of the bank collapse was a matter of justice to innocent, naive black citizens, some of whom had been his slaves. It was also an opportunity to prove his paternalistic concern for blacks as well as criticize Reconstruction carpetbaggers.[23]

While Hampton's version of reconciliation often twitted Republican politicians, it embraced northern soldiers. Hampton strongly supported efforts to reorganize a "Blue-Gray reunion" of veterans at Gettysburg. He supported petitions to Congress on behalf of pensions for Union war veterans who were from the South, including a request from the widow of a North Carolinian who allegedly had spied for the Union. He frequently praised the courage and honest motives of Yankee soldiers, always asserting the same virtues for those of the South. He even supported the nomination of Judson Kilpatrick, his old nemesis, for the post of ambassador to Chile. Unlike William T. Sherman, Kilpatrick had never blamed Hampton for the Columbia fire and had later admitted to Calbraith Butler that Hampton had embarrassed him at Monroe's Crossroads. Hampton might reconcile with a former enemy, but only if the latter gave him his due.[24]

Hampton was still a "moderate" by southern standards. By the end of the 1880s, he was seen as one in the North as well. Yet his opinion of African Americans had changed little, other than his impatience at how slowly the black population as a whole was coming around to supporting the Democratic Party. Christian sensibility and benevolent paternalism still did not allow him to sanction outright disenfranchisement, racial violence, or forced emigration, and he was concerned with the South's image in the North. Yet he protested little as the rights of his black constituents gradually disappeared. In fact, by asserting again and again that Reconstruction had been a mistake, that the South was honorable, that he himself wanted reconciliation with the North, Hampton indirectly ensured continued black oppression. By the time he retired from the Senate, Hampton's image in the northern mind had transformed from that of a dangerous Rebel to that of an honest and honorable old soldier. The success of his Senate career and his increasing national popularity helped persuade many in the North that those "old rebels" might be trusted after all.

HAMPTON VERSUS TILLMAN

By 1889 Wade Hampton was tired of public life. As early as 1882, there had been rumors that he would retire from the Senate. Hampton never got pleasure from his Senate obligations, and we can probably believe his claims that he served mainly from a sense of "duty." The great battles of his life seemed to be waning or closing, since much had been redeemed. He had returned his state to its "rightful" rulers. By the end of the decade, there were signs that the North was willing to acknowledge the honor and honest motives of its former southern foes. On a personal level, Hampton had not recouped even a fraction of his former wealth, but his living conditions were tolerable. He was still able, in fact, to vacation in the Virginia mountains once a year. Though he had not recovered all of his former lands in Mississippi from the Duncans, or even paid all of his debts, his son McDuffie managed both well enough after the deaths of son Wade and brother Kit.

Hampton much preferred hunting with McDuffie at Wild Woods to politicking in Washington. In 1889, for example, he missed the opening of Congress's fall session because he was in Mississippi negotiating the sale of some of his land. He wrote Calbraith Butler to explain his absence, adding that the hunting had been excellent—he and McDuffie had killed seven deer. After all, he wrote, "There is much more fun in doing that, than in listening to dry speeches!"[1]

Outdoor activity like hunting gave moments of exhilaration to an aging Hampton, who felt that much of life was a struggle to deal with the ravages of past blows. He still rode tall in the saddle at Confederate reunions and publicly projected pride and dignity. Privately, though, he acknowledged his growing frailty and fatigue. Just seven months before killing seven deer with McDuffie, the seventy-year-old Hampton had written to his youngest son Alfred explaining the terms of his will and the division of his estate. "I wish that all of you were provided for," he lamented, "but I can do very little toward that end." He also confessed that he "suffered terribly from neuralgia in my wound" and that his heart had given him trouble lately. "Time, sorrows, wounds, & troubles have taken from me, much of my recuperative power, & I must look for the end before very long."[2]

Yet unknown to Hampton, there was still one more great battle to   463

George "McDuffie"
Hampton (1858–1917).
Hampton's first son by
Mary McDuffie Hampton.
South Caroliniana Library.

fight, one more humiliation ahead that would have to be undone. The
new challenge came from Benjamin Ryan Tillman, an Edgefield planter
who had been a follower of Martin Gary. Tillman had been a teenager
during the Civil War. He had enlisted at the age of seventeen, but immediately contracted a severe eye infection, preventing further Confederate
service and resulting in the loss of his left eye. During Hampton's 1876
campaign, Tillman had led a company of Red Shirts.

Though the movement he led in the 1880s and 1890s is often considered to have had class overtones, Tillman was no poor yeoman farmer.
His parents were moderately well-to-do slaveowners. Like most southern planters, Tillman struggled financially for several years after the
war, but by 1881 he was one of Edgefield County's leading planters and
the owner of a 2,000-acre estate.[3]

Tillmanism, however, fed off very real resentments and divisions
464 lying under the surface of white unity, many of them existing since

colonial times. There had long been a rivalry between up-country and low-country districts, resulting in long-standing feuds over apportionment and representation. This battle traditionally had class implications, sometimes portrayed as a conflict between fabulously rich low-country rice planters and yeoman farmers of the up-country.[4] Resentment also festered in many quarters that an elite few—the "courthouse clique," or the "ring" of leaders put in place by Hampton—still dominated political offices and the inner workings of the state Democratic Party. Tillman made this charge even more vehemently, and profanely, than Gary.

Additionally, Tillman enjoyed support from men who felt that the tide of black disenfranchisement had not gone far enough. The "Conservative" faction of the party, led by Hampton's former lieutenants, felt concern about the possible return of black-Radical rule, but not as acutely as did the "Tillmanite," or "Reform" faction of the party. Nearly fourteen thousand black men managed to vote in 1888 despite the Eight-Box Law, and a handful of black legislators still helped govern the state. More ominously, there remained the danger of a breakaway faction of Democrats uniting with black voters and threatening white Democratic control of the state. As Francis Butler Simkins noted, "a full policy of reaction" against black citizenship had met several obstacles— "a sense of responsibility toward the Negro, whose suffrage Hampton had sworn to protect . . . the fear of the intervention of the national government . . . and . . . the inertness of the conservative leaders of the lowcountry."[5]

Tillman, though not a poor farmer, also made himself the representative of angry white farmers struggling against low cotton prices, high interest rates, a tight money supply, and exhausted soil. The failure of the state's conservative Redeemers—the men who came to power with Hampton—to address the plight of farmers made it easier for Tillman to position himself as the leader of the "Farmer's Movement" in the state.[6]

By 1888, the animosities between the Tillman wing of the South Carolina Democratic Party and the Conservative wing led by Hampton's protégés had become serious. Hampton remained above the fray until the 1890 campaign, when Tillman made a bid to become the Democratic nominee for governor. Hampton and other Conservatives found almost nothing in Tillman to admire. His dress was slovenly, his speech profane. His political stock-in-trade consisted of outlandish accusations, insinuations, epithets, and name-calling that delighted some rural audiences but shocked and enraged those who still considered politics a gentleman's game. Worse still, Tillman attacked the integrity and manhood of fellow Democrats, not Radicals—the usual targets.[7]

The state Farmers' Association nominated Tillman for governor in March 1890. His Democratic opponents were former Confederate general John Bratton and Judge Joseph Earle, both of whom were close to Hampton. At Democratic stump meetings across the state, there was little intellectual debate; instead, Tillman and his supporters rudely interrupted and insulted Bratton and Earle, making it difficult for them to speak. The Conservatives planned a similar ambush of Tillman at the June 24 meeting in Columbia, Hampton's hometown and the Conservatives' stronghold. They invited Hampton and Butler to attend to lend weight to their rebuke of Tillman. Fifteen hundred veterans, as well as Columbia residents, were there to cheer Hampton and heckle Tillman.[8]

Hampton spoke first. He began by asking the audience to show respect to all the speakers and allow all to be heard. He was not about to gag Tillman, but neither did he want Tillman to threaten party unity. Hampton expressed shock at the very idea that Tillman and his followers would insult their elders who had fought valiantly for the Confederacy. "When I saw that a South Carolina audience could insult General Bratton, I thought, good God, have all the memories of '61 been forgotten?" In an indirect rebuke to Tillman's attacks on fellow Democrats, Hampton said: "Shoulder to shoulder I implore you men of South Carolina, not to forget the past. . . . It is useless to contend that you are Democrats when you do anything to divide your own, the Democratic party." Hampton denied the charge that Conservatives were arrogant aristocrats: "I do not know what aristocracy is, God knows I do not know. . . . If there is any man here who followed me during the war, I appeal to him to bear me witness that I treated the man in the ragged jacket as well as I treated the man with stars on his coat." Hampton's old soldiers in the audience cheered in affirmation.[9]

When Tillman spoke, it was his turn to face the abuse suffered by Bratton and Earle. Tillman hurled insults back at his tormenters, but several times the crowd's jeers were loud enough to drown out part of his sentences. Confusion reigned, especially after Tillman successfully fended off an accusation from Alexander Haskell about his lack of Confederate service. At that point Hampton rose to remind the audience of his earlier request and "to give Capt. Tillman a silent and respectful hearing."[10] Tillman, however, did not change his tactics. While Hampton's rebuke criticism of Tillman had been moderate and indirect, Tillman went for the jugular as he turned on Hampton—"The grand mogul here, who ruled supremely and grandly, cannot terrify me," he shouted. "I do not come from such blood as that."[11]

Tillman's followers determined to avenge him at a meeting in Aiken, to which they invited Hampton. Hampton refused to ride in the same carriage with Tillman, and when he rose to speak for Democratic unity, the unthinkable happened. For the first time in his political career, Wade Hampton was shouted down by a South Carolina audience and forced to take his seat. Some in the audience even cried, "Put him out!"[12]

At seventy-two, Hampton apparently decided that he no longer had the stomach for such a fight. Though he despised Tillman, he stepped out of the fray to let the Democratic Party work out its own destiny. Unfortunately for him, it was too late for the Conservatives to stop Tillman. Tillman's followers had spent the first half of the year solidifying their position in the party while Conservatives were still indecisive. At the state convention, Tillman won the Democratic nomination.[13]

A disgusted Alex Haskell refused to accept the inevitable and ran as an Independent. His candidacy created a dilemma for Hampton, first because Haskell had served alongside Hampton in the war, been wounded four times, and lost an eye in combat. He had also helped direct Hampton's gubernatorial campaign in 1876 and had supported him loyally ever since. Finally, he was the older brother of John Haskell, who had married Hampton's daughter Sally. On the other hand, it was Hampton himself who had once warned that an Independent was "if possible, worse than a Radical" and a "traitor to his state." Hampton still believed that Democratic unity was critical to prevent a return of Negro-Radical rule, but his denunciation of Independents was now coming back to haunt him.

Haskell appealed to black voters and pledged to protect them, but his promises were vague and transparent. He would not promise to ensure that more black men could vote, nor would he agree to appoint black men to office as Hampton had done. In the end, he got only lukewarm support from blacks and from the Republican Party; even white Democrats who disliked Tillman found it safer to vote for him rather than risk dividing the party. So did Hampton. He made it clear that he reluctantly intended to vote for Tillman, though he refused to renounce Haskell as he had other Independents—"I shall not denounce the man who was my comrade in war . . . and my trusted friend in 1876."[14] In the general election, Tillman defeated Haskell by a vote of roughly 59,000 to 15,000.[15]

As soon as the election of Tillman was confirmed and a pro-Tillman legislature was in place, Conservatives were shocked to realize that, at Tillman's insistence, the lawmakers planned to oust Hampton from the U.S. Senate rather than reelect him to a third term. Everyone understood that there was no love lost between Hampton and Tillman, but Conservatives naively assumed that not even Tillman would dare dishonor South Carolina's hero and savior.[16]

Too late, Hampton's friends recognized the danger and tried to stem the tide against him. "God grant that some revolution will hurl from power those who forget their duty to Wade Hampton," cried one legislator. Other Conservatives furiously denounced the very idea of rejecting Wade Hampton, South Carolina's great Redeemer. On the day of the Senate election, friends went to Hampton's house and begged him simply to make an appearance at the statehouse, to walk through the corridors, just like the days in December 1876 when even his presence in the same building with Governor Daniel H. Chamberlain was enough to make all men recognize his moral authority. Would it not be like Napoleon returning from exile in Elba, silently reminding the people of their past loyalty to him? Hampton quietly refused to play the role, saying that "the Senatorship" was "not to be sought or begged for."[17] If the people no longer considered him worthy to be their senator, he would accept their will. Besides, active campaigning for the position would be akin to seeking a handout, since everyone knew of Hampton's relative poverty and the importance of his Senate salary.[18]

The first vote put Hampton behind Tillman's campaign manager, John L. M. Irby, and the legislature postponed subsequent tallies until the next day. Meanwhile, the *Charleston News and Courier* declared that "[Hampton] has not been hanging around the State House begging for votes. . . . There he stands, out in the open field, his body covered with the scars of honorable warfare, ready to serve his people, as he has ever served them, faithfully, loyally . . . while the politicians cry out to the freemen who they would make their slaves, down with him! It is a sad, sad spectacle which no true South Carolinian ever expected to witness."[19]

After the third day of voting, December 11, 1890, the verdict was out: Wade Hampton would no longer be South Carolina's senator after the following March. P. M. B. Young, one of Hampton's former officers, said that nothing in the history of the last century could compare to such an event, nothing but the murder of Marshall Ney at the hands of the French people. Veterans in Columbia wore black armbands in mourning, and the *News and Courier* predicted a "casting up of accounts" when the people demanded of their representatives why Wade Hampton had been kicked out of public life.[20]

Hampton's strategy in 1890 was the most unfortunate one he could have taken. The most politically expedient (and cynical) course would have been an unqualified endorsement of Tillman and abandonment of Haskell in the name of Democratic Party unity. This would have induced the Tillmanites to spare Hampton's Senate position. Hampton's political career might have been damaged, but not ruined. Eventually Tillman would have been able and willing to use Hampton's prestige to bolster his own claims to legitimacy among South Carolina Conservatives, and Hampton might have been able to temper Tillman's extremism.

Such a course, though politically shrewd, was personally impossible for Hampton. The demands of honor and loyalty to an old comrade would not allow him to stab Haskell in the back. A full-fledged defection to Tillman, moreover, would fly in the face of Hampton's convictions that the state should be led by gentlemen, not rabble-rousers.

The opposite approach would have been to denounce Tillman to the end and stand by Haskell, the Independent, without qualification. This was the path of honor as well as political suicide. A younger, more stubborn Hampton might have followed that course. It is easy to imagine the Hampton of 1868 or 1876 stubbornly adhering to it. But those had been the days when he had nothing to lose. To white southerners of that period, there had been nothing left except honor. By 1890, Hampton believed there was much more to lose. A Democratic Party that was still united on a superficial level now controlled South Carolina, and Yankee Republican influence was nil. The threat of Republican-bolstered "Negro rule" was smaller than it had been since the war. To Hampton and others, the major current threat to that reality was factionalism within the party. At least Tillman, as a South Carolinian and a Democrat, was no Sherman, no Governor Moses, not even a Chamberlain. A Tillman-controlled state would never be a Republican-controlled state, while a Haskell victory might conceivably bring about that very nightmare.

So Hampton sought the middle ground, one that was neither totally honorable nor ensured his political survival. Moreover, his nod to Tillman sealed the fate of black South Carolinians, who had once seen Hampton as their best hope within the Democratic Party. Hampton could not foresee how completely the Tillmanites would exclude blacks from political life, nor comprehend how serious Tillman was in his rhetoric of race hatred. Tillman's most rabid pronouncements on race, in fact, were still in the future. Still, Hampton's announcement that he would vote for Tillman was, at best, a dangerous concession to racial fanaticism and, at worst, a betrayal of South Carolina blacks, whom Hampton had repeatedly referred to as "our people." Admittedly, this is of more concern to us than it would have been to his white contemporaries. Also, it is another reminder that Hampton had always sought social and political stability through southern white unity more than racial equality.

Hampton left Columbia for Mississippi immediately after the vote. For a time at least, he was bitter, despite the fact that he had long been tired of public life. "Base methods," he wrote Butler, "were used to defeat me: the ordinary methods of Tillman and his followers:—misrepresentation, detraction, & lying, but I prefer defeat at their hands, rather than to have been successful, by sacrificing my independence & self-respect." At least he could leave Washington—"I must now resume the life of a planter, although late in the day to do so. But I can make enough to live on, & I shall at least, be free." Most of all, he told his old comrade, "I am hurt that the old soldiers turned against me, for I did not expect that at their hands."[21]

While Hampton felt betrayed by his people and northern newspapers reported that a "political and social revolution" had occurred in the state, both were only partially right.[22] It was true that Hampton's "Redeemer," "Bourbon," or "Conservative" faction had lost control of the state to Tillman's "Reformers." Hampton's ouster from the Senate was only the most startling event symbolizing the change. And Tillman had generated great excitement and a loyal following. But it is unlikely that the "people's" love of Hampton had greatly waned. It will be seen that after his defeat, he was deified all the more, and Tillman never became the beloved figure that Hampton was. Tillman's election, explains one historian, was "a factional coup masquerading as a mass movement."[23] Hampton's rejection was the result of an internal revolution in the state Democratic Party, not a grassroots rejection of Hampton himself. William Watts Ball, a postgraduate student and future newspaper editor, remembered that "some of us who voted against Haskell in the general election could not anticipate that Wade Hampton was to be defeated in the General Assembly."[24] State legislators who had urged Hampton's reelection as senator also asserted convincingly that had the Tillman movement revealed that unseating Hampton was one of its goals, the voters would never have elected Tillman.[25]

A few weeks after complaining to Butler that the "old soldiers" had turned against him, Hampton too seemed to realize that he was more the victim of a political coup than a popular rebuke. To Theodore Barker, Hampton confided that he had received many sympathetic letters calling his defeat the "disgrace of the State." He said he would be content "if the people will rebuke the representatives, who misrepresented their constituents."[26]

Hampton devoted much of his remaining strength to fighting Tillman and his followers, whom he considered "unscrupulous demagogues."[27] At first, however, he still could not bring himself to threaten Democratic unity. In March 1892 Hampton and several allies organized a "Peace and Harmony" convention, designed to organize the Conservatives in a fight to recapture the Democratic Party. Supporting Hampton were the Haskells, Butler, News and Courier editor J C. Hemphill, and Narciso Gonzalez, editor of The State, a paper founded in 1891 largely for the purpose of opposing Tillman. Hampton's faction in 1892 agreed not to stoop to Tillman's methods, resolving not to "stir passions by general accusations which we cannot prove."[28] His followers also pledged to respect the Democratic Party's choice of nominees. Obviously believing that they still had the support of most of the white population, the Conservatives tried to have the party select its nominees through a direct primary, rather than a primary that only selected delegates to a state convention, which they suspected the Tillmanites could control.[29]

Tillman responded by painting members of the Hampton-Haskell faction as white traitors who were willing to stoop to seeking black votes, dividing white men so they could return to power. Tillman and his supporters were able to control the election and reelect him in 1892, and Hampton tried again to organize a party coup in 1894. Gonzalez was ready to support Hampton in an all-out fight. Hemphill and others, however, taking note of squabbling within the Tillman camp, declined to nominate candidates in the hope that dissension would wreck Tillman's movement. Once again the Conservatives were foiled. Tillman took over Calbraith Butler's U.S. Senate seat, and John Gary Evans, the nephew of Martin Gary, became Tillman's hand-picked successor to the governor's chair. A disgusted and ailing Hampton could only write: "We have gone to the Devil in this State & the Natl. Democracy seems marching in the same direction."[30]

It was not just Tillman's personality and style that Hampton disliked. In his second term as governor, Tillman had managed to push through a "dispensary law" by which the state controlled the sale of alcohol. Tillman-appointed dispensary agents were empowered to enter the homes of "independence-loving South Carolinians" to seize illicit liquor, sometimes resulting in the shooting death of homeowners.[31] Many dispensary agents were guilty of corruption and gross misman-agement. Hampton's response to the dispensary system may not be on record, but it undoubtedly offended his conservative constitutional principles.[32]

Tillman also preached a brand of white supremacy that offended Hampton's paternalism, as well as his older, but fading, vision of a South Carolina jointly ruled by elite whites and loyal black and white voters. Hampton had always tried to stem racial violence, or at least to distance himself from it when it occurred. Tillman, on the other hand, was determined that no man could accuse him of being "soft" on Ne-groes. In the summer of 1892 he pledged that, "Governor as I am," he would personally lead a lynch mob against any "negro who ravishes a white woman."[33] In the following spring, the first lynching of Tillman's second term occurred. John Peterson of Denmark, Barnwell County, accused of raping a white woman, protested his innocence and appealed to Tillman for protection. Tillman sent him back to Denmark, sup-posedly to prove his innocence, with a single armed guard for protec-tion. Predictably, Peterson was "tried," hung, and shot by a mob of five hundred whites. Outraged South Carolinians, both white and black, condemned Tillman for complicity in murder. Rather than acting as a force of law and order, the state's chief executive seemed to be under-mining it.[34]

Tillman was also brutally frank in his determination to eliminate black voting. For years, he pushed for a new state constitution that would destroy that possibility once and for all. When South Carolinians went to the polls in the fall of 1894, they voted on whether to call a new constitutional convention to address the suffrage question. Officially, the measure passed by a vote of 31,402 to 29,523, but it almost certainly would have failed without widespread cheating and fraud by Tillmanite precinct officials and election boards.[35]

Hampton, of course, opposed any return to "Negro rule," as well as any divisions among white men that might bring it about. Tillman's determination to eliminate black suffrage completely, however, struck Hampton and other Conservatives as unnecessary and vindictive. Most of all, they thought, Tillman's calls for protecting white supremacy were a trick intended to keep his faction in power. Hampton, Butler, and others believed that there was no real threat to white supremacy—it was only the excuse Tillman used to write a new constitution designed to gain control over the election process. In the spring of 1895, before the election of convention delegates, Hampton made his views clear in an open letter to the *Spartanburg Herald*:

> I have no fear of negro domination, a cry used only to arouse race prejudices and to put the coming convention under control of the Ring which now dominates our State. The negroes have acted of late with rare moderation and liberality, and if we meet them in the same spirit they have shown, they will aid in selecting good representatives for the convention. I, for one, am willing to trust them, and they ask only the rights guaranteed to them by the Constitution of the United States and that of our own State.[36]

This statement strongly resembled ones Hampton had made in the late 1860s and 1870s. It cut against the grain even then; in the racially charged atmosphere of 1895, it was the most racially enlightened comment that a white man in South Carolina politics could conceivably utter. Other letters to the editor agreed that Conservatives should seek black votes rather than go over to their hated Tillmanite enemies. It was too late—if Hampton and other Conservatives had taken that course in 1890, it might have stalled Tillman's rise.[37]

In any event, pro-Tillman newspapers responded by accusing Conservatives of appeal[ing] to the negro" to reassert elite dominance over "the white majority."[38] The *Edgefield Advertiser* accused Conservatives of manipulating the black vote to ensure control of the constitutional convention, charging that they "only wish to see how far Edgefield County will permit them to go niggerwards without rebuke, and this rebuke will come sharp, and strong, and soon, and will drive them to cover."[39] These attacks echoed Tillman's obvious reference to Hampton and his allies the previous year—"white men of acknowledged character and decent reputation [who] are willing to use the Negro in politics with the hope of regaining lost supremacy."[40] Martin Gary had made virtually the same charge against Hampton sixteen years before.

The South Carolina Constitutional Convention of 1895 achieved virtually all of Tillman's goals. Despite Hampton's advice, the new constitution was never submitted to the people for a vote; it went into effect as soon as the delegates approved it. New restrictions and regulations regarding registration and voting nullified the black vote and instituted less democratic ways of selecting candidates for state and local offices. By 1900, the number of black South Carolinians who voted could not have been more than 3,500 out of a voting-age black male population of over 100,000. Local school boards acquired the power to apportion public school funds and could now more easily discriminate against black schools. Hampton and the Redeemer state legislatures had provided roughly half of the state's education funds to black schools. By 1899, though, black schools received only two-sevenths of the state's funds; in 1920, just over one-tenth. Thus, Hampton paternalism, if waning in the 1880s, was clearly dead by the turn of the century. Hampton himself had retreated from it by the end of his career in the Senate; by the 1890s it was fully routed in South Carolina. The Constitution of 1895 was its death knell.[41]

Recently, some scholarship has described Hampton's paternalism essentially in the same way that Reconstruction-era Republicans did. Hampton's so-called moderate stance was, some argue, a sham, a deliberate cover for terrorism and racial oppression. Stephen Kantrowitz contends that despite differences in rhetoric, Tillman's and Hampton's programs were virtually one and the same. Both men were white supremacists, insists Kantrowitz, and Hampton's "paternalism" and Tillman's violence "were in fact complementary and mutually necessary strategies."[42]

Despite the important contributions of Kantrowitz's fascinating study of Tillman, there are serious problems with equating Hampton with Tillman. Like Tillman, Hampton was definitely a racist, and he did believe that positions of social and political leadership should largely be left to the white elite. But asserting that Hampton and Tillman were both white supremacists is not very useful. White supremacy was a big tent in the late nineteenth century—few white southerners (or Americans) did not ascribe to most of its basic tenets. Within this big tent, there was room for wide differences in ideology and political action. Thus, whereas Hampton acted to protect the black franchise and appointed black men to office, Tillman led the movement for total black disenfranchisement. Whereas Hampton consistently eschewed violence, Tillman openly advocated lynching. Whereas Hampton continued to claim that "just treatment of the negro" and benevolent paternalism had been the key to restoring and maintaining white control since 1876, Gary, and later Tillman, always insisted that violence alone had saved South Carolina from "Negro rule," and white men must always be ready to resort to it again. Whereas Hampton sought to create a biracial, but white-led, Democratic Party, Gary's, and later Tillman's, followers sys-

tematically and openly excluded blacks from party meetings and prima-
ries. And whereas Hampton favored education for both races as a means
to cultivate responsible citizenship, Tillman represented the segment
of the white population that asserted that education of a black child
"ruined a good field hand." It is ahistorical for us today to lump Hampton, Tillman, and Gary together simply as white supremacists, for contemporaries, black and white, clearly understood the differences between them. Years after Hampton's death, leading black Republican
leader Thomas E. Miller observed: "If the people of our State had taken
[Hampton's] advice after he was elected Governor, the politician [sic]
tension between the races would have been destroyed." Writing to a
white conservative, Miller added that if white Democrats had followed
Hampton's course, Tillman would have never won power, "because
Negroes . . . including myself, would have come to the rescue of the men
who made and saved South Carolina."[43]

Yet it is true that Hampton's paternalism, and Hampton himself,
were not up to the task of stemming the tide of racial extremism that
swept the South near the turn of the twentieth century. First, Hampton's
paternalism rested on the fundamental assumption of black inferiority,
on the belief that blacks could only be junior partners in reconstructing
constitutional government in the South. He simply believed that white
men had a duty to be kind protectors of inferior blacks. Hampton's
speeches and writings in the latter part of his senatorial career only
made this clearer. Second, Hampton's opposition to Tillman was not as
fierce as it had been to carpetbaggers and scalawags; even the resistance
he did mount sprang only partly from his racial paternalism. His opposition also grew out of personal dislike, a desire for personal vindication, and a belief that Tillmanism was a disgrace to the state. After the
ratification of the Constitution of 1895, Hampton gave up the fight
altogether and withdrew completely from state politics.

The reasons he withdrew are many. Former political allies seemed,
one by one, to be submitting tamely to the Tillman regime. Once the
constitutional convention finally was held, in fact, Conservatives participated in achieving the goals of the "Reformers." Hampton was nearly
alone in saying that further restrictions on black voting were unnecessary and that the constitution should be submitted to the voters prior to
ratification. Hampton felt old, wounded, sick, and tired. A federal appointment as U.S. railroad commissioner from 1893 to 1897 would
consume much of the energy he did have. But fatigue and infirmity were

not the only reasons Hampton's opposition to Tillman waned. Something else was happening as well. From the time of Hampton's retirement from the Senate in 1891 until his death in 1902, he finally achieved what he had sought for much of his life—vindication. As Hampton became more and more politically irrelevant, his deification in South Carolina, and reconciliation with the North, became all but complete.[44]

TIME MAKES ALL THINGS EVEN

In the last decade of his life, Wade Hampton completed his final transformation from warlord and politician into mythical hero. Old enemies
fell silent, or forgot that they had once opposed him. Even his bitterest
critics of the past, such as *Harper's Weekly* and the *New York Times*, came to
regard him as a symbol of values that belonged to the past. The timing
of the process differed, however, between North and South.

In South Carolina, Hampton was still a political figure, or the leading
symbol of a political faction, until 1895. Between his ouster from the
U.S. Senate in 1890 and the ratification of the 1895 South Carolina
Constitution, Hampton enjoyed several moments of personal vindication against the Tillmanites, but his final deification as the patron saint
of South Carolina would have to wait until he was all but irrelevant in a
political sense. In the North, on the other hand, Hampton was virtually
irrelevant politically as early as March 1891. His final rehabilitation in
the eyes of former northern foes could therefore begin earlier. He never
enjoyed the same level of hero worship on the national stage that he
enjoyed at home in 1876–77 and after 1895, but northern newspapers
and even Republican leaders eventually treated him with respect and
even affection. By 1894, northern newspapers, like South Carolina Conservatives, had already come to regard Hampton as a symbol of virtues
that were fast disappearing from national life. He also became a symbol
of reconciliation, not only between North and South but between war-
ring factions in his own state.[1]

In South Carolina, Hampton's first post-1890 tastes of vindication
had decidedly political overtones, or else were deliberate shots at his
past foes. In the spring of 1891, for example, the city of Columbia
celebrated the centennial of the first meeting of the South Carolina
General Assembly, and the undoubted highlight of the first day's ceremonies was the personal appearance of Hampton. He had just retired
from the Senate and returned from Washington, to be welcomed home
as a hero. "The day was strictly Hampton's Day," announced *The State*,
"and the intense enthusiasm with which he was received . . . indicated to
the grand old warrior-statesman that the people of South Carolina,
taken as a whole, considered him as their greatest hero." No defeat

engineered by political tricksters, in other words, could lessen the people's "undying love and esteem" for Hampton.[2]

As the old "warrior statesman" left his carriage and walked to the speaker's platform, old soldiers with empty sleeves and wooden legs followed him, "acting as his escort." Hampton received an ovation that lasted "fully five minutes." Tears filled his eyes. Following a prayer, a playing of "Dixie," and effusive praise of Hampton by the mayor, Hampton rose to speak, to another vociferous round of cheers.[3]

Hampton spoke on themes that were patriotic and others that were political. In both cases, however, the themes were also personal. Governor Tillman was sitting on the platform behind Hampton, remaining quiet and smiling occasionally. Hampton thanked the crowd for a reception that "assured me that you still held me worthy of your esteem and confidence."[4] Again playing the role of a man who had redeemed his people's honor, he presented to the city the original seal of the "Town of Columbia," cast in 1786 and found among Columbia's ruins just after the fire of 1865. Hampton had received it from a friend, and he now proudly presented it to his fellow citizens. Hampton rebuked Tillman, though in his own dignified fashion. "No public office, however high, can of itself confer honor," Hampton lectured. "That obtained by falsehood, or misrepresentation, or trickery, brands its possessor with dishonor." Hampton signed off by saying that his "public work" was over and that abler hands might now take it up, but that no son of South Carolina would ever "serve her with a more loyal devotion, a more willing hand or a more loving heart than I have done. My prayer shall ever be . . . God bless our State!"[5] Wild cheers and applause erupted once again; another speaker later declared that "Wade Hampton was to South Carolina in 1876 what George Washington was to the colonies in 1776."[6] In Columbia, at least, it was clear that the real hero would always be Hampton, not Ben Tillman. At this point Hampton was still a political figure, and the crowd could not have missed his digs at Tillman.

The state's Conservative newspapers went out of their way to portray Hampton as the symbol of South Carolina's honor and of Old South virtues. At first this effort reflected not only love for Hampton but also opposition to Tillman. The *Charleston News and Courier* complained that Tillman "makes no attempt to being a gentleman. He scorns refinement of manner and speech and prefers 'damn you' to 'if you please.' "[7] The *State* began a series of articles called "The Book of Zerrachaboam" that ridiculed the Tillman faction in biblical language. The passages traced the rise of an evil king, "one Benjamin, a man haughty of spirit and subtile [sic] of heart, who greatly deceived the people. The same as was spoken by the Prophet, saying 'a one-eyed man shall be king among the blind.' "[8] In 1893 another passage from the "Book of Zerrachaboam" ridiculed the behavior of John L. M. Irby, Hampton's replacement in the Senate and a notorious drunkard. Irby had just disgraced himself and embarrassed Tillman, his mentor, after some drunken exploits on a train ride and further adventures in Columbia. "Then were the Tillmanites much troubled," smirked *The State*'s chronicler, "and reasoned one with another, while many repented them that they had despitefully treated Wade, the just, and set an evil man in his stead to rule over them."[9]

Other events in 1891 gave Columbians the sense that old wrongs had been righted. One was the death of William T. Sherman. *The State* published its inaugural issue on February 18, 1891, in Columbia's centennial year and on the anniversary of the great fire of 1865. Sherman had just died four days before, and *The State* gloated:

"1865 and 1891"

Twenty-six years ago this morning Columbia was a heap of smoking rubbish, and Gen. Sherman was in command. This morning Death commands Gen. Sherman, and the press of *The State* [by publishing its inaugural issue] sends out a new evidence of Columbia's resurrection of ruin. "Time makes all things even."[10]

This was language that Hampton would never have used publicly, but he must have agreed with the sentiment that time was making things even.

In the U.S. Senate and in the North, the process of reconciliation and vindication had begun even earlier, and the northern press had toned down its criticism of Hampton by the mid-eighties. Hampton's last Senate speech in 1891 was against the so-called Force Bill, which would have sent federal election supervisors to monitor elections in southern states. Southern congressmen, of course, angrily denounced this latest threat to white (and Democratic) supremacy as unconstitutional. When Hampton rose to speak on it, he predicted that such a measure would bring a resurgence of racial tension and great evil to both races. Hampton was condescending concerning the intelligence and political ability of blacks, though he once again conceded that they were not to blame for their lack of either. No one, of course, expected the former Confederate warlord to sanction this latest threat to states' rights, and he did not. What contemporaries noted most, though, was the conciliatory, rather than angry, tone of his speech. Hampton concluded with the observation that his "public career" was now ending. He had not, he asserted, ever sought office, and he had no regrets about going into retirement other than "the severance of the many ties of friendship" he had made in the Senate:

> During the time I have had the honor to represent my State in this body not one word of recrimination, nor one calculated to keep alive sectional animosity, has escaped my lips. The thunders of war had scarcely ceased to reverberate when I, in opposition to the feelings . . . of many of my fellow-citizens, urged them, not only to deal justly with the negroes, but to accord to them all the rights which would necessarily follow their enfranchisement. From that day to the present I have steadily . . . advocated the same policy.

Appealing to the "conservatism," "patriotism," and "sentiment of fraternity" among his fellow senators, Hampton said that his last public duty to his state and to the country was to ask them to pause before passing this bill until "the people can deliver their deliberate verdict."[11]

Applause erupted not only in the galleries but also on the floor among his fellow senators. Hampton took satisfaction in the fact that he parted from his Republican Senate colleagues on good terms and in the thought that he had been a force for sectional reconciliation. In a letter to his old adjutant Theodore Barker, he boasted that none of the hundreds of Senate reports he had helped prepare ever failed to pass, and this he regarded "as a recognition by the Republicans of my fair dealing." Looking back on his Senate career, Hampton concluded that Republicans had often used "insolent language" deliberately "to provoke sectional debates, [and] I determined never to be led into the trap prepared for us. The course pursued has met the approval of our most conservative men, & it gave me an influence in the Senate, even with the Republicans. Nearly all of them have expressed sincere regret at my defeat."[12]

Hampton indeed appeared as a symbol of reconciliation in the North. In June 1891 a New Jersey paper reported that Hampton was joining a month-long fishing expedition in Canada with Senator John R. McPherson, a New Jersey Democrat (who owned the salmon stream), and George F. Edmunds, a Vermont Republican. The story, reprinted in the New York Times, asserted that the three men were "great chums."[13]

Even more than reconciliation, though, Hampton represented the virtues of a dying generation. Shortly after his Senate retirement, the

Washington Herald lamented:

There is a martial and historic figure and a kindly, noble face missing from the old Senate Chamber. His has been a career that has always inspired the esteem of even the bitterest foes of rebellion who have hurled scathing anathema at him, but not one has ever insinuated that he did not nobly perform the duties that he believed incumbent upon him. Not one has been known to disparage his honor or his bravery. Not a human soul can point the finger of scorn at him. A gentleman to the heart's core—foremost among the last surviving generals—he is one of the few great and good men left standing.[14]

This editorial conveniently forgot the blistering attacks on Hampton in the northern press and charges by John Sherman and other Republican foes of only ten or fifteen years before. But its tone matched many others. T. Thomas Fortune, an African American reporter for the *New York Sun*, interviewed Hampton a few days after he left the Senate. As the interview ended and Hampton boarded a train "Southward," Fortune concluded that he "could not but think pleasantly of the fine old type of Southern gentlemen."[15] *Harper's Weekly* sounded similar themes once it took the measure of Tillman and Irby. Tillman's rise and Hampton's fall, said *Harper's*, were startling evidence in the decline in wisdom and ability among "public men" in the South, respect for the rule of law, and even deficiencies in southern education. The newspaper claimed that sadly, particularly in the South, "there is very little virtue among the successful politicians of the day."[16] Even Daniel Chamberlain, Hampton's Republican opponent in 1876, praised his character and leadership in an article in the *Atlantic Monthly*.[17]

The *New York Times* now delighted to portray Hampton in heroic terms. It reported that on a Sunday morning in February 1899, a fire ignited on the roof of Hampton's house, Southern Cross. A servant informed Hampton, who, without awaking anyone else in the house, climbed on the roof with his cork leg. He and the servant doused the fire. Under the headline, "Plays Fireman and Climbs to a Roof at the Age of 81," the newspaper observed that Hampton had "lost none of his old-time dash and courage."[18] An 1897 article in the *Times* related three incidents from the war in a tone sympathetic to Hampton. One was the story of Frank's death at Brandy Station and how duty prevented a grief-stricken Hampton from going to his brother's bedside. The second was the story of Preston's death and Wade's wounding at Burgess's Mill. Finally, there was a story of Hampton showing mercy to a thief in the ranks who had just been drummed out of camp. Hampton gave some of his own money to the despised soldier before he was sent away. The *Times* called the stories proof of Hampton's "devotion to duty" and "heroic generosity."[19] Such praise could never have appeared in a Republican newspaper while Hampton was still a Democratic senator.

Nostalgic references to Hampton and statesmen of his generation represented several national trends in the 1880s and 1890s. In American culture as a whole, patriotism and honor were being redefined in terms of martial valor and physical courage, much as southerners had defined it throughout the nineteenth century. This trend muted old arguments about states' rights and calls for racial equality, but it also fostered sectional reconciliation. If the war had proved that both northern and southern men were valorous rather than self-righteous abolitionists on one hand, or greedy, violent slaveholders on the other, both sides could find common ground on its meaning and greater respect for veterans on the other side. Also, many Americans expressed growing concern with the alleged decline in character and honesty among public officials —a concern that would help fuel the Progressive movement around the turn of the century. They often became nostalgic for a dying breed of statesmen, whose courage had been tested in battle and who supposedly adhered to Old World standards of honor and fair dealing. Men like Hampton, while sometimes appearing obsolete and out of touch with current issues, seemed to match that description.[20]

Back home in South Carolina, and in the South as a whole, Hampton's stature as a Lost Cause Confederate hero only grew as his direct role in political affairs faded. A transitional event occurred on May 14, 1895, only a few days before Hampton publicly expressed his opposition to Tillman's plans for the constitutional convention. Though South Carolinians still recognized Hampton as a Tillman opponent, much of the Conservative leadership had already broken with him on how best to oppose Tillman's plans. Obviously the old hero's direct political influence was waning fast. Yet Hampton was the guest of honor in Charleston at a joint meeting of the local Sons of Confederate Veterans and the Daughters of the Confederacy. Comments by one of the meeting's leaders, Theodore Barker, showed that Conservatives were still apt to use such occasions to express their resentment of Tillman. What emerged even more clearly, however, was that the name and image of Hampton were beginning to transcend the mundane world of petty politics. He was becoming less a symbol of a political faction and more that of soldierly, civic, and Christian virtue.

As Hampton appeared on the stage of the Academy of Music, leaning on Barker's arm, the crowd went wild with applause, giving "such a
demonstration as has never before been seen in Charleston."[21] A clergy-
man offered a prayer. On a political note, Barker then introduced Hampton as "the stone which the builders of 1890 refused, but who remains
and will ever remain the headstone of the corner in the temple of
a grateful people's heart."[22] But Barker went on to claim that gratitude
to Wade Hampton was not so much loyalty to a political program as it
was respect for honor and valor. Secession was dead, and states' rights
was not the burning issue it once was. "Indeed the farther we are removed . . . from the days of the great War for Southern Independence,
the more thoroughly the burning issues of those days have become dead
issues of the past," Barker explained. Meanwhile, "the more absolutely
our new conditions are accepted, the more intense and vivid seems to
grow the interest and the more tender the reverences for that sacred
past, which was illumined by the splendid valor and heroic suffering
of our dead soldiers and the patriotic devotion of the women of the
South." Hampton's presence at the meeting, Barker proclaimed, was
an inspiration. "Loyalty to, and love for Wade Hampton," Barker explained, was simply gratitude from South Carolinians "who will not let
the memory of good deeds die, who are true to their own highest ideals,
and who deem ingratitude a base sin."[23] As he concluded, and Colonel
Zimmerman Davis rose to propose three cheers, Barker's words were
drowned out with cheers as Hampton rose and limped to the podium.[24]

Hampton was now a cultural hero more than a political one, and this
became even clearer after the Constitution of 1895 was ratified. By that
time, there was no longer a possibility that Conservatives from Hampton's "clique" could retake control of the state Democratic Party. Gradually the Tillmanites themselves began to divide and compete with one
another, and the statesmanship of political elites declined further. Tillman distanced himself from Irby. Irby's Senate successor, John L. Mc-
Laurin, grew so dissatisfied with Tillman's power that he committed the
cardinal sin of moving toward an alliance with the Republicans. In
March 1902 Tillman and McLaurin, formerly allies, traded punches on
the floor of the Senate. In 1896 Conservative Joseph Earle became so
exasperated with the personal insults of John Gary Evans that he slapped
his face on the speaker's stand at a meeting in Florence. Politicians in
South Carolina retaliated against each other with the sort of demagogu-
ery and base insults they had once reserved for Republicans, and rou-
tinely charged each other with corruption. The difference was that now

that the Republicans were out of the picture, the targets were fellow white South Carolinians—men who had voted for Hampton in 1876 and sons of the soldiers who had stood shoulder to shoulder in the ranks of Hampton, Butler, and Gary in what seemed, in hindsight, a nobler time.[25]

Hampton and other veterans became symbols of what had been lost—the selfless virtue, courage, and self-control it took to withstand Yankee shot and shell in 1861. True, some of the white population still hailed Hampton simply as the original standard-bearer for white supremacy in 1876. They conveniently forgot that Hampton's version of white supremacy was far milder than the one they now pursued. Forgetting his indignant demands that they preserve the black man's basic political rights, they remembered only that he had put white Democrats back in charge—an event that now allowed the crushing of any moves toward racial equality. Many more saw him not only as the original white hero, but also as the savior who had defeated Yankee arrogance and black rule and restored the pride of a humiliated people. To them, he was more than just a white supremacist, but also a noble Redeemer. Finally, there was the sentiment that increasingly regarded Hampton as a martyr—not only of the southern cause but of the social ideals of antebellum paternalism and chivalry. All that was best, or that white South Carolinians imagined that was best, about the Old South—gentlemanly deportment, kindness to social inferiors, dignified self-respect, courage, and honesty—they ascribed to Hampton.[26]

W. Scott Poole has noted that the culture of the Lost Cause in the South included a sense that "the truth lives among ruins," that whatever was defeated or dead represented the best traditions of the past.[27] Hampton's political demise in 1890, likewise, only enhanced his reemergence as a Confederate hero of yore. That last defeat, supposedly at the hands of an unprincipled foe, clarified his image as the noble fallen hero of antebellum virtue. As he became more and more politically marginalized, the romantic Confederate legend surrounding his image only grew. The most eloquent expression of this nostalgia appeared a few years later in a eulogy of Hampton in the *News and Courier*: "The people loved him because he represented them as they knew they should have been, rather than as they knew they were."[28]

In 1895 Hampton was unanimously elected commander of the Department of the Army of Northern Virginia of the United Confederate Veterans (UCV). In 1896 his appearance at a large veterans' reunion in Richmond provoked spontaneous applause from former soldiers from all over the South; the ovation drowned out other speakers and interrupted the proceedings. Three years later one of his old soldiers, Edward Wells, published the first biography of the former general, entitled *Hampton and His Cavalry in '64*. It was as much a work of hero worship as history. In May 1899 Hampton was the most honored celebrity of the national reunion of the UCV held in Charleston. When he stepped onto the stage of Memorial Hall on the night of May 9, the crowd showered him with "a storm of cheers" that lasted for five minutes. Mayor Smyth resorted to Shakespearean verse as he attempted to define what Hampton meant to Charleston and his state:

> I do not think that a braver gentleman
> More active valiant, or more valiant still,
> More daring or more noble, is now alive
> To grace this latter age with noble deeds.[29]

As Hampton rose to speak, there were five more minutes of cheers and waving of hats and handkerchiefs. Hampton made a short, rambling speech that few could hear. It did not matter—he was Wade Hampton. The auditorium filled with cheers again until "the rafters echoed back the sound."[30] The next day, he rode in the parade and was "its distinctive hero."[31] So many ladies waved handkerchiefs and applauded that he was compelled to ride hatless along the entire route, bowing constantly. Hampton made no other speeches during the convention, took no part in the meetings, offered no political advice.[32]

With internal strife dividing the South Carolina Democratic Party, its leaders decided that a hero like Hampton could once again be a source of unity. In October 1901, only six months before Hampton's death, state Democratic chairman Wilie Jones announced his withdrawal from the Democratic primary in the U.S. Senate race. He proposed that other candidates, including McLaurin, do the same so the way would be clear for Hampton to return to the Senate unopposed. (By this time, senators were popularly elected in South Carolina.) Such a result would not have revived Hampton's old Conservative faction or thwarted Tillman, but it aimed to prevent "a bitter political campaign." Even Tillman agreed to the plan, though it did not affect him directly since his term was not due to expire. *The State* claimed that this was the least that South Carolina owed to its greatest hero. The *New York Times* stated that "all factions now acknowledge" that Hampton "was treated unfairly when Tillman first came into power."[33]

Hampton, of course, was not only an object of Lost Cause adoration

Hampton prepares to deliver a speech at a Confederate monument dedication in the 1890s. Several men in the crowd, obviously veterans, wear military caps. South Caroliniana Library.

—he was also one of its messengers. This biography has argued that the Lost Cause was not always part of the larger scheme of reconstructing white supremacy. For Hampton it was not that at all. Hampton rarely, if ever, mentioned race or African Americans in his speeches dealing with the Confederacy. He seemed, instead, to share the concern that once southerners had ceased honoring the sacrifices of Confederate soldiers, moral decay would set in. The 1895 meeting of the Sons of Confederate Veterans and the Daughters of the Confederacy reassured Hampton that perhaps the next generation had not yet forgotten what he and his comrades had done. He feared, though, that the values of the "New South, the cardinal principle of which seems to be . . . the accumulation of riches," would eventually make his people forget his generation's sacrifices and accept the notion that they had been wrong. The war was over, the Union was indivisible, and the South had to abide by the terms that it accepted in 1865, but "we shall [not] brand our heroic dead as well as the living as traitors. . . . Will the living soldiers who followed the Starry Cross on hundred[s] of battle fields ever consent to denounce their dead comrades as traitors?" he demanded. Would the "sons of these veterans" or "the women of the South" do such a thing? "Ah! no; these things can never be as long as truth, patriotism, honor, virtue . . . and courage, are respected."[34]

Hampton said much the same in Columbia in 1901, long after there was any foreseeable threat to white supremacy in the South. When a throng of Confederate veterans greeted him with Rebel yells at the UCV convention that May, he asked them to tell their "children's children" about that yell—not so they would ever use it in battle, but so they would understand "how [the yell] always told of men who were willing to die for their southland, to die for truth, for honor, for manhood, for chivalry."[35] This was how Hampton had always interpreted the Confederate experience, ever since the battle flags had been furled in 1865. The difference was that in 1901, no one, whether in Columbia, Washington, or New York, cared to dispute him.

CHAPTER 36

GOD BLESS THEM ALL

Hampton's public career was not entirely over in 1891. In 1893 sympathetic friends found him a position in Grover Cleveland's administration as commissioner of railroads for the Department of the Interior. The Senate approved the nomination unanimously. His job was to oversee the accounts of railroad companies operating west of the Mississippi that had received federal land grants or other federal assistance. When Hampton took the job, many of these companies were deeply in debt and suffering from the panic of 1893. Later the Pullman strikes and natural disasters would cripple them further, and they were in danger of defaulting on their loan repayments to the government.

Hampton took his job seriously. He spent several months each year traveling on the western railroads, examining account books and inspecting railroad facilities. Each year he submitted detailed reports and recommendations over one hundred pages in length. He made thoughtful recommendations to Congress on how to resolve the crisis in a way that would keep the companies solvent. Hampton knew very well what it was like to be a debtor, and a defunct railway did nothing for the public interest and wasted the government's investment. He also recommended against federal ownership of the lines, citing previous examples of public ownership of rail lines as failures.[1]

Hampton enjoyed his work, especially since it gave him ample opportunity to explore the American West and enjoy some excellent fishing. Though he frequently suffered from colds, pain in his leg, grippe, erysipelas, and failing eyesight, his trips to the West seemed to rally him. Returning from such a journey in 1897, seventy-nine-year-old Hampton boasted to his good friend Bradley T. Johnson that he was in excellent health. He teased Johnson: "It will mortify you to know that all the ladies say that I 'look splendid.' No 'picturesque wreck' about me now & if you doubt that assertion, come here & I will polish you off in two or three rounds!"[2]

Besides traveling, fishing, and spending time with his children and grandchildren, Hampton remained close with his old comrades, especially Johnson, Thomas Munford, and Theodore Barker. He and Johnson visited one another and fished together often. Hampton communicated often with Edward Wells, the former Confederate private who was now writing a book on him. These men continually reminisced about the war years, refighting old battles with the Yankees and even old disputes with other old Confederates. Hampton was polite to Fitz Lee and even went hunting with him, but never fully forgave him for his behavior at Trevilian Station. He was also friendly with Joe Wheeler, but privately scoffed at Wheeler's tendency to refer to himself as a lieutenant general. Once he publicly, but gently, corrected Wheeler in print when Wheeler published an account of the last days of the war that offended Hampton. Wheeler had written that, after the surrender to Sherman, the escort of men with Hampton deserted him as he rode southward to rescue Jefferson Davis. Hampton, "jealous . . . to keep the honor of my own command untarnished," asserted that none of his brave followers left him until he ordered them to do so.[3]

Hampton delighted in speaking with old comrades, whether fellow officers or enlisted men. Confederate reunions were one of his favorite activities. Though he claimed that his proudest moment was when he took control of the statehouse in 1877, he rarely dwelled on the battles of Reconstruction. The legacy of that fight was messier. Now that his victory had wrought a racially proscriptive, money-grubbing South Carolina rather than a harmonious, paternalistic society, there was less moral clarity in it. Instead, he preferred to dwell on the war, where no one dared question the motives and bravery of Preston, Frank, Hampton's beloved comrades, or himself. Always proud of his martial achievements, Hampton still managed to maintain a veneer of modest reserve. When one of his former troopers asked his former general how many Yankees he had personally killed, Hampton simply answered "Eleven, two with my sword and nine with my pistol." As the interview progressed, however, the younger man protested, remembering the charge he saw Hampton lead at Trevilian Station to save the guns of Hart's battery. "What about the two at Trevillian?" he asked. "Oh, I did not count them," replied Hampton. "They were running."[4]

Hampton lost his government job as well his $4,500 salary in 1897, after Republicans recaptured the White House. He complained of being "dead broke."[5] He still was a vice president of the Metallic Cotton Baling Company of Virginia and owned stock in a western gold mine. He asked his son Alfred's help, though, in selling his shares in the mine, "as I need funds greatly."[6]

The octogenarian still followed political affairs closely. He particularly disapproved of the U.S. declaration of war on Spain in 1898 over the situation in Cuba. It was a "sinful war," he wrote Bradley Johnson.[7]

Perhaps unaware of his father's attitude, Alfred, living in El Paso, Texas, sought a commission in the volunteer forces, hoping to get a position in a unit to be commanded by Fitz Lee. When Hampton learned of it through his daughter Daisy, he rebuked his son for not consulting him first. "I regard the war as an unjust one," he told Alfred, "but of course every state was bound in honor, to give the quota called for. . . . I would not wish a son of mine to serve, in any case, under Fitz Lee."[8] He was also aware of the continuing dissension within the ranks of South Carolina Democrats. John L. McLaurin, the man who had seconded the nomination of John Irby in 1890 for U.S. Senate as opposed to Hampton, won the Senate seat himself in 1896. By 1901, McLaurin's resentment of Ben Tillman had led him to make overtures to Republicans and participate in an effort to rebuild the Republican Party in the South by offering patronage to prominent Democrats. Emissaries from McLaurin even approached Hampton to ask if he were interested in the job of postmaster in Columbia under the Republican administration of Theodore Roosevelt. The promised salary would be welcome to the impoverished Hampton. According to one account, Hampton listened politely for awhile before finally saying, "Please tell them I am not for sale."[9] When curious reporters went to his house to ask what course he would take, he replied, "The people of South Carolina ought to know by this time that I cannot be bought."[10] Reconciliation could only go so far.[11]

Stories like these make the aging Hampton sound like a curmudgeon, but, interestingly, almost no one remembered him that way. Probably the reason was that he was usually very kind in person, especially to children and animals. A surviving letter from Hampton to his granddaughter Corrine illustrates the point. Corrine had just suffered some "painful accident," and Hampton hoped to cheer her up by inviting her to spend some time at Southern Cross:

I wish that you [would] come here, where you would have Aunt Daisy to nurse you all the time & read to you. Dr. Taylor would cure you very soon, & you could feed my game chickens. I have the most beautiful game cock you ever saw, & a great many pretty hens. If you could bring [your sister] Mary with you we could have a fine time. I hope that you received the dolls and that you admire them. . . . We have a great big dog, named Brenda, a great Dane, & she is so playful that if you & Mary were here, she would probably knock both of you down several times a day. Your letter was a very nice one & you must write to me again.

Corrine and her parents, McDuffie and Heloise Hampton, soon moved back to Columbia from Mississippi and lived down the street from Grandfather Wade.[12]

Misfortune continued to stalk Hampton in his declining years. Only weeks after climbing on the roof with a servant and extinguishing a fire at Southern Cross, another fire broke out, mocking Hampton's heroic efforts to prevent disaster. Before dawn on the morning of May 2, 1899, Hampton discovered the fire and roused Daisy. Once again tragedy had struck, and once again the aging Hampton emerged as a tragic hero. State newspapers reported the incident sympathetically, and the *New York Times* took up the story:

> [Hampton] strapped on his cork leg, and gathering up the swords of himself, his father, and his grandfather, escaped from the house.
>
> There were family jewels, plate, and priceless old books in the house, but the General did not attempt to re-enter it till he heard the cries of a pet collie dog. In his efforts to save the dog he made, as he said, more desperate efforts than ever in battle. He lost his eyebrows, had part of his mustache and hair singed off, and his skin scorched before he fell back. In the loss of the finest private library in this section, Gen. Hampton sustained a severe blow.
>
> The house, Southern Cross, was of peculiar value to its owner, having been built by his old slaves from the wreck of the mansion burned by the Union Army.[13]

The tale of his reentry to the house was vintage Hampton, both as his people delighted to see him and as he was. Riches meant little to him, the story suggested, and he lost most of them. But he did salvage the symbols of martial honor and family pride—the swords of three Wade Hamptons. He had emerged, it seemed, only with the clothes on his back and with his sword, with nothing of value intact except his honor. And, in heroic paternalistic fashion, he suffered wounds and risked his life to save dependents under his authority, in this case a beloved puppy. The courage, the sacrifice, the disregard for material wealth—this is what the people wanted to remember about Hampton and about the generation that had fought the Yankees.

But there was more to the story. Hampton had failed, in fact, to save the puppy despite his best efforts. And actually he had saved a little more than the swords. Some family jewels and plate also survived. While he and Daisy lodged in an outbuilding, Hampton wrote Edward Wells that he had also saved a gun and some fishing tackle. "We are in an outhouse, quite comfortable. If I had only saved my tent, I would be all right."[14]

Strangely, the disaster seemed to rally Hampton's spirits. Only weeks before, he had complained to Bradley Johnson of chronic illness and begged him to come to Charleston for the veterans' reunion in May, "to ride with me for the last time. I want some of my old comrades to be with me on that occasion."[15] Now, though, he exuded confidence: "Well, I have had many hard knocks in my life, and I do not know any one better to stand it than I am."[16] A week after the fire he was leading the parade in Charleston, enjoying the raucous applause of thousands.

Even before he left for Charleston, citizens in Columbia started a fund-raising campaign to buy Hampton a new house. Editors and letter writers exclaimed that it was the least the people could do to honor and reward him for his selfless public service. Within days, donations were pouring in from all over the state. For Hampton, this would not do. It had always been his role to be the provider, and he objected to being a charity case. He published an open letter in *The State* thanking his citizens for their generosity but declining the gift. He did not deserve his fellow citizens' gratitude for only doing his duty, he said, but if they wished to thank him they had already done so by their verdict of "Well done, good and faithful servant."[17] *The State* published the letter "with regret," insisting that some way must be found to help the grand old man of South Carolina. A committee formed and sent out flyers to communities across the state, hoping that Hampton would not learn of the campaign until it was too late. "His magnanimous and characteristic request that his friends cease their well-meant efforts need not affect our plans," the committee insisted. After raising a respectable sum, "we can then show General Hampton that it his duty to accept what the conscience and love of the people prompt them to offer." The people of the state had no other way to shield "their good name from the reproach of neglecting a noble patriot" who had given so much.[18] Hampton finally relented. He and Daisy eventually moved into the new structure on the corner of Senate and Barnwell streets, though relatives later said privately that he never liked the house.[19]

Now the recipient of charity, Hampton began his final decline. His eyesight grew so poor that he could barely read or write. He rarely rode. Columbians became accustomed to seeing him sitting on the front porch of his new residence, often with a dog in his lap. A grandnephew remembers that Uncle Wade would watch a strip of flypaper hanging in the corner. Whenever a fly was caught, he would exclaim, "There goes

Hampton sitting at home on his front porch, with a dog in his lap. South Carolina Historical Society.

another Yankee!"[20] Dr. Tom Taylor, his physician and old friend, gave orders that he was not to have more than one cup of coffee a day. The wily strategist was not to be foiled by these orders. "He'd drink about half the cup, then say, 'I think it needs a little more cream,'" remembered Harry Hampton. "Then it would be, 'I think it's getting a little cold.' Next time he'd want a little more sugar, and so on, until he'd downed perhaps three cups of coffee."[21]

Dr. Taylor recognized that Hampton was suffering from valvular heart disease. His last horseback ride was at the age of eighty-three during the veterans' reunion in Columbia in May 1901, when he led the procession to Elmwood Cemetery. For two days, contingents of veterans marched to his house to pay their respects. Hampton stood on his porch, his voice choked with emotion, to say a few words to them and shake each hand as the men filed past.[22]

In December 1901 Hampton attended a reunion of alumni of the South Carolina College. Hampton, as the oldest living alumnus, was the guest of honor. It was his last public appearance. He caught a cold from which he never fully recovered.[23]

On April 1, 1902, not long after his eighty-fourth birthday, he felt well enough to take a carriage ride through town. Weakened by the adventure, he took to his bed. Another lifelong friend, Episcopal bishop Ellison Capers, went to see him. Hampton, widely regarded by white citizens as the savior of his state, obviously had been preparing to meet his own Redeemer. He told Capers that although he knew he was unworthy, he was assured that God had forgiven him all his sins. "From my heart I forgive all my enemies," he said, "if there are any men in South Carolina who are my enemies."[24]

Over the next few days the family gathered. Hampton gave orders concerning his funeral. He wanted a simple ceremony with no martial display. He wished for his favorite hymn, "Lead On, Guiding Light," to be sung. One of the sins for which Hampton may have thought he needed forgiveness was pride, for it was the subject of one of the hymn's verses:

I loved to choose and see my path; but now
   Lead thou me on.
I loved the garish day, and spite of fears,
   Pride ruled my will: remember not past years.[25]

For several days he took little nourishment other than milk and pain relievers. Alfred Hampton kept a log:

Hampton's youngest son, Alfred, recorded Hampton's nourishment and medications on his deathbed. Library of Congress.

On the back of his log, Alfred recorded Hampton's last words. Library of Congress.

Sunday, April 6. 3 P.M.—Hot milk.
4:30—Tablets & drops.
5:40—Half glass cold milk . . .
8:00 Whiskey.[26]

By Thursday, April 10, he was floating in and out of consciousness. Half-delirious, his mind drifted back to the gloomy, damp battlefield that haunted him still, and he whispered. Two familiar forms, his beloved sons, lay bleeding and prostrate, and that old feeling of hopelessness, of wretched misery, returned. "All is black—My children on the field—Heroes forever! forever!"[27] When asked if he was speaking of Preston and Wade, he nodded yes.[28]

Later that evening he spoke again. "All my people, black & white. God bless them all." Finally, Wade Hampton released his soul into the hands of his God:

My children, my Jesus, my friends, my country.
My Jesus, my Jesus, my Christ, my Redeemer.

Jesus will not deceive me.[29]

Hampton had accepted, it seems, that his ultimate vindication was not within his own grasp. He was silent the rest of the night. His pulse weakened and his breathing became nearly imperceptible. At 8:50 A.M., April 11, 1902, Dr. Taylor turned to Hampton's children and sisters and told them he was dead.[30]

EPILOGUE

Wade Hampton had once told South Carolinians that all he wanted from his state was "a grave in yonder churchyard." Now he was getting that and much more. His funeral was the largest in the history of South Carolina. Twenty thousand mourners thronged the streets of Columbia. Though Hampton wanted no military display at his funeral, state troops guarded his remains in the preceding days and hours, as did contingents of the United Confederate Veterans. Old soldiers stooped to weep over the open coffin. Black servants of the family did so as well, as they laid on his chest flowers taken from the grounds of Millwood and Diamond Hill. The funeral procession wound through the city streets to Trinity Church, where members of five Hampton generations were buried. Joining the column were Daughters of the Confederacy, Citadel cadets, students from South Carolina College, and militia units, civic organizations, and veterans from every corner of the state. Mourners of both races thronged the route and crowded outside the church, where only fifteen hundred of them would be able to enter. Driving the horse-drawn hearse was Kit Goodwyn, Hampton's ex-slave and lifelong servant.

The entire state paused to grieve. Shops and businesses in Columbia closed on Friday, the day of his death. Bells tolled and flags were lowered to half-mast in towns throughout the state. Newspapers the next day were edged in black. For days, tributes to Hampton poured in from all over the nation—from friends, enemies, and those who had been both. John B. Gordon, Joe Wheeler, James Longstreet, Fitz Lee, J. E. B. Stuart Jr., northern and southern politicians, President Theodore Roosevelt, Ben Tillman, John L. McLaurin, and veterans from North and South expressed their grief and admiration.[1]

Many tried to find symbolic or moral significance in the circumstances of his death. Some noted that he died on April 11, the twenty-fifth anniversary of his taking possession of the statehouse from the carpetbagger Daniel H. Chamberlain—the anniversary of his delivering the people of the state from foreign rule, of restoring native white supremacy. In white southern memory, however, April 11 was not only the anniversary of a political victory, but also of the restoration of peace and of a new reign of virtue. Most saw him, therefore, not only as a 499 political or white race hero, but also as a saint, savior, redeemer, and peacemaker. The common impression at the time, and for long afterward, was that his final words were "God bless all my people, black and white."[2] To many, then, Hampton's last words were his final "benediction, his prayer for South Carolina."[3] It was a notion that highlighted Hampton's paternalistic instincts, his patriotism, his basic goodness, while softening the fact that he never considered all of his "people" to be equal.[4]

Still another mutation of his last words appeared in an African American newspaper in Ohio. The *Cleveland Gazette* quoted Hampton's "last utterances" as "All my people are black and white." The *Gazette* found in his words a rebuke to the tide of proscription, segregation, and political marginalization of black people that was then sweeping the nation, particularly the Jim Crow South. It was testimony, the editor said, of Hampton's "brave conviction that the people of every nation are his people." It was true that Hampton had spent much of his political career preaching adherence to what the *Gazette*'s editor called "the spirit of liberty and justice and of mutual good-will and fellowship." But the Ohio newsman misunderstood Hampton. Hampton had sought harmonious social relations, but that did not include racial equality or the extent of universalism that the *Gazette* article implied.[5]

All agreed in 1902, however, that a great man had died, a fierce warrior who was yet a symbol of peace, reconciliation, and unity. Strolling through Columbia on the beautiful spring morning of Hampton's funeral, Edward Wells remembered seeing nothing but blackened ruins in those same streets in the spring of 1865. That was "Sherman's work," he mused. But the rebuilt, peaceful, and relatively prosperous Columbia before him now was "Hampton's work, the peace of God."[6] A northern Republican newspaper praised Hampton's role in the "rehabilitation of a people" and in his restoration of South Carolina to "governmental order and financial prosperity."[7] *Harper's Weekly* later praised his "policy of conciliation between the North and the South."[8] Ironically, this one point that contemporaries agreed on—Hampton as a peacemaker—was the most problematic. Hampton had been a divisive figure from the time he donned a Confederate uniform until the mid-1880s. He had briefly become one again as late as 1890. Before his death, his fellow Democrats had ultimately decided that even the "peace" he brought to his state in 1877 could be maintained only through oppression.[9]

For several more generations, Hampton continued to be a hero to white South Carolinians, and their black neighbors rarely dissented.

Equestrian statue of Hampton on statehouse grounds, Columbia, erected in 1906. South Caroliniana Library.

His name appeared on schools, buildings, and streets statewide. A large equestrian statue of him was raised in 1906 on the statehouse grounds in Columbia, just across from Trinity Church, appropriately facing north. For at least half a century, he remained one of South Carolina's greatest heroes, a towering symbol of heroic resistance, chivalry, statesmanship, and patriotism.

In the field of race relations, though, white leaders often disagreed over what Hampton's legacy actually was. In the 1932 Senate primary between James F. Byrnes and "Cotton Ed" Smith, for example, South Carolina Democrats fought each other over who had the right to wear Hampton's mantle. Byrnes was the pro-Roosevelt, pro–New Deal candidate, whom Smith accused of "catering" to blacks.[10] Several Byrnes supporters, however, pointed out that since Wade Hampton himself had appealed for black votes, it was no sin for modern Democrats to do the same. When Smith won the 1938 primary, he too tried to appropriate Hampton's legacy, but it was a different one than that embraced by Byrnes supporters. Still playing the race card, Smith posed beneath the Hampton monument beside the statehouse in a red shirt and urged whites to protect the state "from the mongrel breed who would take us back to the horrid days of reconstruction." "We conquered in '76, and we conquered in '38," he boasted.[11]

Hampton's form of paternalism became the model for white moderates of the 1930s and 1940s who supported concessions to blacks that did not include social equality or integration. Hard-liners, meanwhile, used Hampton's name to oppose these moderates. As ex-governor Strom Thurmond ran for the U.S. Senate in 1950, an opponent attacked him for appointing a black man to a minor office, thereby undermining "Wade Hampton's era of segregation."[12] No governor since Reconstruction, of course, had appointed more black men to office than Hampton had. Yet one must conclude that anyone who looked, or looks, to Hampton as the model of one or another racial policy distorts who he was. It is akin to an architect studying one of the columns of a mansion to the neglect of the mansion itself. The forces that drove him were pain, tragedy, a thirst for redemption and vindication, the desire for peace and stability, personal religious faith, and the social ideals of the antebellum aristocrat—not dreams of either racial equality or racial proscription.

★ Hampton is gone, and so is his world, including many of the ideals he fought for. Most Americans outside South Carolina no longer know who he was, unlike the cases of Robert E. Lee, J. E. B. Stuart, or even

Nathan Bedford Forrest. His model of racial paternalism no longer
exists. States' rights doctrine too is nearly dead, except among a few
hard-core modern Confederates.

And yet the courage with which he fought for those ideals still in-
structs, even for those whom it does not inspire. Hampton refused to
renounce a lost cause. Partly this was due to conviction, but it was also
because his loyalty to those close to him was so deep that he could not
disown the cause for which they died—mainly out of the fear that, by
doing so, he would be renouncing them personally. But in his quest to
vindicate, redeem, and restore from the past what he deemed honorable, he was unable to confront squarely what was ugly and wrong. He
did act often to help or protect those whom society had placed under
him. Yet in asserting his rights and his state's rights against the North
and against federal power, he unintentionally became part of the machinery of oppression of others in his midst.

Edward Wells, his white contemporaries, and later generations of
South Carolinians always insisted that Hampton was the savior of his
people. But Hampton was an imperfect savior at best. His moral and
physical courage supplied the need of South Carolinians at one point
in their history when they needed to feel good about themselves. His
personal example and prestige brought an end to a period of political
and social turmoil in 1877. It is difficult to deny that he was probably
the only figure who could have brought outward stability and peace to
his state after the chaos of Reconstruction. For a brief moment, he
seemed to have achieved the best that was realistically possible for post–
Reconstruction South Carolina—a white-led regime that nevertheless
protected black civil rights and limited political participation. He was a
useful symbol of national reconciliation afterward. But he could not
rescue South Carolina from the economic malaise that brought him
down along with his fellow citizens. And his model of racial paternalism could only be a temporary, stopgap solution to chaos, not a model
for the future. Even before he left the governor's seat, it was clear that
the peace he brought could only be sustained by electoral fraud, violence, and the subordination of black South Carolinians.

This was due partly to the racial hatred of other men and partly to
Hampton's own inability to escape the racial and paternalistic assumptions of the antebellum world in which he came of age. Hampton was
indeed one of the best examples of what antebellum southern paternalism and chivalry could produce. But because of inherent flaws in that
aristocratic, paternalistic ethos, he was incapable of bringing true racial 503

and social justice to South Carolina. He was admirably suited for fighting "Yankees," restoring order in times of chaos, restoring confidence and hope to his own "people," and occasionally even checking their worst impulses. But it was simply not in him, and not part of paternalism, to fight for the ideals of racial justice that were just emerging in his own day and that are so fully entrenched now.

Some modern scholarship regards Hampton as a villain, not a savior. Several prominent historians insist that Hampton was a "moderate" only because he preferred maintaining white supremacy through "fraud and intimidation" rather than "meticulously planned multiple murders."[13] Another observes that no "gangster's racket" could have been more effective than the combination of Hampton's promises of "protection" to African Americans with Martin Gary's and Calbraith Butler's threats.[14] These comments, like Edward Wells's, are oversimplifications and distortions. They illustrate how educated people—scholars and laypersons alike—still often study southern history and southern heroes like Wade Hampton already sure of what they will find. Many will find in Hampton exactly what they came for—proof of either virtue or hypocrisy in white southern leaders. Some people who wish to learn about Hampton's story lose interest shortly after the Confederate battle flags are furled. Others do not tune in until later, starting with Reconstruction, assuming that Hampton's early life, personal tragedies, and battlefield heroism have nothing to do with their modern concerns. But it is the complete story of Hampton's life that teaches us the most about our own failings, our limitations, and our narrowness of vision—as well as our potential for greatness.

APPENDIX
THE FABLE OF HAMPTON,
"MAJOR S," AND A UNION
PRIVATE

One modern historian after another has uncritically repeated the bizarre tale of Hampton's adventures with the Union sharpshooter and the Yankee lieutenant near Gettysburg.[1] There are many ways to prove that it never happened. First, it was uncharacteristic of Hampton. He never lacked physical courage, but neither was he foolish enough to ride two hundred yards ahead of friendly troops to engage in one-on-one combat, especially when it had nothing to do with his larger mission. Clearly the story was meant to portray Hampton in a chivalrous light, as well as to highlight his well-known marksmanship. Yet Hampton was enough of a marksman and sportsman to know that an accurate pistol shot from 125 yards—on horseback, no less—would be more than improbable; it would be miraculous. A duel at that range between a rifle shooter and a pistol shooter was not gallantry, but that species of romantic foolishness that Hampton usually shunned.

One must also trace the source. The only primary source for the story is an 1894 article published in the *Southern Historical Society Papers* over the name of T[homas] J. Mackey. Curiously Mackey was a native South Carolinian at one time considered a scalawag by other white southerners. He served as a judge in the Republican administrations of the Reconstruction era, only to switch sides and reingratiate himself with Hampton and other Democrats as they regained control of the state. Mackey never served in the Confederate army. And though the narrative is told from the Confederate perspective, no other Confederate witnessed the event and Hampton never mentioned it. There were plenty of veterans in the postwar period, such as Ulysses Brooks and Edward Wells, who loved to publish heroic accounts about Hampton. None of them mention the story, nor does any other ex-Confederate. Additionally, Wells, Hampton's first biographer, communicated frequently with Hampton in the 1880s and 1890s on stories concerning Hampton's military career, and none of the voluminous correspondence between the two men mentions the incident.[2]

So how did Mackey learn of the story, particularly since he claimed that when Hampton stopped at the fence, he was in a fold in the terrain that shielded him from the view of any other Confederate? Mackey claimed that years after the war, the Yankee lieutenant—later "Major S." —approached "Colonel Frank Hampton, a younger brother of the General's," while on a visit to Mobile, Alabama. Supposedly "S" told Frank Hampton that he regretted taking a cheap shot at Hampton and wished Frank to express his regrets to Hampton. A courteous exchange of letters supposedly followed, by which the Hamptons learned that the Union private was Frank Pearson, a farmer in Kalamazoo, Michigan. Hampton allegedly communicated with Pearson as well. This part of the story stresses reconciliation between honorable warriors of North and South, a common theme in postwar literature on the Civil War. No such correspondence between Hampton and a Frank Pearson survives, however, in Hampton's papers. And, of course, the alleged meeting between Frank Hampton and Major "S" never took place, since Frank Hampton was killed before the Battle of Gettysburg.[3]

Clearly, the entire tale is a fabrication by one of Hampton's contemporaries, repeated by none of his others. It is modern historians who have given it the most credence.

NOTES

Persons

JHH   James Henry Hammond
MFH   Mary Fisher Hampton
MPH   Margaret Preston Hampton
REL   Robert E. Lee
SBH   Sally Baxter Hampton
WH   Wade Hampton III

Sources and Repositories

CLS   Charleston Library Society, Charleston, S.C.
CSR   Compiled Service Records of Confederate Generals and Staff Officers. Microfilm M331, roll 115. National Archives, Washington, D.C.
HFP   Hampton Family Papers, South Caroliniana Library, University of South Carolina, Columbia
HJ   South Carolina General Assembly. House. *Journal of the House of Representatives of the General Assembly of the State of South Carolina.* South Carolina Department of Archives and History, Columbia.
HL   Huntington Library, San Marino, Calif.
LOC   Library of Congress, Washington, D.C.
LR-CSW   Letters Received by the Confederate Secretary of War. Microfilm M437. National Archives, Washington, D.C.
NA   National Archives, Washington, D.C., and College Park, Maryland
OR   U.S. Government. *The War of the Rebellion: A Compilation of the Official Records of the Union and Confederate Armies.* 128 vols. Washington: GPO, 1880–1901. OR citations take the following form: volume number (part number, where applicable): page number. Unless otherwise indicated, all volumes cited throughout are from series 1.
PL   William R. Perkins Library, Duke University, Durham, N.C.
SCDAH   South Carolina Department of Archives and History, Columbia
SCHS   South Carolina Historical Society, Charleston
SCL   South Caroliniana Library, University of South Carolina, Columbia

SHC   Southern Historical Collection, Louis Round Wilson Library, University of North Carolina, Chapel Hill

SJ   South Carolina General Assembly. Senate. *Journal of the Senate of the General Assembly of the Senate of South Carolina*. South Carolina Department of Archives and History, Columbia.

Testimony   U.S. Congress. *Testimony Taken by the Joint Select Committee to Inquire into the Condition of Affairs in the Late Insurrectionary States*. 42nd Cong., 2nd sess. Washington, D.C.: GPO, 1872.

PREFACE

1   Earlier, doting biographies of Hampton include Wells, *Hampton and His Cavalry* and *Hampton and Reconstruction*, and Wellman, *Giant in Gray*. Meynard's *The Venturers* is an excellent work in genealogical and family history that also is very complimentary of Hampton. Longacre's *Gentleman and Soldier* aims for a more objective tone, as does Cisco's *Wade Hampton*, though both often gloss over contradictions and neglect larger questions about Hampton's life. Ackerman's recent *Wade Hampton III* is a useful, balanced portrayal, though it skims over Hampton's pivotal Civil War experiences and does not emphasize the themes of personal loss, humiliation, and vindication that I believe are so critical to understanding Hampton and many of his contemporaries. The dozens of other works that attempt to come to grips with Hampton's racial views and policies will be cited later.

2   A small sample of scholarship dealing with antebellum southern paternalism includes Genovese, *Roll, Jordan, Roll* and *The World the Slaveholders Made*; Dusinberre, *Them Dark Days*; Clinton, *Plantation Mistress*; McCurry, *Masters of Small Worlds*; Faust, *Hammond*; Walter Johnson, *Soul by Soul*; and Hartman, *Scenes of Subjection*, 46, 52–54, 88–89.

3   Wyatt-Brown, *Southern Honor*; Greenberg, *Honor and Slavery*.

4   Anderson, *Blood Image*, passim, esp. xiii–xvi.

5   Another advantage of the term "vindication" is that it captures the deep sense among white southerners that they were the victims of gross injustice and humiliation at the hands of the North. I certainly do not intend to revive the "Dunning thesis" of Reconstruction or write a pro-Confederate tract in my chapters on the Civil War and Reconstruction. I do wish to convey Hampton's own sense of victimhood, rage, and humiliation. It is imperative to do so to understand the latter half of his life.

CHAPTER I

1   "Wade Hampton on Old Cayce House: Incident He Related 44 Years Ago in Columbia Centennial Oration," clipping from *Columbia State*, June 30, 1935, box 4, folder 100, HFP.

2 Bridwell, "Wade Hampton I," 2, 10–23, 78I; Meynard, *The Venturers*, 62–63; Leyburn, *The Scotch-Irish*, 256–72.

3 Bridwell, "Wade Hampton I," 32–35, 50; Meynard, *The Venturers*, 67–68.

4 "The Hampton Family," *Charleston Mercury*, Aug. 4, 1843; Bridwell, "Wade Hampton I," 54–55; Edgar, *South Carolina*, 227–29; Meynard, *The Venturers*, 71–72.

5 "The Hampton Family."

6 Ibid.

7 Ibid.

8 Ibid.; Bridwell, "Wade Hampton I," 52–57. Meynard (*The Venturers*, 72–73) relates a slightly different version.

9 Bridwell, "Wade Hampton I," 69.

10 "The Hampton Family"; Bridwell, "Wade Hampton I," 67–73; Meynard, *The Venturers*, 73, 78–100; Edgar, *South Carolina*, 222.

11 Bridwell, "Wade Hampton I," 77–80, 90, 93, 96, 101–2 (quotation, 101).

12 WH to Lyman C. Draper, Jan. 14, 1870, Draper Collection, 12VV107, SCDAH.

13 Bridwell, "Wade Hampton I," 140, 141 n. 20, 146.

14 Ibid., 148–53, 160–63, 208.

15 Bridwell, "Wade Hampton I," 175–83; John W. Gordon, *South Carolina and the American Revolution*, 164.

16 Bridwell, "Wade Hampton I," 90–91, 151 (quotation), 155–56, 222–23, 197–98, 203–4.

17 Ibid., 194, 211–12, 220.

18 Ibid., 215–18, 226, 256, 268; Meynard, *The Venturers*, 142–43.

19 Bridwell, "Wade Hampton I," 505–744.

20 Ibid., 235, 247–49, 270, 273, 278–378, 386–90, 421, 435–95, 770, 781; Meynard, *The Venturers*, 110, 113–14. On the Yazoo Land frauds, see Coleman, *History of Georgia*, 96–99.

21 Genovese, *Roll, Jordan, Roll*, 1–7. Cash (*The Mind of the South*) sketched a similar portrait of southern planters as ambitious capitalists. Walter Johnson (*Soul by Soul*) emphasizes that, to masters, slaves were capital assets, but that they often tried to disguise the harshness of that reality when selling their slaves.

22 Bridwell, "Wade Hampton I," 771.

23 Ibid., 772.

24 Censer, *North Carolina Planters*; Fox-Genovese, *Plantation Household*; Oakes, *The Ruling Race*, 153–91. The debate on the character of the antebellum planter class and its social relations is neatly summarized in Young's *Domesticating Slavery*, 3–6.

25 Bridwell, "Wade Hampton I," 764.

26 Ibid., 763.

27 Kate Hampton to Means Davis, July 8, 1902, box 4, HFP; Bridwell, "Wade

Hampton I," 403–4, 497–98, 764, 780–82; Meynard, *The Venturers*, 140; Censer, *North Carolina Planters*; Fox-Genovese, *Plantation Household*.

28 Bridwell, "Wade Hampton I," 768. Wade I's daughter Caroline married John Smith Preston, younger brother of William C. Preston. Years later, Wade III wed William Preston's younger sister Margaret (Meynard, *The Venturers*, 138–39, 197). For more on Hampton's unpopularity, see Bridwell, "Wade Hampton I," 247–49, 394, 767–70.

29 Bridwell, "Wade Hampton I," 644, 731–48.

30 Meynard, *The Venturers*, 146–47; Bridwell, "Wade Hampton I," 747–48.

31 Bridwell, "Wade Hampton I," 748; Meynard, *The Venturers*, 147–48.

32 Meynard, *The Venturers*, 151–84.

33 Ibid., 150, 164, 167; Bridwell, "Wade Hampton I," 780–82.

34 Meynard, *The Venturers*, 167, 182.

35 Obituary clipping from *Southern Christian Advocate*, Feb. 13, 1858, box 3, HFP; Genovese, *A Consuming Fire*.

36 Wade II to MFH, Nov. 17, 1855, box 3, HFP.

37 WH to MFH, Feb. 14, 1857, ibid.

38 WH to MFH, Nov. 2, 1857, ibid.

39 WH to MFH, Aug. 26, 1857, ibid. On "Mom Nelly," see Wellman, *Giant in Gray*, 16, 257.

40 Meynard, *The Venturers*, 190.

41 Ibid., 178.

42 Ann Fripp Hampton, *Divided Heart*, 79.

43 Wellman, *Giant in Gray*, 257.

CHAPTER 2

1 Harry R. E. Hampton, "Some Hampton Notes," typescript in Meynard Papers, box 1, folder 87, SCL.

2 Harry R. E. Hampton, "About the General," 1, typescript in ibid., folder 81; Meynard, *The Venturers*, 196. Over a century after Hampton's encounter with the gander, an overenthusiastic historian claimed that the boy determinedly and "grimly" hacked and hacked his assailant until it was dead (Wellman, *Giant in Gray*, 17–18).

3 Meynard, *The Venturers*, 195.

4 See Hampton's letters to Mary Fisher in HFP, esp. WH to MFH, Feb. 12, 1858, box 3.

5 Meynard, *The Venturers*, 156.

6 Wells, *Hampton and Reconstruction*, 17.

7 Wade II to MFH, Dec. 12, 1856, box 3, HFP. For other examples of Wade II's reporting on his son's hunting successes, see Wade II to MFH, Apr. 22, Nov. 17, 1855. See also Meynard, *The Venturers*, 175, 198.

8 Harry R. E. Hampton, "About the General," 2.

9 Ibid., 4. See also Wells, *Hampton and His Cavalry*, 38–43, 47, and Paul Schullery, *The Bear Hunter's Century*, 77. Harry Hampton thought that Roosevelt had claimed eighty knife-slain bears for Hampton. Wellman's 1949 biography of Hampton repeated the exaggerated figure of eighty knife-slain bears (Wellman, *Giant in Gray*, 44).

10 Meynard, *The Venturers*, 199. See also Harry R. E. Hampton, "About the General," 6–7; Meynard, *The Venturers*, 198; and Wellman, *Giant in Gray*, 21.

11 Proctor, *Bathed in Blood*, 21.

12 Ibid.

13 Ibid., 23 (quotation), 37–39, 44–45.

14 Ibid., 61–75 (quotation, 75). Kenneth Greenberg (*Honor and Slavery*, 124–35) makes similar points about hunting, mastery, and white manhood.

15 WH to MFH, Nov. 8, 1857, box 3, HFP.

16 Proctor, *Bathed in Blood*, 60.

17 Wells, *Hampton and Reconstruction*, 17; Wellman, *Giant in Gray*, 39. For descriptions of the other three men's good looks and Wade II's prominence as a socialite, see Meynard, *The Venturers*, 158, 162, 172–74, 176, 187, 190, 201, 226–27, 230, and Chesnut, *Mary Chesnut's Civil War*, 50, 289.

18 Wells, *Hampton and Reconstruction*, 17.

19 Ibid.

20 Ibid., 17–18; Wellman, *Giant in Gray*, 3, 38–39, 139.

21 Meynard, *The Venturers*, 138–39, 141, 163, 194, 197.

22 Ibid., 197.

23 Bleser, *Secret and Sacred*, 8–9.

24 Faust, *Hammond*, 221, 228, 235, 241; Bleser, *Secret and Sacred*, 21–22; Meynard, *The Venturers*, 173.

25 JHH Diary, Dec. 9, 1846, JHH Papers, SCL.

26 Ibid.

27 Ibid.

28 Faust, *Hammond*. 241; Byron, "Beyond the Traditional Code of Honor," 53, 60.

29 JHH Diary, Jan. 23, 1847.

30 Ibid.

31 Ibid.

32 See also JHH Diary: "Records of Antebellum Southern Plantations," Jan. 31, 1844.

33 Matthew Adam Byron ("Beyond the Traditional Code of Honor," chap. 3) has paid special attention to the peculiar way in which the Hampton-Hammond feud unfolded. He uses the term "shadow duel" in an attempt to explain the two men's efforts to conduct an affair of honor—by nature a public event—virtually in private.

34 JHH Diary, Dec. 9, 1846.

35 Ibid., Jan. 31, 1844.

36 Faust, *Hammond*, 289.

37 Ibid., 243–45, 288–89, 302, 314–15, 338–39; Meynard, *The Venturers*, 174.

38 For further comments on the girls' behavior, see Faust, *Hammond*, 242.

39 Ibid., 314; Bleser, *Secret and Sacred*, 17–18.

40 WH to James Conner, Apr. 11, 1869, box 4, HFP.

41 Meynard, *The Venturers*, 198.

42 Ibid., 198–99.

43 WH to MFH, July 27, 29, 30–31, Aug. 1, 10, 12–13, 1846, WH Papers, SHC.

44 Ibid.

45 WH to MFH, July 31, 1846.

46 WH to MFH, Aug. 1, 1846.

47 WH to MFH, Aug. 10, 1846.

48 WH to MFH, July 27, 1846.

49 WH to MFH, Aug. 1 (quotation), 10, 13, 1846.

50 Meynard, *The Venturers*, 562.

51 Ibid., 562, 527.

52 Ibid., 562, 577, 200, 204.

53 WH to MFH, Sept. 2, 1855, WH Papers, SHC.

54 Ibid.

CHAPTER 3

1 HJ (1854): 35, 37, 56, 84–85, 123, 125–29, 147, 163; HJ (1859): 56–57; Meynard, *The Venturers*, 200.

2 SBH to George Baxter, Dec. 29, 1855, in Ann Fripp Hampton, *Divided Heart*, 29–30.

3 Ibid., 30. Sally's letter uses the word "indifference" rather than "indifferent."

4 Meynard, *The Venturers*, 202.

5 WH to Mary S. McDuffie, Mar. 1, 1853, folder 1, WH Correspondence, PL.

6 For an eloquent discussion of planters' abilities to excuse their own inhumanity in the selling of slaves, see Walter Johnson, *Soul by Soul*, esp. 24–30.

7 Meynard, *The Venturers*, 203.

8 WH to Mary S. McDuffie, Feb. 14, 1857, box 3, folder 69, HFP.

9 Meynard, *The Venturers*, 206.

10 Ibid., 190. Meynard states that Hampton did not arrive at New Orleans and learn of his father's death until February 14. Yet his February 12 letter to Mary Fisher was written from New Orleans and discusses the family's loss.

11 Ibid. See WH to MFH, Feb. 12, 15, 17, 24, 27, Mar. 14, 27, Apr. 2, 10, 16, 24, 1858 (box 3), and Mar. 8, 1858 (box 2) HFP.

12 WH to MFH, Feb. 12, 1858, box 3, HFP.

13   WH to MFH, Mar. 8, 1858, box 2, folder 64a, HFP.

14   WH to MFH, Feb. 27, 1858, box 3, HFP.

15   Meynard, The Venturers, 163, 192, 976–85; Hampton Family Legal Records, box 7, folder 28, ser. II, Abney Papers, SCL.

CHAPTER 4

1   Meynard, The Venturers, 204, 976–84.

2   WH to MFH, Apr. 10, 16, 24, May 1, 1858, box 3, HFP; WH to MFH, Apr. 11, 1859, folder 2, Hampton Family Papers, LOC.

3   WH to MFH, Nov. 6, 1859, box 3, HFP. See also WH to MFH, May 15, June 5, 12, 1859, ibid.

4   WH to MFH, Nov. 4, 1860, box 3, HFP. See also WH to MFH, Oct. 22, 1860, box 2, folder 64a, HFP.

5   As Anderson (Blood Image, 2, 33–35, 71–72, 175–76) explains, home defense was at the core of the nineteenth-century chivalric ideal.

6   WH to James Chesnut Jr., June 5, 1852, box 2, folder 89, Williams-Chesnut-Manning Family Papers, SCL.

7   WH to MFH, Dec. 17, 1861, box 3, HFP.

8   Haskell, Haskell Memoirs, vii. Edmunds (Pickens, 116–18, 121–23, 131–32, 152) traces Pickens's journey from advocating cooperation to unilateral secession, to cooperation, and back again.

9   Sinha, Counterrevolution of Slavery, 180; Schultz, Nationalism and Sectionalism in South Carolina, 20–23; Edgar, South Carolina, 348.

10   Sinha, Counterrevolution of Slavery, 131–32 (quotation), 129.

11   Ibid., 100.

12   Ibid. For the best summary of Pettigrew's speech, see Wilson, Carolina Cavalier, 99–104.

13   Wilson, Carolina Cavalier, 105; Sinha, Counterrevolution of Slavery, 145–49.

14   Sinha, Counterrevolution of Slavery, 147, 180; "Speech of the Hon. Wade Hampton on the Constitutionality of the Slave Trade Laws . . ., December 10, 1859," 1–2, 22, SCL (hereafter Hampton's Slave Trade Speech).

15   WH to Francis Lieber, Aug. 14, 1859, LI 1601, Lieber Papers, HL.

16   Sinha, Counterrevolution of Slavery, 154–61 (quotations, 154).

17   Hampton's Slave Trade Speech, 23.

18   Sinha, Counterrevolution of Slavery, 174.

19   Ibid., 179.

20   Hampton's Slave Trade Speech, 22–23.

21   Ibid., 1–3; SJ (1858): 39, 109, 119–20; SJ (1859): 5.

22   SJ (1859): 3.

23   Ibid.

24   Ibid., 14.

25   Ibid., 3.

26 Ibid., 3–4.

27 Ibid., 19.

28 Ibid., 19–20.

29 Ibid., 17–18.

30 Ibid., 9.

31 Ibid., 20, 18.

32 Ibid., 19.

33 Ibid., 25.

34 Meynard, The Venturers, 208.

35 Charleston Mercury, Dec. 12, 1860; Wellman, Giant in Gray, 36; Sinha, Counterrevolution of Slavery, 181.

36 Chesnut, Mary Chesnut's Civil War, 4.

37 Sinha, Counterrevolution of Slavery, 220.

38 Channing, Crisis of Fear, 70.

39 Ibid., 77. See also 18–20, 92–96, and passim.

40 Channing, Crisis of Fear, 96.

41 Edmunds, Pickens, 150.

42 WH to MFH, Feb. 12, 1860, box 3, HFP. A letter to Mary Fisher indicates that Hampton was floating down the Mississippi River from Memphis to Vicksburg by February 2 (WH to MFH, Feb. 2, 1860, folder 2, Hampton Family Papers, LOC).

43 WH to MFH, Feb. 12, 1860.

44 WH to MFH, Feb. 22, 1860, folder 2, Hampton Family Papers, LOC.

45 Edgar, South Carolina, 349; Meynard, The Venturers, 210.

46 WH to MFH, Nov. 4, 1860, box 3, HFP. See also WH to MFH, June 23, 25, 1860, postmarked from Washington, D.C., ibid.

47 WH to MFH, Nov. 4, 1860. See also WH to MFH, Oct. 22, 1860.

48 WH to MFH, Oct. 22, 1860.

49 WH to MFH, Nov. 4, 1860. See also Channing, Crisis of Fear, 240, and Edgar, South Carolina, 351.

50 Edgar, South Carolina, 350.

51 WH to His Excellency, Governor Gist, Nov. 24, 1860, LR-CSW.

52 Charleston Daily Courier, Nov. 26, 1860.

53 Edgar, South Carolina, 351; Ann Fripp Hampton, Divided Heart, 80.

54 Cisco, Wade Hampton, 55.

55 SBH to George Baxter, Dec. 22, 1860, in Ann Fripp Hampton, Divided Heart, 79.

56 Ibid.

57 SBH to Baxter Family, Dec. 10[?], 1860, ibid., 72. The South Carolina elites referred to are Charles Lowndes, William C. Preston and John Smith Preston, former governor John Laurence Manning, Christopher G. Memminger, James L. Orr, and James Johnston Pettigrew.

58 SBH to George Baxter, Dec. 22, 1860.

59 SBH to Baxter Family, Dec. 10[?], 1860.

60 SBH to Samuel B. Ruggles, Jan. 1, 1861, in Ann Fripp Hampton, *Divided Heart*, 86.

61 SBH to Samuel B. Ruggles, Dec. 14, 1860, ibid., 74.

62 SBH to Anna Baxter, Jan. 11, 1860, ibid., 98.

63 Frank Hampton to Anna Baxter, Jan. 10, 1861, ibid., 96.

64 Cisco, *Wade Hampton*, 56.

65 Morrill, *Civil War in the Carolinas*, 34–46.

66 SBH to Anna Baxter, Jan. 11, 1861, in Ann Fripp Hampton, *Divided Heart*, 97.

67 SBH to Wyllys Baxter, Feb. 10 [or 17?], 1861, ibid., 107. See also SBH to Wyllys Baxter, Jan. 18, 1861, ibid., 100–104.

68 SBH to George Baxter, Mar. 19, 1861, ibid., 108.

69 WH to MFH, Apr. 9, 1861, box 3, HFP.

70 Ibid.

71 WH to MFH, Mar. 27, 1861, ibid.

72 On the connections between slavery, honor, and liberty in southern thought, see Cooper, *Liberty and Slavery*.

CHAPTER 5

1 WH to MFH, Apr. 24, 1861, box 2, folder 64a, HFP.

2 Meynard, *The Venturers*, 216. Hampton was officially mustered into Confederate service on June 12, 1861, as colonel of the Hampton Legion, though correspondence between Pickens and Davis as early as May 3 referred to him as "Colonel" Hampton (Wellman, *Giant in Gray*, 340 nn. 16–17; CSR. Longacre (*Gentleman and Soldier*, 35, 280 n. 11) writes that Hampton returned from Mississippi via steamer and went first to Charleston, mentioning neither of the stops in Montgomery and Greenville. He cites Wellman, *Giant in Gray*, 50, and an April 30 letter, neither of which offers conclusive proof of that chain of events. I rely on Meynard, who presents only circumstantial evidence, but whom I have generally found to be exceptionally reliable in factual details.

3 James Conner to "My dear Mother," June 13, 1861, box 181, folder 3, Military Correspondence, Conner Family Papers, SCHS.

4 Ibid.; WH to MFH, Apr. 30, 1861, box 3, HFP. Longacre (*Gentleman and Soldier*, 39–40) provides useful detail on the extent to which the legion's equipment actually was paid for from Hampton's own pocket.

5 James Conner to "My dear Mother," June 13, 1861.

6 Moffett, *Letters of General James Conner*, 4, 7–8, 25–26; Meynard, *The Venturers*, 216–17; CSR.

7 Coxe, "Wade Hampton," 460.

8 Harry R. E. Hampton, "About the General," 7, typescript in Meynard Collection, box 1, folder 81, SCL.

9 WH to Mrs. Singleton, Sept. 5, 1861, box 3, HFP.

10 Coxe, "Wade Hampton," 462; see also 460.

11 Von Borcke and Scheibert, Brandy Station, 119–20.

12 Freeman, Lee's Lieutenants, 3:xxi–xxii.

13 Meynard, The Venturers, 907 n. 39.

14 Ibid., 218–19.

15 Davis, Bull Run, 142.

16 Ibid., 141–43, 272 n. 20; Longacre, Gentleman and Soldier, 2; Coxe, "Battle of First Manassas," 24–25; James Conner to Mother [July 1861], box 181, folder 3, Military Correspondence, Conner Family Papers, SCHS; WH to P. G. T. Beauregard, June 5, 1885, CW 165, Civil War Collection, HL; James Lowndes to Cousin Mattie, July 26, 1861, Lowndes Papers, SCL; OR 2:487, 566.

17 OR 2:566. My effort to re-create how Wade Hampton and his men must have experienced their part of the battle is based on Davis, Bull Run, 146–238 passim; McDonald, We Shall Meet Again, 34–44, 77–81, 91–93, 127–49, 167; Hampton's official report in OR 2:566–67; Beauregard's report in OR 2:487–500; Johnston's report in OR 2:474; WH to P. G. T. Beauregard, June 5, 1885, CW 165, Civil War Collection, HL; James Conner to Mother [July 1861]; James Lowndes to Cousin Mattie, July 26, 1861, Lowndes Papers, SCL; and Johnston, Narrative. The eyewitness accounts overlap and understandably differ in many details, sometimes significantly. I have favored the accounts that are most detailed when it comes to the legion, that were written soonest after the battle, and seem to be best corroborated by the others.

18 WH to P. G. T. Beauregard, June 5, 1880, CW 165, Civil War Collection, HL.

19 James Lowndes to Cousin Mattie, July 26, 1861, Lowndes Papers, SCL.

20 James Lowndes to Cousin Mattie, July 26, 1861; James Conner to Mother [July 1861]. Conner's account makes it sound as if the legion were on the turnpike, but then turned at right angles to deploy along a wide country lane leading from the turnpike. The lane he mentions also provided good cover. McDonald's excellent secondary account of the battle mentions the lane as well. Hampton's accounts do not (McDonald, We Shall Meet Again, 77–78; OR 2:566).

21 Hampton always maintained, probably with little exaggeration, that "we were fighting on our own hook & fighting the main column of the enemy . . . for two hours" (WH to Mrs. Singleton, Sept. 5, 1861, box 3, HFP; see also WH to P. G. T. Beauregard, June 5, 1880).

22 Hampton's official report, OR 2:567.

23 James Conner to Mother [July 1861]; OR 2:567. Glatthaar ("Battlefield Tactics," 79–80) points out that after firing ten rounds with a black powder weapon, the inside of the barrel would be so fouled with residue that a soldier could not load another round without cleaning the weapon—a fact usually overlooked by Civil War military historians.

24 OR 2:567.

25 Ibid.

26 MFH to Mrs. William Martin, Aug. 12, 1862, box 3, HFP. Days after the battle, Hampton's sister Caroline wrote: "God grant your wound may be as slight as you telegraph it is." (Caroline Hampton to WH, July 1861, ibid.). See also James Conner to Mother, Aug. 14, 1861, box 181, Military Correspondence, Conner Family Papers, SCHS.

27 WH to MFH, Sept. 5, 1861, box 3, HFP.

CHAPTER 6

1 OR 2:500.

2 OR 2:474.

3 Wellman, Giant in Gray, 65.

4 Johnston regretted his inability to procure the brigadier rank for Hampton (Johnston, Narrative, 84).

5 WH to Mrs. Singleton, Sept. 5, 1861, box 3, HFP.

6 Ibid. The fact that some had died is found in WH to MFH, Sept. 4, 1861, ibid.

7 WH to Mrs. Singleton, Sept. 5, 1861 ("prostrated"); James Conner to Mother, Aug. 29, 1861, in Moffett, Letters of General James Conner, 54 ("malarial").

8 WH to Mrs. Singleton, Sept. 5, 1861. In his report to Beauregard, Hampton expressed feelings of "pride" and "unqualified approbation" for the "unflinching courage of [his] brave men" and the "gallantry of the officers" (OR 2:567).

9 WH to John S. Preston, Oct. 7, 1861, and WH to Hon. J. P. Benjamin, Sept. 30, 1861, roll 11, LR-CSW.

10 WH to MFH, Nov. 17, 1861, box 3, HFP. For more on caring for the sick, see WH to P. G. T. Beauregard, Nov. 20, 1861, CW 164, Civil War Collection, HL, and WH to MFH, Oct. 28, 1861, box 2, folder 64a, HFP.

11 WH to MFH, Mar. 2, 1862, box 3, HFP; Moffett, Letters of General James Conner, 82.

12 WH to MFH, Mar. 2, 1862, box 3, HFP. See also WH to MFH, Oct. 28, 1861, ibid. Hampton himself became ill at least twice during the winter.

13 WH to Mrs. Singleton, Sept. 5, 1861 (quotation); Moffett, Letters of General James Conner, 53, 64. See also Freeman, Lee's Lieutenants, 1:133–34; WH to Hon. George W. Randolph, Apr. 26, 1862, LR-CSW.

14 WH to Kate Hampton, Jan. 15, 1862, box 3, HFP.

15 See ibid. and WH to MFH, Mar. 25, 1862, box 2, folder 64a, HFP. For his desire to expand the legion into a brigade, see OR, ser. 4, 1(1):902; WH to Kate Hampton, Jan. 15, 1862, and WH to MFH, Feb. 2, 1862, box 3, HFP. See also Johnston, Narrative, 84.

16 WH to MFH, Oct. 1, 1861, box 3, HFP. See also copy of Hampton's report to Colonel Thomas Jordan, AA Genl 1st Corps Army Potomac, Sept. 24, 1861, box 4, folder 8, HFP.

17 WH to MFH, Jan. 3, 1862, box 3, HFP.

18 WH to MFH, Dec. 17, 1861, ibid.

19 WH to Kate Hampton, Jan. 15, 1862, ibid.

20 WH to MFH, Jan. 15, 1862, ibid.

21 WH to MFH, Nov. 17, 1861, ibid.

22 WH to MFH, Dec. 17, 1861, ibid.; Morrill, Civil War in the Carolinas, 171–75. See also Conner's comments on the matter in Moffett, Letters of General James Conner, 64.

23 WH to MFH, Feb. 2, 1862, box 3, HFP.

24 WH to MFH, Mar. 25, 1862, ibid.

25 WH to MFH, Christmas 1861, ibid.

26 McArthur and Burton, A Gentleman and an Officer, 159–60; WH to MFH, Dec. 30, 1861, Jan. 15, Feb. 2, Mar. 2, 1862, box 3, HFP. Longacre (Gentleman and Soldier, 60) incorrectly states that while his men lived in tents, Hampton had found a nice house to winter in, and that his quarters were so "snug that early in the new year, Hampton's wife and their youngest son arrived to live with him for an extended period." The letters Longacre cites (Nov. 17, Dec. 30, 1861, and Jan. 3, 1862) indicate no such thing— only that Hampton was looking for suitable quarters for his family near him. Indeed, Mrs. Hampton never got closer to the front than Richmond, and only Sally, not McDuffie, was able to go with her. On Dec. 17, 1861, Hampton wrote that he was living in a tent; on Jan. 15, 1862, he was living in a "common little hut." Lieutenant Colonel Griffin noted that Hampton was lying in his tent suffering from the mumps in February (WH to MFH, Dec. 17, 1861, Jan. 15, 1862; McArthur and Burton, A Gentleman and an Officer, 159–60).

27 WH to MFH, May 21, 1862, box 2, folder 64a, HFP; Meynard, The Venturers, 221.

28 WH to MFH, Christmas 1861, HFP; OR 5:1029–32, 1058. The Hampton Legion was an unbrigaded part of Van Dorn's division, then part of Whiting's brigade, then Longstreet's, then Whiting's again. Its area of operations, however, remained fairly constant (OR 5:778–79, 960, 913).

29 This statement is based on Hampton's incredibly detailed discussions on terrain, fortifications, and potential courses of action in his letters of

November and December (WH to P. G. T. Beauregard, Nov. 20, 1861, CW
164, Civil War Collection, HL; WH to Joseph Johnston, Dec. 8, 1861, JO
107, Johnston Papers, HL). See also Freeman, *Lee's Lieutenants*, 1:195, and
OR 5:533–35.

30 Freeman, *Lee's Lieutenants*, 1:135, 138–40; Johnston, *Narrative*, 96, 102; OR
5:1092.

31 Freeman, *Lee's Lieutenants*, 1:195.

32 OR 5:534–35 (quotation); Johnston, *Narrative*, 102–6.

33 Ibid., 530.

CHAPTER 7

1 Freeman, *Lee's Lieutenants*, 1:145–55.

2 Moffett, *Letters of General James Conner*, 87–88; Sears, *Peninsula Campaign*, 51,
366.

3 Moffett, *Letters of General James Conner*, 96.

4 Sears, *Peninsula Campaign*, 85.

5 OR 11(1):629.

6 Sears, *Peninsula Campaign*, 86.

7 OR 11(1):628–32; Moffett, *Letters of General James Conner*, 93.

8 OR 11(1):630.

9 Sears, *Peninsula Campaign*, 86 (quotations); OR 11(1):629–32.

10 Sears, *Peninsula Campaign*, 117–22, 138; Freeman, *Lee's Lieutenants*, 1:221–
43.

11 OR 11(1):991.

12 WH to MFH, June 3, 1862, box 3, HFP.

13 OR 11(1):991; Sears, *Peninsula Campaign*, 137–38; WH to MFH, June 3,
1862; Moffett, *Letters of General James Conner*, 98.

14 WH to MFH, June 3, 1862.

15 WH to Hon. George W. Randolph, June 21, 1862, LR-CSW. The losses
given for the Hampton Legion correspond to Hampton's report to the
secretary of war but not to that of General Gustavus Smith, who indicated
that the Hampton Legion lost 164 killed (OR 11(1):994; Sears, *Peninsula
Campaign*, 126–38). According to Sears, Confederate losses for May 31
were 5,002. That does not include losses for June 1, which brought the
total to 6,134. Union losses for both days totaled 5,031 (Sears, *Peninsula
Campaign*, 138; Freeman, *Lee's Lieutenants*, 1:244 and n. 7). Smith's account
of the battle was yet another that praised Hampton's "coolness, promptness, and decided practical ability as a leader of men in difficult and
dangerous circumstances. In these high characteristics . . . he has few
equals and perhaps no superior" (OR 11[1]:991).

16 WH to MFH, June 3, 1862. Preston was still in the legion, while Wade 519

served on Johnston's staff. After Johnston was wounded and carried from the field, Wade volunteered his services to his replacement, Gustavus Smith, who praised him in his official report (OR 11[1]:993).

17 WH to MFH, June 3, 1862.

18 WH to MFH, May 21, 1862, box 3, HFP.

19 WH to MFH, June 8, 1862, ibid.

20 Chesnut, *Mary Chesnut's Civil War*, 376. Evidence that Hampton had a broken foot appears in WH to George Randolph, June 21, 1862, LR-CSW.

21 Chesnut, *Mary Chesnut's Civil War*, 395.

22 Wellman, *Giant in Gray*, 76.

23 In the fall of 1861 Hampton took pains to assure his superiors that his goal was the increased strength and usefulness of the legion, not his own promotion (see WH to Secretary of War via John S. Preston, Oct. 7, 1861, and WH to Hon. Judah P. Benjamin, Sept. 30, 1861, LR-CSW).

24 Freeman, *Lee's Lieutenants*, 1:118, 218; WH to Hon. Judah P. Benjamin, Sept. 30, 1861 (2 letters), and WH to John S. Preston, Oct. 7, 1861, LR-CSW; WH to William Porcher Miles, Dec. 10, 1861, Miles Papers, SHC; WH to MFH, Jan. 15, Feb. 2, Mar. 2, 25, 1862, box 3, HFP; OR 11(3):543.

25 Moffett, *Letters of General James Conner*, 98.

26 WH to Hon. George W. Randolph, Apr. 26, June 3, 1862, LR-CSW; WH to MFH, Sept. 5, 1861, Jan. 15, Mar. 2, 1862 (box 3), and WH to MFH, May 21, 1862 (box 2, folder 64a), HFP; Moffett, *Letters of General James Conner*, 98.

27 Moffett, *Letters of General James Conner*, 99; CSR.

28 Moffett, *Letters of General James Conner*, 98, 100; "Hampton to His Legion," clipping in box 4, folder 99, HFP; Chesnut, *Mary Chesnut's Civil War*, 393.

29 McPherson, *Battle Cry of Freedom*; 464–65; Sears, *Peninsula Campaign*, 194–95.

30 Sears, *Peninsula Campaign*, 197–201. The Hampton Legion's infantry was assigned to Hood's brigade, with which it fought at Eltham's Landing; the 14th Georgia and the 16th North Carolina were reassigned to brigades in A. P. Hill's division that were made up of regiments from their respective states. The 19th Georgia joined Archer's brigade, also in A. P. Hill's division (ibid., 385–87).

31 OR 11(2):756.

32 Sears, *Peninsula Campaign*, 208; McPherson, *Battle Cry of Freedom*, 466.

33 OR 11(2):592–93; Sears, *Peninsula Campaign*, 236, 385. Wellman (*Giant in Gray*, 76–77) claims that Wade IV also served on his father's staff during the next several days.

34 Sears, *Peninsula Campaign*, 283; Freeman, *Lee's Lieutenants*, 1:541, 566–67.

35 Freeman, *Lee's Lieutenants*, 1:541, 566–67.

36 Sears, *Peninsula Campaign*, 283–85, 287; Freeman, *Lee's Lieutenants*, 1:571, 578–79; Alexander, *Fighting for the Confederacy*, 105–6, 108–9.

37 Krick, "Sleepless in the Saddle," 80–81; Alexander, *Fighting for the Con-*

federacy, 105–6, 108–9; Sears, *Peninsula Campaign*, 287; Freeman, *Lee's Lieutenants*, 1:579–80; McPherson, *Battle Cry of Freedom*, 469.

38 WH to MFH, July 19, 1862, box 3, HFP.

39 Ibid.

CHAPTER 8

1 This particular phrase was used by Calbraith Butler (Brooks, *Butler and His Cavalry*, 562). Colonel John Logan Black (*Crumbling Defenses*, 24) recalled that "Hampton was not much on books or maps but had a really fine topographical head and from his sporting taste well knew how to get through a country and he was hard to rope in as he was as much at home on a haypath with light cavalry as on a broad pike."

2 Wellman, *Giant in Gray*, 80–81; OR 11(3):655.

3 Freeman, *Lee's Lieutenants*, 1:671; Wellman, *Giant in Gray*, 80–81.

4 Wellman, *Giant in Gray*, 43, 88–89; Meynard, *The Venturers*, 196–97, 199. See Marcus Cunliffe's discussion of the "Rifleman" in the American military ethos in his *Soldiers and Civilians*, esp. 415–17, and Anderson, *Blood Image*, xiv, 19, 23–26, 175–80. Hampton also liked being compared to his father. A friend of his overheard some Confederate troops say: " 'There is Wade Hampton: he is a chip off the old block[.]' 'Yes, said another, he is a true son of his father[.]' " Hampton wrote his sister that "this was . . . as high praise as So.Ca. soldiers could give to me" (WH to MFH, box 2, folder 64a, HFP).

5 Wellman, *Giant in Gray*, 85; Longacre, *Lee's Cavalrymen*, 127; CSR. For evidence of Hampton's praise of Butler, see Brooks, *Butler and His Cavalry*, 278. Young's cadetship at West Point is mentioned in *Southern Historical Society Papers*, 25:147.

6 Wellman, *Giant in Gray*, 52, 218, 325; Brooks, *Butler and His Cavalry*, 558; Meynard, *The Venturers*, 216.

7 Longacre, *Lee's Cavalrymen*, 54, 110, 129.

8 Cooke, *Wearing of the Gray*, 52.

9 Ibid., 51; Wellman, *Giant in Gray*, 83.

10 Cooke, *Wearing of the Gray*, 48.

11 Ibid., 52.

12 Ibid., 52, 54; Thomas, *Bold Dragoon*, 139, 201–2, 275–76. Heros von Borcke also commented on Hampton's "calm, dignified nature and friendly but very reserved mien" (Von Borcke and Scheibert, *Brandy Station*, 119).

13 Wellman, *Giant in Gray*, 83; Longacre, *Lee's Cavalrymen*, 105.

14 OR 12(3):920.

15 McPherson, *Battle Cry of Freedom*, 524–28; Longacre, *Lee's Cavalrymen*, 106–11, 114–22.

16 McPherson, *Battle Cry of Freedom*, 529–32.

17 OR 12(3):941–42, 944.

18 "Sketches of Hampton's Cavalry," 75–76 (quotation); Hartley, *Stuart's Tarheels*, 121–22; OR 12(2):744–45; Longacre, *Lee's Cavalrymen*, 127.

19 Hartley, *Stuart's Tarheels*, 124; Longacre, *Lee's Cavalrymen*, 128–29; WH to MFH, May 21, 1862, box 2, folder 64a, HFP.

20 Longacre, *Lee's Cavalrymen*, 128–29; Thomas, *Bold Dragoon*, 160–61.

21 Thomas, *Bold Dragoon*, 166–67; Longacre, *Lee's Cavalrymen*, 130; McPherson, *Battle Cry of Freedom*, 536.

22 Thomas, *Bold Dragoon*, 162–66; Wellman, *Giant in Gray*, 89–90; Hartley, *Stuart's Tarheels*, 126–27. Some sources say the ball took place on September 8, others on September 10 (Hartley, *Stuart's Tarheels*, 131; Wellman, *Giant in Gray*, 90). Stuart's official report, of course, did not mention it at all.

23 OR 19(1):822; Hartley, *Stuart's Tarheels*, 127–29; Wellman, *Giant in Gray*, 90–91; Brooks, *Butler and His Cavalry*, 65 (information on Meighan).

24 OR 19(1):822.

25 Ibid.; Brooks, *Butler and His Cavalry*, 64–65.

26 OR 19(1):823.

27 Letter of Oct. 9, 1862, Munnerlyn Letters, SHC.

28 Ibid. Hampton's men did not hold the position long. Five of the horses pulling the Union gun were killed, so the Confederates left it rather than hitch up a new team to pull it.

29 Wellman, *Giant in Gray*, 9; Brooks, *Butler and His Cavalry*, 64–65; "Sketches of Hampton's Cavalry," 82.

30 Thomas, *Bold Dragoon*, 166–67; Hartley, *Stuart's Tarheels*, 130, 132.

31 Wellman, *Giant in Gray*, 92 (quotations), 344 n. 29; *Southern Historical Society Papers*, 25:148; Wells, *Hampton and His Cavalry*, 71–72.

32 Wellman, *Giant in Gray*, 92, 344 n. 29; *Southern Historical Society Papers*, 25:148; Wells, *Hampton and His Cavalry*, 71–72; OR 19(1):816–18, 822–24; Hartley, *Stuart's Tarheels*, 129–33.

33 OR 19(1):826.

34 Hartley, *Stuart's Tarheels*, 135–39; OR 19(1):823–24.

35 Thomas, *Robert E. Lee*, 262.

36 OR 19(1):815–16. In "The Net Result of the Campaign Was in Our Favor," Gallagher reflects on the impact of the Maryland campaign on Confederate morale. He concludes that this campaign was viewed at the time as one of a series of events in which Lee successfully shifted the focus of the eastern theater from Richmond to the Potomac. It had a relatively positive effect on civilian morale and on the confidence of the Army of Northern Virginia.

37 OR 19(1):820–21, 824; Hartley, *Stuart's Tarheels*, 139–40.

38 Blackford, *War Years with Jeb Stuart*, 154; Von Borcke, *Memoirs*, 1:252–53 (quotation, 253).

39 Hartley, *Stuart's Tarheels*, 140–41; OR 19(1):821, 824.

40 Longacre, *Lee's Cavalrymen*, 139–41; Thomas, *Bold Dragoon*, 168–71; Hartley, *Stuart's Tarheels*, 144.

41 WH to MFH, June 3, July 19, 1862, box 3, HFP; WH to MFH, Aug. 11, 1862, box 2, folder 64a, HFP; Ann Fripp Hampton, *Divided Heart*, xiv, 27–119 passim.

42 WH to Hon. George W. Randolph, Aug. 21, 1862, LR-CSW.

43 WH to MFH, Oct. 5, 1862, box 2, folder 64a, HFP.

44 McPherson, *Battle Cry of Freedom*, 493–94, 505–7.

45 Brooks, *Butler and His Cavalry*, 152 (quotation), 89; Wellman, *Giant in Gray*, 85, 108.

46 Hartley, *Stuart's Tarheels*, 145; OR 19(2):52, 55–56; Longacre, *Lee's Cavalrymen*, 142.

47 OR 19(2):52, 55–56; Thomas, *Bold Dragoon*, 173–74; Hartley, *Stuart's Tarheels*, 144–46.

48 The outline of the following events can be found in OR 19(2):51–58. I have also relied on the excellent narratives in Hartley, *Stuart's Tarheels*, 145–57; Longacre, *Lee's Cavalrymen*, 143–50; Thomas, *Bold Dragoon*, 174–80; and Wellman, *Giant in Gray*, 95–98. Another primary source used here is Brooks, *Butler and His Cavalry*, 80–84. For a picture of Federal officers' desperate, confused attempts to catch Stuart, see OR 19(2):59–76.

49 Hartley, *Stuart's Tarheels*, 147.

50 WH to MFH, Oct. 24, 1862, box 3, HFP.

51 OR 19(2):57.

52 Ibid., 52, 57.

53 Ibid.

54 Wellman, *Giant in Gray*, 96–97 (quotation, 96).

55 Longacre, *Lee's Cavalrymen*, 146–47.

56 OR 19(2):51–76; Hartley, *Stuart's Tarheels*, 157; Longacre, *Lee's Cavalrymen*, 150; Thomas, *Bold Dragoon*, 180; Wellman, *Giant in Gray*, 98. Gallagher (*Antietam Campaign*, esp. 15) agrees that the Maryland campaign tended to reinforce the confidence of the Army of Northern Virginia as a whole and that Stuart's October raid further enhanced civilians' overall assessment of Lee's 1862 Maryland campaign. The phrase "better men" appears in Connelly and Bellows, *God and General Longstreet*, 21–28, though I use it a little differently here.

CHAPTER 9

1 WH to MFH, Oct. 24, 1862, box 3, HFP.

2 WH to MFH, Nov. 22, 1862, ibid.

3 WH to MFH, Nov. 24, 1862, ibid. WH to MFH, Nov. 22, 1862.

4 Longacre, *Lee's Cavalrymen*, 157.

5   WH to MFH, Nov. 22, 1862.

6   OR 19(2):143–44; Hartley, *Stuart's Tarheels*, 162.

7   OR 19(2):143–46. The Union version of this fight is in ibid., 126. See also Hartley, *Stuart's Tarheels*, 163–68.

8   OR 19(2):146; Hartley, *Stuart's Tarheels*, 168.

9   OR 21:15–16.

10 OR 21:1051.

11 OR 21:13–16; WH to MFH, Dec. 9, 1862, box 3, HFP (quotation).

12 OR 21:691. See also Hampton's report in ibid., 690–91, and Brooks, *Butler and His Cavalry*, 85–87.

13 McPherson, *Battle Cry of Freedom*, 572.

14 WH to MFH, Dec. 25, 1862, box 3, HFP.

15 Ibid.

16 OR 21:695–96; Freeman, *Lee's Lieutenants*, 2:399.

17 Brooks, *Butler and His Cavalry*, 89.

18 WH to MFH, Jan. 2, 1863, box 3, HFP.

19 Ibid.

20 Ibid.

21 Ibid.

CHAPTER 10

1   WH to J. E. B. Stuart, Nov. 7, 1862, SA 23, Stuart Military Papers, HL.

2   Ibid. (first quotation); Von Borcke and Scheibert, *Brandy Station*, 119–20; Coxe, "Wade Hampton," 460, 462; WH to MFH, Nov. 22, 1862, box 3, HFP (second quotation).

3   WH to MFH, Nov. 24, 1862, box 3, HFP.

4   WH to Louis Wigfall, Jan. 19, 1863, ibid.

5   Freeman, *Lee's Lieutenants*, 2:399–408; Thomas, *Bold Dragoon*, 195–200.

6   The Confederate system in neatly summarized by former Confederate private Edward Wells in Wells, *Hampton and His Cavalry*, 97–99. See also Starr, *Union Cavalry*, 1:130–31, and Ramsdell, "Lee's Horse Supply."

7   WH to MFH, Jan. 22, 1863, box 3, HFP.

8   Hartley, *Stuart's Tarheels*, 183.

9   Ibid.

10 WH to MFH, Jan. 22, 1863; WH to Louis Wigfall, Jan. 19, 1863.

11 Longacre, *Lee's Cavalrymen*, 167–68; OR 25(2):621–22; OR 25(1):795; Freeman and McWhiney, *Lee's Dispatches*, 71–73; WH to Louis Wigfall, Feb. 16, 1863, box 3, HFP.

12 WH to Louis Wigfall, Feb. 16, 1863.

13 WH to MFH, Nov. 22, 1862.

14 WH to Secretary of War James A. Seddon, Apr. 10, 1863, LR-CSW (quotation); WH to P. G. T. Beauregard, Apr. 6, 1863, CSR; OR 14:890; Morrill,

Civil War in the Carolinas, 321–24; Burton, Siege of Charleston, 136–45. The approximate date of Hampton's return to Virginia can be surmised from his May 25 letter to Mary Fisher complaining that he had received no letters, "though it has been more than a month since I left home" (WH to MFH, May 25, 1863, box 2, folder 64a, HFP).

15 Longacre, Lee's Cavalrymen, 169–80.

16 OR 25(2):622.

17 Ibid., 737–38, 740.

18 Ibid.

19 OR 25(2):823; Longacre, Lee's Cavalrymen, 186–87; WH to MFH, May 13, 19, 1863, box 3, HFP.

20 WH to MFH, May 13, 1863.

21 OR 25(2):849–50.

22 Longacre, Lee's Cavalrymen, 187–89; Thomas, Bold Dragoon, 216–20.

CHAPTER 11

1 Longacre, Lee's Cavalry, 190; Thomas, Bold Dragoon, 220.

2 Longacre, Lee's Cavalry, 190; Thomas, Bold Dragoon, 220; Hartley, Stuart's Tarheels, 199–200.

3 OR 27(2):679–80, 721; Longacre, Lee's Cavalry, 190; Hartley, Stuart's Tarheels, 199–200.

4 OR 27(2):721–22, 727–28, 732, 749.

5 Ibid., 721; Hartley, Stuart's Tarheels, 203; Longacre, Lee's Cavalrymen, 193; Thomas, Bold Dragoon, 222. Years later, Butler and McClellan claimed that Butler moved his command to Stevensburg on his own initiative when he heard about the enemy threat there (Brooks, Butler and His Cavalry, 152; McClellan, I Rode with Jeb Stuart, 268). Yet Stuart reported that he gave Butler his orders (OR 27[2]:680). The important point here is that, at least for a time, Hampton may have thought that one of his regiments had again been ordered away without his being informed.

6 Hartley, Stuart's Tarheels, 206.

7 OR 27(2):721–22; McClellan, I Rode with Jeb Stuart, 272–79; Hartley, Stuart's Tarheels, 205–10. H. B. McClellan, who published the most thorough and reliable eyewitness account of the fighting on Fleetwood Hill, believed that "the magnificent order in which [Hampton] advanced to the attack" on Fleetwood "was the sure harbinger of success" (p. 276).

8 OR 27(2):722.

9 Ibid., 722, 682.

10 Ibid., 719, 723.

11 Ibid., 729–31, 743–44; Brooks, Butler and His Cavalry, 132–33, 152.

12 OR 27(2):729.

13 Ibid., 729–31, 743–44; Brooks, Butler and His Cavalry, 132–33, 152–53.

14 OR 27(2):744.

15 Brooks, *Butler and His Cavalry*, 153.

16 *New York Times*, June 27, 1897.

17 Ibid. (quotation); Brooks, *Butler and His Cavalry*, 165–68.

18 Meynard, *The Venturers*, 225, 227–28. Wade's sister Caroline, who had nursed Sally Baxter Hampton on her deathbed, was named the children's official guardian. Franky, 7, and Caroline, 19 months, stayed at Millwood. Georgia Anna, 5, and Lucy, 4, went to live temporarily with their mother's parents in New York. Georgia Anna died in 1865, and Lucy returned to Millwood (ibid., 228).

19 OR 27(2):722.

20 Ibid., 722 (quotation), 719–20; Thomas, *Bold Dragoon*, 225–29, 231; Longacre, *Lee's Cavalrymen*, 195–96. Pleasonton had 10,981 men south of the Rappahannock on the day of the battle but failed to get all of them into action. His losses were 907; Stuart had slightly over 10,000 effectives, and his losses were approximately 500 (OR 27[1]:905–6, OR 27[2]:719, 846). Stuart did not address or allude to Hampton's criticisms in his own report. Instead, he praised the performance of Hampton and his men (OR 27[2]:681–83).

21 The quotation (reworded to put it in the first person) is from Brooks, *Butler and His Cavalry*, 169. See also ibid., 132, 153, which emphasizes that the 4th Virginia "fled," and OR 27(2):729, 731.

22 Longacre, *Lee's Cavalrymen*, 189, 196–97; Hartley, *Stuart's Tarheels*, 219–20.

23 Longacre, *Lee's Cavalrymen*, 197–201.

24 Brooks, *Butler and His Cavalry*, 177.

25 Ibid., 174, 176; Longacre, *Lee's Cavalrymen*, 201.

26 Brooks, *Butler and His Cavalry*, 176–77 (quotations, 177).

27 Ibid., 177.

28 OR 27(2):690–91; Hartley, *Stuart's Tarheels*, 223; McClellan, *I Rode with Jeb Stuart*, 313.

29 McClellan, *I Rode with Jeb Stuart*, 313.

30 Ibid., 311.

31 Ibid.

32 Ibid., 311–12.

33 Longacre, *Lee's Cavalrymen*, 202. In the several days of fighting around Aldie, Middleburg, and Upperville, Stuart's cavalry had lost just over 500 men killed, wounded, and missing. The Federal cavalry and infantry attacking them had suffered over 800 losses. The Upperville fight on June 20 cost the Confederates a total of 180 troopers killed, wounded, or missing; the Federals lost 209 (McClellan, *I Rode with Jeb Stuart*, 314; OR 27[2]:691; OR 27[1]:172).

34 OR 27(2):691.

35 McClellan, *I Rode with Jeb Stuart*, 313.

36 Longacre, *Lee's Cavalrymen*, 203–5.

37 Hartley, *Stuart's Tarheels*, 230–32; Longacre, *Lee's Cavalrymen*, 204–8.

38 Longacre, *Lee's Cavalrymen*, 209–12.

39 Ibid., 207.

40 Ibid.

41 OR 27(2):696.

42 Ibid.

43 Longacre, *Lee's Cavalrymen*, 213.

44 OR 27(2):724.

45 Ibid.; Nye, "Affair at Hunterstown," 29–30; Longacre, *Lee's Cavalrymen*, 214.

46 Mackey, "Hampton's Duel on the Battle-Field," 123.

47 Ibid., 124.

48 Ibid.

49 Ibid.

50 Ibid., 125–26.

51 The primary source for this unlikely story is T. J. Mackey's article, "Hampton's Duel on the Battle-Field." I explain why this source is flawed and why the event itself almost certainly never occurred in the Appendix. For examples of modern historians who have repeated the story, see Wellman, *Giant in Gray*, 115–16; Longacre, *Lee's Cavalrymen*, 214; and Nye, "Affair at Hunterstown," 29–30. Longacre (*Gentleman and Soldier*, 148) unaccountably decreases the range of Hampton's miraculous pistol shot to the slightly more reasonable range of "within a hundred yards," but he cites no evidence that would explain this change.

52 Longacre, *Lee's Cavalrymen*, 215; Nye, "Affair at Hunterstown," 33; OR 27(2):724; OR 27(1):992.

53 Longacre, *Lee's Cavalrymen*, 215.

54 OR 27(2):697, 724; Longacre, *Lee's Cavalrymen*, 216–17.

55 OR 27(2):697–98, 724.

56 Ibid., 724.

57 Stuart's report states that it was Fitz Lee's 1st Virginia, not Chambliss's brigade, that received help from Hampton. Hampton maintained that it was Chambliss's. McClellan's memoir makes it clear that both Fitz Lee's and Chambliss's men were heavily engaged when Hampton's troops arrived on the scene. See the conflicting reports in ibid., 698, 724–25, and McClellan, *I Rode with Stuart*, 340.

58 OR 27(2):725.

59 Ibid.

60 Wittenberg, *Protecting the Flank*, 96.

61 "Sketches of Hampton's Cavalry," 175.

62 Ibid.

63 Ibid.

64 There are two original accounts of Hampton's role in this melee. One is by Edward Wells, a postwar friend of Hampton's who served under him from 1864 to 1865. Wells was not at Gettysburg, but he spoke and corresponded often with Hampton while writing Hampton and His Cavalry in '64. This was the first biography of Wade Hampton, but it was written in 1899, thirty-six years after the battle. The other version, "Sketches of Hampton's Cavalry," is an anonymous account written in 1864. Internal evidence indicates that the author was almost certainly a member of the 1st North Carolina. It is written in dramatic, romantic prose, but gives such a thorough, detailed rendering of Hampton's fight at Gettysburg that it reads like an eyewitness report. I have attempted to write an account that is a likely combination of the two primary sources. Though the anonymous eyewitness account is more detailed, certain details from Wells's story, like the misfiring pistol, surely came from Hampton's memory. Wells is also the one who insists on the truth of Hampton's saber cleaving through a Federal's skull (Wells, Hampton and His Cavalry, 75; "Sketches of Hampton's Cavalry," 175–77). According to "Sketches," Hampton's hip wound was from a pistol ball, though Hampton himself usually referred to it as a piece of shrapnel (see Wellman, Giant in Gray, 347 n. 31). The other advantage of the anonymous version in "Sketches" is that it accounts for both of Hampton's saber wounds at Gettysburg without mentioning the fantastic legend of the encounter with the Yankee lieutenant at Huntersville. After the war, Hampton replied to an inquiry from Wells in a letter that stated: "I was wounded at 1st Mannasas [sic]; at Seven Pines, & three times at Gettysburg, two saber cuts, & one shrapnell [sic] (WH to Edward L. Wells, June 17, 1898, Wells Correspondence, CLS).

65 OR 27(2):698, 322.

66 Thomas, Bold Dragoon, 300.

67 OR 27(2):312; Hartley, Stuart's Tarheels, 252–53, Brooks, Butler and His Cavalry, 171.

CHAPTER 12

1 Cisco, Wade Hampton, 121; Charleston Daily Courier, Oct. 10, 1866; Surgeon's Note, July 20, 1863, CSR; WH to Louis Wigfall, July 15, 1863, box 2, Wigfall Papers, LOC.

2 WH to MFH, July 16, 1863, box 3, HFP.

3 Ibid.

4 WH to Louis Wigfall, July 15, 1863.

5 Chesnut, Mary Boykin Chesnut's Civil War, 484.

6 Ibid., 452.

7 Meynard, *The Venturers*, 75.

8 MFH to [illegible addressee], Aug. 12, 186[1], box 3, HFP. See also Moffett, *Letters of General James Conner*, 28, 45, 78.

9 WH to MFH, Sept. 10, 1864, box 3, HFP.

10 WH to MFH, June 3, 1862.

11 Wells, *Hampton and Reconstruction*, 40.

12 Ibid.

13 WH to Louis Wigfall, Dec. 31, 1863, Wigfall Papers, LOC.

14 Meynard, *The Venturers*, 219, 225–28.

15 Ibid., 226.

16 Passport to Mississippi for Colonel C. F. Hampton, Dec. 24, 1864, roll 130, LR-CSW.

17 Meynard, *The Venturers*, 226; WH to MFH, Jan. 1, 12, 31, 1866, box 3, HFP. By December 1863 enemy units, including two black regiments, were posted at Skipwith's Landing on the Mississippi, from which Hampton had always shipped his cotton. With his pro-Union neighbor and former friend Stephen Duncan there, Hampton suspected that the Yankees were using local slaves to gain information. He wrote Mary Fisher that "if Genl. Johnston will give me a few good cavalry, I think I could break up the party at Skipwiths. Duncan should be sent away, for I regard him as a contemptible traitor. No negroes should be left near the river as they act as spies for the Yankees" (WH to MFH, Jan. 14, 1864, box 3, HFP).

18 Kate Hampton to "Dear Uncle Manning," Jan. 3, 1864, box 6, folder 181, Williams-Chesnut-Manning Families, SCL.

19 WH to MFH, Feb. 16, 1863, box 3, HFP.

20 Chesnut, *Mary Boykin Chesnut's Civil War*, 330.

21 Ibid., 459.

22 WH to MFH, Jan. 5, 1864, box 3, HFP.

23 WH to MFH, Sept. 10, 1864, ibid.

24 WH to MFH, Sept. 10, 1864; Dec. 8, 22, 1863; Jan. 5, Feb. 15, Aug. 20, 1864—all in ibid. On July 30, 1864, Confederate cavalry led by Jubal Early had advanced to Chambersburg, Pa., and burned the town when the local authorities refused to surrender. Many Confederate troopers (most of whom had never served under Hampton) pillaged and robbed the citizens. Hampton's September 10 letter complained: "Some of our troops, when last there, behaved in the most shameful manner to our friends, stealing their stock & in some cases even taking the jewelry from ladies who had brothers in our service. This was done by some of these rascally cavalry of the Mountains, who prefer stealing to fighting" (WH to MFH, Sept. 10, 1864).

25 WH to MFH, Nov. 29, 1863, ibid.

CHAPTER 13

1 Longacre, *Lee's Cavalrymen*, 241–44.
2 Hartley, *Stuart's Tarheels*, 301; WH to MFH, Nov. 12, 1863, box 2, folder 64a, HFP.
3 WH to MFH, Nov. 20, 1863, box 3, HFP (quotation); Hartley, *Stuart's Tarheels*, 302.
4 WH to MFH, Nov. 20, 29, 1863, box 3, HFP.
5 WH to MFH, Nov. 20, 1863, ibid.
6 WH to MFH, Dec. 8, 1863.
7 Hartley, *Stuart's Tarheels*, 305; Freeman, *Lee's Lieutenants*, 3:269; Thomas, *Bold Dragoon*, 275.
8 OR 29(1):899.
9 Ibid., 901–2.
10 Ibid., 899.
11 Ibid., 902.
12 Ibid.
13 Ibid., 899–900, 902 (details of battle); WH to MFH, Nov. 29, 1863, box 3, HFP (quotation). Freeman (*Lee's Lieutenants*, 3:278–79) and Thomas (*Bold Dragoon*, 275–76) have also faulted Stuart on his micromanagement of Hampton's division during the Mine Run campaign.
14 CSR.
15 Haskell, *Haskell Memoirs*, 26–27.
16 Meynard, *The Venturers*, 230; Haskell, *Haskell Memoirs*, xi.
17 Petition of Officers of the Jeff Davis Legion, Jan. 31, 1864, folder 2, Waring Papers, SHC.
18 Thomas, *Bold Dragoon*, 271; OR 29(2):664–65; Longacre, *Lee's Cavalrymen*, 267; Black, *Crumbling Defenses*, 70.
19 WH to MFH, Jan. 14, 1864, box 3, HFP; OR 29(2):862–63.
20 WH to Louis Wigfall, Dec. 31, 1863, Wigfall Papers, LOC.
21 Hampton's War Reminiscences, 19, HFP (written for Robert E. Lee in 1866–67; page numbers from the typescript version); Longacre, *Lee's Cavalrymen*, 266–67; WH to MFH, Jan. 5, 14, 1864. Hampton also complained to Senator Wigfall (WH to Louis Wigfall, Dec. 31, 1863).
22 Hampton's War Reminiscences, 9–10.
23 OR 33:1154.
24 Ibid.
25 Ibid. See evidence of Lee's earlier efforts to have cavalry transferred to Virginia in OR 33:1117–18.
26 Dowdey and Manarin, *Wartime Papers of R. E. Lee*, 673.
27 OR 32(2):632.
28 Ibid., 632, 681–82.
29 OR 33:1118.

30 WH to MFH, Dec. 22, 1863, Jan. 5, 1864, box 3, HFP.

31 OR 33:19, 103, 559, 606.

32 Hampton's War Reminiscences, 20–21; Longacre, *Lee's Cavalrymen*, 270; V. C. Jones, *Eight Hours before Richmond*, 27, 46, 50; OR 33:182–83.

33 Hampton's War Reminiscences, 21–22; Wells, *Hampton and His Cavalry*, 112–14; Longacre, *Lee's Cavalrymen*, 270–71; V. C. Jones, *Eight Hours before Richmond*, 67–69; WH to Edward Wells, May 10, 1898, Wells Correspondence, CLS. I have deduced Hampton's tactical thinking prior to this raid from his instructions to his men, and from Wells's insistence that Hampton's raid "was not done in a spirit of wild adventure or daredevil recklessness, but, on the contrary, was sagaciously planned and coolly executed, as the best available means for driving off the raid from Richmond" (Wells, *Hampton and His Cavalry*, 123). Wells's main source for his biography of Hampton was Hampton himself—it was an "authorized biography." Wells's (and probably Hampton's) claims of Hampton's prudence correspond with Hampton's tactical style throughout most of the war.

34 V. C. Jones, *Eight Hours before Richmond*, 100; see also 86–91, 96–97.

35 OR 35(2):362, 365, 402–3; OR 33:1231–32.

36 OR 51(2):835–37. The details of the cavalry exchange were hashed out in a long memo from Adjutant and Inspector General Samuel Cooper to his assistant adjutant general on March 14.

37 OR 33:1229–30 (quotation); Hampton's War Reminiscences, 28.

38 Chesnut, *Mary Chesnut's Civil War*, 588.

39 Ibid. Chesnut wrote in her diary that Hampton was angry over Stuart taking "one of Hampton's brigades and [giving] it to Fitz Lee." There is no other indication that this was the case, though it is quite possible it was discussed, as the organization of the cavalry corps was in flux in the spring of 1864.

40 As late as July 26, 1864, Chesnut wrote in her diary of Hampton's "tiff with General Lee," though the two men were clearly moving toward a reconciliation by mid-June (ibid., 625; see also 602).

CHAPTER 14

1 Hampton used the phrase "good spirits" in letters of January 14 and February 14, 1864, and described troop morale positively in his letter of January 29 (WH to MFH, Jan. 14, 29, Feb. 14, 1864, box 3, HFP).

2 The general sense of optimism pervading Lee's Army of Northern Virginia in the spring of 1864 is clear in Power, *Lee's Miserables*, esp. 1–80.

3 WH to MFH, Feb. 28, 1864, box 2, folder 64a, HFP.

4 WH to Mrs. Singleton, Apr. 24, 1864, box 3, HFP.

5 Ibid.

6 WH to MFH, May 6, 1864, box 3, HFP.

7 Wells, *Hampton and His Cavalry*, 125–26; Hampton's War Reminiscences, 29–30, HFP; OR 36(2):953; Longacre, *Lee's Cavalrymen*, 273. Gordon's other regiment, the 5th North Carolina, had not yet returned from recruiting in its home state. For more evidence of Hampton's disgust, see J. Fred Waring Diary, May 2, 1864, Waring Papers, SHC.

8 For a modern, critical appraisal of Sheridan, see Wittenberg, *Little Phil.*

9 Hampton's War Reminiscences, 11–12; Wells, *Hampton and His Cavalry*, 136; Rhea, *Spotsylvania*, 30–37.

10 Thomas, *Bold Dragoon*, 293 (quotations); Wells, *Hampton and His Cavalry*, 137; Longacre, *Lee's Cavalrymen*, 283–88; Rhea, *Spotsylvania*, 96–97; Thomas, *Bold Dragoon*, 288–95.

11 Thomas, *Bold Dragoon*, 297.

12 Longacre, *Lee's Cavalrymen*, 288.

13 Hampton's War Reminiscences, General Order No. 6, 34.

14 Ibid., 35.

15 Ibid., 33.

16 See Hampton's War Reminiscences, 36.

17 Wells, *Hampton and His Cavalry*, 137. See also ibid., 152–54; Hampton's War Reminiscences, 36–37; OR 36(3):816; OR 51(2):956; and Longacre, *Lee's Cavalrymen*, 292.

18 Emerson, *Sons of Privilege*, 64–66; Rhea, "The Hottest Place," 44–45.

19 Rhea, "The Hottest Place," 45–46.

20 Hampton's War Reminiscences, 38; Wells, *Hampton and His Cavalry*, 157; Rhea, "The Hottest Place," 44–46, 49–50.

21 Rhea, "The Hottest Place," 47.

22 Ibid., 51–52.

23 Ibid.; Hampton's War Reminiscences, 38.

24 Hampton's War Reminiscences, 38; Rhea, "The Hottest Place," 52.

25 Hampton's War Reminiscences, 39.

26 Ibid., 38.

27 Wells, *Hampton and His Cavalry*, 158; Rhea, "The Hottest Place," 52.

28 Quoted from Wells (*Hampton and His Cavalry*, 160), who was a member of the 4th South Carolina.

29 Hampton's War Reminiscences, 38–39; "The Battle of Haw's Shop, Va.," *Confederate Veteran* 33 (1925): 373–76; Rhea, "The Hottest Place," 53–54; Emerson, *Sons of Privilege*, 71–77; McDaniel, *Confederate War Correspondence*, 245 (quotation).

30 Rhea, "The Hottest Place," 55.

31 Rhea astutely points out some of these errors (ibid., 45, 55–56). He also seems to think that it was a mistake to withdraw the Confederate brigades "seriatim, rendering the entire Confederate line untenable" (p. 56). But that was precisely the tactic that Hampton had implemented so well at

Brandy Station, Upperville, and elsewhere. It had proved to be the best way for cavalry to disengage. Rhea also faults Hampton for accepting Rooney Lee's unnecessary request to withdraw. Hampton, though, could not have expected an experienced officer like Lee to mistake cavalry for infantry. Accepting that Rooney's assessment must be correct, his choice to withdraw was the right one, since now Hampton had found, he thought, the information he was looking for—the location of Grant's infantry. The presence of infantry columns would have made it foolish to stand and fight, especially since Early had already refused to help Hampton. Rhea is undoubtedly correct in stating that Haw's Shop was a "learning experience" for Hampton and that the future would show that "he learned well" (p. 56). Rhea's excellent account of the Battle of Haw's Shop is also found in Rhea, *Cold Harbor*, 63–89.

32 Longacre, *Lee's Cavalrymen*, 296 (quotation); Wells, *Hampton and His Cavalry*, 170–74; Hampton's War Reminiscences, 38–42; OR 36(3):362; OR 51(2):970, 977.

33 Rhea, *Cold Harbor*, 382.

34 Ibid., 12, 382.

35 Longacre, *Lee's Cavalrymen*, 296–97.

36 Ibid., 297.

37 Longacre (*Lee's Cavalrymen*, 294–95, 297 [quotation]) and Rhea ("The Hottest Place," 56) both mention Hampton's emerging generalship and his men's confidence in him at this stage. For other astute comments on Hampton's tactics, see Wells, *Hampton and His Cavalry*, 149–50.

CHAPTER 15

1 Wittenberg, *Glory Enough for All*, 21; McPherson, *Battle Cry of Freedom*, 737.

2 OR 37(1):754; OR 36(1):1095.

3 Wittenberg, *Glory Enough for All*, 21–23; OR 37(1):753; OR 36(1):1034, 1095. After the war, Sheridan wrote: "There also *appeared* [emphasis added] to be another object, viz, to remove the enemy's cavalry from the south side of the Chickahominy, as, in case we attempted to cross to the James River, this large cavalry force could make such resistance at the difficult crossings as to give the enemy time to transfer his force to oppose the movement" (OR 36[1]:795). Eric J. Wittenberg (*Glory Enough for All*, 23, 34 n. 91) suggests astutely that this was "twenty-twenty hindsight" on Sheridan's part.

4 Hampton's War Reminiscences, 42–43, HFP; Freeman, *Lee's Lieutenants*, 3:516–17.

5 Wittenberg, *Glory Enough for All*, 45.

6 Ibid. See also pp. 25, 44.

7 Brooks, *Butler and His Cavalry*, 238; OR 51(2):1003.

8 OR 36(1):1095; Wittenberg, *Glory Enough for All*, 49, 52, 54.

9 OR 36(1):1095; Wittenberg, *Glory Enough for All*, 61.

10 Brooks, *Butler and His Cavalry*, 239–40.

11 OR 36(1):1095.

12 Wittenberg, *Glory Enough for All*, 97; OR 36(1):1095; Butler, "Trevilian Station," 237.

13 Wittenberg, *Glory Enough for All*, 56, 59.

14 Brooks, *Butler and His Cavalry*, 243.

15 Wittenberg, *Glory Enough for All*, 72–75, 79, 84–86.

16 Ibid., 97–101.

17 Ibid., 101.

18 Wittenberg, *Glory Enough for All*, 105, 108, 110 (quotation). As Private Hayes passed through a group of captured Federals, the Michiganers resorted to an increasingly frequent means of taunting the underfed Rebels: "Buddie, won't you have some chicken?" The furious Georgian replied, "You God damned blue-bellied son of a bitch, I wouldn't have anything you've got!" (p. 10).

19 Ibid., 118.

20 Ibid., 97.

21 Ibid., 112–14, 118; Brooks, *Butler and His Cavalry*, 245.

22 Wittenberg, *Glory Enough for All*, 125, 138, 142, 154.

23 Brooks, *Butler and His Cavalry*, 245.

24 Ibid., 195; Gary R. Baker, *Cadets in Gray*, 100–101; Andrew, *Long Gray Lines*, 28; Wittenberg, *Glory Enough for All*, 142, 145.

25 Wells, *Hampton and His Cavalry*, 200; Wittenberg, *Glory Enough for All*, 142, 155.

26 Myers, *The Comanches*, 301 (quotation); Wittenberg, *Glory Enough for All*, 177–78, 157–58.

27 Longacre, *Lee's Cavalrymen*, 300.

28 OR 36(2):1097.

29 WH to Edward L. Wells, Jan. 18, 1900, Wells Papers, SCHS.

30 WH to Edward L. Wells, Feb. 22, 1900, Wells Correspondence, CLS.

31 Wittenberg, *Glory Enough for All*, 174.

32 Ibid., 173–74, 233; Wells, *Hampton and His Cavalry*, 201–2.

33 Wittenberg, *Glory Enough for All*, 176.

34 Ibid., 195, 199, 200.

35 OR 36(1):1096.

36 Wittenberg, *Glory Enough for All*, 203–4.

37 Ibid., 203.

38 Ibid., 204, 213 n. 93.

39 Wells, *Hampton and His Cavalry*, 212.

40 OR 36(1):785, 1096.

41 Wittenberg, *Glory Enough for All*, 342, 344. Sheridan lost a total of 955 killed, wounded, and captured at Trevilian Station; Hampton lost 813.

42 Ibid., 315.

43 Ibid., 204, 206.

44 Myers, *The Comanches*, 291.

CHAPTER 16

1 Wittenberg, *Glory Enough for All*, 220–23; OR 36(1):1096.

2 OR 51(2):1013–14; WH to MFH, June 14, 1864, Wade Hampton Family Papers, LOC.

3 Longacre, *Lee's Cavalrymen*, 304; Wittenberg, *Glory Enough for All*, 239–42.

4 WH to Braxton Bragg, June 20, 1864, folder 2, WH Correspondence, PL.

5 McPherson, *Battle Cry of Freedom*, 737, 739–40.

6 OR 36(3):901.

7 WH to Braxton Bragg, June 20, 1864.

8 Wittenberg, *Glory Enough for All*, 233.

9 Ibid., 249–59.

10 Ibid., 259, 264–65; OR 36(1):1097.

11 Wittenberg, *Glory Enough for All*, 280.

12 Ibid., 287.

13 OR 36(3):903; Wittenberg, *Glory Enough for All*, 263–83. Wittenberg notes that Hampton's report of the loss in his own division, even excluding Fitz's division and the brigades of Gary and Chambliss, is undoubtedly low. He surmises that by combining reports of losses in individual brigades from various Richmond newspapers, one can assert that Hampton's losses were closer to 200. I consider this method unreliable as well. Civil War newspapers rarely published accurate reports from the battlefield (ibid., 285, 298–99 n. 21).

14 Wittenberg, *Glory Enough for All*, 319–22.

15 Ibid., 309.

16 James B. Ligon to Mother, June 30, 1864, Ligon Papers, SCL. Gary's brigade, to which Ligon and the Hampton Legion belonged, was the only cavalry unit left north of the James by June 30.

17 OR 36(3):903. For examples of Confederate cavalrymen exulting in their victory over Sheridan, see Wittenberg, *Glory Enough for All*, 307–9, 321.

18 Wells, *Hampton and His Cavalry*, 231–35; OR 40(1):620–21.

19 Hampton's War Reminiscences, 55, HFP.

20 Ibid., 56.

21 Wells, *Hampton and His Cavalry*, 236–43; OR 40(1):752; Hampton's War Reminiscences, 57–60. Hampton's report is found in both his Reminiscences and OR 40(1):807–10. For the capture of the Union detachment, see Wells's memorandum of his conversation with Hampton, May 9, 1899, Wells Correspondence, CLS.

22 OR 40(1):809.

23 Hampton's War Reminiscences, 58–59; Wellman, *Giant in Gray*, 151.

24 The figures for Federal losses come from Hampton's Reminiscences and are roughly consistent with the report of Wilson, who estimated his loss at "about 900" killed, wounded, and missing. Wilson said that he lost 16 guns rather than 12, however, reflecting the fact that some of the guns were spiked and sunk in a marsh and the Confederates did not recover them (OR 40[1]:624). Robert E. Lee gave different figures in his report to Richmond (ibid., 752).

25 WH to MFH, July 4, 1864, box 3, HFP.

26 Ibid.

27 Hampton's War Reminiscences, 62; Wells, *Hampton and His Cavalry*, 245–46.

28 WH to MFH, June 14, 1864, Wade Hampton Family Papers, LOC.

29 Ibid.

30 The evidence of this personal meeting between Lee and Hampton is circumstantial, but the discussion almost certainly took place. On June 25 Lee concluded his congratulatory letter to Hampton with the request that he "join" Lee as soon as Sheridan crossed to the south side of the James (OR 36[3]:903). The two had not had a chance to speak face-to-face since Hampton had departed for Trevilian over two weeks before, and Lee now wanted him to coordinate the cavalry's response to Union activity south of the James.

31 Freeman, *Lee's Dispatches*, 268–69.

32 OR 42(2):1171.

33 Ibid.; Longacre, *Lee's Cavalrymen*, 310, 323; WH to Samuel Cooper, Adjutant and Inspector General, July 18, 1864, box 3, HFP; OR 42(2):1195.

CHAPTER 17

1 WH to MFH, Aug. 30, 1864, box 3, HFP.

2 J. Fred Waring Diary, July 7, June 15, 1864, Waring Papers, SHC.

3 Christian D. Owens to Cousin John, July 23, 1864, Owens Letters, SCHS.

4 WH to MFH, Aug. 20, 1864, box 2, folder 64a, HFP.

5 McPherson, *Battle Cry of Freedom* 768 (quotation); see also 750, 756, 760, 762, 766–69.

6 WH to MFH, July 22, 1864, box 2, folder 64a, HFP.

7 Ibid. (quotation); Wells, *Hampton and His Cavalry*, 247, 250; Hampton's War Reminiscences, 61, HFP; Longacre, *Lee's Cavalrymen*, 308.

8 WH to MFH, Aug. 7, 1864, box 2, folder 64a, HFP.

9 OR 42(2):1170–72, 1176–77; Hampton's War Reminiscences, 66–67; Power, *Lee's Miserables*, 143–44; Longacre, *Lee's Cavalrymen*, 309.

10 Hampton's War Reminiscences, 67.

11 Ibid., 67–69 (quotation, 69); Wells, *Hampton and His Cavalry*, 272–74; OR 51(1):1035–36.

12 OR 42(2):1202; Longacre, *Lee's Cavalrymen*, 323; Hampton's War Reminiscences, 70–71; Wells, *Hampton and His Cavalry*, 276–78.

13 Wells, *Hampton and His Cavalry*, 283 (quotation), 277–85; OR 42(1):940, 942–44; Brooks, *Butler and His Cavalry*, 304.

14 OR 42(1):228, 944; Wells, *Hampton and His Cavalry*, 282–83; Hampton's War Reminiscences, 75; Dowdey and Manarin, *Wartime Papers of R. E. Lee*, 845.

15 WH to MFH, Aug. 30, 1864, box 3, HFP.

16 Ibid. (quotations); Power, *Lee's Miserables*, 192–93; Dowdey and Manarin, *Wartime Papers of R. E. Lee*, 845.

17 Hampton's War Reminiscences, 85–86; Cardwell, "A Brilliant Coup," 148.

18 Hampton's War Reminiscences, 78 (Hampton's account here is identical to his report in OR 42[1]:944–47).

19 Hampton's War Reminiscences, 78; Cardwell, "A Brilliant Coup," 150.

20 Hampton's War Reminiscences, 78–79; Wells, *Hampton and His Cavalry*, 90–91; Cardwell, "A Brilliant Coup," 150.

21 Hampton's War Reminiscences, 79–81; Wells, *Hampton and His Cavalry*, 293, 296, 299.

22 Cardwell, "A Brilliant Coup," 153; Brooks, *Butler and His Cavalry*, 321. Union message traffic and reports of the Beefsteak Raid can be found in OR 42(1):26–30, 614–15, 821–25, and OR 42)(2):852–80 passim.

23 Hampton's War Reminiscences, 81. See also Boykin, *Beefsteak Raid*. Though full of factual detail and entertaining, Boykin's account invents so much dialogue that it approaches being a work of fiction.

24 WH to MFH, Oct. 5, 11, 1864, box 2, folder 64a, HFP.

25 Ibid., Oct. 5, 1864; Hampton's War Reminiscences, 36, 40; Brooks, *Butler and His Cavalry*, 351; Wells, *Hampton and His Cavalry*, 321–22; Haskell, *Haskell Memoirs*, xii; Alexander, *Fighting for the Confederacy*, 472, 484; Daly, *Alexander Cheves Haskell*, 150–51.

CHAPTER 18

1 OR 42(2):874, 879; Hampton's War Reminiscences, 93, HFP.

2 Wells, *Hampton and His Cavalry*, 318–21; Hampton's War Reminiscences, 88–91; OR 42(1):947–48.

3 Hampton's War Reminiscences, 89.

4 Ibid.

5 WH to MFH, Oct. 11, 1864, box 3, HFP.

6 WH to MFH, Oct. 16, 1864, ibid.

7 Ibid.

8 Wells, *Hampton and His Cavalry*, 355 (WH to Lee, 352–54).

9 Hampton's War Reminiscences, 95–97, 99–100; Wells, *Hampton and His Cavalry*, 326–36; OR 42:949.

10 Brooks, *Butler and His Cavalry*, 358.

11 Ibid., 359.

12 Ibid., 354.

13 Ibid., 352–54, 358–59; Wells, *Hampton and His Cavalry*, 345–46; Chesnut, *Mary Chesnut's Civil War*, 665; Wells, *Hampton and Reconstruction*, 59). The numerous accounts of Preston's death are remarkably consistent. The fight at Burgess's Mill, or Boydton Plank Road as it was often known, was a Confederate victory at the tactical level, since the Federals withdrew and made no further attempt to cut the railroad until the following spring (Wells, *Hampton and His Cavalry*, 334–35; Brooks, *Butler and His Cavalry*, 354; Power, *Lee's Miserables*, 211).

14 Brooks, *Butler and His Cavalry*, 359.

15 Ibid., 354, 359; Cisco, *Wade Hampton*, 146.

16 Chesnut, *Mary Chesnut's Civil War*, 665.

17 Ibid., 666.

18 Zimmerman Davis added: "It was an ennobling and inspiring sight, to see this grand hero, with the kiss from the lips of his dead son still warm upon his own, while the other son was being borne from the field severely wounded, thus subordinating parental affection to duty to his country" (Brooks, *Butler and His Cavalry*, 354).

19 WH to MFH, Nov. 14, 1864, box 2, folder 64a, HFP. There are no extant letters written by Hampton in the Hampton Family Papers between Oct. 16 and Nov. 14, an unusually large gap.

20 OR 42(1):949 (quotation); Hampton's War Reminiscences, 101.

21 WH to MFH, Nov. 14, 1864.

22 WH to MFH, Nov. 21, 1864, box 3, HFP.

23 Chesnut, *Mary Chesnut's Civil War*, 665.

24 Braxton Bragg to WH, Nov. 2, 1864, box 3, HFP; Meynard, *The Venturers*, 236; WH to MFH, Nov. 20, 1864, box 2, folder 64a, HFP.

25 Chesnut, *Mary Chesnut's Civil War*, 666.

26 Faust, *Mothers of Invention*, 78.

27 WH to MFH, Nov. 14, 1864, box 2, folder 64a, HFP.

28 Ibid.

29 WH to MFH, Dec. 18, 1864, ibid. See also WH to MFH, Dec. 14, 1864, and WH to MFH, Nov. 17, 1864, box 3, HFP.

30 WH to MFH, Nov. 20, 1864.

31 WH to MFH, Jan. 10, 1865, box 2, folder 64a, HFP. See also WH to MFH, Dec. 14, 1864.

32 WH to MFH, Jan. 1[?], 1865, box 3, HFP.

33 For comments on the "plantation myth" of elite southern women, see Clinton, *Tara Revisited* and *Plantation Mistress*.

34 Blight, *Race and Reunion*, 282; Clinton, *Tara Revisited*, 19.

35 Hampton's War Reminiscences, 103–4.

36 Ibid., 104; WH to REL, July 21, Nov. 11, 1866, box 3, HFP; copy of REL to P. G. T. Beauregard, July 31, 1865, forwarded to Hampton, ibid.

37 Hampton's War Reminiscences, 104.

38 Ibid.

39 Ibid., 105.

40 Clipping of obituary, n.d., box 3, HFP. The verse is paraphrased from English poet Thomas Babington, Lord Macaulay (1800–1859), *Lays of Ancient Rome*.

41 Osterweis, *Romanticism and Nationalism in the Old South*.

CHAPTER 19

1   OR 42(2):1173–75; Thomas, *Bold Dragoon*, 110; Von Borcke, *Memoirs*, 2:297–302.

2   In computing these numbers, Hampton included Butler's and Rooney Lee's divisions, as well as Dearing's and Rosser's brigades. Rosser's brigade was with him in August but spent much of the rest of the year fighting in the Shenandoah Valley (Hampton's War Reminiscences, 119–20).

3   Ibid., 119; OR 42(1):854–55, 950–52.

4   Company D Records, 5th South Carolina Cavalry, SCDAH.

5   Ibid.

6   OR 43(2):926.

7   See Hampton's War Reminiscences, 120–26, HFP; OR 46(2):1028; and WH to Jefferson Davis, Dec. 18, 1864, box 3, HFP.

8   Barrett, *Sherman's March*, 40 (quotation); McPherson, *Battle Cry of Freedom*, 808–15.

9   WH to MFH, Jan. 10, 1865, box 2, folder 64a, HFP.

10 WH to MFH, Jan. 10, 1865, and Mar. 9, 1864, ibid. Hampton believed the charges against Dahlgren (see WH to REL, July 21, 1866, box 3, HFP).

11 J. Fred Waring Diary, June 15, 1864, Waring Papers, SHC. In this entry Lieutenant Colonel Waring was actually writing about Union general Hunter's destruction of the Shenandoah Valley, but about the same time he also wrote contemptuously of Sheridan's destruction in Hampton's theater (see ibid., June 16, 26, 1864).

12 Wittenberg, *Glory Enough for All*, 226; OR 42(1):445–46; Longacre, *Gentleman and Soldier*, 221. Both Stephen V. Ash (*When the Yankees Came*, 24–67) and Mark Grimsley (*Hard Hand of War*) trace the growing harshness of Federal policy toward southern civilians. For Grimsley's treatment of McClellan's policy in The Peninsula campaign, see 56, 71–73.

13 Chesnut, *Mary Boykin Chesnut's Civil War*, 678.

14 Ibid., Longacre, *Gentleman and Soldier*, 221; Anderson, *Blood Image*.

15 Longacre, *Gentleman and Soldier*, 222.

16 WH to Daisy Hampton, Jan. 4, 1865, box 3, HFP.

17 OR 46(2):1003–4 (quotation), 1100–1101; Hampton's War Reminiscences, 113–14; REL to Jefferson Davis, Jan. 15, 1865, in Dowdey and Manarin, *Wartime Papers of R. E. Lee*, 881–82.

18 WH to MFH, Jan. 18, 1865, box 3, HFP.

19 WH to Louis Wigfall, Jan. 20, 1865, Wigfall Papers, LOC.

20 Marion Lucas places Hampton's arrival in the state on January 28, though he may have had a personal conference with Governor Andrew Magrath in Columbia on January 27 (Lucas, *Sherman and the Burning of Columbia*, 41 n. 66; A. G. Magrath to Brigadier General Lawton[?], Quartermaster General, Richmond, Jan. 27, 1865, Magrath Papers, 1861–65, SCHS).

21 WH, "Battle of Bentonville," *The Century*, 941.

22 Barrett, *Sherman's March*, 48–49; Lucas, *Sherman and the Burning of Columbia*, 42. Mark Bradley (*Last Stand in the Carolinas*, 21–22) estimates that Beauregard had 17,000 effective troops on February 2. By February 25, he had over 24,000.

23 Wittenberg, *An Infernal Surprise*, chap. 7, p. 7.

24 OR 47(2):1054, 1157; WH to William Porcher Miles, Jan. 21, 1865, Miles Papers, SHC; WH to Louis Wigfall, Jan. 20, 1865, Wigfall Papers, LOC.

25 OR 47(2):1165.

26 The Compiled Service Records give Hampton's date of rank as February 14, but Davis wrote to Hampton on the sixteenth to tell him that the Senate confirmed his promotion "yesterday" (CSR; OR 47[2]:1204, 1207).

27 Wellman, *Giant in Gray*, 167; WH, "Battle of Bentonville," in *Battles and Leaders*, 4:700–701; OR 47(2):1186; WH, "Battle of Bentonville," *The Century*, 940; Lucas, *Sherman and the Burning of Columbia*, 42–46; Longacre, *Gentleman and Soldier*, 225–26.

28 Barrett, *Sherman's March*, 56.

29 Grimsley, *Hard Hand of War*, 201–3 (quotation, 203). See also Barrett, *Sherman's March*, 52–56, and Ash, *When the Yankees Came*, 56.

30 OR 47(2):1198. Beauregard wrote these words to Hampton's subordinate Major General Stevenson, informing him that he had given these same instructions verbally to Hampton an hour before.

31 OR 47(2):1186, 1199.

32 Lucas, *Sherman and the Burning of Columbia*, 39–40; Longacre, *Gentleman and Soldier*, 226; Meynard, *The Venturers*, 238; Chesnut, *Mary Chesnut's Civil War*, 715.

33 Lucas, *Sherman and the Burning of Columbia*, 51–53, 55–64.

34 OR 47(2):1178; Longacre, *Gentleman and Soldier*, 226.

35 OR 47(2):1199.

36 Ibid.; Lucas, *Sherman and the Burning of Columbia*, 47.

37 Lucas, *Sherman and the Burning of Columbia*, 67–69; Chesnut, *Mary Chesnut's Civil War*, 773 (quotations).

38 Lucas, *Sherman and the Burning of Columbia*, 70–71; WH, "Who Burned Columbia? Gen. Wade Hampton Tells the Story."

39 Lucas, *Sherman and the Burning of Columbia*, 93.

40 Ibid., 83–118, 128–62.

CHAPTER 20

1 WH to MFH, Mar. 30, 1865, box 2, folder 64a, HFP.

2 Ibid.

3 OR 47(2):1219.

4 Ibid., 1247.

5 Johnston, *Narrative*, 372 (quotations); Longacre, *Gentleman and Soldier*, 231; Barrett, *Sherman's March*, 112–13; Chesnut, *Mary Chesnut's Civil War*, 711.

6 Johnston, *Narrative*, 377.

7 Wells, "A Morning Call on Kilpatrick," *SHS Papers* 12 (1884): 124.

8 For a snapshot of Hampton's activities over the next few weeks, see his flurry of messages to Beauregard between Feb. 20 and 22 from Winns- boro, Chester, Blackstock, and Chester again in box 3, HFP; also OR 47(2):1224–1447 passim; OR 47(1):1111–15.

9 Barrett, *Sherman's March*, 102–4, 108–12.

10 OR 47(1):860.

11 OR 47(2):546.

12 Ibid., 597.

13 Ibid.

14 Ibid., 1300.

15 Brooks, *Butler and His Cavalry*, 450.

16 Martin, *Kill-Cavalry*, 11–12, 16, 35–36, 49, 57, 61–62, 145, and passim; Barrett, *Sherman's March*, 32, 52, 97, 128, 136; Starr, *Union Cavalry*, 1:417– 18; Bradley, *Last Stand in the Carolinas*, 91.

17 OR 47(1):1111–12; Bradley, *Last Stand in the Carolinas*, 85; Wittenberg, *An Infernal Surprise*, chap. 3.

18 OR 47(1):861; Bradley, *Last Stand in the Carolinas*, 85–88; Barrett, *Sherman's March*, 125; Martin, *Kill-Cavalry*, 220–21.

19 Brooks, *Butler and His Cavalry*, 424 (quotation); Bradley, *Last Stand in the Carolinas*, 88.

20 Brooks, *Butler and His Cavalry*, 443; OR 47(2):786; Wells, "A Morning Call on Kilpatrick," 123–27.

21 OR 47(1):1130; Wittenberg, *An Infernal Surprise*, chap. 4; Wells, *Hampton and His Cavalry*, 400–402; Hugh H. Scott, "'Fighting' Kilpatrick's Escape," 588.

22 Wittenberg, *An Infernal Surprise*, chap. 5, first page.

23 Ibid.

24 Ibid., second page.

25 Ibid., second page.

26 OR 47(1):861.

27 M. C. Butler to Edward L. Wells, Mar. 27, 1900, Wells Correspondence, CLS. See also Brooks, *Butler and His Cavalry*, 446; Wells, *Hampton and His Cavalry*, 403–5; Bradley, *Last Stand in the Carolinas*, 94; and Wittenberg, *An Infernal Surprise*, chap. 5.

28 Brooks, *Butler and His Cavalry*, 445.

29 Ibid., 446.

30 Bradley, *Last Stand in the Carolinas*, 94–100; Barrett, *Sherman's March*, 127–29; Wittenberg, chaps. 5–6.

31 OR 47(1):862; Bradley, *Last Stand in the Carolinas*, 100–104; Barrett, *Sherman's March*, 128–30; Wells, *Hampton and His Cavalry*, 405–8, 410–15; Brooks, *Butler and His Cavalry*, 447. Confederate reports on losses from the battle are incomplete, and Kilpatrick's are suspect; see Bradley, *Last Stand in the Carolinas*, 100–101, Barrett, *Sherman's March*, 129–30, and esp. Wittenberg, *An Infernal Surprise*. Wittenberg gives the clearest explanation of the battle's operational importance. See also Martin, *Kill-Cavalry*, 222.

32 Wells, *Hampton and His Cavalry*, 410. See also Wells, "A Morning Call on Kilpatrick," 127–28; Bradley, *Last Stand in the Carolinas*, 97; Barrett, *Sherman's March*, 128; and Martin, *Kill-Cavalry*, 221–22. Careful students of the battle now assert that Mary Boozer was not with Kilpatrick at the time of the Monroe's Crossroads affair (Wittenberg, *An Infernal Surprise*, app. C).

33 "Glorious Confederate Victory!," Confederate imprint, March 1865, HL.

34 Brooks, *Butler and His Cavalry*, 112.

35 Smith, Smith, and Childs, *Mason Smith Family Letters*, 172.

36 Hugh H. Scott, " 'Fighting' Kilpatrick's Escape," 589.

37 Wells, *Hampton and His Cavalry*, 29–37; Brooks, *Butler and His Cavalry*, 113; OR 47(1):203; Wells, "Hampton at Fayetteville."

38 WH to MFH, Mar. 22, 1865, box 3, HFP.

39 Smith, Smith, and Childs, *Mason Smith Family Letters*, 172. The story of the Fayetteville charge, remarkable in itself, grew somewhat in the telling. Wells initially wrote his aunt that the band of Confederates had killed ten and captured six (ibid.) but later revised this count upward. Hugh Scott claimed thirteen killed and twelve captured. In addition to the two Yankees dispatched by Hampton's saber, another veteran asserted that Hampton shot four with an ivory-handled "grooved-cylinder" pistol (Brooks, *Butler and His Cavalry*, 436, 113).

40 WH to Joseph Johnston, Mar. 3, 1865, JO 110, Johnston Papers, HL.

41 Bradley, 136–37. Johnston officially had less than 16,000 infantry and

artillery on March 17, but the gradual arrival of elements of Frank Cheatham's corps raised his estimate to around 18,000 by the next day (OR 47[2]:622, 1408, 1413, 1424, 1426; OR 47[1]:1054).

42 Hughes, *Bentonville*, 14–15, 45–46; Bradley, *Last Stand in the Carolinas*, 140.

43 OR 47(2):1411; Bradley, *Last Stand in the Carolinas*, 141–42.

44 OR 47(2):1429.

45 Ibid., 1409, 1411, 1414–15, 1429; Johnston, *Narrative*, 384–86; Bradley, *Last Stand in the Carolinas*, 141–42.

46 WH, "Battle of Bentonville," *The Century*, 941.

47 Ibid. (quotation); OR 47(2):1429–30, 1433.

48 WH, "Battle of Bentonville," *The Century*, 942 (quotations); Bradley, *Last Stand in the Carolinas*, 142; Hughes, *Bentonville*, 46; WH to James F. Hart, June 10, 1863, October 12, 1864, folder 8, PlB (oversize), HFP; Hampton's War Reminiscences, 115–17, HFP; "Hart's South Carolina Battery."

49 Johnston, *Narrative*, 386–88; WH, "Battle of Bentonville," *The Century*, 942–43; Hughes, *Bentonville*, 56–166 passim; Bradley, *Last Stand in the Carolinas*, 203–315 passim.

50 Johnston, *Narrative*, 390; Bradley, *Last Stand in the Carolinas*, 323–25.

51 WH, "Battle of Bentonville," *The Century*, 943.

52 Bradley, *Last Stand in the Carolinas*, 340, 343; Hughes, *Bentonville*, 177–78.

53 WH, "Battle of Bentonville," *The Century*, 943.

54 Ibid.; Bradley, *Last Stand in the Carolinas*, 370–80; Johnston, *Narrative*, 391.

55 WH, "Battle of Bentonville," *The Century*, 944.

56 Ibid. Hampton remembered only the presence of the 8th Texas, not the 4th Tennessee, though the latter unit was certainly there. His "Battle of Bentonville" article was republished in *Battles and Leaders*, 4:700–705, over an editor's note that made a point to include the 4th Tennessee in Hampton's narrative (ibid., 705).

57 WH, "Battle of Bentonville," *The Century*, 943–44; Hughes, *Bentonville*, 199–207.

58 WH, "Battle of Bentonville," *The Century*, 944.

59 Ibid. (quotation); Johnston, *Narrative*, 391; Hughes, *Bentonville*, 201, 288 n. 36.

60 WH, "Battle of Bentonville," *The Century*, 944.

61 Ibid.

62 These numbers come from Johnston's memoirs, corresponding closely to his 1865 report to Lee, and from Sherman's official report on the battle (Johnston, *Narrative*, 393; OR 47[1]:1057, 27).

63 WH, "Battle of Bentonville," *The Century*, 941.

64 Ibid., 944.

65 Ibid.

66 WH to MFH, Mar. 22, 1865, box 3, HFP.

CHAPTER 21

1   Johnston, *Narrative*, 394.

2   OR 47(3):2684.

3   WH to Joseph Johnston, Mar. 27, 1865, JO 116, Johnston Papers, HL.

4   OR 47(3):806. See also OR 47(1):614, 618, 626, 630, 634, and Bradley, *This Astounding Close*, 83, 97, 105–6.

5   Johnson, "Memorandum of Conversation with Wade Hampton, October 5, 1895, box 4, Johnson Papers, PL. Hampton also related the story in an article in *The Story of American Heroism*, 605–15.

6   See Hampton's correspondence with Johnston's headquarters, March 25–27, JO 112, JO 114, JO 115, JO 116, Johnston Papers, HL; "Semi-Weekly Report of Effective Strength of Cavalry," Mar. 31, 1865, JO 461, HL; Barrett, *Sherman's March*, 201; Bradley, *Last Stand in the Carolinas*, 96–97; and OR 47(3):181, 261.

7   On April 10, 1865, President Davis made it clear to North Carolina governor Zebulon B. Vance that he believed the rumors of Lee's surrender (OR 47[3]:787).

8   Gallagher, *Confederate War*, 10–12, 58–59, 63, 65, 72, 85–89, 139–40.

9   Ballard, *A Long Shadow*, 78–84.

10 Bradley, *This Astounding Close*, 108–9; OR 47(3):225; Ballard, *A Long Shadow*, 58, 84.

11 Bradley, *Last Stand in the Carolinas*, 109–10; OR 47(3):791. A recent biography of Vance states that he consulted Johnston on the idea of North Carolina obtaining a separate peace, and that Johnston advised the governor that he "should obtain the best terms that he could" (McKinney, *Zeb Vance*, 248). If Johnston knew of Graham's and Swain's mission, he too failed to notify Hampton or other Confederate leaders besides Hardee.

12 Bradley, *This Astounding Close*, 110–11.

13 Ibid., 111–14; Barrett, *Sherman's March*, 212. See also Duncan McRae's letters to Jefferson Davis in Rowland, *Jefferson Davis, Constitutionalist*, 6:329–33, 341–44.

14 OR 47(3):186 (quotation), 797; Bradley, *This Astounding Close*, 116.

15 Saunders, "Governor Z. B. Vance," 164; Bradley, *This Astounding Close*, 114–15 (quotations), 119–21.

16 Saunders, "Governor Z. B. Vance," 166.

17 Ibid.; Bradley, *This Astounding Close*, 147.

18 J. Fred Waring Diary, Apr. 16, 1865, Waring Papers, SHC.

19 OR 47(3):224–25, 233–34; Johnston, "My Negotiations," 658.

20 Bradley, *This Astounding Close*, 158–59; Barrett, *Sherman's March*, 231. Wade Hampton Manning's mother Susan was the daughter of Wade Hampton I and his third wife, Mary Cantey (Meynard, *The Venturers*, 516, 520).

21 Wellman, *Giant in Gray*, 181–82.

22 Ibid., 182.

23 J. Fred Waring Diary, Apr. 17, 1865, Waring Papers, SHC.

24 Bradley, This Astounding Close, 162.

25 Ibid. (quotations); Johnson, "Memorandum of Conversation with General Hampton, October 5, 1895," box 4, Bradley Johnson Papers, PL.

26 Bradley, This Astounding Close, 162.

27 Ibid., 166 (quotation); Barrett, Sherman's March, 235.

28 Johnston, "My Negotiations," 658, and Narrative, 402; Sherman, Memoirs, 2:349–50.

29 Johnston, "My Negotiations," 659; Bradley, This Astounding Close, 166–67 (quotation). See also Bradley's comments on p. 340 n. 28.

30 Sherman, Memoirs, 2:356.

31 The claim that Hampton asked Johnston "not to include me in any surrender" comes from Hampton's April 27 dispatch to Breckenridge (OR 47[3]:845).

32 OR 47(3):814.

33 Ibid., 813.

34 Ibid.

35 Ibid.

36 Barrett, Sherman's March, 269–70.

37 OR 47(3):830.

38 Ibid., 829; WH, "An Effort to Rescue Jefferson Davis," 133.

39 Johnston, Narrative, 410–11.

40 OR 47(3):835.

41 Ibid.

42 Ibid., 847.

43 Ibid., 837.

44 WH, "An Effort to Rescue Jefferson Davis," 134–35.

45 OR 47(3):841.

46 Ibid., 845.

47 WH, "An Effort to Rescue Jefferson Davis," 135.

48 Ackerman, Wade Hampton III, 88.

49 J. Fred Waring Diary, Apr. 27, 1865, Waring Papers, SHC.

50 WH, "An Effort to Rescue Jefferson Davis," 135.

51 OR 47(3):845.

52 Ibid., 851; Wheeler, "An Effort to Rescue Jefferson Davis," May 1898, 85–86.

53 WH, "An Effort to Rescue Jefferson Davis," 135; Ballard, A Long Shadow, 111.

54 Wheeler, "An Effort to Rescue Jefferson Davis," May 1898, 86.

55 Ibid., 87.

56 WH, "An Effort to Rescue Jefferson Davis," 135.

CHAPTER 22

1   Simkins and Woody, *South Carolina during Reconstruction*, 18.

2   Chesnut, *Diary from Dixie*, 404.

3   Clipping from *Washington National Republican*, box 1, folder 98, Meynard Papers, SCL.

4   WH to unknown captain, May 10, 1865, box 3, HFP. Virginia Meynard (*The Venturers*, 244) logically surmises that the captain to whom Hampton wrote was Lowndes.

5   Meynard, *The Venturers*, 245–46.

6   WH to Major General Mansfield Lovell, Cmdg., May 15, 1865, with enclosed parole form dated May 15, 1865, ML 239, Lovell Papers, HL.

7   *Testimony*, 1223–24.

8   Hampton spoke these words at a gathering of the "Soldiers' Association" in Walhalla on September 22 (*Charleston News and Courier*, Oct. 10, 1866).

9   "Introduction" and "Wade Hampton Application for Pardon," in "Case Files of Applications from Former Confederates, 1865–1867," Group I, roll 45, NA. See also Dorris, *Pardon and Amnesty*, 35, 111–12.

10 *Columbia Phoenix*, Nov. 15, 1865. On the evolution of northern opinion on black suffrage, see Carter, *When the War Was Over*, 232–34, 244–46.

11 WH to *Columbia Phoenix*, July 27, 1865, box 3, HFP.

12 WH to Louis Wigfall, May 19, 1867, box 2, Wigfall Papers, LOC. Hampton made the same comment to Thomas G. Clemson, son-in-law of John C. Calhoun, in September 1865. Clemson's daughter Floride wrote in her diary that Hampton "said nothing kept him in the country but a desire to pay his debts" (Floride Clemson, *A Rebel Came Home*, 92–93).

13 U.S. Congress, 71st Cong., *Acceptance and Unveiling of Wade Hampton Statue*, 38; Unknown writer to Lieutenant General Wade Hampton, July 25, 1865, box 3, HFP. On Hampton being expected to lead the emigration movement, see Meynard, *The Venturers*, 248, and Wellman, *Giant in Gray*, 197–98.

14 WH to Hon. James G. Gibbes, Aug. 20, 1865, box 3, HFP.

15 Edgar, *South Carolina*, 383–84; Fleming, *Documentary History of Reconstruction*, 1:296–310; Simkins and Woody, *South Carolina during Reconstruction*, 38–39.

16 Thompson, *Ousting the Carpetbagger*, 2, 19; Meynard, *The Venturers*, 248; Simkins and Woody, *South Carolina during Reconstruction*, 43.

17 Perry, *Reminiscences of Public Men*, 278 (found in John J. Dargan Collection, SCL).

18 Ibid., 277. See also Perry, *Writings of Benjamin F. Perry*, 1:232, 234, 238–39. Hampton's pardon was not signed until Nov. 13, 1865 ("Case Files of Applications from Former Confederates, 1865–1867," Group I, roll 45, NA).

19 Zuczek, *State of Rebellion*, 14.

20 *New York Times*, Oct. 30, 1865.

21 *Testimony*, 1222.

22 *Charleston Daily Courier*, Oct. 10, 1866.

23 WH to REL, July 21, 1866, box 3, HFP.

24 WH to MFH, Dec. 18, 1865, ibid.

25 WH to MFH, Jan. 1, 1866; see also WH to MFH, Dec. 18, 1865—both in ibid.

26 *Testimony*, 1236.

27 Ibid.

28 Ibid.

29 WH to MFH, Jan. 1, 1866.

30 WH to MFH, June 3, 1866, box 3, HFP.

31 WH to MFH, Jan. 31, 1866, ibid.

32 WH to MFH, Jan. 14, 1864, ibid.

33 Scarborough, *Masters of the Big House*, 142–43, 222–24; Meynard, *The Venturers*, 186, 190, 204, 221, 251, 253; Carter, *When the War Was Over*, 102–3, 142.

34 WH to Armistead Burt, Mar. 13, 1868, folder 2, WH Correspondence, PL.

35 Ibid.

36 WH to MFH, Jan. 31, Mar. 28, 1866; copy from Washington County Deed Book X, pp. 114–16, box 1, folder 99, Meynard Papers, SCL.

37 Meynard, *The Venturers*, 255–56; Hampton Bankruptcy Files, box 4, HFP. See also the papers of one of Hampton's lawyers in boxes 7, 8, ser. II, Abney Papers, SCL.

38 Clipping in box 1, folder 98, Meynard Papers, SCL. In its issues of Dec. 23, 1876, and Sept. 22, 1877, the *New York Times* repeated the charge that Hampton was a cheat and a defrauder of widows and orphans.

39 Moffett, *Letters of General James Conner*, 203.

CHAPTER 23

1 OR 47(1):21–22; Lucas, *Sherman and the Burning of Columbia*.

2 Transcript of article from *New York Day Book*, July 15, 1865, 15–16, box 3, HFP. Hampton wrote the article on June 14.

3 Ibid. A later comment by Hampton indicates that although he was known to oppose the custom of dueling, he may have considered demanding satisfaction from Sherman. In 1873 Hampton wrote that he first learned of Sherman's charge "at a time when I was a prisoner of war, under parole, and thus unable to meet it in the only manner it deserved" (WH in *Baltimore Enquirer*, June 24, 1873, clipping, in J. J. Nicholson, *The Burning of Columbia*, 4).

4 WH to P. G. T. Beauregard, Apr. 22, 1866, box 3, HFP; *Congressional Globe*, May 1, 1866.

5   *Congressional Globe*, May 1, 1866.

6   Wellman, *Giant in Gray*, 236.

7   Fellman, *Citizen Sherman*, 231.

8   George W. Nichols, "The Burning of Columbia," *Harper's New Monthly Magazine* 33, no. 195 (August 1866): 363–66; *Congressional Globe*, May 1, 1866.

9   One such northern attempt appeared in the memoir of former Union soldier D. Leib Ambrose, who wrote in 1868: "The impartial historian will tell the world that Wade Hampton burned his own city of Columbia by filling the streets with lint, cotton and tinders, and setting fire to it. . . . But it matters not with the seventy thousand [Union soldiers] who will be charged with the burning . . . for this great army . . . smiled and felt glad in their hearts when they beheld this city laid low in ashes, where rebellion was born, and where pampered and devilish treason first lifted its mad head and made its threats against the Union and freedom" (Ambrose, *From Shiloh to Savannah*, 207–8).

10 James McCarter, "The Burning of Columbia Again," *Harper's New Monthly Magazine* 33, no. 197 (October 1866): 642–47.

11 Trezevant, *Burning of Columbia, S.C.*"

12 Agnes Law, "The Burning of Columbia—Affidavit of Mrs. Agnes Law," *Southern Historical Society Papers* 12 (1884): 234.

13 Sherman, *Memoirs*, 287.

14 Ibid., 288.

15 Calhoun, *Liberty Dethroned*, 290.

16 For other contemporary articles on this controversy, see "The Burning of Columbia" (Charleston, 1888), HL; *New York World*, June 17, 1875; *The Land We Love* 4, no. 5 (March 1868): 361–69; WH to *Baltimore Enquirer*, July 1, 1873; " 'The Burning of Columbia,' A Collection of Pamphlets," HL; clipping from *Metropolitan Record and New York Vindicator*, box 3, HFP; and Scott, *Random Recollections*, 175–92. Hampton complained of Sherman's "lies" in letters to Jefferson Davis, Robert E. Lee, P. G. T. Beauregard, and many others.

17 " 'The Burning of Columbia,' " 12; Meynard, *The Venturers*, 247; *Testimony Taken before the Mixed Commission on American and British Claims*, Dec. 10, 1872, in J. J. Nicholson, *The Burning of Columbia*, 18–20.

18 Carter's *After the War Was Over* best describes southern conservatives' attempts to read the North's evolving, coalescing constitutional understanding immediately after the war.

19 WH to Major General Mansfield Lovell, Cmdg., May 15, 1865, with enclosed parole form dated May 15, 1865, ML 239, Lovell Papers, HL.

20 Sidney Andrews, "Three Months among the Reconstructionists," *Atlantic Monthly* 17, issue 100 (February 1866): 237–46.

21 Ibid. The *New York Times* of Oct. 18, 1866 ridiculed Hampton's claim

that Confederates surrendered under certain terms and conditions. "The South," it said, "*surrendered because it was unable longer to resist. Its armies could no longer keep the field.*" As noted previously, Hampton did not see it that way at the end of April 1865.

22 Simkins and Woody, *South Carolina during Reconstruction*, 57.

23 Clipping from *Metropolitan Record and New York Vindicator*, August 1866, box 3, HFP.

24 Clinton, *Tara Revisited*, 27.

25 Ibid., 19.

26 Blight, *Race and Reunion*, 282. Fred Arthur Bailey, in his studies of Redeemer-era textbooks, argues that the myth of the Lost Cause represented a deliberate effort to justify continued dominance by southern elites in the postwar era. See, e.g., Bailey, "Textbooks of the Lost Cause." See also Cox, *Dixie's Daughters*; Bishir, "Landmarks of Power"; Joan Marie Johnson, "'Drill into Us . . . the Rebel Tradition'"; and Nolan, "The Anatomy of the Myth."

27 Foster, *Ghosts of the Confederacy*, 22–25. Jubal A. Early was another prime example of ex-Confederate generals seeking to vindicate their own reputations and that of fellow Confederates. See Early, *A Memoir*, especially Early's preface, xxi–xvi, and Gallagher's introduction, xii–xvi.

28 *Charleston Daily Courier*, Oct. 10, 1866. Modern secondary literature on the Lost Cause is too voluminous to cite here fully. Other works include Wilson, *Baptized in Blood*; Connelly and Bellows, *God and General Longstreet*; Osterweis, *Myth of the Lost Cause*; Gallagher, *Lee and His Generals*; and Lesley J. Gordon, *Pickett*.

29 Besides the speech cited at the end of this chapter, other Lost Cause orations by Hampton include "Public Ceremonies . . . of the Washington Light Infantry, 6–16, HL, and "Proceedings of the Joint Meeting of Camp Moultrie, May 14, 1895," Jervey Papers, SCHS.

30 WH to REL, July 21, 1866, box 3, HFP; see also WH to REL, Nov. 11, 1866, July 16, 1867.

31 WH to REL (1867), cover letter on Hampton's War Reminiscences, HFP.

32 Constitution of the South Carolina Survivors' Association, SCHS.

33 WH to James Conner, Apr. 11, 1869, box 3, HFP.

34 Washington Light Infantry, "Proceedings on the Occasion of Unveiling the Monument," 14, PL.

35 Ibid., 16.

36 Ibid., 14.

37 Ibid., 19. The quotation is from Shakespeare's *Macbeth*, act 5, scene 8.

38 Wellman, *Giant in Gray*, 257.

39 WH to REL, July 16, 1867, box 3, HFP.

40 Meynard, *The Venturers*, 251.

CHAPTER 24

1 WH to Louis Wigfall, May 19, 1867, box 2, Wigfall Papers, LOC.

2 Hampton's letter was published in the *Metropolitan Record and New York Vindicator* in August 1866. The clipping and Hampton's handwritten original, 41 pages long, are in box 3, HFP (quotations in this and previous paragraph).

3 Ibid.

4 Ibid.

5 Abbott, *Freedmen's Bureau*, 28–29, 52–55, 118–29; Fleming, *Documentary History of Reconstruction*, 1:379–81, 386–89.

6 Ballard, *A Long Shadow*, 157–63.

7 Clipping from *Metropolitan Record and New York Vindicator*, August 1866.

8 WH to Louis Wigfall, May 19, 1867, box 2, Wigfall Papers, LOC.

9 WH, "What Negro Supremacy Means."

10 "Wade Hampton's Speech," typescript of article in *Anderson Intelligencer* [1876], box 3, HFP.

11 Lacy K. Ford, "Republics and Democracy," 121–45; Underwood, *The Constitution of South Carolina*, 4:5; Freehling, *Secessionists at Bay*, 22; Klein, *Unification of a Slave State*, 267.

12 *Testimony*, 1222; Perman, *Reunion without Compromise*, 75, 90, 104, 146, 150, 168, 171, 174, chaps. 9–10 passim. For examples of other white southerners who contemplated black suffrage, see Carter, *When the War Was Over*, 244.

13 Hampton related this event in his testimony at a congressional hearing in 1871 (*Testimony*, 1222).

14 WH to Andrew Johnson, n.d., box 3, HFP (published in *Metropolitan Record and New York Vindicator*, August 1866).

15 WH to James Conner, Mar. 24, 1867, box 181, folder 8, Family and Personal Correspondence, Conner Family Papers, SCHS.

16 WH to John Mullaly, Mar. 31, 1867, box 3, HFP.

17 WH to John Mullaly, Apr. 11, 1867, ibid.

18 Ibid. See also Cisco, *Wade Hampton*, 179–80, and Grossman, *The Democratic Party and the Negro*, 1–10.

19 WH to James Conner, Mar. 24, 1867.

20 Jarrell, *Wade Hampton and the Negro*, 16 (quotations); *Harper's Weekly*, Apr. 6, 1867, 211. See also Dewitt Grant Jones, "Wade Hampton and the Rhetoric of Race."

21 Simkins and Woody, *South Carolina during Reconstruction*, 85.

22 Ibid., 85–86.

23 *Charleston Advocate*, Mar. 23, 1867.

24 WH to Louis Wigfall, May 19, 1867, box 2, Wigfall Papers, LOC.

25 WH to James Conner, July 29, 1867, box 181, folder 8, Family and Personal Correspondence, Conner Family Papers, SCHS.

26 WH to D. W. Ray, W. H. Talley, J. P. Thomas, et al., in *Charleston Mercury*, Aug. 29, 1867, box 3, HFP. Jarrell cites the same letter as appearing in the *Columbia Phoenix* (Jarrell, *Wade Hampton and the Negro*, 19 n. 43).

27 WH to D. W. Ray, W. H. Talley, J. P. Thomas, et al., in *Charleston Mercury*, Aug. 29, 1867.

28 Ibid.

29 Ibid.

30 WH to James Conner, Aug. 1, 1867, box 181, folder 8, Family and Personal Correspondence, Conner Family Papers, SCHS.

31 WH to Armistead Burt, n.d., Burt Papers, PL.

32 Zuczek, *State of Rebellion*, 49. See comments in the Preface on my use of the term "Negro rule."

33 Simkins and Woody, *South Carolina during Reconstruction*, 96–102, 109; Underwood, *The Constitution of South Carolina*, 4:11–13.

34 Zuczek, *State of Rebellion*, 38, 74.

35 Ibid., 74; Simkins and Woody, *South Carolina during Reconstruction*, 109–10; Lou Falkner Williams, *Ku Klux Klan Trials*, 22.

36 Zuczek, *State of Rebellion*, 55.

37 Shapiro, "Ku Klux Klan during Reconstruction," 36.

38 WH to James Conner, June 12, 1868, box 181, folder 8, Family and Personal Correspondence, Conner Family Papers, SCHS (quotations here and in previous paragraph).

39 Clipping from *Metropolitan Record and New York Vindicator*, August 1866, box 3, HFP (emphasis in original).

40 WH to James Conner, Apr. 11, 1869, box 3, HFP.

CHAPTER 25

1 Current, *Those Terrible Carpetbaggers*, 146–48 (quotation, 146).

2 For examples of historians praising Hampton's moderation, see Jarrell, *Wade Hampton and the Negro*, 28–31, and Wellman, *Giant in Gray*, 222–23 and passim.

3 Zuczek, *State of Rebellion*, 54–58. There had been scattered incidents of racial and political violence in 1866 and 1867 as well, before the appearance of the Klan in the state (29–32, 51).

4 Lou Falkner Williams, *Ku Klux Klan Trials*, 9.

5 In his testimony before a congressional subcommittee in 1871, Hampton claimed that he could not be sure of the Klan's existence. "As far as I know I have never seen any man that was identified with that organization, if one exists. I have never been approached upon the subject at all,

and I do not know that there is an organization of that kind at all. That outrages have been committed, I have no question, for that I have seen stated; but whether this is done by any organization extending through the State or merely from some local outbreak, I do not know; but I am inclined to think it is the latter" (Testimony, 1223). Hampton's claim to have no direct personal knowledge of the Klan is plausible, and the words above are probably, strictly speaking, correct. But it is difficult to believe that he was not firmly convinced of the organization's existence.

6 Edgefield Advertiser, Sept. 16, 1868.

7 Testimony (reprinted from Columbia Phoenix, Oct. 18, 1868), 1248.

8 Zuczek, State of Rebellion, 59.

9 Ibid., 58–60.

10 The man Scott called "Gibbs" was probably Columbia mayor James Gibbes.

11 Current, Those Terrible Carpetbaggers, 146–48; Zuczek, State of Rebellion, 60; Testimony (reprinted from Columbia Phoenix, Oct. 23, 1868), 1248 (quotation).

12 Testimony (reprinted from Columbia Phoenix, Oct. 30, 1868), 1264.

13 Zuczek, State of Rebellion, 60; Edgar, South Carolina, 398.

14 New York Times, July 28, 1868; Testimony, 1261.

15 The words quoted here are from a reporter's paraphrasing in "Monthly Record of Current Events," Harper's New Monthly Magazine 37, issue 220 (September 1868), 570. See also Meynard, The Venturers, 254.

16 WH to G. L. Park in Columbia Phoenix, Oct. 23, 1868, reprinted in Testimony, 1262–63.

17 Adams and Hampton spoke from the same stand in Columbia on October 12 ("Massachusetts and South Carolina"; see also partial handwritten transcript of their remarks in box 3, HFP, and Columbia Phoenix, Oct. 11, 1868). And see New York Times, July 16, 1868.

18 New York Times, July 14, 1868.

19 "The Physical Force Programme," Harper's Weekly, Aug. 8, 1868, 498. Harper's made the same charge in its August 15 edition, p. 514, as did the New York Times on July 14, 1868.

20 Harper's Weekly, Nov. 14, 1868, 722. See also, e.g., Harper's Weekly, Aug. 1 (482), Aug. 29 (546—in which the Klan-supporting charge was made even more clearly—and 547), Oct. 31 (690), 1868; and The Nation, July 23 (63), Aug. 6 (101), 1868.

21 "25 Rebel Generals, 30 Rebel Colonels, 10 Rebel Majors, 20 Rebel Captains . . ." (1868), HL.

22 Columbia Phoenix, July 26, 1868, in Testimony, 1261.

23 Harper's Weekly, Aug. 15, 1868, 514. Interestingly, Harper's account of Hampton's speech in Charleston is remarkably more bellicose than the version printed in the Charleston Mercury and Columbia Phoenix and reprinted in Testimony.

24 Dunning, *Reconstruction*; Reynolds, *Reconstruction in South Carolina*; Franklin, *Reconstruction*; Foner, *Reconstruction*; Current, *Those Terrible Carpetbaggers*.

25 Zuczek, *State of Rebellion*, 52 (quotation); Edgar, *South Carolina*, 387.

26 Holt, *Black over White*, chaps. 2–3, app. A, table 5; Hine, "Black Politicians in Reconstruction Charleston."

27 Lou Falkner Williams, *Ku Klux Klan Trials*, 8.

28 "An Appeal to the Honorable the Senate of the United States, in Behalf of the Conservative People of the State of South Carolina, against the Adoption . . . of the New Constitution Proposed for South Carolina," in *Testimony*, 1238–45 (quotation, 1240).

29 Ibid., 1239, 1219.

30 Lou Falkner Williams, *Ku Klux Klan Trials*, 12.

31 Ibid.

32 Edgar, *South Carolina*, 395.

33 Ibid., 394.

34 Williamson, *After Slavery*, 383.

35 Edgar, *South Carolina*, 394–95; Simkins and Woody, *South Carolina during Reconstruction*, 137, 139–40, 148, 203–22; Williamson, *After Slavery*, 381–94.

36 Edgar, *South Carolina*, 394–95; Simkins and Woody, *South Carolina during Reconstruction*, 126–27, 169; Williamson, *After Slavery*, 381–94; Lamson, *Glorious Failure*, 165, 206–11; Miller, *Gullah Statesman*. Miller presents the considerable evidence against Smalls in the printing scandal (pp. 70–73) and appears to believe its authenticity, but he later comments that "historians generally agree that the case against [Smalls] was not strong, and that its motivation was decidedly political" (p. 116). According to David Duncan Wallace, the full extent of Gary's and Butler's involvement was not publicly known until February 1878 (Wallace, "Life of Gary," 38–41, unpublished biography, Wallace Papers, SCHS).

37 *Beaufort Republican*, Nov. 23, 1871, quoting the *Missionary Record and Colored Organ*.

38 *Beaufort Republican*, May 23, 1872.

39 *New York Times*, Feb. 17, 1874. Robert Brown Elliott was an example of a black politician who recognized the danger that Republican corruption was doing to white perceptions of black political abilities (see Lamson, *Glorious Failure*, 184). Later Hampton would trumpet to a national audience that he had been right about universal suffrage, which amounted to "negro supremacy" and thus bad government in black majority states. See, e.g., WH, "What Negro Supremacy Means." For other examples of black Republican newspapers condemning the Republican regime, see *Beaufort Republican*, Nov. 6, Dec. 21, 1871, Aug. 29, 1872; *Port Royal Standard and Commercial*, Jan. 8, 1874; and *Beaufort Republican*, Jan. 8, 1874.

40 Lamson, *Glorious Failure*, 195–97; Meynard, *The Venturers*, 981; Graydon, *Tales of Columbia*, 225.

41 WH to James Conner, Apr. 11, 1869, box 3, HFP. See also WH to Armistead Burt, Nov. 14, 1872, folder 1, WH Correspondence, PL.

42 WH to Col. L. D. Childs, Feb. 22, 1869, box 3, HFP. See also the optimistic letter to Conner, Apr. 11, 1869, ibid.

43 WH to Armistead Burt, Jan. 2, 1871, folder 1, WH Correspondence, PL.

44 Ibid., Dec. 28, 1871.

45 WH to James Conner, Nov. 7, 1873, box 181, folder 13, Conner Family Papers, SCHS.

46 For letters indicating Hampton's involvement in the life insurance business, see WH to Armistead Burt, Oct. 22, 1871, folder 1, WH Correspondence, PL; Jefferson Davis to James Phelan, Aug. 6, 1872, in Rowland, *Jefferson Davis*, 7:326; WH to Colonel William C. Carrington, Aug. 22, 1873, box 162, folder 30, Maury Family Papers, HL; WH to T. L. Preston, Mar. 29, 1873, box 3, HFP; and Jefferson Davis to WH, Sept. 20, 1873, box 3, HFP. For the sale of magazine subscriptions and memberships to the Southern Historical Society, see WH to James Conner, Nov. 7, 1873, box 181, folder 13, Conner Family Papers, SCHS, and letters of Dec. 9, Dec. 28, 1873, Jan. 5, 23, Feb. 18, 1874, all in box 3, HFP.

47 WH to Dr. Trezevant, Dec. 27, 1872, box 3, HFP.

48 WH to REL, July 16, 1867, and WH to John Mullaly, Feb. 18, 1874, box 3, HFP; WH to James Conner, Aug. 11, 1867, box 181, folder 8, Conner Family Papers, SCHS.

49 On Dec. 16, 1871, Hampton wrote that Mary's "last attack was serious. It was not of the same character as her first & Dr. Trezevant thinks indigestion was the cause of it" (WH to Armistead Burt, Dec. 16, 1871, folder 1, WH Correspondence, PL). On Mar. 1, 1872, he noted that Mary could not "write without pain."(WH to Mrs. Parker, Mar. 1, 1872, box 3, HFP).

50 WH to Armistead Burt, Dec. 16, 1871; Meynard, *The Venturers*, 257.

51 WH to Armistead Burt, Oct. 22, 1871, and WH to Dr. Trezevant, Oct. 2, 1872 (quotation), both in box 3, HFP.

52 WH to Anna Preston, Apr. 7, May 28, 1873, and WH to Thomas L. Preston, Mar. 29, 1873, box 3, HFP; Meynard, *The Venturers*, 257–58.

53 W. T. Howard to WH, Mar. 13, 1874, and M. C. Butler to WH, Mar. 16, 1874, box 3, HFP; WH to Armistead Burt, Apr. 12, 1874, folder 1, WH Correspondence, PL (quotation).

CHAPTER 26

1 WH to Armistead Burt, Oct. 22, 1871, folder 1, WH Correspondence, PL.

2 Kantrowitz, *Tillman*, 7–8, 57, 78–79.

3 Though Hampton took little part in the 1870 campaign, he did speak on behalf of the "Reform Party" at a political meeting in Charleston on October 11 (*Columbia Daily Phoenix*, Oct. 13, 1870).

4   Zuczek, *State of Rebellion*, 72–82; *Testimony*, 1219. Hampton cited the education of his children as a primary reason for his absence (WH to Armistead Burt, Oct. 22, 1871, folder 1, WH Correspondence, PL).

5   Zuczek, *State of Rebellion*, 82, 84 n.15; Simkins and Woody, *South Carolina during Reconstruction*, 445–56; Lamson, *Glorious Failure*, 85–89, 113–15; Lou Falkner Williams, *Ku Klux Klan Trials*, 18 (quotation), 14–16.

6   Lou Falkner Williams, *Ku Klux Klan Trials*, 46; Zuczek, *State of Rebellion*, 92–93.

7   Lou Falkner Williams, *Ku Klux Klan Trials*, 41.

8   WH to Armistead Burt, folder 1, WH Correspondence, PL.

9   Lou Falkner Williams, *Ku Klux Klan Trials*, 19, 41–42; Zuczek, *State of Rebellion*, 82, 88–99.

10 *Testimony*, 1219.

11 Ibid., 1197–1265 (quotation, 1228). One bit of Hampton's testimony that does seem dishonest is his claim that whites in the state "are not generally armed now" (1225). Hampton should have known that was not the case, especially since he had played a role in obtaining arms in 1868.

12 WH to Armistead Burt, Jan. 2, 1871, folder 1, WH Correspondence, PL. In a letter to another correspondent written the same day, Hampton apologized for the tardiness of his reply. He explained that the letter had been forwarded to him in Mississippi and had only arrived a few days before, indicating that he had been there for some time (WH to Rev. Mr. Jones, Jan. 2, 1871, box 3, HFP).

13 WH to Armistead Burt, Oct. 22, Nov. 25, 1871, folder 1, WH Correspondence, PL.

14 Zuczek, *State of Rebellion*, esp. ix–x, 4–6. See also Mark M. Smith, "'All Is Not Quiet in Our Hellish County,'" 152–55, and Shapiro, "Ku Klux Klan during Reconstruction," 36. In 1877 Governor Hampton and President Hayes referred to Ku Klux Klan crimes as "political offenses" in their correspondence (Hayes telegram to WH, May 12, 1877, and WH to Hayes, June 24, 1877, WH Papers, SCDAH).

15 *Beaufort Republican*, Nov. 6, 1871.

16 Hampton used the term "criminality of a few" in the Democratic Party's written appeal of October 1868 (*Columbia Phoenix*, Oct. 18, 1868, reprinted from *Testimony*, 1248).

17 *Beaufort Republican*, Nov. 2, 1871.

18 Ibid.

19 *Beaufort Republican*, Nov. 6, 1871.

20 WH to Armistead Burt, Oct. 22, 1871, folder 1, WH Correspondence, PL.

21 Lou Falkner Williams, *Ku Klux Klan Trials*, 46–49.

22 *Charleston News and Courier*, Feb. 21, 1874.

23 Lamson, *Glorious Failure*, 156–63. Hampton was the chairman of the Democratic Party's Central Committee in South Carolina but advocated the

South taking a passive role in selecting national candidates or national platforms. Though favoring Horace Greeley's candidacy, he played almost no part in the national campaign (*New York Times*, Sept. 24, 1871, May 31, 1872).

24 Williamson, *After Slavery*, 407, 407 n. 121; WH to Armistead Burt, Jan. 2, 1871, folder 1, WH Correspondence, PL. For Hampton's activities (an 1874 vacation in the Virginia mountains with his family in the summer following Mary's death, paying closer attention to his Mississippi plantations and investing in a "quarry," the arrival of another grandbaby), see letters of Jan. 31, Apr. 27, and May 12, 1875, box 3, HFP.

25 *Charleston News and Courier*, Jan. 5–8, 1876.

26 *Charleston News and Courier*, Jan. 10, 1876.

27 Simkins and Woody, *South Carolina during Reconstruction*, 477–82; Lamson, *Glorious Failure*, 220–25. For a small sample of the national press's criticism of South Carolina carpetbaggers, see *Scribner's Monthly* 8 (July 1874): 368–69; *Scribner's Monthly* 9 (January 1875): 375–76; and articles from northern newspapers reprinted in *Charleston News and Courier*, Feb. 21, 1874, Jan. 5, 1876.

28 John H. Strous to WH, Jan. 20, 1873, and WH to Anna Preston, July 14, 1875, June 18, 1876, box 3, HFP; Meynard, *The Venturers*, 258, 264; *Minutes of the Proceedings of the Reunion of the Hampton Legion*; *Charleston News and Courier*, June 29, 1876. Other examples of Hampton exhorting fellow southerners to continue the fight for political vindication include "Address of Gen. Wade Hampton," *Southern Magazine* (January 1874): 11–18, SCL; a speech printed in the *Edgefield Advertiser*, Nov. 7, 1872; and Hampton's 1875 speech to the Hampton Legion Reunion cited above. Hampton was also leader of the South Carolina Survivors' Association and a leader in the Southern Historical Society, as indicated elsewhere in this text.

CHAPTER 27

1 Zuczek, *State of Rebellion*, 193–94; Simkins and Woody, *South Carolina during Reconstruction*, 523; *Charleston News and Courier*, Nov. 28–29, 1876; Wellman, *Giant in Gray*, 277; Wells, *Hampton and Reconstruction*, 158; Sheppard, *Red Shirts Remembered*, 168–69; *Edgefield Advertiser*, Nov. 30, 1876.

2 Tindall, *South Carolina Negroes*, 13; Drago, *Black Red Shirts*, 8; Holden, "Is Our Love for Wade Hampton Foolishness?," 64.

3 Passages that question Hampton's sincerity or portray him as an advocate of fraud and intimidation appear in Drago, *Black Red Shirts*, 8; Zuczek, *State of Rebellion*, 175; Lamson, *Glorious Failure*, 245; and Orville Vernon Burton, "Black Squint of the Law," 123. Stephen Kantrowitz (*Tillman*, 78) argues that Hampton "came to believe [his] own rhetoric" about conducting an

honest and peaceful campaign, but that "paternalism and violence were in fact complementary and mutually necessary strategies."

4 The writer of the article claimed that the people of South Carolina "borrowed glory of [Hampton's] achievements, and they were grateful. The ideal of manhood they dreamed, he was." ("Charleston's Greatest Son," *Charleston News and Courier*, Apr. 12, 1902).

5 Poole, *Never Surrender* (first quotation is from title). Charles Reagan Wilson (*Baptized in Blood*) also pays close attention to religious elements in the Lost Cause.

6 WH to Martin Gary, July 25, 1876, box 3, HFP; Williamson, *After Slavery*, 406–7.

7 Words of Governor Chamberlain in Simkins and Woody, *South Carolina during Reconstruction*, 488.

8 Ibid., 489.

9 Summaries of the Hamburg massacre can be found in Edgar, *South Carolina*, 403; Tindall, *South Carolina Negroes*, 11–12; Zuczek, *State of Rebellion*, 159–72; Williamson, *After Slavery*, 268–70; and Simkins and Woody, *South Carolina during Reconstruction*, 486–89.

10 Ackerman, *Wade Hampton III*, 156–61.

11 Simkins and Woody, *South Carolina during Reconstruction*, 490; Wallace, "Life of Gary," 1–31, unpublished biography, Wallace Papers, SCHS; Zuczek, *State of Rebellion*, 167. Later, in 1864, Hampton did recommend Gary for promotion to brigadier general (Cisco, *Wade Hampton*, 132).

12 Kantrowitz, *Tillman*, 78.

13 Wallace, "Life of Gary," 149.

14 *Charleston News and Courier*, Dec. 15, 1879.

15 Ibid., Aug. 15, 1878. Gary recounted this story in a public speech in Anderson in 1878 (Wallace, "Life of Gary," 64). It was a time when he was trying to highlight his associations with Hampton and assume credit for devising the straightout campaign, but no one ever disputed the gist of this story—not even Hampton after the split between the two men became open and bitter.

16 Wellman, *Giant in Gray*, 244–45.

17 Ibid., 247–48 (source of this and next three paragraphs).

18 *Columbia Daily Register*, Aug. 18, 1876; Wellman, *Giant in Gray*, 249; Simkins and Woody, *South Carolina during Reconstruction*, 490.

19 S. W. Ferguson to Theodore G. Barker, Jan. 7, 1876 [copy], Gary Papers, SCL (source of this and next paragraph).

20 "No. 1 Plan of Campaign," folder 2, Gary Papers, SCL.

21 *Columbia Daily Register*, Aug. 18, 1876.

22 Ibid.; Jarrell, *Wade Hampton and the Negro*, 116; Cresswell, *Rednecks, Redeemers, and Race*, 5–7.

23 *Charleston News and Courier*, Sept. 18, 1876. In Abbeville, Hampton said that if any man thought that because he was a Democrat or a white man Hampton would stand between him and the law or give him any privileges or protections not given to black men, "he is mistaken, and I tell him so now that if that is his reason for voting for me not to vote at all" (WH, *Free Men! Free Ballots!! Free Schools!!!*, 4).

24 Jarrell, *Wade Hampton and the Negro*, 58; Zuczek, *State of Rebellion*, 167. See Hampton's and Haskell's testimony in U.S. Congress, *South Carolina in 1876*, 3:815–17, 985; *Columbia Daily Register*, Aug. 18, 1876.

25 *Charleston News and Courier*, Sept. 18, 1876.

26 Alfred B. Williams, *Hampton and His Red Shirts*, 217.

27 Wellman, *Giant in Gray*, 266 (citing Wells, *Hampton and Reconstruction*, 140); *Edgefield Advertiser*, Sept. 7, 1876.

28 Wise, *End of an Era*, 333.

29 Alfred B. Williams, *Hampton and His Red Shirts*, 91.

30 Wells, *Hampton and His Cavalry*, 249; J. A. Hoyt, article, Columbia State, May 9, 1901.

31 *Beaufort Republican*, Oct. 4, 1876.

32 Ibid. See also speech in Abbeville reprinted in WH, *Free Men! Free Ballots!! Free Schools!!!*, 5–6.

33 *Charleston News and Courier*, Oct. 5, 1876.

34 *Columbia Register*, Sept. 20, 1876. See also Wellman, *Giant in Gray*, 258; Drago, *Black Red Shirts*, 32, 149 n. 50.

35 *Charleston Daily Courier*, Mar. 23, 1867.

36 Dewitt Grant Jones, "Wade Hampton and the Rhetoric of Race," 78.

37 *Charleston News and Courier*, Oct. 5, 1876.

38 *Charleston News and Courier*, Sept. 20, 1876.

39 *Charleston News and Courier*, Oct. 2, 1876. See Dewitt Jones's careful and useful analysis of Hampton's rhetoric on race in "Wade Hampton and the Rhetoric of Race," esp. 142–46. Hampton said that not only land and economic power belonged to whites "by title deed from the Almighty," but so did "the government of the State and country" (*Columbia Daily Register*, Sept. 20, 1876).

40 Alfred Williams, "Eyewitness to 1876," Dec. 12, 1926, SCL.

41 Zuczek, *State of Rebellion*, 173; Edgar, *South Carolina*, 143; Poole, *Never Surrender*, 116, 130–31; Alfred Williams, "Eyewitness to 1876," Jan. 2, 1927, SCL; Cisco, *Wade Hampton*, 235.

42 Edgar, *South Carolina*, 407.

43 Wickham, "Wade Hampton, the Cavalry Leader, and His Times," 448; Edgar, *South Carolina*, 404. For the religious zeal that characterized the Hampton campaign, see Poole, *Never Surrender*, chap. 6. For the religious imagery of the Lost Cause in general, see Wilson, *Baptized in Blood*, passim.

44 Williamson, *After Slavery*, 407.

45 *Charleston News and Courier*, Oct. 2, 1876.

46 Poole, *Never Surrender*, 117.

47 Drago, *Black Red Shirts*, 32, 62–67. For information on Delany, see Ullman, *Delany*, 485–89; *Charleston News and Courier*, Sept. 26, Nov. 2, 1876; and Levine, *Delany: A Documentary Reader*.

48 Drago, *Black Red Shirts*, 59.

49 *Charleston News and Courier*, Oct. 2, 1876; Drago, *Black Red Shirts*, 61. Democratic newspapers, especially the *Charleston News and Courier*, reported hundreds of black Red Shirts marching at some Democratic meetings and often mentioned large enthusiastic, or at least respectful, black audiences when Hampton spoke. They undoubtedly exaggerated but, as Edmund Drago (*Black Red Shirts*, 25–28) points out in his detailed study, Republican newspapers likewise deliberately underestimated the number of black Red Shirts and Hampton supporters.

50 *Charleston News and Courier*, Oct. 5, 1876.

51 Drago, *Black Red Shirts*, 26–27; *Charleston News and Courier*, Sept. 8, 18, Oct. 2, 5, 10, Nov. 2–3, 1876; *Abbeville Medium*, Sept. 20, 1876.

52 *Charleston News and Courier*, Sept. 18, 1876; Simkins and Woody, *South Carolina during Reconstruction*, 498–99, 240; Lamson, *Glorious Failure*, 243–44; Zuczek, *State of Rebellion*, 166.

53 Zuczek, *State of Rebellion*, 168; *Charleston News and Courier*, Oct. 4, 1876.

54 Zuczek, *State of Rebellion*, 167–76; Drago, *Black Red Shirts*, 37. For other evidence of black-on-black violence, see Drago, *Black Red Shirts*, 38–43, 58–59, 63, 68, 84, and *Charleston News and Courier*, Sept. 21, Oct. 2, 21, 1876.

55 Mark M. Smith, " 'All Is Not Quiet in Our Hellish County.' " For a heavily biased Democratic version of events, see *Charleston News and Courier*, Oct. 4, 1876.

56 Moffett, *Letters of General James Conner*, 217.

57 *Charleston News and Courier*, Oct. 2, 1876.

58 Zuczek, *State of Rebellion*, 174–75.

59 *Charleston News and Courier*, Oct. 2, 1876.

60 Ibid., Oct. 2, 4–5, 1876; Williamson, *After Slavery*, 103–4, 271; Simkins and Woody, *South Carolina during Reconstruction*, 504; Zuczek, *State of Rebellion*, 177; Chamberlain's testimony in U.S. Congress, *South Carolina in 1876*, 2:16.

61 *Edgefield Advertiser*, Oct. 19, 1876; *Charleston News and Courier*, Oct. 11, 1876.

62 *Charleston News and Courier*, Oct. 20, 1876 (quotation); Zuczek, *State of Rebellion*, 177–78.

63 Zuczek, *State of Rebellion*, 177–78; Simkins and Woody, *South Carolina during Reconstruction*, 509.

64 Moffett, *Letters of General James Conner*, 221.

65 Simkins and Woody, *South Carolina during Reconstruction*, 509; Zuczek, *State of Rebellion*, 179.

66 WH to John Mullaly, Mar. 31, 1867, box 3, HFP.

67 Moffett, *Letters of General James Conner*, 219.

68 Ibid., 220. Actually, the State Board of Canvassers consisted of five men. Three of them—Francis Cardozo, H. E. Hayne, and Dunn—were members of Chamberlain's cabinet and were candidates for reelection (Simkins and Woody, *South Carolina during Reconstruction*, 516).

69 U.S. Congress, *South Carolina in 1876*, 1:894, 2:22–23.

70 Ibid., 1:894.

71 *Charleston News and Courier*, Oct. 21, 1876.

CHAPTER 28

1 Williamson, *After Slavery*, 407.

2 Poole, *Never Surrender*, 120.

3 Harry R. E. Hampton, "About the General," 4, Meynard Collection, box 1, folder 81, SCL. For the importance of prowess, self-control, and mastery over violence and death in the southern masculine ideal, see Proctor, *Bathed in Blood*, 61–75. Greenberg (*Honor and Slavery*, 125–27) discusses the importance in "mastery" of men having the ability to control violence and administer death, though he does not mention the value of forbearance in the use of violence.

4 Zuczek, *State of Rebellion*, 190–92; Ronald F. King, "Counting the Votes," 173, 176–77, 187, 191; Simkins and Woody, *South Carolina during Reconstruction*, 514–15, 515 n. 2; *Charleston News and Courier*, Dec. 29, 1876; *Spartanburg Herald*, Jan. 17, 1877.

5 Drago, *Black Red Shirts*, 29.

6 Ibid., 33.

7 Ibid., 29–33; *Charleston News and Courier*, Sept. 18, 1876; Jarrell, *Wade Hampton and the Negro*, 61. For Hampton's opinion on his black votes, see U.S. Congress, House, Select Committee, *Recent Election in South Carolina*, 333, and *Charleston News and Courier*, Dec. 29, 1879. Chamberlain estimated that Hampton received 3,000 legitimate black votes (U.S. Congress, *South Carolina in 1876*, 2:40).

8 Moffett, *Letters of General James Conner*, 226; *Charleston Republican*, Oct. 26, 1876; *Port Royal Standard and Commercial*, Oct. 15, 19, 1876.

9 Simkins and Woody, *South Carolina during Reconstruction*, 516–22; Ronald F. King, "Counting the Votes," 170–71; Edgar, *South Carolina*, 404.

10 WH to Armistead Burt, Nov. 19, 1876, WH Correspondence, PL.

11 In June 1877 Hampton informed one correspondent that his majority was 1,134, "but had the fraudulent votes been rejected, it would have been much larger" (WH to George M. Johnson, June 9, 1877, box 3, HFP).

12 Zuczek, *State of Rebellion*, 197; see also 1–2, 188, 208–10.

13 Meynard, *The Venturers*, 263, 983. The first newspaper reference I have seen to the fire is an oblique one in Alexander Haskell's open letter published in the *Columbia Daily Register*, Jan. 18, 1877.

14 Zuczek, *State of Rebellion*, 193–94; Simkins and Woody, *South Carolina during Reconstruction*, 523; *Charleston News and Courier*, Nov. 28–29, 1876.

15 *Charleston News and Courier*, Nov. 29, 1877; Simkins and Woody, *South Carolina during Reconstruction*, 523; Zuczek, *State of Rebellion*, 194.

16 *Edgefield Advertiser*, Nov. 30, 1876.

17 *Charleston News and Courier*, Nov. 29, 1876 (quotation); Wellman, *Giant in Gray*, 277; Wells, *Hampton and Reconstruction*, 158). Some sources (Wellman, *Giant in Gray*, 277, and Wells, *Hampton and Reconstruction*, 158) indicate that after the last sentence quoted here, Hampton added: "I have been elected Governor, and so help me God, I will take my seat."

18 *Edgefield Advertiser*, Nov. 30, 1876. William A. Sheppard, the son of a Red Shirt who idolized Gary and saw Hampton as a traitor, wrote that the crowd met Hampton's request with a "groan." "Peace—while the Radicals stole the State! A long minute passed, and another, and a dispirited cheer signified compliance with Hampton's request" (Sheppard, *Red Shirts Remembered*, 168–69).

19 *Spartanburg Herald*, Dec. 6, 1876, reprinting the story from the *Atlanta Telegram*.

20 Wellman, *Giant in Gray*, 279.

21 Ibid., 279–80.

22 Rable, *But There Was No Peace*, 184; Chamberlain, "Reconstruction in South Carolina," 480 (quotation).

23 From Elliott's December 9 letter to Chamberlain in Allen, *Governor Chamberlain's Administration*, 450.

24 *Charleston News and Courier*, Dec. 8, 1876; Allen, *Governor Chamberlain's Administration*, 448.

25 *Charleston News and Courier*, Dec. 8, 1876.

26 Lamson, *Glorious Failure*, 258–59; Allen, *Governor Chamberlain's Administration*, 449–50 (quotation, 450).

27 *Charleston News and Courier*, Dec. 1, 1876.

28 Ibid.

29 Telegram, WH to His Excellency US Grant, Presdt., Nov. 30, 1876, and WH to His Excellency R. B. Hayes, Gov. of Ohio, Dec. 23, 1876, and telegram, WH to Hamilton Fish, Dec. 3, 1876, in "Xerox Copies of Letters from Governor Wade Hampton to President Rutherford B. Hayes," WH Papers, SCDAH; *Charleston News and Courier*, Dec. 4, 1876.

30 *Charleston News and Courier*, Dec. 4, 1876.

31 HJ (Nov. 30–Dec. 4, 1876).

32 Sheppard, *Red Shirts Remembered*, 181; Alfred B. Williams, *Hampton and His Red Shirts*, 418 (quotation).

33 Alfred B. Williams, *Hampton and His Red Shirts*, 418.

34 Jarrell, *Wade Hampton and the Negro*, 110–11; Sheppard, *Red Shirts Remembered*, 179–82; *Charleston News and Courier*, Dec. 9, 1876 (quotation).

35 Alfred B. Williams, *Hampton and His Red Shirts*, 418.

36 Ibid.

37 Zuczek, *State of Rebellion*, 198.

38 *Charleston News and Courier*, Dec. 6–7, 15, 1876; *Springfield Republican*, quoted in Wells, *Hampton and Reconstruction*, 170. See also editorial of *Cincinnati Enquirer* in *Spartanburg Herald*, Jan. 17, 1877.

39 *Charleston News and Courier*, Dec. 9, 16, 1876.

40 *HJ* (Dec. 14, 20–21, 1876); *Charleston News and Courier*, Dec. 15–16, 21, 1876, Feb. 20, 1877 (quotation); *Columbia Register*, Jan. 9, 11, 14, 1877; *Spartanburg Herald*, Jan. 17, 1877; Simkins and Woody, *South Carolina during Reconstruction*, 535.

41 *Charleston News and Courier*, Dec. 29, 1876, Feb. 14, 20, Mar. 3, 1877; Simkins and Woody, *South Carolina during Reconstruction*, 533–34.

42 Wellman, *Giant in Gray*, 289; *Columbia Daily Register*, Jan. 19, 1877; Zuczek, *State of Rebellion*, 198. A temporary court injunction forbade the two banks that served as repositories of public funds from lending money to the Republican government (Simkins and Woody, *South Carolina during Reconstruction*, 534).

CHAPTER 29

1 Quoted phrase borrowed from Williamson, *After Slavery*, 407.

2 Wellman, *Giant in Gray*, 288–89; Ullman, *Delany*, 495. One of the clearest expositions of the extremists' bitterness toward Hampton is found in Sheppard, *Red Shirts Remembered*, 80–322 passim.

3 Letter from "A Tilden Democrat," *Augusta Chronicle and Sentinel*, Jan. 10, 1877.

4 Ibid.; Wellman, *Giant in Gray*, 288. The letter from "A Tilden Democrat" contains a broad sample of criticism of Hampton's move in the national press.

5 Letter from "A Tilden Democrat," *Augusta Chronicle and Sentinel*, Jan. 10, 1877. "A Tilden Democrat" did not originally mention all these Democrats by name, but the names came out in a subsequent controversy over the issue between 1878 and 1880. There was some general agreement on who was present, though most of the participants specified that Hampton did not attend the original meeting in Columbia, only a subsequent one in Abbeville (Wallace, "Withdrawal of the Democratic Electors," 374–

85, manuscript, Wallace Papers, SCHS; Jarrell, *Wade Hampton and the Negro*, 117).

6 *Columbia Daily Register*, Jan. 18, 1877.

7 Wallace, "Life of Gary," 91, 121–25, unpublished biography, Wallace Papers, SCHS. See, e.g., *Spartanburg Herald*, Jan. 17, 1877; *Columbia Daily Register*, Jan. 9, 11, 18–19, 1877; *Augusta Chronicle and Sentinel*, Jan. 11, 1877; and *Abbeville Press and Banner*, Jan. 24, 1877.

8 *Columbia Daily Register*, Jan. 18, 1877.

9 Ibid.

10 Ibid.

11 Ibid. The most thorough refutation of the letter from "A Tilden Democrat" charges is found in Wallace, "Withdrawal of the Democratic Electors."

12 Letter from "A Tilden Democrat," *Augusta Chronicle and Sentinel*, Jan. 10, 1877.

13 *Columbia Daily Register*, Jan. 18, 1877.

14 Ibid.

15 Moffett, *Letters of General James Conner*, 214, 216–17; Wells, *Hampton and Reconstruction*, 147. Conner's determination to avoid an armed clash in Charleston can be seen in his orders to the rifle clubs there dated Sept. 12, 1876, box 181, folder 15 (Rifle Clubs), Family and Personal Correspondence, Conner Family Papers, SCHS.

16 Haskell also claimed that when South Carolina Democrats were considering whether to withdraw Tilden's name from the ticket, they would do so "under a protest" while exposing the plot cited by Mackey and Cooke and "announcing that we withdrew to prevent the intervention of military force, which would rob us of the exercise of our constitutional rights." The logic of the claim is unclear, but it does support the interpretation that Hampton had tactical as well as philosophical and cultural reasons for portraying himself as a defender of peace and lawful order (*Columbia Daily Register*, Jan. 18, 1877).

17 *Spartanburg Herald*, Jan. 17, 1877.

18 *Columbia Daily Register*, Jan. 19, 1877.

19 HJ (Dec. 15, 1876): 42.

20 *Spartanburg Herald*, Jan. 17, 1877. Chamberlain, meanwhile, tried to convince Washington that black civil rights would not be safe under a Hampton regime (Chamberlain to [incoming] Secretary of State Maxwell Evarts, Mar. 6, 1877, Chamberlain Papers, SCL).

21 HJ (Dec. 15, 1876): 42.

22 WH to Hayes, Dec. 23, 1876, and Mar. 29, 31, 1877, WH Papers, SCDAH.

23 Wellman, *Giant in Gray*, 289–90.

24 Proclamation of Feb. 20, 1877, Governor Wade Hampton Miscellaneous Letters, WH Papers, SCDAH.

25 Hampton to Hayes, Dec. 23, 1876, ibid.
26 WH telegram to T. J. Mackey, Mar. 17, 1877, ibid.
27 WH telegram to R. B. Hayes, Mar. 26, 1877, ibid.
28 Wellman, *Giant in Gray*, 291.
29 *Beaufort Tribune and Port Royal Commercial*, Apr. 12, 1877.
30 Wellman, *Giant in Gray*, 291.
31 *Charleston News and Courier*, Apr. 3, 1877.
32 *Charleston News and Courier*, Apr. 7, 1877; see also issues of April 5–6.
33 *Beaufort Tribune and Port Royal Commercial*, Apr. 12, 1877.
34 Printed in *Beaufort Tribune and Port Royal Commercial*, Apr. 26, 1877.
35 " 'Jane Washington Day' " (quotations from cover), PL.
36 Ibid., passim.
37 Ibid., 1.
38 Ibid., 10.

CHAPTER 30

1 Edgar, *South Carolina*, 408–9 (quotation, 409); Cooper, *Conservative Regime*, 16–19, 23, 43, 208–10.
2 Clipping from *Washington National Republican*, box 1, folder 98, Meynard Papers, SCL.
3 "25 Rebel Generals, 30 Rebel Colonels, 10 Rebel Majors, 20 Rebel Captains . . ." (1868), HL.
4 Tindall, *South Carolina Negroes*, 22.
5 *Charleston News and Courier*, Apr. 20, 1877.
6 Hampton's inaugural address, Dec. 14, 1876, HJ (1876): 39–42; Message from the Governor No. 1, Extra Session, Apr. 24, 1877, SJ (1877–78); "Message from the Governor, No. 1," Nov. 28, 1877, SJ; Governor Wade Hampton to Hon. W. D. Simpson, President of the Senate, June 8, 1877, WH Papers, Executive Messages, SCDAH. Traditional sources, such as Tindall, *South Carolina Negroes*, state that Hampton appointed 86 blacks to office, based on a survey by the South Carolina Historical Commission in the mid-twentieth century. A more recent tabulation shows the figure of 116, with four names added afterward (Tindall, *South Carolina Negroes*, 22, 22 n. 28; "Negroes Appointed to Public Office by Gov. Wade Hampton," folder 48, WH Papers, SCDAH); Simkins and Woody (*South Carolina during Reconstruction*, 548) wrote in 1932 that "Governor Hampton in most instances refused to give Republicans representations on the boards of election." But the document mentioned above indicates that Hampton appointed 26 black elections commissioners (ibid.). See also *Charleston News and Courier*, Apr. 20, 1877, and *Yorkville Enquirer*, Apr. 26, 1877.
7 Proclamations of Mar. 3, May 11, 1877, Proclamation Books, 1877–78, WH Papers, SCDAH.

8   Ullman, *Delany*, 497.

9   Tindall, *South Carolina Negroes*, 38. Another high-profile black appointment by Hampton was that of former lieutenant governor Richard Gleaves, a black Republican, as a trial justice in Beaufort (Cooper, *Conservative Regime*, 88; Tindall, *South Carolina Negroes*, 17).

10 SJ (1877, Special Session): 24.

11 Tindall, *South Carolina Negroes*, 266–67; Mancini, *One Dies, Get Another*, esp. 198–99, 202–3.

12 "Message from the Governor, No. 1," Nov. 28, 1877, SJ (1877): 16. After Hampton's veto of the chain gang bill the following February, the *Charleston News and Courier* praised his wisdom but, like Hampton earlier, hoped that some means could be used to defray the expense of the penitentiary by hiring out convict labor. In light of the passage of the convict lease bill the preceding June, both the newspaper's and Hampton's urgings in November are curious (*Charleston News and Courier*, Feb. 16, 1878).

13 *Charleston News and Courier*, Feb. 15, 1878.

14 Message from Governor Wade Hampton to House of Representatives, Feb. 14, 1878, WH Papers, SCDAH; Meynard, *The Venturers*, 263; Wellman, *Giant in Gray*, 299.

15 Tindall, *South Carolina Negroes*, 267–76; Megginson, *African American Life*, 376–77, 399, 410–11; Mancini, *One Dies, Get Another*.

16 Cooper, *Conservative Regime*, 45–46.

17 Edgar, *South Carolina*, 410; Cooper, *Conservative Regime*, 46.

18 *Charleston News and Courier*, June 26, 1877.

19 *Charleston News and Courier*, June 25, 1877.

20 *Charleston News and Courier*, Nov. 5, 1877.

21 "Message from the Governor, No. 1," Nov. 28, 1877, SJ (1877): 14. See also *Charleston News and Courier*, June 26, 1877.

22 *Charleston News and Courier*, Feb. 14, 1878.

23 Cooper, *Conservative Regime*, 48.

24 Ibid., 47–50; Perman, *Road to Redemption*, 212–13; Edgar, *South Carolina*, 410.

25 WH to Hon. W. W. Evarts, May 13, 1877, box 4, HFP.

26 Cooper, *Conservative Regime*, 51.

27 *Charleston News and Courier*, Apr. 20, 1877.

28 Cooper, *Conservative Regime*, 50–53.

29 *Charleston News and Courier*, June 25, 1877.

30 *Harper's Weekly*, Oct. 6, 1877, 783.

31 WH to Hayes, Sept. 25, 1877, Jan. 9, Mar. 25, June 4, June 14, July 15, 1878, WH Papers, SCDAH.

32 Lou Falkner Williams, *Ku Klux Klan Trials*, 46–46, 100–101, 109–13; Cooper, *Conservative Regime*, 18–19; Simkins and Woody, *South Carolina during Reconstruction*, 542–43. Hayes used the phrase "political offenses" in his

telegram to Hampton, May 12, 1877, WH Papers, SCDAH; Hampton used the terminology in the letters cited in n. 33 below.

33 WH to Hayes, Mar. 25, 1878. See also Tindall, South Carolina Negroes, 18–19; Simkins and Woody, South Carolina during Reconstruction, 542–43; Jarrell, Wade Hampton and the Negro, 136, 136 n. 37; WH to Hayes, June 24, Sept. 25, 1877, L. D. Pillsbury to WH, June 22, 1877, and Hayes to WH (telegram), May 12, 1877, WH Papers, SCDAH; Charleston News and Courier, July 29, 1878. Tindall (South Carolina Negroes, 19) states that Simpson pardoned Carpenter also, but Hampton's Mar. 25, 1878 letter to Hayes, cited above, indicates that Hampton gave the pardon. Hampton named two of the three convicted Klansmen. One was Pinckney Caldwell, who is mentioned by name in the testimony of James B. Porter of Yorkville in Testimony, vol. 3. Porter testified that Caldwell was one of the three men whipping him the night the York County treasury was raided by Klan members. For Hampton's efforts to secure amnesty for accused Klansman Dr. Rufus Bratton, brother of ex-Confederate general John Bratton, see WH to John S. Bratton, June 14, 1878, folder 154, Bratton Family Papers, SCL.

34 Ullman, Delany, 456.

35 WH to Hayes, Aug. 5, 7, 1878, WH Papers, SCDAH; Charleston News and Courier, Aug. 28, 1878; "South Carolina v. John J. Patterson," box 198, folder 2, South Carolina Attorney General Papers, Conner Family Papers, SCHS; Simkins and Woody, South Carolina during Reconstruction, 542, 546.

36 "Message from the Governor, No. 1," Nov. 28, 1877, SJ (1877): 17. See also Charles Richardson Miles to WH, Nov. 1, 1877, box 4, HFP, in which Miles alerted Hampton to the "hard trial to ignorant and timid negroes" tricked into paying taxes to Chamberlain.

37 Edgar, South Carolina, 394; Charleston News and Courier, Jan. 21, 28, 30–31, Feb. 2, 1878. The Citadel returned to state control in 1879 (Bond, Story of The Citadel, 90–92).

38 Edgar, South Carolina, 392, 424; Meynard, The Venturers, 256; Williamson, After Slavery, 232; "Message from the Governor, No. 1," Nov. 28, 1877, SJ (1877): 15–16.

39 Edgar, South Carolina, 412; Perman, Road to Redemption, 244–45. Hampton's veto message on the usury bill is found in box 4, folder 11, HFP, but does not appear in state legislative records; he signed the anti-usury bill on Dec. 20, 1877 (see South Carolina General Assembly, House, Acts and Joint Resolutions [1877–78], 325; also Manuscript Acts of the General Assembly of the State of South Carolina, 1877–78, Act #296, SCDAH).

40 Cooper, Conservative Regime, 94; Simkins and Woody, South Carolina during Reconstruction, 548; Tindall, South Carolina Negroes, 18.

CHAPTER 31

1 *Charleston News and Courier*, Oct. 3, 1878.
2 Ibid.
3 *Charleston News and Courier*, July 6, 1878.
4 Ibid.
5 *Charleston News and Courier*, Sept. 20, 1878.
6 Ibid.
7 *Charleston News and Courier*, July 8, 1878.
8 Edgar, *South Carolina*, 413; Cooper, *Conservative Regime*, 92; Dewitt Grant Jones, "Wade Hampton and the Rhetoric of Race," 197.
9 Cooper, *Conservative Regime*, 54–55.
10 *Charleston News and Courier*, Aug. 15, 1878.
11 Cooper, *Conservative Regime*, 90.
12 Wallace, "Life of Gary," 105, unpublished biography, Wallace Papers, SCHS; Cooper, *Conservative Regime*, 90; *Charleston News and Courier*, Aug. 29, 1878 (quotation).
13 Wallace, "Life of Gary," 107.
14 Ibid., 107–8; Cooper, *Conservative Regime*, 91; Tindall, *South Carolina Negroes*, 31. Some of the details above come from correspondence in David Duncan Wallace's notes (Notes, Martin Gary Biography, n.p., Wallace Papers, SCHS).
15 Wallace, "Life of Gary," 108.
16 Henry S. Farley to Martin Gary, Sept. 23, 1878, folder 16, Gary Papers, SCL; see also Farley to Gary, Oct. 11, 1878, folder 18, and Thomas Rosser to Gary, Sept. 29, 1878, folder 17, ibid.; Wallace, "Life of Gary," 106, 108; Cooper, *Conservative Regime*, 91.
17 WH to James Conner, Sept. 5, 1878, box 3, HFP.
18 Cooper, *Conservative Regime*, 60 (Hampton wrote Bonham on Sept. 28—ibid., n. 59); Wallace, "Life of Gary," 105–6.
19 *Charleston News and Courier*, Sept. 10, 1878.
20 Ibid.
21 *Abbeville Medium*, Apr. 3, 1878. For other examples of enthusiastic Hampton crowds, see *Abbeville Medium*, Mar. 27, 187, and *Charleston News and Courier*, July 6, Oct. 3, 30, 1878.
22 *Columbia Daily Register*, Aug. 1, 1878.
23 *Charleston News and Courier*, Aug. 29, 1878; Cooper, *Conservative Regime*, 60–62.
24 Simkins and Woody, *South Carolina during Reconstruction*, 85–86.
25 *Columbia Daily Register*, Apr. 5, 1878. Cooper (*Conservative Regime*, 59, 59 n. 54) identifies the Spartanburg *Carolina Spartan* and the Columbia *Straightout* as other pro-Gary papers, while also asserting that most of the state press supported Hampton.

26 Tindall, *South Carolina Negroes*, 25 (quotations); Ullman, *Delany*, 497.

27 *Charleston News and Courier*, Mar. 28, 1878.

28 *Charleston News and Courier*, July 29, 1878.

29 *Yorkville Enquirer*, Aug. 8, 15, 1878; *Charleston News and Courier*, Aug. 8–9, 1878; Tindall, *South Carolina Negroes*, 32–33.

30 Tindall, *South Carolina Negroes*, 34.

31 *Charleston News and Courier*, Nov. 15, 1878, quoting *National Republican*.

32 *New York Times*, Nov. 5, 1878.

33 *Columbia Daily Register*, Jan. 17, 1879.

34 Ibid.; *New York Times*, Apr. 22, 1881; *Charleston News and Courier*, Apr. 23, 1881. Hampton believed that he received almost 45,000 black votes in 1878 (*Charleston News and Courier*, Dec. 29, 1879). A careful study by William J. Cooper (*Conservative Regime*, app. B, 215) concludes that while fraud makes such claims impossible to substantiate, it seems clear that more blacks voted for Hampton in 1878 than in 1876.

35 On November 16 and 30, the *New York Times* printed harsh criticism of Hampton and his alleged connection with fraud in South Carolina's election. For most of December, the *Times* reported on Hampton's medical condition. On December 30, it resumed its charges against him (*New York Times*, Nov. 5, 16, 30, Dec. 8, 10–11, 14–15, 17–20, 22, 27, 30, 1878).

36 Cisco, *Wade Hampton*, 287; *Columbia Daily Register*, Jan. 17, Feb. 2, 1879.

37 Wellman, *Giant in Gray*, 301–4.

38 Tindall, *South Carolina Negroes*, 38; Wellman, *Giant in Gray*, 303; Jarrell, *Wade Hampton and the Negro*, 153–54; Alfred B. Williams, *Hampton and His Red Shirts*, 130.

39 Jarrell, *Wade Hampton and the Negro*, 152–53; Cooper, *Conservative Regime*, 81.

CHAPTER 32

1 *Greenville Weekly News*, Dec. 24, 1879; WH to Anna Preston, Mar. 20, 1880, box 4, HFP (quotation).

2 WH to Bradley T. Johnson, Sept. 6, 1899, Johnson Papers, PL.

3 Meynard, *The Venturers*, 269. In 1888 Hampton would lose another grandson, Wade Hampton V, son of McDuffie Hampton and his wife Heloise (ibid., 562). For other genealogical information on Hampton's descendants, see ibid., chap. 19.

4 Foster, *Ghosts of the Confederacy*, passim; Blight, *Race and Reunion*, 104, 107, 137–38, 264–99; Bruce E. Baker, "Devastated by Passion and Belief," 56 (quotation).

5 *Charleston News and Courier*, Dec. 15, 20–21, 24, 1879; *Greenville Weekly News*, Dec. 18, 24, 1879; *New York Times*, Dec. 26, 1879. Gary hoped that the

Democratic nomination for governor would go to him rather than Johnson Hagood, the Hampton-backed candidate (Cooper, *Conservative Regime*, 60–64).

6 *Charleston News and Courier*, Dec. 15, 1879.

7 *Abbeville Medium*, Jan. 28, 1880.

8 *Carolina Spartan*, Feb. 11, 1880.

9 Ibid.; *Abbeville Medium*, Jan. 28, 1880; *Charleston News and Courier*, Dec. 17, 20–21, 24, 1879; *Greenville Weekly News*, Dec. 18, 24, 1879; Wallace, "Life of Gary," 120–38, unpublished biography, Wallace Papers, SCHS.

10 "Proceedings of the Joint Meeting of Camp Moultrie," 35, Jervey Papers, 28/291/13, SCHS.

11 *New York Times*, Nov. 30, 1878.

12 For straightforward or cautious praise of Hampton, see *New York Times*, Mar. 15, 1878, Nov. 23, 1879; *Harper's Weekly*, Apr. 6, 20, 1867, Oct. 6, 1877, June 1, 1889. For denunciation, see, e.g., *Harper's Weekly*, Oct. 7, 1865, Nov. 3, 1866, Aug. 8, 15, 29, 1868, Nov. 6, 1880; and *New York Times*, Aug. 24, Sept. 27, Oct. 16, 21, 31, Nov. 5, 16, 1878, Apr. 6, 1879, Sept. 24, Oct. 19, 25, Nov. 6, 1880, Feb. 18, 1881.

13 *New York Times*, Nov. 6, 1880.

14 U.S. Congress, *Congressional Record*, 46th Cong., 1st sess., vol. 9, 1779.

15 *New York Times*, June 6, 1879.

16 U.S. Congress, *Congressional Record*, 46th Cong., 1st sess., vol. 9, 1780.

17 Ibid.

18 Ibid., 1781.

19 Ibid.

20 Ibid.

21 *New York Times*, Nov. 21, 1879.

22 *New York Times*, Nov. 23, 1879.

23 *Charleston News and Courier*, June 25, 1880; see also June 23.

24 *New York Times*, Oct. 25, 1880; *Harper's Weekly*, Sept. 11, 1880; Cisco, *Wade Hampton*, 292–93.

25 *New York Times*, Sept. 24, 1880.

26 *New York Times*, Oct. 19, 1880.

27 The correspondence between Hampton and John Sherman is reprinted in "Wade Hampton in a Rage," *New York Times*, Oct. 19, 1880.

28 Ibid.

29 "Wade Hampton Wants a Fight," ibid. See also *New York Times*, Dec. 16, 1880, and "Chivalry," *Harper's Weekly*, Nov. 6, 1880.

30 *New York Times*, Dec. 16, 1880.

31 Longacre, *Gentleman and Soldier*, 16; Meynard, *The Venturers*, 268; WH to Peter D. Torre, Jan. 6, 1836, box 1, folder 65, HFP; WH to E. B. C. Cash, Nov. 13, 1880, Jan. 29, 1881, Cash Papers, SCL.

32 *New York Times*, Dec. 15, 1880; *Charleston News and Courier*, Dec. 16, 1880.

33 U.S. Congress, *Congressional Record*, 46th Cong., 1st sess., vol. 9, 1780.

CHAPTER 33

1 Charleston News and Courier, Dec. 29, 1879; Tindall, South Carolina Negroes, 68; Cooper, Conservative Regime, 80–81.

2 Tindall, South Carolina Negroes, 68; Charleston News and Courier, Apr. 23, 1881 (quotation).

3 Tindall, South Carolina Negroes, 50–51; Kantrowitz, Tillman, 99–109; Cooper, Conservative Regime, 69–72.

4 Tindall, South Carolina Negroes, 68–71; Cooper, Conservative Regime, 98–103. The Democrats also gerrymandered the state's congressional districts to ensure easy Democratic victories in six of the seven districts and concede Republican victory in the heavily black Seventh District (Cooper, Conservative Regime, 103–5).

5 See Hampton's open letter to the state in Charleston News and Courier, June 20, 1882.

6 Poole, Never Surrender, 152. For more of Hampton's assurances to black voters, see Charleston News and Courier, Sept. 27, 1884; New York Times, Nov. 3, 1884; Columbia Register, Nov. 16, 1884; and Cooper, Conservative Regime, 80–81. The number of blacks who voted in 1876 was greater than 91,000; in 1890 it was less than 14,000, fewer than the number that had voted for Hampton in 1876. The number of black legislators decreased from 96 in 1872 to 7 in 1890 (Edgar, South Carolina, 415).

7 WH et al., "Ought the Negro to be Disfranchised?," 241.

8 Ibid.

9 WH, "What Negro Supremacy Means," 387.

10 U.S. Congress, Congressional Record, 51st Cong., 1st sess., vol. 21, part 1, 971–74 (first quotation 972; second quotation, 971).

11 Ibid., 971.

12 Ibid. (first quotation, 971; second quotation, 973).

13 Henry McNeal Turner to M. C. Butler, Apr. 10, 1890, Butler Papers, SCL; WH to James R. Doolittle, Nov. 12, 1889, Wade Hampton Family Papers, LOC.

14 U.S. Congress, Congressional Record, 47th Cong., Special Session, vol. 12, 373.

15 Ibid.

16 Ibid., 372.

17 Ibid.

18 New York Times, Apr. 22, 1881.

19 Charleston News and Courier, Oct. 30, 1882.

20 "Speech of Hon. Wade Hampton, of South Carolina, in the Senate of the United States, May 13, 1880," PL.

21 SJ (April 1877, Extra Session): 25.

22 "Speech of Honorable Wade Hampton, of South Carolina, in the Senate of the United States, on Senate Bill No. 398 . . ., March 27, 1884," 5, PL.

23 U.S. Congress, *Congressional Record*, 49th Cong., 2nd sess., Feb. 26 1887, vol. 18, part 3, 2326; Abbott, *Freedmen's Bureau*, 109–11.

24 Bruce Baker, "Devastated by Passion and Belief," 57–58 (quotation, 58); OR 47(1):861; M. C. Butler to Edward L. Wells, Mar. 27, 1900, Wells Correspondence, CLS; Brooks, *Butler and His Cavalry*, 446.

CHAPTER 34

1 Cisco, *Wade Hampton*, 295; WH to M. C. Butler, Nov. 16, 1889, Butler Papers, SCL (quotation). See also WH to Jefferson Davis, Apr. 9, 1888, Nov. 4, 1889, in Rowland, *Jefferson Davis*, 10:48, 161–62.

2 WH to Alfred McDuffie Hampton, Feb. 3, 1889, Wade Hampton Family Papers, LOC.

3 Simkins, *Pitchfork Ben*, 27–29, 32, 45–46, 66–69, 70–105 passim.

4 Freehling, *Secessionists at Bay*, 220–22; Klein, *Unification of a Slave State*, 1–8, 257–58, 261–62, 266–68, 303–5; Ford, *Origins of Southern Radicalism*, 106–8.

5 Tindall, *South Carolina Negroes*, 54–67, 73; Simkins, *Tillman Movement*, 14.

6 Simkins, *Pitchfork Ben*, 70–168 passim; Kantrowitz, *Tillman*, 87–155.

7 Simkins, *Pitchfork Ben*, 1–2.

8 Simkins, *Tillman Movement*, 113–18.

9 Quotations from ibid., 119, and Wellman, *Giant in Gray*, 315. The wording of Hampton's quotes is slightly different in the *Charleston News and Courier*, June 25, 1890, but identical in substance.

10 *Charleston News and Courier*, June 25, 1890.

11 Simkins, *Tillman Movement*, 121; *Charleston News and Courier*, June 25, 1890.

12 Simkins, *Tillman Movement*, 122.

13 In an open letter to the *Spartanburg Herald* in 1895, Hampton referred to this public rebuke to himself as a partial explanation of why he would no longer run for office (*The State*, May 25, 1895).

14 Simkins, *Tillman Movement*, 132.

15 Edgar, *South Carolina*, 427; Tindall, *South Carolina Negroes*, 51–53; Reece, "Pure Despotism," 43–48.

16 *Charleston News and Courier*, May 15, 1890. For reasons why Tillman resented Hampton, see Simkins, *Pitchfork Ben*, 186; B. R. Tillman to J. G. Guignard, Sept. 2, 1912, Tillman Papers, SCL; and Ball, *The State That Forgot*, 232.

17 Wellman, *Giant in Gray*, 319.

18 Ball, *The State That Forgot*, 232.

19 Wellman, *Giant in Gray*, 318–19; Simkins, *Pitchfork Ben*, 185–87; Ball, *The State That Forgot*, 232; *Charleston News and Courier*, Dec. 10, 1890.

20 Cisco, *Wade Hampton*, 304.

21 WH to M. C. Butler, Dec. 13, 1890, Butler Papers, SCL.

22 *New York Times*, Dec. 12, 1890. See also *Harper's Weekly*, Apr. 14, 1894.

23 See Orville Vernon Burton's Introduction to Simkins, *Pitchfork Ben*, 2002 ed., xxii. Burton is summarizing here much of the argument found in Kantrowitz, *Ben Tillman*.

24 Ball, *The State That Forgot*, 22. A perceptive modern work dealing with Tillmanism is Reece's "Pure Despotism," which treats the rise of Tillmanism as largely generational or as the replacement of the older Lost Cause veterans by younger men (p. 42).

25 *Charleston News and Courier*, Dec. 10, 1890.

26 WH to Theodore Barker, Jan. 29, 1891, box 4, HFP.

27 WH to William H. Vilas, July 30, 1892, Vilas Papers, Wisconsin Historical Society.

28 Simkins, *Tillman Movement*, 159.

29 Ibid., 159–60; *New York Times*, Mar. 24, 1892.

30 WH to Bradley T. Johnson, Dec. 15, 1894, Johnson Papers, PL (Hampton was suffering from erysipelas and had been confined to bed for weeks (ibid.); Lewis Pinckney Jones, *Stormy Petrel*, 213–14; Simkins, *Tillman Movement*, 180–84; WH to Narciso Gonzalez, Aug. 30, 1893, Feb. 9, 1894, box 4, HFP; WH to James C. Hemphill, Mar. 13, 29, Apr. 9, 25, May 11, 1894, Hemphill Family Papers, PL. In the last letter cited here, a frustrated Hampton wrote Hemphill: "I was willing & anxious to aid in an aggressive & straightout fight, but as our people prefer to submit, I shall let them take their own course."

31 Edgar, *South Carolina*, 441.

32 Poole, *Never Surrender*, 164, 174; Simkins, *Tillman Movement*, 189–99; Ball, *The State That Forgot*, 243–58.

33 *Charleston News and Courier*, July 7, 1892.

34 Kantrowitz, *Tillman*, 177–79; Simkins, *Tillman Movement*, 179.

35 Reece, "Pure Despotism," 68–71; Kantrowitz, *Tillman*, 198–99.

36 WH to *Spartanburg Herald*, reprinted in *The State*, May 25, 1890.

37 See, e.g., letters by "A Hampton Democrat," *The State*, May 25, 1890, and M. C. Butler, ibid., May 27, 1890.

38 *Columbia Daily Register*, June 25, 1895; see also June 19.

39 *Edgefield Advertiser*, June 5, 1895.

40 Simkins, *Tillman Movement*, 205.

41 Ibid., 213–28; Tindall, *South Carolina Negroes*, 214; Cooper, *Conservative Regime*, 112; Edgar, *South Carolina*, 445–47.

42 Kantrowitz, *Tillman*, 78. See also Drago, *Black Red Shirts*, 8, and Orville Vernon Burton, "Black Squint of the Law," 169.

43 Tindall, *South Carolina Negroes*, 25 (first quotation), 53 (second quotation); Poole, *Never Surrender*, 160–61; Kantrowitz, *Tillman* (on Gary and Tillman's

view of violence being the key to maintaining white supremacy), 2, 78, 92–95, 113, 120–21, and passim.

44 For evidence of how Hampton's views differed from other conservatives by the spring of 1895, see Reece, "Pure Despotism," 75; Simkins, Pitchfork Ben, 286–87; and Lewis Pinckney Jones, Stormy Petrel, 217–20.

CHAPTER 35

1 Charles J. Holden ("Is Our Love for Wade Hampton Foolishness?," 61, 71–81) brilliantly describes this process, though with slightly different periodization and more emphasis on economic class.

2 The State, May 14, 1891, p. 1. See also "Proceedings of the Centennial Celebration."

3 The State, May 14, 1891, p. 1.

4 Ibid.

5 Ibid., p. 5.

6 Ibid.

7 Charleston News and Courier, June 14, 1892.

8 The State, Aug. 15, 1892; Lewis Pinckney Jones, Stormy Petrel, 195.

9 Simkins, Pitchfork Ben, 187–88, 329; Lewis Pinckney Jones, Stormy Petrel, 200; The State, Sept. 23, 1893 (quotation).

10 The State, Feb. 18, 1891.

11 "Speech of Wade Hampton, a Senator from the State of South Carolina, . . ., Friday, January 16, 1891," 8, SCHS.

12 WH to Theodore Barker, Jan. 29, 1891, box 4, folder 94, HFP.

13 New York Times, June 28, 1891.

14 Meynard, The Venturers, 271–72.

15 Cisco, Wade Hampton, 307–8 (quotation, 308).

16 Harper's Weekly, Aug. 14, 1897, 798. Harper's also praised Hampton and condemned Tillman on Apr. 14 and 21, 1894. On the death of Senator Francis Bayard of Delaware, Harper's (Oct. 8, 1898, 997–98) mentioned Hampton and a few others as men "of whose services the country is deprived in order that vulgar men may serve themselves in places once filled by patriots and statesmen."

17 Chamberlain, "Reconstruction in South Carolina," Atlantic Monthly, 480.

18 New York Times, Feb. 28, 1899.

19 New York Times, June 27, 1897.

20 Blight, Race and Reunion, passim; O'Leary, To Die For, passim.

21 "Proceedings of the Joint Meeting of Camp Moultrie," 22, Jervey Papers, 28/291/13, SCHS.

22 Ibid., 25.

23 Ibid.

24 Ibid., 25–26.

25 Simkins, *Pitchfork Ben*, 329–30, 8–9, 385–90; Meynard, *The Venturers*, 275; Lewis Pinckney Jones, *Stormy Petrel*, 226.

26 Poole, *Never Surrender*, 122–23.

27 Ibid., 19.

28 *Charleston News and Courier*, Apr. 12, 1902.

29 WH to Mr. Curtins, June 12, 1896, and Theodore Barker to WH, July 8, 1896, box 4, folder 95, HFP; *The State*, May 25, 1895, July 1, 1896; *Charleston News and Courier*, May 10, 1899 (quotation, paraphrased from *King Henry IV*, part 1, act 5, scene 1).

30 *Charleston News and Courier*, May 10, 1899.

31 *Charleston News and Courier*, May 11, 1899.

32 Ibid., May 11–12, 1899.

33 *The State*, Oct. 7, 1901; *New York Times*, Oct. 7, 1901.

34 "Proceedings of the Joint Meeting of Camp Moultrie," SCHS, 29.

35 *The State*, May 10, 1901.

CHAPTER 36

1 U.S. Congress, House, *Report of the Commissioner of Railroads to the Secretary of the Interior*, 1893, 1894, 1895, 1896, 1897, House Ex. Docs. 53–2, 53–3, 54–1, 54–2, 55–2.

2 Cisco, *Wade Hampton*, 309–18; WH to Bradley Johnson, Oct. 2, 1897, Johnson Papers, PL (quotation).

3 WH, "An Effort to Rescue Jefferson Davis," 27, 135; WH to John H. Wyeth, Feb. 18, 1899, and WH to Joseph Wheeler, Aug. 16, 1899, box 306, folder 34, Maury Family Papers, HL; Wheeler, "An Effort to Rescue Jefferson Davis"; Cisco, *Wade Hampton*, 297. For Hampton's correspondence with surviving veterans, see Johnson Papers, box 1 passim, PL; Theodore G. Barker to WH, July 8, 1896, box 4, folder 95, HFP; letters between Hampton, Wells, Butler, Thomas Rosser, and Theodore Barker, Wells Correspondence, passim, CLS; WH to Henry B. McClellan, June 22, 1883, CW 166, Civil War Collection, HL; WH to Thomas T. Munford, July 25, 1888, Jan. 25, Nov. 11, 1898, Munford-Ellis Family Papers, PL; WH to Bradley Johnson, Nov. 9, 1899, folder 1, WH Correspondence, PL. Much of this correspondence involves these men rehashing their old battles and campaigns.

4 Brooks, *Butler and His Cavalry*, 548.

5 WH to Bradley Johnson, Mar. 3, 1899, Johnson Papers, PL.

6 C. E. Griffith to George McDuffy [sic] Hampton, Oct. 24, 1896, box 4, folder 96, HFP; WH to Alfred Hampton, Apr. 6, 1898, WH Family Papers, LOC (quotation). Hampton is listed on company stationery as vice president of the Metallic Cotton Baling Co. in WH to Edward L. Wells, Jan. 16, 1900, Wells Correspondence, CLS.

7   WH to Bradley Johnson, Mar. 3, 1899.

8   WH to Alfred Hampton, May 7, 1898, box 4, HFP. As a young man, Alfred had been present when Hampton and Fitz Lee had visited pleasantly together in 1887 while on vacation in Daggers Springs, W.Va. Alfred had been impressed with Lee, who was then governor of Virginia (Meynard, *The Venturers*, 270; Speech of Alfred Hampton in Galveston, Tex., 1910, box 4, folder 99, HFP).

9   Wells, *Hampton and Reconstruction*, 224.

10 "The Truth of the Matter," *The State*, May 9, 1901, part 2.

11 Meynard, *The Venturers*, 277; Wells, *Hampton and Reconstruction*, 220–24.

12 WH to Corrine Hampton, Jan. 2, 1899, box 4, folder 96, HFP; Meynard, *The Venturers*, 269, 276.

13 *New York Times*, May 3, 1899. A longer account of the disaster and Hampton's losses appears in *The State*, May 3, 1899.

14 Wells, *Hampton and Reconstruction*, 216.

15 WH to Bradley Johnson, Mar. 3, 1899.

16 *The State*, May 3, 1899.

17 Hampton's letter appeared in *The State*, May 17, 1899.

18 "South Carolina's Testimonial to Hampton: The Loving Tribute of a Grateful People," flier dated May 22, 1899, box 4, folder 11, HFP.

19 "Wade Hampton's Homes," box 4, folder 102, HFP; Meynard, *The Venturers*, 276.

20 Harry R. E. Hampton, "About the General," 9, Meynard Collection, box 1, folder 81, SCL.

21 Ibid., 9–10.

22 Cisco, *Wade Hampton*, 323; *The State*, May 10–11, 1901; George McDuffie Hampton to Miss Annie Laurie Rogers, May 4, 1911, box 4, folder 99, HFP.

23 Wells, *Hampton and Reconstruction*, 224; *Charleston News and Courier*, Apr. 12, 1902.

24 Capers's account of his discussion of spiritual matters with Hampton appeared in the *Charleston News and Courier*, Apr. 12, 1902. Hampton's words have been put into the first person here.

25 Cisco, *Wade Hampton*, 3; Wellman, *Giant in Gray*, 332–33.

26 A fragment of Alfred Hampton's log is in WH Family Papers, folder 5, LOC.

27 Wells, *Hampton and Reconstruction*, 225.

28 *Charleston News and Courier*, Apr. 12, 1902.

29 Alfred Hampton, "Last Words of Father. Gen. Wade Hampton," folder 5, WH Family Papers, LOC. Alfred recorded the time that these words were spoken as "Thursday, Apr. 10th. 5:30? P.M."

30 Wells, *Hampton and Reconstruction*, 225; *Charleston News and Courier*, Apr. 12, 1902.

1 *Charleston News and Courier*, Apr. 12–14, 1902; Wells, *Hampton and Reconstruction*, 228–31; Meynard, *The Venturers*, 277. A detailed account of the funeral services drawn from the above sources is in Cisco, *Wade Hampton*, 2–4.

2 See Ellison Capers's letter in *Charleston News and Courier*, Apr. 12, 1902; Wells, *Hampton and Reconstruction*, 225–26; Wellman, *Giant in Gray*, 333; *New York Times*, Apr. 20, 1902, quoting from *Savannah News*.

3 Cisco, *Wade Hampton*, 324.

4 R. Means Davis, "Hampton the Civilian," *Charleston News and Courier*, Apr. 12, 1902.

5 "Last Great Words of Gen. Wade Hampton," *Cleveland Gazette*, May 3, 1902, www.ohiohistory.org/resource/audiovis/repro.html.

6 Wellman, *Giant in Gray*, 334.

7 "Wade Hampton," clipping in box 4, folder 97, HFP.

8 *Harper's Weekly*, Dec. 1, 1906, p. 1717.

9 See also clippings in box 4, folder 97, HFP; *New York Times*, Apr. 12, 1902.

10 Bruce E. Baker, "Devastated by Passion and Belief," 273.

11 Ibid., 268–88 (quotation, 282).

12 Tindall, *South Carolina Negroes*, 306; Holden, "Is Our Love for Wade Hampton Foolishness?," 81. Excellent treatments of the competing uses of Hampton's legacy appear in Bruce E. Baker, "Devastated by Passion and Belief," 267–92, and Holden, 60–62, 76–81.

13 Orville Vernon Burton, "Black Squint of the Law," 169.

14 Kantrowitz, "One Man's Mob," 81.

APPENDIX

1 For examples of modern historians who have repeated the story, see Wellman, *Giant in Gray*, 115–16; Longacre, *Lee's Cavalrymen*, 214; and Nye, "The Affair at Hunterstown," 29–30. In *Gentleman and Soldier* (148), Longacre unaccountably decreases the range of Hampton's shot to the slightly more reasonable range of "within a hundred yards," but he cites no evidence that would explain this change.

2 Mackey, "Hampton's Duel on the Battle-Field"; Wells Correspondence, CLS.

3 Mackey, "Hampton's Duel on the Battle-Field," 125–26.

BIBLIOGRAPHY

PRIMARY SOURCES

Manuscript Collections

Chapel Hill, North Carolina
    Southern Historical Collection, Louis Round Wilson Library,
        University of North Carolina
        Wade Hampton III Papers
        Alexander Cheves Haskell Papers
        John Cheves Haskell Collection
        William Porcher Miles Papers
        James Keen Munnerlyn Letters
        Joseph Frederick Waring Papers
        Webb Family Papers
Charleston, South Carolina
    Charleston Library Society
        Edward Laight Wells Correspondence
    South Carolina Historical Society
        Joseph W. Barnwell Papers
        Conner Family Papers
        F. W. Dawson Papers
        Wade Hampton III: "Speech of Wade Hampton, a Senator from
            the State of South Carolina, Delivered in the Senate of the United
            States, Friday, January 16, 1891"
        Charles Thomson Haskell Papers
        Theodore D. Jervey Papers
        Andrew Gordon Magrath Papers
        Christian D. Owens Letters
        Sons of Confederate Veterans, Camp Moultrie Chapter, Readings and
            Addresses, 1895
        South Carolina Survivors' Association Collection
        David Duncan Wallace Papers
        Edward Laight Wells Papers
Clemson, South Carolina
    Strom Thurmond Institute
        Original Letters Collection
        Benjamin Ryan Tillman Papers

Columbia, South Carolina
  South Carolina Department of Archives and History
    Daniel H. Chamberlain Papers
    Company D Records, 5th South Carolina Cavalry
    Lyman C. Draper Collection
    Wade Hampton Papers
    Robert K. Scott Papers
  South Caroliniana Library, University of South Carolina
    Benjamin L. Abney Papers
    Bratton Family Papers
    U. R. Brooks, ed. *Stories of the Confederacy*, loose collection including
      "Sketches of Hampton's Cavalry" and "Record of Hart's Battery."
    Matthew Calbraith Butler Papers
    Daniel H. Chamberlain Papers
    Ellerbe Bogan Crawford Cash Papers
    John Gary Evans Papers
    Martin Witherspoon Gary Papers
    Narciso Gener Gonzalez Papers
    James Earle Hagood Papers
    Hammond, Bryan, and Cummings Family Papers
    Edward Spann Hammond Papers
    James Henry Hammond Diary: "Records of Antebellum Southern
      Plantations from the Revolution through the Civil War," series A,
      part 1, reel 13. Selections from the Holdings of the Library of
      Congress (Plantation Journals, Diaries, and Scrapbooks): Part 1: The
      Papers of James Henry Hammond, 1795–1865 (can be found in local
      filing number R1068m).
    James Henry Hammond Papers
    Hampton Family Papers
    Wade Hampton III: "Speech of the Hon. Wade Hampton on the
      Constitutionality of the Slave Trade Laws, Delivered in the Senate of
      South Carolina, December 10, 1859" and "Speech of Wade Hampton
      at Columbia Centennial, 1891"
    James Blackman Ligon Papers
    James Lowndes Papers
    Virginia Gurley Meynard Papers
    Benjamin Franklin Perry Papers
    Benjamin Ryan Tillman Papers
    Alfred B. Williams, "An Eyewitness Reporter" (scrapbook of newspaper
      clippings covering the 1876 campaign)
    Williams-Chesnut-Manning Family Papers
Durham, North Carolina
  William R. Perkins Library, Duke University

Alfred Adams Papers
Ulysses R. Brooks Papers
Armistead Burt Papers
Wade Hampton III Correspondence
Wade Hampton III and Mary Singleton McDuffie Hampton Papers
Hemphill Family Papers
"Jane Washington Day: Grand Military Parade." *Charleston, S.C. News and Courier Job Presses*, 1877.
Bradley T. Johnson Papers
Munford-Ellis Family Papers
Madison, Wisconsin
Wisconsin Historical Society
William H. Vilas Papers
San Marino, California
Huntington Library
William Marshall Anderson, "Pocket Diary of a Trip to Mississippi, Dec. 31, 1870–Mar. 23, 1871"
Civil War Collection
Wade Hampton, "Who Burned Columbia? General Wade Hampton Tells the Story." *Boston Globe*, July 15, 1889. In "Who Burned Columbia," a pamphlet of articles.
Joseph E. Johnston Papers
Francis Lieber Papers
Mansfield Lovell Papers
Maury Family Papers
J. E. B. Stuart Military Papers
25 Rebel Generals, 30 Rebel Colonels, 10 Rebel Majors, 20 Rebel Captains . . . Nearly One Fifth of the Whole Number, of the Late Democratic National Convention of July 4, 1868 . . . N.p., 1868.
Washington, D.C.
Library of Congress
Thomas Francis Bayard Collection
P. G. T. Beauregard Papers
Wade Hampton Family Papers
Louis T. Wigfall Papers

Newspapers and Magazines

Abbeville Medium
Abbeville Press and Banner
Anderson Intelligencer
Atlantic Monthly
Augusta Chronicle and Sentinel

Beaufort Republican
Beaufort Tribune
Beaufort Tribune and Port Royal Commercial
Carolina Spartan
Century Magazine
Charleston Advocate
Charleston Chronicle
Charleston Courier
Charleston Daily Courier
Charleston Mercury
Charleston News and Courier
Charleston Republican
Cleveland Gazette (http://www.ohiohistory.org)
Columbia Daily Phoenix
Columbia Daily Register
Columbia Phoenix
Confederate Veteran
Easley Messenger
Edgefield Advertiser
Greenville News
Greenville Weekly News
Harper's New Monthly Magazine
Harper's Weekly
The Land We Love
New York Herald
New York Times
New York Tribune
North American Review
Port Royal Standard and Commercial
Scribner's Monthly
Southern Historical Society Papers
Spartanburg Herald
The Nation
The State
New York World
Yorkville Enquirer

Published Letters, Memoirs, Diaries, Pamphlets, and Speeches

Alexander, E. P. Fighting for the Confederacy: The Personal Recollections of General
    Edward Porter Alexander. Edited by Gary W. Gallagher. Chapel Hill: University
    of North Carolina Press, 1989.

Ambrose, D. Leib. *From Shiloh to Savannah: The Seventh Illinois Infantry in the War.* Dekalb: Northern Illinois University Press, 2003.

Ball, William Watts. *A Boy's Recollections of the Red Shirt Campaign of 1876 in South Carolina: Paper Read before the Kosmos Club of Columbia, S.C.* Columbia: The State Co., 1911.

Beauregard, P. G. T. "The First Battle of Bull Run." In *Battles and Leaders of the Civil War,* 1:196–227. New York: Thomas Yoseloff, 1956.

Black, John Logan. *Crumbling Defenses, or Memoirs and Reminiscences of John Logan Black, Colonel, C.S.A.* Edited by Eleanor D. McSwain. Macon, Ga.: Eleanor D. McSwain, 1960.

Blackford, W. W. *War Years with Jeb Stuart.* New York: Scribner, 1945.

Bleser, Carol A., ed. *Secret and Sacred: The Diaries of James Henry Hammond, a Southern Slaveholder.* New York: Oxford University Press, 1988.

Brooks, U. R., ed. *Butler and His Cavalry in the War of Secession.* Columbia, S.C.: The State Co., 1909.

The Burning of Columbia. Charleston, S.C.: Walker, Evans, and Cogswell, 1888.

Butler, M. C. *Address of General M. C. Butler on the Life, Character, and Services of General Wade Hampton before the General Assembly of South Carolina, on the 23d of January, 1893.* Washington, D.C.: Gibson Bros., 1903.

——. "The Cavalry Fight at Trevilian Station." In *Battles and Leaders of the Civil War,* 4:237–39. New York: Thomas Yoseloff, 1956.

Calhoun, C. M. *Liberty Dethroned: A Concise History of Some of the Most Startling Events before, during, and since the Civil War.* N.p., 1903.

Cauthen, Charles E., ed. *Family Letters of the Three Wade Hamptons, 1782–1901.* Columbia: University of South Carolina Press, 1953.

Chamberlain, Daniel H. "Reconstruction in South Carolina." *Atlantic Monthly* 88 (April 1901): 473–84.

Chesnut, Mary Boykin. *A Diary from Dixie.* Edited by Isabel D. Martin and Myrta Lockett. Gloucester, Mass.: Peter Smith, 1961.

——. *Mary Chesnut's Civil War.* Edited by C. Vann Woodward. New Haven: Yale University Press, 1981.

Clemson, Floride. *A Rebel Came Home.* Edited by Charles M. McGee Jr. and Ernest M. Lander Jr. Columbia: University of South Carolina Press, 1961.

Constitution of the Survivors' Association of the State of South Carolina. Charleston: Walker, Evans, and Cogwell, 1870.

Cooke, John Esten. *Wearing of the Gray.* Bloomington: Indiana University Press, 1959.

Coxe, John. "The Battle of First Manassas." *Confederate Veteran* 13 (January 1915): 24–26.

——. "Wade Hampton." *Confederate Veteran* 12 (December 1922): 460–62.

Dowdey, Clifford, and Louis H. Manarin, eds. *The Wartime Papers of R. E. Lee.* Boston: Little, Brown, 1961.

Early, Jubal A. *A Memoir of the Last Year of the War for Independence in the Confederate States of America.* Edited by Gary W. Gallagher. Columbia: University of South Carolina Press, 2001.

Final Report of the Commission to Provide for a Monument to the Memory of Wade Hampton. Columbia, S.C.: Gonzalez and Bryan, 1906–7.

Freeman, Douglas Southall, and Grady McWhiney, eds. *Lee's Dispatches: Unpublished Letters of General Robert E. Lee, C.S.A., to Jefferson Davis.* New York: Putnam, 1957.

Glorious Cavalry Victory! Hampton Whips Kilpatrick! Broadside by Confederate States Government, 1865.

Green, James. *Personal Recollections of Daniel Henry Chamberlain, Once Governor of South Carolina.* Worcester, Mass.: Worcester Antiquity Society, 1908.

Hagood, Johnson. *Memoirs of the War of Secession.* Columbia, S.C.: The State Co., 1910.

Halliburton, Lloyd, ed. *Saddle Soldiers: The Civil War Correspondence of General William Stokes of the 4th South Carolina Cavalry.* Orangeburg, S.C.: Sandlapper Publishing Co., 1993.

Hampton, Ann Fripp, ed. *A Divided Heart: Letters of Sally Baxter Hampton, 1853–1862.* Spartanburg, S.C.: Reprint Co., 1980.

Hampton, Wade. *Address on the Life and Character of Gen. Robert E. Lee, Delivered on the 12th of October, 1871, before the Society of Confederate Soldiers and Sailors in Maryland.* Baltimore: J. Murphy and Co., 1871.

———. "The Battle of Bentonville." In *Battles and Leaders of the Civil War,* 4:700–705. New York: Thomas Yoseloff, 1956.

———. "The Battle of Bentonville." *The Century* 34, issue 6 (October 1887): 939–45.

———. "An Effort to Rescue Jefferson Davis." *Southern Historical Society Papers* 27 (1899): 132–36.

———. *Free Men! Free Ballots!! Free Schools!!! The Pledges of Gen. Wade Hampton, Democratic Candidate for Governor, to the Colored People of South Carolina, 1865–1876.* N.p., 1876.

———. "Negro Emigration: Speech in the Senate of the United States," Thursday, January 30, 1890. Washington, D.C.: N.p., 1890.

———. *Reply of Wade Hampton, Governor of South Carolina, and Others, to the Chamberlain Memorial.* Columbia, S.C.: Presbyterian Publishing House, 1877.

———. "What Negro Supremacy Means." *The Forum* (June 1888): 383–95.

———. "Who Burned Columbia?" *No Name Magazine* 2, no. 7 (April 1891): 90–93.

Hampton, Wade. *The Race Problem.* Boston: Arena Publishing Co., 1890.

Hampton, Wade, et al. "Ought the Negro to Be Disfranchised? Ought He to Have Been Enfranchised?" *North American Review* 128, issue 268 (March 1879): 239–44.

"Hart's South Carolina Battery—Its War Guidon—Addresses by Major Hart and Governor Hampton." *Southern Historical Society Papers* 6 (1878): 128–32.

Haskell, John Cheves. *The Haskell Memoirs*. Edited by Gilbert E. Govan and James W. Livingood. New York: Putnam, 1960.

Johnston, Joseph E. "My Negotiations with General Sherman." In *Battles and Leaders of the Civil War*, edited by Peter Cozzens, 5:653–66. Urbana: University of Illinois Press, 2002.

——. *Narrative of Military Operations Directed during the Late War between the States*. New York: Appleton, 1874.

"The Lesson of the Recent Strikes." *North American Review* 159, issue 452 (August 1894): 188–95.

"Letter from General Hampton on the Burning of Columbia." *Southern Historical Society Papers* 7 (1879): 156–58.

"Massachusetts and South Carolina: Correspondence between John Quincy Adams and Wade Hampton and Others of South Carolina." Boston: J. E. Farwell, 1868.

McArthur, Judith N., and Orville Vernon Burton, eds. *A Gentleman and an Officer: A Military and Social History of James B. Griffin's Civil War*. New York: Oxford University Press, 1996.

McClellan, H. B. *I Rode with Jeb Stuart: The Life and Campaigns of General J. E. B. Stuart*. Bloomington: Indiana University Press, 1958.

McClure, Alexander Kelly. "Colonel Alexander K. McClure's Recollections of Half a Century." Salem, Mass.: N.p., 1902.

McDaniel, Ruth Barr, ed. *Confederate War Correspondence of James Michael Barr and Wife Rebecca Ann Dowling Barr*. Taylors, S.C.: Faith Printing Co., 1963.

Message No. 1 of His Excellency Wade Hampton, Governor of South Carolina, 1877.

Miller, William E. "The Cavalry Battle near Gettysburg." In *Battles and Leaders of the Civil War*, 3:397–406. New York: Thomas Yoseloff, 1956.

Minutes of the Proceedings of the Reunion of the Hampton Legion Held in Columbia, South Carolina, July 21, 1875. Charleston, S.C.: Walker, Evans, and Cogswell, 1875.

Moffett, Mary Conner, ed. *Letters of General James Conner*. Columbia, S.C.: R. L. Bryan Co., 1950.

Mosby, John S. "The Confederate Cavalry in the Gettysburg Campaign." In *Battles and Leaders of the Civil War*, 3:251–52. New York: Thomas Yoseloff, 1956.

Myers, F. M. *The Comanches: A History of White's Battalion, Virginia Cavalry, Laurel Brigade, Hampton Division, A.N.V., C.S.A.* Baltimore: N.p.,, 1871.

Nicholson, J. J., ed. *The Burning of Columbia: A Collection of Pamphlets*. N.p., n.d.

Nicholson, William Alexander. *The Burning of Columbia*. Columbia, S.C.: N.p., 1895.

Northrop, Theodore F. "The Other Side of the Fayetteville Road Fight." *Confederate Veteran* 20 (1912): 423.

Perry, Benjamin Franklin. *Reminiscences of Public Men and Addresses*. Greenville, S.C.: Shannon and Co., 1889.

——. *The Writings of Benjamin F. Perry*. 3 vols. Edited by Stephen Meats and Edwin T. Arnold. Spartanburg, S.C.: Reprint Co., 1980.

Preston, Thomas L. *Historical Sketches and Reminiscences of an Octogenarian*. Richmond: B. F. Johnson Co., 1900.

"Proceedings of the Centennial Celebration of the First Meeting of the General Assembly of the State of South Carolina, Convened in the Town of Columbia in the Year 1791, Celebrated in the City of Columbia, South Carolina, May 13th, 14th, and 15th, 1891." Columbia, South Carolina, Centennial Committee, 1893.

"Proceedings of the Joint Meeting of Camp Moultrie, Sons of Confederate Veterans and the Daughters of the Confederacy Held on Tuesday Evening May 14th, 1895, at the Academy of Music, Charleston, S.C."

"Public Ceremonies in Connection with the War Memorials of the Washington Light Infantry, with the Orations of Gen. Wade Hampton . . . Charleston, S.C.: E. Perry and Co., 1894.

Ramage, James B. "Local Government and Free Schools in South Carolina." *Johns Hopkins University Studies in Historical and Political Science* 12 (1883): 1–39.

Rodenbaugh, Theodore F. "Sheridan's Trevilian Raid." In *Battles and Leaders of the Civil War*, 4:397–406. New York: Thomas Yoseloff, 1956.

Rowland, Dunbar, ed. *Jefferson Davis, Constitutionalist: His Letters, Papers, and Speeches*. 10 vols. New York: AMS Press, 1973.

Saunders, W. J. "Governor Z. B. Vance: Story of the Last Days of the Confederacy in North Carolina." *Southern Historical Society Papers* 32 (1904): 164–68.

Scott, Edwin J. *Random Recollections of a Long Life, 1806–1876*. Columbia, S.C.: C. A. Calvo, 1884.

Scott, Robert K. *Special Message of His Excellency Robert K. Scott, Governor of South Carolina, in Reply to Charges Made against Him*. Columbia: Republican Printing Co., 1872.

Selby, Julian A. *Memorabilia and Anecdotal Reminiscences of Columbia, S.C. and Incidents Connected Therewith*. Columbia: R. L. Bryan Co., 1905.

Sheridan, Philip H. *Personal Memoirs of P. H. Sheridan*. 2 vols. New York: Charles L. Webster Co., 1888.

Sherman, William T. *Memoirs of General William T. Sherman*. Bloomington: Indiana University Press, 1957.

Simms, William Gilmore. *A City Laid Waste: The Capture, Sack, and Destruction of the City of Columbia*. Edited by David Aiken. Columbia: University of South Carolina Press, 2005.

——. *Sack and Destruction of the City of Columbia*. 1865. Reprint. Edited by A. S. Salley. Freeport, N.Y.: Books for Libraries Press, 1971.

"Sketches of Hampton's Cavalry, 1861-2-3: Being a Reprint of a Pamphlet Published in Columbia Latter Part of 1864, Author Unknown . . ." In *Stories of the Confederacy*, edited by U. R. Brooks, 67–218. Columbia, S.C.: The State Co., 1912.

Slocum, H. W. "Final Operations of Sherman's Army." In *Battles and Leaders of the Civil War*, 4:754–59. New York: Thomas Yoseloff, 1956.

Smith, Daniel E., Alicia R. Huger Smith, and Arney R. Childs, eds. *Mason Smith Family Letters, 1860–1868.* Columbia: University of South Carolina Press, 1950.

Smith, Gustavus W. "Two Days of Battle at Seven Pines." In *Battles and Leaders of the Civil War*, 2:220–63. New York: Thomas Yoseloff, 1956.

"South Carolina: Her Wrongs and the Remedy: Remarks of Col. Richard Lathers, Delivered at the Opening of the Taxpayers' Convention, in Columbia, S.C., Tuesday, Feb. 17, 1874." Charleston, S.C.: News and Courier Job Presses, 1874.

Tillman, B. R. "Speech of Hon. B. R. Tillman in the Constitutional Convention of South Carolina, October 31, 1895."

———. "The Struggles of '76: Address Delivered at the Red Shirt Reunion, Anderson, S.C., August 25th, 1909." N.p., 1909.

"Transactions of the Southern Historical Society: Minutes of the Southern Historical Convention." *Southern Magazine*, January 1874.

Trezevant, D. H. *The Burning of Columbia, S.C.: A Review of Northern Assertions and Southern Facts.* Columbia: N.p., 1866.

Von Borcke, Heros. *Memoirs of the Confederate War for Independence.* 2 vols. New York: P. Smith, 1938.

Von Borcke, Heros, and Justus Scheibert. *The Great Cavalry Battle at Brandy Station 9 June 1863.* 1893. Reprint, Winston-Salem, N.C.: Palaemon Press, 1976.

"Wade Hampton." *The American Missionary.* 42, issue 7 (July 1888): 179–80.

Washington Light Infantry. "Proceedings on the Occasion of Unveiling the Monument Erected in Memory of Their Comrades who Died in the Service of the State, June 16, 1870." Charleston, S.C.: Walker, Evans, and Cogswell, 1870.

Wells, E. L. "Hampton at Fayetteville." *Southern Historical Society Papers* 13 (1885): 144–48.

Wheeler, Joseph. "An Effort to Rescue Jefferson Davis." *Century Magazine* 56, no. 1 (May 1898): 85–91.

———. "An Effort to Rescue Jefferson Davis: A Correction by General Wheeler." *Century Magazine* 56, no. 3 (July 1898): 477–78.

Who Burnt Columbia? Charleston: N.p., 1873.

Wise, John S. *The End of an Era.* Boston: Houghton Mifflin, 1899.

Witcher, J. C. "Shannon's Scouts—Kilpatrick." *Confederate Veteran* 14 (1906): 511–12.

Wright, Mrs. D. Giraud. *A Southern Girl in '61.* New York: N.p., 1905.

Yetman, Norman R., ed., *Life under the "Peculiar Institution": Selections from the Slave Narrative Collection.* New York: Holt, Rinehart, and Winston, 1970.

Government Documents

Case Files of Applications from Former Confederates for Presidential Pardons, 1865–67. Microfilm, Group I, roll 45. National Archives, Washington, D.C.

Compiled Service Records of Confederate Generals and Staff Officers. Micro-film M331, roll 115. National Archives, Washington, D.C.

Letters Received by the Confederate Secretary of War. Microfilm M437. National Archives, Washington, D.C.

Proceedings in the Ku Klux Trials, at Columbia, South Carolina in the United States Circuit Court, November, Term, 1871. Columbia: Republican Printing, 1872. Reprint, New York: Negro University Press, 1969.

Richland County, South Carolina. Probate Records. South Carolina Department of Archives and History, Columbia.

South Carolina General Assembly. House. Acts and Joint Resolutions of the General Assembly of the State of South Carolina. South Carolina Department of Archives and History, Columbia.

South Carolina General Assembly. House. Journal of the House of Representatives of the General Assembly of the State of South Carolina. South Carolina Department of Archives and History, Columbia.

———. Senate. Journal of the Senate of the General Assembly of the Senate of South Carolina. South Carolina Department of Archives and History, Columbia.

U.S. Congress. Congressional Globe.

U.S. Congress. Congressional Record, 1879–91.

———. House. Report of the Commissioner of Railroads to the Secretary of the Interior. 1893. 53rd Cong., 2nd sess., House Executive Doc. 1, microform sheet 3211, pp. 73–170. National Archives, Washington, D.C.

———. Report of the Commissioner of Railroads to the Secretary of the Interior. 1894. 53rd Cong., 3rd sess., House Executive Doc. 1, microform sheet 3307, pp. 85–213. National Archives, Washington, D.C.

———. Report of the Commissioner of Railroads to the Secretary of the Interior. 1895. 54th Cong., 1st sess., House Executive Doc. 5, microform sheet 3383, pp. 87–195. National Archives, Washington, D.C.

———. Report of the Commissioner of Railroads to the Secretary of the Interior. 1896. 54th Cong., 2nd sess., House Executive Doc. 5, microform sheet 3490, pp. 87–189. National Archives, Washington, D.C.

———. Report of the Commissioner of Railroads to the Secretary of the Interior. 1897. 55th Cong., 2nd sess., House Executive Doc. 5, microform sheet 3642, pp. 65–160. National Archives, Washington, D.C.

———. Select Committee on the Recent Election in South Carolina. Recent Election in South Carolina. 44th Cong., 2nd sess., 1877. Misc. Doc. 31.

U.S. Congress. Acceptance and Unveiling of the Statue of Wade Hampton. Presented by the State of South Carolina. 71st Cong. Washington, D.C.: GPO, 1929.

———. South Carolina in 1876: Report on the Denial of the Elective Franchise in South Carolina at the Elections of 1875 and 1876 . . . 44th Cong., 2nd sess, 1876. Misc. Doc. 48, 3 vols.

———. Testimony Taken by the Joint Select Committee to Inquire into the Condition of

Affairs in the Late Insurrectionary States. 42nd Cong., 2nd sess. Washington, D.C.: GPO, 1872.

U.S. Government. *War of the Rebellion: A Compilation of the Official Records of the Union and Confederate Armies.* 128 vols. Washington, D.C.: GPO, 1880–1901.

Works Projects Administration. Federal Writers' Project Papers: Ex-Slave Narratives. South Caroliniana Library, University of South Carolina, Columbia.

Other Published Primary Sources

Fleming, Walter L. *A Documentary History of Reconstruction.* 1906. 2 vols. Reprint, Gloucester, Mass.: Peter Smith, 1960.

Levine, Robert S. *Martin R. Delany: A Documentary Reader.* Chapel Hill: University of North Carolina Press, 2003.

SECONDARY SOURCES

Books, Dissertations, and Theses

Abbott, Martin. *The Freedmen's Bureau in South Carolina, 1865–1872.* Chapel Hill: University of North Carolina Press, 1967.

Ackerman, Robert K. *Wade Hampton III.* Columbia: University of South Carolina Press, 2007.

Allen, Walter. *Governor Chamberlain's Administration in South Carolina.* 1888. Reprint, Freeport, N.Y.: Books for Libraries Press, 1969.

Anderson, Paul Christopher. *Blood Image: Turner Ashby in the Civil War and the Southern Mind.* Baton Rouge: Lousiana State University Press, 2002.

Andrew, Rod, Jr. *Long Gray Lines: The Southern Military School Tradition, 1839–1915.* Chapel Hill: University of North Carolina Press, 2001.

Ash, Stephen W. *When the Yankees Came: Conflict and Chaos in the Occupied South, 1861–1865.* Chapel Hill: University of North Carolina Press, 1995.

Baker, Bruce E. "Devastated by Passion and Belief: Remembering Reconstruction in the Twentieth-Century South." Ph.D. diss., University of North Carolina, 2003.

Baker, Gary R. *Cadets in Gray: The Story of the Cadets of the South Carolina Military Academy and the Cadet Rangers in the Civil War.* Columbia, S.C.: Palmetto Bookworks, 1989.

Ball, William Watts. *The State That Forgot: South Carolina's Surrender to Democracy.* Indianapolis: Bobbs-Merrill, 1932.

Ballard, Michael B. *A Long Shadow: Jefferson Davis and the Final Days of the Confederacy.* Athens: University of Georgia Press, 1997.

Barrett, John G. *Sherman's March through the Carolinas.* Chapel Hill: University of North Carolina Press, 1956.

Benedict, Michael Les. *A Compromise of Principle: Congressional Republicans and Reconstruction, 1863–1869.* New York: Norton, 1974.

Beringer, Richard E., et al. *Why the South Lost the Civil War.* Athens: University of Georgia Press, 1986.

Bleser, Carol. *The Promised Land: The History of the South Carolina Land Commission, 1869–1890.* Columbia: University of South Carolina Press, 1969.

———, ed. *The Hammonds of Redcliffe.* New York: Oxford University Press, 1981.

Blight, David W. *Race and Reunion: The Civil War in American Memory.* Cambridge: Harvard University Press, 2001.

Bond, O. J. *The Story of the Citadel.* Richmond, Va.: Garrett and Massie, 1932.

Boritt, Gabor, ed. *Why the Confederacy Lost.* New York: Oxford University Press, 1992.

Bowers, Claude G. *The Tragic Era: The Revolution after Lincoln.* New York: Blue Ribbon Books, 1929.

Boykin, Edward. *Beefsteak Raid.* New York: Funk and Wagnalls, 1960.

Bradley, Mark L. *Last Stand in the Carolinas: The Battle of Bentonville.* Campbell, Calif.: Savas Publishing, 1996.

———. *This Astounding Close: The Road to Bennett Place.* Chapel Hill: University of North Carolina Press, 2000.

Brazy, Martha Jane. *An American Planter: Stephen Duncan of Antebellum Natchez and New York.* Baton Rouge: Louisiana State University Press, 2006.

Bridwell, Ronald E. "The South's Wealthiest Planter: Wade Hampton I of South Carolina." Ph.D. diss., University of South Carolina, 1980.

Brundage, W. Fitzhugh, ed. *Where These Memories Grow: History, Memory, and Southern Identity.* Chapel Hill: University of North Carolina Press, 2000.

Burger, Nash K., and John K. Bettersworth. *South of Appomattox.* New York: Harcourt, Brace, 1959.

Burton, E. Milby. *The Siege of Charleston, 1861–1865.* Columbia: University of South Carolina Press, 1970.

Byron, Matthew Adam. "Beyond the Traditional Code of Honor." M.A. thesis, Clemson University, 2002.

Carter, Dan T. *When the War Was Over: The Failure of Self-Reconstruction in the South, 1865–1867.* Baton Rouge: Louisiana State University Press, 1985.

Cash, W. J. *The Mind of the South.* New York: Vintage Books, 1969.

Censer, Jane Turner. *North Carolina Planters and Their Children, 1800–1860.* Baton Rouge: Louisiana State University Press, 1984.

Channing, Steven A. *Crisis of Fear: Secession in South Carolina.* New York: Simon and Schuster, 1970.

Chesnutt, David R. and Clyde N. Wilson, eds. *The Meaning of South Carolina History: Essays in Honor of George C. Rogers, Jr.* Columbia: University of South Carolina Press, 1991.

Cisco, Walter Brian. *Wade Hampton: Confederate Warrior, Conservative Statesman.* Washington, D.C.: Brassey's, 2004.

Clark, E. Culpeper. *Francis Warrington Dawson and the Politics of Restoration, 1874–1889*. University: University of Alabama Press, 1980.

Clinton, Catherine. *The Plantation Mistress: Woman's World in the Old South*. New York: Pantheon Books, 1982.

———. *Tara Revisited: Women, War, and the Plantation Legend*. New York: Abbeville Press Publishers, 1995.

Coclanis, Peter. *The Shadow of a Dream*. New York: Oxford University Press, 1989.

Coleman, Kenneth, ed. *A History of Georgia*. 2nd ed. Athens: University of Georgia Press, 1991.

Connelly, Thomas L., and Barbara L. Bellows. *God and General Longstreet: The Lost Cause and the Southern Mind*. Baton Rouge: Louisiana State University Press, 1982.

Cooper, William J. *The Conservative Regime: South Carolina, 1877–1890*. Baltimore: Johns Hopkins Press, 1968.

———. *Liberty and Slavery: Southern Politics to 1860*. Columbia: University of South Carolina Press, 2000.

Cox, Karen L. *Dixie's Daughters: The United Daughters of the Confederacy and the Preservation of Confederate Culture*. Gainesville: University Press of Florida, 2003.

Cresswell, Stephen. *Rednecks, Redeemers, and Race: Mississippi after Reconstruction, 1877–1917*. Jackson: University Press of Mississippi, 2006.

Cunliffe, Martin. *Soldiers and Civilians: The Martial Spirit in America*. Boston: Little, Brown, 1968.

Current, Richard Nelson. *Those Terrible Carpetbaggers*. New York: Oxford University Press, 1984.

Daly, Louise Haskell. *Alexander Cheves Haskell: The Portrait of a Man*. Norwood, Mass.: Plimpton Press, 1934.

Davis, William C. *Battle at Bull Run: A History of the First Major Campaign of the Civil War*. New York: Doubleday, 1971.

Dorris, Jonathan T. *Pardon and Amnesty under Lincoln and Johnson: The Restoration of the Confederates to Their Rights and Privileges, 1861–1898*. Chapel Hill: University of North Carolina Press, 1953.

Drago, Edmund L. *Hurrah for Hampton! Black Red Shirts in South Carolina during Reconstruction*. Fayetteville: University of Arkansas Press, 1998.

Dunning, William A. *Reconstruction: Political and Economic, 1865–1877*. New York: Harper, 1907.

Dusinberre, William. *Them Dark Days: Slavery in the American Rice Swamps*. New York: Oxford University Press, 1996.

Edgar, Walter. *South Carolina: A History*. Columbia: University of South Carolina Press, 1998.

Edmunds, John B., Jr. *Francis W. Pickens and the Politics of Destruction*. Chapel Hill: University of North Carolina Press, 1986.

Edwards, Laura F. *Gendered Strife and Confusion: The Political Culture of Reconstruction*. Urbana: University of Illinois Press, 1997.

Emerson, W. Eric. *Sons of Privilege: The Charleston Light Dragoons in the Civil War.* Columbia: University of South Carolina Press, 2005.

Faust, Drew Gilpin. *James Henry Hammond and the Old South: A Design for Mastery.* Baton Rouge: Louisiana State University Press, 1982.

———. *Mothers of Invention: Women of the Slaveholding South in the American Civil War.* Chapel Hill: University of North Carolina Press, 1996.

Fellman, Michael. *Citizen Sherman: A Life of William Tecumseh Sherman.* Lawrence: University Press of Kansas, 1995.

Foner, Eric. *Reconstruction: America's Unfinished Revolution, 1862–1877.* New York: Harper and Row, 1989.

Foote, Shelby. *The Civil War: A Narrative.* 3 vols. New York: Random House, 1958–74.

Ford, Lacy K., Jr. *Origins of Southern Radicalism: The South Carolina Up-Country, 1800–1860.* New York: Oxford University Press, 1988.

Foster, Gaines. *Ghosts of the Confederacy: Defeat, the Lost Cause, and the Emergence of the New South, 1865–1913.* New York: Oxford University Press, 1987.

Fox-Genovese, Elizabeth. *Within the Plantation Household: Black and White Women of the Old South.* Chapel Hill: University of North Carolina Press, 1988.

Franklin, John Hope. *Reconstruction: After the Civil War.* Chicago: University of Chicago Press, 1961.

Freehling, William W. *Secessionists at Bay, 1776–1854.* Vol. 1 of *The Road to Disunion.* New York: Oxford University Press, 1990.

Freeman, Douglas Southall. *Lee's Lieutenants: A Study in Command.* 3 vols. New York: Scribner, 1942–44.

———. *R. E. Lee: A Biography.* New York: Scribner, 1934–35.

Gallagher, Gary W. *The Confederate War.* Cambridge: Harvard University Press, 1997.

———. *Lee and His Generals in War and Memory.* Baton Rouge: Louisiana State University Press, 1998.

———, ed. *The Antietam Campaign.* Chapel Hill: University of North Carolina Press, 1999.

Gallagher, Gary W., and Alan T. Nolan, eds. *The Myth of the Lost Cause and Civil War History.* Bloomington: University of Indiana Press, 2000.

Genovese, Eugene D. *A Consuming Fire: The Fall of the Confederacy in the Mind of the White Christian South.* Athens: University of Georgia Press, 1998.

———. *Roll, Jordan, Roll: The World the Slaves Made.* New York: Pantheon Books, 1974.

———. *The World the Slaveholders Made: Two Essays in Interpretation.* New York: Pantheon Books, 1969.

Gordon, Asa H. *Sketches of Negro Life and History in South Carolina.* 2nd ed. Columbia: University of South Carolina Press, 1971.

Gordon, John W. *South Carolina and the American Revolution: A Battlefield History.* Columbia: University of South Carolina Press, 2003.

Gordon, Leslie J. *General George E. Pickett in Life and Legend.* Chapel Hill: University of North Carolina Press, 1998.

Graydon, Nell S. *Tales of Columbia.* Columbia, S.C.: R. L. Bryan Co., 1964.

Greenberg, Kenneth S. *Honor and Slavery.* Princeton, N.J.: Princeton University Press, 1996.

Grimsley, Mark. *The Hard Hand of War: Union Military Policy toward Southern Civilians, 1861–1865.* New York: Cambridge University Press, 1995.

Grossman, Lawrence. *The Democratic Party and the Negro: Northern and National Politics, 1868–92.* Urbana: University of Illinois Press, 1976.

Hamer, Phillip M. *The Secession Movement in South Carolina, 1847–1852.* 1918. Reprint, New York: Da Capo Press, 1971.

Hartley, Chris J. *Stuart's Tarheels: James B. Gordon and His North Carolina Cavalry.* Baltimore: Butternut and Blue, 1996.

Hartman, Saidiya V. *Scenes of Subjection: Terror, Slavery, and Self-Making in Nineteenth-Century America.* New York: Oxford University Press, 1997.

Holden, Charles J. *In the Great Maelstrom: Conservatives in Post–Civil War South Carolina.* Columbia: University of South Carolina Press, 2002.

Holt, Thomas. *Black over White: Negro Leadership in South Carolina during Reconstruction.* Urbana: University of Illinois Press, 1979.

Hughes, Nathaniel Cheairs, Jr. *Bentonville: The Final Battle of Sherman and Johnston.* Chapel Hill: University of North Carolina Press, 1996.

Jarrell, Hampton M. *Wade Hampton and the Negro: The Road Not Taken.* Columbia: University of South Carolina Press, 1949.

Johnson, Walter. *Soul by Soul: Life in the Antebellum Slave Market.* Cambridge: Harvard University Press, 1999.

Jones, Dewitt Grant. "Wade Hampton and the Rhetoric of Race: A Study of the Speaking of Wade Hampton on the Race Issue in South Carolina, 1865–1878." Ph.D. diss., Louisiana State University, 1989.

Jones, Lewis Pinckney. *Stormy Petrel: N. G. Gonzales and His State.* Tricentennial Studies, no. 8, published for the South Carolina Tricentennial Commission. Columbia: University of South Carolina Press, 1973.

Jones, V. C. *Eight Hours before Richmond.* New York: Holt, 1957.

Kantrowitz, Stephen. *Ben Tillman and the Reconstruction of White Supremacy.* Chapel Hill: University of North Carolina Press, 2000.

Kibler, Lillian Adele. *Benjamin F. Perry: South Carolina Unionist.* Durham, N.C.: Duke University Press, 1946.

King, Alvy L. *Louis T. Wigfall: Southern Fire-Eater.* Baton Rouge: Lousiana State University Press, 1970.

Klein, Rachel N. *Unification of a Slave State: The Rise of the Planter Class in the South Carolina Backcountry, 1760–1808.* Chapel Hill: University of North Carolina Press, 1990.

Kousser, J. Morgan. *The Shaping of Southern Politics.* New York: Oxford University Press, 1974.

Lamson, Peggy. *The Glorious Failure: Black Congressman Robert Brown Elliot and the Reconstruction in South Carolina*. New York: Norton, 1973.

Leemhuis, Roger P. *James L. Orr and the Sectional Conflict*. Washington, D.C.: University Press of America, 1979.

Leyburn, James L. *The Scotch-Irish: A Social History*. Chapel Hill: University of North Carolina Press, 1961.

Litwack, Leon F. *Been in the Storm So Long: The Aftermath of Slavery*. New York: Knopf, 1979.

Longacre, Edward G. *Gentleman and Soldier: The Extraordinary Life of General Wade Hampton*. Nashville, Tenn.: Rutledge Hill Press, 2003.

——. *Lee's Cavalrymen: A History of the Mounted Forces of the Army of Northern Virginia*. Mechanicsburg, Pa.: Stackpole Books, 2002.

Lucas, Marion Brunson. *Sherman and the Burning of Columbia*. College Station: Texas A&M University Press, 1976.

Mancini, Matthew, J. *One Dies, Get Another: Convict Leasing in the American South, 1866–1928*. Columbia: University of South Carolina Press, 1996.

Martin, Samuel J. *Kill-Cavalry: The Life of Union General Hugh Judson Kilpatrick*. Mechanicsburg, Pa.: Stackpole Books, 2000.

——. *Southern Hero: Matthew Calbraith Butler: Confederate General, Hampton Red Shirt, and U.S. Senator*. Mechanicsville, Pa.: Stackpole Books, 2001.

McCurry, Stephanie. *Masters of Small Worlds: Yeoman Households, Gender Relations, and the Political Culture of the Antebellum South Carolina Low Country*. New York: Oxford University Press, 1995.

McDonald, Joanna M. *We Shall Meet Again: The First Battle of Manassas (Bull Run), July 18–21, 1861*. Athens, N.Y.: Oxford University Press, 1999.

McKinney, Gordon B. *Zeb Vance: North Carolina's Governor and Gilded Age Political Leader*. Chapel Hill: University of North Carolina Press, 2004.

McPherson, James M. *Battle Cry of Freedom: The Civil War Era*. New York: Oxford University Press, 1988.

Megginson, W. J. *African American Life in South Carolina's Upper Piedmont, 1780–1900*. Columbia: University of South Carolina Press, 1996.

Meynard, Virginia G. *The Venturers: The Hampton, Harrison, and Earle Families of Virginia, South Carolina, and Texas*. Greenwood, S.C.: Southern Historical Press, 1981.

Miller, Edward A., Jr. *Gullah Statesman: Robert Smalls from Slavery to Congress, 1839–1915*. Columbia: University of South Carolina Press, 1995.

Moore, *Columbia and Richland County: A South Carolina Community, 1740–1990*. Columbia: University of South Carolina Press, 1993.

Morrill, Dan. *The Civil War in the Carolinas*. Charleston, S.C.: Nautical and Aviation Publishing Co., 2002.

Nelson, Jack, and Jack Bass. *The Orangeburg Massacre*. New York: World Publishing Co., 1970.

Oakes, James. *The Ruling Race: A History of American Slaveholders*. New York: Knopf, 1982.

Oates, John A. *The Story of Fayetteville and the Upper Cape Fear*. Charlotte, N.C.: Dowd Press, 1950.

O'Leary, Cecilia. *To Die For: The Paradox of American Patriotism*. Princeton, N.J.: Princeton University Press, 1999.

O'Reilley, Francis Augustin. *The Fredericksburg Campaign: Winter War on the Rappahannock*. Baton Rouge: Louisiana State University Press, 2003.

Osterweis, Rollin G. *The Myth of the Lost Cause, 1856–1900*. Hamden, Conn.: Archon Books, 1973.

——. *Romanticism and Nationalism in the Old South*. New Haven: Yale University Press, 1949.

Parrish, Michael T. *Richard Taylor: Soldier Prince of Dixie*. Chapel Hill: University of North Carolina Press, 1992.

Perman, Michael. *Reunion without Compromise: The South and Reconstruction, 1865–1868*. Cambridge, England: Cambridge University Press, 1973.

——. *The Road to Redemption: Southern Politics, 1869–1879*. Chapel Hill: University of North Carolina Press, 1984.

Pike, James S. *The Prostrate State: South Carolina under Negro Government*. New York: Appleton, 1874.

Poole, W. Scott. *Never Surrender: Confederate Memory and Conservatism in the South Carolina Upcountry*. Athens: University of Georgia Press, 2004.

Power, J. Tracy. *Lee's Miserables: Life in the Army of Northern Virginia from the Wilderness to Appomattox*. Chapel Hill: University of North Carolina Press, 1998.

Powers, Bernard E. *Black Charlestonians: A Social History, 1822–1885*. Fayetteville: University of Arkansas Press, 1994.

Proctor, Nicolas W. *Bathed in Blood: Hunting and Mastery in the Old South*. Charlottesville: University Press of Virginia, 2002.

Rable, George C. *But There Was No Peace: The Role of Violence in the Politics of Reconstruction*. Athens: University of Georgia Press, 1984.

——. *Civil Wars: Women and the Crisis of Confederate Nationalism*. Urbana: University of Illinois Press, 1989.

Reece, Lewie. "Pure Despotism: An Evaluation of Ben Tillman's Role in Suffrage Restriction, 1890–1895." M.A. thesis, Clemson University, 1994.

Reynolds, John S. *Reconstruction in South Carolina, 1865–1877*. Columbia: The State Co., 1905.

Rhea, George C. *The Battle of the Wilderness, May 5–6, 1864*. Baton Rouge: Louisiana State University Press, 1994.

——. *The Battles for Spotsylvania Court House and the Road to Yellow Tavern, May 7–12, 1864*. Baton Rouge: Louisiana State University Press, 1997.

——. *Cold Harbor: Grant and Lee, May 26–June 3, 1864*. Baton Rouge: Louisiana State University Press, 2002.

———. *To the North Anna River: Grant and Lee, May 13–25, 1864*. Baton Rouge: Louisiana State University Press, 2000.

Rose, Willie Lee. *Rehearsal for Reconstruction: The Port Royal Experiment*. Indianapolis, Ind.: Bobbs-Merrill, 1964.

Royster, Charles. *Destructive War: William Tecumseh Sherman, Stonewall Jackson, and the Americans*. New York: Knopf, 1991.

Rubin, Anne Sarah. *A Shattered Nation: The Rise and Fall of the Confederacy, 1861–1868*. Chapel Hill: University of North Carolina Press, 2005.

Rubin, Hyman III. *South Carolina Scalawags*. Columbia: University of South Carolina Press, 1996.

Saville, Julie. *The Work of Reconstruction: From Slave to Wage Labor in South Carolina, 1860–1870*. New York: Cambridge University Press, 1994.

Scarborough, William Kauffman. *Masters of the Big House: Elite Slaveholders of the Mid-Nineteenth Century South*. Baton Rouge: Louisiana State University Press, 2003.

Schullery, Paul. *The Bear Hunter's Century: Profiles from the Golden Age of Bear Hunting*. New York: Dodd, Mead, 1988.

Sears, Stephen W. *A Landscape Turned Red: The Battle of Antietam*. New Haven: Ticknor and Fields, 1983.

———. *To the Gates of Richmond: The Peninsula Campaign*. New York: Ticknor and Fields, 1992.

Severance, Benjamin Horton. "Legitimizing a Usurpation: The Campaign of 1876 and the End of Reconstruction in South Carolina." M.A. thesis, Clemson University, 1995.

Sheppard, William Arthur. *Red Shirts Remembered: Southern Brigadiers of the Reconstruction Period*. Atlanta: Ruralist Press, 1940.

———. *Some Reasons Why Red Shirts Remembered*. Greer, S.C.: Charles P. Smith Co., 1940.

Schultz, Harold S. *Nationalism and Sectionalism in South Carolina, 1852–1860: A Study of the Movement for Southern Independence*. 1950. Reprint, New York: Da Capo Press, 1969.

Simkins, Francis Butler. *Pitchfork Ben Tillman*. Baton Rouge: Louisiana State University Press, 1944. Reprint, Columbia: University of South Carolina Press, 2002.

———. *The Tillman Movement in South Carolina*. Durham, N.C.: Duke University Press, 1926.

Simkins, Francis Butler, and Robert Hilliard Woody. *South Carolina during Reconstruction*. Chapel Hill: University of North Carolina Press, 1932.

Simpson, Brooks D. *Let Us Have Peace: Ulysses S. Grant and the Politics of War and Reconstruction*. Chapel Hill: University of North Carolina Press, 1991.

Sinha, Manisha. *The Counterrevolution of Slavery: Politics and Ideology in Antebellum South Carolina*. Chapel Hill: University of North Carolina Press, 2000.

Starr, Stephen Z. *Union Cavalry in the Civil War*. 3 vols. Baton Rouge: Louisiana State University Press, 1979.

The Story of American Heroism: Thrilling Narratives of Personal Adventures during the Great Civil War as Told by the Medal Winners and Roll of Honor Men. Philadelphia: B. T. Calvert and Co., 1897.

Stowe, Steven M. *Intimacy and Power in the Old South: Ritual in the Lives of the Planters*. Baltimore: Johns Hopkins University Press, 1987.

Taylor, Alrutheus A. *The Negro in South Carolina during the Reconstruction*. Washington, D.C.: N.p., 1924.

Thomas, Emory. *Bold Dragoon: The Life of J. E. B. Stuart*. New York: Harper and Row, 1986.

———. *Robert E. Lee: A Biography*. New York: Norton, 1995.

Thomason, John W., Jr. *Jeb Stuart*. New York: Scribner, 1930.

Thompson, Henry T. *Ousting the Carpetbagger from South Carolina*. Columbia: R. L. Bryan Co., 1927.

Tindall, George Brown. *South Carolina Negroes, 1877–1900*. Columbia: University of South Carolina Press, 1952.

Trelease, Allen. *White Terror: The Ku Klux Klan Conspiracy and Southern Reconstruction*. New York: Harper and Row, 1974.

Ullman, Victor. *Martin R. Delany: The Beginnings of Black Nationalism*. Boston: Beacon Press, 1971.

Underwood, James Lowell. *The Constitution of South Carolina*. 4 vols. Columbia: University of South Carolina Press, 1986–94.

Walker, Clarence E. *Deromanticizing Black History: Critical Essays and Reappraisals*. Knoxville: University of Tennessee Press, 1991.

Wallace, David Duncan. *The History of South Carolina*. 4 vols. New York: American Historical Society, Inc., 1934.

———. "The Life of Martin Witherspoon Gary." Manuscript. David Duncan Wallace Papers, South Carolina Historical Society, Charleston.

Wellman, Manly Wade. *Giant in Gray: A Biography of Wade Hampton of South Carolina*. New York: Scribner, 1949.

Wells, Edward L. *Hampton and His Cavalry in '64*. Richmond: B. F. Johnson Publishing Co., 1899.

———. *Hampton and Reconstruction*. Columbia, S.C.: The State Co., 1907.

Williams, Alfred B. "Hampton and His Red Shirts." Bound volume of clippings, South Caroliniana Library, University of South Carolina, Columbia.

———. *Hampton and His Red Shirts: South Carolina's Deliverance in 1876*. Charleston: Walker, Evans, and Cogswell, 1935.

Williams, Lou Falkner. *The Great South Carolina Ku Klux Klan Trials, 1871–1872*. Athens: University of Georgia Press, 1996.

Williamson, Joel. *After Slavery: The Negro in South Carolina during Reconstruction, 1861–1877*. Chapel Hill: University of North Carolina Press, 1965.

———. *The Crucible of Race: Black-White Relations in the American South since Emancipa-tion.* New York: Oxford University Press, 1984.

Wilson, Charles Reagan. *Baptized in Blood: The Religion of the Lost Cause, 1865–1920.* Athens: University of Georgia Press, 1980.

Wilson, Clyde N. *Carolina Cavalier: The Life and Mind of James Johnston Pettigrew.* Athens: University of Georgia Press, 1990.

Wittenberg, Eric J. *An Infernal Surprise: The Cavalry Battle at Monroe's Crossroads, North Carolina, March 10, 1865.* Celina, Ohio: Ironclad Publishing Co., forth-coming.

———. *Glory Enough for All: Sheridan's Second Raid and the Battle of Trevilian Station.* Washington, D.C.: Brassey's, 2001.

———. *Little Phil: A Reassessment of the Civil War Leadership of Gen. Philip H. Sheridan.* Washington, D.C.: Brassey's, 2002.

———. *Protecting the Flank: The Battles of Brinkerhoff's Ridge and East Cavalry Field, Bat-tle of Gettysburg, July 2–3, 1863.* Celina, Ohio: Ironclad Publishing Co., 2002.

Woodman, Harold D. *New South: The Legal Foundations of Credit and Labor Relations in the Postbellum Agricultural South.* Baton Rouge: Louisiana State University Press, 1995.

Woodward, C. Vann. *The Burden of Southern History.* Baton Rouge: Louisiana State University Press, 1960.

———. *Origins of the New South.* Baton Rouge: Louisiana State University Press, 1951.

———. *Reunion and Reaction: The Compromise of 1877 and the End of Reconstruction.* Boston: Little, Brown, 1951.

Wyatt-Brown, Bertram. *Southern Honor: Ethics and Behavior in the Old South.* New York: Oxford University Press, 1982.

Young, Jeffrey Robert. *Domesticating Slavery: The Master Class in Georgia and South Carolina.* Chapel Hill: University of North Carolina Press, 1999.

Zuczek, Richard M. *State of Rebellion: Reconstruction in South Carolina.* Columbia: University of South Carolina Press, 1996.

Articles

Bailey, Fred Arthur. "The Textbooks of the Lost Cause: Censorship and the Cre-ation of Southern State Histories." *Georgia Historical Quarterly* 75, no. 3 (Fall 1991): 507–33.

Barnwell, Robert W., Sr. "Bentonville: The Last Battle of Johnston and Sher-man." *Proceedings of the South Carolina Historical Association* 13 (1943): 42–54.

Benedict, Michael Les. "Southern Democrats in the Crisis of 1876–1877: A Reconsideration of Reunion and Reaction." *Journal of Southern History* 46, no. 4 (November 1980): 489–524.

Bishir, Catherine W. "Landmarks of Power: Building a Southern Past in Raleigh and Wilmington, North Carolina, 1885–1915." In *Where These Memories Grow:*

History, Memory, and Southern Identity, edited by W. Fitzhugh Brundage, 139–
68. Chapel Hill: University of North Carolina Press, 2000.

Burton, Orville Vernon. "The Black Squint of the Law: Racism in South Caro-
lina." In The Meaning of South Carolina History: Essays in Honor of George C.
Rogers, Jr., edited by David R. Chesnutt and Clyde N. Wilson, 161–85.
Columbia: University of South Carolina Press, 1991.

——."Race and Reconstruction in Edgefield County, South Carolina." Journal of
Social History 12 (Fall 1978): 31–56.

Cardwell, David. "A Brilliant Coup: How Wade Hampton Captured Grant's
Entire Beef Supply." Southern Historical Society Papers 22 (1894): 147–56.

Clark, E. Culpepper. "Sarah Morgan and Francis Dawson: Raising the Woman
Question in Reconstruction South Carolina." South Carolina Historical Magazine (January 1980): 8–23.

DeSantis, Vincent P. "Rutherford B. Hayes and the Removal of the Troops and
the End of Reconstruction." In Region, Race and Reconstruction: Essays in Honor
of C. Vann Woodward, edited by J. Morgan Kousser and James M. McPherson,
417–50. New York: Oxford University Press, 1982.

Ford, Lacy K. "Republics and Democracy: The Parameters of Political Citizen-
ship in Antebellum South Carolina." In The Meaning of South Carolina History:
Essays in Honor of George C. Rogers, Jr., edited by David R. Chesnutt and Clyde
N. Wilson, 121–45. Columbia: University of South Carolina Press, 1991.

Ford, N. P. "Wade Hampton's Strategy: An Attack on Richmond Foiled." Southern Historical Society Papers 24 (1896): 278–84.

Gallagher, Gary W. "The Net Result of the Campaign Was in Our Favor: Confederate Reactions to the Maryland Campaign." In The Antietam Campaign,
edited by Gallagher, 3–43. Chapel Hill: University of North Carolina Press,
1999.

Glatthaar, Joseph T. "Battlefield Tactics." In Writing the Civil War: The Quest to
Understand, edited by James M. McPherson and William J. Cooper Jr. Columbia: University of South Carolina Press, 1998.

Hampton, Wade, II. "The Hampton Family." Charleston Mercury, August 4, 1843.

Hennessey, Melinda Meeks. "Racial Violence during Reconstruction: The 1876
Riots in Charleston and Cainhoy." South Carolina Historical Magazine 86 (April
1985): 100–112.

Hine, William C. "Black Politicians in Reconstruction Charleston, South Carolina." Journal of Southern History 49 (November 1983): 555–84.

Holden, Charles J. " 'Is Our Love for Wade Hampton Foolishness?': South Carolina and the Lost Cause." In The Myth of the Lost Cause and Civil War History,
edited by Gary W. Gallagher and Alan T. Nolan, 60–88. Bloomington: Indiana University Press, 2000.

Johnson, Joan Marie. " 'Drill Into Us . . . the Rebel Tradition': The Contest over
Southern Identity in Black and White Women's Clubs, South Carolina,
1898–1930." Journal of Southern History 66 (August 2000): 525–62.

Kantrowitz, Stephen. "One Man's Mob Is Another Man's Militia: Violence, Manhood, and Authority in Reconstruction South Carolina." In *Jumpin' Jim Crow: Southern Politics from Civil War to Civil Rights*, edited by Jane Daily, Glenda Elizabeth Gilmore, and Bryant Simon. Princeton, N.J.: Princeton University Press, 2000.

King, Ronald F. "Counting the Votes: South Carolina's Stolen Election of 1876." *Journal of Interdisciplinary History* 32, no. 2 (Autumn 2001): 169–91.

Krick, Robert K. "Sleepless in the Saddle: Stonewall Jackson in the Seven Days." In *The Richmond Campaign of 1862: The Peninsula and the Seven Days*, edited by Gary W. Gallagher. Chapel Hill: University of North Carolina Press, 2000.

Logan, S. Frank. "Francis Warrington Dawson, 1840–1889, South Carolina Editor." *Proceedings of the South Carolina Historical Association* (1952): 13–28.

Longacre, "The Long Run for Trevilian Station." *Civil War Times Illustrated* 18 (November 1879): 28–39.

Mackey, T. J. "Hampton's Duel on the Battle-Field at Gettysburg with a Federal Soldier." *Southern Historical Society Papers* 22 (1894): 122–26.

Mercer, P. M. "Tapping the Slave Narrative Collection for the Responses of Black South Carolinians to Emancipation and Reconstruction." *Australian Journal of Politics and History* 25, vol. 3 (1979): 358–74.

Monaghan, Jay. "Custer's 'Last Stand'—Trevilian Station, 1864." *Civil War History* 8 (1962): 245–58.

Moore, James Tice. "Redeemers Reconsidered: Change and Continuity in the Democratic South, 1870–1900." *Journal of Southern History* 44, no. 3 (August 1978): 357–78.

Nolan, Alan T. "The Anatomy of the Myth." In *The Myth of the Lost Cause and Civil War History*, edited by Gary W. Gallagher and Nolan, 11–34. Bloomington: University of Indiana Press, 2000.

Nye, William S. "The Affair at Hunterstown." *Civil War Times Illustrated* 9, no. 1 (February 1971): 22–34.

Peskin, Allan. "Was There a Compromise of 1877?" *Journal of American History* 60, no. 1 (June 1973): 63–75.

Pessen, Edward. "How Different from Each Other Were the Antebellum North and South?" *American Historical Review* (December 1980): 119–49

Rable, George C. "Bourbonism, Reconstruction, and the Persistence of Southern Distinctiveness." *Civil War History* 29, no. 2 (1983): 135–53.

Ramsdell, Charles W. "General Robert E. Lee's Horse Supply, 1862–1865." *American Historical Review* 35, no. 4 (July 1930): 758–77.

Rhea, Gordon C. " 'The Hottest Place I Ever Was In': The Battle of Haw's Shop, May 28, 1864." *North & South: The Magazine of Civil War Conflict* 4 (April 2001): 45–57.

Scott, Hugh H. " 'Fighting' Kilpatrick's Escape." *Confederate Veteran* 12 (1904): 588–89.

Shapiro, Herbert. "The Ku Klux Klan during Reconstruction: The South Carolina Episode." *Journal of Negro History* 49, no. 1 (January 1964): 34–55.

Smalls, Robert. "Election Methods in the South." *North American Review* 151, no. 408 (November 1890): 593–600.

Smith, Mark M. " 'All Is Not Quiet in Our Hellish County': Facts, Fiction, Politics, and Race—The Ellenton Riot of 1876." *South Carolina Historical Magazine* 95 (April 1994): 142–55.

Wallace, David Duncan. "The Constitution of 1790 in South Carolina's Development." In *History of South Carolina*, edited by Yates Snowden, 1:505–23. Chicago: Lewis Publishing Co., 1920.

——. "The Question of the Withdrawal of the Democratic Presidential Electors in South Carolina in 1876." *Journal of Southern History* 8, no. 3 (August 1942): 374–85.

Wickham, Julia Porcher. "Wade Hampton, the Cavalry Leader, and His Times." *Confederate Veteran* 36 (1928): 448–50.

Woodward, C. Vann. "Communication: Yes, There Was a Compromise of 1877." *Journal of American History* 60, no. 1 (June 1973): 215–23.

Zuczek, Richard M. "The Last Campaign of the Civil War: South Carolina and the Revolution of 1876." *Civil War History* 42, no. 1 (1996): 18–31.

INDEX